BARKLEY

BARKLEY

BARKLEY

A BIOGRAPHY

TIMOTHY BELLA

HANOVER
SQUARE
PRESS

HANOVER
SQUARE
PRESS™

Recycling programs
for this product may
not exist in your area.

ISBN-13: 978-1-335-48497-0

Barkley

Hanover Square Press
22 Adelaide St. West, 41st Floor
Toronto, Ontario M5H 4E3, Canada
HanoverSqPress.com
BookClubbish.com

Printed in U.S.A.

To Betsy and Teddy.

You can't start a fire without a spark.

TABLE OF CONTENTS

PROLOGUE

Looking down from the roof of his housing project, Charles Barkley believed he could fly. Wearing a homemade Superman cape made from one of the family's bathroom towels, the seven-year-old launched himself from twenty feet off the ground, knowing in his heart he could match the majestic superpower of television's George Reeves.

"He felt like he could do just about anything," grandmother Johnnie Mae Edwards said.

On this day, Charles's plan was inevitably derailed by gravity. When his mother, Charcey Glenn, ran outside, she thought Charles was dead. He was unconscious, bleeding profusely, and suffered a mild concussion.

"When I found out he was all right... I could have killed him myself," she said.

Barkley chalked up the near-death experience as another afternoon in the life of a wild child in Leeds, Alabama.

"When you're a poor kid in the projects, you'll do anything for excitement," he said.

It was part of the blessing of Barkley.

★ ★ ★

Charles Wade Barkley is as transcendent as he is irreverent, a foul-mouthed, bald Peter Pan in Nikes who never grew up. His basketball legacy is as close as someone without a championship can get to being unassailable. He was an eleven-time All-Star, selected to every game from 1987 to 1997. He was an All-NBA selection for eleven years. He earned two Olympic gold medals—including one in 1992 as part of the Dream Team, considered by many as the most dominant assembly of basketball talent ever. He was the 1993 MVP and finished in the top ten in voting nine times. He has enough nicknames to make Apollo Creed blush. The six-foot-six player we've known as the Round Mound of Rebound, Sir Charles, the Incredible Bulk, the Leaning Tower of Pizza, or just Chuck remains the shortest player to ever win a rebounding title. He was named as one of the greatest players in NBA history as part of the league's fiftieth and seventy-fifth anniversaries. By the time he retired in 2000, he was only the fourth player in league history to score 20,000 points, grab 10,000 rebounds and dish out 4,000 assists.

"These new generations don't understand because they can't believe it," said Chuck D, the legendary lyricist and leader of Public Enemy, "but Charles Barkley was the biggest problem."

He has been inducted into the Naismith Memorial Basketball Hall of Fame an unprecedented three separate times—one for his career, one for his role with the Dream Team, and one for winning the Curt Gowdy Media Award as part of *Inside the NBA*, the first award of its kind for a studio show. His games were must-see TV for fans, and networks benefited from the bump in ratings that came with his unpredictability.

He helped change not just how fans watched the game but also how they talked about it. When he isn't discussing race or politics on the basketball show, Charles, who isn't on social media, regularly goes viral for sound bite after sound bite—suggesting former Vice President Mike Pence shut the hell up, joking about Draymond Green being the worst member of a boy band, admitting that he mistook symptoms of a prolonged hangover for signs that he might have the coronavirus. He can befriend anyone anywhere—from Ric Flair and Guy Fieri to Ryan Smith, a college basketball player who valiantly fought against leukemia, and Lin Wang, the cat-litter scientist in Iowa who reminded us that the unlikeliest of bonds are just as special as those we see on TV every Thursday.

His place in basketball lore will forever be linked to Michael Jordan, the best player the game has ever seen and a contemporary that both he and his peers could never topple. Whether it's fair, there's a question to his basketball story that gets brought up repeatedly: Is he the greatest player to never win a ring? Possibly. Tune in on any given Thursday to *Inside the NBA*, and you'll hear Shaquille O'Neal mention it unmercifully if he feels like he's losing an argument against his friend.

Whenever Chuck's asked how much better he could have been if he dedicated himself to conditioning for the entirety of his career, like he had during the '92 Dream Team and his subsequent MVP season, he laughs at the notion that avoiding the extra Reese's Pieces would have done him any good.

"What the fuck else could I have done if only four guys did the shit I did?" he asked *Sports Illustrated*'s Jack McCallum in 2012.

At the height of his career, he was treated more like a rock star than a basketball player. A pitchman for two of the biggest brands in the world, Nike and McDonald's, Charles appeared in movies and iconic TV commercials, and graced magazine covers that became collector's items. Everyone wanted a piece of him: presidents and pundits, actors and activists, even Madonna. Images of him getting mobbed by fans in Spain during the Dream Team's 1992 Summer Olympics drew comparisons to Beatlemania. He's hosted *Saturday Night Live* the most times of any athlete in the show's history. And he says he makes tens of millions of dollars annually between his job at TNT and endorsements for brands like Subway and Capital One.

We've been hearing him for a long time, but he's contended that hearing him doesn't necessarily mean people have understood him. He doesn't like being called controversial, but sometimes there's no other word to better sum him up. To many, he resurrected what it meant to be the provocative voice of the American athlete not seen for decades in a world he considered too politically correct, too guarded, and too uncomfortable. For others, he is, and always has been, a blowhard with an inflated opinion of himself and his perspective, an inflaming figure in a culture fractured by race and politics. The same goes for basketball, like when LeBron James responded to Chuck's criticism of him by listing off all the things Barkley had done as a player: "I'm not the one who threw somebody through a window. I never spit on a kid. I never had unpaid debt in Las Vegas. I never said, 'I am not a role model.' I never showed up to All-Star Weekend on Sunday because I was in Vegas all weekend partying." Kevin Durant echoed James in 2021: "I don't know why they still ask for this idiot's opinion."

An altercation with Charles could involve an opponent or an official, a coach or an owner, a teammate or an announcer, a fan or a bar patron, or anyone who dared get in his way. His 329 technical fouls are good for second all-time, ranging from fighting with Bill Laimbeer to poking a ref in the nose and drawing blood. His arrests and the millions he's lost gambling made headlines, and the bar fights are shared like old war stories. So, why is now the time to tackle the long, full life of Charles Wade Barkley? Bob Costas succinctly summed him up: "If you go looking for the next Charles Barkley, you'll be looking from now until doomsday."

"I see his picture every day and I'm like, 'I need to be a motherfucker just like Charles was on the court.' That's who I'm like," said Diana Taurasi, the Phoenix Mercury star and one of the greatest women's players ever.

Charles cemented this legacy not only through basketball, but by also speaking out, for better or worse, at every turn, living an unfiltered existence filled with amusement and anger, philanthropy and faults, triumphs and tragedies.

"He won the lottery of fame and charm and learning and excellence and sculpted his finest skills honestly so that he could be relevant across four decades," said Dan Le Batard, the media personality and a longtime friend of his. "Charles mattered. What he said mattered. What he did mattered."

Over a period of less than two years, I conducted interviews with 374 people from every walk of Charles's life, from his childhood friends and first coaches in Leeds to teammates and about forty Hall of Famers to vice presidents and senators to golfing buddies and even cops who've arrested him. There are original interviews from some of the biggest names in sports, culture, media, and politics from Julius Erving, Shaquille O'Neal, and Sue Bird to the Reverend Jesse Jackson, Adam Sandler, and Jemele Hill. I found that some of the most valuable insights came from those who had previously not spoken at length about Charles, whether it was a close female confidant in Leeds, a guidance counselor, Miss Alabama 1980, his college roommate, an Auburn University tutor, the Tennessee student who ordered pizzas delivered to Barkley before a game, the girl he accidentally spit on in New Jersey, a bodybuilder who got into a bar fight with Charles, or the man underneath the Barney suit from his first *Saturday Night Live* monologue. While I was optimistic about speaking with the man himself, Charles, through his agent, Marc Perman, declined to be interviewed for the book.

I tried to be as comprehensive as possible in my reading, which is why I devoured every book of significance related to Barkley, such as the four he co-wrote or contributed to with authors Michael Wilbon, Roy S. Johnson, and Rick Reilly, and another by David Casstevens that captured one of his seasons in Phoenix. Included in that list of books were works of the journalists who I've long admired, such as David Halberstam, Jack McCallum, Jackie MacMullan, Bob Ryan, Sam Smith, Roland Lazenby, and Ernie Johnson. It would be negligent of me if I didn't specifically single out the 1992 autobiography *Outrageous!* coauthored by Roy S. Johnson. Roy's work offered the most comprehensive look at Charles's early life, and it also might be the only autobiography in the history of publishing in which one of its authors initially claimed to have been misquoted.

I reviewed thousands of newspaper and magazine pieces and watched and listened to hundreds of TV interviews and podcasts. Many of them came from outlets like *Sports Illustrated*, the *Philadelphia Inquirer*, the *Arizona Republic*, the *Houston Chronicle*, the *Washington Post*, the *New York Times*, and ESPN. Invaluable information was highlighted in several documentary-style and home-video features, including *Sir Charles* from NBA Entertainment in 1994, an ESPN *SportsCentury* episode from 2001, the *Dream Team* documentary from NBA Entertainment in 2012, and *The Last Dance* docuseries from ESPN and Netflix in 2020. I pored over hundreds of video clips from *Inside the NBA* uploaded on YouTube and many others from Turner Sports and the NBA. With the help of a researcher, we watched and transcribed every significant broadcast interview and late-night TV appearance involving Charles since the '80s, as well as every episode of *The Steam Room* podcast he cohosts with Ernie Johnson. Through the assistance of HBO, I was able to view three pieces on Charles from *Real Sports with Bryant Gumbel* that are not publicly available online. The same goes for ESPN, which granted me access to watch a rare television interview with Frank Barkley on *Up Close* from their archives.

In addition to my reading on basketball, I reflected on works about Alabama, the city of Leeds, the civil rights movement, the '60s, '70s, '80s, and '90s, Auburn, Philadelphia, Phoenix, Houston, Nike, television, and pop culture. During one of my trips to his hometown, I was given access by Leeds High School to read through each of the four yearbooks he was listed in from 1978 to 1981. The same goes for the three yearbooks he's featured in at Auburn University between 1982 and 1984, as well as the student newspaper articles written about him and the Tigers in the *Auburn Plainsman*. During the course of the research, I also constructed a comprehensive timeline of Charles's life, dating back to the birth of his great-great-great-grandfather in the early 1800s, the earliest public record of a Barkley family descendant in the United States.

For someone who hasn't played in more than two decades, says whatever he wants, and abhors and abstains from all social media, he remains one of the most popular people in America. There has never been a comprehensive biography spanning the entirety of Charles's life to date, a book that offers a look at the crucial role his mother and grandmother played in raising him to go from the Russell Heights projects in Leeds to a cultural icon out of Studio J in Atlanta. What I found was a subject who's been a part of my life for decades, someone I aggressively booed sitting in the nosebleeds with my dad at The Summit only to become a Barkley believer when he came to town in hope of winning a ring. The moment he told me, wearing shorts on a forty-degree day in Houston, to "put on some damn pants" when I was about twelve is forever burned into my memory. My hope from the beginning was to deliver a fresh look at his live-and-in-living-color, only-in-America tale and capture the true, and thunderous, spirit of one of the biggest bolts of lightning to ever strike basketball and television.

"Charles thought he was bigger than life," his friend and former coach Cotton Fitzsimmons once said. "And sometimes, he was."

1

The undersized man was from Central Alabama. What he lacked in height he made up for in width, speed, and grit. He vowed long ago to his family that no one was going to beat him ever again.

The battle between John Henry and the steam hammer is believed by some to have taken place at Oak Mountain Tunnel near Leeds, Alabama, almost twenty miles east of Birmingham. The tall tale goes that Henry, a freed slave, challenged a steam drill engine to a race on September 20, 1887. He believed he could build the railroad faster than his machine replacement.

The steam hammer was no match for Henry and his fourteen-pound hammer. He defeated the machine and maintained the livelihoods of his friends and family, yet his achievement came at the ultimate price. Henry died shortly after winning the race, a busted blood vessel in his brain costing him his life.

Nearly a century later, another Black folk hero of sorts would emerge from Leeds. Charles Barkley, the transcendent basketball star and irreverent media personality with a penchant for Krispy Kreme doughnuts, would come of age in the projects, just four miles from John Henry's tunnel.

"There will never be another player like me," Charles once joked. "I'm the ninth wonder of the world."

Located along a trail that would later become a stagecoach route following the War of 1812, Leeds, originally known as Cedar Grove and then Oak Ridge, blossomed thanks to the discovery of iron ore and minerals. Looking to reap the riches of the land, European woodsmen came from Tennessee to live with Cherokees who inhabited the Cahaba Trail. Leeds transformed into a hub for cement workers during the Industrial Revolution, as the railroads expanded. After the Civil War, slaves freed by four local families formed their own farming community. Other newly freed Black families followed, yet Leeds was not immune to the region's entrenched racism.

On August 2, 1901, Charles Bentley, a Black man, was found guilty by an all-White jury of killing a White man in Leeds named Jim Vann. The verdict, like most verdicts leveled against Black defendants at the time, hinged on scant evidence. Soon after the verdict was given, a White mob dragged Bentley to the border between Jefferson and St. Clair Counties. "Members of the mob learned of the verdict and a crowd quickly gathered around the prisoner," the *Pine Belt News* wrote at the time, "and unheeding his pleas for mercy, hanged him to the limb of a tree."

On November 30, 1901, Jas B. King, a sawmill owner, was arrested for Bentley's death, and a grand jury later convicted him. The result was an unlikely piece of justice for one of the only recorded lynchings in Leeds's history.

Charles Barkley's family line in Leeds dates back to a time when cotton was king in Alabama. In the region that would eventually become Talladega County, a green, rural area east of Birmingham, the first members of the Barkley family appeared in public records in the early 1800s.

Charles's great-great-great-grandfather, Henry Barkley—spelled "Barcley" and "Barclay" in the 1870 and 1880 US Census, respectively—was born sometime between 1805 and 1820 in either South

Carolina or Tennessee. (Discrepancies in federal records were not uncommon in the nineteenth century.) The 1870 Census is the first to include Black people by name after the Civil War and is often considered the first official record of surnames for former enslaved people, according to the National Archives and Records Administration. Henry Barkley is not listed in the 1860 Census, but his father was born in North Carolina and his mother in South Carolina. Henry, who couldn't read or write, settled in Talladega County as a farm laborer, raising a family of roughly seven children with his wife, Harriet, whose job was "keeping house."

Among those children was Simon Barkley, Charles's great-great-grandfather. In November 1880, Simon, who also worked as a farm laborer, and his wife, Janc, welcomed Wade Barkley into the world, their third child.

Wade, Charles's great-grandfather, could neither read nor write by the time he was twenty-eight, but he and Charles's great-grandmother, Willie Lee Stamps, both maintained steady work as farm laborers to support their three kids. One of them was Simon William Ernest Barkley, who arrived on June 20, 1908.

Having dropped out of school after the seventh grade, Simon Sr., Charles's grandfather, and wife, Ruby Bledsoe, with an eighth-grade education of her own, stuck to farming.

By the time Frank Howard Barkley was born in September 1942, Simon and Ruby had moved to Leeds, a suburb fifteen minutes outside downtown Birmingham.

That same year, fifteen-year-old Johnnie Mae England gave birth to Charles's mother, Charcey. Johnnie Mae was the undisputed backbone of the family. She worked at Lumber Jacks, a local meatpacking house, for decades. She operated a beauty salon behind her house for twenty-five years and later transitioned into nursing.

"I was spoiled rotten," Charcey said of her childhood. "But Johnnie Mae always preached to me about maintaining my sense of independence, and to be beholden to no one. 'Not even your husband,' she told me."

But Charcey's mother also ran a tight ship.

"My mother was a strict disciplinarian—could whoop harder than any man could ever whoop," Charcey said.

From the time the first Black families began to settle in Leeds, education access was an issue. The original Leeds Negro School was built in 1920 on land purchased for $200. For nearly three decades, the separate trustee boards agreed that Black students in Leeds who wanted to attend and graduate high school would be bussed more than a half hour west to Rosedale High School in Homewood. That changed in the late 1940s when the Leeds Negro Trustee Board called on the Jefferson County Board of Education to build a Black high school. It was to be built in the Russell Heights community, home to an overwhelming number of Black families, many of whom lived in low-income shotgun houses while working at the cement plant or in the coal mines.

By the time the school opened in 1948 as Robert Russa Moton High School, named after the second president of the Tuskegee Institute, the Leeds school would become a refuge not just for young Black people in town but also for students bussed in from nearby Irondale, Overton, and Trussville.

In this setting, Charcey—raised on the tenets of God, family, and community—had to grow up quickly during one of the most tumultuous periods in the nation's history. When Charcey was thirteen, Rosa Parks was arrested one hundred miles south of Montgomery for refusing to give up her bus seat to a White passenger. Over the next few years, the Freedom Rides, the series of integrated bus trips through the Deep South, ignited violence and hatred in Montgomery, Anniston, and nearby Birmingham.

In high school, Charcey was popular, even crowned homecoming queen on multiple occasions. At roughly six feet tall, she was a commanding presence in her class and reminded some of Pearl Bailey, the stunning Tony- and Emmy-winning entertainer.

"Charcey Mae was a beautiful woman, very statuesque," classmate Raymond Marbury noted. "I thought she looked like a movie star."

Whether it was a football game on Friday nights, a make out party in the woods, or a jaunt to the bowling alley in the Black part of Birmingham, Charcey found ways to have fun and stand out.

They were a no-nonsense family and unafraid of confrontation—a streak Charles would inherit.

Athleticism also ran in the family. Years later, Sandra McGuire remembered playing with Charcey on the local women's softball team.

Charcey may have been slow in the outfield, but with each swing of the bat, her moon-shot home runs left her opponents slack-jawed.

Not much of the same could be said of Frank Barkley during or after that period in high school. He wasn't that opinionated or nearly as vocal as Charcey, mostly keeping to himself.

"He was just trying to get out of school to graduate and do his life," Raymond Marbury remembered. "He wasn't a scholar or anything like that. He was just kind of a regular guy."

The two would find each other during a turbulent time in the country's history—and the eye of the storm was just down the road.

In the spot where Jefferson Davis was sworn in as president of the Confederacy, George Wallace approached the microphone in the portico of the Alabama state capitol on January 14, 1963, and promised to lawmakers and the throngs of White men standing behind him in approval—part of the 96 percent of voters who catapulted him into the governor's office—to make race not just the basis of government for Alabama, but the foundation of politics in the United States.

"Let us rise to the call of freedom-loving blood that is in us and send our answer to the tyranny that clanks its chains upon the South. In the name of the greatest people that have ever trod this earth, I draw the line in the dust and toss the gauntlet before the feet of tyranny," he told the feverish crowd. "And I say: Segregation today! Segregation tomorrow! Segregation forever!" As Peggy Wallace Kennedy, the governor's daughter, recalled years later Wallace's frothing screed was "probably the most racist speech ever given."

The vulgarity of his vow, one rooted in the Ku Klux Klan, would further fuel the racial tumult in the state, illustrated in images of high-pressure water cannons, police dogs, and a prolonged string of senseless violence against Black people.

This is the turmoil that Charles Wade Barkley was born into.

Charles was just six pounds when he was born on the chilly morning of February 20, 1963. Even at birth, he made history, the first Black baby delivered at Leeds's segregated hospital. Grandfather Adolphus Edwards was a janitor at the hospital and called in a favor so that Charles could be delivered. But from the start, baby Charles was in danger. The baby was suffering from severe anemia, resulting in a full blood transfusion when he was just six weeks old. Charcey would later insist that there was something magical in the blood transfused into her boy.

"My mom used to always joke around—'I have no idea what blood they put in your body,'" he remembered.

In life, he'd later joke about his lighter Black complexion. "I told you," he said to comedian George Lopez, "I'm lighter because I had a slave-owner creeper."

Living in the projects with a newborn son, the couple found themselves young, impoverished, and overmatched, without a real sense of how to make a life for their growing family. Life around them was not easy either. By 1963, Birmingham had cemented itself, in the words of Dr. Martin Luther King Jr., as "probably the most thoroughly segregated city in the United States." The social unrest in Alabama heightened that September, when four members of the KKK bombed the 16th Street Baptist Church in Birmingham, killing four Black girls between the ages of eleven and fourteen and injuring twenty-two others. King would call the heinous act "one of the most vicious and tragic crimes ever perpetrated against humanity."

But the couple had each other, Charcey thought.

That is, until they didn't.

Burdened by the pressures of supporting a young family, Johnnie Mae remembered times of uneasiness between the two and at least one physical incident.

"I know one time he hit her, and I told him that I'd take his wife and baby home with me," Johnnie Mae said years later to ESPN. "And I did."

Frank Barkley left the family in the spring of 1964, moving to Southern California. He remarried and had four children.

"Like me, he was young and untrained, not for skilled work nor for marriage, and he simply couldn't cope with the responsibilities of fatherhood," Charcey recalled of Frank.

Charcey then married Clee Glenn and together they had two sons: Darryl in 1966 and John 1970.

"[Charles] was a father to his younger brothers because he grew up without a father," his grandmother recalled.

"Frank Barkley was one of the few mistakes I've ever made in my life," Charcey said. "The only good thing that came out of it was Charles."

BARKLEY

★ ★ ★

Through the dissolution of Charcey's marriage it was Johnnie Mae Edwards who held the family together. Known affectionately as "the chairman of the board" by those closest to her, Johnnie Mae had an outsized influence on her grandson. "Momma, I know I had Charles, but sometimes I don't know whether he's your child or mine," Charcey would tell her mother. "I'm 100 percent like her," Charles agreed.

She was also the guiding voice the chubby young boy needed early on—an aggressive, strong-willed matriarch who took on all the tough decisions. Johnnie Mae often left Charles's more passive and sensitive mother bewildered.

"With her, what comes up from the gut just about comes out of her mouth," Charcey said of her mother. "So, I guess Charles got that from his granny, too."

Money was tight and times were hard around Russell Heights. Inside a one-story, reddish-brown housing project, the family relied on government assistance. At the dinner table, the menu was cold and far from extravagant, featuring government bologna and cheese sandwiches one night, mayonnaise sandwiches the next. Vegetables were a luxury they could not afford. (Charles never had a taste for vegetables anyway.) So, when the opportunity arose, Charles rarely turned down a decent meal. Adolphus and Johnnie Mae separated and eventually divorced, but the man known as "Little Daddy" remained a present figure in Charles's life on the weekends. Charcey remembered one morning in which Adolphus kept offering Charles more and more eggs for breakfast, and the boy didn't decline.

"After a while, he said, 'I'd better not go any higher because Charles'll eat every egg in the house,'" his mother recalled.

In his grandfathers, young Charles found the kind of mature male voices he lacked without his father around.

"My grandfathers were spectacular," Charles said. "I was probably too immature to understand at the time how necessary they were to a kid's success."

At home, the family did not have much furniture and the boys shared clothes, but they were never hungry. And Charles still could not believe how he was the first kid in his neighborhood to own a pair of Chuck Taylors.

There was no shame about their lifestyle.

"I never had any sense, though, that we were doing without," he said. "There were no luxuries, but we had everything we needed. The holidays were cool because the three of us knew our mother and grandmother were going to find a way to get you one really nice thing you really wanted." Reflecting on his family in his 1994 documentary, *Sir Charles*, he acknowledged, "That's probably the greatest thing that I learned from them, just do whatever it takes to make yourself successful."

Even in the times when Charcey couldn't get her boys the best or most stylish clothes or toys, she knew Charles would be okay doing without.

"He didn't ask for things that other kids had, because we didn't have the money," she said. "I knew he wanted those things. You know how kids are about things that are in style, but he didn't grumble."

With her employment options limited, Charcey worked multiple jobs to stay afloat, mainly at the high school cafeteria and as a housekeeper, cleaning homes in the town's White, middle-class neighborhoods.

To Charles, the other side of town "might as well have been a fantasy island in the middle of the Pacific." His mother, however, thought of the setup a little differently. Charcey recognized early on that she not only had to work hard to get ahead, but she needed to get along with her White employers to survive. She was lucky, she said, as the work wasn't "straining, or demeaning" and she could be her own boss. Charles sometimes joined his mother as she worked, so that he could play inside some of the homes, many of them with spacious rooms and oversized backyards. She'd bring home $15 for a day's work, a decent take at the time.

"Scrubbing people's toilets and floors just to take care of four boys, you know, that's not an easy thing to do," he said. Charcey's fourth boy, Rennie, died during infancy.

Leeds was still largely segregated, but Charcey was treated well by her friendly employers. Charles said he never despised the families his mother worked for, mostly because they treated her as a human and never looked down on her. The admiration shown toward his mother from these White families was eye-opening for young Charles.

"I always respected them for the way they treated my family, almost like members of their own," he said. He added, "That's how I ultimately learned that you shouldn't judge people by their color or race."

Early on, Charles shouldered the responsibilities as the oldest brother. Charcey would often tell him how much she was struggling to provide for her boys and maintain a home of her own. He was the one she could always come to, often speaking to young Charles like an adult. She even called him her "little man."

"If loving and respecting your mother and being proud of her makes you a momma's boy, then that's what I am," Charles said.

Yet his father's absence inevitably would come up, and it bugged him.

"He just couldn't understand why his own father was not around, even though I tried to explain it to him at an early age," his mother remembered. "I didn't want him to hear rumors and whispers from the other kids in the neighborhood."

What she needed from Charles, a father figure to his brothers and a momma's boy to his friends, was help.

In turn, Barkley, a neat freak of a kid who never had to be told to pick up his room, cleaned their house, urging his brothers to follow his lead. He washed and dried everything—well, almost everything.

"I would come home dead tired, and he would have the house superclean," his mother said. "He could clean up the kitchen as good as I could, but he hated to wash dishes. He would wash the floors, the cabinets and sink, but then he would stack all the dirty dishes very neatly in the sink and put a clean towel over them."

Though all the adults in the home worked, they were barely making ends meet. So, they came up with a solution for a side hustle: bootlegging. Alabama's preachers vowed to keep alcohol from public consumption, using county police to conduct raids on any illegal booze. Decades earlier, Alabama implemented a statewide prohibition in 1915 before the nation went dry. Even when Prohibition ended in 1933, the state remained dry for another four years. In the decades that followed, however, bootlegging became a way of life.

"How much money can you make working in a meatpacking factory? Or working as a maid? So, we sold alcohol," Barkley said. "The house was like a casino on the weekend. Guys would come on Friday and drink and gamble until Sunday."

Years later, Charcey remembered how one of Barkley's associates called Johnnie Mae to make sure she was comfortable being outed as a bootlegger in her son's 2002 book, *I May Be Wrong but I Doubt It*. Her reaction: "Why the hell should I be embarrassed?"

"She said, 'Everybody already knows I was a bootlegger,'" Charcey recalled to ESPN. "'The ones reading the book came to the house and bought some whiskey. I did what I had to do to help my child.'"

Right before deciding between ribs and pulled pork, the cashier at Rusty's Bar-B-Q tells me how Charles helped corral a runaway dog scrambling across the parkway. "Just last week, he stopped in the middle of the road and hopped out of his truck to get the dog," she tells me, ringing up my order of ribs and spicy baked beans, wisely advising me to save room for coconut cream pie, a family recipe. "People are still talking about him getting the dog."

It's the end of another sweltering summer in Leeds and the signed photo on the wall of Charles with Rusty Tucker, the proprietor of the best barbecue spot in town, is starting to fade. He first came to the spot for the 2009 Iron Bowl, when he knew no one would be around to distract him from pork and Auburn football.

In the adjoining dining room, Leslie Blair points to the supermarket parking lot next door where she hung out with Charles and their friends in high school. Known as "The Lot," she explains how her dad would drive by several times a night to make sure no one was getting into trouble. She carries a photo album of her friends, flipping through the pages of a smiling Charles, a brother to her from another part of town.

Leeds was almost like growing up in Mayberry. Everybody knew everybody. There was a soda fountain where you got milkshakes and ice cream. Everybody did the church thing on Sundays, and Wednesdays was the youth group night.

Charles's parents were real poor and everything. In the Heights, people talked about how it was such a bad area, but it was just as much the White people as it was the Black people. Later on, Charles tried to get his momma to move, but she wanted to stay over there. Charcey was just a gem. She would tell me about people shooting guns down the street, but she was never scared living over there.

His grandmother, she didn't play with anybody. She was all serious about Charles. I only met her one time before she passed, but she always sat out on the front porch and that school over there was the junior high. When I rode the bus, his grandmother was always on the porch, waving at us every day. Charcey and granny were all about Charles. They just loved him. Charles is like a female Charcey, that's where he gets his outgoing spirit.

He's a big ol' teddy bear. When I first got a divorce, he was calling and checking on me every week—you doing okay?

He's always been my best friend.

A different kind of excitement came in the summer of 1972. Charcey picked up the phone to hear a familiar voice on the other line. It was her ex-husband.

He was coming home to Leeds that summer. He wanted to see Charles. It would be the first time the nine-year-old boy would meet his father, and it couldn't have come sooner.

But instead, that missing love and need for a father would turn into something else: anger. That wrath helped bring Charles toward the game that would change his life.

2

The sleepy small town has come alive to the point that it's now being forced to shut down.

The audience rises from their lawn chairs, cheering the teens in gowns and crowns who toss out beads for homecoming. Riding atop a white and blue Hummer, Greeny, the oversized mascot of the Leeds High Green Wave, throws candy to the hundreds of children and families pleading for his attention along Parkway Drive. The band's rendition of the *SportsCenter* theme bounces off the buildings, each of which are flying US flags. Behind Greeny, Ford pickup trucks and Jeep Wranglers escort the young women who make up the homecoming court, fire trucks carrying cheerleaders and the Leeds High football team.

It doesn't matter that it's ninety-three degrees in early October or that the team is having a rough start to the season. Residents and alums transform Parkway Drive into a celebratory tailgate filled with pompoms, food trucks, and soaring footballs tossed in the street.

At the law firm across the street is Lee Barnes Sr., a longtime friend of Charcey's who would travel with her around the state.

"We were in Mobile for a conference on a dinner break at Wintzell's Oyster House, and the waitress somehow dumped Charcey's salad in her purse. We joked, asking her if she needed a longer fork to eat her salad," Barnes said. "Instead of getting upset, she was gracious and nice to the lady. That's how Charcey was, a beautiful person."

Charcey thought it was important for her firstborn to know the father who abandoned him. Frank would call to speak with Charles from time to time, which excited the young boy. They picked up right where they left off.

"I promised him a lot of things. I promised to call him a lot of times," Frank said. "He looked forward to these things, and when I didn't do it he just [got] mad about it."

Any excitement Charles had in speaking to his father would soon change once the calls ended.

"As long as I was talking to him I was content. On the phone he was my father. He was what he was supposed to be. But as soon as we hung up, it was like everything went quiet, like I was suddenly alone," Charles explained in *Outrageous!* "After a while, he didn't call very often. I didn't have anything to say to him anyway."

Now Charles desperately wanted to know more about the man who left his family behind. *Why did he leave? Did he not want to be his father?*

Frank visited the family in Leeds and then invited Charles to join him for the summer in Los Angeles. Charcey hoped the invitation might signal a shift toward more support from Frank, both emotionally and financially.

"It wasn't long before Charles and I both realized that it was a wasted visit," Charcey said. "Charles took his first plane ride for the visit, but he didn't enjoy himself one bit... Over the next few years, his dad sent me $10 to $12 on a couple of occasions.

"When Charles got home, he was more hurt and upset than I had ever seen him in his life. Lord forgive me, but I think if I could have gotten my hands on Frank that night, I think I could've killed him." She added, "Charles said he would never ask his father for anything else as long as he lived. He never did."

Barkley could not escape the emptiness of not having a father. "When I was young, I would see other kids with their fathers and felt empty, like I was being cheated," Charles said in 1992. "I missed his companionship. I missed having an older friend."

The disappointment with his dad came at a time when Charles was still adjusting to life at school with White students.

When it came to homecoming, Leeds had two young women atop the throne each year: the traditional homecoming queen from the White school and a "basketball queen" from the Black community, specifically Russell Heights. It was a tradition that continued into the '90s.

"That was one way we had representation for both Black and White," said Margaret Little. "Nobody had a problem with that. The kids thought it was fair. We had parents who thought it was okay, and the teachers didn't mind it either. Everyone just got along."

The same could not be said for the rest of Jefferson County. In a 1971 order, Judge Sam C. Pointer allowed White communities to secede from districts placed under school desegregation orders. It came years after high school student Linda Stout, the daughter of the head of the local chapter of the NAACP, wanted to leave her all-Black school for an all-White one. In Pointer's order, the judge also forced the White communities in Jefferson County to bus in Black children from other areas so that there was a ratio of at least one Black child for every three White children in the newly formed school district. A Supreme Court ruling in 1972 would reaffirm that precedent. Significant demographic shifts in the population, namely the spike in Black communities, have created other school desegregation questions connected to Pointer's order for the county and other parts of the state in recent years.

"When it came to mixing the Blacks and Whites, well, everyone was very leery of each other," Charles recalled. "When they integrated the all-White Leeds Elementary School when I was young, very few Black families had the guts to send their kids there rather than to the all-Black school that all of us had been attending—even though everyone knew that the kids at Leeds Elementary were getting a better education."

Charcey felt that Leeds Elementary had better resources, better books, better everything. She didn't think twice.

By the time Charles entered the first grade in early 1970, he was among the first Black students to integrate the elementary school. Johnnie Mae walked him to school each morning. Uncertain of what might happen, she carried a pistol in her purse in case the situation called for it.

The move proved to be something of an adjustment for Charles. He found himself between two worlds. "It wasn't easy for us," Charles said. "We took heat from some of the White kids at school, then caught more shit from the Black kids back home in the neighborhood who said we must have thought we were too good to attend the Black school."

Charles needed a distraction. He wouldn't have to go far to find it.

The Leeds Civic Center is an unremarkable place. There are tennis courts and baseball fields covered in dead grass along Park Drive. Gravel and dirt roads push up against the woods that surround the miniature fieldhouse. The equipment and facility are lackluster.

Yet the civic center, with its chipped-paint cement walls and scratched hardwood floor, was where Charles learned to play the game of basketball.

Wanting to keep her son out of trouble, Charcey scrounged together $30 to purchase a membership to the civic center. The White kids at Leeds Elementary, Charles's new friends, would often fill the place after school and on the weekends. You rarely saw a Black child there at the time. Soon, Charles was on his first team, joining two other Black kids among an otherwise all-White squad.

"It was a big sacrifice for me, but Charles was eight years old and he was a good kid," his mother said of the membership.

The financial burden would become more pronounced when Clee Glenn, Charcey's second husband, died in a car accident at the age of twenty-six. Charles was nine.

Back on the court, Charles was not very good. He was a five-foot-nothing dribble-heavy point guard—a black hole of a player who would jack up shots from midcourt if given the chance.

And before long, the boy's insatiable appetite for breakfast, lunch (and maybe second lunch), dinner (and even second dinner), and dessert helped round out Charles.

"He was on the chubby side, and he was just about as tall as he was chubby," Johnnie Mae said. "Kids used to pick at him."

What he lacked in a jump shot, defense, athleticism, and overall skill he made up for with his mouth.

"If something came up, he was honest about it," childhood friend Travis Abernathy said to *USA Today*. "He would tell us when we need a bath, anything. Somebody else would be thinking that person needed a bath. He would actually tell them." Abernathy said, "He used to talk so much, we used to call him Ali."

Abernathy, who lived nearby, had vivid memories of Charles, around age eight or nine, telling anyone within earshot that he was "going to play pro ball."

The worn-in baseball field across the street is a stone's throw away from Charles's boyhood home. Walk another hundred yards and you'll see the pavement is torn up, and the heat in the summer makes staying out there for more than a few minutes a challenge.

It's on these dilapidated courts where the boy known by his friends as Wade honed his flawed but promising game.

Before the rebounds came the half-court shots. There were a lot of them.

"That was my 'rep' among the players," Charles said. "I'd come across half-court and just throw it up. That's not the best way to help your popularity."

When Victor Campbell first heard from Travis Abernathy about the kid who would take almost all of his shots from half-court, he knew he had to meet him. "I thought that was unbelievable," Campbell said. "I was like, 'Nah, man, that can't be true.' But he would just throw it up from there every time."

With a wide grin and full afro, Campbell had a similar energy to young Charles. Like Charles, Campbell lost a parent at a young age—his mother died when he was four—and was mostly raised by his grandparents. They'd soon be in the same homeroom in the fourth grade at Leeds Elementary, and Campbell would let the boy he called

Wade do most of the talking. They shared a love of basketball, even making an elementary school all-star team.

When they were ten, they traveled with their teammates to Montgomery for an all-star exhibition, Campbell said. They might have been only one hundred miles away, but staying in a hotel for a night in 1973 felt like the kind of foreign luxury enjoyed by a class of people who felt much further away from their impoverished reality.

Yet the racial tension that they were largely shielded from in Leeds was more evident in Montgomery. On their way there, Campbell remembered a parent overseeing the trip telling the boys on the mixed team that they had to go to the back of the bus. It was the first time Campbell had been the focus of the racism that had sadly come to be expected throughout the state.

"The guy in charge of taking us to Montgomery told us we had to sit in the back," Campbell said. "I didn't understand, and never experienced, racism or why we had to sit in the back. I didn't understand it at the time."

By the time Charles got to Leeds Junior High School in the mid '70s, he had mostly played with White players and been coached by White fathers. That was about to change with Wallace Honeycutt, his first real basketball coach.

"The basketball coach was Black, which I thought would be good for Charles after being at a predominantly White elementary school," Charcey said.

A coach at an all-Black school in Graysville, Wallace Honeycutt was transferred to Leeds after Alden High was converted to an elementary school during integration. He was the only coach at the school for any sport when he was first hired. The structured way of life around Leeds left Honeycutt, who lived eighteen miles away and was relatively disconnected from the town, feeling that he didn't belong.

"I just didn't like it," he said. "I kind of resented it."

His frustration toward Leeds began to change once he got to know the kids. The bachelor would stay after school and keep the gym open for a couple extra hours. He wasn't getting paid to do so, but it didn't matter. He started an informal program for kids between the ages of six and twelve to come play. It didn't take long before adults would come by to volunteer, with Honeycutt organizing games for the kids to play each other.

A hands-on coach, Honeycutt pushed his players, both figuratively and literally. Campbell remembered days in which Honeycutt chased them down with brooms to get them to push the ball faster. His style was fast-paced and aggressive.

The player who was there more than anyone else was Charles, who lived just a half block away from the school. The boy was so wide that Honeycutt was surprised that he hadn't even hit the sixth grade yet. Charles was a gym rat, wanting to stay and work on his game with Honeycutt, who accommodated him as long as the boy didn't cut classes. His handles were good enough, but the coach converted Charles to a role on the low block, teaching him how to score underneath the hoop, as well as a selection of reversal moves to get past his overmatched defender.

"You don't have that many kids to pull from," Honeycutt once said. "So, if you see a kid with size and potential, you start working on him right away. 'Cause you're gonna need him."

While Charles picked up on Honeycutt's up-tempo style, it didn't stop him from repeatedly inquiring about the meaning behind the drills. *Why do you want me to do this? What's the purpose? What will I get out of this?* Charles's pushback got him on Honeycutt's bad side.

"I would tell him all the time to shut his mouth," he said, laughing. "He had an idea that once he learned how to play basketball, he could tell every kid on his team what to do—you go there, I'll go here. I told him that was my job, and that most of the time he didn't know what he was talking about anyway."

As Charles would find out, Honeycutt wasn't afraid to bench him whenever he started shooting from midcourt. But when it came to the games, Honeycutt needed every bit of Charles's dramatic flair to win at a high level. In the final seconds of a tie game in Pinson, in which his undefeated junior high team was playing a squad of high school freshmen, Charles wanted the ball.

"He was telling the team out on the floor to get him the ball and he'd go up and shoot," Honeycutt said.

After a tipped inbounds pass, Charles was the first to the ball and, much like he had done throughout his childhood, he launched it from a different area code.

"He threw the ball up from almost half-court when the buzzer went off," he noted. "And it went in and we won the game. He kept us undefeated."

Honeycutt kept things together in the summertime. Nearly every day, he'd drive about thirty-five minutes east from Adamsville to organize pickup games and weekend activities for the kids in hope of keeping them occupied.

"Mr. Honeycutt didn't belong to the neighborhood, but he was so instrumental in our era, because he helped a lot of children stay out of the streets and kept them from doing stupid stuff," said Berderia Spence, one of Charles's childhood friends.

The results from those years spoke for themselves. Seasons of thirty or more wins were regular. When Honeycutt took Charles and a busload of his teammates to play more prestigious basketball powers in Birmingham, the days would regularly end with the boys singing to celebrate another victory.

"We showed them what Leeds was made of," Honeycutt said.

The incentive for winning remained the same among the junior high players: Big Macs at McDonald's. No one subscribed to this more than Charles, who wouldn't let the ongoing taunts of being short and round stop him from snacking.

Charles and the others didn't have a lot of spending money, so Honeycutt told whoever didn't have cash to come to him privately and he'd cover them. He never wanted a child to go hungry as their teammates enjoyed celebratory Chicken McNuggets.

Even though the coach encouraged a spending limit for how much each player should buy, Charles's hunger always won out.

"I can tell you he had an appetite," Honeycutt recalled. "If he had money, whenever the bus stopped he'd be the first one in line at McDonald's. He would not just order one but two or three burgers, French fries, and drinks. We'd also stop at Wendy's and a pizza place." He added: "It didn't matter where we stopped, he was eating it."

Athletic success in junior high came naturally for Charles, and the trust between him and Coach Honeycutt deepened. The relationship resonated the most during Honeycutt's weekly team pep talks.

"I would always tell them that whatever they want to go out for, they should always have a plan B," Honeycutt said. "I didn't want them to be someone who was living under the freeway."

In doing so, Charles got a message he had yet to receive from an adult to that point in his life: the coach wasn't worried about him. Why? He knew young Charles was going to be successful.

The voice on the other end of the phone is older now, but a mere mention of his most decorated pupil from nearly a half century ago injects life into Wallace Honeycutt.

I called him my son. It was like a father-son relationship.

He was always larger than the rest of the kids. He was stouter. He always had a bald head. I remember the first time I saw him I asked him why he didn't have any hair.

He was about four feet tall in the sixth grade and after that he began to grow. As he grew, the weight came with it. He could just jump, too. He was such a good rebounder. It was very seldom that I took him out, but he would let you know when he was tired. He would always run his mouth. He was a great talker.

Charles was a good kid back at home, following strict orders from his mom and granny: get home before dark or you're going to get your butt whipped. But that didn't stop him from excelling as one of the town's best petty thieves. In fact, he was thriving.

Bored out of his mind, Charles would steal candy, pens, and other small items from the stores downtown. The next step up from pens? Obviously, it was cakes.

Charles got good at the game. Every Sunday at around ten or eleven at night, he and a group of like-minded friends waited for the delivery trucks to drop off boxed cakes in front of the Winn-Dixie. Sitting on a curb nearby the store, Charles would gorge a couple cakes by himself before taking some home. A boy could only eat government bologna and cheese for so long.

Charles's first interaction with police was over stolen cake.

"Kids do stupid things late at night," said Ricky Moore, who was among the group of cake thieves.

About a month into the new Sunday routine, police got wind of the cake bandits of Leeds, and wanted to see where all the baked goods were going. One night, the boys, upset with the cake selection, started throwing the cakes at each other. Soon, cakes were whizzing across the parking lot, the boys driving grocery carts as bumper cars, clanging into one another. When one of the grocery carts crashed into one of the store's windows and set off the alarm, it triggered a high-speed police chase for several blocks, forcing Charles into the woods.

Charcey's son was running for his life. The police went off-road, driving down a narrow trail in the woods in pursuit of the cake boys.

"I could hear the cops saying, 'Freeze!'" Charles remembered, "and we were crawling on the ground. I probably crawled about 100 yards on my knees in the woods. It scared the hell out of me, to be honest with you."

Crawling was not going to do it. He had to run. It was so dark, and Barkley was going so fast, that he couldn't see his feet. Then, he ran face-first into a tree.

"When I hit the ground, I thought I was dead," Barkley said.

He was more dazed than dead. The cops might have abandoned their search, but the chase changed Barkley in more ways than one. He was scared straight, terrified that the cops were bearing down on him. Charles and the other boys dodged a bullet with the cops, but the court of public opinion among their peers was a different story.

"When classmates found out about what happened, they called us the Cake Bandits. Even our teachers made fun of us," Moore remembers with a laugh. "But they didn't have any proof."

"It was only a matter of time before my petty thievery turned into something more serious," Charles said. "From that point on I said, 'I've got to find something else to do.'"

The question remained if there was ever going to be room on the high school team in Leeds for a short and fat kid with a big mouth. It would take years before Charles would get his answer.

3

As Charles Barkley goes up to pull down a one-handed rebound, he does so with white bird shit covering his head, hands, and jersey.

Next to an empty parking lot, a replica of the statue erected for him at Auburn University stands proudly in front of Leeds High School. Charles, with a full head of hair, jumps from the exploding floorboards of the court. The statue is also skinny, something the man himself likes to loudly point out in public settings.

A few blocks away sits the Jerry N. Oxford Gymnasium, the former home of the Green Wave basketball team. The dimly lit auxiliary court is a relic of American high schools of the '70s and '80s, with a parquet floor and decades of gym musk seeped into the wooden bleachers. The floor reads, "Home of Charles Barkley."

Rayford Williams can't even begin to estimate how many millions Charles has given to the high school over the years, donating no less than a projected $100,000 each year to various causes, he said. Williams, the high school principal who coached one of Charles's nieces, talks about Charles paying for new shoes and equipment for the basketball teams, refurbishing the court and setting up a four-hour, online educational program on African American history.

It's almost as if he's the role model he didn't intend to become.

The incident with the cops shook Charles, who knew he had to do right by his family and friends. Though life could be difficult in Russell Heights, he credited his newfound straight-and-narrow approach to the families struggling alongside them in the neighborhood.

"The community feeling in the projects probably kept me from hanging with the wrong crowd. Everybody knew everybody else's kids, and they all looked after one another when someone had to work or be away from home," Charles recalled. "But make no mistake: the projects were also someplace you wanted to leave."

His way out, he thought, was through basketball. The fat point guard recognized he had to get stronger. He had grown from around five feet to five-foot-seven, but he was still wide and stocky, and couldn't stay away from free McDonald's burgers whenever the opportunity arose.

When he asked his mom to buy him a jump rope, Charcey swore her son was going to pass out during the sweltering ninety-degree days.

"I thought he was going to jump that rope to death," she said.

His focus had sharpened around the time the former cake thief narrowly escaped police custody. It was now all basketball, all the time. Still trying to gain an edge, he turned to an unlikely structure for his training.

A fence surrounded his family's home. Charles took a standing start and propelled himself over it. As his feet hit the ground, an unfamiliar high came over him. It looked impressive, but it wasn't hard, at least not for him. Charles didn't know it at the time, but jumping over a fence would be the exercise that eventually differentiated him from his peers on the court.

"He'd jump from one side to the other—I mean flat-footed," Johnnie Mae said. "And he'd do it over and over again, maybe fifteen or twenty times. Then he'd rest and do it again. He did that just about every day."

Honeycutt remembered the day he got a call from his pupil. The junior high coach had a hard time believing that Charles could now dunk the ball.

"I said, 'I bet you a soda you can't,'" said Honeycutt, noting how Charles knew there was a soda machine in the lobby of the gym. "He got in the middle of the floor after school and he dunked the ball. He turned around and asked me, 'How do you like that?!' Of course, I smiled."

In the empty gym, Honeycutt warned him against dunking or letting anyone know he could. The coach thought the short eighth grader was too young to be slamming the ball, urging him to save his long-term health, even if it looked cool.

"He dunked it without anybody knowing it," Honeycutt said.

Charles didn't lose his "basketball virginity" until high school. "To me, that dunk was the moment when I reached manhood."

By the time Charles started at Leeds High School in the fall of 1977, he was still trying to find his place.

Though he was bright, academics were not a priority for Charles. He may have been a self-described math whiz, even tutoring some of his classmates. But his performance in school was, he described, "probably the most disappointing thing about my life."

"As a student, I was a loser," he said. "In high school, I did just enough to get by in the classroom. I never pushed myself academically."

Jeff Falletta, the class president, said Charles found himself the target of bullying in the first couple of years at Leeds High. It got so bad a couple times that Charcey had to pull the crying teen out of school early.

To take his mind off the uneasiness of early high school, he leaned on basketball. He found, however, that whatever talent he had in junior high was not going to cut it under Billy Coupland.

A former college basketball player at Birmingham Southern, Coupland wasn't one to cuss or fuss at you if you screwed up. In fact, the mild-mannered coach didn't say much at all, preferring to let the culture he had built at Leeds High speak for itself.

Coupland, who accepted the job at Leeds after teaching at a junior high while working on his master's, came to the program with a basic version of UCLA's high-post offense under John Wooden. Coupland didn't need much else, really, as he'd usually find a way to get the best player the ball at all times.

"He didn't go overboard with running fancy plays or defenses, and he didn't try to change guys' games to the way he wanted them to play," Charles remembered. "Coach Coupland just gave us the ball, drew up a few plays, and said, 'Fellas, it's yours.'"

He was not strict by any means, but Coupland had his own form of discipline. There was an understanding among the players that if you were to dunk during warmups, he'd make you do ten pushups right there and then. You were to not show up your opponents, even if you had the talent. Punctuality was a pillar, too, which meant you'd get left behind if you were a minute late.

"It didn't matter if it was Charles or anyone, he would leave me and my friends off the bus," teammate Brent Reese said. "Sometimes, we'd be running across town to catch the bus, and knew when he had to come across a red light to hopefully let us on."

He went against a culture in the high school athletics system that had some coaches valuing an athlete's race over their talent, Victor Campbell said. The no-nonsense style was part of why the players loved him. It also put Charles in Coupland's crosshairs. Despite growing another three inches, Charles was still nothing more than a chunky shoot-first point guard who could at least try to post up much taller defenders down low.

"It was just hard for him to compete," Coupland said. "Plus, his shot in high school wasn't that good."

That uneven mix of size and style didn't work for Charles in his first two years, and he was cut from the varsity team both times, spending his first couple years on JV.

"There's really not much use for a 5-10 fat point guard," Charles realized.

Getting cut twice was a blow to Charles's confidence. His dreams of playing in the NBA had failed to even launch. At home, the man of the house felt as if he was letting down his mother and grandmother.

When Charles relayed the message to Honeycutt that he wasn't going to play in high school, and was thinking about getting into wrestling or throwing the shot put, his junior high coach thought that was impossible.

"I said, 'No, you can't do that, you have a future,'" Honeycutt recalled. "I don't think he tried to really make the team until we got on his case."

Rejection left Charles uncomfortable. Much like he had done with Honeycutt, Charles gravitated toward Coupland, a basketball lifer, constantly picking the brain of a guy he wanted so desperately to please.

"He wanted to be around Coach Coupland all the time. He would push him," Campbell observed. "It had gotten to the point where he would tell Wade to go away and leave him alone."

To no one's surprise, Wade didn't go away. Instead, he was picking up some stuff from his peers. There was Travis Abernathy, his cousin and friend, a six-foot-four scoring guard who skipped JV as a freshman and enjoyed success as the top dog on the varsity team. Forward Bernard Lockhart had the silkiest jump he had seen to that point. But it was Moore and his elite-level rebounding that most caught his attention for how he could make the most immediate impact.

"I realized the only way I was going to get the ball was get rebounds," he said.

That realization was coupled with an ultimatum from the head coach in 1979 heading into the summer before Charles's junior year.

"I told him he wouldn't make the varsity unless he grew," Coupland said.

It was the summer before his junior year, and the sixteen-year-old had dedicated himself solely to the game, jumping rope and fences for hours on end as well as playing pickup games at Russell Heights. Each time he jumped, he had Coupland's words in his ear: get taller or jump higher or you'll never make it.

After hours, Barkley walked down the street to the same tattered basketball court where he first started playing when he was younger. If he had to do this, he had to get better on his own, without any distractions deep into those Leeds summer nights. Friends? Maybe later. Girls? Yeah right. Anything else not related to basketball or family? Forget it.

Soon, Charcey and Johnnie Mae were concerned, yet proud, about their boy making a thoughtful decision on not just the volume of his training but also its timing to maximize his quest.

"He never liked to go down there during the day when all of the other kids were there and people were standing around watching," his mother said. "He waited until night, after everybody had gone home, and he would play by himself for hours."

To Charcey, her eldest's commitment to the game showed a level of determination she had been waiting to witness from her boy.

"He became obsessed with basketball," she said. "That's all he did the whole summer. He'd run and run and run."

Sometime that summer, Charles traveled back to California to see his father. When he returned to Leeds, his body was changing in ways he couldn't imagine.

Leslie Blair was standing in line when she ran into her best friend, who she says, "grew overnight."

"I was like, 'What the hell happened to you?'" Blair recalled. "He was like, 'What do you mean?' I'm like, 'You're ten feet tall!' I felt like a midget next to him."

Berderia Spence heard over and over how badly the five-foot-ten Charles wanted to be on the varsity team, and she mostly brushed it aside. But this was different: he stood now at around six-foot-two.

At the high school, all Coupland could do was smile about how Charles took his ultimatum to heart.

"How's that for coaching?" Coupland joked.

With that, Charles had finally made it to varsity.

The first time Margaret Little laid eyes on young Charles, she thought he was a typical ninth grader. Little, a guidance counselor at the school for years, would meet with underclassmen to introduce herself and go over what they had in mind for high school and plans for once they graduated. But when she met with him, Little learned that he hadn't taken, or planned to take, any college prep classes. He expressed to her that he didn't think college was for him. His lack of algebra or chemistry credits worried her, especially when it came to his future.

Yet the teen thought nothing of it.

"I remember Charles specifically saying when I came in, 'I'm not going to raise my kids on welfare,'" Little said. "He just didn't see himself going to college."

Even when he finally made the varsity team, Charles's footprint at the school through his first three years was barely noticeable. Thumbing through the yearbooks, Charles's photo isn't posted with the JV for his freshman or sophomore seasons. He's not in any other clubs or groups, and isn't listed anywhere else throughout. His sophomore photo was used for his junior year portrait. In the junior year group photo with the class of 1981, the black-and-white image in front of the school shows Charles, towering over his classmates following his growth spurt, giving a half smile and joining a couple hundred of his classmates in squinting at the camera.

"He was not like the most popular guy," said Paige Phillips Parnell, who was a year older and was eventually crowned Miss Alabama 1980. "But you could tell there was something about him."

His mother remembered him being popular among his female peers—"The girls were on him like white on rice"—but that the momma's boy couldn't care less. In an interview many years later with *Real Sports with Bryant Gumbel*, Charcey recalled how "some of the kids used to call him sissified," wondering why the boy was so quiet and shy and not more into girls. There was still some mystery to Charles. The booming personality was reserved for those closest to him.

Amy Shorter, his first girlfriend, was among that group. A freshman when he was a junior, Shorter knew the boy she called Wade from growing up around her aunt, who, like Johnnie Mae, was a beautician on the weekends. They weren't officially introduced to one another until high school, when they got to know each other through mutual friends. She was drawn to the boy who talked of basketball, but was mostly "really, really shy" whenever he'd walk her to class and her locker. Shorter brushed off the teasing from her godbrothers over dating Wade Barkley, whom they referred to as "the little waterhead boy."

"They used to tell me, 'That boy can't walk straight. Every time he straightened his head he would fall over.' But I told them I liked him a lot," Shorter said. "He used to hold my books, and we had that kind of puppy love."

She would tease him about how well he cleaned his own house and how his grab-bag fashion style had him closing his eyes to pick a shirt to wear that day. He talked about basketball a lot, but Shorter still didn't know if he was any good. Wade encouraged her to join the women's team so they could ride the same bus to and from the games. After she finished her games, he would meet her with a Hardee's roast beef sandwich and a strawberry milkshake, which made her fall for him even more.

Whatever it was that intrigued his peers was about to become more transparent. It took another player's fall for Charles to get a real look.

For someone who eventually would exhibit some bad practice habits, Charles was a coach's dream in high school. If you gave him the attention, he'd bust his ass to make whatever you asked of him work.

"Charles was always a hard worker," Coupland said. "If you showed him something, he'd go work on it until he got it down right. That has something to do with who raised him and where he grew up."

Later into high school, Charles was feeling himself. He could no longer hold back on the physical gifts that started manifesting as early as junior high.

"Everybody was like, 'Hey, come down to the gym, Charles Barkley can touch the rim and slam a basketball,'" remembered Todd Burkhalter, one of his teammates. "I thought, there's no way Charles Barkley can dunk a basketball. He's six foot."

His athleticism alone wasn't good enough to crack the starting lineup, and Charles was just another guy on a squad brimming with talent.

Charles and teammates saw Austin Sanders as a legitimate Division I prospect, who averaged about 21 points a game and was one of the best players on the team.

Coupland's team was hitting new heights during the 1979–80 season, blowing out teams every week. With Abernathy leading the way with his shooting, Sanders was the perfect scoring complement on the other side of the floor. Mix in Ricky Moore pulling down every board and big man Gary Clark jumping out of the gym at a moment's notice, and you were in for a long night.

But Sanders played with an attitude that could be detrimental at times, Charles recalled in his autobiography. That culminated one night, when Sanders and Coupland got into a yelling match at half-time. Coupland, whose squad was undefeated at that point, believed any of his players could start for any other team, and wanted to play guys he thought could benefit from starting against opponents who weren't as good. Sanders didn't like not starting and let the coach know about it, Campbell remembered.

Charles and the others thought their teammate was going to the bathroom to cool off. Instead, he had his clothes on and told them he had quit the team before the start of the third quarter, Charles said.

"Just like that, he was gone. Everyone sat there stunned, including the coach," Charles described. "After a few moments, Coach Coupland turned to me and said, 'Charles you're starting.' Suddenly, *I* needed to go to the bathroom."

Coming off the best year in school history, which ended in defeat at the 3A state title game, the Green Wave wanted to finish what they started. Charles got into foul trouble in the title game in Tuscaloosa, and the team couldn't overcome Wetumpka, losing 74–66.

To make the jump from runner-up to state champion, they would have to lean more on their rising senior, who averaged 13 points and 11 rebounds the previous season. It didn't hurt that he grew another couple inches and now stood at six-foot-four. The group that had grown up playing with each other since junior high—Charles, Abernathy, Campbell, Reese, Burkhalter, Pep Mock, Thomas McDonald, and Stanley Mink—was ready to plant their flag as the best in Leeds history and the top team in Alabama.

On a team already loaded with gunners and scorers, Charles knew again that the only way he was going to get the ball was to clean up everyone's mess.

"Going into my senior year, I wanted to get 20 rebounds a night. That was my goal," he said.

The team's confidence in Charles was crystallized one day when the teammates were playing pickup during an open gym run at the high school. In a down moment in between games, Charles jumped flatfooted from underneath the hoop and touched the top of the square on the backboard, eleven and a half feet from the ground. The nonchalant leap left his teammates dumbfounded.

"I don't think any of us knew how to respond," Reese noted. "We were just playing around the gym, and he jumped up and touched the top of the square. All of us were like, what did he just do?"

The increased confidence was apparent to Moore, who would come back to Leeds to see the team after he graduated. This Charles was different than the one who looked up to him when he wasn't playing. Moore had known Charles long enough to figure out the effect of not having his father around was having on his mentee.

"I guess he had that anger for not having a father figure in his life, and he knew something had to happen," Moore said. "He knew God had something for him."

What God had in store for him in December 1980 wasn't just something. It was a matchup against a high school phenom who was one of the most highly recruited players in the nation.

Standing at nearly six-foot-ten and weighing 242 pounds, Bobby Lee Hurt was the bruising, chiseled standard for S.R. Butler High School in Huntsville and the rest of the state in the late '70s and early '80s, gaining attention when he was still at Westlawn Middle School. By the end of his sophomore year, he was named MVP of the 4A state tournament in a losing effort.

Everywhere they went, the Rebels' games were sold out, fans curious as to how the defensive force called Bobby Lee Hurt would single-handedly influence games with a rare combination of strength and speed.

Averaging 20 points and 13 rebounds a game on 69 percent shooting, Hurt, with a "thousand-watt smile" that reminded some of Magic Johnson, was a wanted man. Growing up with a mechanic for a father and a homemaker for a mother, Hurt basked in the attention and chance at a free education. And he'd do it all by playing roughly half of a game for the state's most dominant team.

"I was as tall as a tree, and the coach would say, 'Throw it up and he'll grab it up and slam it down. Just throw it to Bobby Lee, he'll go and get it,'" Hurt said. "It was that simple."

But alleged recruiting violations would soon follow Hurt throughout high school and college.

In a series of stories published in the *Birmingham Post-Herald*, Hurt was accused of being paid to play at Butler after threatening to transfer and signing a letter of intent to play at the University of Alabama because he was under financial pressure from a Crimson Tide fan who he cosigned an automobile loan for between $500 and $600.

Paul Finebaum, the reporter at the *Post-Herald* on the series who would later become one of ESPN's most recognizable college football personalities, reported that Hurt took cash from vending machines at Butler High for two years, grouped in bills ranging from $5 to $50, and that $1,100 in home basketball receipts was taken to help pay for some of Hurt's dental fees.

Hurt has repeatedly denied all the allegations and ended up suing the newspaper in an unsuccessful $800,000 libel lawsuit, but the questions surrounding his recruitment remained.

By the time of a Christmas tournament outside of Birmingham, Leeds and Butler were on a collision course set for Minor High School. Everyone on the Green Wave knew about Butler and Hurt, the undefeated ass kickers from Huntsville. No one on the Rebels knew about Leeds and Charles, the unbeaten enigma of a team from the hick town.

Knowing he'd be matched up with Hurt, Charles, a relative unknown nearing 300 pounds, understood that if he "was ever going to have an opportunity to earn a college scholarship, this was it." And Charles was feeling some relatable queasiness leading up to the Christmas tournament game.

"I was scared, intimidated by the prospect of playing Bobby Lee Hurt," Charles recalled in *Outrageous!* "The realization of the magnitude of the encounter was almost too much to bear. I damn near threw up."

Coupland, a disciple of John Wooden's teachings, wasn't changing the game plan for their high-profile opponent: they were running the "UCLA High Post Offense" to take advantage of Charles's passing and shooting and playing man-to-man defense. Playing Hurt was an in-game tutoring session from a McDonald's and Parade All-American.

"I tried to stop him and learn at the same time," Charles said. "He's such a good player that I couldn't stop him all the time."

But those sitting in the stands that day saw something different. On Hurt's first shot, Charles blocked the star recruit.

He did the same thing for the second.

And the third.

And the fourth.

By the end of the game, an upset win for Leeds, Charles outclassed Hurt. The chunky center, en route to MVP honors for the tournament, finished with an eye-opening 25 points, with about 14 of those coming on dunks, and 20 rebounds against one of the nation's best.

"Barkley ate his lunch," Moore remembered. "He just dominated this guy. Barkley had, like, air shocks in his shoes."

Bobby Lee Hurt is a hard man to track down. When I do find the man who is partially responsible for Charles's breakout game, he points to how he bounced back, especially in a state tournament game in which he scored 32 points, with 20 of those on dunks, and pulled down 16 rebounds. Yet for all his triumphs as a high school star in Alabama, it's the game against Charles that keeps coming up forty years later.

That game kind of paved the way for Charles. That particular game was probably the turning point in his career.

I had never heard of Leeds, Alabama. I had no idea about it. Later on, it meant Charles Barkley. But you really didn't know Charles Barkley or Leeds High School. We kind of heard about this team in Birmingham who has a great player. We watched a couple films on him and he was definitely an exciting player to watch.

The thing about him was he didn't say much. I think he came ready to play.

I had heard Charles over the years mention how I was one of the toughest and most difficult players to play against him. And I can echo that for Charles. His butt was so big, it was just so hard to get around him. He could get off the ground in a heartbeat. When he caught the ball, he could create a major problem—and he did.

He did a lot of gorilla dunks. It was nothing fancy—he would catch them off the rim and slam it down.. If you didn't box him out, he was going to slam it all over you.

Most people thought he was the standout in that game, because they didn't expect him to play that great until he played against me. That's when college scouts started to watch him like, "Oh man, who is this guy?"

I think the game was a plus for the both of us. I really think it was a great advantage for Charles because it helped put him on the map. He had a great game and played well, so I give Charles all of the props.

Sitting in the stands that night with the college coaches and scouts was Jack Doss, the head coach of Birmingham's Hayes High School who was there to scout Butler.

The coach came away from that December night in Birmingham with an unlikely takeaway.

"That was the time that the world knew about Charles Barkley," Doss said.

4

The shrine to Charles inside the Jonathan Bass House Museum is across the hallway from the memorial for those in the area who served for the Confederate States of America.

The historical landmark, which was the home of a lifelong resident who fought for the Confederacy in the 1860s, sits on the side of the old stagecoach road to honor the veterans and early settlers who hailed from the "City of Valor." There, you see photos of the old White men from the area who served as captains, commanding officers, and soldiers for the Confederate Army. They are remembered with other veterans, from World War I to the Iraq War. The other side of the home takes on a different tone, with a Nike poster of Charles holding a rim ripped off from a basket. Below it is a white basketball emblazoned with his name and two matching framed jerseys—one of the 1992 Dream Team and the other from high school.

Deeply Rooted in Leeds' Heritage And Never to Be Forgotten. Thanks for the Memories!

Down the road, Macy Vandergrift and Molly Rutledge take refuge from the brutal humidity after the homecoming parade at Leeds First United Methodist Church. Separated by a dozen years, the Leeds

High alums have little in common, but both the teacher and aspiring educator are grateful to Charles for helping them pay for their college. Set up in the mid-nineties, the Charles Barkley Foundation, overseen by Charcey and Johnnie Mae before it was handed off to Glenn Guthrie, has awarded hundreds of Leeds High School students with millions of dollars in college scholarship money. It didn't matter if you were the valedictorian or getting by with a 2.5 GPA, you were going to get something from the renewable program, which gives out anywhere between $50,000 to $100,000 annually.

"Charcey and granny would put Charles on the cell phone during our meetings, and he would say, 'Mom, I just want to give this money,'" said Lisa Hudson, the high school counselor who helped oversee the scholarship program for decades. "Charcey would say to the kids, 'Charles wants to help and will continue to help as long as you go to college, but don't go and party this money away and expect more next year.'"

Years after her brother relentlessly followed the star around town for an autograph, Rutledge couldn't get over the computer lab Charles donated to the school.

"If it wasn't for him, my student loan debt would have been way, way more than what it was," said Rutledge, a second grade teacher with the Leeds City Schools district. "But he believed in me."

Vandergrift doubts she would have been able to go to college without the help of the Barkley scholarship. Raised by a single mom who went to school with Charles, Vandergrift used the scholarship funds to get her degree in elementary school education at the University of Alabama at Birmingham.

Charles's performance against Bobby Lee Hurt, a hurricane of dunks, blocks, and aggression, inspired wonder and opened eyes. Almost overnight, the question among coaches, scouts, and boosters around the state shifted from, *Who is Charles Barkley? To What did we just witness?*

Stan Cook had seen Charles and Leeds play that season. Cook, the head coach of Gadsden State Community College, was arguably the most dominant junior college coach in the state, winning 535 games and eventually getting inducted into the Alabama Community College Conference Hall of Fame. But what little Cook saw on his scouting trip to Pell City was more than enough. The two hit it off, with Charles even taking a visit to the school, an hour away from Leeds. Cook saw the recruiting landscape and got the feeling that Auburn and Alabama didn't know how they would use him or if he would even have the grades to qualify.

"He was just a total diamond," he said.

Cook's pitch to Charles was not uncommon for a junior college coach to a potential star: you'd get immediate playing time at a place close to home and have the chance to get your grades up for a four-year school.

The pitch wasn't as appealing to Charcey, who made it clear that she wanted her boy to go to a four-year school, Cook said. The coach was honest with her, recognizing that it would be a stepping-stone to wherever Charles played next.

The triple-threat recruiting showdown between Alabama's flagship institutions was something normally reserved for the football programs. When it came to Charles, there was Wimp Sanderson, the Alabama head coach with the oversized personality, Southeastern Conference rival Norm Sloan of Florida, and Gene Bartow, who was still in the early years of building UAB into a perennial power.

Recognized for his guile on the sidelines, Bartow, who went 52-9 at UCLA before bouncing to Birmingham, was the clean-cut figure of the group. In another corner was Wimp Sanderson, the self-described hard-ass known as much for his plaid sport jackets, concave shoulders, and midcourt scowl as he was for turning around Alabama basketball.

After twenty years as an assistant coach in Tuscaloosa, Sanderson, a self-deprecating and folksy hang who once claimed to have "flunked English in four states," took over the big chair when C.M. Newton left to become assistant commissioner of the SEC.

Charles "Sonny" Smith of Auburn, the coach who could recruit kids to play anywhere, got a call about Barkley in the summer of 1978. From the time he was a boy in Roan Mountain, Tennessee, Smith and his mother would sing hymns and strum the guitar to the drunks who came by the house on Saturday nights.

"All my thoughts in those days was I wanted to be a coach or an entertainer of some kind," Smith said.

The relationship between the three for basketball supremacy in the football state was a mixed bag. When they weren't trying to beat the crap out of each other on the court, Smith and Sanderson were close friends. Between Smith and Bartow, there was a deep, mutual respect, with the Auburn coach calling his adversary, "the real deal in all aspects."

That was not the case with Sanderson and Bartow, a situation in which the disdain between the two was evident. It would culminate in the early '90s, when Bartow sent a letter to the NCAA accusing Sanderson of widespread recruiting violations—and urging the governing body to blow the whistle on the Crimson Tide.

That tension played out throughout the recruiting battles. "Crap no, it wasn't civil," Sanderson said.

Charles's ascent paralleled that of Birmingham as the basketball mecca of Alabama. Whether it was Hurt, Ennis Whatley, Buck Johnson or any of the other all-Americans, the attention was high and the talent was deep. The latest prize fight between the three for the chunky kid escalated quickly. A look ahead to the next season saw UAB returning two big men, Auburn bringing back none, and Alabama close to signing Hurt, seen as the top player in the in-state recruiting war.

Yet it was Bartow who jumped out to an early advantage. After the Christmas tournament, Charles said he gave a verbal commitment to UAB. Sanderson wasn't as quick to pull the trigger on an offer.

"In my eyes, he was more suspect rather than prospect," Sanderson said. "He was going to be a good player, but you didn't know. He was overweight and not in good condition, to the point that you wanted to see how many Big Macs he could eat in one sitting."

"Wimp said, 'I don't know where I'd play him,' and Sonny didn't say anything," Cook recalled. "I kind of knew Sonny was going to be able to get him to Auburn."

Deep into spring, Sanderson was able to convince Charles for an in-person visit. The senior was skeptical as to why the coach was going so hard after him. To Charles, it was a foregone conclusion that Hurt, who Sanderson was recruiting with greater interest, would end up in Tuscaloosa. And Charles was at least the third player on Sanderson's wish list, behind Hurt and Ennis Whatley, the top guard in the state.

"I could play against anybody, anywhere, and at any level," Charles said. "But to some schools, I was the bottom man on the totem pole. I wasn't even worth a used Chevy."

Charcey and Johnnie Mae still welcomed the Alabama coaches into their home in Russell Heights. The pitch was in the living room, the coaches on one side, Charles and Charcey on the other. It didn't take long for the head coach to quickly figure out that it was Johnnie Mae, listening from the next room over, who was the one he needed to impress.

"You have to find the keys to open the door, and his grandmother was the key that opened the door," Sanderson said.

He painted Alabama as the perfect porridge for Charles—not too close and not too far, but just right. Johnnie Mae had an opinion of that from the other room.

"The grandmother from the backside of the room said to us, 'Coach, it's just as close to Auburn over the mountain,'" Sanderson recalled. "Well, bullshit. I didn't want to say to her, 'I didn't want you as a travel guide,' I didn't want to say anything that ugly. I said, 'Just as close to Auburn over the mountain? And she said, 'Oh yeah, it's just as close over the mountain.'"

The rest of the conversation was polite, but Sanderson knew he was out.

"I punched my assistant coach and said, 'Let's get out of here. I think Sonny bought him a car,'" he said, repeating a long-running joke between the two.

Dan Sims said he and Glenn Guthrie, colleagues at Southern Natural Gas Company in Birmingham and Auburn alums separated by a year, were perhaps the first unofficial basketball boosters for the school. Now they had an idea.

Guthrie was in the stands with the coaches and recruiters that night at Minor High. Sims had to leave early, assuming Hurt and Butler rolled the rest of the way. Days later, Guthrie looked down at the *Birmingham Post* and saw that Leeds was playing at Pell City that same day. Sims proposed a dinner date with their wives and families at Pell City Steak House. Unbeknownst to their spouses, they were going right down the road for dessert.

"As we were paying our bill, I asked the little lady taking care of us, 'Hey, where is the high school?'" Sims said. "My wife looked at Glenn's wife and said, 'Well, I figure we're about to go to a basketball game.' And we did."

Guthrie and Sims left at the end of the third quarter of the rout in Pell City. Sims urged his friend to get Herb Greene on the phone. Yet the Auburn assistant had already started on the biggest assignment of his life.

The Tigers had blown the earlier opportunity to get to know Charles the season prior, and Greene didn't want to repeat the mistake. To make good on his efforts, he found himself in Leeds regularly in pursuit of Charles.

"He camped out," said Jan Greene, his wife. "When Sonny okayed Charles's recruitment, Herb started working harder and harder. He did whatever he could to outsmart the other coaches."

Smith knew they were late to Charles, but not as late as the other schools, so Auburn had a real shot. With Herbert in Leeds all the time, Auburn was laying it on thick.

"He lived in Leeds. He was there by as many rules allowed him to be there," Smith said in June 2019. Later in the conversation, Smith, in his thick drawl, joked, "We might have broken a few rules. He was *there*."

Like Charles, Greene liked to sleep in, which worked to his advantage. Charles had a study hall every morning from 8:00 a.m. to 9:00 a.m. Knowing this, the Alabama and UAB coaches would call him at 7:00 a.m. to catch him before school, showing him that they wanted him. The problem was that Charles and the principal had an understanding that he wouldn't have to show up to school until 9:00 a.m. The rival recruiters either got no answer or a very groggy Charles—a losing proposition no matter how you cut it. Greene knew better and would wait until around 3:00 p.m. to go see him at practice, where he got to see an awake prodigy show off his competitive streak.

"Herb hated to lose, and I think he saw that in Charles," Jan Greene said.

The Auburn assistant was there for each of Leeds's remaining games. The persistence was noticed by Charles, who took a liking to the newfound attention from Greene.

"I have always had a great admiration for Herbert because he was the first guy who actually thought I could play," Charles said. "I will always be in debt to him for that."

The work Greene was doing on behalf of the team was supplemented by the efforts of Guthrie and Sims, who wondered how much the program had budgeted for recruiting.

"We decided what we'd do is put together a few guys and kick in to take care of whatever recruiting needs," Sims said in December 2019. "The statute of limitations has run out now and it was probably a violation at the time, but it was a good thing to do."

"It was a different deal back then," said Sims, a Sunday school teacher of fifty-plus years.

We got involved. I started traveling and I'd call Sonny and say, for example, "If there's somebody in Nashville you're looking at, tell me who they are and if they are playing I'll look at them." I'd find me a basketball game and watch that.

Granny was definitely the head honcho. Charcey was there, but as long as granny was alive, she was calling the shots.

Let me tell you a story that I bet you hadn't heard. Charles wanted a car. His granny, who ran a beauty shop behind the house, told Glenn that he needed a car. Two of the guys in our group, like me, traveled a lot and drove a '78 Oldsmobile, which was a really nice car. They put a lot of miles on them, but they were easy miles. When they got so many miles on them, they sold them for $3,000 or $4,000. I told them, "Charles needs a car." And granny said that he wanted more of a sports car. I was like, "Well okay then," and started laughing.

My little secretary where I worked had a Buick and it was kind of a hybrid, but it was more like a sports car. It was more than she needed. I said, "How much do you want for that thing?"

"$4,800," she said. She said, "I'm going to take that and buy me a Volkswagen." I took that thing over and Charles said, "I like this!" Granny said,

"How much?" After she heard it was $4,800, she said, "Alright, I want you to meet me at the Leeds bank Tuesday and I'm going to make a loan and bring the car over to the bank."

So, I got over there, and I witnessed granny's signature to sign the loan. We gave them the keys, and me and that gal came back and ordered a Volkswagen.

It was a lot easier then to do that stuff than compared to now. You would hear about the $100 handshakes. What we would do was innocent. The players would get four tickets to every game, and we would go get those tickets and sell them. They were like $5 apiece and you'd come back to them with $20 and they'd buy a pizza.

With his granny, we ain't never figured out why a 60-year-old Black gal in Leeds was an Auburn fan, but she was.

UAB's surprise run in the NCAA Tournament in March 1981 turned out to be what pushed Charles Barkley away.

The Blazers' first Sweet 16 appearance, with an upset over Kentucky in the second round, made UAB the place to be if you were a top high school player in Alabama. That coupled with UAB returning four starters the next season made staying at home not a realistic possibility for the guy who wanted to play immediately.

"Most teams use the kind of success UAB enjoyed in the 1981 NCAA Tournament to *attract* recruits, but that year's success *cost* UAB," Charles said. "It cost them Charles Barkley."

Now, with Charles making his way to Auburn on US-280 East, the verbal commitment he had made months earlier to the in-state rival was no good.

In the middle of his third consecutive losing season to start off his career at Auburn, Smith knew he had to make some inroads fast when it came to recruiting. That meant convincing the state's best Black players to come play at the most racially segregated school in Alabama, with just around 3 percent of the student population being African American.

"It was truly a school of White people," said Steve Wallace, an offensive tackle at the school during that period.

In a federal ruling that decade, a district judge decided that "except for the presence of Black athletes and the changes mandated by Federal laws and regulations, Auburn's racial attitudes have changed little since the '50s," and that the widespread perception of African Americans throughout the state had been supported in the ruling.

When Charles came to campus for his official visit, he didn't want to have fun. Instead, he was looking for a coach for the next four years.

"Charles said all he wanted to do was get to know me, to make sure he knew everything about me," Smith said.

Jan Smith, Sonny's wife, didn't pay much attention to him as a recruit until the coach brought him to their home. And Charles didn't leave their home for the whole visit to Auburn. At some point, Charles, as an excuse for staying, told Jan he wasn't feeling well, "which wasn't true," she said.

The bars and college women were replaced on this visit with TV on the Smiths' couch, hangouts with Jan, and pimiento-stuffed olives.

"He hung out on the couch with two jars of olives with red pimentos in them. I gave him the first bottle of olives and he ate the whole thing. He said, 'Do you have any more?' and gave him the other one, too," she said. "He said he wanted pizza for dinner.

"I said, 'Charles, I don't think you're sick.' He goes, 'I know, I just wanted to stay with you.'"

Said Smith, "I'd never had a recruit do that before."

With that, Charles signed with Auburn back at his home in Leeds with Charcey, Johnnie Mae, his brothers, and a grinning Billy Coupland.

Before his arrival on campus, he had two goals in mind: win a state title and graduate high school with his peers. But dismay was on the way.

5

If not for his growth spurt at the start of the '80s, the changes and opportunities happening in Charles Barkley's life would have looked very different.

"I'd be fucked," Charles admitted to ESPN.

Instead, the fat kid from Leeds was rolling.

His mother and grandmother knew something was beginning to change earlier that same season. The stands were as packed and loud as they were during that two-year run, but the hooting and hollering was mostly directed at their baby.

"His grandma and I sat in the stands one night and were stunned at how, all of a sudden, everybody was cheering Charles like he was some kind of hero," his mother said. "It was pretty unbelievable how much he had learned about basketball, and how good he'd gotten."

The home court advantage at Oxnard helped the Green Wave rout opponents for the better part of the 1980–81 season, and their following on the road grew with each team Charles left decimated in his wake.

"There was some kind of excitement that I can't even begin to describe," said classmate Lydia Smith. "I wasn't even that big of a basketball fan, but he would come down the court, jump up and dunk the ball, and hang on the rim, and that place would go wild. We had never seen anyone play like that before."

Classmates now recognized Charles, with his afro and full frame, as "the school celebrity."

"He made a transformation from whiny little fat kid with a smart mouth to this big, really good athlete," classmate Jeff Falletta said.

Teachers were also soon hearing the buzz around Wade, the kid whose only goal at one time was to not raise his future children on welfare.

As he was becoming more popular at school, Charles, a senior contestant for the homecoming court, vowed to abstain from the drinking and pill-popping that some of his classmates engaged in each weekend. He would joke throughout his life that the only thing he ever got out of smoking weed was an appetite.

"I smoked pot like five times in my life. All it did was [make] me want to eat potato chips," he said. "It was a waste of my time. I didn't feel no euphoria, it didn't take me to no special place."

This was also around the time Charles, one of the only guys in home economics class, was becoming more attractive for the young women of Leeds High. Girlfriend Amy Shorter broke up with him, but admittedly got back together with him once she realized how good he had gotten at basketball. A few months later, young Charles got her back shortly after his eighteenth birthday. This time, *he* was the one breaking up with her.

"I was so heartbroken, but we still ended up going to prom," Shorter said. "That's teenage drama for you."

Love life aside, basketball was as good as it ever had been to him. In practice, Coupland felt that Charles had hit a turning point in his development.

"Dumb me tried to give the ball to a guard every time," said Coupland, calling it a mistake on his part. "There was a point guard in his body."

In Pell City, a main rival for Leeds, the crowd was ready to boo the hell out of the chubby teen, recalled Doug Turner, a freshman playing for the opposing team's varsity. But what started as a tight game evolved into a defensive clinic.

"He scored 60 by himself and they beat the crap out of us," Turner said. "He was a pretty brash guy, but I remember it was more about the aura of this guy's coming, so he filled up the gym. He was this oddity you wanted to see." He added, "People were just in awe of not only what he was doing that night but of what we thought he was going to do in the future."

Charles wore the same pair of shoes to every game that year. Money remained tight, and even his newfound stardom didn't mean he had more pairs of kicks than he needed.

"My mother would bring the shoes to the game, and after the game was over she came and waited at the locker room door, and I handed her the shoes and she took them back home," Charles said. "That one pair of basketball shoes had to last the whole season."

That one pair turned out to be shoes you didn't mess with. At 26–3, Charles lifted the Green Wave to a second consecutive state tournament appearance. By the time the regular season had ended in 1981, Charles averaged 19.1 points, 17.9 rebounds and 5 blocks a game, piling up MVP honors at tournaments and being named all–Jefferson County. He did it by shooting an eye-popping 59.7 percent from the floor.

In the process, he put Leeds on the map.

After handling their first two playoff opponents, Leeds squeaked by their next opponent by just 3 points to punch their ticket back to Tuscaloosa.

At the state quarterfinals in late February 1981, the Green Wave was up by as much as 16 against Sylacauga late in the third period. An aggressive full-court press from the Aggies brought them all the way back to force overtime. With Sylacauga's starting center and leading scorer, Troy Morris, fouling out, Charles looked to take advantage of Jon Hand, the junior backup big man. Not even Hand, a six-foot-seven, 280-pound specimen who would go on to play defensive end at Alabama before being drafted fourth overall by the Indianapolis Colts in 1986, could bully Barkley in the extra period.

Before you could blink, Charles dropped in two buckets in the first minute of overtime. There wasn't a possession he didn't touch the ball. After the 82–76 win, Charles, who finished with 20 points and 12 rebounds, admitted he had to show off some of the point guard speed against the future football star to give them a chance.

"I knew we had to get ahead early in the overtime," Barkley told the *Anniston Star*. "I thought I could move on Hand, because he was kinda slow."

They were now a game away from getting back to the title game and avenging the previous year's defeat. Coupland instilled in them a fear of the underdog. What Coupland and the team didn't account for in their semifinal matchup against Colbert County on February 27, 1981, however, was Charles fouling out in the *third quarter*.

As the final horn sounded on a 73–61 loss, Charles lowered his head and wailed; the tears rolled down his face inside the home of the Crimson Tide. His high school career was over with two state tournament appearances and no state titles. He was left inconsolable. For the second time in two years, Charles's team came up short on the biggest stage in Alabama.

"All of us were brokenhearted that we left something undone. We were starstruck by all the traveling and going to Tuscaloosa," Reese said. He paused before continuing about the what-if from nearly three decades ago: "I just wish we would have won a state championship."

Nearly a month went by before Charles made his decision to go to Auburn. What seemed like nothing more than a pipe dream just two years earlier when he was jumping over the fence repeatedly, was now a reality. Flanked by a grinning grandmother and a proud mother, as well as his brothers and Coupland behind him, Charles leaned over from his spot on the living room couch and put pen to paper to sign his letter of intent in late March.

"Charles Barkley, a six-foot-six, 230-pound forward from Leeds, has become the first high school basketball player to accept an Auburn grant-in-aid in 1981," according to the announcement from athletic director Lee Hayley on March 25, 1981.

The decision came as a surprise to UAB and Bartow, as Charles, on the basis of his verbal agreement, was supposed to report to classes in Birmingham in only a few short weeks' time. As it turned out, Charles never got around to telling them he wasn't showing up after all.

"Bartow was pissed, and he had every right to be," Charles remembered in *Outrageous!*

"But I didn't really give a damn. I wasn't going anyplace where I wasn't going to play."

Around the time Charles signed with Auburn, Sanderson, the Alabama coach, gave his friend and rival at Auburn a ring. They hated losing to each other, but Sanderson said he couldn't stay mad at Smith for long.

"Wimp tells the story about how he got beat by Auburn for Charles—'What did Sonny do?'" said Smith, setting up a long-running joke between the two. "He said, 'Sonny bought him a car.' I said, 'Yeah, but it was an old one.'"

With his future on the Plains in place, Charles mentally checked out of his academics in the latter part of his senior year.

Charles found himself in a Spanish class taught by Raquel Caiñas Gomez. Shortly after coming to the US from Havana in 1961, the same year as the Bay of Pigs invasion, Gomez earned her master's in Spanish at Samford University in Birmingham and went on to teach at Leeds High for almost two decades.

The Cuban immigrant called "Saint Raquel" by her family was sweet and kind, but kept high expectations for all her students.

"She was tough and didn't give an inch," classmate Ronie Langston said.

Charles was in trouble. His friends and classmates felt he didn't have much of a chance of passing, and Coupland and the coaching staff recognized it as well.

"Ms. Gomez, she was not going to let him pass," Blair said. "The coaches begged and pleaded, and she said, 'No, he's going to be treated like the rest of the class.'"

For years, Charles has pointed to him flunking Spanish as the reason why he didn't graduate from Leeds High with the rest of his classmates. Yet it was his refusal to turn in his senior English paper that was another catalyst for him not walking on graduation day.

Betty Nash was a long-standing English teacher at Leeds High. A lifelong Alabamian, Nash was respected and even feared, and you couldn't goof off and expect to get by. This approach was embraced by many, including Charles, who told the *Leeds News* during his senior year that she was his favorite teacher.

"She explains things so the student can understand," he said. "She is also the fairest teacher I ever met. I think she is a great person."

His friends saw him struggling to make it through Nash's class. One day, she even called him out, wondering why he couldn't get his grades up. His response? *Ms. Nash, I'm going to be playing basketball at Auburn.* Nash wasn't one to let that kind of reply go unchecked, especially in her classroom. Her answer? *Oh no you won't.*

"I know I could speak for most people," Victor Campbell said. "I didn't hear anyone speak anything against our teachers."

It was why Charles's stubborn rebuke was so maddening, with weeks to go before the end of high school.

Charles didn't want to do his final paper in English. He just didn't want to turn it in. One of the teachers came to me and said, "All Charles has to do is turn it in." The teacher came to me and told me, "Please talk to him about why he's not turning it in." His response was just like, "I'm not turning it in."

Charles was very smart, and I copied his notes all the time at my house. All of my notes I ever got from Charles were great and I got good grades because of it. I knew he could write the paper, but he just didn't want to write it.

I was contemplating telling his mother, as I knew he would do it then. But the only reason why I didn't do that was because it was our senior year and we were told that we had to learn to be more independent.

The teachers weren't trying to make an example out of him or flunk him. He already knew he was going to college. He could be stubborn, and he was very stubborn at that time.

Berderia Spence, a self-proclaimed bookworm in school, didn't want her friend to screw this up. The senior English paper was straightforward: write a report on any subject. Spence did hers on fish, looking at the different types of fish, where they live, what they ate, that kind of thing.

"This was at the height of him being Mr. Charles Barkley," Spence recalled. "I remember telling him, 'Wade, you've got to do the work, she is not playing.'"

Her efforts to help him with the report fell on deaf ears, as Charles had already said goodbye to high school—even without the diploma.

"I told him he was making a big mistake," she said. "Unfortunately, my worst fear came true."

The question of whether Charles Barkley, the star basketball recruit for Auburn, would own a high school diploma turned into a real question. While his scholarship standing was not in doubt—his jumping and brute force mattered more to Auburn than his ability to speak Spanish or eloquently break down the intricacies of Shakespeare's *Macbeth*—it was still a major blow just before graduation. Smith even came by Leeds again to make sure that his gem would graduate from summer school in a few weeks.

Nowhere was the disappointment of Charles not graduating on time more palpable than at home. When Charcey and Johnnie Mae came to the school, the counselor feared that she was about to get ripped a new one like most parents do when their children come up short in the classroom. That never happened.

"His mother and grandmother blamed him instead of the teachers," Little said. "It was his decision and his fault, they said, and that was the end of it."

While he has not publicly talked about failing English, Charles has repeatedly pointed to his F in Ms. Gomez's Spanish class as a motivating factor for life.

"I was mad at Ms. Gomez, my Spanish teacher. I didn't realize till later it wasn't her fault, it was my fault I flunked my Spanish exam," he said.

It was a lesson he took with him in the decades to come, often telling any young person who would listen to take advantage of the educational opportunities he admittedly took for granted. Years later, he would be the voice pushing academics that he said he never got from his family, teachers, or coaches.

"I should've been a better student," he said. "I should have expected more of myself, but it would have been nice if someone had told me that *they* expected more of me, too."

The end was indeed near, but not before one last wrinkle from two thousand miles away. Frank Barkley was back in town to watch the son he left graduate.

In the spring of 1981, it was time to celebrate the senior class, a group not solely defined by their academic achievements but by good people who looked out for one another.

"Our graduation song was 'Celebration' by Kool & the Gang, so that's all that needs to be said about us," Langston said.

The guy who helped make them exceptional was nowhere to be found.

"Everyone was talking about the F...but we didn't realize he didn't graduate with us," Falletta said.

Instead, Charles was dealing with his father. What was meant to be a peaceful return to Leeds for Frank grew uncomfortable with the news that he had flown cross-country to watch his son not earn his diploma. Marching into the principal Jerry Oxford's office with his son, an infuriated Frank demanded an explanation for his son failing—the opposite approach Charcey and Johnnie Mae had taken.

"Mr. Oxford turned to Charles and said, 'Tell your daddy about Ms. Nash,'" Little said. Charles, reiterating to his dad what he had told the *Leeds News* about Nash, said, "She's a very fair teacher and she's my favorite teacher."

Back at home, Frank couldn't shield his anger over what amounted to a wasted airplane ticket.

Already devastated about not graduating with his classmates, Charles remarked how he couldn't believe his father, the man who left him and his mom when he was thirteen months old, had the audacity to get mad at him over his academic predicament.

"He ripped me a new asshole," Charles recalled in 2022.

On the night of graduation, Charles disappeared. He had to get away from the disappointment he'd created. Without telling anyone, he drove over to the stadium for the commencement ceremony. As the sea of green caps and gowns was settling in at the football stadium, he quietly walked over to the adjacent baseball field. Climbing to the top row of the bleachers on the first base side, he had an unobstructed view of the major life event that was going on without him.

"I just stood there for two hours straight, just crying," he said. Charles later recalled to Dr. Phil, "I was so distraught."

Years would pass before Charles would get over the sting of not walking across the stage with his classmates. He'd eventually finish summer school and would earn his diploma sans the pomp and circumstance.

"It taught me that you aren't going to be given anything in life, that you have to earn what you get," he said. "It was my life and my fault."

6

It's 4th and 2 at the Auburn 35, and the 87,000-plus inside Jordan-Hare Stadium are yelling, taunting, and doing everything necessary to make the last play of the game absolute hell for the freshman quarterback of Ole Miss and hold on to a 6-point lead.

On a windy fall night on the Plains, the No. 11 Tigers, sluggish for the first hour of a game against a hapless 3–6 opponent, are in survival mode.

Even coming off a close loss to eventual national champion LSU, not much could keep down the Auburn fans in the tailgating hours before the 7:00 p.m. kickoff. Over by Foyer Hall, bites of brisket, ham, and chicken tenders are washed down with glugs of Miller Lite, Truly, and whatever bourbon you want. Tents blaring Kenny Chesney, The Ramones, and Kanye West take over dozens of blocks surrounding the stadium, filled with everyone from the eager freshmen who have painted their bodies to spell out "AUBURN" to the smiling septuagenarians who've been coming to the same party for decades.

There are enough tales of Charles Barkley's legend at Auburn to fill a bottomless well, but only Rob Shuler can say that he was there in 2004 when his friend convinced a group of Alabama guys to park on the front lawn of their fraternity house during the Iron Bowl. When Shuler, an Auburn offensive lineman in the '80s, knocked on the front door and explained the dire situation minutes before kick-off, the fraternity brothers lost it at the sight of Sir Charles exiting the car on their lawn. They let them park there with one condition: they wanted to have a beer with Charles after the game.

"We beat them, and Charles comes back and has a beer with them and takes pictures with the frat boys," Shuler remembered. "On the day of the Iron Bowl when everybody hates everybody, those Alabama kids who hate Auburn never said a word about Auburn; it was all about Charles Barkley. They realized he's an icon above Auburn and Alabama. If I parked my car there without Charles, it would have been on fire."

Other than the traditional War Eagle flight and the special pre-game flyover by a local F-35 Lightning II aircraft unit, these final seconds at Jordan-Hare are the most deafening it's been all game. The crowd lets out a collective sigh when the Tigers defense picks off the overmatched quarterback as the clock expires for another win.

By the time you get to the intersection of College Street and Magnolia Avenue, fans have already rolled Toomer's Corner, covering the trees with toilet paper. When students aren't figuring out the next round of libations and grub, magic can happen here, too. Take gymnast Samantha Cerio, who got engaged after wrapping Toomer's Corner on the night of her last home game as a student. Cerio gained national attention after suffering career-ending leg injuries at a competition in April 2019, and the coverage got to a point where she pleaded with people to stop sharing the viral video of the worst moment of her life. Still groggy and recovering from surgery, she was taken aback when she was told that Charles, who had never met her before, sent her well-wishes to the millions watching during the March Madness broadcast.

"That was one of the biggest things I needed at the time," Cerio said. "People like Charles Barkley who do that…because it's Auburn."

The line for Skybar, a rooftop establishment and go-to spot in the heart of town, now stretches around the corner as young and old alike pour in.

Welcome to the loveliest village on the Plains.

Charles Barkley found himself in an unfamiliar place but in relatively familiar territory when he arrived at Auburn in the fall of 1981.

The unfamiliar: he was more than one hundred miles from the only home he knew to that point. The familiar: a majority White school, with only about 430 Black students among the more than 18,000 on campus. Although he had experiences at a predominantly White elementary school and a mixed high school, "the sea of White faces was pretty intimidating at first."

"One of my first reactions when I got to Auburn was, 'Jesus, there's no Black people here,'" he once said. In his autobiography with Roy S. Johnson, he noted, "I didn't know what was going to happen. I didn't know whether these farm kids would be able to deal with me and my outrageous attitude and become my friends, or whether they would turn on me because I was Black."

So, what exactly was he walking into? Not unlike other areas throughout the Deep South, the feelings of fear and uncertainty were rooted in the school's history to that point, which largely reflected a cold approach to Black people in the classroom. In the late 1800s, when the school was Alabama Polytechnic Institute, its president, William Leroy Broun, a New South educator who had previously led the Confederate States Army in Richmond, Virginia, during the Civil War, had considered Black people to be better suited for manual training than college. This was in addition to the school's stance against women in the classroom, who were denied from higher learning at Auburn until 1892. While Ralph Brown Draughon, who led the university between 1947 and 1965, didn't agree with Governor George Wallace on segregation, some Auburn graduates remained staunchly opposed to ending segregation, with one writing how "desegregation would victimize foolish White girls, subject them to thought control, and result in a half-breed population," according to *The Village on the Plain*.

Harold Franklin, who sued the school to gain admission in January 1964 and was Auburn's first Black student, remembered being stopped by a state trooper who demanded to see his student ID. The looks he got from his classmates on that first day tickled him to some extent.

"They didn't really want me there as Auburn wanted to delay desegregation for as long as they could," Franklin said. "The thing that stood out to me was the students who looked at me as if I might be an alien or something. They had seen African Americans before, but maybe not at Auburn."

The reception was similar for Black student athletes. As the Southeastern Conference began to fully integrate, Thom Gossom Jr. came to Auburn in 1970 as a walk-on wide receiver and left as the first Black student athlete to graduate from the school. In *Walk-On: My Reluctant Journey to Integration at Auburn University*, Gossom recounted a mostly good experience with his teammates and coaches, but a life of isolation and loneliness for the man referred to by some as the N-word walk-on.

"Auburn was not an inclusive environment at that time, but I can't say there was a meanness to it," said Gossom, the school's oldest living Black athlete. "You were just kind of ignored."

Elements of the culture trickled over into the '80s, said Vern Strickland, a forward for the men's basketball team. "Everybody got along, but you had the rich White kids freaking out about who they're hanging out with and who they're standing next to in line at school," Strickland said. "If you weren't a sports fan, they just weren't interested in us."

Any initial fear he had of not being accepted at the almost all-White school was quickly put to rest when Charles got on campus, saying he never had any problem with racism or racists during his time there.

"I understand that much of the way they treated me was because I was an athlete, but the atmosphere at Auburn was truly like one big family," he told author Roy S. Johnson. "It was also an experience that added to my belief that Blacks have to be able to deal with Whites, and vice versa, in every situation. It doesn't matter how they feel about each other, because, in the end, neither of them is going to change colors."

For a program that hadn't had a winning season in five years, enthusiasm was understandably nonexistent when Charles came to town.

Then at 251 pounds, Charles's appearance concerned people in the athletics department, especially Dennis Wilson, the head of the university's department of health and human performance. Charles was weighed underwater to measure his body fat percentage before the start of the season.

In a five-hundred-gallon converted milk tank, Wilson, using Archimedes' principle of displacement to measure the density of a body, had Charles lie facedown in the 104-degree water and blow out all his air while remaining still in the frame holding him. The results he got after six trial runs on October 15, 1981, surprised Wilson.

"His percent body fat was 17.3, which is pretty high for a college-aged athlete and is more like a normal college-aged male who was not involved in athletics," Wilson said. "But my recommendation to Sonny was not to put him on any program to lose weight since he was working so hard that he was going to be OK."

As the first official days of practice got underway in mid-October, Sims, the Auburn booster, would get reports back from the student manager about how Charles was doing. "His eyes got big," Sims recalled. "He said, 'Mr. Sims, we've never seen anything like that.'"

While writing for the *Auburn Plainsman*, the student newspaper, Vince Thompson landed a job working for the school's sports information director. The assignment that day was to be present for the vertical tests for all the players. Charles's turn is the one Thompson still remembers.

"I saw him literally leap onto a 42-inch wooden box with absolute ease," Thompson said.

During five-on-five runs, Sonny Smith put the freshman with four of the lesser talented players to go against the starting unit—and Barkley's team would always win. No battle with a teammate was fiercer than with Darrell Lockhart, the highly recruited six-foot-nine physical presence. In a scene eerily similar to that of his matchup with Bobby Lee Hurt less than a year prior, Charles rejected the first few shots of Lockhart's, putting his teammates, coaches, and any students who mistook him for a football player on notice.

"Charles intimidated Darrell so bad that I ended up with a vegetable," Smith said. "Finally, I had to stop Charles from guarding him."

Lockhart wasn't aware of it at the time, but his new teammate wanted to send a message to the tallest target available.

"What I learned later was that he came to Auburn with a chip on his shoulder. He knew if he could take the best player out that he could be top dog," Lockhart said. "He came in and focused on me, and I'm not going to lie, he went to work on me. He was blocking my shots; he did all that. He made me work, which made me better."

Assistant coach Mack McCarthy acknowledged that the coaching staff "kind of pitted them against each other" with mixed results.

"They were so good that they impacted the other player's game," McCarthy said. "Charles couldn't deal with Darrell's physicality and skill, while Darrell couldn't deal with Charles's athleticism and rambunctiousness."

After one of those first practices, Barkley caught up with Sims. When he signed with Auburn, he had laid out a series of goals he wanted to accomplish on a car ride with the booster.

"'Mr. Sims, do you remember those goals we talked about? I've changed them,'" Sims said Charles told him. "He said, 'I *know* I'm going to start. I still want to make the All-Freshman team.' He says, 'I don't want to be one of the top three rebounders in the SEC—I want to lead the SEC in rebounds for three years.' And he said, 'I want to leave Auburn after my third year and be a Top-5 pick in the Draft.'"

The team had easy outings in its exhibition and season opener, with Charles the leading rebounder in both games and a 5-block performance to start the regular season. But on December 2, 1981, the Tigers were down by three to Stetson with less than a minute to go, and on their way to an embarrassing home defeat in front of less than three thousand fans. When Smith looked at his freshman forward, however, he got something else—and he couldn't get a word in.

"He was so confident it was funny," Smith said to the press afterward. "He never stopped talking, even when I was trying to say something."

In a moment that would foreshadow the next four decades, Charles wouldn't stop talking, rattling off the perennial powers the Auburn Tigers could beat if they wanted to—Indiana, Kentucky, North Carolina, Notre Dame. To Charles, the same Auburn program that had never made March Madness could easily play with some of the sport's true blue bloods.

"He picked some winners to compare us to, but I think we all started to believe him after a while," Smith confessed. "He made us believe we could beat Stetson, anyway."

They did just that, beating Stetson, 60–59, and Charles, with 10 rebounds, led the team in boards for the second consecutive game off the bench, despite playing less than half of the game. Writer Rick Bragg covered the game for the *Anniston Star* and scribed the unusual early effect the kid from Leeds was having early on.

"But, conceded Smith, for a 17-year-old kid who has yet to play more than seventeen minutes in a college basketball game, Barkley makes his presence known," Bragg wrote in the *Star*.

Yet getting excited over double-digit rebounding performances against the Mississippi Colleges and Tennessee Techs of the world hardly reflected how he would fair boxing out an SEC rival at a time when the conference was the most interesting in the nation.

"What was happening in the SEC in the '80s was an incredibly fun, exciting conference," said *Sports Illustrated* writer Alexander Wolff. "It wasn't just Kentucky and a bunch of Washington Generals. Aside from the talent, it was largely driven by coaches with real personalities, who made sportswriters want to cover basketball."

The added attention was just another element to Auburn's early-season loss to Tennessee on December 12, 1981. But the loss was almost secondary considering their young freshman had gone for 21 points and 11 rebounds off the bench. After the game, Smith was quick to name Charles to the starting lineup.

Although it was the first loss of the season, Charles was accustomed to winning—and it showed.

"I sat in the locker room and cried like a baby. One of my teammates saw me and came over to where I was sitting. 'Why are you crying?' he asked. 'Man, I'm not used to losing. I hate the feeling,'" Charles recalled saying after the game. "He started laughing. 'Man, you'd better not be crying around here after every loss. You'll flood us out of here.'"

When he wasn't bawling, he was the conference's newest tormenter. He would put together a string of dominant performances not seen from a freshman anywhere, including a 25-point, 17-rebound outing in a loss to No. 3 Kentucky in front of more than 23,000 fans at Rupp Arena that immediately made him a force to recognize in major college basketball. However, his first stretch of magnificence at Auburn would trigger the taunt that would follow Charles for the rest of his playing days.

Hey, Fatso, do you work at Burger King?
The fans in Baton Rouge were going to make sure that Charles Barkley knew that they thought he was a fat-ass. A talented one, but a fat-ass, nonetheless.

In response, Charles did not yell or give them the middle finger. Instead, he blew kisses at the LSU student section. He scored 24 in a 1-point loss, but he refused to let the opposing fans get in his head as he was finding success.

"Ahh yes, I hear everything they said. That just means they love me," he said to reporters after a game. "They're just part of the family."

When he said he heard everything they said, the forward could have also been referring to what his coaches and teammates called him: "Fatso." In one of the first stories about him written by a state newspaper, *Alabama Journal* columnist Darryal Ray's piece on January 20, 1982, titled, "It Isn't Over Until the Fat Boy Sings," gave Charles the chance to clarify that he embraced his love handles.

"It doesn't bother me," he said to the *Journal* of his "Fatso" persona. "They called me that in high school. I am fat, but I don't have any plans to lose any weight right now. Things are going too well for me."

The preseason concerns of Smith and a coaching staff over Charles's 17.3 percent body fat and inability to keep the weight off lingered throughout his freshman year. This was confirmed in accounts by people closest to the program, like Auburn play-by-play announcer Jim Fyffe, who once remembered how Charles would smuggle three giant pizzas into his room even after eating a postgame sandwich.

As he was about to turn nineteen, Charles was stumped in describing how he had gotten so big while also increasingly comfortable talking about his specific eating habits and how much he missed his mother's cooking, especially her fried chicken.

"I only eat twice a day," the freshman forward said. "It's the snacks that do me in. I'm always eating candy, cookies, cakes, or something. But I've got this little refrigerator back in the room. I've got a turkey back in there now, but mostly I keep cold cuts and things like that. Darrell [Lockhart] has a hot plate in his room and we use that to fix snacks a lot of the time."

When it came to monitoring Charles's conditioning, the little fridge in his dorm at Sewell Hall would be a consistent bane of the coaching staff's existence. The Auburn coaches weighed Barkley every day during his freshman year. Coaches would run him from baseline to baseline, sideline to sideline, to the top of the coliseum and back. It even extended into running after dark throughout the town.

Smith mused that since X-rays of his wrists indicated that he still might be growing that he could only hope that didn't mean his eating would continue, too.

"You couldn't get it off of him," Smith said. "You could break the plate, you could monitor his eating habits. I even sent coaches with him to class and to the dining hall."

As the media picked up on their freshman's budding stardom, Smith and Auburn sports information director David Housel had an idea: what if Auburn marketed Charles's weight as a way to get attention and help put butts in the seats of the largely empty Memorial Coliseum. Years later, Smith fully accepts that he used Charles's weight to the program's advantage—*Step right up, folks, and come see this small, big guy who plays bigger than the big guys.*

"We were getting attention out of the fact that Charles was so heavy," Smith said. "We worked hard to get publicity any way we could, and that was one way to get it. We were selling fat, we were selling anything, and Charles was a sellable item, he really was."

Reflecting on the promotions Auburn ran to drum up interest for a football-thirsty crowd who thought of basketball as the activity you did in the winter before spring football, Housel said it probably wasn't necessary given that Charles sold himself.

"Charles did not need any promotion. Auburn basketball just followed on his coattails," Housel said. "He was a show."

Don't get it twisted though, because Auburn lost in stretches that first season and it happened often. For a team not used to winning, their freshman's individual success felt just as good.

"You're talking about a guy that was around 280 pounds and could stand flat-footed under the basket and jump up and put his hands over the square," noted Phillip Marshall, the sports editor at the *Montgomery Advertiser*. He added of the team, "They still weren't very good, but he became a very popular guy very quickly."

Charles had come a long way since the days of being told by Wallace Honeycutt to hold back from throwing it down in junior high.

"I try to dunk as soon as possible and as many times as possible," he said. "It lets the other team know I can score and take it to the hoop."

There is both aggression and joy to a Barkley jam. The ascent is sudden. On the fast break, his hips and legs can get so far up that it looks like the Incredible Hulk is on a swing set. The comedown is the wild card, offering an array of options, ranging from the roar that reverberates through an arena or shit-talking of an opposing crowd to the mischievous grin that tells you he not only enjoys dunking on you but that he's about to try it again.

In practice, Smith asked Charles over and over: don't dunk on the breakaway rims.

"Every time he would dunk, he would break that rim down and look at me like, 'What are you going to do about this, Sonny?'" Smith said. "I said, 'If you break the rim down one more time, you're out of here.' And he broke it down and I ran him out of practice."

The dunks would soon give way to some wins. Opponents were starting to take Auburn more seriously, especially after Charles went for 18 points and 12 rebounds in the Tigers' overtime win against No. 9 Kentucky at home, avenging the earlier loss at Rupp Arena. Now he was both winning and looking good doing it, even if the two weren't always in lockstep.

He was, however, grabbing the attention of Georgia's Dominique Wilkins, the reigning SEC Player of the Year and a consensus top prospect in that year's NBA Draft. As one of the most exciting players in the nation, the man whose breathtaking dunks and unworldly athleticism earned him the moniker "the Human Highlight Film" was puzzled when the "little" center, who was more like six-foot-four than six-foot-six, decided he was going to challenge Wilkins the first time they met on January 23, 1982.

"When I first saw him play, I was like, 'Who is this big fat kid?'"

Wilkins said. "The next play, I realized who he was when he went up on our whole frontline and dunked it." He added, "He could move so graciously, so easily at that size, and I knew right away what I was looking at."

By all accounts, Charles's freshman year was one of wild individual success and some team improvement. He finished the year averaging nearly 13 points, 10 rebounds, and 2 blocks, leading the SEC in rebounding as a freshman. He was awarded the SEC's Freshman of the Year, while also being tabbed to the Freshman All-America Third Team and the All-SEC Second Team. The team finished at 14–14, bowing out in the second round of the SEC Tournament. The nearly three-game improvement from the previous season, with wins against ranked opponents in Kentucky and Tennessee, offered some momentum heading into the off-season.

But underneath all that promise, the familial and personal stress had caught up to Charles. His first year at Auburn was the longest he had ever been away from home, and he was regularly homesick, missing his mother and grandmother. Around that same time, his brother Darryl was struggling in school and eventually dropped out after the ninth grade. Charcey and Johnnie Mae grew worried that him staying out late with the wrong people would lead to trouble.

While he was all smiles in public about his weight, his relationship with Smith had become strained over the coach badgering Barkley about his body. By the end of his freshman year, Charles was at 278 pounds, gaining about 27 pounds throughout the season.

"Charles was never a discipline problem. He was never one to mouth back at you or voice his opinion on the court," Smith said. "He handled all the abuse he had to take from me verbally until it got so bad around that time."

It was a point of contention throughout the year, and nearly crumbled before Charles even started a game. With Smith yelling at him again for not working hard in practice early in the season, the teen had enough.

"Fuck it. I'm gone," Charles remembered telling Smith.

Back in his living room in Leeds, Charles was met by a crying mother and a grandmother who understood where he was coming from but was still stunned that her baby had packed his bag and returned home five games into his freshman season.

Charcey pleaded with her son to go back to college for a chance at a better life; a chance to help turn around the family's quality of life was why she cleaned homes for all those years.

"You've got to stay at least one year," she said. "I don't care what you do after that, but you've got to go back to Auburn and finish the first year. At least. You've got to stay. You've got to just stay."

He listened to Charcey because he knew that no matter how stubborn he was, she was right. His family needed him, just not in Leeds.

The season ended, but the feelings he harbored toward Smith remained mostly unchanged. And a resolution was nowhere in sight.

"I was beginning to wonder if I had made a big mistake, a real big mistake," Charles recounted to Johnson in 1992. "And it had nothing to do with our regular contributions to the loss column.

"The mistake was Sonny Smith."

7

Why don't I go over the top?

With Auburn football staring down the barrel of another loss that would cap off a decade's worth of defeats to Alabama, Bo Jackson reminded Coach Pat Dye that he—a running back doing his best impersonation of Kratos, the Greek god of strength and power, in pads—could high-jump seven feet in high school. The freshman prodigy's question to the coach in the waning minutes of the 1982 Iron Bowl in Birmingham was concise—it needed to be.

It's anything but a hot take to say that Auburn University had long harbored an inferiority complex when it came to the University of Alabama. In Tuscaloosa, the school is populated by wealthy lawyers and doctors, multigenerational family traditions that earn or at least expect to be at the top of the state's food chain. At Auburn, the blue-collar vibe is loud and clear at a place that was considered the rural land grant, farmer school.

"It used to be the old joke that the last person out at Auburn should lock the gate, because we were the cow college," Vince Thompson said.

So the rivalry, likened by Auburn's David Housel as having Christmas with in-laws you can't be in the same room with, hit differently when Jackson, a two-sport athlete, made his way to campus. Unbeknownst to many, Barkley and Jackson would mark the beginning of an athletic renaissance for the blue and orange. They'd soon be joined by a tight end and heavy hitter named Frank Thomas, three transcendent athletes on campus in only a few years.

Filmmaker Jonathan Hock described the era led by Barkley and Jackson as a joyous one.

"In the post-integration era, the era that became entrenched in the years of Barkley and Bo Jackson in the '80s, you have a phenomenon in college sports in Alabama that is the great unifier," said Hock, executive producer of *Bo, Barkley and The Big Hurt*.

Charles, who had seen Jackson run over his Leeds team in high school, suddenly had a peer wearing No. 34 with both the athletic gifts to match him. "Bo was in college with me, let's get that correct," Charles said, jokingly. "I was there first." Jackson didn't need Charles to tell him he was there first—he had already seen him play. "When he came down the lane, nobody got in his way," Jackson said of Charles. "He would slam on 'em and step on 'em and break guys' collarbones, and you'd have to be an idiot to get in front of Charles Barkley."

The pair developed one of the more captivating comparisons of two athletes from the same school that there's ever been. On one hand, you had a chiseled, two-sport, all-natural Adonis, quiet, and generally more reserved in nature (partially due to a speech impediment) who was the chosen one the day he stepped foot on the Plains.

"It was such an honor and privilege to watch Bo Jackson play in college," Charles said.

On the other, there was the minivan with the Ferrari engine, lacking an ability to say no to anything except sprints and salads who came to Auburn almost as anonymous to students as the kid in your economics class. Together, they've gone back and forth over who is the top athlete in Auburn history, with them jokingly calling the other "No. 2."

"No matter how you look at it, he's No. 1 'cause he was a star on campus before I was," Jackson said. "He will always be No. 1 in my heart when it comes to Auburn University." After a short pause, Jackson, who showed off his "Mine Is Bigger Than Yours" T-shirt to Charles during Barkley's statue unveiling, added, "I'll accept No. 2 because I'm generous like that."

Jackson also had the appetite to match his friendly rival. In the pecking order of student athlete food at Auburn, there was football and then there were sports not named football. To accommodate the athletic cash cows of the university, the other student athletes were forced to eat earlier in the day before the football team came in.

"We'd get sandwiches, we'd get hamburgers, we'd get hot dogs, and as they're moving the stuff out of the way, you see the steaks and the lobsters coming in," Charles said.

Barkley would get the football players back in his own way, preferably through Godfather's Pizza. His late-night ordering got to a point where he'd order the pies "just to make 'em mad, to be honest with you." Jackson soon saw what his friend was doing.

"Barkley got smart," Jackson said. "Barkley would order three pizzas and he would give the football players one pizza and he'd keep the other two, so he got smart. His teammates never caught on."

Sonny Smith didn't recognize it at the time, but Jackson was pushing his star player in mostly good ways, even if it meant eating an extra slice when he was full.

If Bo was the myth, then Charles was the man. They were the teen royalty the community had been waiting to serve.

"When you would see Bo Jackson in the stands at the Coliseum, fans were coming because they knew Bo was going to be there," said Charlene Thomas, a forward for the women's basketball team.

By the time Jackson stretched across the goal line, you could feel the culture he and Charles inherited beginning to change. As the final seconds ticked off the clock, a half-naked Auburn fan straddling the goal post at Legion Field held on for dear life as it came tumbling down. The scoreboard read, Auburn 23, Alabama 22, the first time in a decade that the final tally favored the Tigers.

"It was like the Berlin Wall coming down," Paul Finebaum said. "They had been freed from the rule of Bear Bryant." (Paul "Bear"

Bryant, considered to be the greatest coach in college football history, died only two months later after suffering a massive heart attack.)

The hope instilled after the 1982 Iron Bowl victory, a feeling that they could compete on the other side's level, would form the foundation for what happened thirty-one years later, when Chris Davis ran back a missed field goal 100 yards for a touchdown as time expired.

Hours after the Tigers shock the world, Charles Barkley, Bo Jackson, and Frank Thomas walk into a bar. The ink on the phrase "Kick Six" had yet to dry when Charles gets on stage, grabs the mic, and announces to the watering hole that for the next three songs, drinks for everyone were on him. In his long-sleeved "Save the World" shirt he sported when he picked Auburn on *College GameDay* hours earlier, Charles, standing in front of a crowd decades younger, spits the lyrics to "Ni★★as in Paris" from Jay-Z and Kanye West. He grins from ear to ear, pointing to the crowd as he speaks Yeezy's lines on fish fillet and Prince William.

After a minute, he knows it's time to get off the stage. Besides, it's time to pay the tab on his three-song promise.

The first time the *Louisville Courier-Journal*'s John McGill typed the most important of Charles's many nicknames, it almost felt like an afterthought.

"With starters back including The Round Mound of Rebounds (6-6, 260-pound Charles Barkley, the league leader with 9.8 per game), Auburn looms as a dark horse," he wrote on November 21, 1982, the first documented instance of the fabled moniker.

Not long after, Charles, at the behest of the push made by the athletics department, would look into the camera and introduce himself to the world on NBC.

"Hello, I'm Charles Barkley of the Auburn Tigers," he said before a game. "Here are a few of my nicknames…

The Bread Truck.

The Love Boat.

Food World.

The Crisco Kid, which is my second favorite.

The Wide Load from Leeds.

Ton of Fun.

The Goodtime Blimp.

But my favorite is the Round Mound of Rebound."

Expectations were high before the start of Charles's sophomore season, and it wasn't only because of a deep catalog of sobriquets not seen since Muhammad Ali. The summer between his freshman and sophomore year saw the nineteen-year-old compete in Indianapolis at the National Sports Festival, the country's largest amateur sporting event held in between Olympic years.

Charles's spirit was contagious and a welcome change of pace from the sometimes-stuck-up environment of the festival. One moment, he's jumping up and down to celebrate his team running a flawless fast break. The next, he's beaming like a Christmas tree when he gets a dunk or a block on Stuart Gray, a seven-footer from UCLA. And in another, he's playfully squirting water at one of the water boys on the bench.

"I like to do things to keep me excited because I play better when I'm excited," he said.

As Bo Jackson was quickly becoming the second coming for Auburn football, Smith needed Charles's excitement and momentum from Indianapolis to carry over to the 1982–83 season if the Tigers had any shot to build on the relative success of the previous year. Smith found some recruiting help in the form of Chuck Person, a nice, quiet kid from small-town Alabama who had averaged 33 points and 20 rebounds a game as a senior. Person was the kind of player who wouldn't have thought twice about Auburn before Barkley showed up on campus, but the team was now beginning to see how attractive it was to play with their sophomore sensation.

"Chuck was recruited to be the designated scorer who would complement my rebounding, and we worked well together precisely because our games were exact opposites," he said.

They were also able to land Vern Strickland, a transfer forward from South Carolina. Strickland, who became Charles's roommate after Barkley couldn't put up with teammate Greg Turner's snoring, plainly broke down the differences between Chuck and Charles.

"One of the hardest-working brothers was Chuck Person, but he really wasn't that naturally gifted," Strickland said. "But with Charles, the Lord closed his eyes and waved his wand and said, 'Make this fat boy a basketball player.'"

Yet Charles was changing. On campus, students were starting to take notice of the different-looking basketball player. Not many of them went to the games at Memorial Coliseum, but word of mouth at Auburn had made him the biggest local celebrity not named Bo Jackson. The media attention had spiked considerably from the start of his freshman year to the beginning of his sophomore season.

"I was always really quiet, and then when they put you in the limelight at the age of 18, you go to college and everybody's talking to you all the time—your personality changes," he said.

The changes didn't alter the marketing around Charles. If anything, they were enhanced with Jackson's arrival. Charlene Thomas, a star of the women's team, would show up to the men's games and see how Smith, Housel, and the rest of the program would play off the "Bo Knows" slogan that would later anchor one of Nike's most influential campaigns of the late '80s and early '90s. Instead of knowing how to score touchdowns, Charles knew food.

"Auburn tweaked it and said, 'Charles Knows How to Cook,'" said Thomas, pointing to the nightly promotions for hot dogs and popcorn. "It was kind of like a 'Bo Knows, Charles Knows' kind of thing. The fans loved it and they embraced it."

But they still needed to win. And while Charles's personality was changing, his issues with Smith lingered into the start of the season.

With Charles and Lockhart forming the conference's best rebounding pair and guard Odell Mosteller scoring at will, the Tigers were proving to be a tough out. They would upend UAB in the season opener and suffer their first loss of the season to Stetson before the program's most important non-conference game in years. Auburn was about to meet the new hotness of college hoops.

On December 8, 1982, the Tigers traveled to Texas to play the

University of Houston, home of Phi Slama Jama, the state's tallest "fraternity." The team, more like a monster headed by the likes of local guard Clyde Drexler and a Nigerian big man named Hakeem Olajuwon, used the dunk as both a central part of their offense and a way to intimidate and humiliate. "The team with the most dunks wins the game," Guy Lewis, the team's coach, said repeatedly. Around Cougartown, the cultural phenomenon of the team made the city of Houston cool for possibly the first time ever, captured in T-shirts, caps, buttons, and a catchy track from DJ Captain Jack that was in heavy rotation on the radio stations.

When the Tigers arrived in Houston, one of the skycaps asked if they were the Auburn basketball team. After Greg Turner confirmed they were who he thought they were, he got an earful while the man helped with his luggage.

"He said, 'You guys got the fat guy on the team who can jump, right?'" Turner recalled. "He said, 'You guys are going to get your asses handed to you tonight by Phi Slama Jama.' We didn't say anything."

Near tip-off at a packed Hofheinz Pavilion, the fans didn't know or care too much about Auburn—and the same could be said of the No. 9 Cougars, the sport's newest collection of stars. "To tell you the truth, I don't know where Auburn is located," Drexler said. "All I've heard about Auburn is that they have a big center named Barkley who is 6-6 and weighs about 260." He added, "Barkley sounds like an offensive lineman to me."

As the game started, Smith called 4-Down, a play designed to get Charles an easy layup. After the big man pinned his defender, Turner threw a bounce pass to Charles for the finish.

"Charles lays that thing up and all you heard was the block sound from Olajuwon," Turner said. "It sounded like everyone in the arena blocked him."

Stubborn and looking to make a point after Houston easily scored on the other end, Smith's play call was easy: run it for Charles again.

"All you heard the next time was whoosh when Charles hammered it down," Turner said.

Despite being down only by 5 at the half, Houston eventually started off the second half on an 18–4 run before winning 77–65. But Charles's 14-point, 8-rebound outing against a national power was another moral victory for a program thirsty for recognition.

"We ended up losing, but he got the respect," Turner remembered. "He put Olajuwon and all of them in the basket."

Following the game, Drexler praised the physicality of Barkley—"He put a couple of legs to me, but he got a couple back, too." He was also baffled by his jumping and mobility.

"He's the best fat guy around," Drexler added afterward.

Charles respected Phi Slama Jama so much that he made a friendly bet inside his dorm that Houston would win the 1983 national championship. Al Del Greco, a kicker for Auburn, had been watching the game between Houston and NC State in the dorm when Lorenzo Charles's putback dunk completed the miracle win.

"I don't remember what the amount was, but in the dorm watching the game, you could hear this one person screaming and running around in sheer agony that he had lost the bet," said Del Greco about what's perhaps one of the earliest instances of Barkley gambling. "He was so sure Houston was going to win that he had put some money on the game, and he was upset it got ripped out from under him."

With Houston on the schedule in December 1982, Syracuse coach Jim Boeheim assigned assistant Bernie Fine to scout the Cougars. When he returned, Boeheim didn't learn as much about Houston as he would have liked because someone else who he hadn't heard of was distracting from the scouting process.

"I said, 'What do you think about Olajuwon?'" Boeheim said. "He goes, 'I don't know, but this other guy from Auburn is unbelievable. He was dunking on everybody.'"

In conference play, opponents were curious to see if Charles could possibly repeat what he did the previous year or if it was an aberration—and it didn't take long for Butch Pierre to get an answer. Pierre, a point guard for Mississippi State, was backpedaling on defense as Charles came tumbling down on the fast break. He saw an Auburn player throw an alley-oop to Charles that he could see was going to soar out-of-bounds. Then, Charles reached his paw to above the top of the square and pounded it home, and Pierre didn't know what to think.

"I thought there was no way he was going to catch it," Pierre said. "Except he did."

Two games in eleven days would define what had been a disappointing sophomore season for Charles. Though the team was winning, the brutish big man had fouled out in three straight games and there were clear signs of a slump.

Looking to turn his individual fortunes around in the first half against fifth-ranked Alabama on January 5, 1983, he went up for a wide-open dunk. Instead of an easy throwdown, Charles ended up slamming the ball off the side of the rim. His powers, however, returned in the second half, where he unleashed a barrage of bruising dunks, box-outs, and blocks in front of the home crowd. Charles scored 21 of his 27 points in the second half. There was one stretch of defensive possessions where he took a charge on a fast break, blocked a shot, and stole the ball, a one-man wrecking crew destroying all plans for a Crimson Tide comeback.

"All I can remember, especially with Charles in those years, was total domination," said Buck Johnson, an Alabama guard.

Guarding Charles was Bobby Lee Hurt, the same big man who Barkley outplayed in the Christmas tournament a couple years earlier to help launch his rise. Hurt, who said Charles was stronger than Georgetown center Patrick Ewing, was held to just 10 points in a 91–80 defeat.

"That matchup down low with him and Bobby Lee, it wasn't really a matchup," Johnson recalled. "I was on the perimeter, so I was lucky I didn't have to go down there and take the abuse Charles was giving Bobby Lee. It was like a man against a child."

While he insisted his matchups with Bobby Lee weren't personal, he showed his delight in dominating the player everyone wanted over him. But he was more concerned in beating the name on the front of Hurt's crimson jersey.

"Going against Bobby Lee fires me up, but going against Alabama fires me up more," he said. "Alabama beat us twice last year and I didn't want that to happen again."

The same could be said about Kentucky, the conference standard who Charles saw as their biggest roadblock. Charles was tabbed as the "Wildcat Whipper" in just his second season at Auburn, and much of that was due to his matchups with Mel Turpin, Kentucky's much-ballyhooed big man. An All-SEC selection in '82 and '83 and the conference's leading scorer, the six-foot-eleven Turpin was a force. But to Charles, he was another talented skyscraper to leap over. That was terribly apparent to Derrick Hord, Turpin's teammate at Kentucky.

"I remember the first time we went up against him and Mel was guarding him, and he just dunked so easily on Mel," Hord said. "I took the ball out-of-bounds and I kept saying to myself, 'This guy just dunked on our seven-footer.' Needless to say, he was in Mel Turpin's head for the rest of his college career."

Wins against two top-6 teams in less than two weeks catapulted Auburn into the Top 25 for the first time since 1976. The once anonymous team from the football school was now the toast of the nation.

"It gives us confidence that we can play anywhere," Charles said after the win. "The feeling's so good it's hard to express."

Auburn's arrival in the Top 25 meant more exposure to a national media already captivated by their circular attraction—part carnival strongman, part *The Little Engine That Could*. In a *Sports Illustrated* profile of the conference, Curry Kirkpatrick laid eyes on the humongous, plump sophomore and concluded that we were witnessing "quite possibly the most amazing, dynamic and fun-to-watch collegian in all of the land."

The Tigers, who were ranked No. 21 but would soon drop from the rankings after alternating wins and losses in conference play, knew their best shot to reenter the Top 25 was to beat Kentucky during their rematch in Auburn.

In the locker room before the Saturday game, Smith barked out instructions to his team. Turpin or Sam Bowie weren't on the coach's mind as much as Charles Hurt. Each time Auburn played them, Hurt, Kentucky's resident enforcer and instigator, would do whatever he could to get you to lose your cool—he'd hold you, elbow you, and ram his butt into you. Smith thought the message was clear: *Don't let Charles Hurt get to you.*

The advice didn't stick for Charles. On Auburn's first possession of the game, Charles was cutting from the wing on a fast break for an easy bucket until Hurt, as the *Louisville Courier-Journal* described it, ran at Barkley and "blasted forth like a pulling guard on an unsuspecting cornerback." After briefly recovering on a press table of exasperated reporters, Barkley picked himself up and chased his aggressor. Seconds later, he cocked back and smacked the back of Hurt's head. The retaliatory gesture proved to be too much for referee Paul Galvan, who tossed Charles 113 seconds into the game.

Auburn kept it close, but fell to No. 13 Kentucky, 71–69. Turpin powered the Wildcats to 25 points in Charles's absence—and no one was more thrilled to see his adversary leave the floor.

"I started feeling sorry for the kid, but yeah, I was happy to see the kid go," Turpin said.

The prevailing theory after the game was that Kentucky had intentionally tried to get Charles ejected. When asked whether he set up the man named "Porkley" by opposing fans, Hurt, who had never guarded Charles until that game, said it was simply "my time to guard Barkley."

"We at Kentucky never set out to do that kind of thing," Hurt said to reporters.

Two hours later, Smith was still infuriated playing back the replay. Years later, he maintains Charles's dominance over Turpin was what set in motion Kentucky's plan to target his hefty hoss.

"He had destroyed Turpin, it was unbelievable," Smith said of Barkley. "Then Joe Hall came up with this deal that led to Charles being ejected. Joe will deny it, and has denied it, but it's true: they knew they couldn't win unless Charles wasn't playing."

Galvan, one of the most respected refs in the conference, didn't consider Charles to be belligerent, but rather someone who lost it in that one moment. That was confirmed the next time he had an Auburn game.

"Before the tip-off of the next game I had him, he came over and said, 'Mr. Paul, I'm sorry about that; I didn't mean to get tossed.

We'll have a good game, right?' I said, 'You'll bet we'll have a good game,'" Galvan said.

While it might not have been apparent in the moment, the sudden ejection and Kentucky loss would portend the trouble that awaited the rest of the year.

Not even a barrage of 20-point, double-digit rebounding games from Charles and a breakout stretch from Person could save Auburn from going 5–10 in the rest of SEC play. Alabama's Bobby Lee Hurt, regularly a target for Charles's ire on the floor, ended up rejecting shot after shot against his adversary, outscoring Barkley, 23–10, in the last game of the season.

The slump came at a time when Smith, who noted that Charles still was very hard on himself after losses, was looking to get weight off his star. The publicity was nice, but he simply thought Charles wasn't in shape.

The coach cited the words of Jack LaLanne, the fitness guru who referred to nutrition and exercise as "the salvation of America," in warning Charles to avoid unhealthy foods. "I told him if it tastes good, spit it out," Smith said. That was not the case during the taping of a thirty-minute television show, when teammate Mark Cahill witnessed Charles consume an entire bag of bite-sized Snickers. There was no spitting out that many peanuts, caramel, and nougat, leaving Cahill aghast. "There was nothing left but this little pile of wrappers," he said. "It was inconceivable."

As someone who didn't meet a meal he didn't finish, Smith's suggestion was one of many that were soundly rejected during practice and throughout a regular day. Herbert Greene, the assistant who recruited Charles from Leeds, knew that the forward needed the needling, even if he didn't realize it could be beneficial.

"Sonny pushed Charles in places he had never been and didn't want to be pushed in," Greene said.

Pat Dye, the football coach who got to know Charles, also noticed from afar that something wasn't working. "It was pretty well documented… Charles didn't work hard enough for Coach Smith and was lazy early on," Dye said.

If Charles wasn't going to listen to the coaches, Smith thought an outside voice could assist. He reached out to Dick Vitale, the college coach–turned–ESPN personality. The endlessly enthusiastic Vitale sat in on a practice before calling one of Auburn's games. What he saw was a star going through the motions, in half of the speed of his teammates and half of the conditioning, which is something he wanted to help change.

"Sonny Smith came over to me and said, 'You need to motivate this kid and inspire him because he has a tendency to not be as intense,'" Vitale said. "I remember grabbing Charles and said, 'Son, you have a chance to make a lot of money, man. Bust your gut, listen to your coaches, don't let it go to waste.'" He added to Charles, "Your coach loves you. Your people here love you. Listen to them. They're trying to help ya, man!"

Vitale saw what he called Charles's special bounce off the floor and realized Smith was in an unenviable position of potentially squandering a player with worldly gifts.

"It's one of the worst things when someone with that talent level is not where they should be," Vitale said. "Sonny cared so much about Charles, and he wouldn't have reached out to me the way he did if he didn't care. Some kids just never get it, but for others all of a sudden, the light just turns on."

The light remained off in the first round of the SEC Tournament, a rematch with Alabama the day after the regular season finale. With a 1-point lead and 1:12 to go, Charles inadvertently stumbled into Alabama's Ennis Whatley, resulting in two made free throws. In the final 17 seconds, Smith drew up a lob play for Charles, who had been held to 4 points, over Person, who had dropped 23. Guessing the team wasn't going to Person, the freshman's defender helped double Charles—and Barkley never got his hands on the ball.

Alabama won; Auburn lost.

What looked to be the start of a breakout year fizzled to a 15–13 campaign, a one-game improvement from the previous year. While Charles dominated again, leading the SEC in rebounding a second straight year, averaging 14 points and almost 10 rebounds, and making the All-SEC 2nd Team, the Tigers fell way short of once lofty prospects.

The nicknames, magazine articles, and aura around Charles was there. What wasn't there were the wins. And by the end of the year, Charles's happiness with his coach had dissipated.

"I said, 'Coach, I'm leaving here. I want to thank you, but this is not fun for me right now,'" he said.

The twenty-year-old everyone thought would bring Auburn to the promised land was on the verge of leaving.

8

Not long after fans walk past Charles's statue and the white tailgating tents around campus with names like "Make Auburn Great Again," the howls inside a three-quarters-full Beard-Eaves-Memorial Coliseum on a Friday in November nearly echo that of a lathered-up Bruce Springsteen crowd at the old Giants Stadium.

But instead of the E Street Band, it's the Auburn men's basketball team, coming off the first Final Four appearance in the history of the football school. The band's rendition of Nirvana's "Smells Like Teen Spirit" gives way to the roar of "Brrruuuuuuuuuuuuuce" that welcomes their boisterous boss, Bruce Pearl.

If Charles was able to take the Tigers to the next level, then Pearl brought them to the final level. In a blue suit with orange-and-white-striped tie, Pearl, strutting to the court with a wide grin that says he knows he can no longer surprise anyone, can do no wrong here after the No. 5 seed upset the three winningest programs in the history of the game—Kansas, North Carolina, and Kentucky—in consecutive rounds on their way to Minneapolis. In fact, he had called his shot of a Final Four berth while dancing with his daughter to "One Shining Moment" at her wedding the previous summer.

"One of the highlights for me as a coach is taking Charles Barkley's school to the Final Four," Pearl said.

When Pearl was in a different shade of orange at Tennessee about a decade ago, his secretary said he needed to hear a certain message on his voice mail. It was from Charles. He had not met or talked to him before. Pearl didn't call him back, mainly because Charles told him there was no need to do so, but he kept the message on a phone and would listen to it whenever he got down on himself.

Much like his time on the Plains, Pearl was revered at Tennessee, bringing in recruits and donor dollars, winning games, and devoting himself to his school, including painting his chest orange and jumping around in the student section during a women's basketball game. His arrival at Auburn came after he was dismissed from Tennessee for violations of unethical conduct regarding a high school junior recruit attending a barbecue hosted by Pearl, and then lying to the NCAA about it.

When he was hired, he vowed to turn Auburn basketball around. Fans, players, and alums took to Pearl immediately, celebrating with him outside the arena upon his arrival.

Just as Pearl's program began to show signs of life for one of the first times since the days of Barkley and Sonny Smith, the activities of another person from that past threatened the present and future. Chuck Person, an associate head coach under Pearl, was arrested in September 2017 on multiple charges, including bribery conspiracy, as part of an FBI investigation regarding Adidas and several college basketball programs accused of corruption, including Auburn. (Person, who was dismissed from the program, was indicted, and later pleaded guilty to a count of conspiracy to commit bribery.)

Even with the team enjoying its best season in years, there were questions of how long the enthusiastic coach could stay at Auburn amid the allegations. A devout Jewish man who often speaks of his faith, Pearl once said of the investigation that while his faith in God had never been stronger, his faith in man had never been weaker. Yet when it came down to it, whatever concerns mounted in the days of the investigation were almost immediately squelched by his most honest supporter.

"Listen, Auburn would be idiots to let Bruce Pearl go," Charles said in 2018. In March 2019, Auburn made the Final Four and Barkley played the nation's cheerleader, with pom-poms and stuffed Tigers lining his studio desk during coverage of March Madness.

The bond between Pearl and Charles was built on not only a love of school but food, golf, family, and deep conversations on politics and religion. Pearl repeatedly harps on the generosity and patience for the common man of an individual he calls the most recognizable person on earth. Decades after Charles devoured Godfather's Pizza, the outgoing Pearl's appetite could be summed up in a 2007 *Sports Illustrated* profile in which he said it was hard to beat a Krispy Kreme in one hand and a Bud Select in the other. The Bruce, Barkley and Basketball Golf Classic, the annual tournament to benefit Auburn, features Charles's swing-stop-swing motion as its logo. They shared in the pain of the Final Four defeat to Virginia. Months later, Charles was awarded a Final Four ring from the team.

"I don't know anybody that's more accomplished or more grateful for the position they're in than Charles," Pearl said.

He added, "And he's truly grateful for Sonny Smith."

You had to be ready to bust your ass when you stepped foot inside the "Sweat Box," the full-court auxiliary gym Smith's teams would use for practice. And Smith had to see what else he could get out of Charles.

One drill in particular, the War Eagle Special, he grew to hate. Starting at the free throw line, you ran and jumped to grab the rim and once you hit the ground, you went back up again, trying to get in as many reps as you could in about sixty seconds. While it was easy for him, conditioning was not.

The contentiousness between Charles and Smith reached a boil during his sophomore year. The coach was eager to push his star forward, while Charles had his own ideas, and was going to accomplish them at his own pace and force. After Charles had dunked the ball so hard that he moved the entire basket support, weighed down by two three-hundred-pound cement blocks, Smith was cursing out people to fix it. As Smith recalled it in *Outrageous!*, Charles pushed him out of the way and moved 600 pounds back and straightened out the goal himself. (Who needs four men when you've got one Charles Barkley?)

With Charles having the highest upside of any player Smith had coached, that meant the Wide Load from Leeds was also going to incur a lot of his coach's criticism. That was evident to Byron Henson at practice when Charles was going half speed. Henson remembered Charles telling a peeved Smith, who wondered why he didn't want to be a great player in practice, that "when the bright lights come on, I play. That's all that counts."

Smith had enough of Charles's indifference in practice, and that frustration came through one day. During a five-on-five run, Charles knocked a teammate up into the stands. Tired of his star player's reckless tendencies, Smith recalled in *Outrageous!* how he ran up to Charles and swung at him at half force, hitting him square in his chest. Charles backed off then and there, but he made it clear to the head coach that he wouldn't let Smith hit him anymore.

"Over the years, Charles had said if he had an O.J. Simpson jury while he was at Auburn, he would have killed Sonny," said Jan Smith.

By the end of his sophomore year, Charles was embarrassed and feeling unappreciated. He entered Sonny Smith's office and told him that he was transferring. Walking out the door, he told him where he wanted to go: *I'm going to Alabama.*

As tantalizing as it might have been to team up with Bobby Lee Hurt and Ennis Whatley, Alabama was never a serious option. But seemingly everything else was on the table. Mack McCarthy remembered Smith handing Charles the NCAA blue book and offering him a chance to go anywhere, and he'd make the call to help facilitate it. "He literally made that offer," he said, adding that there was no chance in hell Smith was going to deliver Auburn's star to the Crimson Tide and frenemy, Wimp Sanderson.

Charles let the coaches sweat it out as he hid out at a friend's girlfriend's apartment, making them think he was bolting for good. When he finally called Smith, it was time to put all their cards on the table.

For as confrontational as Charles would become, he was still thin-skinned in the standoff with a coach who had become one of the chief father figures in his life. He was asking for positive reinforcement, and Charles, as hard as it is to believe, had difficulty putting it into words until they sat down with each other.

"He said, 'Well, tell me what you want me to do,'" Charles said. "I said, 'I want you to tell me, "Son, you're doing good, but you can do better."'"

Clearing the air helped, but there were other people working to keep him on campus. One of them was Joe Ciampi, the women's basketball coach who he had befriended while sitting in on their practices. What started as Charles being in the gym at the same time turned into Ciampi giving him pointers on where his elbow should be on his free throws. Ciampi remembers a young man who wanted to be heard and accepted by his coaches, while also maintaining his pride.

Ciampi raised the question: What would it look like if Charles quit now and walked away from his teammates? For as flashy and exciting as Charles was, he was still a team player.

"We got to the point where he believed he didn't want to let his teammates down," Ciampi said. "I told him that sometimes your coaches will say things to you that make it sound like they're denouncing how you play the game, but I promise you they're praising you as much as they're denouncing you. You're just hearing the denouncing part."

Much like she had done during his recruitment two years earlier, Jan Smith played a critical role in keeping him there. She had become a maternal figure to Charles, cooking dinners for him and the rest of the team and being the gentler half of their coach.

"I was just always there for him if he needed me and vice versa," she said. "It just worked out okay... He just needed a mom figure here." That was clear when Jan, then only forty-seven, suffered what the coach describes as a devastating stroke around 1983. Sonny Smith remembers that Charles had developed such a fondness for Jan that he was the first player to arrive at the hospital to check on the woman he told his coach was "the greatest wife ever."

Now in his eighties, Sonny Smith is proud of his relationship with Charles. And he'll be the first to tell you the bond he has with Charles today looks far different than their relationship decades ago.

We sat down and I realized I had to coach him better after that. I was reluctant to change at first, but I realized I had to do it to make this work.

It was certainly a stale situation at one time. It was never personal with me and I don't know if it was with him or not. I just wanted to make him better and I didn't think he was cooperating. If I was coaching today, I'd do it totally different.

I never felt pressure to leave if Charles left. It would have been very difficult had I lost him. We would have gone back to losing and the same old things we had been doing. The league was so good, everybody had good players. It was never said, but I think I never would have made it at a high level after that if he left.

Now, he looks at me like a father figure. Our relationship got better every year. But it had to grow.

I would like Charles to say that he realizes I meant well and that I tried to get him there. Not that it would validate anything for me, but when I read the book, I'd like to see him say he realizes that.

Now that Sonny Smith had regained Charles's trust, could they win together?

For what felt like the first time in his two-plus years at Auburn, the Tigers finally belonged to Charles. The player who had been described in newspapers as "Fred Astaire in Orson Welles' body," "the Pillsbury Doughboy who plays like Superman," and "Baby Huey in shorts and tennis shoes" had turned Auburn into one of the main attractions of college basketball for the 1983–84 season. This was not all clear to Charles, who as a twenty-year-old remained starstruck by the idea of asking Pat Sullivan, the school's Heisman-winning quarterback, for an autograph and not realizing he was arguably the most-written-about athlete for the school since Sullivan himself.

No amount of mouthwash could possibly rinse away the sour taste of his sophomore season. Sure, he got headlines, ate pizza, won another rebounding title, beat Kentucky, ate more pizza, and cemented himself as a potentially transformative player, but the campaign was empty. The narrative had already formed for the upcoming season: *the only person who could stop Charles Barkley from reaching the greatness everyone wanted him to achieve was Charles Barkley.* Pundits like Dick Vitale loved what Charles could be, but declared that he was only a teaser, someone who was solely motivated by playing time and attention and couldn't empty the tank for his team night after night after night.

From that disappointing sophomore campaign came a third-year recommitment to the game and to himself. This was no more apparent than Charles removing the famed fridge from the dorm, hoping to limit any late-night temptation to eat before bed. No more chicken nuggets or Subway sandwiches. The pizza was still there, but two new words entered his vocabulary: moderation and vegetables. The expanded lexicon came with Charles running three miles a day and trimming down to about 258 pounds, more than 30 pounds lighter than his playing weight the previous season. The summer league runs back in Birmingham helped keep it off him. He returned to school at 14.5 percent body-fat, one of the lowest on the team and a considerable drop from when he entered as a freshman.

So, why the diet for the doughboy? Before that summer's World University Games in Edmonton, pro coaches told Charles, labeled by national media as "Fat Man," that his game was as good as any NBA player if he gave a damn. Summertime players like Oklahoma's Wayman Tisdale regarded him as his favorite player in college basketball and gifted him a name of his own: "the Eighth Wonder of the World."

Missouri's Norm Stewart, the US coach, still thought he was thirty pounds overweight, but expressed throughout a silver-medal performance in which Charles averaged 14 points and 9 rebounds that only he could decide how much he wanted to weigh and how good he wanted to be at the next level.

"This doesn't mean I'm still not going to have fun," Charles said of his change in approach in June 1983. "It just means I'm going to play harder than I ever have before."

Back at Auburn, incoming freshman guards Gerald White and Frank Ford were ready to stabilize a backcourt light on depth outside of Paul Daniels. Add in Charles, Person, Vern Strickland, and senior Greg Turner, and Auburn, picked to finish fourth in the conference, was poised to compete—if they didn't screw it up.

In a sign that the "Charles for Change" campaign was no fluke, McCarthy, the Auburn assistant, was wondering what the junior was doing with the rest of his teammates who had done something to warrant being at the baseball field at 5:30 in the morning.

"Well, what did you do?" McCarthy asked.

"I didn't do anything," Charles responded.

"Well, why are you here?" the coach replied.

"Coach, I feel one coming on," Charles said. "I'm going to hang out with my guys, and I want to put one in the bank if that's OK."

In what was potentially his final year, Charles was not only feeling in control of the team but also becoming a fixture at Auburn, almost as much as the chicken at Rusty's or a 3:00 a.m. nightcap at the War Eagle Supper Club. That feeling trickled over to the faculty, too, specifically with Edward H. Hobbs, the dean of the School of Arts and Sciences, who named his dog Barkley after the junior.

The reality of Charles's reach was felt in everyday situations, big and small. The renovation of the athletics dorm meant that the basketball players would live in off-campus apartments right behind the Fiji fraternity house. For Ron Anders, the three-on-three games among the fraternity brothers inevitably became a lot more interesting whenever Charles walked by, put down his backpack, and called for the next game. Though he was clearly going at maybe 10 percent speed against the defensive scheme concocted by the gentlemen of Phi Gamma Delta, Anders, then an Auburn cheerleader whose family founded Anders Bookstore in town, still marveled whenever Daniels threw alley-oops to Charles that he finished with the same ease some fraternity brothers would have had shotgunning a beer. In Charles, Anders found that he could call the folk hero both a pickup adversary and friend.

"He became chummy to many of the guys in the fraternity," recalled Anders, who would eventually be elected as mayor of the city of Auburn.

Pat Dye Jr. was always up for pickup games at the "Sweat Box" with Charles and Person. With Charles at shooting guard, he would jokingly launch shots just past half-court, a callback to his days heaving up those shots for Leeds Junior High and Wallace Honeycutt. Dye Jr. was surprised when Charles passed him the ball and saw that he did his best to not dunk the ball off every rebound.

Those runs inside the non-air-conditioned auxiliary gym had a hint of hilarity when Bo Jackson walked in. Jackson's vast and profound athletic talents did not fully extend to basketball, said Dye Jr.

"Bo had problems hitting the backboard, let alone the rim," he recalled. "He could jump and dunk it, don't get me wrong, but Barkley would laugh at Bo trying to shoot a basketball. Charles was talking a lot of trash to Bo about that."

Charles might have been thriving socially, including a girlfriend he lovingly called "Knucklehead," but the coaching staff were consistently concerned about whether the physical education major could stay eligible in the classroom. His best classes were the electives—"I was on the non-mandatory dean's list"—and the athletics department didn't want to stretch the limits of his academic motivation. He was deterred by the department and Smith from switching his major from physical education to business management, worrying he would flunk challenging courses like business law. (He passed.)

Smith knew from his time at Leeds High that Charles wasn't particularly big on class time, so he assigned assistants to accompany him to class. Minutes after dropping him off at his classroom and seeing Charles walk inside, McCarthy was left befuddled when he would receive phone calls from professors who said that he wasn't there. McCarthy thought it was impossible—*I saw him go inside the classroom.*

The day after one of these calls, McCarthy, thinking the professor obviously had to have been blind to overlook the nearly three-hundred-pound student athlete in the room, accompanied Charles to another class. He would show that professor what's up, the assistant thought.

"I walk him to class and I kind of hang around, and there's Charles, going in the front door and out the back," McCarthy said. "And he was beating me back to the dorms."

Charles was going to class. He just wasn't staying in it for more than a minute. Keeping Charles on the court meant assigning him tutors in several subjects. Mark Stevenson, an Auburn native, was assigned as his economics tutor. Stevenson, who finished up his degree at Auburn after "not bothering to graduate" from Princeton in five years, was enrolled in grad school and wanted to make some extra cash tutoring basketball, football, and track athletes. As an assistant sports editor for the school newspaper, Stevenson had marveled at what Charles was able to do with his body, comparing his joyful exuberance on the court to that of a little kid who just found out he can walk on his hands and was sharing that happiness with his friends.

The tutor realized quickly that working with him in a public space near the library came with people waving at the star and Charles taking time to chat with friends and strangers passing by. It was evident to Stevenson in the two weeks of economics tutoring that Charles stayed for a lot of his classes and had absorbed enough material to make the sessions more of a confidence booster than anything else.

"He made it clear that he never touched the textbook. He had soaked up enough listening to the lectures that it became clear he didn't need tutoring and he was going to pass," Stevenson said. "I went to the academic counselor and told him there's no value in this because they were spending money on tutoring when Charles knew his stuff."

On a team flight back after a conference game, Phillip Marshall was sitting across the aisle from Charles when he noticed that he was writing a letter to Charcey. When a reporter asked about it, Charles let on that he was telling her that he loved her in case "I don't make it home." As it turned out, Charles was casually dating a White girl from the northern part of the state, Marshall said, at a time when interracial relationships were not looked too kindly upon in that area of Alabama. The worst part? Her daddy was apparently going to be at the airport when the team landed. Charles turned to Mark Cahill, the only White guy on the team, for a last-ditch request in case the situation turned from funny to tense.

"He says to Cahill, 'When we get back, we're switching cars,' and Cahill goes, 'Bullshit, we're not!'" Marshall recalled. "I asked him one time later if the father was there and he was actually there, but obviously nothing happened."

In town to cover Maryland's football game against Auburn, Michael Wilbon wandered over to the coliseum for an intra-squad scrimmage open to the media before the game. Smith wanted national journalists to get a look at what they had on the Plains in November 1983. It was the first time Wilbon met Charles, or even laid eyes on him, and the *Washington Post* reporter left the gym staggered and mesmerized, almost as if he'd seen the future of basketball.

"I just remember going there for one reason and then just you could not take your eyes off Chuck. You couldn't take your eyes off him," Wilbon remembered. "You're just like, 'I'm sorry, who is this guy again?'... I saw him in that scrimmage and then I became obsessed."

But before anyone could declare Auburn to be back (or to have arrived at all), the more pressing concern was *Charles's* back.

Ten minutes into the first half of an exhibition that same month against US amateur champion Marathon Oil, Charles pulled his back coming down for a rebound, and dropped to his knees in pain. Nagging injuries to Charles and other starters would delay the launch of Auburn's promising season, as the Tigers dropped three of their first five. When Smith couldn't hold him out, Charles, still suffering from muscle spasms and severe pain of a lower-back sprain, suited up and just walked up and down the court. He could barely walk, but the Tigers won the game with the loudest and roundest decoy in college basketball.

Charles would end up sitting three games and played limited minutes off the bench for another ten. He couldn't benefit from the electric therapy because he was still too thick for the impulses to have any effect on his bones. He started showing signs of life against hapless Eastern Kentucky, scoring 18 points in a tiring fifteen minutes on a series of thundering yet ill-advised dunks to help stretch out his back.

He had returned to form. In his custom-made shorts to fit his tree-trunk legs, he was no longer lumbering. Off a steal against LSU at the free throw line, Charles took five dribbles and threw down a one-handed jam for the and-1 on the other end, clapping and pumping his fist to the roof of the coliseum. The LSU fans that once taunted Smith about whether he was going to send "Charlie" to the A&P supermarket had been shut up. Against Ole Miss, he dropped a left-handed bounce pass on the fast break to Person for the easy deuce. Moments later, an Ole Miss defender darts past him to get out of the way of what would be a perfect poster to capture a flat-out angry fast-break dunk. "Incidental contact with that guy over the speed limit could give you terminal whiplash!" a color commentator proclaimed one game.

After each win, kids rushed the court for a chance to say hi or touch their hometown hero. Knowing this, Charles started to wear six sweatbands, three on each arm, to hand out to young fans.

The love wasn't everywhere, especially not at Vanderbilt. In Nashville, he skied so high to reject a shot that his head nearly grazed the rim. Seeing Charles repeatedly dominate against the Commodores brought about at least one racist rant from the stands, Smith remembered.

"Some guy behind our bench—I'm absolutely sure he wasn't a Vanderbilt student—stood up and said, 'Why don't you coach those damn N— before they get up here!'" Smith recalled. "Our bench stood up and I told that guy to sit down because he wouldn't hear that crap at Auburn."

The casual racism mattered little to Charles, a product of the Jim Crow South whose mother taught him to rise above the bigotry. Smith said people would even find out where he was staying on the road and call his room at all hours of the night. But he still had some scores to settle on the court.

Hurt, the man who unintentionally helped put Charles on the map, was on the end of one last gorilla dunk. Facing foul trouble, Hurt saw Charles coming down the court with reckless abandon. As he was going up for the block, Charles gave a slight push-off to Hurt to create separation and flush the ball with his right hand as both his legs jutted out in the air as if he were on a swing set for giants.

"That kind of became a highlight photo," Hurt said. "He pushed off, but it looked good on his part so it's okay. It's a thing that happened."

For as much as he relished victories over Hurt and Alabama, he *needed* to win against Turpin and Kentucky. On January 13, 1984, the top-ranked Wildcats came to town, nearly a year removed from squeaking out a win after Charles got himself ejected shortly following tip-off. Vince Thompson, a friend and member of the sports information office, remembered Charles's fight the year before as a watershed moment of sorts in Auburn's clashes with Kentucky, saying it reminded him of when Apollo Creed realizes he has hands full with Rocky Balboa. And as long as Charles Barkley was in the blue and orange, Thompson said, Kentucky was going to be in for a fight—a true tussle where Charles throws someone wearing a blue jersey to the floor.

After going down 10–0 to start a Friday the 13th matchup promoted on TBS as Twin Towers versus Twin Towers, Charles came off the bench to help ignite a comeback within minutes. Sam Bowie, Kentucky's other much-celebrated center, often called games that unfolded involving Barkley as "a scary situation," and this meeting in front of a rare sell-out crowd at Beard-Eaves-Memorial was even more spooky than the others. Whatever back pain Charles had in the first couple months of the season had left town for one night, as he went to work early on Turpin, dunking and leaping over his old rival in a must-have game.

It's hard to envision a more difficult opponent for Turpin than Charles, a human isosceles triangle. As Charles himself described the advantage he had on the Dipper, "I can put my butt on Melvin's legs, but Melvin can only put his legs on my butt." That's a Charles way of saying I've got you in my pocket. His attempts to talk to Turpin during the game were unsuccessful, leading the Kentucky big man to say that Charles has a "lotta loose lip."

They did a lot more than just talk. The triangle-and-two zone defense stifled the Wildcats, and Charles finished with 21 points and 10 rebounds to go along with Person's 25 points and 9 rebounds. Turpin got his 22 points, but was neutralized on the glass with only 5 rebounds. The death knell came not on a dunk or block but on a rebound and left-handed outlet pass to Person who found Strickland for the and-1 that sent the fans into a tizzy. Intimidated no more, the Tigers dismantled Kentucky, 82–63, their first-ever win against a No. 1 team and the biggest victory in program history.

"Isn't that how it works? Don't you get No. 1 if you beat No. 1?" Charles asked amid the pandemonium. "Who said Friday the 13th was bad?!" Despite being the leading scorer in the conference, Person knew Charles was something different that night, calling it a joy to watch him perform and operate. "After that game, I knew he was one of the best, if not the best, college basketball player in the country," Person said.

Two weeks and a couple underwhelming losses passed before they beat another top opponent in No. 10 LSU. The win, which catapulted them into the Top 25 for the first time that season, was the first time it seemed like Charles might not return for his senior season. He insinuated for the first time that it would be one of his last games at Auburn.

He credited the success to Smith and their unusual but now stable relationship.

"I'm going to drive him crazy before I leave, but we're having a lot of fun together," Charles said of his coach.

It was the beginning of one of the most important years of his life, one filled with hellos and goodbyes as well as burgundy suits and Denny's pancakes.

9

By the time March Madness approached, Charles Barkley had figured out what it meant to be great at the college level. In the process, everyone wanted a piece of him.

Before a March 1 game against Mississippi State, Ohio senator
John Glenn stopped by Auburn and said hi to Charles during his
1984 presidential campaign. Charcey was in the stands, delighted.

Alexander Wolff was there to profile Charles for *Sports Illustrated*.
Glenn's campaign wasn't going anywhere, Wolff realized after seeing how Charles had fifteen times the charisma of the senator. After
meeting Glenn, Charles blurted out to no one in particular that his
goal in life was to become president of the United States, which
would mean he would "lock up everybody over twelve and let kids
rule the world."

"He had total trust in what he said and the integrity of human
interaction, and he was going to look you in the eye and be completely confident with how the interaction would turn out," Wolff
said. "It was all natural."

Though he had largely reshaped his diet, pizza was not included in that food furlough, and the photos of him scarfing a supreme pie at his dorm would be the first visual evidence of the love affair. In one set of photos, Charles, sporting a practice jersey from the summer, a pair of tight blue jeans and Chuck Taylor All Stars, is sitting on the doorstep of his apartment, grinning at the pizza from Godfather's. In another, dressed in what looks to be a burgundy velvet tracksuit, he is joined by Strickland, Chuck Person, and other teammates in the kitchen to chow down on some more pizza.

The photos gave a window to a national audience of what regional fans already knew. At Tennessee, student David Grim had twelve empty pizza boxes from Domino's delivered courtside to Charles before a game in Knoxville, which left both Charles and his coach laughing.

"We really liked Barkley," Grim said. "We always bonded with anyone who could stick it to Kentucky."

The additional attention would be a boon for Auburn, which was still expanding its national profile outside of just Bo Jackson.

"P.T. Barnum didn't need anybody to be his publicity guy. He was his publicity guy. That's how Charles was," David Housel said. "P.T. Barnum did it with smoke and mirrors. Charles did it himself."

The doting on Charles bugged Person, the team's leading scorer. While Charles was playing himself into shape, Person was the team's best player for most of the '84 season after coming off hernia surgery and an appendectomy in the off-season. Called "Mr. Smooth" by TBS's Joe Dean, Person strived for attention and thought he had earned it. He recognized Charles's talent, but wanted fans and the media to give him his due, too.

But whatever tension there was between the two was quelled for the SEC Tournament, where the Tigers were the No. 2 seed and considered favorites to get to the title game against Kentucky. They'd do so behind Barkley, who was named the SEC Player of the Year after averaging 15 points, nearly 2 blocks, and 9.5 rebounds, clinching his third consecutive rebounding title. In a year of honors, Person, who had the second-most first-place votes for Player of the Year, joined Charles on the First Team, and Smith was named the conference's Coach of the Year.

The first two games of Auburn's tournament in Nashville were defined by lethargy and last-second prayers. It was essentially a home game for seventh-seed Vanderbilt at Memorial Gymnasium in the quarterfinals. Though the Tigers shot well from the field, Vanderbilt's 2–3 zone took some shine off the Auburn stars, limiting Charles and Person to a combined 26 points. With a shot to win it, a thirty-foot heave from Vandy fell short and Auburn survived, 59–58.

The semifinals the next day against sixth-seed Tennessee had nearly a mirror result. They would win 60–58, setting up a rubber match with top-seed Kentucky.

By the time the two were set to meet for the conference title, Auburn's 19-point blowout two months earlier had felt like a distant memory. The rematch in February 1984 saw the Wildcats return the favor. During the pregame introductions in Lexington, Charles shook hands with everyone except Mel Turpin, resulting in deafening boos from the rabid crowd. The retribution came in the form of a 20-point rout of the Tigers.

The stakes couldn't get any higher on March 10, 1984, in a conference championship game involving two teams that had been entangled in the SEC's premier rivalry that season. Auburn, the mom-and-pop shop of the conference, had one more shot to topple Kentucky, a corporate juggernaut likened to IBM. Unlike their previous meetings, Charles and Turpin shared a forceful high five during the introductions, an acknowledgment of mutual respect .

The back-and-forth affair tipped Auburn's way in the second half. Charles and a banged-up Person still poured in a combined 28 points and 13 rebounds matched up against Turpin and Sam Bowie, but the team stalled, not scoring in the last four minutes after going up by 3.

As Kentucky was set to in-bound the ball with 1:46 left, Charles broke from the huddle, clasped his hands together in a praying position, looked to the ceiling of the arena and mouthed one word: *Please*. After calling the final timeout with fourteen seconds left in the title game, Hall had the play set up to exploit Smith's man-to-man, a chess match between opponents who knew each other too well.

At the top of the key, Kentucky guard Jim Master looked at the crowded lane and began to penetrate to the free throw line. He would wait till four seconds were left on the clock to dish it off to Kenny Walker near the left elbow. The anxiousness inside the gym intensified as Walker took one dribble to his left. From there, Walker skied in the air for a high-release jumper over the six-foot-ten Person with two seconds remaining.

Much like Walker's shot, the fate of the Auburn team hung in the air and hinged on a bounce off the front of the rim. By the time the ball came back down to earth and fell through the hoop, it looked like half of the Bluegrass State had covered the court. Kentucky won 51–49.

Getting named SEC Tournament MVP, and outplaying Turpin one final time, was a small consolation. The moment has stuck with Charles for years, and it's one that Walker remembers fondly. Whenever he sees Charles, you can bet that he's bringing up the shot that crushed him and Auburn. "He is still feeling it after all these years, too," Walker said. "I think it still hurts him and I get that."

The loss was even more difficult to accept given that he had already made up his mind that he would be leaving Auburn at the conclusion of the NCAA Tournament.

"I wanted that to be my gift to Auburn," he said of a conference championship. "That took a lot out of me."

As Al Del Greco kicked the field goal that won Auburn the Sugar Bowl in front of a raucous crowd at the Louisiana Superdome, Auburn was set up for an athletic renaissance in 1984. And on Selection Sunday of that year, all eyes were on the fat guy who defied gravity.

While one postseason goal went by the wayside, another was realized: Auburn was officially going dancing for the first time in school history. In a CBS segment on Charles, the network flashed a video of Charcey, in her blue and orange shirt with a way-too-big button of Charles's face, standing and wildly cheering for the eldest son she raised in the Heights. "The big reason for Auburn's success is this woman's son: Charles Barkley," said the announcer.

"One of the greatest accomplishments of my life was getting Auburn to the NCAA Tournament," Charles said. "When I got here, it was not good. I tell people that was one of the great things in my life. When you take a team to the tournament that hasn't been to the tournament, it's pretty special."

BARKLEY

A five-seed in the East Regional, Auburn was placed in the same part of the bracket as former national champion North Carolina, led by Dean Smith, Sam Perkins, and a junior guard named Michael Jordan. They also had a potential second-round matchup with four-seed Indiana and Bob Knight. Before all that, however, they had to win a first-round date with the twelve-seed Richmond Spiders, the champions of the Eastern College Athletic Conference who were also making their first NCAA Tournament appearance.

What Richmond lacked in star power they made up for in discipline, experience, and familiarity. The five starters played almost the entire game time with a sixth man that entered sparingly. They fit into their traditional roles nicely, with Johnny Newman as the guy to get you a bucket, Kelvin Johnson as the wing scorer, Greg Beckwith at point, John Davis as the big to crash the boards, and center Bill Flye doing a little bit of everything.

The coaches didn't give the Richmond players too much tape to watch of Auburn, fearing they'd be intimidated by Charles. Beckwith remembered how in one of their scouting reports Charles was listed as "the most dominating player you'll play against at this level."

Matching up with Barkley was Flye, the resourceful, redheaded post presence who considered Charles to be on the Mount Rushmore of college basketball at the time.

"I was expecting some big monster to be out there, and he still had that star appeal," Flye said. "There are people in this world who have an aura about them and he had it then."

If the Richmond players were given little to go on about Auburn, then the Tigers were somewhat clueless about the Spiders. As Richmond took the floor for an open practice, Charles had an odd request for Dick Tarrant, the Spiders' head coach.

"He goes, 'Coach Tarrant, I'm Charles,'" said Tarrant, who told the junior he had heard of him. "He said, 'Would you mind if some of my teammates and I could watch some of your practice? We know nothing about you.' I told him it was an open practice and open to the public—and he thanked me."

The scouting session didn't last long. After five minutes, Charles and the rest of the team left, with Tarrant believing that they weren't impressed. Charles even laughed the first time he saw Flye, whom he regarded as a stiff.

The common knock against Charles was that he would be motivated to play against the best teams and players, but dialed it in when it came to the lesser-known programs.

"If you played someone with a name, Charles would destroy them," Smith said. "They didn't believe me when I told them how good Richmond was."

Flye insists that he owes Charles a drink, cigar, round of golf, or all three for years of making him sound more talented than he was at the time. To be linked in such a way to Charles, as you can imagine, remains a bit odd for Flye, a business development sales manager.

The coverage on him back then wasn't nearly what it would be like today if he was playing. He had dark circles around his eyes, so he would come off looking like a villain. We didn't know anything about Charles.

Everyone I talked to, we're talking about hundreds of people before the game, said, "Hey, you're playing Barkley." None of them said I was playing Auburn. They all mentioned that I was going up against Barkley. I didn't know what I was going to be getting into.

I don't know this for a fact, but I would venture a guess that Charles didn't put a whole lot of credence into what Sonny said to prepare for us.

I was a guy who'd like to keep a conversation during the game, and Charles and I had some nice conversations. We would talk about the coaches and players, the crowd, the good-looking girls in the stands. When one of his teammates had two turnovers, he'd tell me, "That bozo doesn't know what he's doing."

Charles and I are completely connected at the hip. Just a month ago, the best man at my wedding was waiting for a taxi when he saw Charles and introduced himself. Charles tells him, "Bill Flye, he kicked my ass in that game in 1984."

Venus, Mars, and Jupiter all had to align that day for us to have a shot to win.

It might have been a sign of things to come when the first-round game was promoted on TBS to the tune of Michael Jackson's "Thriller." But closer to the game on March 15, 1984, Tarrant delivered different messages to his team: *Don't worry about the accolades.*

We're going to score on them because those guys don't like playing defense. We can win. It's unclear whether the Auburn players were still recovering from the gut punch of the Kentucky loss five days earlier, but what was transparent was that Richmond had other plans. The Spiders wanted to kick Auburn in the groin before they knew what hit them—and they did just that.

Exposing Auburn's passive 3–2 zone, Richmond scored at will, going 12-of-16 in the first ten minutes and 64 percent for the first half. Despite the media hype before the game, Charles, limited by foul trouble, was nowhere to be found in the tightly packed zone, mustering 6 points and 6 rebounds to go along with his 3 fouls. When he was coming out of the game, the Richmond fans who made the trip used a Wendy's slogan to send him off: "Where's the beef? On the bench!"

By the half, Richmond was up 39–22 and were on their way to being the turd in the punch bowl at Auburn's first dance.

With an upset in the making, Barkley was sent back to the bench with less than fifteen minutes to go in the game after committing his fourth foul. The catalyst would have to take a seat, but not before relaying a message to Smith.

"He walked over to the bench and, he had never done this before, he said, 'Coach, give me the ball,'" Smith said. "When he realized Richmond was going to beat us, in his mind he said, 'No way.'"

The Tigers were down 15 when Charles reentered with 9:12 left in the game. Barkley was back and so was the hope of an Auburn win. Tarrant could only do so much to stop him from ripping his team apart with four minutes to go.

"He's stealing the ball, knocking guys down, dunking it everywhere," Tarrant said. "He was a man possessed, and wasn't about to be denied."

But was it too late? The teams exchanged 15 free throws in the final 1:31 until Charles pulled down a rebound with eighteen seconds to go. He hesitated for a half second before taking the ball himself down the other end with his team down by 3. Charles whipped it to Greg Turner who bobbled it before recovering and putting up a missed shot.

Charles rebounded, and put it up at eight seconds. Miss.

He rebounded it again, put it up at six seconds. It was good. Down 1 with four seconds left. They needed one more shot.

But that would be the last play for the '84 Auburn Tigers. Richmond wisely never threw the ball inbounds and let the running clock hit 0:00, winning 72–71, completing the upset while simultaneously holding off the collapse. Guarding the inbounder, Charles gazed on helplessly as he looked up at the clock and then his man, realizing he wouldn't have a chance to escape the Spiders' web.

The Richmond players admit that if there'd been more time on the clock, the result might've been different. "If there were five more seconds left, we might not have won," Beckwith predicted.

"I don't know why whenever I watch the game on ESPN Classic I think the result will be any different," Turner said. "All we had to do was throw the ball up to Charles. He would have outjumped anybody and you wouldn't have been able to stop him."

Smith publicly expressed confidence that his star would return for his senior season, but many believed that would never be the case.

The immediate future was even more of a toss-up. Between the loss in the SEC title game and the early departure from the tournament, Charles was searching for ways to increase his stock. Then he received a telegram from USA Basketball. For the first time, he'd be on the same court with the nation's best college players for a chance to represent his country.

While the others might have been fighting for a spot on the Olympic team, Charles couldn't care less about representing the country at the '84 Games in Los Angeles. Nevertheless, he would look oh so good doing it.

10

Bob Knight was late, and Charles Barkley could not wait to fuck with him.

A loud proponent of being on time to meetings and practices, Knight, the legendary and controversial Indiana coach tabbed to lead the 1984 USA men's basketball team, was late for one of the squad's nightly sessions with the coaching staff during the Olympic Trials. After Knight entered the room about ten minutes late, Charles jumped and shouted in front of everyone, "It's ten after five, where the hell have you been?"

For as much as Charles's reputation of being a talented, free-spirited wild card preceded him, the same could be said surrounding the perception of Knight—a basketball savant whose fury regularly crossed the line separating teacher from tyrant. So it was no surprise that the coach did not take it well.

"Let me tell you something, Charles, you fat son of a bitch!" yelled Knight, according to an account from Alvin Robertson of Arkansas, one of the players in the room. "There's only one chief in this army, and that's me!" He added, "Your fat ass won't be around here much longer!"

While there was one chief to be seen, there was also one Charles to be heard. The banging noise was so sudden and booming that Jim Boeheim scurried back inside the sprawling fieldhouse to see what the commotion was about. It would be easy to take for granted the constant quality of play among the seventy-two collegiate players going at each other at the 1984 Olympic Trials for a chance to represent their country, a who's who of NCAA stardom. But all of that was thrown out the window when Charles dunked on Patrick Ewing and everyone else.

"I heard another bang and looked over, and Charles was dunking on all of them," Boeheim said. "I mean, he was *tearing* the basket down."

From a Bear Bryant–style tower Knight was closely inspecting his favorite players. This time, he was scowling and shaking his head at the demolition below. Plays like that were not what the Trials were about, or at least not what Knight believed they were trying to achieve. The Indiana coach was a controversial pick to lead the program. With an innovative and demonstrative personality, Knight was tabbed to instill discipline, respect, and fear into a USA Basketball program that had been knocked off by Russia for the gold medal in controversial fashion twelve years earlier and whose touring Soviet team steamrolled college teams during a 1982 American tour.

While it remained unclear at the time whether the Cold War foes would again boycott the '84 Games, Knight organized a program of rules on top of rules as if the nation's basketball future depended on it. That meant doing it in his own no-frills, no-coddling, all-crass way—yelling, cursing, belittling, and mentally abusing players by any means necessary in the pursuit of perfection.

It also included giving a look to the young man who went against a lot of Knight's rigid and controlling tendencies, but whose talent could not be ignored.

"Charles Barkley was a RPIA: Royal Pain in the Ass," Knight said.

Charles wasn't sending him a Christmas card either. "I hate the son of a bitch," Charles said of Knight.

If selecting the intemperate Knight to lead the team into battle was considered a provocative choice, then what would it mean to arm him with one of college basketball's baddest and most unpre-. dictable warheads? Charles, who had previously voiced his disdain for the Russians and their place in the basketball landscape, publicly praised the chance to play for Knight, saying that he and Chuck Person being picked for the Trials for the Los Angeles Games was a "great honor." Knight, who later said that no one wanted Charles on the team more than him due to the matchup problems he presented to the world, suggested that the invitation to the SEC Player of the Year came with a message he wanted to send to a potential threat to America's dominance.

"When those Russians come over here, I want them to know they've been hit," Knight said.

Given the publicity surrounding his weight, and the back-and-forth with Smith over conditioning during that time, Charles correctly predicted in the spring that his figure would be an issue for Knight, who hilariously requested that he weigh 215 pounds. Knight then thought better of it: "Barkley at 215 would be like asking Raquel Welch to undergo plastic surgery."

"I went to the Trials intending to change everyone's mind about Charles Barkley," Barkley said. "I was going to, as Muhammad Ali used to say, 'shock the world.' That's what excited me most about the Olympic Trials—that, and the prospect of making money."

The athletes that showed up for the '84 Olympic Trials were considered the most accomplished collection of American amateur basketball talent ever assembled. Pete Newell, the 1960 Olympic coach and one of Knight's closest mentors, had "never seen anything like these guys." To the left, there's Ewing, Michael Jordan, and Sam Perkins, the smooth lefty big man. To the right, you see the sharp-shooting Chris Mullin of St. John's, the worldly Wayman Tisdale of Oklahoma, and Indiana's own fundamentally sound freshman point guard, Steve Alford. Joining them were lesser-known talents who all had a shot to make it professionally, from John Stockton and Karl Malone to Joe Dumars and Terry Porter.

They each had their own quirks. Antoine Carr took time away from a $225,000 annual salary with his Italian league team as well as a pasta-making job in Milan. Danny Manning was still in high school. You hoped to learn a new phrase from the pithy vernacular of Malone, the statuesque Louisiana Tech forward. Tisdale's terrible impression of Richard Nixon was not to be missed. As many were first starting to learn, Jordan had a bit of a competitive streak in all non-basketball activities and enjoyed some time alone at The Chocolate Moose ice cream shop, his favorite haunt in town.

But Charles was the story of the camp, intriguing scouts, executives, players, coaches, and media members, as well as the fans who were getting their first glimpse of the mostly regional talent. Among those in attendance was Duke coach Mike Krzyzewski, a former point guard and assistant under Knight who could only join everyone else in awe of the Auburn ace.

"I had never seen anyone with that physique be able to play at the level he was playing at," Krzyzewski said.

As Charles's profile increased in stature, so did talk around his girth and diet. Some of the nicknames were insulting, and he worried the discourse around his body would overshadow his talent on the court. One *San Francisco Examiner* article said Charles "handles a fork as well as anybody in the world."

Shortly after arriving for the Trials, Charles was asked again by reporters about his weight and his eating habits, and again he was ready with a sound bite to satiate their appetite. "I really don't eat that much. I just, more or less, tend to eat all the time," he told reporters. "If I could go into a room and peel some of this stuff off of me, I'd come out looking like Hercules."

Writing for the *Washington Post*, Michael Wilbon predicted that when, not if, Charles made the team that summer, "he might just cut the first exercise album with lyrics that encourage a snack after every jumping jack."

When it came to his on-court presence, however, players started forming their own opinions. UCLA's Kenny Fields noted Charles's politeness, how he regularly said, "I'm sorry," when accidentally crashing into him. Tulane's John Williams, who was still sore from the crunching jab Charles gave him with his elbow during the Trials, often thought when he came down the lane, "Oh, no, anybody but him." Stockton, the unknown Gonzaga guard, had to cool off after cocking a fist at Charles for a blindside collision. Illinois guard Bruce

Douglas had considered taking a charge until he thought, "Wait a minute. This guy is going *too* fast."

Once the workouts and smaller games had wrapped up, Joe Kleine and some of the other players gravitated toward wherever Charles was inside the fieldhouse to watch him. While playing on another court, Cal State-Fullerton's Leon Wood would look out of the corner of his eye to see if he could catch a glimpse of Charles dunking on some unsuspecting dude. Kleine, the Arkansas center, was regularly in the crowds that went three or four deep to admire the show put on by Charles. "He never disappointed," Kleine said. "He wasn't big like Karl Malone, who looked like a sculpted weightlifter. He had a big butt and a huge gut, but he was killing everybody."

In between the three-a-day practices, Larry Krystkowiak often found himself hanging with Charles, Kleine, and SMU's Jon Koncak. The big man from Montana might have been the most obscure prospect there, but he found comfort in Charles's energy. One day at the cafeteria, Charles proclaimed to Krystkowiak that he wanted to lead the camp in points, rebounds, and assists. "I thought he was nuts," Krystkowiak said, "but I'll be damned if he didn't end up doing just that."

There was, however, another player on the verge of entering the NBA Draft that even Charles had to keep an eye on. A player who Charles would admit to Smith might even be able to outperform him.

"I had to tell him, 'Coach, there was one guy up there who's the best player I've ever seen. It's Michael Jordan,'" Charles said. "'He was the only guy better than me.'"

By the time Jordan had finished his third year at Chapel Hill—a run featuring a national championship in 1982, a consensus choice as National Player of the Year in 1984 and twice being named a consensus first team All-America—North Carolina assistant Roy Williams surmised that the guard was the only player he had seen who could turn it on and off on the court.

"And he never freaking turned it off," Williams concluded.

For as much as Knight rode Charles, he lauded Jordan—much like him, a creature of habit and system—as "the best basketball player

I've ever seen play" before he ever stepped on the court for his first professional game.

It's one reason why Charles insisted on guarding Jordan during the Trials. But Jordan, who tried to convince reporters that he couldn't relax in fear of getting cut, was one of five locks to make the team—along with Ewing, Perkins, Mullin, and Tisdale—and was already a given to go in the top-3 of the summer's NBA Draft.

That didn't make it any less weird for Jordan to go virtually unnoticed and unmentioned during the Trials.

"Michael wasn't setting out to wow people like that," recalled Mark Heisler, the decorated NBA writer for the *Los Angeles Times* who was covering the Trials. "No one was talking about Jordan or Patrick Ewing or Chris Mullin. It was all Charles."

The matchups between the two were very one-sided, in that there was no way in hell Jordan was going to guard Charles on the other end of the floor. Every drive to the hoop seemingly ended with Jordan out-of-bounds, which the Carolina guard found to be funny. But Jordan appreciated the physical challenge Charles posed, using it as motivation to keep his own game even sharper.

In the spring of 1984, the friendship between the two most important basketball luminaries of the '90s began to blossom. Off the court, they got to know each other at the Student Union pool room. Unsurprisingly, there was betting involved, and their eight ball games were almost as competitive as those on the parquet floor. Alford said that while Charles was good, Jordan was next-level, thinking three shots ahead and jumping balls and playing spins like a natural. Jordan was going to let you know about it, too. But Charles would get him back each night in their head-to-head matchups in Tonk, the fast-paced matching card game that combined elements of knock rummy and conquian, a game popularized by Southern blues and jazz musicians of the 1930s. Eight years after the Trials, Charles remained convinced that Jordan still owed him money for his Tonk winnings.

Born three days apart and raised about 550 miles from one another, their paths felt both familiar and distinct. While Charles's father, Frank, was not in the picture, James Jordan Sr. was a present figure in his son's life, working at General Electric and raising the family with Deloris, who worked at a bank. Instead of fighting for his father's attention like Michael did with his brother Larry, Charles became a father figure himself early on for Darryl and John to alleviate the stress on his mother and grandmother.

Like the others at the Trials, their excellence created a burden of expectation and pressure surrounding the looming NBA Draft. Their shared experiences, and Charles's contagious spirit, made Jordan want to open up to him in ways he rarely allowed.

"I can relate very well to him because I can relax around him," Jordan said of Charles at the time. "With Charles, I don't have to be anybody but Michael. In that sense, he's like a brother to me."

The Michael and Charles Show had a special Saturday night display in front of a sold-out crowd of 17,182 at Assembly Hall in late April 1984. By the end of the second game of an intra-squad doubleheader, the crowd, which roared for the grinning pair during the introductions, saw them score 19 each. These were the guys you came to see for different reasons: Jordan steals the show and Barkley takes your breath away.

While guarding Charles, Duke's Mark Alarie, standing at six-foot-nine and weighing 222 pounds, found himself looking up from the floor and nearly sliding into the band after colliding with "the Incredible Bulk." The play continued without a foul called and an easy eighteen-foot jumper, a sight so hilarious to USA assistant George Raveling that he howled into Knight's shoulder and nearly fell into his lap. Alarie's attempt to hack Charles across the arm on the other end would only backfire and result in a 3-point play.

"Charles was already not Bobby Knight's favorite player or personality, and he went out there that night and absolutely dominated that game and destroyed everyone put in front of him," said Fran Blinebury, the NBA writer and columnist for the *Houston Chronicle* who was in attendance that night. "Assembly Hall just went crazy."

On his finest night of the Trials, Charles owned Knight's house.

In his decades covering the NBA, the '84 Trials remain one of the most fun highlights for Heisler. He has Charles to thank for that.

In this Bobby Knight production, he was just another guy and not a guy you expected to make it. Yet he was this sensation who couldn't be held down.

He told us the story about how he tried to lose weight before the camp and went on a diet of nothing but fruit juice and wound up in the hospital. He then said how he ended up gaining all the weight back, which was fabulous.

There really wasn't a relationship between Knight and Charles. Knight didn't have relationships with his players; they were his employees. Even if Charles had gone to high school in Bloomington and was dying to be a Hoosier, I don't know if Knight would have taken him. Knight was never going to bend enough to put up with Charles's hijinks. Charles was outside of Knight's vision.

Knight hating him was kind of a compliment for him, showing what a one-man juggernaut he was.

Despite making it through the first couple of player cuts at the Trials, some figured Charles was on borrowed time. His weight had become the lead story in Bloomington, and his volatile relationship with Knight, whom he called "crazy man" behind his back, was now a close second. Ewing, who credited Charles for lightening up the mood, cracked up over how his teammate could turn his coach a shade of red darker than that of the Indiana crimson. Charles himself remembered the media framing his potential inclusion on Knight's team as "the most explosive and controversial coach in the country versus the most explosive and controversial player in the country."

"They say if the coach screams and hollers a lot he likes you," Charles observed. "I guess he likes me."

The assistants, however, were in agreement: If Knight was going to cut Charles, he would have to do it himself. After one rim-rattling dunk, Boeheim had a suggestion for Dave Gavitt, chairman of the selection committee. "I don't know if they're going to cut him, but they better do it by mail," he offered.

Despite the talk of his weight, Charles took the coach's words to heart and had lost nine pounds in six days of camp, getting down to 274, according to Knight. C.M. Newton, an assistant with Knight's staff, remembered how the Indiana coach asked him to return to mini-camp within five pounds of his ideal playing weight. Knight, who saw how the Auburn star had connected with Knight's thirteen-year-old son, Pat, wanted to bring Charles back, but he had to prove to the coach that he could lose nine additional pounds in eighteen days.

When Charles returned, he hadn't even touched a basketball. He had gone the other way on the scale, too. He not only failed to lose nine additional pounds, but he *gained* eleven back.

Yet his signature boldness was on full display for the day of the team photo. As documented in *The Jordan Rules*, the team was getting organized for the shoot when Knight walked over in an old pair of wing tip shoes. Naturally, Charles thought they were some of the ugliest kicks he'd ever laid his eyes on and proceeded to ask Knight where he got his granddaddy's shoes.

"Everyone falls over and Knight's not laughing and Barkley's still going on about those shoes," Jordan said. "Knight said something about Charles being a jackass and started cussing. I've never heard anyone talk to Coach Knight like that."

The day after Charles laughed at Knight's wing tip shoes, the coach recalled how Alford was working the big man's ass off in a drill, saying Charles appeared so tired that he looked like he was doing a version of "the Stepin Fetchit routine," referencing the vaudeville actor who often portrayed the painfully racist stereotype of the lazy Black man. But Knight, apparently, had seen enough.

"I looked at the chart and said, 'Charles, maybe nobody else has ever told you anything that they meant, or they were going to stick by, but when I told you that you had to lose nine pounds, that was something that you had to do,'" the coach said. Knight then told Charles that he had his plane ticket home and wished him good luck.

The top performer of the Trials, and arguably the most exciting, matched only perhaps by Jordan, would not be representing his country in Los Angeles. Also going home in the rounds of cuts included the likes of Malone, Stockton, Dumars, Porter, Person, and Carr, who agreed with Charles when he said that Knight preferred players he could control—a group dubbed by then–Arkansas coach Eddie Sutton as "the Bobby types." Jordan, his running mate at the Trials, thought Charles should have been at the Olympics with him and guessed that his mouth did him in.

Two years after Charles told the *New York Times* that he hated the SOB, Charles walked back his criticism of the coach in an interview with *Playboy*, saying that he now appreciated and loved Knight because he didn't bullshit him. He confirmed in his 2002 autobiography in *I May Be Wrong but I Doubt It* that his disdain for Knight and his need to raise his stock made leaving the program easy.

"In a way, it was a relief: a big part of me didn't want to make the Olympic basketball team in 1984," he wrote. "Seriously, I didn't."

But Knight, who detailed in his own 2002 autobiography *Knight: My Story* that he was trying to do Charles a favor by getting him to drop to a reasonable playing weight before going to the NBA, has not minced words regarding the Auburn star in recent years. He's gone so far as to tell audiences that he had "developed a total disuse for Charles Barkley."

In a van ride from the Indiana campus to the airport dubbed "the bus of shame," Charles commiserated with Stockton, Porter, and Maurice Martin of Saint Joseph's about what went wrong. Stockton, who had dreamed of a scenario in which the four future pros could challenge any quartet on the US team, bonded with Charles on the trip. What was supposed to be a bummed-out ride turned into Charles holding court, talking most of the way to Indianapolis and hyping up his van mates about how they were going to prove Knight wrong. That meant more to Stockton than even he realized at the time.

"He was undaunted, as if he knew he wasn't the right flavor for Coach Knight," Stockton said. "He was just so undaunted by everything, and he made that van so much fun."

What was more fun for the Olympian-that-should-have-been? The answer: all the money Charles was about to make for himself after a week's worth of work.

11

For a forty-eight-hour period in 1984, Charles engaged in an eating binge in hopes of dissuading the Philadelphia 76ers from selecting him in the draft. He began with two Denny's Grand Slam breakfasts—six pancakes and bacon totaling around 1,660 calories, and a vanilla milkshake to wash it down. The lunch offerings, which have varied in the decades' worth of repeat tellings, included either Kentucky Fried Chicken, mashed potatoes, and coleslaw; half of the menu at Red Lobster; two McDonald's fish fillets, a large fries, and a Diet Coke; or two Texas-sized barbecue sandwiches. The dinner menu at a steakhouse included a T-bone, baked potato, and, of course, three desserts.

Charles repeated it all the next day, gorging, as he described, "everything I could get to my face, everything that wasn't nailed down or poison." During a night of heavy drinking with his agent, the sight of Charles crushing beers might have made people think that Prohibition was about to be reinstated, he said.

This excess consumption was never the plan, but the league's unstable footing complicated Charles's financial future.

The NBA was struggling. On top of the rampant cocaine abuse

among players, TV executives and advertisers felt the league was not marketable to mainstream America because it was too Black. Critics supported the notion that by pointing to Marvin Gaye's rendition of "The Star-Spangled Banner" at the 1983 All-Star Game, a groundbreaking, funky version of the national anthem meant to reflect the Black excellence of the players on the court. All of this came as salaries had spiked too quickly and several franchises were in danger of folding. "We were a pretty struggling organization in 1984," said Russ Granik, the league's deputy commissioner who was in his first year. "There was a lot of skepticism about how long the NBA would survive."

To address the escalating problems plaguing the league, the collective bargaining agreement announced for the 1984–85 season helped institute a salary cap, the first long-term deal of its kind in all of US professional sports, one that averted a strike and saved teams like Cleveland and Indiana from going under. Teams with payrolls at or above the salary cap could only offer their first-round picks a one-year deal worth $75,000. (The player would become a restricted free agent in their second year.) In other words, whoever was getting picked by Philadelphia, a franchise capped out at around $4.5 million, would not have the security of a multiyear, multimillion-dollar deal.

Charles had already lost about ten pounds that summer, a request made by the 76ers before a pre-draft weigh-in. Then, Charles's agent, Lance Luchnick, had some tough news to deliver to his prized client.

"You do know if the Sixers draft you they are going to give you $75,000, right?" Luchnick said to Charles.

"I didn't leave college for $75,000," Charles replied to his new agent in a not-so-calm tone.

By Charles's standards, the caloric clinic worked: he gained roughly twenty pounds in two days, putting him at nearly 300 pounds.

At a weigh-in, Harold Katz, the 76ers' owner who made his fortune as founder of Nutrisystem, the national chain of weight-loss centers, flew off the handle as Charles tried not to laugh. *Are you nuts or just fat and lazy?* Pat Williams, the team's loquacious general manager, was rendered speechless and alarmed by "this enormous girth."

"Whatever he did before he came to Philadelphia for the weigh-in, it was scary," said John Nash, an assistant with the team.

On the Amtrak train to New York for the draft, Charles and Luchnick high-fived each other on a job well done. There was no way the 76ers would take Charles Barkley now. No way.

That's what they thought anyway.

The worst-kept secret in basketball was out and all that was left for Charles to do was say goodbye.

In declaring himself eligible for the NBA Draft on April 28, 1984, Charles acknowledged his self-doubt. If coming to Auburn was the biggest decision of his life, then leaving the Tigers would be the most important. On the heels of the sensational performance at the Olympic Trials, Charles, who years later would be named the SEC's Player of the Decade for the '80s, reflected on what he accomplished on the Plains and what was left on the table.

Throughout his farewell news conference, he reiterated that there was a fair chance in a few years' time that leaving early would have been the wrong decision. With Person and Charles, both probable All-Americans, Auburn would be set up to flatten the SEC and make a potential Final Four run. (The Tigers would make the Sweet 16 in 1985 and the Elite 8 in 1986.)

Included in those regrets was not finishing his degree. During the decision-making process, Johnnie Mae made him promise he would return to school in the summertime to complete his college education. Charles stubbornly agreed after his grandmother kept riding him about following through on the promise. "It's not like I'm going to be a brain surgeon," he joked.

But the need to provide for his mother, grandmother, and brothers reaffirmed his decision. And this choice was his to make and his alone.

"I don't know if I'll make it in the NBA, but at least I helped control my own destiny," he said while making his announcement. "I'm going to do my best."

At the time Charles was weighing his options, Lance Luchnick had quickly established himself as an agent who got deals done. Born in Brooklyn and based in Texas, Luchnick's persona as the young, hip basketball junkie was attractive to NBA prospects. Charles was enamored with the thirty-something New Yorker who had "mastered the art of 'street talk' and was well versed in Black music and other forms of Black culture."

"He seemed like he could be one of the fellas," Charles said. "He was a White guy who acted like he was Black." And unlike the other agents who pressured Charles to sign up with them after he received their money, Luchnick stayed away entirely, never giving funds to Charles and preferring to come in with a clean slate.

There was, however, a dark side to Luchnick, who represented five first-round selections from the 1982 NBA Draft alone. He'd been accused of reeling in clients through payments to coaches and relatives of the players. When the players were on board, as former clients alleged in an investigation published in the *Atlanta Journal-Constitution*, Luchnick improperly used their funds via a broad power-of-attorney clause included in their contracts.

NBA agent Steve Kauffman, who provided some accounting and legal services to Charles in his early years, said Luchnick "wasn't a guy I would have hired back then." The sentiment was shared by several former clients who ended up suing him.

But Charles's bond with Luchnick grew stronger with each nightclub Luchnick took him to. When Luchnick made the visit to Leeds to meet with Charcey and Johnnie Mae, they met at the home in Russell Heights at 6:00 p.m. to go over the details of Charles signing with him. Within ninety minutes, Charles was snoring on the couch, Luchnick said. At around 9:30 p.m., Charcey called it a night as well. That left Johnnie Mae to hammer out the details with him into the early-morning hours.

"At 1:30 in the morning, his grandmother pushed her glasses up on her nose and said, 'All right, tell me again: What do you mean by full power of attorney?'" Luchnick recalled.

Smith was against Charles hiring Luchnick, but he ultimately failed to stop the union. "The most important thing to him was taking care of his family," Luchnick said, "and I was telling him he could do that."

That is, of course, if a team could pay him.

To this day, World B. Free insists Charles Barkley owes him $25. Then known as Lloyd Free, the twenty-four-year-old who never met a shot he didn't take, wasn't the best fit for Billy Cunningham's 76ers. Before the start of his second season at the helm, Cunningham, a Philadelphia legend who brought the city glory as a player with the 1967 NBA title, approached Pat Williams to see what they could get for Free. Any move would also trim down the bloated roster and free up more playing time to a promising rookie named Maurice Cheeks. The only bite they got was from the San Diego Clippers, who in exchange for a first-round draft pick wanted the Sixers to essentially give Free away for, well, free.

On paper, the trade on October 12, 1978, between the 76ers and Clippers did not warrant more than a fifty-six-word wire story in the Associated Press. Free was on his way to the Clippers. In exchange, Philadelphia received the first-round pick they were looking to land, but with one caveat: it would not be until the distant future of 1984. "The best I could get was six years down the road," Williams said. "I'm sure the Clippers were thinking, 'Ehh, six years may never even get here.'"

After going 43–39 for the 1978–79 season, the Clippers went on to average about twenty-nine wins a year for the next five seasons. By the 1983–84 season the Sixers were making plans to be in the draft lottery's coin flip between the teams with the four worst records to decide the top picks. Philadelphia desperately wanted a shot at either North Carolina's Michael Jordan or Houston's Akeem Olajuwon, considered by them and the rest of the league as the two potential franchise cornerstones of the draft. Katz acknowledged that the Sixers' pick at No. 1 would have "absolutely" been Jordan. Williams added that if the Sixers landed Jordan, the plan was to initially have him back up Julius Erving and Andrew Toney. "There was a sense that the Draft was going to drop off pretty radically after Olajuwon and Jordan," said the general manager.

But after both the Houston Rockets and Chicago Bulls tanked terribly, the Sixers, with the fifth-worst record in the league, couldn't join the coin flip proceedings. Houston got the first pick, while Philly was locked in at No. 5.

Charles was certainly not a secret to the Sixers. Months earlier, Jack McMahon, the team's director of player personnel, described the Auburn star to *Sports Illustrated* as having the body of Wes

Unseld and the ups of Erving, while also noting that any team that took him on would "have to put a weight clause in his contract." But the owner, Harold Katz, spoke of Charles glowingly.

"Harold was in awe of Charles Barkley," Nash said.

A lifelong basketball fan from South Philadelphia who lived fifteen minutes away from The Spectrum growing up, Katz got his start at the family business, a fair-sized grocery store in the Germantown neighborhood. He'd eventually move on by going door-to-door, selling dozens of products, from vacuum cleaners and brushes to TVs and lawnmowers. After hawking insurance for John Hancock and building a successful burglar/fire alarm and intercom company, Katz was baffled to hear his mother had to spend $60 a week for her dieting—the behavioral counseling, spa treatment, and special food. Seeing the potential of bundling everything into an all-in-one package, he founded Nutrisystem in 1971 at a time when millions of Americans were looking to drop some pounds. Almost a decade later, Katz, then forty-four, turned a $20,000 investment in the weight-loss chain into a personal wealth of around $100 million. In a profile of Katz, *Inc.* magazine noted his taste for the finer things in life, from a $56,000 customized Cadillac Seville to a McMansion that some dubbed "the castle."

"If the word ostentatious had not existed before, it would have been coined for Katz," the magazine reported.

The entrepreneur bought the 76ers from F. Eugene Dixon for more than $12 million in 1981, inheriting a pricy payroll, low attendance, and significant financial losses. Katz, a ball of fire who acknowledged it was "bananas" to take on a franchise in peril, vowed to turn it around. To him, the only thing worse than losing money, no matter how much of it you have, was getting beat on the basketball court. In 1983, less than two years later, the Sixers won their first NBA championship in sixteen years behind Erving and league MVP Moses Malone, sweeping the Los Angeles Lakers and bringing pride back to the hoops haven.

Ed Rendell, who at thirty-three had become the youngest district attorney in the city's history, remembered Katz as a respected but aloof figure with a reputation and edge that earned him admiration throughout Philadelphia.

"Harold was a guy who got things done. I don't think the fans loved Harold, but they respected what he did with the title in '83," said Rendell, a Democrat who later served as mayor. "If you asked the average 76ers fan about Harold Katz, they'd say he did some good, but that he was a real SOB, because he was very tough."

And now, Katz was all-in on Charles. But Cunningham had some hesitation. The coach worked out the prospect at Saint Joseph's University in Philadelphia six weeks before the draft. Within five minutes of Charles jumping from a standing position to effortlessly grab rebound after rebound, Cunningham too was all-in.

"The one great gift Charles had was that it was an easy game for him," said the Hall of Fame player–turned-coach. "It wasn't complicated."

Scouting reports from draft experts echoed what the Sixers saw. "If he ever gets down to 250, fasten the seatbelts and clear the runway," *Sports Illustrated* declared.

The weight still presented a hang-up for the organization ahead of the June event, so Katz and Williams challenged the 282-pound Charles to lose about 10 pounds. Working out in Leeds and Houston, Charles jogged and lifted weights to get to around 272. "Mostly, I just stopped eating," Charles joked. Then, Charles went the other way, employing a man-versus-food approach never before seen by an elite athlete trying to convince a team to avoid drafting him—both the tastiest and most painful to date.

Decades later, Free, the centerpiece of the '78 trade, said he's still waiting on his money from Charles: "Every time I look at Charles, I say, 'You owe me $25. You would not have gotten picked if it wasn't for me.'"

For reasons that remain unclear, burgundy was Barkley's favorite color growing up. He was all smiles in a burgundy tuxedo when he took Amy Shorter to the prom his senior year. The burgundy tracksuit he rocked in the pizza-centric photoshoot for *Sports Illustrated* never looked better on someone with a mouthful of a supreme slice.

On the day of the NBA Draft, he wore a double-breasted burgundy suit with gold buttons

"When you're poor, you get that one suit and that was it," he said.

"Man, burgundy was my favorite color. I wanted to have a nice suit for the Draft, and we went out and got it."

The outfit was just one element of what's considered by many the greatest NBA Draft in the history of the game.

"The Draft was the start of my amazing journey through life," Charles said. "I've had an amazing life and it all started that night."

Coming back from a pre-draft party among rookies and their families at a small Italian restaurant near Madison Square Garden, Charles had a feeling his two-day stint as a competitive eater wasn't enough to stop Philadelphia. On the day before the draft, Cunningham assured Charles that the team would pick him at No. 5 if Sam Perkins went to Dallas at No. 4. Katz didn't care how much Charles weighed—just as long as he was wearing Philadelphia's red, white, and blue.

The four at the top went according to plan: Olajuwon to the Rockets, Sam Bowie to the Trail Blazers, Jordan to the Bulls, and Perkins to the Mavericks. But the new salary cap had put Charles and the Sixers in an awkward position hours before the draft. Three months earlier, Luchnick told the *Dallas Morning News* that no players of his, including Charles, would sign the one-year, $75,000 deal without moving forward with legal action against the NBA for the rule.

In his first draft as league commissioner, the mustachioed David Stern announced Charles Barkley as the Sixers' pick. The grin on the commissioner's face turned to a smirk as the dozens inside the Felt Forum went crazy.

In truth, Charles was half listening to Stern until the commissioner uttered his first name. The announcement was not a total surprise, but still just as disappointing. He took a deep breath and bit his bottom lip before sauntering to the podium. Visibly dejected, he lowered his head and walked to meet Stern. What had he just done?

"The look on my face is, 'Are you kidding me?'" Charles said of his reaction on Draft Night. "I wasn't smiling because I was like, 'I left college for $75,000.'"

Many decades later, Charles pointed out how seemingly everyone around him was savoring the moment—that is, except him. "When people go back and look at me walking, and they see that awful burgundy suit, everybody else is happy and Charles isn't happy," he said.

BARKLEY

★ ★ ★

There was no stopping Katz from getting his man in the '84 Draft, even if it meant butting heads with the porky prodigy.

I had told Charles since then that it wasn't going to be a problem to bring him in. I'm not sure what his agent told him.

I really didn't care how much he came in weighing. I knew he was going to lose the weight. We did have to fine him three or four times for his weight. He still tells me about how I fined him.

What stood out to me, frankly, was that he had a personality stronger than 99 percent of the total population. He was so strong-willed when he was young. Charles's reputation was a little different then. He's the opposite now, and he's the most pleasant person to be around. When I got him at twenty-one years old, he was so different then. He didn't get it at that point about what it meant to be him.

By the end of his time here, the fans loved him; they absolutely adored him. I loved him. Christ, I sure loved him after I drafted him.

One of the most exciting players in all of college basketball was going to play alongside Erving and Malone. The frustration of his contract situation faded behind his genuine excitement.

"It's got to be every kid's dream to play on the same team with Dr. J and Moses," he said. "This is better than a dream. I'm on top of the world right now."

He was saying all the right things, but in reality, he kept thinking: *What have I done?*

Notes about his weight did not go unnoticed among the announcers. Lou Carnesecca, the longtime St. John's coach who was announcing the '84 Draft, said he'd like to open a pizza concession stand in Charles's vicinity and see if it would do as well as he envisioned.

The questioning continued moments after he was drafted. Veteran broadcaster Eddie Doucette asked him about the reputation he had for being able to inhale a couple pizzas in one sitting, which produced a cackle from a couple members of the crowd that was captured during the broadcast. "I get a lot of talk about my weight, but I think that I can control my weight and I feel like I'll go to camp and lose a lot of weight," he said through a forced smile. Tiptoeing past another weight-related query, he thanked God and the women who got him there.

"I'd like to thank my mother and grandmother, who I think are the two greatest ladies on earth," he said. "I just like to say hello to my mother and grandmother 'cause they're great."

When Barkley was asked about the $75,000 payday that was staring the newest 76er in the face, Charles said all he had to do was work hard and money would handle itself. He had accomplished a once-impossible dream of making it to the NBA, and as a top-5 pick no less. But with his agent suggesting legal action against any team unable to offer him a competitive wage, his dream of supporting his family was temporarily uncertain.

But whether Philadelphia knew it or not, the Charles Experience was about to come at the city with the force of a runaway 18-wheeler. And Charles would soon care little about what people thought along the way.

12

The doctor saw a rookie who was built like a bear and could run like a cat. The chairman thought the kid he named "fathead" was lazy. And the coach jokingly wondered whether the player would undo his career.

While Philly had little inkling of what it was getting itself into, the same could be said of Charles, who hadn't lived anywhere outside of Alabama and was now jumping headfirst into a rabid, blue-collared city that demanded greatness. For Geno Auriemma, who emigrated to the city from Italy in the '60s, he could only laugh when reflecting on what it meant to have Charles Barkley come to Philadelphia.

"The way I would describe Charles in Philadelphia was that it was a Charles Dickens marriage—it was the worst of times, it was the best of times," said the Connecticut women's basketball coach. "To be that good in Philadelphia comes with a lot of responsibility. But he did it 'cause he was that good and that loud."

But how would Charles's game translate to the next level? Julius Erving saw with his own two eyes on the first day of training camp that he was the right guy for a team hoping to make another title run.

On Draft Night, Charles said he was excited to learn from Marc Iavaroni, the team's starting power forward. But on the court, Charles saw the veteran much like he did Darrell Lockhart during the start of his freshman year at Auburn: *This is the guy in front of me who I have to beat out and beat down.*

What was a common rebounding drill turned into something else with Charles inside the gym at Franklin & Marshall College.

"When the ball bounces off the rim, we see Marc flying into the stands and it was because of Charles and his girth," Erving said. "He just took a step or two forward and hit him with his body, and suddenly it was no contest."

Erving turned to Maurice Cheeks and asked if he thought Charles was going to injure Iavaroni. If that play wasn't enough evidence, Erving himself nearly ended up in the eighth row in a failed attempt to box him out at the free throw line. Charles went from stressing out about not knowing how to address Erving—he settled on "Doc" only after the veteran introduced himself as such before the first practice—to throwing him around with ease. From that day on, Doc joked, he stayed out of Charles's way.

But before Charles could send anyone into retirement, he had to first be on the team. In an effort to convince the organization that a one-year, five-digit deal would not suffice for a top-5 pick, agent Lance Luchnick had an idea to have the unsigned Charles play for the 76ers' team of rookies and free agents during the Princeton Summer League.

"They thought I was going to be a bust in that rookie camp," Charles said. "[Luchnick] told me, 'If you go and mess up, we're in a lot of trouble,' so that was real pressure."

The contract standoff with Philadelphia lasted more than three months until a flurry of moves created cap space. The 76ers, one of five teams to go over the cap, traded Leo Rautins and Tom Sewell and cut Franklin Edwards. In all, around $280,000 had been freed up to put toward Charles.

The four-year deal came out at about $2 million. It was only finalized after a ten-hour marathon negotiation session with Katz. All the while, Leon Wood, the tenth overall pick, was still set to make $75,000 after he and his agent filed an unsuccessful lawsuit in the US District Court against the NBA to challenge the salary cap.

A news conference on September 25, 1984, officially welcomed Charles to the team. Charles, dressed in a suit more befitting a future millionaire, was soft-spoken, as he described himself as a God-fearing child of a single mother and grandmother. He was also polite, replying to reporters' questions with "ma'am" or "sir." Expectations were low for Barkley, whose goal had always been to average 10 points and 10 rebounds for his career.

But the endless string of fat jokes from Williams continued, which made Charles unhappy as he sat by Charcey and Johnnie Mae. "Charles stepped on a scale the other day and a little card popped out of the slot, saying, 'One [person] at a time, please,'" Williams told reporters. If there was ever a time to start anew and move away from the fat jokes, it was during Charles's introduction to the team. But the weight clause in his contract kept attention on the franchise's concern. The clause was designed to keep Charles between 255 and 265 pounds. Not meeting the weight would result in fines as high as $12,000. Charles, who dropped fourteen pounds ahead of the news conference from 280 to 266, expressed optimism at playing at that weight, even though he had never done so before.

"It just makes me play harder to show I can do the job," Charles said. "I have that God-given ability."

The Sixers would need every ounce of that ability to recapture their former glory.

Two years had passed since Erving tasted the champagne at the Forum and felt the ticker tape rain down on him. They had finally slayed the Kareem-and-Magic Lakers—the basketball bogeyman that had won NBA titles against them in two of the previous three seasons—and the party was worthy of such an occasion. Irene Cara's "Flashdance… What a Feeling" blared on a loop as crowds gathered on the sidewalk along Broad Street. They'd won that elusive ring, but Erving wanted another championship. Just one more.

The Sixers' victory in 1983 was a thing of beauty for a city longing for respect. The honeymoon would come to an end in 1984 when the championship defense ended in a surprise first-round exit to the

New Jersey Nets. Losing three times on their home floor, the Sixers were slowed by Erving's groin and stomach issues, and overwhelmed by Micheal Ray Richardson in his finest performance before he was banned from the league for violating its drug policy three times.

That put the 1984–85 Sixers in win-now mode, with much of the core still in its prime. Malone continued to dominate every time they stepped on the floor. Maurice Cheeks, a defensive dynamo at point guard, and Andrew Toney, one of the most underrated offensive players of the era, improved by leaps after the championship experience. But there was still concern about everyone else. Although he could still average 20 a game, the thirty-four-year-old Erving was no longer the dominant force of years past. The same could be said for Bobby Jones, a virtuous defender who personified the city's lunch pail work ethic.

It can be argued that no two legends had more of an influence on a player than Malone and Erving had on Charles in his first year. And Charles, the ball of clay, needed shaping.

"Charles viewed them both as the kind of stardom that he wanted to try to reach as a person," said Jim Lynam, a Sixers assistant who later became head coach during the decade.

As basketball's first true artist of the air, Erving had reached icon status by the time Charles arrived. A singular talent with a balletic style and an iconic afro, Erving legitimized the American Basketball Association, revitalized the NBA, and popularized the dunk in mainstream America.

While Charles reveres the legend today, that wasn't always the case during his time in Philadelphia. Erving was on a pedestal for young Charles, who had been entranced by him back in Leeds. The thirteen-year age difference between Charles and Erving made for uneven interactions in Charles's early years. Erving's form of leadership was not necessarily what young Charles looked for at that age.

"What the public saw of Julius on the court—the all-business, charismatic Dahk-tah, Julius *Errrrrr-ving*, as the 76ers' late great public address announcer Dave Zinkoff used to call him—was pretty much the person that he allowed his teammates to see. Nothing more," Charles wrote in *Outrageous!* "To us, there is no other side to Julius Erving."

The most crucial moment, though, came as Charles was still figuring out what to do with his money. Looking toward his post-playing career, Erving already had an office for his company for five years before Charles arrived.

At this point, Charles would not have been mistaken for fiscally responsible. Working on a $10,000 monthly allowance from Luchnick, Charles had few plans for what to do with his newfound fortune. Sticking to his promise, he renovated his mother and grandmother's home back in Leeds. He'd offered to move his mother out of the neighborhood entirely, but Charcey, a matriarch of the area, couldn't and wouldn't leave. (She also refused to stop cleaning houses.) When that was complete, Charles had an early appetite for cars, at one point owning several vehicles, including a couple of BMWs, a Mercedes, and a Porsche. The prudent Erving pulled him aside to offer some advice.

"You don't need six fancy cars to be somebody," Erving said. "It's not about the car, it's about the brother driving it." The advice stuck with him—but so did the cars.

A potential playoff preview at the Boston Garden would set the tone for the season, and give Charles a window into a side of Erving he had yet to see. The 76ers and Boston Celtics had one of the fiercest rivalries in the sport. The playoff matchups had been dominated by Philadelphia, which ended Boston's run in four of the previous six seasons. Toney with his twenty-foot dagger fadeaways, had been dubbed the "Boston Strangler."

Both teams came in undefeated and with something to prove, whether it was Philly showing its championship window hadn't closed or Boston trying to reverse their fortunes against their rival.

Charles went off against the Celtics, going for 27 points and 7 rebounds off the bench under the bright lights in Boston. But one of the worst defensive performances of the year and an offensive dud from Erving—6 points in twenty-three minutes—put the Sixers down 20 late in the third quarter. Larry Bird, one of the pillars of the league's revival in the '80s, scorched the 76ers en route to 42 points. As Bird and the struggling Erving were running down the floor, they pulled and tugged at each other. Given that the two had done Converse and Spalding ads together, Erving thought they were cool. (He was wrong.)

Robert Parish could see the tension bubbling over between Erving, Bird, and Celtics' big man Kevin McHale, whose chirping grew louder and louder.

"Everything Larry threw up went in and he was talking trash up and down the floor, and Kevin was chiming in," Parish said. "I used to tell them that sooner or later you'd be talking trash to the wrong person at the wrong time, and lo and behold it manifested itself."

When the Sixers star tried to hold Bird back, his hand slipped down and ended up on his neck. Then, an infuriated Bird reached for Erving's neck. The fight was on.

Charles, who said he thought he saw Erving getting whaled on, responded by running up behind Bird and placing the Celtics legend in a headlock as Erving delivered three straight right jabs to the face and chest. "Nice going, guys," Celtics color man Tommy Heinsohn said sarcastically of Charles and Malone after players and coaches broke up the melee.

The fight made history: the $30,500 in fines among seventeen players and coaches was believed to be the most expensive fight-related penalty in the history of the league.

Charles was slapped with a $1,000 fine for his role in the fight, which he claimed was an unjust punishment. He even called into the league office in an effort to clear his name. Years later, Charles repeatedly said he was trying to be the peacemaker in what looked to be a three-on-one WWE style attack, and that the NBA owes him money for fining him.

"I was trying to break the fight up," he said. "I thought somebody had Doc. I didn't know Doc was punching Bird when I was holding him."

Every year at Erving's golf tournament, Charles and NFL great Marcus Allen take a few minutes onstage to become Abbott and Costello. It's one of Erving's favorite exhibitions of one-upmanship, a friendly comedic rivalry between two legends who won't put down the mic until they've had the last word.

One of the main things I first noticed about Charles was his zest for life, but he was still a guy who would show you the ultimate respect. At the same time, he had a lot of mouth on him. His sense of humor and sense of timing were so good that even when he said things people didn't like, they wouldn't get mad at him or stay mad at him. He's a hard individual to stay mad at.

His rookie year was a blur. The question was whether everyone was up for the chase. The younger guys on the team, their agenda was, "Yeah, we want it all and we know what to do." I thought, "You'll find it out." It's easier said than done. It's a rare and precious opportunity to get into the Finals, so it was not anything you should take for granted.

In terms of legacy, the media sometimes will look at how many championships you won. The players you went against will view how many times you got on the court and kicked ass. The fans will look at it as, "Man, I was thoroughly entertained every time I saw this guy play and I would not leave my seat in fear that I would miss something that nobody else has done."

For me, he's with the top of the heap.

If Erving was comparable to royalty, then Malone was more like a father figure. From the moment Malone first met Charles in the summer of '84, the pair had a kinship: "Hey, fathead," Malone greeted him, "welcome to the team."

"Moses was in Charles's mind, and I don't want to put words in his mouth, but he was iconic to Charles," said Howard Eskin, a stalwart of Philadelphia sports radio for decades and Charles's friend.

You couldn't have asked for a better influence for Charles than Malone, a normally close-mouthed but funny giant who valued his family and finances. While responding to questions about the league's widespread issues with cocaine, Malone, an intimidating person for most, joked that the closest he came to using drugs was drinking a Coca-Cola: "Look at me: I'm 6'10"—high enough."

Malone, less than eight years Charles's senior, understood what it was like to be lonely in a new place. Right as he turned nineteen, Malone became the first high school player in the modern game to go pro when he was selected in the third round by the ABA's Utah Stars in 1974. He'd been homesick, and initially faced intimidation from his teammates. While he wasn't shy, Malone was reticent with press, preferring to be the best paid player instead of the most well-known. Del Harris, his coach in Houston, said Malone was "often embarrassed by the attention he receives."

Malone could joke with Charles, too. Big Mo would warn him during training camp to "watch out for the freaks" who would inevitably try to take advantage of his newfound fame. In a CBS segment on Charles, the rookie acknowledged how post players are, in general, ugly. "I consider myself ugly," said Charles, "but I consider Moses uglier."

Charles never understood why Malone took him under his wing, but he went on to become the most important figure in his career.

"Moses filled a gap in my life that had burdened me since my father abandoned my family," Charles said.

It came at a moment of aimlessness. For the first time since his junior year of high school, Charles wasn't the biggest star in the room. Bouts of insecurity plagued him during his rookie year, and the usually upbeat Charles felt a rare sense of self-doubt on some nights. The nerves came out through needless fouls, which got on the nerves of Cunningham, who hoped the pupil would stop relying so much on emotion.

Charles's first game on October 26, 1984, turned out to be more about surviving the Cleveland Cavaliers than stealing the show. The 11-point, 6-rebound outing, which included a team-high 5 turnovers, did not live up to the big expectations placed on his broad shoulders. Yet Phil Hubbard, a veteran power forward and member of the gold medal team from the 1976 Olympics, felt the excitement.

"You didn't know for sure what he was, but he showed flashes in that first game," Hubbard remembered. "You knew they had something decent in the right situation."

The limited action—twenty-seven minutes of playing time—frustrated Charles. Like he did with most things, he turned to Malone.

"I pulled Moses aside and asked him, 'Why am I not playing more?'" Charles said. After looking the young man up and down, Malone had a simple answer.

"You're fat and you're lazy, that's why," Malone said. "You can't play basketball if you're not in shape."

"I said, 'I don't understand that,'" Charles recalled. "He said, 'Which part, the fat or the lazy part?'"

To Malone, the young man wanted a job, but he didn't want to work for it. After Charles got over being called fat and lazy—"It took me a little bit to get over that"—Malone put the three-hundred-pound Charles to work before and after practice. Even in the rain, Malone would run with Charles on a nearby track. Every week, Malone would give the same goal: lose ten pounds. And Charles would do just that. The weight loss coincided with more playing time.

To make sure he kept the weight off, Malone had to be a noisy neighbor. After convincing Charles to move into the same condominium building as him, Malone quickly figured out that his mentee would order pizza at night. A startled Charles didn't know how Malone correctly guessed about his delivery habits. "I was like, 'How you know I got pizza in here?'" Charles recollected. "He says, 'Charles, you can't lose weight eating pizza.'"

"Moses was disgusted with him, really," said Jackie MacMullan, the award-winning NBA writer and commentator, "but he said things like that because he liked Charles, and Barkley listened."

Once 300 pounds, Big Mo's Big Workout brought Charles down to 255. The rookie was finally ready. Cunningham understood he couldn't keep his super sub out of the starting lineup for long. Katz, an ardent supporter of Charles, would reportedly come down to the locker room early in the season to argue with Cunningham about why the top-5 pick wasn't starting. Before the tenth game of the season against Washington, Cunningham pulled aside Charles with an incentive: play well and you're the starter. By the end of the game, a 17-point, 9-rebound performance, Charles had officially displaced Iavaroni from the starting lineup. (Iavaroni was traded to San Antonio a couple weeks later.)

His first start on November 30, 1984, turned out 16 points, 13 rebounds and the first of a long string of wins that elevated the Sixers to the top of the standings. The move turned out to be a revelation for the team, which went 22–2 over the next month and a half.

"Here's the key about Charles: he didn't know he was as good as he was," Katz said. "Once he got into great shape, then he finally realized he was a superstar, not just a star. Previous to that, I don't think Charles understood how good he was."

Hope had returned to The Spectrum. The Sixers were bona fide contenders once more.

Civilized people go home for Christmas, Charles thought, which is why he wanted to return to Leeds for a day. The schedule might have said that the team had a game in Detroit on Christmas Day, but the question came up repeatedly to the team: *Can I go home for the holidays?*

"I've never been away for Christmas," he insisted.

There would be no Christmas miracle for Charles. In consolation he hosted Charcey, his brothers, and girlfriend, Donna, before the holiday at his condo on the edge of the city in Bala Cynwyd. If not for Charcey cooking up fried chicken, corn, and greens in the kitchen, the only semblance of the holiday ritual would come in the form of an undecorated Christmas tree in the corner of the dark bare-walled apartment.

His home, minimally decorated with a pink ceramic lamp and a dull print of a blue flower pot, was the only place he felt safe in Philadelphia. In fact, Charles took on the social tendencies of a hermit— and a large one at that—often reclining on his sofa in his sweats and sneakers while watching TV. His mother said as much, even if he denied it. Charcey guessed it had something to do with how she raised him in Leeds, most of the time protecting her firstborn from the harsh realities of an often overwhelming world.

"I think he's still a baby in a lot of ways," she said of her son. "Charles was very sheltered as a child, and I think that has a lot to do with why he's such a private person now."

The twenty-one-year-old was alone in the biggest city he had lived in. But thanks to an unlikely encounter at a Hertz car rental location during his first week, he began to build a community, according to Larry Platt, a Philadelphia journalist who later befriended Charles. When Charles told the woman at the counter, who didn't know much about sports, that he was new to the city and was probably going to pick up some Popeyes on his way home, she insisted he come over for dinner. Her name was Diane and her husband,

John, was a police officer. Charles accepted the invite and they remain friends to this day.

Bob Ford, longtime columnist for the *Philadelphia Inquirer*, reflected on the ways Charles grappled early on with his celebrity.

"We think of him completely owning every situation and room he's in, but that was not necessarily the case coming out," Ford said. "I wouldn't say he was a loner, but he was easily entertained by the smaller things that didn't involve bright lights."

The court became a refuge, an escape from the loneliness of his life outside of basketball. But even that wasn't easy. Games were one thing, but practices could be contentious. Williams said it wasn't irregular for Charles to go off-script from Cunningham's instruction. He'd pull a rebound off the iron, dribble into traffic, fire a behind-the-back pass and get the ball back for a two-handed flush. Erving was in awe of Charles's on-court imagination.

"Charles didn't process getting better through repetition, so each time down the floor he would innovate and each time was different," he said. "It was very hard to practice because we were trying to practice repetition and offensive and defensive sets over and over and over, and Charles just wasn't cut out for that.

Something was off if Cunningham wasn't almost hoarse after yelling at Charles. The normally reserved Erving, who had Charles carrying his bags during his rookie year, begged for the "biscuit head" to pass the rock. Cunningham said it was part of the gift and curse of coaching Charles.

"Charles was not an easy person to coach," Cunningham said. "I used to have open practices for the media, but when Charles came along I saw this was going to be a battle of wills, and it was. Charles liked the way he did things."

Despite the back-and-forth with Cunningham, Charles wanted to be liked by his coaches, teammates, and most certainly the public. He'd give interviews early on about how he wanted to learn and listen, and how lucky and blessed he was to be in this position. But he also remembered one television interview in which he thanked God for the life he'd had to that point. The next day, Charles got a call from the Sixers, who asked him to stop talking about God on camera after the organization received a flurry of complaints from atheists and agnostics. But he saw a double standard in how another athlete talked about the same subject. Realizing this, Charles grew more comfortable speaking out. It was the first time he understood that it was okay not to be liked by everyone, and that he'd likely face criticism no matter what he said.

"It doesn't matter what you say, you can't make everybody happy... half of these people are gonna like it and half of them gonna hate you," he said. "I made up my mind and said, 'Okay, I've got to be able to look myself in the mirror.' That don't mean I'm right all the time, but I'm gonna try to speak my truth and my rightness."

This newfound openness helped him with his teammates, although it didn't have an impact on the hazing. Walking through the airport with a dozen bags around his neck was not his idea of a good time. Toney was particular about having warm milk around 11:00 p.m. Malone, Erving, and the others wanted their morning newspapers at 7:00 a.m., a time Charles probably didn't typically see.

The mood eased up more on road trips. In the days of bus rides for away games in New York, New Jersey, and Washington, teammates learned that Charles would provoke anyone. He found a sparring partner in Clemon Johnson, the team's dependable backup center. During the pair's witty exchanges, Erving would joke that neither of them were allowed to sit toward the front of the bus as their over-sized heads prevented anyone from seeing out the window. The personality traveled by air, too.

"When he got on a plane, he'd say, 'I don't know why we need a seat belt if this plane goes down. Everybody is gonna die,'" Erving said through laughter. "Who says that?"

Fans were wondering something else on Charles's birthday. In a February 20, 1985, game against the Golden State Warriors, he hung on the rim after a dunk to avoid crushing an opponent below him. But in doing so, Charles displaced the rim and backboard—and moved the 2,240-pound basket support by six inches.

He celebrated his twenty-second birthday with a twenty-two-minute game delay as the basket got fixed. Teammate George Johnson mused that the basket didn't outweigh Charles by much, and team trainer Al Domenico cracked that he should be put in jail for what he did to that poor hoop. Bobby Jones had another idea.

"To fix the basket," he concluded, "they should have just let Charles dunk from the other side."

In the spring of 1985 the team held a meeting to discuss their losing streak. In a suit and tie, Erving said his peace. Leon Wood, the team's other top rookie, kept silent. He couldn't say the same for Charles.

"He says, 'I got something to say. No disrespect, but I need to be involved in the offense more. You're getting up in years.' I had my head down, thinking, 'Are you kidding me?'" Wood remembered. "Everybody says how Charles speaks his mind. Well, it started that first season."

By the end of his rookie season, one in which the Sixers soared to 58 wins, there was a good chance Charles would do something new each night—pushing the fast break, a razzle-dazzle dish, a thunderous throwdown, or all of the above. His first year was largely exhilarating, averaging 14 points and 8.6 rebounds on nearly 55 percent shooting in 82 games played. The twenty-two-year-old would be named to All-Rookie First Team, joining the four players selected in front of him in the draft, including Michael Jordan, who won Rookie of the Year.

But issues with his defense and erratic jumper occasionally overshadowed his moments of brilliance. Cunningham made the call before the playoffs to bring Charles off the bench in favor of Jones, the heart of the team.

Eight games later, after routing Washington 3–1 and sweeping Milwaukee, Charles was giddy while icing his ankles. "Shout" by The Isley Brothers still rang in everyone's ears as the raucous Philly crowd helped their new hero send the Bucks packing. The Sixers were going to play for a shot at the NBA. A sign inside The Spectrum during the deciding fourth game summed up the state of the Eastern Conference semifinals: CHARLES IN CHARGE.

The media compared his playoff run to that of Bird or Magic Johnson in 1980. He joked that coming off the bench was good for him as it allowed him to learn and watch. What did he learn exactly? "I should be out there," he replied.

If there was ever a time Philadelphia needed Charles's charisma, it was in May 1985. As tensions mounted between MOVE, the anti-establishment Black liberation group, and Philadelphia police, a state police helicopter dropped four pounds of Tovex and C-4 explosives in a satchel bomb (a demolition device used in combat), without warning on a row house occupied by MOVE members and their children. When the smoke rose from 6221 Osage Avenue, a fire that police commissioner Gregore J. Sambor acknowledged he wanted to keep burning, neighbors of the quiet, largely middle-class Black residence watched in horror as one of the worst tragedies in the city's history played out in front of them. Eleven people died, including five children. Sixty-one homes were burned and decimated, and more than 250 residents were left homeless due to the blast.

In the city's collective failure, it had burned a neighborhood to the ground and shown no regard for Black life. With the mood of the city at a low, the Sixers were seemingly the one bright light peeking through the remnants of the C-4. But any excitement from the Washington and Milwaukee wins was short-lived. The Celtics quickly vanquished the Sixers in the next round.

It was a macabre ending for a team that felt like it had more left in the tank. Yet as long as Charles was there, the Celtics' Robert Parish thought it would be the first of many playoff matchups with Philadelphia. "Even as a rookie, Charles wasn't afraid of the moment. I thought if he could keep the weight down, he was going to be a monster," Parish said. "We expected the Sixers to be back."

Walking out of the Garden, Charles could hold his head high knowing he had taken care of his family in his first season, accomplishing his No. 1 goal in life.

"I think everything else is just icing on the cake," he said. "That's what I'm striving for is more icing."

13

In a year, Charles Barkley had solidified his legends in Philly. Dawn Staley saw his effect on the projects of North Philly, where his brash attitude and blue-collared approach appealed to a neighborhood desperate to latch on to someone who not only looked like them but acted like them.

"We could really relate to him," said Staley, the women's basketball legend and coach at South Carolina. "Everything that Charles did was from working hard. Him being undersized and overweight resonated with us Philadelphians."

DJ Jazzy Jeff, who was around twenty when he first met Charles at an auto store, recalled how his star quickly rose. "It didn't take long before that team belonged to Charles," said the Grammy Award–winning artist. "Some of the stuff he did made Charles the prototypical Philly person. It didn't matter how big he was, because he was still gonna jump out of the gym and dunk on dudes."

He was also now without a coach. Billy Cunningham became a prophet of sorts when he announced his retirement about a week after the team was bounced by the Celtics. Departing with an NBA title and 520 career coaching wins, including 66 playoff wins, Cunningham stressed that the decision had been made around Christmas.

Looking for someone who could leave their mark on a team with aging stars and a potential one in the making, owner Harold Katz wasn't sure that Matt Guokas wanted the job. A member of the 1967 title team and an assistant for four years under Cunningham, Guokas was considered an easy successor, someone who would keep things afloat. Unlike his former boss, he was more of a players' coach, a nice guy with an even disposition. "If you could not get along with Matt Guokas, something was wrong with you," said GM Pat Williams.

News of the change in coaches couldn't cramp the party Leeds held for their favorite son. They honored him with "Charles Barkley Day," including an autograph session and a parade. The mayor thanked him for putting the town of eight thousand on the map.

The family was humbled by the change in lifestyle and notoriety that accompanied Charles's ascent. Johnnie Mae got a new Lincoln on her birthday. Their boy bought them a satellite dish that covered most of the compact backyard so they could see all of his games. After Charcey and Johnnie Mae vowed to stay in the neighborhood, the house was about to be remodeled with five bedrooms, including one for the oldest son, a three-car garage, two dens, and a sun deck. Residents and strangers would take the winding roads to the back of town for a chance to say they saw Charles Barkley's home.

"I'm not a bragful woman," Charcey stated, "but I couldn't help thinking, 'Look at what my baby's done.'" She said of the celebration, "I don't think there's ever been a mother as proud as I was that day."

"We're playing like shit," Charles told Doc. "We need to talk."

Another loss to the Celtics dropped the Sixers to 6–8, with almost immediate calls for Guokas to be fired. Even owner Harold Katz suggested the team was boring home crowds.

The foot and ankle problems that plagued Andrew Toney at the end of the previous year knocked him out for all but six games of the 1985–86 season. Without their most reliable perimeter scorer, Guokas's new offensive scheme called for Charles to shift more of his game to the perimeter to open up the floor. Philadelphia's backcourt depth was in shambles, too. Erving was about to turn thirty-six, and

Bobby Jones had signaled that he was on the verge of retirement at thirty-four at the end of the season.

It's why the Sixers needed their second-year player to come in focused, which is exactly what he did. Breaking the silence in the locker room, Charles, conferring with Erving, held a forty-five-minute closed-door session in which he urged everyone to call for corrections, not alibis. When word got out that Charles and not Erving or Malone called the meeting, Philadelphia media minted it in two ways: either you were in the camp that Charles, the entertainer, had become Charles, the leader, or you questioned whether a young player was attempting a coup.

Regardless, Barkleymania had arrived in Philadelphia. And with it came added on-court responsibility.

While he was publicly doubting his ability to lead, others were putting the finishing touches on Charles's crown. *Sports Illustrated* promoted him as "a star of epic proportions."

"He's the power forward in the league now," Milwaukee's Terry Cummings, who is believed to have coined Barkleymania, told the magazine. "And please tell Charles I said so."

The franchise's attempts to steer Charles from volatile wild card to even-keeled cornerstone lacked subtlety. Williams, who had stopped talking about his weight, implored Charles to read up on newspaper articles about Larry Bird in hope that he would adopt a work ethic similar to that of the Celtics' forward. Such attempts were lost in translation: Charles took that to mean the Sixers would sign him to a lifetime contract if he played well, a suggestion that Katz rebuffed.

A significant part of those efforts were about keeping Charles's mouth from costing them. Baby Barkley could now walk and talk, a dangerous proposition for any who heard him at Auburn. But with each technical foul, he got louder and louder. The tantrums, which Charles touted as "a clear indication that my career was in full swing," were frowned upon by Katz and the media.

"He didn't wordsmith anything, and he didn't, or couldn't, hold anything back," said John Gabriel, who worked in the front office before becoming an assistant coach. "He was still doing some growing up and had some ways to go."

The emotion Charles bottled up under Cunningham could not be contained under Guokas. In some ways, the forward preferred a player-coach relationship that wasn't a daily test of wills. Charles wanted to be a shot of adrenaline for the fans. "Sometimes I need the crowd to get me going," he said. "When I do some showboating or something spectacular, I do that to get myself motivated. What's wrong with that if it gives you an emotional lift? People want to see that."

And by the end of the season, Charles had been vindicated. At 54 wins, the Sixers were overachievers in a first year for Guokas. The team had a looseness and easygoing outlook that made them considerably different from the workaholic squad that won in '83, but Cheeks, a member of that group, said it was a good thing. The catalyst was the stat-stuffing Charles, who was second in the league in rebounding at nearly 13 a game to go along with 20 points, 3.9 assists, 2.2 steals, 1.6 blocks, and 57.2 percent shooting. Snubbed for the All-Star Game, Charles would make the All-NBA 2nd Team, win the Schick NBA Pivotal Player Award for all-around excellence, and finish sixth in MVP voting.

But Malone broke the orbital bone around his right eye toward the end of the season, putting a deep playoff run in peril. Jones, however, knew Malone's protégé gave them a chance. "Charles is the heart of this team right now," he said.

For as much as he was still discovering the extent of his powers on the floor, Charles was only just beginning to test out the range of his voice. And the side effects of fame would wear on him.

By 1986 his increased celebrity was weighing on him more than he let on. He didn't trust his power and reach, and often kept people at arm's length to maintain some semblance of normalcy. During games, the trash talking on the floor seemed minimal compared to some of the vileness being spewed from the stands. The racial remarks worsened when he was in public with girlfriend Donna, who is White.

"That stuff cuts deep because I know how it makes her feel," Charles remarked. "There are two sides to being a celebrity. The one side is what everybody sees...the money and the TV. The other side is having to deal with ignorant people who think you're public property.

"I might learn to deal with the one side, but I won't never learn to deal with the other."

If Charles wasn't playing basketball, he was staying at home.

He wasn't exactly a loner but being around people wasn't a top priority. A good night for Charles usually meant grabbing food at Chili's or Friendly's, staying in, and watching *The Cosby Show* and *Miami Vice*, and unwinding to Whitney Houston and Luther Vandross. At twenty-three, Charles yearned for the days of being home in Leeds with Charcey, Johnnie Mae, Darryl, and John—"five peas in a pod," as Charcey put it—eating a chicken dinner with them and balling with the neighborhood kids at the playground of his youth.

One of the people who saw him socially was Eagles' cornerback Herm Edwards, who was in his last year with the club and lived down the street from Erving and Cheeks. Edwards, who felt firsthand the depth and intensity of the city's connection to their teams after his "Miracle at the Meadowlands" scoop-and-score in 1978, got to see for himself that the new kid on the block was more reserved than he was on TV, but maintained that same intensity in his interactions off the court. As their friendship progressed, Edwards realized Charles would always ask about his family. He cherished their life chats.

"There was no letdown in Charles Barkley. He was all about trying to win," Edwards said. "And when you're a friend of Charles Barkley, he's got you. He's your friend. When he decided to let you into that circle, you were his friend and that was that."

After struggling to get past Washington in five games, Charles would find no friends in Milwaukee. They had faced off in four of the previous five seasons in the conference semifinals, and Philadelphia ended Milwaukee's season each time. "The Sixers were our kiss of death," said Paul Mokeski, a center with the team.

From the moment the ball first touched Charles's fingertips, the entire city of Milwaukee was calling him an asshole. Deafening chants of "Barkley sucks!" reverberated throughout the MECCA Arena and didn't stop for four games. Charcey and Johnnie Mae were disgusted at some of the other obscenities that they could hear on the broadcast. Maybe the Barkley backlash was due to him describing the Bucks, with the exception of Sidney Moncrief and Terry Cummings, as a team of role players. (That was true, but the locals weren't having it.) After telling Milwaukee fans that they were in the arena to harass him instead of cheer for their team, he ordered them to "kiss me where the sun don't shine." This ramped up the Bucks fans to the point where even Moncrief became concerned.

"I went up to him and said, 'Hang in there, man, just keep playing,' just trying to give some encouragement," remembered Moncrief, who missed most of the series with heel and foot injuries. "It can be lonely when people would go at you a certain way. I don't know what the fans were saying, but it wasn't very nice."

Barkley's barbs coupled with Philly's dominance set up a bitter series in the spring of 1986. Charles, at 30.8 points and 15.5 rebounds a game, played impeccably. Malone's absence was obvious, but the hole he left in the low block allowed Philadelphia to spread things out and play through Charles, as evident by the 31 points, 20 rebounds, 6 assists, 6 steals, and 2 blocks he put up in Game 1.

Guarding him in Game 5 was Paul Mokeski, a journeyman center who had learned he would have an advantage on the block by playing a physical, borderline dirty brand of basketball. As Cheeks drove to the hoop, Mokeski sneakily delivered a cheap elbow to Charles. After, he turned around at midcourt to feel the Sixers' star push him back two steps.

Leaning in with his hips, Charles delivered a wild left hook to the seven-footer that missed its mark by such a wide margin that his forearm ended up rocking the right side of Mokeski's face, dropping the big man on his butt. The game stopped and both were assessed technical fouls, but neither was tossed, even though NBA commissioner David Stern was sitting at midcourt. Don Nelson, the coach of the Bucks, remarked that it was the first time he had ever seen a player not get ejected for throwing a punch. Charles could only smirk. "If you knock a guy down with one punch, you gotta laugh," Charles said.

The Bucks took Game 5. As Charles was leaving the floor, one bespectacled heckler got Charles's attention. The Sixers' star insisted he take off his glasses so he could give the fan a gift. "If he had, I'd have popped him dead in the face," he said angrily.

The fans had gotten to Charles in a way no other crowd had to that point, but that didn't stop him from venturing out to a Brewers game, buying a cap, and sitting in the upper deck as people walked up to him to say hi and ask for autographs. Some of them, maybe even a few who tossed expletives his way, apologized for the behavior of the fans at the MECCA.

Picking up the phone to speak to his grandmother, Charles thought for sure Johnnie Mae was going to give him an earful. The critiques of her grandson's game had become standard fare by now, but the call had a different result. She was proud of him for hitting "McClatchy."

"I'm only sorry that Charles didn't give him a good lick and knock him out so they'd have to dump water on him to wake him up."

When a clip of the fight aired on *Inside the NBA* in 2019, Mokeski's phone couldn't stop blowing up. He wasn't going to out-skill or out-work Charles, he thought, so the Bucks' center pivoted to the next best option: out-crazy.

Half of my fouls back in the day would have been flagrant 1s or flagrant 2s… I think I got respect for the way I played.

Against Charles, I'm in survival mode, trying to do the best I can. One thing I remember was that every time I was guarding Charles, I was saying stupid shit. I said, "I'm crazy, man. I don't know what I'll do." He would look at me like, "Who is this crazy guy?" That was my defense mode. I was saying some crazy stuff and he was looking at me like, "What the hell?" At that point, my thought was, "I'm just trying to win this playoff game, so what can I do now?" So I thought, "Maybe I can act crazy?"

When we squared off at half-court, it was my fault. Things don't happen for no reason. I don't think they called a foul. I don't think anyone shot free throws. Whoever the ref was, they kind of brought us together and said, "Cut that shit out." And then we went back at it.

I'll tell you what though: he punched me in the face and I still like him.

Cummings had grown sick and tired of Barkleymania, saying that it was Milwaukee's time to finally beat the big brother who never let them win. When word got back to Charles about the supposed discontinuation of Barkleymania, he suggested that the Bucks' forward "go bleep himself," noting that the message should be relayed to the ordained Pentecostal minister "in a religious way." After forcing Game 7 with 23 points and 21 rebounds, Charles said that his career in public speaking had come to an end after fielding calls from his mother and grandmother convincing him to shut up. (This did not last for long.)

Although he said he wasn't tired, Cunningham, who was on the call for CBS, noted that Charles was nowhere to be found in the first half, failing, even, to score a field goal. "That's not Charles Barkley," Cunningham said on the broadcast.

Down 1 with seven seconds left, the plan was for Charles to post up off after inbounding the ball to guard Sedale Threatt. On the pass, however, Threatt saw a better option in Erving, who was wide open at the elbow. When the ball hit off the front rim, Milwaukee finally defeated Philadelphia. Moncrief could only sum up the win with one word: "Lucky."

On June 17, 1986, history repeated itself, and for the second time in three years Philadelphia was poised to draft one of the best players in college basketball to join a dominant big man and a talented but aging core.

The odds-on pick had to be Brad Daugherty, the seven-foot All-American from North Carolina who terrorized college basketball and would be an easy fit into the team's big man–centric scheme. Ahead of the draft, Williams suggested the team would be hard-pressed to trade the first overall pick, saying a decision would need to be "a blockbuster of a trade." Charles himself was excited by the prospect of running roughshod over the East with Daugherty for the next ten years.

The problem was Katz didn't like what he saw from a private workout he held for Daugherty at his home basketball court, said Mike Missanelli, the longtime Philadelphia sports radio host.

"That put the wheels in motion to change the plan they had in place because Harold didn't like the workout at his house," Missanelli said. "Charles thought it was crazy."

A telex sent from the Sixers to the league was hoping to gauge interest for the twenty-first pick, which Philadelphia owned. When Cleveland reached out about No. 21, the discussion swerved toward the first pick and Cleveland forward Roy Hinson, a three-year veteran and solid open-court asset. The offer came up hours after a New Orleans courtroom found John "Hot Rod" Williams to be innocent on all five counts of sports bribery in the Tulane point-shaving scandal, thus making Hinson expendable.

When it was announced that the Sixers had traded the first overall pick for Hinson and cash considerations, the dedicated crowd gathered at the Felt Forum at Madison Square Garden booed lustily. Daugherty, who went to bed thinking he would be joining Charles, Erving, and Malone, was confused.

"I don't know what's going on," he said, unsure of the name of the Cleveland owner he had just met.

Lenny Wilkens was considering taking the job as coach of the Cavs around this time. When he heard news of the Daugherty trade, he said it was one of the main reasons he ended up taking the gig. "They used to call that team the Cadavers, but that helped change that around," Wilkens said of the trade. "I could understand why Charles wanted to play with a guy like Brad Daugherty because Brad was a great passer, could score down on the low block and was very team-oriented, and those are the kind of guys that help you become better."

There was, however, another move in the works. Rumors of the team trading Malone gained strength ahead of the draft. While his numbers had dipped slightly since his MVP years, few other players could put up 23.8 points and 11.8 rebounds a game. Charles still looked to him as the focal point and voiced his displeasure about the possibility of his trade. So did Malone, who stressed the Sixers didn't need to spend the top pick on a center. "I'm still one of the top players in the league," he said.

The championship window for the aging team was short and rapidly closing, so a Malone trade was thought to be the most efficient way to extend that period for Charles, Lynam said.

The rumors became reality on Draft Day when Malone found out from his home in Houston that he had been traded to the Bullets. In exchange for Malone, forward Terry Catledge, and two first-round picks in '86 and '88, the Sixers received from Washington Jeff Ruland and Clifford Robinson, two big men who came with concerns over their health and consistency. Katz didn't consult with Charles over the move, a practice he said he never did with star players. The move devastated Charles, who credited Malone for turning his career around in two years and being the strong male influence he had been seeking since his dad left.

"Mentally, it screwed me up a great deal for some time because in losing Moses, I lost another father figure, someone who was more important to me than anyone in my life, except for my mother and grandmother," Charles wrote in *Outrageous!*

The relationship between Malone and Katz had deteriorated after the owner criticized the big man while he was playing on a fractured ankle. Malone said he saw the same thing play out with the "cocky" Katz and his approach to Toney's injury. On the way out, Malone, a business-smart mercenary who thought he found his last stop in Philly, told the *Inquirer* that after going through his experience with Philadelphia, his pupil would have a similar fate shortly down the road.

"When Charles Barkley gets to be about my age...not my age, but after he's played about five years, I think they might do the same thing to him," Malone said.

In one day, the Sixers had traded a three-time MVP still averaging almost 24 points and 12 rebounds, a rotation player, the first and twenty-first picks in the '86 Draft and a first-round pick in '88 for three veterans that management thought could help Charles win now. The deals were not received well.

Williams, who would depart the team the next morning to take the general manager job in Orlando, said there was a shared hope among those in charge that the move would help take the Charles-led team to the next level.

"We thought as that night ended that we had created a nice team that would allow Charles to excel," Williams said.

"Then, everything went wrong. None of it worked."

One play into training camp and Charles measured up Hinson. Charles remained angry over the trades.

"He knocks him over, dunks on Roy Hinson, and says for everyone to hear, 'Anybody got any questions?'" said the *Inquirer*'s Bob Ford. "He had laid Harold Katz's strategy out on the floor."

Ruland, who had come over in the trade for Malone, called Charles's soaring dunk on Hinson one of the greatest plays he'd ever seen. The play was a tough beat for the newcomer.

"Oh my God, I don't know if Roy ever recovered," said Ruland, the Bullets big man who previously matched up with Charles and Malone in the playoffs. "He was just tough on Roy. He destroyed him personality-wise. Charles would test you and if you crumbled, it was not good."

What was supposed to be the happiest day of Hinson's basketball life turned out to be the most disappointing. A Sixers fan growing up in Trenton, New Jersey, he couldn't contain his excitement. Then, he met with Guokas. Despite being on board with trading Malone, the coach was opposed to dealing the top pick, Hinson said. "The first words out of his mouth were, 'I never wanted you here,'" the forward recalled. "He saw my face and said he was only kidding, but he didn't shake my hand, so I knew he wasn't. Some things you can't get over and I just didn't get over that."

Changes abounded in Philadelphia and Charles suggested that the group looked more like an expansion team than a contender. Aside from the reliable Cheeks, the whole franchise was seemingly in flux. Guokas was on thin ice entering his second season. Toney's foot injuries lingered, an ugly point of contention with Katz. The owner had also sold the majority of his stake in Nutrisystem after it stalled out in the marketplace. And Erving announced that the next season would be his last, triggering one of the NBA's great farewell tours.

Then, there was Charles, whose nightly brilliance and ascendance into stardom coincided with a growing ego.

I think I should win the MVP.

I'm more talented than Larry Bird.

I don't feel the fans and media know anything about the game.

At the age of 30, I'm going to retire and never get out of bed before noon again.

Realizing Charles's increasing importance, Katz came to terms with him on an eight-year deal worth $13 million and locking him up through his prime. But the long-term agreement did not fully quell the looming issues Charles had with Katz. And there was also the intimidating prospect of inheriting the mantle from Erving, an American icon.

"It put a tremendous amount of personal pressure on Charles during this developmental period of his in which he mentally knew he was a star who was physically putting up the numbers of a superstar," Erving said. "In Philly, he was in a situation that was spiraling down."

As his star grew brighter and his wallet widened, interest in Charles's personal life was coming into sharper view. Charcey and Johnnie Mae would often tell the stories of him inhaling honey buns and Orange Crush soda from Ramsey's Grocery in Leeds, even if his mother said he had now "graduated a little bit to Twinkies."

Charles's third year in the league also came with the added burden of trying to reconnect with a father who had been all but scrubbed from his life. Charles avoided all mentions of his father in his first years in the league, which was something that struck Roy Firestone as he interviewed the son, mother, and father separately over the years. Firestone's interview with Frank on ESPN's *Up Close* remains the only known televised interview with Charles's father.

"One person was all about the responsibility and all about the business of raising Charles and the family, and the other was not," Firestone said. "Charcey was sassy as hell, and that's where Charles came from. Frank was sort of a heel who had this regret that was noticeable."

The absent father wrote letters to his son trying to explain why he had to go and wasn't a part of his life. He would do the same with the missed calls and voice mails. None of it worked. It wasn't until Charcey spoke with Charles about not being able to avoid his father forever that he was able to relent.

"To say Charles hated his father is not an exaggeration," Charcey said. "He called his father 'scum.'"

The early attempts for Charles to reconcile with Frank Barkley were awkward at best. He had started over in Los Angeles with a new family, and Charles, it seemed, had finally move on. Yet whenever Charles went out to Los Angeles, he would leave a ticket for Frank, his way of extending an olive branch. He even skipped out on the Slam Dunk Contest during his rookie year to spend time with his father in Southern California. When they would hang out, Charles said his father almost treated him as if he was a "show pony," an object of interest.

Victor Campbell made the trip out to Los Angeles during this period to watch his high school friend in an NBA game for the first time. Seeing his friend go from getting treated poorly on a school bus in Leeds to having his name on the marquee at the Forum was a point of pride for Campbell, one he still talks about to this day. After the Lakers game, Campbell said he went to see Charles in the locker room, which is where he saw Frank for the first time. Things soon got awkward when Campbell razzed his former teammate about missing a couple dunks. Though Charles laughed it off, hearing Campbell's quip set off Frank.

"His father was ready to fight me. Charles had to pull him away, the dad talking to me like I don't know what the fuck I'm talking about," Campbell recalled. "I was like, 'You've never been around him all this time, why are you here now?'"

Around the same time, Charles admitted that his love of basketball was waning, saying that he used to enjoy the game but that he now played it for the money. Though the team looked deep on paper, injuries and poor chemistry made them remarkably average. Charles, Erving, and Cheeks missed fifty games among them—Charles was out with a bruised spleen. Ruland missed all but five games. Toney played the most he had in two years but was no longer the offensive weapon he was before.

In February 1987, Charles summed up his brand of leadership in a few words. It was the equivalent of a thwacking in the face with a frying pan. "We've got so many bitchers and complainers on this team," Charles said to reporters. "We've got guys who have complained, complained, and complained… We've got a lot of pussies on this team. They don't realize that we're all in this together."

He'd identify one of those people as World B. Free, the man who was traded out of Philadelphia for the draft pick used to take Charles. Returning to the team as a free agent about halfway through the year, Free gathered pretty quickly that things had changed since he was last with the 76ers. Charles asserted himself in his dealings with Guokas, who did what he could to appease the star, Free said. If

Charles said something, it was going to be done. In fact, this dawned on Free while he was taking a shower, wondering why he was the only one washing up one day. Unbeknownst to Free, Charles had his own shower—and Free was standing in it.

"I came in there and the next thing you know, I see a shadow, a big ol' shadow behind me, and I was like, 'What the heck? This is Charles's shower?'" Free said. "About three weeks later, I was cut. I don't know if the shower had anything to do with it."

Coming into his role as leader didn't mean he couldn't still have fun. After a loss around Christmastime, Charles invited some teammates out for steaks and beers at the TGI Friday's on City Line, two blocks away from his place. Tim McCormick was skeptical that Charles, the team's highest-paid player, would pick up the tab. Toward the end of the night, McCormick was surprised when Charles told his teammates that he had to run out to his car to get them their Christmas presents. McCormick thought for sure they were going to get hooked up with good gifts after Charles inked his new deal.

"He came back and put these beautiful presents in front of me and my teammates," McCormick said. "He then said, 'I'll see you guys tomorrow.' We opened up our boxes and they were empty. We were very confused. We saw the Friday's manager coming at us angrily, saying that the restaurant's Christmas tree was without any fake presents underneath." He added, "Charles casually snuck out and left without paying the bill."

At the end of a lunchtime parade through downtown Philadelphia featuring nine college and high school marching bands and a dozen antique cars carrying Sixers' players was the doctor who twenty thousand people came to see. Julius Erving had scored his 30,000th point and was being escorted in a 1928 Packard Roadster through the throngs of fans in the middle of a workday. It was an honorable goodbye in a season for which there would be no sending Erving off with a championship.

It was no fault of Charles's, named to his first All-Star team, a repeat performance on All-NBA 2nd Team and another top-6 finish in MVP voting. For as unstoppable of a rebounder as he was, his first and only rebounding title came that year with him pulling down 14.6 a game to go along with averages of 23 points and 4.9 assists.

"Coaches would question you about how you let Charles Barkley get 20 rebounds," the seven-foot-two Dikembe Mutombo recalled, "and sometimes you just didn't have an answer."

When the Sixers were about to lose their first-round playoff rematch with Milwaukee, all the attention shifted to Erving. From luxury cars and memberships at elite golf clubs to a piece of the parquet floor at the Boston Garden, the love shown for the ambassador of the game during his final season was bottomless. Erving exited the game to a standing ovation from the Milwaukee crowd, Charles gave him a hug.

A towel around his neck and the game ball in his hands, Erving walked off the court with his head high while "Going the Distance" from *Rocky* played in the arena to pay tribute to Philadelphia's champion. Decades later, he'd say walking off with a loss to those guys was a fitting ending. Palming the ball with his right hand, he lifted it above his head to the delight of fans going crazy for the man who taught the game how to fly.

"I took the ball, and it was like, 'Okay, Charles, it's your turn,'" Erving said.

14

Philadelphia was changing, and Public Enemy gave voice to a city where hip-hop was exploding, including referencing Charles Barkley in their song "Rebel Without a Pause."

"I namechecked Charles because he was relentless, brash, bold, and fast and furious, without a pause. Barkley fit all that," Chuck D said. "Charles was the hero of the moment."

Being referenced in a triumphant way in a Public Enemy song in the late '80s was the kind of street cred you couldn't buy. But Charles feared that he would become so popular that he'd lose his freedom and never regain it. He looked at Julius Erving and saw how Doc had lost all sense of privacy. He didn't want that, he thought, but he might not have a choice.

Phil Knight reasoned that any company wanting to work with Charles would know within ten minutes of sitting down with him what he was all about. And Nike was ready to give him an open mic.

"Nike absolutely helped magnify the personality and marketing power of Charles Barkley," Knight said. "He would have been big without us. We just made him bigger."

For the Nike chairman, the company was in a painful spot. In addition to significant layoffs, Nike was facing the emergence of upstart Reebok.

In hope of turning around the company's struggles, Nike returned to a core strategy of building products around successful and popular athletes. More importantly, the brand looked to broaden and diversify its focus beyond athletic shoes. There were several niche markets identified as areas of growth, including running, tennis, and water sports. The fourth area was basketball.

The executives gathered at the McMansion in the Pacific Northwest in 1984 asked whether the most fun young player in basketball could be the signature athlete to help lead Nike's march into the future. The weekend jaunt marked what Sonny Vaccaro considered the start of the second phase of that quest. The early takeaway was that Nike would sign at least one player coming out of the '84 Draft, and up to three. From the start, Knight wanted to sign Charles, who he saw as a potential game changer. The company was the No. 1 basketball brand in the world, but Knight acknowledged his business had been dealing with really good players instead of the great ones. The great ones, like Larry Bird and Magic Johnson, were with Converse, the official shoe of the NBA.

But Vaccaro, who journalist Armen Keteyian said "basically owned college basketball" through the executive's dealings with coaches and the sport's major programs, suggested that Nike give all the dedicated funds to the rookie class to one person: Michael Jordan.

Charles described signing with Nike in July 1984 as a blessing both he and the company would never forget. "It was truly an honor for a growing global company to sign a small-town kid from Leeds, Alabama," he said.

Knight, who signed Charles before he even came to an agreement on his rookie deal with the 76ers, laughed at the discussion surrounding just having one star when he could also sign Jordan.

"There was some argument early on that since we had Charles that we did not need Michael. That was not a winning argument," Knight said. "We worked very hard to sign Michael, which was not easy. Then, we had the two of them."

As the Bulls star was about to launch a new line at Nike called Air Jordan, the company had plans for Charles to help lead the Air Force series. In one of his first known print campaigns, Charles looks all too serious teaming with his mentor, Moses Malone, in space-aged black-and-silver mesh outfits. In "Men at Work," one of the earliest TV ads featuring Charles, he's joined by Malone and other stars in short shorts as they sweat profusely and don't say a word during three-on-three games in a crappy gym in New York.

Jim Riswold, the former creative director at Wieden+Kennedy, the Portland-based advertising firm known for its work with Nike, remembered young Charles, not accustomed to what shooting a commercial fully entailed, was having a hard time taking direction during the shoot for "Men at Work."

"The early version of Charles, to be blunt, was a fucking pain in the ass to work with," Riswold said. "He hadn't quite refined himself, and he'd often say, 'I'm not doing that, that's stupid.'"

Through a series of sharp taglines—*The meek may inherit the earth, but they won't get the ball*—the Air Force series took off under Charles, who had quickly become the company's No. 2 basketball star behind Jordan. By 1987, the Air Force was the No. 1 shoe at the company ahead of Air Jordan. Within five years of signing at Nike, Charles's endorsement deal was worth $500,000 a year.

Charles's rise coincided with Nike overtaking Reebok in annual sales toward the end of the '80s. Knight lauded the success of the Air Force and its instrumental role for Nike's turnaround. "In some ways, Charles was unlucky that it came along at the same time as Michael Jordan, because there's been nothing like Michael's shoe in the history of sporting shoes," Knight said.

Vaccaro emphasized that Nike would've been just another shoe company if Air Jordan didn't take flight the way it did. It would have affected everyone, including Charles.

"If Jordan doesn't hit at Nike, there is no Charles Barkley," Vaccaro said. "I think Michael gave Charles a whole new life in that regard. But Charles and everyone else who followed him to create a mystical brand of shoes would have never had a chance without Michael."

Simply known as "Barkleys," Charles's kicks were hot. Dawn Staley had Barkleys on her feet when she was named national high school player of the year during her senior season at Murrell Dobbins Tech High School in North Philly. Jerry Stackhouse was attracted to the style and feel of a shoe promoted by someone whom the McDonald's All-American modeled his own game after in high school. It extended beyond Philadelphia to Northern California, where Matt Barnes grew up with pretty much nothing until he got his pair of Barkleys, the first basketball shoes he ever wore, when he was nine years old. "I wore them until I had holes in them," he said. Bakari Sellers, the CNN commentator, saw his parents save up money to buy him a pair when he was growing up, but he didn't want to wear them on the court, in fear of scuffing his colorful prized shoes. In Detroit, Jalen Rose, the Michigan recruit out of Southwestern High School, wore Barkleys because he also knew how it felt to be ostracized for being a strong and opinionated Black athlete.

"I lived it by wearing Barkleys," Rose said. "We wore his shoes and embraced his struggle of talking about things that permeated throughout basketball culture when no one was saying that."

As a kid who loved shoe culture, DJ Jazzy Jeff wanted, and needed, to get a pair of Barkleys, partially because of the connection between Charles and Philadelphia.

The funny thing is I think the first guy to get revered for a shoe was probably Dr. J. I remember the first pair of shoes I wanted were the Converse Dr. J's, the high-top leather ones.

People bought Barkleys because of Charles. I had Barkleys and I still have Barkleys. When you looked at Charles, you were kind of looking at your friend who just made it to the NBA.

That's the time Nike was really on fire because it was all so new to us. You knew who had what shoe.

I think that effect was just as much about him being the man and not just in basketball. This was Charles Barkley and he was from Philly. He was around, you know?

Chuck D wrote in one of his first albums, "I'll slam it down your throat like Barkley." When you get your name cemented in something like that, that's it. That's it!

★ ★ ★

His effect on basketball culture was not only on feet but also on bedroom walls. Charles didn't know what to think of John and Tock Costacos when he walked into the Greek family's garage in Seattle in 1987. The brothers with the infectious personalities had developed a series of distinctive, original sports-themed posters with NFL stars like Lawrence Taylor, Jim McMahon, and Brian Bosworth that were must-have items in '80s pop culture.

"The poster made you look cool," Charles said. "You didn't make the poster cool."

Seeing that Charles had come in all businesslike, the brothers, and sister Marianne, needed to break the ice with the quiet and shy kid who wasn't prone to open up to strangers. When the four-foot-ten Marianne was heading out to get a jockstrap for the shoot, she succeeded by asking Charles what size he wore: Small or extra small?

The clean poster titled "Get Off My Backboard," the first Costacos piece to feature an NBA athlete, showed the forward with his arms crossed, showing a protective scowl as he stands on the rim. "I thought it captured who he was pretty well, which is funny since people always point out the short shorts," John Costacos said.

Charles remained close with the family, particularly Marianne. When she once asked him why he had been ejected from a game in Philadelphia one night, Charles recalled the insult that did him in.

"I told the ref his mom gave lousy head," he told her, according to Costacos.

The friendship between Charles and the family got to a point where he showed up to their Christmas party one year. As he walked around in John's Santa hat, the host insisted the 125 guests not ask for autographs or photos. Well, Charles found out three hours later and proceeded to sign whatever, take any photos, and record voice mail greetings on people's cell phones. *This is Charles Barkley. You've reached John Costacos's phone. I don't know why you're calling him, but leave a message.* When one guest's young children stopped by the party, Charles came out to see them in their minivan. After Charles introduced himself to the youngest child, a five-year-old girl, she had a question for her new acquaintance: Why does everybody say you suck?

"The girl's mother was horrified, but Charles chuckled a little bit and smiled," Costacos said. "And he said, 'Because I want them to.'"

No longer round or a mound, Barkley had earned respect. He'd become basketball royalty in Philadelphia. He was Sir Charles.

It's unclear when the moniker started or who started it, but the name was popularized to a national audience in the *New York Times* in 1987. The title would make the Round Mound of Rebound and the other nicknames obsolete. One nickname for Charles to rule them all. "Charles Barkley, known increasingly as Sir Charles, a Knight of the Round Ball, may still be a blimp to some…but he's some blimp," wrote Ira Berkow.

Anticipation couldn't have been higher for Charles's ascent into the upper echelon of the league's elite. Entering his fourth year, Charles was a superstar waiting to be certified. In his mind, he could dunk like Jordan, score in the clutch like Bird, and dazzle in the open floor like Johnson. In fact, he could do it as well, if not better. "I'm definitely as good as those guys," he said in 1988. "I don't think anybody could say who's better, but I know for a fact that I'm as good as they are."

But there was one problem: the undisputed leader and face of the Philadelphia 76ers had entered his personalized version of basketball hell. The Inferno was at the Boston Garden, a familiar realm of failures past. Down by as many as 49 to Bird's Celtics, Charles, endlessly frustrated, kicked a folding chair that slid toward a row of fans. When an elderly female fan told him that it wasn't very nice to kick the chair their way or curse at his teammates, Charles replied, "Shut up, you bitch."

"She'll get over it," he said afterward.

Referee Mike Mathis—a longtime nemesis who Charles angrily pursued on the court before being restrained by teammates the previous season—ejected Charles for the third time in two seasons. Afterward, it didn't take much for Charles to give an honest assessment of his team.

"The team is just bad. We got a bad fuckin' team," he said to the media. "Unless we play a perfect game, we can't win." Knowing what Charles had just said was going to get attention, Phil Jasner of the *Philadelphia Daily News* gave the Philadelphia firebrand a chance to clarify his stance. "I posed the question among a group of reporters: 'Do you mean that you have a team that didn't play well tonight?'" Jasner remembered to ESPN in 2001. "And he looked us all in the eye and said, 'No, man, we got a bad team.'" The Sixers fined Charles $3,000 for the remarks, one headache in a season full of them.

Andrew Toney played his final pro game in February 1988. The nagging knee injury that cost almost all of the previous season for Jeff Ruland had also forced him into early retirement. Roy Hinson and Tim McCormick got traded halfway through the year to New Jersey for Mike Gminski and Ben Coleman. At 20–23, Matt Guokas, who Charles had once begged for management to bring back as coach, was fired right at the All-Star break and replaced by assistant Jim Lynam.

The disappointment of the 36–46 season contrasted with Charles's brilliance on the court. In that fourth year, the twenty-five-year-old had more than doubled his scoring since his rookie season, putting up 28.3 points per game to go along with 11.9 rebounds. Charles, an all-star who would lead the league in free throw attempts for the only time in his career, made his first All-NBA 1st Team.

There was no real interest in trading Charles, who the Sixers felt was the best player in the league not named Michael Jordan, John Nash said.

While they returned to the playoffs in the 1988–89 season—thanks to wise deals for Hersey Hawkins, Ron Anderson, and Derek Smith—the Sixers were swept out of the first round by New York. Charles was dominant again—25.8 points and 12.5 rebounds, including first in total offensive rebounds for a third consecutive year—but his ascendance came at a low point for the team, not having won a playoff game in two seasons.

Frustration on the court, however, gave way to moments of joy away from it. Scott Brooks, an undersized, undrafted guard who Charles invited to live with him for two months, remembered being awakened in the middle of the night by a loud vibrating hum. "What the fuck do you think it is? I'm vacuuming!" the clean freak told Brooks. "I can't sleep if the lines in the carpet aren't straight." Charles took a liking to the five-foot-eleven guard from the CBA. In addition to his roommate urging him to watch Oprah Winfrey instead of going to the arena early and sending him off in his Porsche to pick up $100 worth of Popeyes, Brooks saw the quiet and giving side of his friend. After Charles piled up groceries from every aisle in the store, Brooks thought Charles was living up to his previous Round Mound reputation. Then, after directing Brooks to drive underneath an underpass, Charles got out of the car and proceeded to hand out the groceries from his trunk to the dozens of homeless people who converged on the vehicle.

"That day right there," said Brooks, "that made such a lasting impression on me—on who he is, and what it is to be a professional athlete."

The summer of discontent started in handcuffs and continued with lost money.

Pulled over on the shoulder of the Atlantic City Expressway, Charles stepped out of his car as a New Jersey state trooper began to search his black '88 Porsche, with reason to believe he was in possession of drugs or a weapon. What prompted that suspicion was unclear. He was on his way home that morning after speaking to hundreds of children at a basketball clinic about the dangers of drug abuse. In the search, trooper Desiree Simon found a loaded 9mm Heckler & Koch semiautomatic handgun located on the floor behind the passenger seat. Since the Pennsylvania resident did not have a New Jersey permit for the weapon that was loaded with thirteen rounds, Charles was arrested on one count of possession of a controlled dangerous weapon on August 17, 1988—a charge carrying a maximum penalty of five years in prison.

Lynam, who joined Charles for the clinic, couldn't have been happier with how the talk went. His star looked like a role model, he thought. But just as he pulled into his home, his wife asked if he had heard about the gun charge, which left the coach dumbfounded. *How could he do this?* The *Philadelphia Daily News* among others ran with "BARKLEY BUSTED" as the standard headline for what was believed to be his first-ever arrest. "I don't know why the media should make a big deal out of this," Charles argued. "It's not an Al Capone kind of thing."

In truth, Charles carried a gun in fear of racism, in fear of the worst-case scenario that could happen to him as an athlete and Black man. Using the gun, however, presented a whole other set of questions and considerations. The weapon provided him an undeniable sense of comfort, he said, but pulling the trigger would've taken extraordinary circumstances.

"I would never want to kill anyone, but I would never let anyone hurt me," he said. "I feel I can handle myself without a gun, but most people would be intimidated by me and they might use a weapon. I've had guns for years, but nobody ever knew. It's not as if I pull a gun every time I lose my temper or get into an argument."

The next day at practice, Lynam confronted him about what happened. Charles had cooperated with police and was released from custody under his own recognizance, and Charles helped him understand why he and other athletes like him carried a firearm, the coach said. The conversation offered him a window into the realities of life for Black men in America.

The weapons charge was dropped after a judge ruled that the trooper's search was illegal.

Financial stability mattered to Charles from an early age, and there was truth to how his political views were shaped by it. The most notable example came in 1988, when he told Charcey he was considering voting for George H. W. Bush in that year's presidential election. In Bush, the vice president promised a continuation of Ronald Reagan's '80s with his famous guarantee not to raise taxes: "Read my lips: no new taxes." This appealed to Charles, but his interest in the Republican befuddled his mother. He scolded her son, saying, "He'll only work for the rich people." Charles, in a lighthearted comment with a heavy dose of truth, replied, "Mom, I *am* rich."

The context of the period, and Charles's recognition of his own wealth, is critical to understand how the audit he ordered that summer of his own finances, one triggered by his agent's alleged underhanded tactics, affected him. As part of the *Newsday* investigation that documented in April 1988 how his agent had allegedly paid high school and college coaches tens of thousands of dollars to persuade big-name prospects to sign with him, Lance Luchnick's history of bad business dealings with NBA players was brought to light. Litigation threats came from former clients, including Charles's former teammate Terry Catledge. Cliff Levingston of the Atlanta Hawks was awarded $17,325 in damages in 1987 after a judge found that Luchnick did not provide adequate "guidance, counseling, and advice in relation to yearly tax planning and preparation." Another lawsuit from Robert Reid of the Charlotte Hornets accused the agent of using his finances as if they were "his own private pocketbook." Terry Teagle, a swingman for the Golden State Warriors who fired Luchnick as his agent in 1987, compared Luchnick running his financial portfolio to "letting an alcoholic trying to kick the habit be a night watchman at a whiskey factory."

Among the players to dump Luchnick was Maurice Cheeks, who parted ways due to bad investments. Like Cheeks, Charles signed an agreement granting Luchnick the power to deposit and withdraw money as well as borrow funds. Charles and Cheeks both had the NBA send their paycheck directly to Luchnick, which meant he took a 10 percent cut.

Luchnick defended his body of work in a 1990 interview with the *Atlanta Journal-Constitution*. "Nobody I know has gone through life without making a mistake or two, and I'm no different," he said. "But I'd prefer not to get into that."

It's difficult to wrap your head around how badly Luchnick allegedly screwed up Charles's money. Approximately $200,000 was invested in hotels, a car dealership, and a bank that went belly-up, Charles claimed. A similar poor investment transpired with a raw land deal that was appraised at little more than a third of the $900,000 in cash Charles had put into it. His investments as part owner of a couple of Texas farms focusing on cattle and pecans, respectively, cost him hundreds of thousands of dollars.

"I built this whole life on not being poor," he said to *PhillySport* magazine. "We were so dirt poor when I was growing up that we didn't have a shower. I decided long ago never to be poor again."

Charles maintained to *Newsday* that while Luchnick was an excellent contract guy, "that should be the extent of his involvement." But the uneasiness hit a breaking point in June 1988 when the NBA Players Association suspended Luchnick from representing any of its athletes, citing the questionable payments. Charles had no choice but to audit the books that summer. To get a clear picture of the extent of his losses, he'd also turn to an old friend, someone who had seen him play when he was still the lightly recruited fat kid from Leeds High.

When Charles picked up the phone to call Glenn Guthrie, he remembered how the Auburn booster stood by him when he was injured his junior year. The respect and kindness he showed to Charcey and Johnnie Mae long was also paramount to Charles. Guthrie, a financial planner in Birmingham, had no experience in NBA contracts, but when it came to investments and planning, Charles trusted no one more. That's exactly what he needed now: trust. By the time Charles first mentioned of "having a lot of problems" with Luchnick to the media, Guthrie had already essentially taken over his finances. Dan Sims, an Auburn booster and Guthrie's friend, went with him to Philadelphia later in the year to help pore over Charles's tax returns. But, as Charles put it, the shit had already hit the fan.

"Lance had Charles in big, big debt," Sims said. "That's when Charles and Glenn found out for sure that something was going on."

Given that Luchnick's investments for Charles were described as "nuclear waste" by an attorney brought on to examine the tax returns, the audit results were distressing. Though Charles was far from broke—he had more than $9 million left on his contract at the time in addition to his lucrative Nike endorsement deal—he had basically nothing to show for the $1 million he had already made.

In digging into the returns, it was discovered that the Philadelphia star had four years' worth of back taxes and penalties due to either not paying them or paying them late, Charles said. Three months later, it was confirmed that a large sum of money was missing from Charles's account. Luchnick was fired in March 1989. Charles had pursued legal action until Luchnick filed for bankruptcy and lost his NBA clients. In not pursuing a lawsuit, Luchnick would also forfeit all claims against his former client. There was also the reported $5-million judgment Charles won against Luchnick, which was hard to collect considering the former agent didn't have any money.

"I left my affairs totally in his hands," Charles said of Luchnick. "I won't make that mistake again."

The drama in his life from the summer of '88 had seemingly settled, and Charles avoided both jail and losing any more of his money.

While this was unfolding, few knew Charles, a little older and wiser, was also trying to settle down.

The love story of his life was born at TGI Friday's.

The chain restaurant by his City Line apartment was a security blanket. He was there for lunch and dinner after practices and games. If it was open for breakfast, the pancakes and bacon better be ready. It was his office for interviews and business meetings, just as long as his desk came with a burger and Diet Coke.

After finishing one of his regular meals at Friday's in October 1987, Charles was about to head to the bank when he passed in the doorway a stunning woman with long blond hair. She was coming, he was going. The meeting between Charles and Maureen Lynn Blumhardt was one of chance, but love at first sight, it was not.

"She grabbed my arm," Charles said to the *Philadelphia Daily News*.

"I didn't grab your arm," she replied. "I was holding the door open for my boss and you came through. I said hello."

"You tried to stop me," he retorted, "and I told you, 'Sorry, I've got to go to the bank before it closes.'"

"You're exaggerating again," she said.

A legal aid and part-time model, the five-foot-ten Maureen looked down and expected to see her five-foot-four boss following behind her. Instead, she said, it was a "big Black thigh" belonging to Barkley. She had seen his immaturity on the court, and had heard he was a jerk. He was polite in their brief interaction, but she didn't think much of him. Charles, on the other hand, was curious. The next day, he returned to his second home to ask a Friday's employee who she was and for a way to contact her.

He called her. Then he called again. And again and again for about a month. The phone had been Charles's best friend in his first couple years in the city, the tool to connect him to those he needed to stay connected to amid a period of loneliness, so this courtship felt natural.

"He chased me like a dog," Maureen said.

One of five children born into a middle-class family in January 1964, Maureen considered herself one of the guys growing up in Bucks County outside of Philadelphia. Her big Irish Catholic brood was kind and so was Maureen. She was the designated driver for her group of friends and dreamed of being a teacher. A self-described beanpole as a kid with big funny feet, she preferred be called Mo. "I was the biggest tomboy on this earth," she said. "I wanted to be a boy and tried to convince myself I was a boy."

After a month of chatting, Charles built up the courage to ask her out on their first date—well, kind of. Come to a Sixers game, he said, and I'll leave you two tickets. Upon accepting, Charles reached out to a couple female friends to see if they could scout her out from afar.

Complications would soon arise. Maureen had asked her twenty-year-old brother Michael to the game. The scouts sitting in front of the Blumhardt siblings mistook the brother for a boyfriend. In turn, Maureen noticed the women looking back and shooting daggers at her so often that she believed one of them had to be a jealous girl-friend. Charles hands out tickets to women every game, she thought. After he noticed her in the stands with another guy, Charles was all but through with her when she gave him the cold shoulder following the game.

"I thought she was stuck up," Charles remembered. "I never wanted to see her again."

If not for Maureen's friend, the one who gave Charles her number without asking, their story would have ended then. She convinced him to give Maureen a second chance.

Though Charles had dated, Maureen was striking in more ways than one—smart, warm, trustworthy. Charles had hardened since coming to Philadelphia, but he warmed up with Maureen, finding in her a quiet, patient partner who gave him the stability he craved. She played to the opposing sides of Charles's personal life, whether it was staying in and watching TV or entertaining friends over lively dinner parties. In Maureen, he saw a person who made him, on the brink of sainthood in Philadelphia, better and complete.

"Sometimes," he said to the *Daily News*, "I think she's too good."

Maureen could keep up with Charles in a way no one had before. When Charles would show up to the restaurant Bridget Foy's after the games to drink some Miller Lites with a group of beat writers, Maureen shared her opinions and hot takes. Media members who got to know her suspected Charles got some of his best material from Mo.

Ten months into dating, Charles had marriage on the mind. It wouldn't take long for their relationship—the smitten bad-boy bachelor gets serious with a local woman—to be in the public eye. Charles vowed he would take the relationship slowly, but Dave Coskey, the spokesperson for the team, indicated to local media that the Sixers forward had been talking about marrying Maureen as early as August 1988. Billy Cunningham, Charles's former coach, witnessed over dinners with the couple how the kid he had as a rookie was far different from the mature adult he saw when he was around Maureen.

"One of the things that changed Charles was Maureen," Cunningham said. "Just being in her presence, you could tell she was the one who got him pointed in the direction of being the man he wanted to be."

That was also around the time the couple found out that Maureen was pregnant. The news delighted Charcey. The pair were engaged by the end of the year, maintaining that marriage was always part of the plan, even before the pregnancy. Charles, in the most honest way possible, interpreted what for better or for worse meant when it came to marrying him.

"I said, 'You know I'm difficult to be with at times, that sometimes I'm a jerk, I'm cocky, arrogant, and spoiled, but I think you're the person I'd like to spend the rest of my life with,'" Charles recounted of the convincing argument.

Though the couple was having fun—Charles had actor Rob Lowe call Maureen to wish her a happy New Year, even though she didn't believe it was him—there was an unjust level of attention paid to the interracial marriage of the Black man from Leeds and the White, blonde woman from Bucks County. In Philadelphia, a vocal minority was trying to tell Charles who he was supposed to like. Maureen heard it, too. She recalled how people would follow her into the bathroom to try to intimidate her: *Why don't you stick with your own kind?*

The basement of the courthouse seemed like a good place to get married and avoid all media attention. Before Charles was on his way to Houston for his first time starting in an All-Star Game, the couple decided there was no better time to elope. Fearing a circus of paparazzi and autograph hounds, they opted for a private civil ceremony on the morning of February 9, 1989, in the basement of the Cecil County Marriage Bureau in Elkton, Maryland, about an hour away from Philadelphia. Days shy of his twenty-sixth birthday, Charles, in a black-and-white checked jacket, dark slacks, and tie, stood next to his twenty-five-year-old bride-to-be, Maureen, six months' pregnant, in her peach-colored dress. It was so intimate that they brought no witnesses to their nuptials. "I really think he just didn't want any publicity," said Janice A. Potts, the deputy clerk of courts for the marriage bureau, of Charles. "She wanted a quiet ceremony."

Moments after they were pronounced husband and wife, the couple were met with applause by about twenty people in the waiting area of the courthouse. They paused for photographs and Charles signed a court employee's game program from the previous night. That evening, the couple made their first public appearance as husband and wife at a benefit for Armenian relief in New York, a commitment Charles had made to the team's orthopedic surgeon before they decided to tie the knot. Arriving in Houston, Charles explained the need for him to separate his public persona from his private life, namely his wife. "This has nothing to do with playing ball," he said of the quiet wedding, adding that he never believed weddings should be a contest of who can have the biggest or the best.

As Maureen was sleeping back at the hotel room, Charles spoke with reporters.

"I felt I was with a special woman—we've been together about a year—and if it turned out I wasn't completely ready, I decided it was worth the sacrifice," he said. "I told myself, if I waited, if I let her go, that wouldn't have been right."

Charles was enjoying the first twenty-four hours of marital bliss. But five years into his time with the 76ers, he was beginning to wonder if he needed Philadelphia to release him. One of his best chances to lead Philadelphia back to the promised land would be on the way. The problem was another player and team wanted to win a title as well.

Michael Jordan and the Chicago Bulls.

15

Even if he didn't immediately admit it, Charles was worried as hell while Maureen was in labor in May 1989.

"You were a nervous wreck," his wife told him.

After Charles stubbornly pushed back, Maureen had heard enough.

"Charles was white if that's any indication," she rebutted.

He laughed before finally relenting: "Okay, maybe I was a *little* nervous."

On May 15, 1989, Christiana Barkley was born at eight pounds, twelve ounces, and life changed on a dime for the newlywed couple only three months into their marriage. Instead of summer vacations and golf, Charles's schedule now included middle-of-the-night baby feedings and exterminator appointments. In the first known public photo of the happy family in the *Philadelphia Daily News*, one-month-old Christiana, a sleepy bundle of cheeks and hair, is held by her glowing mother and more concerned-looking father. Maureen's face says, *We're in it, this is great.* Charles's mug reads more like, *So I hold it like this?*

If he was nervous about the birth of his daughter, then he was pretty much terrified about the idea of marriage. Before Maureen, he had not seen a successful marriage in his own home, still scarred by the actions of Frank. Yet it was these moments with Christiana, hanging by the pool while barbecuing with Maureen, that helped ease some of the fears ingrained in him since childhood.

For the first time in his life, he thought, he had his priorities in order. Charles was growing up and it felt good.

"I realize there is more to life than basketball," the twenty-six-year-old said. "I want to have a good marriage. I want to have a big, happy family. I want to build something permanent."

But the same month he started building his family, there was trouble back in Leeds. Charles's younger brother Darryl Barkley was growing resentful of his brother's success, so much so that he wouldn't watch his games on TV. A high school dropout who struggled in one year of vocational school, Darryl bounced around and couldn't hold a significant job. Meanwhile, his older brother nearly nine hundred miles away could do no wrong.

"Darryl had to follow a star here in Leeds," said Margaret Little, the guidance counselor at the high school.

It's unclear when Darryl started using cocaine or for how long, but the family suspected the twenty-two-year-old started using around 1988. Charles recounted how Darryl grew depressed and started hanging with the wrong people. After seeing this pattern play out with other families of famous people, Charles feared this could happen.

"I had an enlarged heart since birth, so I didn't play sports like my brother," said Darryl, referring to Charles.

A drug culture had always existed in and around Leeds, one that Charcey warned her boys about for years. Much later, Darryl told the *New York Times* that he had been a part of the drug community "for a while."

A week before Christiana was born, Darryl was on his way to pick up beer at the FoodMart near Leeds Junior High, when police arrested him on a charge of selling crack.

Leeds police had been investigating the town's underbelly for months. The area of specific concern was Leeds Junior High, a stone's throw away from the family's house. Every sale tracked by police occurred within one mile of the school. To help with the investigation, Leeds police brought in an undercover cop from Montgomery to start buying cocaine and crack from dealers for about five months. At least one of Darryl's transactions was to the undercover officer at a local club. He was among fourteen people arrested in the largest drug roundup in the small town's history.

Charcey and Johnnie Mae wanted to believe that Darryl wasn't using cocaine. But when he declined his grandmother's offer to take a drug test, Charcey, finding all the strength she had left, gave an ultimatum: take the drug test or I'm throwing you out of the house.

After making the drive of about one hundred miles north to a drug-testing center in Decatur, Charcey said the doctor gave her and Johnnie Mae the news before he shared it with Darryl. The urine test showed traces of cocaine and marijuana. The results devastated Charcey and her mother. Darryl denied using drugs once more before he was shown the results.

In Philadelphia, Charles, who learned what had happened days after the Sixers were swept by the Knicks, was infuriated. People told him there were helicopters flying over the house and local TV stations covering his brother's arrest. The next day, a version of the same headline ran in the Associated Press and nationwide: "Barkley's Brother Arrested in Drug Sweep." Charles cared about him, but this was beyond unacceptable.

"I love my brother, but I told him if he [sells drugs], he is out of our lives forever. He will be my brother in name only. I mean it," Charles said at the time. "I've got no sympathy for anyone who gets involved with drugs. I told him if he did this, he deserves to go away for a long, long time. Maybe he'll wake up if he hears those [prison] doors slam behind him."

Although police announced that each arrest would be enforced under a special Alabama law mandating a minimum five-year sentence for drug deals within a mile of a school, it's unclear if Darryl was convicted or faced any prison time. (The Alabama Department of Corrections does not have any records of Darryl in its system.)

Despite Darryl's short stay in rehab, Charles was convinced his brother had taken his message to heart. Then, five months later, Darryl suffered a stroke that left him partially paralyzed. A blood clot on the right side of the brain had manifested. Charles noted how doctors found that his enlarged heart was unable to pump blood fast enough to get to the brain.

When Charles left training camp to see his brother at a Birmingham hospital in October 1989, Darryl was in serious condition. He couldn't move or talk. He was out of it.

"I just can't imagine being paralyzed at age twenty-two. It shakes me up. I think about him a lot during the day," said Charles, who called him every day during this time. "But I have to be an example for him, to show him he can come back if he works hard in rehab. My whole family needs me. So I have to be strong."

Thankfully, Darryl survived the stroke. Charles had some advice for him: Don't be consumed by money. Don't chase it.

"That's what got him in trouble," Charles said.

The seven-word note given to the Detroit ball boy to pass along to Pistons' center Bill Laimbeer was one of the more efficient messages delivered by Charles at any point in his life.

Dear Bill,
Fuck you.
Love,
Charles Barkley

For many watching basketball in the late '80s, the Detroit Pistons were reviled. Michael Jordan expected them to be dicks. Scottie Pippen hated them to death. The same went for Patrick Ewing. But the team simply called themselves world champions, the squad that dethroned the reigns of Boston and Los Angeles.

"Nice guys finish last. You know, sometimes the villain wins," said Pistons' big man Rick Mahorn. "It's kind of fun being the villain."

Titles were the furthest thing from Philadelphia's mind at the start of the 1989–90 season. A return to relevance would be a good start. Mired in two years of miserable mediocrity, the Sixers needed help fast if they planned on not wasting the prime of Charles's career. Building on the promising moves of the previous season, John Nash got younger by trading stalwart point guard Maurice Cheeks, who was on the decline, to San Antonio for Johnny Dawkins, a heady player with elite athleticism. Lynam, a Philadelphia native entering his first full season as coach after taking over the previous year, had the full support of the organization, a player's coach who could say something to Charles if he did something wrong, but not embarrass him.

Luckily for the Sixers, Charles was about to find a noggin-knocking, body-bashing basketball brother to further take his mind off things.

Mahorn thought the Pistons were joking when they told him on the day of the championship parade that he was no longer with the team. Still in his championship hat and T-shirt, he was informed he had been selected by the Minnesota Timberwolves in the Expansion Draft that afternoon. The unanimous decision to keep him unprotected was made during the NBA Finals, with the franchise thinking Mahorn, a dominant enforcer and vicious rebounder and screener, was the most replaceable. Concern about Mahorn's back also arose, but his agent denied any issue, saying that his client "had more tests than Ronald Reagan this year, and he didn't fall off any horses."

Unwilling to go to an expansion team, the thirty-one-year-old Mahorn threatened to play in Italy. When that hit a snag, the Timberwolves finally traded him to the Sixers for three draft picks. The move was twofold. In addition to playing Charles less minutes, Lynam knew Mahorn would clean up whatever lapses their 25-point scorer had on the defensive end. A frontline of Mahorn, Mike Gminski and the 242-pound Charles shifting to small forward was too enticing to pass up.

In Mahorn, Charles found a physical contemporary who could show him what it meant to win at the highest level. It was also a good excuse to show people that Mahorn, not Charles, had the biggest butt in the league, the star joked.

"The connection he had with Rick Mahorn was unparalleled," Howard Eskin said.

They were Bump and Thump—Charles bumped 'em and Mahorn thumped 'em—and the league was about to feel their pain. Mahorn liked to knock people down and so did Charles. The elbows, holding, and psychological tricks were fair game as long as you didn't get arrested for it, Charles claimed.

"The team was a reflection of the city," Dawkins said. "We had some of the toughest guys in the league. We put our hard hats on and got to work."

Charles was having fun again. In year six, this was the best team he'd had since his rookie season with Julius Erving and Moses Malone. It was also the healthiest, as each of the five primary starters—Charles, Mahorn, Gminski, Hawkins, and Dawkins—all played at least seventy-five games that year. He'd punch mascots on the road, chuck the ball into the stands after wins at home, and laugh when Mahorn replied to a taunting fan with a comment about their mother. Sometimes, it would be a little too much fun for his wallet. While the technicals were down, his donations to the league office had spiked since Mahorn's arrival, a costly year in fines totaling at least $35,000, from cursing to shoving and slapping.

Meeting with commissioner David Stern was as harsh of a punishment as the $5,000 fine leveled against Charles and New York Knicks point guard Mark Jackson after they made informal bets between themselves during a game. Throughout a career of technical fouls, suspension, and fine-worthy actions, Charles recounted how the chats with Stern in his office, a catch-up between star employee and big boss, were "one of the most uncomfortable things that could ever happen to you in your life."

"When you screwed up, he let you know it," he said. "But always, at the end, after he kicked you out of his office, he gave you a hug and [said], 'Son, you made a mistake. We're going to get past this.' And I'll never forget that." Of course, the meeting with Stern didn't stop Charles from walking into the locker room and joking if anyone knew the line for that night's game.

While the edge remained, this was a friendlier Charles. Earlier in 1989, Mary Walsh, a seventy-six-year-old fan from Trenton, New Jersey, called into a radio station to complain how Charles was "mean" and a ball hog. Well, Charles was listening and proceeded to record a message played on the station all throughout the following day in an attempt to get in touch with her. Walsh, who thought she had imagined hearing Charles's voice reach out to her on a loop, finally accepted, and was greeted with a limousine and four seats to a game. Upon seeing her, he gifted her with flowers. Walsh, who immediately changed her tune, responded by giving him a Valentine's Day card and a wedding card. "My wife and my momma told me that I'd better shape up," he told Walsh. "They don't want nice ladies like you to be mad at me."

Allen Lumpkin was struck when Charles walked up to him during practice and asked him if he'd seen the news. A local church conducting a toy drive for underprivileged families and children was broken into and left without a single gift. Charles told Lumpkin he wanted to use his own money to pay back everything that was stolen, plus some extra. Lumpkin did just that, giving the church the money on Charles's behalf. "The only stipulation was the church couldn't say where they got the gifts from," said Lumpkin, a friend of Charles's who was then the team's equipment manager. "It had been nothing I had ever seen before."

His humanitarian episodes had become so commonplace that Dave Coskey, then the team's publicity director, recalled how Charles would "kill me if I publicized it." Coskey grew so fond of Charles that he asked him to be the godfather to his first child.

"Most athletes are bad guys who want you to think they are good guys," Coskey said. "Barkley's a good guy who wants people to think he's a bad guy."

Charles felt a true connection to that year's team, a hodgepodge group of mismatched personalities that fit well together. That was especially the case for Gminski, one of his best friends during his time in Philadelphia. Gminski remembered how much it meant for him and the person he knew as Charlie to go see *Mississippi Burning*, the 1988 film with Gene Hackman and Willem Dafoe, loosely based on the abduction and murder of three civil rights workers in 1964. As a White guy who grew up in Connecticut, the experience of seeing the film with Charles, and hearing about Charles's life as a Black man in Leeds, were both powerful and eye-opening for Gminski. When the Sixers had an exhibition game in Birmingham, Gminski and the team also got to visit Leeds for a home-cooked meal from Charcey and Johnnie Mae. Being in Alabama with his teammates was the most nervous Gminski had seen Charles, as Charles realized the responsibilities he faced in coming home.

Changing Charles's palette, however, proved to be more difficult.

A lover of wine and fine dining, Gminski grew tired of repeatedly going to Friday's and Chili's, and suggested there was a much bigger culinary world Charles needed to explore. Gminski figured he'd start by trying to adjust Charles's pregame meal from McDonald's: two fish fillet sandwiches, large fries, and a Coke. Knowing Charles had the same meal before each game, Gminski recommended he have pasta as his pregame meal like he did, as well as a bagel beforehand as part of his carbo-loading. During a pregame shootaround, Charles voiced his displeasure at his teammate for screwing up his gastronomical routine.

"We're warming up and he's like, 'Goddammit, I'm so hungry. That pasta went right through me. That's the last time I do that,'" Gminski said. "The fried food laid in his stomach and that was the end of the pasta experiment."

To Charles, an MVP favorite on one of the league's best teams, the Bad Boy Pistons were that in name only, a charade that had gone on long enough. Aside from Isiah Thomas and Joe Dumars, he proclaimed that no one else on the team could really fight. You could push them around and he intended to do just that in late April 1990, with the team trying to clinch its first division title in seven years.

"The Sixers had the real Bad Boy, and the Pistons knew it," he said of Mahorn. "Bill Laimbeer knew it, too."

Known as the Darth Vader of the NBA, Laimbeer could be calculating. "I don't know in my time…of covering the NBA that there was ever a more loathsome character than Bill Laimbeer," Michael Wilbon said to ESPN in 2020.

Charles had his eye on Laimbeer. Hawkins said that when he walked into the Palace at Auburn Hills, he sensed that something bad was going to happen.

"You just tried not to get hurt," Hawkins said.

For as physically imposing as the Pistons were during the period, the Sixers had their number. Charles dunked his way to 36 points, and Isiah Thomas was ejected for taking a swing at Mahorn and grazing him, much to the delight of his former teammate. That's when Charles and Mahorn started to have fun, Gminski recalled.

"Mahorn leans across Laimbeer and sniffs the air and says, 'Charlie, do you smell something?' Charles leaned across Laimbeer and sniffed and said, 'Yeah, what is that?' [Mahorn] leaned back across Laimbeer and says, 'It smells like pussy,'" Gminski remembered. "You could just see the smoke coming out of Laimbeer's ears at this point."

As Mahorn went up for a fast-break dunk in the final seconds of a Sixers' win, Dennis Rodman pushed him for the foul. Laimbeer took the ball and stuck it into Mahorn's teammate's chin. Then, Laimbeer took a swing at an interceding Charles. Charles retaliated, thwacking Laimbeer with a left so off-balance that he stumbled backward.

Laimbeer shoved teammate Vinnie Johnson to the side to make room for the showdown. Charles took a moment to square up before missing wildly with another overhand hook. Laimbeer, a student of the scuffle, pulled his opponent under for a couple uppercuts as the heavyweights tumbled to the floor amid a roaring crowd.

John Salley, the Pistons' center, lunged into the donnybrook to see what he could do to help.

"Charles is not realizing this is about to be a fight. So, I grabbed him, and he couldn't see who was behind him. I go, 'Charles, it's Sall.' He goes, 'Sall, pull me out of this,'" Salley remembered. "I literally pulled him and moved him out of the fight."

After a shouting match with Rodman, Charles walked to the locker room by himself, a decision one of the announcers noted was not a good idea. Seconds later, the entire Sixers bench ran toward the tunnel. Dozens of fans crowded the barrier and one attempted to slug Charles. The fan was detained, but Charles declined to press charges. He punished the man in his own way.

"He swung at me for no reason," Charles said of the fan. "I spit in his face; I got him good."

About six minutes later, the fight ended. In response, the NBA levied a total of $162,500 in fines, then a league record. Only three players were suspended one game each: Charles, Laimbeer, and Detroit reserve Scott Hastings. Among the fourteen players fined, Charles lost more than $50,000 total from the fine and a missed game check. Katz and Pistons' owner Bill Davidson were informed a couple days later that they were each getting fined for $50,000. "I called David Stern and asked him why he was fining me since I was watching the game from my bed through my toes," the owner recalled.

In the locker room, the Atlantic Division champions celebrated with champagne and laughter. A proud Lynam repeated some of the criticisms leveled at his players from a doubting public: *Mahorn, you're nothing but a thug. Ron Anderson and Hersey Hawkins, you're too soft. Charles Barkley, you're not going to make anyone better.*

While Laimbeer was deriding the Philadelphia star, Barkley, with scrapes and red marks on the left side of his face, joked that he had defended his heavyweight title, winning in a decision against a worthy contender. The two would later take their rematch, a bar-room brawl, to the big screen in the 1991 comedy *Hot Shots*. But the night in Detroit wasn't a joke. Walking into the bathroom amid the celebration, Gminski noticed a stream of water shooting out of the wall.

"Charlie was so pissed he ripped the urinal off the wall," Gminski said. "Maintenance had to come down to shut down half the water and only three shower stalls were working at the time. We were partying and drinking champagne, and we could only go in three at a time to take a shower."

Charles didn't give it a second thought when he nearly disemboweled a helpless Craig Ehlo as part of the Sixers' first-round win against Cleveland. The coast-to-coast dunks had more emphasis, the blocks were more forceful, the shoulders packed more of a sting. Charles was a runaway train to start the playoffs, and the 53-win Sixers were along for the ride. Or in Ehlo's case, he was taking a ride to the floor.

"My body collided with his, and I just lost my body very easily," Ehlo said. The violent hit on the Cleveland guard was one of the examples used by the league to change their rules. Such fouls could now result in ejection.

Hard fouls weren't the only thing the Sixers were dishing out. Charles had help in the form of Hawkins going off for 39 points on 26 shots in a win-or-go-home showdown with Cleveland. They'd need him for what was next. With a gold chain around his neck and an earring dangling off his left lobe, Hawkins was looking forward to a deep playoff run. "We're going to Chicago thinking we can win," he said.

The second-round matchup between Michael Jordan's Bulls and

the Sixers was a showcase event. Two of the league's MVP candidates and old friends, about to face each other in the playoffs for the first time.

The talking point that would follow Charles for the rest of his career first emerged toward the end of that season: *If you don't win a championship, you're not a success.* The narrative had trailed some of the game's best, and now it had grafted itself to Charles.

"I can live with whatever happens, if we do our best," he said.

Going down 2–0, the best was far from good enough. Despite a 30-point, 20-rebound exhibition from Charles in Game 1, Jordan was averaging 42 points in the first two games of the series. Not even shoves and elbows from Mahorn could stop the run. Chicago center Will Perdue could see this coming. "They had some good players, but they didn't have a Scottie Pippen. And as good as Chuck was, Mike was still better."

The Sixers were without Derek Smith, the strong wing off the bench who they had planned to defend Jordan for most of the game. Jordan overheard in the Philadelphia huddle how Charles was going to step up and guard him. He started to salivate, never knowing his friend as a defensive stopper.

"The first thing he does is break down in this defensive position, with hands up—everything looks technically, technically right. And I just laughed. I said, 'When in the hell are you gonna start playing defense? And who taught you how to get in a defensive stance?'" a smiling Jordan said in his retelling of a play that ended in him passing the ball. "Even though he was not up to the challenge, he didn't care."

But it was Charles's animated flare-ups with Gminski and Anderson that had gained attention. Since he was getting double-teamed as soon as he touched the ball, he needed more out of his teammates, including their shallow bench. "Barkley's teams were still so diminished by the time the Bulls got going that they really weren't a great competitor like the Pistons were," said Sam Smith, author of *The Jordan Rules.*

The drama came as Charles's right shoulder acted up. He'd soon learn he'd been playing with bone spurs the entire year. "By the time we went to Chicago for Game 1 of the conference semifinals, the Bulls knew I was hurting," Charles said. "So did I."

Charles tried to squelch any rumor that he had issues with two of his guys, accusing the media of trying to pull the team apart. He responded by going for 34 points, 20 rebounds and 8 assists in a Game 3 win back in Philly.

Despite the win, Jordan put Lynam on edge when the Sixers were up by 20 at the end of the third quarter.

"As he turns away, he says something to Pippen and he nods in response. I swear to you, I went, 'That ain't good,'" Lynam recalled. "We were up by 20 and they came out and stormed back like you can't believe. We had to win the game twice. As the final buzzer went off, I looked down the sideline and saw those two bitches walk off exactly how they were earlier. He told something to Pippen, they looked up the sidelines, and left. My wife goes, 'What's wrong with that?' I said, 'Tomorrow, we're going to be in trouble.'"

The series took a different tenor prior to Game 4 when Scottie Pippen returned home for the funeral of his father in Arkansas. A man down, the Bulls turned to backup Ed Nealy, a six-foot-seven journeyman whom Smith likened to a "plow horse among thoroughbreds." He would wear out Charles on the defensive and on the glass, earning CBS Player of the Game honors. The look threw off Sir Charles, who still put up a 22-and-13, but missed 6 consecutive free throws down the stretch in a 111–101 loss. At 3–1, Philadelphia was facing the inevitable.

Jordan empathized with what Charles was going through, trying to carry a team.

"He didn't have any legs left," Jordan said of his friend. "He wasn't talking much down the stretch. When he's talking, that gets him motivated, energized. But his batteries started decreasing and we took that as a good sign."

Jordan also knew that his 45-point showing in the win might have taken the heart out of Charles and the Sixers for good. They were playing six or seven guys already, Mahorn was playing on an MCL sprain in his left knee, and Charles had difficulty lifting his arm above his head.

Pippen's emotional return to a thunderous Chicago Stadium fueled his 29-point barrage off the bench that helped send the Sixers home with a whimper. His defense on Charles resulted in Charles's worst game. Even by Jordan standards, the conference semis against Philadelphia were awe-inspiring. He averaged 43 points in the five-game series to go along with 7.4 assists and 6.6 rebounds. Each game was more masterful than the next, expanding the notion of what excellence could look like on a nightly basis in the playoffs. Jordan's 37-point spree in Game 5 was his lowest scoring game of the series.

"I never played four consecutive games like I did against Philly," Jordan said.

Charles saw his best chance to compete for a title evaporate. His averages in the series—23.8 points, 17 rebounds, 5 assists—would have gotten top billing any other time. Instead, they're a forgotten footnote in history.

The same could be said of Charles coming in second in MVP voting despite finishing with the most first-place votes. In one of the closest votes in league history, Magic Johnson won his third MVP despite having eleven fewer first-place votes than Charles, thirty-eight to twenty-seven. Johnson's wide margin on second-place votes, thirty-eight to fifteen, helped the Lakers guard pull away with the award. Jordan, who finished in third in voting with twenty-one first-place votes, also secured more second-place votes than Charles.

Charles has remained sensitive about the year that could have been.

"I haven't let it go," he said of the snub. "I'm never letting it go."

Eight-year-old Lauren Rose had no idea who Charles Barkley was on the night of March 26, 1991. She'd soon become the only regret of his career—and a turning point in his life.

Growing up in the shadows of New York City in Short Hills, New Jersey, Rose, now Lauren Porreca, was raised by a loving middle-class family, who enjoyed swimming, playing tennis, and watching *Garfield and Friends* on Saturday mornings. She listened to the Beach Boys because they were her dad's favorite, and dreamed of getting slimed on Nickelodeon.

The family also had season tickets to the New Jersey Nets, seats in the front row along the baseline. Though the second grader enjoyed going to the games, the best part for Porreca was getting to know the arena staff and adults she'd see at every game, and the face time with Duncan the Dragon, the googly-eyed, anthropomorphic mascot who could pass for the Phillie Phanatic's cousin.

"It was more like a playground for me," she said of going to Nets games.

Watching the game from her mom's lap, she heard the men around her heckling the Sixers and their star player with the bald head. Some of it was harmless, some of it was far from wholesome. One of the hecklers was Craig Pistilli who would regularly give Lauren pom-poms and gifts whenever he'd see her, Porreca said. A car dealer in North Jersey with a love for the New York Yankees, conservative politics, and restoring old cars, Pistilli was trying extrahard to get under Charles's skin, she recalled. Taunting and yelling was one thing, but the child thought he was being straight-up mean.

Charles could see the jerk out of the corner of his eye, and certainly heard him for forty-eight minutes of play. The game was close, and Charles was in the middle of putting another hurting on the Nets to the tune of 32 points and 17 rebounds.

The verbal abuse, including, as Charles reported, racial slurs, continued deep into the game. Charles fired back with some vulgarities of his own. After Mahorn fouled New Jersey's Derrick Coleman with 1:38 left in the game, Pistilli ran up and down the aisle while Charles and Mahorn did their Bump and Thump chest-butt routine, Lauren remembered.

What happened next would mark Charles's worst night in the NBA. Only two known camera angles exist, but they do not offer a full view of the scene.

At the line, Coleman hit his first free throw. When the ball dropped through the hoop, Lauren's father saw Charles start to gather his spit together. Cheeks puffed out, death glare in his eyes, Charles spit toward the ground. Long after the night, he'd repeat that it wasn't his intention to spit on anyone. The trajectory of the saliva, however, had other ideas.

The cameraman on the baseline immediately reacted as if he was hit by the spit. Several fans grew enraged, including the heckler who instigated the chaotic scene in the first place. One of the fans looked to be squared up, ready to fight someone, even if he looked ridiculous. Charles could be seen yelling in his general direction in footage.

But the superstar's spit meant for the ground, or the heckler, had landed on Lauren Porreca's face.

"All of a sudden, I felt wet and gross, like, 'This is disgusting,'" she recalled. "I remember actually laughing, mostly in shock, because I didn't know what was going on."

Her father was so incensed that he walked onto the edge of the court and yelled at Charles for spitting on his daughter. People kept coming up to her throughout the game to ask if she was all right. Given the uncertainty and lack of information surrounding HIV at the time, Porreca said her mother later told her that she was worried about the possibility of contracting the virus through Charles's spit.

When Charles realized what had happened, Hersey Hawkins saw his face shift from rage and defiance to deep hurt about the misfire from his mouth.

"As a teammate, all you could do was console him," Hawkins remembered. "All you could do was just say, 'We know that's not you. We know that's not your personality. That's something that just happened.'"

The wild circumstances didn't surprise Jim Lynam, who categorized the spitting incident as another "Charles being Charles" moment. For him, they'd deal with it and move on, because he knew Charles didn't mean it. "The spitting incident never changed my opinion that Charles Barkley was a caring, good guy," he said.

Following the game, an overtime loss for the Sixers, Porreca was approached by Philadelphia big man Armen Gilliam. Acquired two months earlier, Gilliam, who clashed with Charles on occasion, put his arm around the girl and apologized for his behavior: *I'm very sorry for my teammate. We're not all like that.*

"It really hit me because I wondered why he was apologizing for someone else," she said.

The local and national backlash toward Charles, who called his action "a stupid mistake" due to him not getting "enough foam in my mouth," only intensified in the days that followed. Charles was now Public Enemy No. 1 for spitting on an eight-year-old girl. Some form of "Spit Happens" appeared in most newspaper headlines of the incident. Columns and local TV ran a steady stream of coverage on the rogue saliva. Callers on talk radio were vicious.

The worst, however, was reserved for Charles's wife, Maureen. In April 1991, while at a Philadelphia bar, Maureen was approached by a White man asking how Charles and Christiana were doing. When she smiled in her reply, the man spit in her face, saying, "How do you like that, [N-word] lover?" Maureen held off telling Charles until that night, which was the right decision since he later said he would have blown the man's head off.

The league suspended Charles for a game and fined him $10,000 for the spitting incident. (The mistake would cost him about $50,000 with the lost game check.) In announcing the punishment, Rod Thorn, the NBA's vice president of operations, acknowledged that they were seeing a pattern in mess-ups involving Charles, and advised the star to "cut it out."

Charles had done plenty of crazy stuff in the past, but this hit differently. The unfair stereotype of him being another angry Black man, and the idea that he was capable of harming a child, ate at him. Reports of the heckler using the N-word and other slurs against Charles were mostly brushed aside in the larger narrative playing out in the media. Instead Charles was perceived as a celebrity who had gone off the rails and was considered a threat. He was in a crisis.

"I didn't think I was going to make it," he said. "I will truthfully admit that I thought I was gonna go crazy, because everyone in the world was against me and rightfully so."

Finding a horse big enough in Charlottesville, Virginia, to carry a 250-pound man shooting a deodorant commercial had become a pressing concern for Neil Tardio. As part of a thirty-second spot for Right Guard, Charles, the bad boy who wasn't really a bad guy, would be surrounded by about a dozen barking dogs before a day of fox hunting. Catching the eye of a pretty female rider—"Well, off to the foxes"—he would ride off saying the product's tagline: "Anything less would be uncivilized."

By the time Raymond the horse made his way on set, scores of people had gathered to witness Charles attempt to mount the creature, the must-see event of the two-day shoot. The same person who tried to fend off the city of Detroit by himself was appropriately intimidated by a horse. Once he was on, the intentionally stuffy dialogue tripped him up, Tardio said.

Seeing Charles out of his comfort zone for the sake of a funny idea indicated to Tardio how much marketing influence he could have down the road.

"He still had that round, nice, well-balanced face and good look about him, but at that time he was really a shining example of the entire sport," Tardio said. "He was so young, so bright, and so funny."

The deal was the first major endorsement for Charles under Marc Perman, who had taken over as his agent following the collapse with Lance Luchnick. A reformed New York litigator, Perman was transitioning into being an agent when he made his pitch in 1989 to Charles and Glenn Guthrie over a burger at a sports bar in Birmingham. In Charles, Perman saw someone who could become a potent commercial spokesman, fueled by a self-deprecating nature and a willingness to let loose.

"I knew he'd have an enduring career after basketball," Perman said.

His rising celebrity did not mean he was avoiding gaffes. After an overtime win in November 1990 against the hapless Nets, he pointed to his wife's presence at the game.

"This is a game that, if you lose, you go home and beat your wife and kids," Charles said to reporters. "Did you see my wife jumping up and down at the end of the game? That's because she knew I wasn't going to beat her." When asked if he wanted to clarify his statement, Charles replied, "Naw, print it. Piss off those women's groups."

His words set off a firestorm. At a time when there were around one million annual attacks on women by intimate partners, hearing an athlete of Charles's caliber joke about domestic violence was infuriating. Leading the charge was Women in Transition, the Philadelphia organization which called on him to make a public apology. The Los Angeles Commission on Assaults Against Women also condemned the comment. "I'm sure the estimated 6 million women who are brutally beaten every year wouldn't find what he said funny," said Roberta L. Hacker, the Philadelphia group's executive director.

In his apology, Charles said he regretted the misunderstanding and seemingly downplayed the weight behind what he intended to be a joke. If you knew him, you'd realize he didn't mean it. "This ain't no big controversy. I don't really remember even saying that," he insisted. "But when I say things after a game and I'm smiling about it, people should understand that it's a joke."

There was a make-it-or-break-it vibe to Charles's seventh season in Philly. On Howard Eskin's radio show in the preseason, Charles promised at a beef ribs restaurant in Cherry Hill, New Jersey, that the team would be even better than the 56-win squad from a year ago. But Rick Mahorn's back and Mike Gminski's elbow injuries were of particular concern, and Charles's recovery from off-season shoulder surgery remained a question mark. Once Charles had the procedure done in Birmingham, Dr. James Andrews was struck by how easy it was to take care of him.

"He was an excellent patient who worked hard and wanted to get well quickly," remembered Andrews, the renowned orthopedic surgeon. "He thought he was invincible."

Gene Shue had been promoted to general manager following John Nash leaving for Washington. A Draft Day trade landed them Jayson Williams, who could help on the boards. Charles took a shine to Williams, which, in retrospect, he wished wouldn't have been the case. Williams enjoyed the structure he had in college—class, practice, study hall, game—and was struggling to adapt to the NBA lifestyle. So, when the time came to head to practice, Williams looked at Charles for guidance. But Charles had practiced twice in two years, and Williams soon learned he wasn't the best example to follow.

"He used to come in and get on the stationary bike and he would ride one mile an hour, and he would take McDonald's and would take the hotcakes and sausage and the butter and the syrup, and fold it like a tortilla and squoosh it—and it would all come out. It would look so good, especially when you're hung over," Williams said. "And he'd be eating, and he'd be like, 'Y'all run the floor!' And he'd be peddling 1 mile an hour and we'd be running up and down practicing, and he'd be just sitting on the side saying, 'That's why we ain't ever gon' be shit, 'cause you guys don't run the floor! Man, practice harder!' And pancakes would be spitting out."

Another addition would give Charles the rim protector he was missing. At seven-foot-seven, Manute Bol was unable to fit into the front seat of the company sedan that assistant general manager Bob Weinhauer had driven to pick him up from the airport after the trade with Golden State. Bol, who would end up sprawled in the back seat of the Buick, was said to have killed a lion with a spear. According to legend, one day in his family's home village in Turalei, Sudan, a teenage Bol saw a lion running across the pasture toward the cattle he was charged to protect and launched the spear that killed the lion in midair. The myth repeated over time drew skepticism and razzing from Charles, who had read about it in the newspaper.

"Man, you didn't kill no lion," Charles told his new teammate. "That lion was old and dead when you showed up."

Bol was a walking entertainment center. He wouldn't eat at a restaurant if they didn't serve Heineken, the beer of choice he drank to gain weight. For as funny and inquisitive as he was, he was a room-service guy, sharing the same hermit tendencies as Charles. He watched CNN and read the *New York Times* to try to learn about his new home. Bol, who squeezed milk directly from the cow back home, was deeply skeptical of low-fat and 2 percent milk. When he was learning to speak English, he'd try to pick up phrases from watching American television. Tony Harris, a guard who was with the team during the 1991 season, explained how Bol would often come to practice reciting taglines from *The Price Is Right* and Miller Lite ads—"Tastes Great, Less Filling."

Bol also became a target for the team's lighthearted abuse and pranks. Hardly a day went by where Charles and Mahorn didn't chase, wrestle or tape up Bol; or, in one case, stuff Bol inside of an equipment bag meant to hold a dozen balls. ("Charlie, let me out of the ball bag!")

Bol was as curious as he was comical, once telling Charles that the problem with Black men in America is that they didn't have any tribes and belonged nowhere as a result. Charles appreciated his perspective, once remarking that "if everyone in the world was a Manute Bol, it's a world I'd want to live in."

The question remained, however, whether the team could win with Bol and the other additions.

Months before the spitting incident, Charles's uncle, Simon Barkley Jr., was dying of terminal cancer. Tragedy marked Simon's life. He and wife Barbara lost two young children within a year—a son at sixteen months old, and a daughter in childbirth. The last time Charles saw his uncle, he was urged to reconcile with his father. "Uncle Simon told me that it was time for me to start trying to forget the past because you never know what turns life takes," Charles said. His uncle died two weeks later at the age of fifty-five.

Shortly after the spitting incident, alone in a hotel room in New Jersey, Charles said out loud the four words he never thought he'd articulate: *I forgive my dad.* "He wasn't there, we grew up poor, it sucked," he said, "but I gotta play basketball for me." Charles added, "I got to move on."

Howard Eskin called his friend the next day to ask what happened. Charles felt remorse, Eskin recalled, but there was also a sense at the time that Charles wasn't entirely sure what really happened. "He didn't know whether the spit did or did not hit her, but he accepted that it did," said the radio host.

Two days later, Lauren's mother informed her that she had a call. It was in the middle of dinner and she was watching TV at her grandfather's desk. On the other line was an apologetic Charles. Lauren was happy he called, but remembered being distracted as he had dialed her right as she was watching an episode of Nickelodeon's *Wild & Crazy Kids.*

"He was like, 'I'm sorry, I got upset and I overreacted.' I remember thinking, 'Oh my God, stop talking. I'm watching my show and just want to see who wins,'" Porreca recalled of her eight-year-old self. "My dad came down and was like, 'What did he say?' I was like, 'I don't know, he was apologetic.' Charles tried and made an attempt."

The apology tour continued with an interview with Pat Riley on the *NBA on NBC* that weekend. Charles acknowledged he snapped, but pushed back against the backlash, reminding people that he didn't kill the heckler or beat him to a pulp. He wasn't making excuses—it was wrong and stupid, he said—but he also wasn't going to let a fan who paid $35 for a ticket call him every name in the book and get away with it. To Charles, the only thing that's truly yours, he said, is your soul. In his soul, he said he hurt for Porreca and himself, but also for his family and friends. The personal responsibility to his loved ones resonated with *USA Today*'s David DuPree and was consistent with what Charles prioritized.

"He didn't give a crap about what people thought of him, but when it came to how his actions reflected on other people, he cared about that and it did bother him," DuPree said. "I've never seen an athlete more sincerely sorry and try to make amends than he did with the spitting incident."

Though Charles claimed to be profoundly changed by the incident, Riley, who acknowledged Charles's otherworldly talents, questioned in his NBC interview whether a lack of maturity would ultimately prevent the public from celebrating him for the right reasons. "His greatness as a player is obvious, but his sometimes crude and outlandish behavior overshadows that greatness," Riley said. "Emotional stability is a characteristic of a champion and until Charles harnesses that, part of his personality will continue to embarrass him and everybody around him. He will continue to be one step removed from true greatness."

A mother and social worker in North Jersey, Porreca's life revolves around her son. Inevitably, one of his friends will ask about the story behind the signed jersey that hangs in their home.

I didn't know he had anger issues. I hope it's true that this silly, little incident changed his life. I don't feel like it was such a big deal, but I hope that's the truth.

My husband shares the story with any new person he meets. It comes up a lot more than you think. And my dad still shares it a lot.

The older I get, the cooler the memory is because it's not as embarrassing. It's something that my son will tell his kids and their kids.

I wouldn't want anything else from him. Even now, I wouldn't want a hello. It happened, it's in the past, and it's over.

It's all kind of ludicrous.

Back in New Jersey, Porreca was the most popular eight-year-old at her school. All of the boys wanted to talk to her and touch the face spit on by their basketball hero, which understandably grossed her out. Her mother drove her around town looking at newspapers to make sure her name wasn't printed or that her dad was not misidentified as the heckler.

She eventually met Charles before a game, and her and her family were surprise guests at the Easterseals benefit roast of him later that year. The event was filled with predictable spit-related jokes and other more amusing barbs at Barkley. (Villanova coach Rollie

Massimino guessed that Charles's idea of a good time was "sitting on the toilet until his legs get numb.") Sitting at a table in the back of the ballroom, Porreca and her family heard Charles as he opened up about the spitting incident, telling the gala attendees that the moment broke him and later helped him to become a better person. At some point, he realized two things. The first was he couldn't play basketball angry. The second was that the purpose of being successful wasn't to shove it in others' faces. From that night on, Charles didn't play angry.

The public would soon forgive him, which would become a pattern in the years to come.

"He stretched the boundaries of the things he would do," said biographer Roy S. Johnson. "When he apologized, it was sincere and wasn't fake. For that, those incidents are less held against him compared to other people."

When Porreca was announced as the special guest at the roast, she said Charles looked shocked before greeting her.

"Lauren taught me a great deal," he said years later. "And I think the best thing that ever happened was the way she treated me."

The notion that she taught Charles still befuddles Porreca, who never wanted an apology even though the public vehemently disagreed. As the years passed, rumors persisted that Charles not only paid for the family's season tickets but also helped put Porreca through college. Porreca said that neither were true, laughing at the long-held myths. She and her parents would occasionally run into the heckler, either at games or around Seaside Heights. She said the heckler, who Porreca believed to have passed away in recent years, was in the wrong for using such ugly words. She has pondered what took him to that place.

"Now that I'm a mom," she said, "I do wonder why he would say those awful things in front of an eight-year-old."

The Gulf War had begun and Charles couldn't sleep. The news of Operation Desert Storm kept Charles up till five in the morning. As he watched coverage of the US response to Iraq's invasion of Kuwait for oil purposes in January 1991, Charles had Pep Mock on the brain. His close friend and the starting center from his days at

Leeds High had gone into the air force and was now being called to duty. He was scared for Mock, whose family helped show Charles that White people could be accepting and kind.

"It's a little different being at war, when you don't know whether the sun's going to shine tomorrow," he said. "Basketball's nothing compared to real life."

He had become one of the five best players in professional basketball and undoubtedly the league's most controversial figure. At an All-Star Weekend in Charlotte that featured a special message from President George H. W. Bush about a month after the start of the Gulf War, Charles donned a blue hat that read "FUCK IRAQ," which nearly caused Glenn Guthrie to have a heart attack. He'd eventually remove the hat to talk to reporters, but not without some convincing from his financial adviser. Charles had missed three weeks with a stress fracture in his left foot, but reluctantly made the trip to Charlotte after the league threatened to suspend him. The goal, he said, would be to distract people from "Sadamn Insane" for two hours.

The game's MVP with 17 points and 22 rebounds on the night, Barkley's performance was extra meaningful with his family in the stands, including Darryl and new wife, Melanie.

The MVP trophy would be a high point in a year of lows. The fallout from the spitting incident was still fresh in people's minds in the final weeks of a rocky season. Bill Lyon of the *Philadelphia Inquirer* hoped that the incident could push Charles—whose frequent escapades and lapses and losses of control had nearly overshadowed his brilliant play—and help him refocus on the title. After another 27-and-10 season, another All-NBA 1st Team, another top-5 MVP finish, could the team make a run? To do so, the Bulls' buzz saw awaited them.

The Sixers swept the Bucks, giving them the momentum they needed going into the conference semifinals against Chicago. The Bulls coach Phil Jackson used a quote from Thomas Jefferson to lead the scouting report for the 76ers: *Nothing can stop the man with the right attitude from achieving his goal, but nothing on earth can help the man with the wrong attitude.* Harold Katz felt the Bulls had their number from the jump.

"What stood out about that period against Chicago was that we always lost," Katz said. "That was the problem whenever we went to the Windy City. We always wound up losing."

After Game 1, it was clear to Charles that the Sixers had no shot of winning. Charles was brilliant with 34 and 11, but the other four starters scored 17 points *combined*. That was the plan all along for Jackson and the Bulls, who had been in a similar position with Jordan feeling he had to carry the whole load to lead them to a win. Sam Smith explained how Jordan's experience with such a mindset proved to be useful in his matchup with Charles. "Michael came to believe, and accept, that you have to have discipline to be successful. Charles was completely undisciplined," Smith said. "Michael always thought he could take advantage of that."

Even with a little more help in Game 2, Charles and the Sixers were stuck and down 2–0. Throughout Game 3, Bump and Thump upped the physicality on screens and in the paint. Jordan, who finished with 46 points despite suffering from tendonitis, missed three free throws in the final two minutes of the game. When Charles was double-teamed and the team down by one, he kicked it to Hawkins for a game-winning 3 in the final seconds.

Spending the day with Jordan and Ahmad Rashad playing craps and blackjack in Atlantic City, Charles returned hoping to build on the success of Game 3. Instead, the Sixers, for all intents and purposes, rolled over at home. The team, with one of the best rebounders of the era, was getting crushed on the boards.

"With Jordan and Pippen, they weren't going to let us have a chance," Lynam said.

As the clock hit zero, Jordan raised his arms in delight and ran over to Charles for a hug in the lane. The embrace ended and they'd soon go their separate ways, Jordan back to the conference finals, Charles back to the off-season.

His friend would soon win his first title. Charles wondered if he could do the same in Philadelphia. But in his heart of hearts, he already knew the answer.

17

The wind chill was -10, snow covered Milwaukee before Christmas, and the Sixers were below .500, but the Jägermeister was flowing all night long for Charles and Larry Krystkowiak. Along with Milwaukee guard Frank Brickowski they were unwinding after another tight game, a Bucks' win.

Charles's next stop was Rosie's Water Works, the longtime watering hole of Water Street in downtown Milwaukee. A city that had once detested him was now clamoring to be around him.

"That's the irony of the fight he got into in Milwaukee," Krystkowiak remembered. "You had to say something stupid to have Charles ever want to hurt you."

Sitting at the bar, James McCarthy was bummed out after seeing the girl he liked chatting up Charles. A twenty-five-year-old army veteran and student at the University of Wisconsin-Milwaukee, McCarthy was a nice guy who never wanted to fight but could still hit someone so hard that they'd fly backward off their feet, said Bob Trednic, a friend who met him through their bodyguard work and weightlifting. Trednic didn't know what to say to McCarthy, who he could tell was growing more upset seeing Charles and the woman leave Rosie's before 2:30 a.m. The pair was on their way to Krystkowiak's home to keep the party going. Trednic had an idea of who Charles was, but he believed McCarthy only knew of him as a professional basketball player of some sort. Toward closing time, Trednic, the Coke-drinking bodybuilder, thought about what he could eat before waking up for an early-morning workout. McCarthy finished his beer and had other more immediate ideas: *Let's go outside and mess with him. But I don't want to fight him.*

As Charles and Lee Anne Wooten were leaving, McCarthy, who appeared to be intoxicated after going to four bars that night, began to yell at them from about a block away, shouting at the woman about whether she was going to have sex with Barkley. (In a telling of the story in 2020, Charles said the woman he was with was Brickowski's wife.) Wooten later testified in court that racial and sexual slurs were made toward them. While Trednic wasn't entirely sure what his friend said, he recalled McCarthy making a joke about the height disparity between the woman and the basketball player. Charles said he remembered he could hear running behind them, which included someone saying, "Fuck Charles Barkley." Charles then remembered the three men—McCarthy, Trednic, and Tony Mehrtens—saying they didn't like him and wanted to kick his ass. Charles grew concerned once he realized the numbers were against him.

"Charles," said the five-foot-eleven McCarthy, "I hear you're one of the baddest dudes in the NBA."

At this point, Charles thought he was probably going to get his ass kicked. Trednic said he never wanted any part of Charles from the outset, and made it verbally clear to him that he would not fight him. But whatever was or wasn't clear to Charles, it was a bad situation and the Sixers' star was running short on answers and time. Then, in the early-morning hours, he came up with an unorthodox solution he could transfer over from the basketball court: make them think you're crazy.

Charles stripped down to his boxers and socks in ten-degree weather and positioned himself for a crane kick from *The Karate Kid*. He also found a triangular parking sign that he waved wildly above his head and would use to thwack the trio, Trednic said. If he was going to get beat down, he thought, it would happen while channeling his inner Ralph Macchio.

"I was like, 'Is he going to start doing karate right now? What is this karate stuff?'" Trednic said. "He was ready to karate-chop my ass down."

McCarthy, still holding his fists in fighting position, provoked Charles with a gesture of some kind. Moments later, Charles delivered a straight left jab to McCarthy's nose, a perfect punch that drew blood immediately. Although Trednic was surprised his friend didn't fight back, he thought to himself how Charles threw a pretty punch.

"He's down, and he's like, 'You fucking hit me!'" Charles recalled. "And I said, 'You damn right, and there's plenty more where that came from.'"

At St. Mary's Hospital, nurses and doctors urged the college student with a broken nose and lacerations on his face to press charges. Hours after getting dropped off at his downtown hotel, Charles heard a knock at his door from a coach. Police had gotten word of the altercation outside the bar. He would be arrested at his hotel room for battery and spend about four hours in Milwaukee County Jail before posting a $500 cash bond shortly after 10:00 a.m. that same day. The battery charge was punishable by a maximum of nine months in jail, a maximum fine of $10,000, or a combination of both.

Bob Ford was on his way to the airport until his cab driver mentioned to him that "police came and got the big boy last night." As the Milwaukee bar fight story progressed, Charles, the former hermit, wasn't afraid to keep going out. All he needed was a ride back. "Can you give me a ride?" he asked Ford. "I haven't been doing very well walking lately." Krystkowiak had been curious why his friend didn't stop by his home. He turned on the TV to watch football on a Sunday when he saw Charles's mug shot take up the entire big screen. Another Jägermeister night for the books, he thought.

"That guy apparently had made a comment about how the woman was going to find out what it was like to be with a big Black cock," Krystkowiak said. "When Charles went apeshit and whipped this guy's ass, he said, 'This is what it's like to be with a big Black cock.' It's the thing of folklore."

BARKLEY

★ ★ ★

The request to Allen Lumpkin was swift: *I want to wear 32 to honor Earvin.* The gesture to switch numbers for the season came not long after Magic Johnson announced he was HIV positive. Shattered by the news, Charles quickly touched base with Lumpkin, the equipment manager, to see what could be done. The number worn by Billy Cunningham had been retired, but his former coach had already given Charles his blessing to wear it for the year.

"As soon as Magic announced he was HIV positive, Charles was adamant about changing the number," Lumpkin observed. "Charles wanted it done and you had to make it work."

The bitter rivalry between the 76ers and Celtics subsided for a night when Charles first wore the number, a strangely emotional sight at the Boston Garden. Magic's announcement was so painful for Larry Bird, Johnson's greatest rival and one of his closest friends, that he barely spoke of it. That night, he'd whisper to Charles his appreciation for what he was doing.

But Charles's attempt to honor his friend set off another firestorm. When asked before the season whether players were concerned about coming into contact with someone like Magic who was HIV positive, Charles reminded people that they were merely playing basketball. "It's not like we're going out there on the court to have unprotected sex with Magic," he said. Critics and media members in the fall of 1991 wondered if wearing No. 32 was such a good idea.

The questions about his tribute, one he said was to help raise awareness surrounding AIDS, set Charles off, wondering why he should care about the opinions of the clueless.

"You really think I give a flying FUCK what the people on the radio calls say?" an irritated Charles fired back during practice. "I really don't give a fuck what they say on the call-in shows. It's not about the fans, it's about a friend. I really don't give a flying fuck..." He paused to correct his coarse language. "I really don't give an F.F. what they think.

"People are stupid," he continued. "For them to make a big deal out of this is ridiculous. This is about me and Earvin, it's not about anything else. I don't have time to play any mind games with people.

I don't have any time to worry about getting criticized. If people like it, that's good. If they don't, fuck 'em."

All Charles had wanted to do was play basketball, but the fraying bond between a city and its twenty-eight-year-old star was making that impossible. After seven years in Philadelphia, a love-hate relationship with the media, and double standards over his interracial marriage, Charles grew tired of the city's racism in ways big and small. Though not a unique dynamic to Philadelphia, the perceived racist politics of his home in the early '90s upset him.

Around this time Charles conferred with Reverend Jesse Jackson, the civil rights activist and former politician. Jackson applauded Charles whenever he spoke out on race or inequality.

"Some athletes had courage on the court but would shrivel off the field of play. Charles did not shrivel," Jackson said. "He was a light beyond the playing field."

The team called Rick Mahorn, Charles's running buddy who was working with him at a youth camp in the Poconos, to inform him that he would not be re-signed. Later, over dinner, Katz informed Charles that the team had signed Charles Shackleford, a much-maligned center who had upped his value after leading the Italian league in rebounding. "I said, 'Dude, if I want Italian, I'll have pasta or something. I'm not looking for no basketball players,'" Charles remembered. In the years that followed, he would needle Katz's decision. "I wanted Shaq and they gave me Charles Shackleford," he joked.

Years of trading first-round picks for minimal returns had finally caught up to with the team by the 1991–92 season. To Charles, Katz had sent him to war against Jordan's Bulls with a BB gun.

"You liked to have your star come up and have the team come up at the same time. The effect of the team going down as he went up was tough to watch," Julius Erving said. "They'd be competitive and could get into the playoffs, but they weren't set up to contend."

Charles, who had now become the subject of a 2:30 a.m. *Sports-Center* rumor that he was getting traded to Portland, had seemingly rubbed off on some of his teammates, namely Jayson Williams. At around 2:00 a.m. at the bar of the Chicago Hyatt Regency following a blowout loss to the Bulls, Williams, joining Charles and a couple other teammates for an after-hours drink, ended up cracking a thirty-four-year-old man in the head with a beer mug after he believed the man was reaching for a knife. In the fallout, Charles, who was not involved in the incident, got heat for just being in the vicinity. "I had met John Cusack, the actor, in there," he said. "Yes, I was at the bar with some of my teammates, but I resent people saying that I was talking to women."

Such media attention soon became unavoidable.

Charles proclaimed his grandmother, Johnnie Mae, could score more points in a game than Bol, the team's seven-foot-seven backup center.

The takes from Charles were spicy and numerous. Gilliam, referred to as "Mr. Macho," had a rebounding game that was too weak and inconsistent. Hawkins would be illegal in twenty-five states if he had anything resembling a killer instinct. Shackleford was tossed aside by the lowly Nets, so what good would he be here? And Katz, well, he knew less than the average basketball fan and needed to trust his basketball people. "I've got three more good seasons left, so get a clue," Charles wrote.

But when these opinions dropped in late 1991 ahead of the release of his autobiography, Charles protested that he didn't say what he had said. In fact, he claimed he had been misquoted in his autobiography.

When he heard his teammate's defense, Hawkins reacted how anyone would: "I don't know how you can be misquoted in your own autobiography."

The book went far beyond bulletin board material. The self-realization of Charcey's son, a shy, poor boy from the Jim Crow South who grew into a loud multimillionaire icon, was provocative as it was a hard truth for many. He'd tell readers in *Outrageous!* that if he wasn't getting paid $3 million a year to jump and dunk a basketball as well as he did, most people would probably run in the other direction at the first sight of him. It's a sentiment that hit home for his co-writer Roy S. Johnson that this was someone who was grounded in his own Blackness.

A *Sports Illustrated* senior editor, Johnson had authored *Magic's Touch*, the biography on the Lakers' star that was a critical and financial success in 1989, by the time he connected with Charles. The way Charles built relationships with Black journalists hit home with Johnson. At a time when there were only a handful of Black NBA writers—Michael Wilbon, David Aldridge, David DuPree, Roscoe Nance, and Johnson to name a few—the star had set out to make sure he got to know the reporters of color who were so few and far between in the locker rooms. Jemele Hill saw how, years later, maintaining access to Charles helped keep up her professional value. "He understood the bar was much higher to cover guys like him, and keeping that access was all by design," she said. "Charles knew how important it was for us to succeed."

That level of support and awareness fascinated Johnson, especially when he'd inevitably end up at the same restaurants and bars as Charles after the game. When he did get to speak to him, Johnson was impressed by the amount of questions Charles would ask about topics he had little knowledge of. His curiosity about everything outside of basketball made talking to him easy.

"Charles always had a strong conscience," Johnson recalled. "As things were changing in the world and in the culture, he would ask me about them. It was easy for us to have a bond beyond talking about the pretty women we'd see at the club."

For hours at a time in the summer, Johnson would take the train down from New York and hit Record while the twenty-something Charles left nothing on the table: his father, growing up in poverty, racism, Sonny Smith and Bob Knight, Moses and Doc, fighting Bill Laimbeer, the cocaine epidemic. Not to mention the scorched-earth offensive against the Sixers.

"Charles was speaking against maybe what he perceived as mediocrity," Johnson said. "Charles was frustrated and the only way it comes out of Charles is unfiltered and honest. It hit some people the wrong way and he felt bad about it, but he was speaking the truth."

An issue came when, much to Johnson's surprise, the *Inquirer* broke the embargo on publishing material from the book and ran Charles's criticism of Katz and his teammates on the front page. No one—Johnson, Charles, publisher Simon & Schuster—knew the lines would run well ahead of when the embargo was to be lifted. The story with his *Outrageous!* criticisms caught Charles off guard, as he didn't know where they had come from, Johnson said. The tense situation led Charles to rebuke his co-author in the media as well as instruct Glenn Guthrie to see what could be done to kill the book altogether. His tune changed once he learned at least sixty thousand copies of the book had been printed, leading him to reverse course and offering support to the book.

Charles would apologize to his teammates, but Katz, at the time, remained miffed. "How many times can you hit someone over the head before you say you won't accept an apology?" the owner asked. "He hasn't learned his lesson." (He said in 2019 that he didn't recall any book coming out on Charles.)

Charles's criticisms of his own team in the autobiography was a watershed moment of sorts, Ford explained.

"The public started to turn a little bit and Charles's fatigue had set in, so the book was a dividing line," he recounted. "The organization was constantly gauging whether there would be real backlash if they traded him. Then they started to get the sense there wouldn't be."

Charles might be a few pounds heavier since Johnson co-wrote his autobiography in the early '90s, but otherwise he hasn't changed much.

Charcey really was a role model for him and created the level of intensity and hard work he strived for. When you see Charles barreling down the floor from one end to the other, a six-foot-four bowling ball, that comes from those projects and seeing how hard his mother worked. To him, she was going to give her best every day.

His upbringing was not too much different than any boy would have when you have a sense of rejection from your father. His mother and grandmother mitigated some of that. I think even his agent, Glenn, was the father he didn't have to some degree.

Early on in their careers, Michael was the standard. Charles did everything he could in Philly to match that standard. There wasn't any animus, as he totally respected Michael and did his best to emulate what Michael had.

Obviously he's grown as a man since that time, but I don't think he's changed much. Now, he's trying to have an effect on the world through activism. He's woke, so to speak. But I don't think he's much more fundamentally different than the person he was then.

★ ★ ★

The twenty-five-footer from the portly power forward clanked off the rim and the Bulls won yet again at The Spectrum.

Following the loss, Lynam had commented that Charles's long ball had been "ill-advised" and word got back to him in the locker room. As reporters surrounded his locker, Charles pushed back against the media's criticism of his judgment and why he took the shot. To him, it was also a good time to get a few things off his chest.

"I'm a '90s N——," he proclaimed. "The [*Philadelphia*] *Daily News*, the *Inquirer* has been on my back. Everything I do is wrong. They want their athletes to be Uncle Toms. I told you White boys you never heard of a '90s N——. We do what we want to do." He'd give a high five to Ahmad Rashad, the *NBA on NBC* sideline reporter who laughed through the brittle silence of a room of White writers. "It's always a racial thing," Charles said. "Racism always exists. I'm going to be a little more vocal now. Striking back at you guys. I'm going to do what I want to do. And you've got two choices: you can kiss my behind or you can try to get me traded."

The year since the spitting incident remained a period of self-reflection. In a city hysterical with condemnation, journalist Larry Platt took a different tack, stepping back to look at the broader phenomenon of Charles and his ability to engage in the world around him. After his story on Charles was published, Platt's editor told him he had a message. Charles wanted to thank Platt and invite him over Sunday to watch football. They'd slam beers together and solve the world's problems from the comfort of Charles's study.

Charles asked him what he was reading, while Platt took notes on the best vacuum cleaners, according to Charles. The basketball star would repeatedly challenge Platt to a tennis match until his friend destroyed him. (Charles later reasoned that he could beat Platt because of what he said were two words: "Gold fucking medal.")

"He was powerfully influenced by Ali's courage and willingness to say stuff," Platt said. "The media played it as Barkley being either just crazy or trying to force a trade. It was more like a young athlete expressing a social conscience. I think it was much more genuine than it was manipulative."

Charles's pointed declaration of who he was and what he represented to a room full of mostly White reporters came amid a year of backlash following Los Angeles motorist Rodney King getting brutally beaten by four police officers. Their acquittals on charges of assault with a deadly weapon set off the LA Riots that killed fifty-five people, and resulted in thousands of arrests and $1 billion in property damage during one of the most racially volatile moments in American history.

As hip-hop culture was having a renaissance at the start of the decade through groups like N.W.A, Public Enemy, and A Tribe Called Quest, conversations that were once private were now becoming increasingly more public, said Dr. Todd Boyd, chair for the study of race and pop culture at the University of Southern California. "Charles's point was basically, 'I'm my own man and I do what I want,' which is a statement of independence," Boyd said. "The language he used was the language popular amongst young Black men at the time. Charles was saying the things you were starting to hear more of in music."

Sharing a 1992 cover of *The Source* with Spike Lee under the article headline "Nineties N—," Charles didn't see his words as being controversial. Society would never totally change to bend to Black people like them, Charles said, but it was shifting.

"I think Blacks are making progress, but it will never be equal," he told the filmmaker. "We'll never be on the same page."

Charles shared with Howard Stern that he had recently shared a hot tub with Donald Trump and some women. He'd been flattered by the shock jock complimenting him as an "Adonis" with "big shoulders, strong muscles, tight ass."

"That's from working hard, Howard," he replied. "One day you'll get a job and have to work hard."

As with many of the Stern interviews of the '90s, the conversation inevitably got around to Charles's sex life. In this case, it was Maureen, the "hot, White blonde" otherwise known as his wife. Stern was curious: *How tall is she? How much does she weigh? Does your wife wear miniskirts?* When Charles was unsure whether Maureen was a C or D cup, he replied that he'd get the answer by checking for himself in their bed.

Naked in bed on a Friday morning, Charles passed the phone to Maureen for some pillow talk with the self-proclaimed "King of All Media." *Is Charles an animal in bed?* "Like an ant or a fly, something little," she joked. *Do your parents give you flak for marrying a Black guy?* "They don't care. He makes $3 million a year," she said.

On the topic of Charles not having her sign a prenuptial agreement, Maureen played with Stern about feeling fine financially if they were to split. "If I do leave him," she laughed, "he says he's gonna dish out the bucks big-time."

The discussion reflected the tumult facing the couple. In early April 1992, a week after the appearance on Stern, reports surfaced that the pair had separated. Stu Bykofsky of the *Philadelphia Daily News* reported that the rumors of a split had been floating for a couple months, with Charles taking residence at the Adam's Mark Hotel on City Avenue.

Any personal troubles coalesced with a dismal 35–47 season. Charles, who was under contract through 1995, already vowed to sit out training camp unless something was done with the roster. But Hawkins knew that Charles had likely played his last game with the Sixers.

"It had just gotten to the point where Charles needed a change in scenery," Hawkins said. "It was unfortunate, but we just weren't good enough."

For three years, one of the main questions surrounding Charles was which team would trade for him. At one point, the *Sporting News* had him on the cover with six different uniforms.

Charles had actually tried to plot out his own move in the previous summer with a trip to Portland to meet with the team's general manager, Geoff Petrie. He saw a team of all-stars led by Clyde Drexler with an exciting up-tempo offense that struggled in the half-court against the league's elite. Charles stressed he could change that in his three-hour pitch to Petrie. The dream was short-lived when he was informed the next day that they wouldn't be trading for him. ("I told them they were never gonna win a championship.") He'd joke in 2018 that the Trail Blazers owed him a check for $1,197 to reimburse him for the roundtrip ticket from Philadelphia to Portland. Days later, Damian Lillard presented him with a check, nearly twenty-seven years following the trade that never was.

But then a deal seemed promising with the Lakers. The trade reportedly would have sent James Worthy, a Hall of Famer in his twilight, and Elden Campbell, a promising big man, to Philadelphia in exchange for Charles. To celebrate, Charles started drinking around noon. Then, around 3:30 p.m., he got another call from Guthrie. The deal with Los Angeles had fallen through, as Philadelphia was fearful of the blowback the organization would incur from trading its franchise player.

"I'm drunk as fuck and we got a game that night," he recalled thinking.

Lynam, who by then moved from coach to GM, had barely gotten settled into the front office, when he received a letter from a fan. The note was about ten lines, each one the same as the next.

Dear Coach Lynam,
Never trade a super.
Never trade a super.
Never trade a super.
Never trade a super.
Never trade a super.
Never trade a super.
Never trade a super.
Never trade a super.
Never trade a super.
Never trade a super.

It's a message the first-year GM would remember for the rest of his life.

The greasy spoon on Milwaukee's North Side was a comfortable choice for Charles to avoid large swaths of crowds demanding to talk to him or sign a ball. Yet Tom Halloran, his attorney in the bar fight incident, was struck by how seemingly everyone inside knew Charles as if he'd been coming in for twenty years. They left him alone too, which helped.

"He said, 'You know, Tom, I'm tired of being Charles Barkley, not as a person, but how I'm portrayed,'" Halloran remembered. "He was always perceived to be a part of the WWE. He understood that and always played his part; he was a marketer. But at that moment, he was tired of being marketed that way. He got a chance to not be Charles Barkley."

Charles's case would only be the second-most high-profile court saga in Milwaukee that year. Earlier in 1992, the trial of Jeffrey Dahmer, the serial killer who killed and dismembered seventeen men and boys, gripped the country. Interest in the case grew even more with it being shown on Court TV, the upstart cable channel. The cases were significantly different, of course, but John Franke, the Milwaukee County circuit judge in Charles's case, said the publicity and complications that came with both of them being on Court TV that year were unlike anything the city had seen—or could handle.

The decision to not have Charles testify would bring the trial to quick completion in June 1992. Franke remembered how McCarthy basically acknowledged he was drunk and acting like a jerk. There was also the $125,000 fee that McCarthy testified he would take in exchange for going away and dropping charges. "Once the jury heard that, there was no way they were going to convict him," Franke said.

Driving to court, Trednic had told McCarthy that he would not lie on the stand for him, which he said he did not. But Charles said he began to worry when he believed that the guys were lying about being fans and wanting autographs.

"If these dudes had beat me to a pulp, I'd be Charles Barkley with his ass kicked," he said.

After a three-day trial, the jury of nine women and three men needed about ninety minutes to acquit Charles of the two misdemeanor charges. He looked noticeably relieved.

"He's a good showman and he put on a really good face for it all," Halloran said. "He told me, 'Tom, this has been a long week.'"

His legal troubles had come to an end. With it, Charles asked Glenn Guthrie to draft a letter to send to the Sixers, informing the organization that he didn't want to play for them again. He had also called Philadelphia and listed the five teams he had interested in being dealt to: Orlando, Phoenix, Portland, San Antonio, and Seattle. But the letter from Guthrie never got there—the team didn't need it. Less than five hours after the court's decision, Charles's time in Philadelphia had come to an end with a trade to the Phoenix Suns.

18

The Dream Team might have been, as commissioner David Stern put it, a legendary combination of the Kirov Ballet, the New York Philharmonic, and the Beatles. Still, the question asked to Charles Barkley had to be answered: *How much do you know about Angola?*

After gaining independence from Portugal in 1975, the country, a prominent producer of oil and diamonds in sub-Saharan Africa, had been entrenched in a years-long civil war at the time of the 1992 Olympic Games. Angola, which was nearly twice the size of Texas, was eagerly awaiting its first multiparty elections as part of its democratization and peace process. The nation's unrest proved to be one of the more prominent proxy wars of the Cold War, which meant the United States had a keen interest in funneling hundreds of millions of dollars in weaponry and aid to the National Union for the Total Independence of Angola to help offset the Soviet Union's funding of the ruling power, the Popular Movement for the Liberation of Angola. The fact that Angola was at the Olympics at all was a stunning triumph.

All of this is to say Charles Barkley was unaware of the affairs of the faraway nation at the beginning of the '92 Olympics. There was gold to be won.

"I don't know anything about Angola," he replied, "but Angola's in trouble."

Trouble looked like a 46–1 run in the first half of the opening match of the Olympics and staring back at your opponent, USA Basketball, the greatest team ever assembled in the history of the sport. A portion of the sold-out crowd inside Palau d'Esports were waving American flags and covered in stars-and-stripes face paint, cheering for every pass by Magic, jumper by Larry, and slam by Michael. Yet Charles, who was dunking, diving, and dominating the overmatched opponent, was growing tired of all the elbows he claimed to have been hit with in the first half. Charles barked at an official to say that Herlander Coimbra had elbowed him in the back.

"I told old boy—I don't know if he understood—I said, 'Hey, man, ease up on the elbows,'" Charles recalled.

At twenty-four years old, Coimbra thought he was the luckiest guy in the world to play against Charles and the Americans. The nerves of playing their heroes got to them before the game started. But asking the Americans for autographs before the game removed the competitive edge. Coimbra, a soft-spoken college student studying economics, was especially fond of Charles, his favorite forward, who he watched every Wednesday in Luanda on the country's weekly NBA broadcasts.

"Other players in Angola who play against Charles Barkley, they told us there's like a kid, a fat boy who is very aggressive in the paint," Coimbra said.

Off a Patrick Ewing rebound, Scottie Pippen took one dribble before zinging a one-handed, full-court strike to Charles, barreling in stride for the easy left-handed layup to give them a 38–7 lead. On the way up, Coimbra had gone for the block. Charles said he felt the Angolan hit his head—even though video of the game shows that to be debatable.

That's when Charles, grinning and bouncing his way back down the floor, reared back his right elbow and cracked the spindly Coimbra square in his sternum, stunning him. He'd be called for a flagrant foul. David Robinson and Karl Malone told him there was no need to make them into the bad guys. Clyde Drexler said Charles did the one thing they were trying not to do. Soon, whistling filled the arena. Michael Jordan would tell him that the whistling was not because they were happy; it's because they were booing. Commissioner David Stern remembered all too well how Charles turned them into "the US bullies."

"We said to Charles, 'Look, man, you're a reflection of all of us, so if you do it, they're not going to write the article that Charles Barkley did it. They're going to say, the Dream Team,'" Johnson recalled.

It wasn't even halftime of the first game and Charles Barkley had become the Ugly American of the 1992 Olympics, with all the aggression, arrogance, and entitlement that accompanied the decision to allow NBA players to compete at the Games.

Two weeks later, he had taken over Barcelona.

"He was the most memorable person of the 1992 Olympics," said Michael Wilbon.

Sometime after he took off the "FUCK IRAQ" cap and before he won MVP at All-Star Weekend '91, Charles was already planting the seeds for his inclusion on what was expected to be a once-in-a-lifetime team.

For Boris Stankovic, it would be considered something of a crime for the head of basketball's worldwide governing body to communicate with the NBA. Still, a meeting was worth it if it meant that FIBA's secretary general would successfully rid the basketball body of the hypocrisy surrounding pro players. The international basketball community had long been skeptical of the trustworthiness and motives of the Americans, who were not part of the official organizational structure of basketball for the rest of the world. If the game was to be lifted to the highest possible level of competition, including professional athletes would undoubtedly raise the perception of Olympic basketball. This was painstakingly obvious when a Soviet Union team led by Arvydas Sabonis and Šarūnas Marčiulionis defeated the collegians that made up the US squad en route to a 1988 gold medal in Seoul. A 1989 resolution from Stankovic allowing all pros to participate in the Olympics hoped to change that.

As more players began to signal their willingness to play in Barcelona, no star made his case harder than Charles, who recognized that his personality could overshadow talent and tenacity. He saw it play out firsthand in MVP voting during the 1990–1991 season when two writers left Charles, the leader in first-place votes, off their ballot entirely. Before becoming director of USA Basketball, C.M. Newton had been an assistant under Bob Knight during the '84 Games. He witnessed Charles steamrolling college basketball's best at the Trials. Newton also saw him come back to camp overweight and his daily sparring with Knight. Ahead of Barcelona, Newton, the athletic director for the University of Kentucky, stressed that the selection process overseen by the committee and coach Chuck Daly would be one predicated on the content of a player's character, and would largely stay away from loud personalities.

"Don't hold 1984 against me," Charles said to Newton during All-Star Weekend. "I really want to be on this team!"

He echoed as much in a *Sports Illustrated* cover story that same month, which previewed what an all-NBA Olympic starting five would look like, a group that could restore the glory lost in '88. Smiling in a photo with Jordan, Johnson, Ewing, and Karl Malone, the magazine had included Charles in a group that it deemed to be an ideal starting lineup. Years later, no one looks happier to be included than Charles.

Donnie Walsh, the general manager of the Indiana Pacers, believed the honesty in Charles's unfiltered responses could prove to be too problematic on an international stage unfamiliar with how he spoke or approached the media.

"He was so outspoken," Walsh said. "If he were to walk down the street and someone would have asked him a question, he'd certainly give a totally honest answer, which wasn't in vogue then."

Russ Granik, who would serve as Stern's deputy commissioner for twenty-two years, said that even though Charles was featured on the *SI* cover, he was not among the first six or seven players initially selected by the committee. They were to be American ambassadors abroad, and his record gave them pause, Granik said. To some, Charles Barkley did not fit with the Olympic ideal. The staunchest of defenders of that perceived perfection might have considered that a strong enough reason to never consider him.

When Granik and Rod Thorn, the two most prominent voices on the committee, volunteered to reach out to Charles, their fellow members offered a path forward: *If you both stick your necks out and vouch for him, the rest will follow.* They reached out to Charles and had what Granik simply described as "a very straightforward conversation with him." By the end of the talk, Thorn, struck by Charles's appreciation for the consideration, was sold. The same went for the more skeptical Granik.

"Right away, he said he would love to be on the team and that he understood everything we were saying and that we should not worry about him," Granik said. "We decided he was serious and went back to the committee with the decision. I think Charles more than lived up to what he said."

In an NBC show in September 1991 revealing the first ten players, Charles's was the second name announced, only after Johnson. On-air, an excited Charles would let Bob Costas know that aside from it being an honor, being picked for the Olympics meant he could potentially land some more endorsements. Also on the roster were Larry Bird, Magic Johnson, Patrick Ewing, Chris Mullin, Karl Malone, and John Stockton all of whom were friends, rivals, or both. David Robinson played the angel to Charles's devil both in Nike ads and on the court. And Michael Jordan and Scottie Pippen, the reigning back-to-back champions, were the standards he strived for. Walking down the hall with Jordan that summer, he joked about it by singing the first few lyrics of his friend's catchy Gatorade anthem from that year. "Sometimes I dream that he is me," Charles began. "I just wanna be like Chuck—I mean, Mike."

They were statesmen of basketball, but also of the US, Mike Krzyzewski said. The historical significance of the event was not lost on Charles. When asked whether the US needed to redeem itself following '88, Charles would say what he thought Robinson couldn't utter.

"We're gonna have a little revenge in our hearts for '72 and '88," he said to the media. "David, he can't say that, because he's a Christian."

★ ★ ★

Up to that point, the day the select college all-stars defeated the Dream Team in a scrimmage in La Jolla, California, was the greatest of Bobby Hurley's life. Fearful of going against the best in the world the Duke point guard with the braces had one goal heading into the practices with his basketball heroes: don't embarrass yourself. By the end of his team's unlikely 62–54 scrimmage victory (Jordan didn't play much), he had done more than survive; he and his teammates dominated. To celebrate, he and Chris Webber took joy rides on golf carts at a nearby golf course.

But Charles passed along a warning shot to Hurley and the others.

"I remember Charles walking by at lunch and he could tell we were feeling good," Hurley remembered, "but he was clear in reminding us that they had our asses for the rest of the week."

The next day, the Dream Team, which now had Jordan actually on the floor, proceeded to shut out the college all-stars. Not a single point. The individual embarrassment Hurley avoided the day before had become a team discomfort. Charles had stuck to his word.

Butt-kicking aside, the future pros were entranced by Charles. Grant Hill saw Charles as a central figure in a larger movement for Black athletes, even if he didn't realize it himself.

"He was almost like *the* conscience for us," Hill said. "Athletes were mindful of image and perception at a time in Black culture, and in sports, where there was this sort of almost acceptance of Black athletes as household names. They were becoming very conscious of the big picture and it was almost like Charles didn't care what everyone thought. In the process of doing that, it became very endearing."

Around his fellow Dream Teamers, a trip he lovingly described as "spring break in the ghetto," Charles learned new things about the men he called peers. The first was to not drink beer with Bird, a Budweiser man, who could drink him under the table. "My head hurt for like two days," Charles said of his Bud Heavy session. He wasn't shy to give advice to Robinson, who he thought didn't talk honestly enough to the media. But his teammates were also discovering there was more to Charles than met the sound bite. When Stockton suffered a severe leg injury that threatened to knock him out of the entire Olympics, Charles was one of the first people to come see him in his room to see how he was doing. The Jazz point guard said he never expected the kind of instantaneous sincerity from Charles. He was also taken aback seeing what he'd do in public for the less fortunate.

"He'd pick up homeless people on the street and invite them to stuff, and then he'd follow up with them," Stockton said. "He'd look them in the eye and treat them with respect. All of us are probably guilty of walking by those people, but he had time for them. He would just give his time to complete strangers."

Excellence and egos created a haves and have-nots basketball hierarchy. As Jack McCallum reported in his 2012 book *Dream Team*, Jordan and Johnson were particularly brutal toward Charles if he tried to join them, whether it was shooting at the gym ("This is a ring basket") or simply sitting down at a table ("This is a ring table").

But Jordan would have time for one of his best friends and the Abbott and Costello routine they'd pull at the expense of Drexler and Malone, their two closest contemporaries at their respective positions.

"Hey, Charles, who's the best two-guard in the world?" Jordan asked.

"That would be Michael Jordan," Charles replied. Without missing a beat, he'd ask a question of his own.

"And who's the best power forward in the world?" he asked.

"That would be Charles Wade Barkley," Jordan replied.

But they all cared for each other, that much was clear. In *I May Be Wrong but I Doubt It*, Charles remembered a late-night card game in which an HBO comedian started going in on Johnson while he was in the hotel room. "Can you believe that Magic Johnson has the AIDS virus?" the comedian said. "Man got all that damn money and too cheap to spend $2 to buy a box of condoms." The room went silent, sensitive to the seriousness of the health crisis Johnson was going through. They had never talked about Johnson's HIV diagnosis, nor did they want to go down that road. After a few seconds of uncomfortable silence, Johnson said it was some "funny shit," and urged the others to laugh. The respect Charles had for Magic grew even more that night.

The sentiment extended to coach Chuck Daly as well. This was a man who once noted how he owned two hundred blue suits because "nobody ever looks bad in a blue suit." His main goal of blending the talent and egos was no easy task, but Daly was a respected personality in a locker room that needed a guide. "He coached the Bad Boys," said Charles, "and if you can coach those assholes, you can coach anybody."

He had taken a liking to Charles, the conference rival who had fought Bill Laimbeer, tangled with Dennis Rodman, and turned Rick Mahorn from a Bad Boy to his BFF. Daly knew what he was doing, but even he was blown away in the opening round of the qualifying tournament in Portland, Oregon, when the Cuban team spontaneously dropped to its knees. Before the game even tipped, the Cubans showed the Americans the same level of respect as if "12 Popes had come by on Easter Sunday," McCallum said. Seeing their opponents bow down before them was a surreal sight to Charles. They'd win by 77 points and go on to easily sweep the tournament, winning by an average of 52 points a game. Charles said they really didn't know they'd win games like that. The expectations for each game had quickly shifted to "Blow Out or Bust."

Charles could give the response Daly couldn't imagine offering. Answering a question from a foreign journalist during the Tournament of the Americas about why US players were superior at basketball, Daly gave a measured and thoughtful answer detailing how young people were able to develop their skills at an early age. That sounded good and all, but Charles had a slightly different take.

"Can I answer that?" asked Charles, who was going to reply regardless. "What he was trying to say diplomatically was he got brothers from the 'hood on his team, and they can flat out hoop all day long in the ghetto, and he's got some athletic brothers out there and they're going to have trouble keeping us with us."

When they got to Monte Carlo for a few days of practices, gambling, and golf, the only issue, aside from the $21 beers, would be their privacy. Craig Miller, the director of public relations for USA Basketball, remembered an exchange he had with the manager of the hotel. "I remember the manager saying, 'This is Monte Carlo, we have kings, queens, and rock stars,' and then we pulled up at night and the parking lot was so full of people that we couldn't pull the bus in," Miller said. "We walked up to the manager and he goes, 'I have never seen this before.'" The dinner protocol implied that when

Prince Rainier and Prince Albert put a fork down and stopped eating, then the team had to follow suit and end their meal. Such guidelines did not fly with Sir Charles.

"Well, I hope he stops when I'm done eating my meal, because I'm eating my meal," he said.

One thing that would not be a problem? The topless women hanging by the pool. J.A. Adande, who was about to start an internship at the *Miami Herald*, ended up getting a credential to cover the Monaco run during his European vacation. As he arrived, he headed over to Charles, who joked about his post-career plans in Monte Carlo. "He goes, 'I'm retiring from basketball. We were hanging out by the pool today and there were all these topless women. I'll be Mark Spitz after this. As long as there are topless women, I'll be in the pool,'" Adande said.

Scrimmages were a daily test of your ranking among the world's elite. This would be the turning point for the Dream Team and years later, would become the subject of a documentary, *The Greatest Game Nobody Ever Saw*, featuring footage from one of the lost games. Pete Skorich, the Pistons' video man who followed Daly to the Olympics, said he didn't understand the full magnitude of what was going on until he watched it later and saw the performances. The individual matchups during practice were delicious. Jordan and Drexler couldn't stand each other, and the feelings from the '92 Finals two months prior remained raw. Ewing and Robinson were out to see who really was the best center in the world. Johnson had something to prove against Pippen after he shut him down during the '91 Finals.

The only other power forward in the world Charles would consider putting in his class was Utah's Karl Malone. Their battles in practice in Monte Carlo were poetry. In the scrimmage, Charles, with a perpetual chip on his shoulder, bullied his superstar peers. At one point, he blew past Jordan and Bird and finished with the and-1 after Jordan grabbed his wrist. Soon thereafter, he stole a Pippen pass and went coast-to-coast to beat Bird for the layup. After that, Mullin tapped the ball away from Jordan and Barkley rolled down the court again, beating Malone and Ewing to the rack for another easy layup. Setting up on the low block, Johnson found Charles backing down Malone for a turnaround jumper.

The performance was one of many things that struck Christian Laettner, the only college player on the team. He was amazed that Charles, who he thought was skinny given his frame, still had so much power in his legs. "I've never seen anyone 6 foot 4 defend the rim like he can," Laettner said. "He would let people get all the way to the hoop and then at the last second block their shot."

Inside the recreation room with the ping-pong and pool tables, Don Sperling would camp out with the rest of his NBA Entertainment crew to capture life with the greatest team ever assembled. From the time he started as senior vice president and executive producer of NBA Entertainment, Sperling held tight to a piece of advice he'd received from David Stern when he first began: *It's better to be lucky than smart.* That luck meant building relationships with the biggest stars in the world at a time right as the game was about to explode for the rest of the world.

On the heels of *Come Fly with Me*, the Jordan feature that became the highest-selling sports home video in history, he looked to feature other stars on their new afternoon show, *Inside Stuff*. He set the film of Charles to "Hit Me with Your Best Shot" by Pat Benatar.

I would go out and spend personal time with him, we developed a trust. I remember going out to dinner with him during the 1990 Finals. Then, we go out again the next year during the Lakers and the Bulls in '91. Him going to that, he began to salivate. He'd say, "When's my time?"

That setup in Barcelona will never happen again. Jordan loved him. Barkley was like his teddy bear. Charles saw us shooting Michael and he walked up and started singing how he wanted to be like Mike. That wasn't planned.

They always played together and always had a great relationship—playing cards, smoking cigars, gambling, doing what men do. They always had that relationship. The thing about Jordan was he always loved to beat his friends in big games. Jordan wanted to beat you and everyone else.

He ended up changing the entertainment business. He was so organic compared to everyone else from that period. You were always going to believe that you were sitting down at a bar and talking to him. His humor has also given him a permanent hall pass—a lifetime hall pass—in that he can say anything he wants.

Because of that, he's never been compromised.

BARKLEY

★ ★ ★

In the early minutes of that first game against Angola, Marv Albert asked a question to Mike Fratello while Charles was at the free throw line.

"Do you get the idea that, one way or another, he might cause an international incident?" Albert said of Charles.

Then, the hit on Coimbra turned into the talk of that first game. Charles brushed aside the coverage on Coimbra, someone who he guessed "hasn't eaten in a couple weeks," as nothing more than "a figment of the American media's imagination." When asked by Bob Costas about whether the elbow was keeping with the ideals of the Olympics, Charles, who had joked how he thought Coimbra was "going to pull a spear on me," said the hit was more like the ideal of the playground.

"His answer was it would be almost disrespectful to them if we didn't play at the level that they expected," Costas said. "He was right because you remember that some of these guys were literally asking to have their picture taken while the ball would go out-of-bounds, and they would want to put their arm around Charles Barkley, Michael Jordan, or Larry Bird and have their pictures taken with them."

The same went for Coimbra, who had refuted Charles's claim that he elbowed him before the incident, but still got a photo with him afterward. The two developed something of a bond in the years that followed, as the elbow made Coimbra a big deal in Angola.

Charles had already come to the conclusion that no matter what he did, his image was going to remain intact. He would no longer let the judgment and criticism get to him. He'd live by the 50 percent rule, knowing that half of the public was going to like him and the other half wouldn't want anything to do with him.

The moment with Coimbra, however, also presented a pivotal shift in how people looked at and responded to Charles. Bob Ryan, the legendary basketball writer for the *Boston Globe*, pointed to the Coimbra elbow as an event that signaled how Charles's actions would no longer face the same level of scrutiny as before.

"With Coimbra, that's when it was becoming evident that Charles Barkley could say or do anything and get away with it," Ryan said.

"That's still true to this moment: Charles Barkley can say anything and get away with it.

"And he totally intimidated and scared the shit out of those teams. He knew what he was doing, and it worked."

¿Dónde está Charles Barkley en Las Ramblas?

David DuPree asked himself this question after every bar and restaurant he planned to meet Charles at was instead one he had just left. The *USA Today* journalist convinced Charles to talk for ten minutes after every game for a newspaper column that would be his during the Olympics. But keeping Charles in one place was nearly impossible at that time of night.

"I was supposed to meet him at a restaurant at 10:30 and Charles wouldn't be there, but there'd be a note from Charles saying to meet him at this place at 11:00," DuPree recalled. "Then, I'd go to that place at 11:00, but I'd find another note saying to meet him at another place. This would go on until 3:00 in the morning. He always had stuff to do, but he was responsible enough to say, 'This is where I will be.'"

While most of the team was holed up at the Ambassador Hotel, Charles made it clear he was not spending all night in his room. Johnson could always go by the sudden roar of the crowd to figure out whether Charles had exited the building. P. J. Carlesimo, an assistant coach for the team, joked that he took it upon himself to walk Las Ramblas at 4:00 in the morning to see if Charles was there so he could get him back to the hotel. Skorich, the video man, remembered joining Charles on Las Ramblas after the star offered anyone to join him. He recalled a motley crew following Charles one night, from Thorn's assistant to a PR person, and how Charles became one with the people. "He didn't care, man," Skorich said. "He was so part of the people and so part of the scene. Those were late nights."

Charles's turn as a journalist was not taken kindly by Mike Moran, the US Olympic public relations chief, who warned both the basketball star and track phenom Carl Lewis to stop writing their respective columns. Predictably, Charles didn't agree with the request. "They're just jealous of the attention this team is getting, and they have an ego problem," he said of the committee.

There was also criticism of the team not staying in the Olympic Village with the rest of the athletes. The difference between nearby luxury hotels and the Village was stark.

"I was mad at him," said Indiana Pacers forward and German team player Detlef Schrempf through laughter, referring to Charles. "I wandered out of the Village to try to find a nice restaurant around the Ritz-Carlton area, and a couple guys came out and said Charles was playing cards upstairs and that I should go up. Mind you, we were four guys to a room with no A/C in the Village."

USA Basketball's dominant run to gold left room for few if any surprises. Their opponents lost by an average of almost 44 points. Jordan, never one to show mercy to an opponent, compared their performance to that of a killer. "When you hire twelve Clint Eastwoods to come in here and do a job, don't ask them what bullets they're putting in the gun."

Along the way, Charles went from the Ugly American to Captain America, roaring down the floor, swatting shots, hanging on the rim after dunks and, in one instance, tossing a stunning two-handed touch pass over his bald dome to Pippen for the throwdown. Surrounded by the best collection of talent he ever played with, Charles led the team in scoring with 18 a game and put on an eight-game clinic that would reshape how the public saw him. Vince Carter, the fifteen-year-old high school basketball star in Daytona Beach, Florida, was mesmerized at what Charles had done on a team with Jordan, Magic, and Larry.

"You looked at him as among the stars of the game, but I feel like '92 solidified him with everyone else on what was the best team ever formed," Carter said. "You think back on those highlights, and it's truly amazing."

On a team of Clint Eastwoods, Charles was the biggest gun. Johnson called him the MVP of the team. Charles recalled decades later how Daly pulled him aside to tell him how much of an honor it was to coach him, calling him "the second-best player here" after Jordan, which, to the forward, was "the greatest compliment I ever got in my life."

A perfect 8–0 brought the US back to the podium as gold medalists. Even that didn't come without some controversy: While blowing kisses to the crowd, Charles joined Jordan and Johnson, loyal Nike clients, in draping an American flag over his right shoulder to block the Reebok logo on his jacket. For Charles, he proclaimed he had "two million reasons not to wear Reebok," referring to the inflated total from his Nike deal. While Phil Knight said he didn't mind if the Nike athletes wore Reebok on the podium, draping the flag over the logo, which he described as something of a stubborn move, showed how committed Charles, Jordan, and the others were to elevating the brand on a global stage by blocking another.

As the national anthem hit for the gold medal ceremony, the twenty-nine-year-old got goose bumps for one of the first times in his life. By the end of the Olympics, Charles had become one of America's best ambassadors, a wide-ranging character arc unlike any other at the Games. What he'd find out in later years was how those two weeks in Barcelona helped shape the world's feelings toward the game and inspired generations of international talent to enter the sport. For now, though, the anthem belonged to Charles. He whispered the same three words to himself: "I made it."

"If I never win a championship, at least no one can take this away from me," he said later on.

Looking back on the accomplishment thirty years later, McCallum, the foremost historian of the Dream Team, pinpointed one night in particular when Charles found a balance between authenticity and maturity. It was another early morning on Las Ramblas, maybe 1:00 or 2:00, and McCallum could see Charles looking around. The gold medal outcome was all but a foregone conclusion, but Charles chose to call it a night rather than stay out until all hours.

"It didn't look like it was getting dangerous, but there were too many people, and too many drunk people throwing themselves at him. It looked like a situation that started to get a little bit out of control," McCallum recalled. "Charles looked at it and, I think he was glad he was [almost] thirty instead of twenty, and said, 'I gotta get the fuck out of here.' He made his way through the crowd and diffused it."

McCallum paused before revealing what the situation said to him. "I think at that moment he became the best version of himself."

BARKLEY

★ ★ ★

The Olympic comedown tasted like KFC.

Calling from the car phone of his red Mercedes two-door convertible, Charles approached his friend's home near W. C. Longstreth Elementary School and wanted to know where he should park to come watch the big fight. Exiting the car at around 5:00 p.m., Charles drew the gaze of the guys playing pickup ball across the street. They must have told the whole neighborhood, because seemingly everybody showed up to see Charles for themselves.

When Anthony Martin mentioned to Charles that he'd be screening the title bout between Julio Cesar Chavez and Hector "Macho" Camacho, he didn't plan on having a gold medalist over at the home. He thought it was the polite thing to do for a friend who was not only a big boxing fan but also helped legitimize him in the business world. After meeting Charles through the brother of Philadelphia teammate Perry Moss, Martin had made gold-tipped shoelaces worn by Eagles quarterback Randall Cunningham that were of interest to Charles. Once the shoelaces gained popularity, Martin partnered with him on a kids' basketball hoop branded with Charles's name, which was a launching point for him to work with other NBA stars, like Anfernee Hardaway.

Philadelphia's former favorite son requested two things for the watch party: a case of beer and fried chicken. Three $100 bills should cover beer and poultry for the house, and probably any stragglers who were there for Charles. The KFC employee had already shut down the grill at the store a half mile away when Martin's friend stormed inside with a desperate plea: *Charles Barkley is over at the house and we need a bunch of fried chicken.* Facing a skeptical employee who thought there was no way Barkley could be in Southwest Philly, Martin's friend got Charles on the phone and passed the call to the manager. Charles spoke to the man for five minutes and convinced him to turn the grill back on: "This is really me."

Martin's mother's house was filled with Miller Lite, chicken legs, and biscuits. Little kids walked up to the porch on that Saturday night to say hello and ask for autographs. On this night, a unanimous decision for Chavez, Charles could do no wrong.

19

Charles had only been in Phoenix a few minutes, but one thing was already clear: it was too damn hot. Riding shotgun in Cotton Fitzsimmons's two-door convertible back from the airport, Charles was baking in what had to be a 105-degree day. He was glad to be out of Philly, but would it always be like this?

"Look, Charles, everybody knows that eventually you're going to hell," Fitzsimmons said to his new star. "We're just getting you used to the heat."

As the news conference began, hundreds of fans had gathered outside the arena, many of whom pressed their faces up against the glass for a chance to see the grinning guy in the Nike polo who was going to bring them a championship. Bob Young of the *Arizona Republic* remembered the buzz.

"That was the first sign of, 'Oh this is different,'" Young said. "This was kind of like a rock concert."

Finishing a fourth consecutive season with at least 53 wins, the Suns found themselves stuck in the upper middle tier of the NBA—good, but not exceptional enough to compete with the top contenders. A core of Kevin Johnson, Dan Majerle, and Jeff Hornacek led one of the most prolific offenses in the league during the 1991–92 season, restoring pride to the Madhouse on McDowell and ingratiating themselves as one of the only professional teams in the community. The problem was the pretty-boy team that owned the passing lanes had hit their ceiling. Despite the recent conference title appearances, they had not made it out of the second round for two years. The Blazers had manhandled them into the off-season.

"We're walking out of the arena and we're bemoaning where we are as a team. We can't get over the hump," Lionel Hollins, an assistant at the time, recalled. "We walk out and we're talking, and I'm like, 'We need a Charles Barkley type. We need someone to rebound and dominate inside.'"

Phoenix was one of the five teams Charles was considering, in part, because they had what he described as a "super," or superstar in Johnson. When negotiations began, Philadelphia tried to get Phoenix to throw Johnson in the deal, which was a nonstarter. The teams would settle on Hornacek, a fan favorite and 20-point scorer, which left Johnson and Tom Chambers with mixed feelings about the deal. Billy Cunningham, Charles's former coach in Philadelphia, also cast doubt on the deal. Shortly after the trade was announced, Phoenix Suns owner Jerry Colangelo said he received a call from his friend about his former player.

"I wish we had spoken in advance," Cunningham said, according to Colangelo's 1999 autobiography *How You Play the Game*. "I'm afraid he's going to come in and give you a great year, and then he's going to break your heart."

Whatever heartbreak lay ahead seemed minor compared with what Colangelo had already faced. Born into an Italian American working-class family in Chicago Heights, Illinois, Colangelo went from tuxedo salesman to head of marketing for the Bulls. Taking a chance on a new expansion team in Phoenix, he left with $200 in his pocket to be the youngest general manager in professional sports in 1968. After making the Finals within the first ten years of the team's existence, the subsequent decade had been trying. The team had entered a rebuild that didn't get off the ground. Nick Vanos, a young center for the team, died in a Northwest Airlines crash that killed 154 passengers and crew. Then, in April 1987, the Suns faced the single biggest drug scandal ever to hit a pro sports franchise at the time. Five past and active Suns players were accused of conspiring to provide cocaine and other drugs to teammates. Six other past or active Suns were linked to the case. Included in that group was Walter Davis, the team's leading scorer and a six-time All-Star who testified against his own teammates in exchange for immunity in a case known as "Waltergate."

For a league already struggling with the perception of it being too drug-infested and too Black, the Suns' scandal was specifically troubling. It also coincided with rumors of a move to Columbus, Ohio. The future of professional basketball in Phoenix was in peril and Colangelo, intent on keeping the Suns in the city, had six weeks to put together a deal to buy the team.

"Out of that situation, I wasn't going to walk away from those circumstances," Colangelo said. "I believe that God had a plan, and the plan was to keep moving forward and things were going to work out."

The team was sold to a group headed by Colangelo for $44.5 million in October 1987, and in the years since the owner came to embody what the city hoped to be in sports, business, and culture, said Len Sherman, a writer who helped co-write *How You Play the Game*. "Jerry became an overarching figure in Phoenix," Sherman said. "It's hard to imagine how big he was in the city, but he was definitely a dominant figure in providing sports."

Lowell "Cotton" Fitzsimmons was a fast-talking kid from Mark Twain's hometown of Hannibal, Missouri. Called "Cotton" by classmates for his wispy and fluffy hair, Fitzsimmons, through his gravelly voice and Midwestern drawl, would often say that he never had a bad day in his life. He'd come to Phoenix from Kansas State as the franchise's second coach, taking over for Colangelo, who saw a young, flexible, and enthusiastic figure the team desperately needed in its first years. Colangelo made the right choice, as Fitzsimmons built the Suns into a winner two years in. The familial approach he instilled in the organization rippled from the top brass down to the interns, like David Griffin, who was there in the '90s as part of the marketing department. "Cotton Fitzsimmons was everything to us.

He had as big of an impact on Charles as he did on those who worked with him," Griffin said.

Though Charles joked early on how hard it was for Fitzsimmons to want him to be Superman all the time—"I have to remind him that Superman was actually Clark Kent more often than he was Superman"—the two talkers shared an immediate bond as men raised by single mothers. (Fitzsimmons's father died when he was in the fifth grade.) Possessing the gift of the gab, they both had a quick wit and biting tongue that gave Charles a suitable sparring partner for conversations outside of basketball.

"I told him I was a Bill Clinton man and a Black multimillionaire. He was a Bush man," Charles said. "He said if Clinton got elected, I'd be just a Black millionaire by the time Clinton got through. And then he said if I got divorced from Maureen, I'd be just Black. I liked that."

Colangelo, in need of a stabilizing force amid a tidal wave of negativity, brought Fitzsimmons back to the organization in 1987, first as director of player personnel and eventually as coach until Paul Westphal, the coach-in-waiting, was ready to take over.

His first major move would come in February 1988 when the Suns traded Larry Nance, their all-star big man, for a package of three players and a first-round draft pick. Among those players was a sparsely used rookie point guard out of Cal named Kevin Johnson.

Then, there was Dan Majerle, a little-known swingman from Central Michigan who was Midwestern strong and an excellent slasher but came with questions surrounding his shooting and level of competition. The pick was wildly unpopular, and those attending the draft party at the Phoenix Civic Center were quick to voice their discontent.

In one of the most dramatic turnarounds in NBA history, the Suns went from a 28-win team to a contender. Colangelo and Fitzsimmons had turned the franchise's fortunes around quickly. The Suns had come out of nowhere, but there was more to be done.

As the legend goes, Fitzsimmons walked Charles through America West Arena on his first day at the new arena. *You see this building? It was built without your services,* Fitzsimmons told him. *You see all these seats? Well, you didn't put one person in the seats; they were already sold out.* Then, he looked up.

"What don't we have? Championship flag. That's what we want from Charles Barkley," he recalled saying to the star. "If you don't bring that championship to us, then don't be telling us what you did for us."

To Charles, the only pressure he said that existed was the pressure you put into your tires. But how would Phoenix take to him? Coming off an Olympic performance for the ages, his arrival in Phoenix inspired awe. Yet some worried how the brash loudmouth would fit into a conservative, mostly white-bread community. The state had been embroiled in issues surrounding Martin Luther King Jr. Day, namely that it wouldn't recognize it as a paid holiday. In fact, Phoenix lost the right to host the Super Bowl after the state voted the measure down. The state would pass the measure to recognize MLK Day in 1992, and eventually hosted the Super Bowl in 1996.

Then, something happened: He was everywhere. *You saw Charles at Chili's? What was he doing at Fashion Square Mall? Was Michael Jordan really at his house?* Wherever he went—bars, restaurants, golf clubs— the fans were there for him to sign their cards, dollar bills, and panties. In Phoenix, Charles had become relaxed. He was always a man of the people, but in Phoenix he found a welcome contrast to the scrutiny he faced in Philadelphia. Whether it was buying drinks for strangers or flirting with Hooters waitresses, Sir Charles was getting situated in his new kingdom.

Hollins remembered the moment vividly: "It had this feel as if we had already won the championship."

Colangelo quickly took a liking to Charles, despite the warnings.
What Billy Cunningham said was to do your due diligence, and I think we did. We spoke to people associated with coaches and management, and even players in the league who he had relationships with to get as much information as we could. We were committed to leaving no stone unturned to make it a very easy transition and protect everyone involved so that it would be a good circumstance.

He had a swagger, no question about it. He became somewhat controversial due to his comments or off-court things. But we took Charles in a trade because we felt he could get us over the hump and we knew exactly what we were getting in a player and person.

We wanted to begin the Barkley era with a new building, a new superstar, and an opportunity to get over that hump.

Everyone in the city embraced him in every regard. He had already lived up to the expectations.

Now known as Chuck by Westphal, he began to test his teammates at training camp. His level of physicality forced Westphal to implement a rule specifically for Charles: if you lower your shoulder on a fast break, it's going to be a foul. Among those in Charles's ongoing testing was Cedric Ceballos, the defending Slam Dunk champion entering his third season in Phoenix. Feeling like he got hacked on the other end, Charles ran back down and delivered a love tap that sent Ceballos, who didn't have the ball, off the court. An infuriated Johnson ran up to Charles and, in his own way, told him that's not how it goes in Phoenix. "That's bogus, Chuck!" he exclaimed. Danny Ainge, the bench specialist who only signed to the Suns to play with Charles, joined in, "You didn't get touched! Play the game!" Chuck came away impressed by the pushback.

Though the core had been together for years, Charles was getting used to the mishmash of personalities on what would be the deepest team he ever had. Westphal was well-liked and young, a players' coach who saw basketball as "a chess game with soul." Johnson was perceived as the nice guy who went to church. Majerle, once maligned by Suns fans, had opened up a sports bar and become the city's favorite son as well as its most eligible bachelor. A dependable teammate, Ainge was chasing the championship glory he had in Boston in the '80s. Ceballos was the X factor. Mark West did the dirty work, while Tom Chambers, a rancher in Wranglers, sacrificed to come off the bench for a chance at a title. Frank Johnson was a crunch-time performer when he wasn't Charles's chaperone, and Richard Dumas, coming off a yearlong suspension for violating the league's substance abuse policy, had something to prove to himself.

Then, there was Oliver Miller, the six-foot-nine, 280-pound rookie center out of Arkansas who was also booed on Draft Night and faced immediate questions about his weight from Charles. "He needs to lose weight. He needs to lose weight. He needs to lose weight!" Charles said to reporters. "If y'all are going to write how... good he is, he's never going to lose weight. The only thing for you to write is he has to lose weight."

While Miller didn't recall some of the weight-related barbs, he did remember how Charles would often ride on the stationary bike while reading *USA Today*.

"I just want God to know that there's a Charles on the court and a Charles off the court. I know he loved his momma and grand-momma and his daughter and his wife—and his Miller Lite," Miller said. "After every game, he would crack a Miller Lite and put some salt on it. I don't know why he did that."

His teammates soon learned he was better than advertised— especially since he was about to enter the season in the best shape of his life after playing in the Olympics. "He pulls the ball off the glass and dribbles down the court faster than most people can run," Ainge marveled. In a game against Charlotte, Westphal was astounded at seeing Charles soar above Alonzo Mourning and Larry Johnson for a rebound. "That right there is why we put up with his crap," he said to Hollins.

Charles knew for the team to have any shot at a run that he and Johnson had to be great. As he worried about Johnson's health, the point guard remained curious about his new star teammate's person-ality. Johnson never wanted to be one of the guys. He'd read works from MLK, Plato, and Erich Fromm in his free time, and highlight passages from *Pascal's Pensées*, the collection of fragments written by the seventeenth-century philosopher and mathematician. Living and adjusting to life as Charles's teammate proved interesting for John-son, who needed time wrapping his head around what it meant to play with him from a historical perspective.

"It's like [what] Malcolm X wrote about LBJ and Goldwater in his autobiography," said Johnson, referencing the 1964 presidential elec-tion. "LBJ was like a fox. You had to watch him because you couldn't trust him. On the other hand, you knew Goldwater was going to bite you. Chuck is like Goldwater. We knew what we were getting."

Goldwater, the Republican senator from Arizona, lost in a land-slide.

The only thing that could distract Godzilla from again decimating downtown Tokyo was hooping against Charles.

The monster, a sucker for basketball, threw on some pink goggles in preparation for the battle of the century. With a left elbow to the face that sent Godzilla helplessly falling backward into a skyscraper, Charles claimed dominance with what had to be the first-ever recorded dunk over a monster. Walking away from the monster jam, the two became friends, with Charles asking Godzilla, "Have you ever thought about wearing shoes?"

The ad, a memorable cultural touchstone, didn't look all that different from his first official game in Phoenix on November 7, 1992. You saw the best of Barkley—feasting around the rim as if he were back in Leeds, rumbling downcourt on a coast-to-coast dunk like an Auburn Tiger, roaring and raising his arms after a big play in a Philadelphia-style celebration. The debut outing of 37 points, 21 rebounds, and 8 assists kicked off what was about to be the most fun season in Suns history.

"That first year in Phoenix was about as good as it gets between an athlete and a city," Colangelo said.

Paul Johnson, the Democratic mayor of Phoenix from 1990 to 1994, also saw how attitudes were changing in a city that now had a talent no other place in the world had at the time.

"It was like watching Babe Ruth going to play baseball," Johnson said. "He just became this character that Arizona fell in love with."

The *Arizona Republic* carved out a daily column titled, "The Barkley Beat." Jumping off the success of his radio show in Philadelphia, he had a weekly TV show in Phoenix called "Jam Session," where he reviewed movies and picked out his "Geek of the Week." His face was splattered across city buses. A Claymation version of Charles with way-too-thick eyebrows encouraged people to exercise through the "Don't Be a Spud" public service announcement for the Arizona Heart Foundation. Fans were so enamored that he was named to the franchise's twenty-fifth anniversary team despite only playing a half season.

"Only one guy gets to be Elvis," Westphal quipped. "Same thing with Charles."

Jude LaCava believed it was the first time in the modern age of the city that a personality had owned Phoenix like Charles did. A longtime sportscaster with Phoenix's Fox affiliate, LaCava remembered how people would drop everything they were doing if he was in the vicinity. "He could show up at a nightclub or a restaurant and people just wanted a glimpse—'By God, it's him,'" LaCava said.

After a while, the team absorbed Charles's confidence, too.

"He brought that role of being Mr. Big Tough Guy all the time and he made sure everybody knew that when the Suns are coming to town there's a possibility of you getting blown out, you getting your butt kicked," Ceballos said.

No team would test them more than the New York Knicks. Led by Patrick Ewing, Charles's Dream Team center, the Knicks inherited the title of the roughest and toughest team in the league from the Bad Boy Pistons, elbowing and trash talking their way to 60 wins that year, becoming the most legitimate Eastern threat to Jordan's Bulls. "That team was as primal of a group as I had ever had," said Pat Riley, New York's coach at the time. If they were to get past Chicago and chips fell the right way for Phoenix, the teams were looking at a possible Finals preview and they knew it. Phoenix's up-and-down style inevitably led to questions of whether the Suns could play in a half-court, grind-it-out game against an Eastern power like the Knicks that frustrated the best teams by making them look boring and plodding. The Suns had been reminded the whole year how they only owned one victory against the East's best teams. The first game with the Knicks in January 1993 left Charles so incensed with the lack of calls that he tried to vault over the scorer's table. The incident cost him nearly $40,000.

The bad blood carried over to their return engagement at America West Arena on March 23, 1993. Right before the half, Johnson and Knicks guard Doc Rivers were in a chest-to-chest shouting match after Rivers elbowed the Suns guard for an offensive foul. In trying to separate the two, Ainge yelled at John Starks and Riley. After four players were assessed technical fouls, Rivers brought the ball up the court for a chance at one more shot. Upon passing it to Starks, Rivers was met by a blind screen set by Johnson, who dropped him on his butt with a surprisingly stiff right forearm shot to the chest. Rivers got right up and chased Johnson until he could take a swing at him at midcourt, sparking a bench-clearing brawl going into the half. Charles had to yank Rivers away from Johnson. When things were seemingly about to cool off, Greg Anthony, dressed in a flower-patterned shirt while sitting out with an ankle injury, belted Johnson with a cheap shot as the Suns guard was being restrained. In trying to break up the fight, Riley ended up tumbling on top of Johnson in the second wave of mayhem, ripping his Armani pants in the process.

"You can't let somebody come into your house, move furniture and other stuff," Johnson said. "The house owner has to take some kind of stand. We did."

The melee resulted in six ejections and $160,000 in player fines (then the costliest incident in NBA history), and caused the league to rewrite the rules regarding the punishments for players fighting and leaving the bench. The second half belonged to Charles, ironically a peacemaker in the brawl, who led the team to a 29-point statement win. "I've gotta go home and see *SportsCenter*. There should be some good highlights," he said proudly of his team.

Decades after their clashes, Riley, president of the Miami Heat, wishes he could have had Chuck on just one of those Knicks teams, believing they would have gotten to the promised land together as the game's odd couple. "I really mean it when I say that if any one of my teams in New York had Charles Barkley, we would have won a title," he said. "To be able to coach a player like that who had that kind of greatness would have made a difference on one of my good teams."

In the first meeting against his old team in Phoenix, Charles took the first cortisone shot of his career to make sure his left big toe was ready to go. If he was breathing, he was playing, and if they didn't win, Charles joked that he'd be left with no other choice but to shoot his teammates. The 36-point, 17-rebound, 9-assist mauling in the win was nice, but Charles admitted he was disappointed in himself for playing with so much rage. He stressed that he was not the same angry young man he was in Philadelphia, and he wanted to prove that in his first trip back to Philly later that month.

While Charles was enjoying the best team of his career, his old one was experiencing its worst in years. Dysfunction and despair plunged the Sixers deep into the abyss in Year 1 A.C. (After Chuck). Coach Doug Moe, who was brought on in hope of running a more run-

and-gun offense, was fired a couple games after the first matchup with the Suns, going 19–37 in only a half season. After Hawkins and Hornacek in the pecking order was Clarence Weatherspoon, the six-foot-six, 240-pound rookie given the moniker of "Baby Barkley." Despite a promising first couple of seasons, the comparison was laughable. Fans refused to watch a team without Charles, evident by the second-worst attendance numbers in the league. But on March 28, 1993, a sold-out crowd at The Spectrum roared for Charles's return. Charles acknowledged ahead of the game that such warmth would actually hurt more than the boos.

"When you walked into the old Spectrum, you could just feel it in the air," recalled Matt Donovan, one of Charles's friends who was at the game that day. Donovan, who befriended his basketball hero a few years earlier in Philadelphia, added, "He was so laser focused coming home. He treated it like a playoff game."

By the time the Suns won, he looked relieved after going for another 35 points and 7 rebounds, the emotion of the day catching up with him. He was happy to sign autographs, hand out high fives, and catch up with Manute Bol. Exiting the game with seventeen seconds left, his former home crowd doused their departed son in chants of "M-V-P! M-V-P! M-V-P!" There was only one thing left to do now in Philadelphia. "I haven't eaten anything today," he said to reporters.

Before Charles pulled away in the limo, he reached out to grab his father's arm. After another Phoenix win in Los Angeles, Frank Barkley was overwhelmed by the chaotic attention surrounding Charles at all times—the autograph hounds, people asking for pictures, fans grabbing and yelling, all of it was an everyday ritual. "It's a madhouse," Frank said of the scene in Southern California.

About to turn thirty, Charles had hit the point where he was afraid of few things. Actually, there was only one. "There ain't nothing for me to fear except failing...making a serious mistake," he told *Esquire*. For Charles, that meant alienating family or friends in a way that's deemed unforgivable. It's why making an effort with his father, one of his uncle's dying wishes, is something he wanted to do, even if it wasn't easy. Pulling away in the limousine, he touched his father's arm and thanked him for coming out. "See you, Dad," he said. Then, he was off, leaving Frank curious as to how his son got there.

"You just never know how things are going to turn out in this world," said Frank, shaking his head.

At Dutch Johns in suburban Scottsdale, Debbie Hartel was having lunch at a sport bar with her husband on a Sunday in April 1993 when Charles, Frank Johnson, and a couple other teammates sat at a table across the aisle. Hartel, a nurse at a nursing home, had no idea who Charles was, but thought it would be cool to get some autographs to bring back to her Suns-loving patients at Forum Pueblo Norte. She said she asked Johnson if he and his teammates could sign five napkins for her patients, which he agreed to do. When Johnson turned around to return the signed piece of paper, Hartel noticed that Charles had only signed one—a personal policy he had of one autograph per fan—and asked Johnson again if the star could sign the others. This is the point where Hartel claimed her husband heard Charles refer to her by a vulgar term used toward women. (The claim was not reported in coverage of the incident.) In response, Hartel said she went up to Charles's table and said, "This is what I think of your autograph," before tearing it into shreds and dropping the signed remains in front of him. Charles was quick to respond with his beer mug, she said.

"He immediately took his beer and threw it in my face. It was close enough that the impact of the beer knocked me back a little bit," Hartel said. "My husband stood up to go after Barkley, and someone held Barkley back. Frank Johnson was so nice. He was like, 'Gosh, I'm so sorry this happened to you. I guess you shouldn't have torn up his autograph.' I said, 'He shouldn't have called me the c-word.'"

No charges were ever filed, but Hartel was left humiliated and dripping in beer. She ended up quitting her job at the nursing home after she gave her side of the story to local media and told outlets where she worked, with her employer reading articles about how she was drunk and belligerent. (She said she was neither.) Hartel noted that she did receive a letter of apology from Colangelo, but nothing from Charles, who remained unapologetic. "If she'd been really upset, don't you think she would have sued me?" he said. Years later, Hartel, then a flight attendant for America West Airlines, had

Charles sitting in first class on one of her trips. He had no idea who she was, but she admitted she had plotted possible payback. "It did cross my mind to walk by with a sugary drink and spill it on him, but I held back," she said.

In Milwaukee, Phoenix trainer Joe Proski remembered getting a page from Charles. As Charles was walking down the street, a couple guys who were a few drinks in yelled at him, "Barkley, you're a fucking bum!" After repeating their statement in the form of a question, he walked inside the bar, asked the question again—"So I'm a fucking bum?"—and grabbed the inebriated men and chucked them onto the sidewalk, Proski said.

"He goes, 'I need some help and cash,'" Proski said.

Amid his incredible season, rumors also swirled around his love life. Charles and Maureen were separated at the time, and the reasons were never made public.

There was a separate matter in which gossip columnists reported how Connie Colla, the morning news anchor with Phoenix's NBC affiliate, had been seeing Charles. Years later, Colla maintained that was never the case. The two were working with each other on the weekly Suns show, and a couple times each month, they would shoot stories about everyday life and goofy bits, such as, "What if Charles had hair?" featuring Barkley in a Mohawk or Princess Leia buns. They had grabbed lunch one day as they often did, but this time, a gossip entry reported them as having an "intimate lunch." The Montana native called Charles to see if he was rattled. He wasn't. "Listen, Montana, when you're in the spotlight, people are going to say all kinds of things about you. As long as they spell your name right, it's all good," he said to her, she recalled. "It means you're important enough to sell their paper."

But those two lines ended up changing everything for Colla. The rumors had hit a point where she had to end the friendship with him, and hasn't spoken to him in nearly twenty years.

"After a while, it became obvious people really believed this, so I told Charles, 'This is nuts.' I'd never in my life told someone to go away and not be my friend, it was really painful," Colla recalled. "I think he was stunned by it, too."

Despite the beer dowsing and gossip rags, Charles became the most popular athlete the city had ever seen. At 62–20, the league's best record, Charles, who was the MVP frontrunner, had given the team and Phoenix exactly what it needed at exactly the right time. And now it called for a championship.

Two games into the first round and the best team in basketball was already on life support. The top-seed Suns had just lost the first two games at home to the eighth-seed Lakers, and the home crowd had turned catatonic. Kevin Johnson missed the first game of the series after he strained his MCL in the postgame celebration. His return in Game 2 wasn't enough to stop James Worthy, Byron Scott, and Vlade Divac. The Lakers were now poised to pull off one of the biggest upsets in NBA history.

At the podium after the game, Westphal knew the next question was whether his team was dead. To that point, only three teams in the history of the league had come back to win a best-of-five series after trailing 0–2.

"We're gonna win the series," he proclaimed. "We're gonna win one Tuesday. Then, the next game is Thursday, we'll win there. And we'll come back and we'll win the series on Sunday. And everybody will say what a great series it was."

Charles responded with 27 points, 11 rebounds, and 5 assists to help the Suns stave off elimination at The Forum. He followed that with one of his best shooting games of the series (13-of-21 to go with his 28, 11, 4 assists, and 3 blocks) to send it to a deciding Game 5. When asked what he did differently to get his shot on track, he gently reminded reporters of what he'd done. "I've got 16,000 [career] points," he bragged. "No sense tinkering with it now."

The wild crowd that awaited them back at America West on Mother's Day was thankful to be there. With 1:10 left, the Lakers up by 4, a quick baseline jumped by Charles cut it to 2. After getting a stop, Charles skied for the offensive rebound off a Johnson miss that went out-of-bounds. Majerle took a wild, off-balance eighteen-footer that dropped to tie the game with thirteen seconds remaining. Sedale Threatt, Charles's former teammate in Philadelphia, acted as if he was about to throw the ball to Divac in the post. Instead, he swung it around to Scott, who had a good look at a catch-and-shoot 3 on the right wing with one second on the clock and Ainge lunging desperately to close out. With no time remaining the ball had bounced off the front rim and the crowd released a collective sigh of relief before the start of overtime.

By the time the horn sounded on a 112–104 victory, the Suns had learned a lesson in pride.

Although the semifinals series against San Antonio had been tied at one point, the Spurs never felt like a true threat against a Phoenix team that would not be caught flat-footed again. Charles's Game 5 of 36 points and 12 rebounds reflected what the team needed from him all year.

A 4-point lead for Phoenix in the waning moments of Game 6 was cut to 1 after a Dale Ellis 3-ball. On the other end, a missed free throw from Ainge resulted in a loose-ball foul on Charles, sending the Spurs to the free throw line with about ten seconds remaining. Robinson connected on both to tie the game. On the bench, Charles, who had two anti-inflammatory injections for his aching hamstrings during the series, bit down on his clear mouthpiece. Frank Johnson can still hear the ringing noise in his ears from the crowd at Hemis-Fair Arena. The coach's plan was to create as much spacing as possible for their star to cook.

Holding the ball at the top of the key, Sir Charles stared into the eyes of the Admiral as the clock winded down. At five seconds, Charles gave two hard dribbles and shifted to his left for a third before going up over Robinson from inside the 3-point line.

Silence came over the arena as the ball fell through the hoop. Looking back on it, Frank Johnson said the collective hush of the crowd was "pretty amazing." Running back to the other end, Charles held his arms up, realizing his shot was about to send him back to the conference finals for the first time since his rookie year. "He turns around to us like, 'Did you doubt what I was about to do?'" Ceballos remembered.

"Chuck wasn't afraid of the moment, wasn't afraid of the shot," observed Chambers, adding that he didn't want him to take the shot from that range. "That's Chuck, that's just the way he was. He was unpredictable a lot of times about the way he did things and what he did, but man, he was good."

The 28 points and 21 rebounds again wowed a national audience in a season full of breathtaking moments. For his efforts, he was named MVP of the 1993 season, averaging 25.6 points, 12.2 rebounds, 5.1 assists, 1.8 blocks—the best player on the best team in the regular season. He said often that this was his best chance to win a championship, and he wasn't going to do anything to screw it up. He'd repeat it more to anyone who would listen. Or it was to himself.

"If you want to be successful in life, you have to make yourself successful," he said. "I want Charles Barkley to be a great basketball player."

20

Charles wasn't in the mood to rebound on the day of the commercial shoot.

Exiting the white limousine to the air-conditioned trailer in the parking lot behind North High School in Phoenix, Charles had five sentences to memorize for the hour-long shoot for his latest Nike commercial. There'd be a teleprompter in case he stumbled. A crew of dozens ran around the high school gym in the spring of 1993 to make sure everything was just right, including a man dedicated to spraying Charles's bald head with mist to mimic sweat. Stuffed chicken and tenderloin of beef were on the menu, and a stack of twenty CDs was next to a black boom box for his own personal entertainment.

Off to the side were children awaiting his autograph and a man named Buddy Cheeks who was waiting to meet Charles after winning a lookalike contest on a local radio station. During the shoot, Charles had two requests of the young admirers: call me Chuck and buy my shoes.

"They only cost $140. Get it from your parents," he joked to the children.

Charles's first season in Phoenix coincided with his unlikely rise as one of the most bankable pitchmen in the country.

"I've seen him get better at everything he's done," said Glenn Guthrie, his financial adviser. "Charles knew that the NBA was an entertainment business long before I did."

On that day, entertainment meant looking straight into the camera for a black-and-white, thirty-second spot. He began:

I am not a role model.

I'm not paid to be a role model.

I'm paid to wreak havoc on the basketball court.

Parents should be role models.

Just because I dunk a basketball doesn't mean I should raise your kids.

In May 1993, the ad was a milestone in how culture saw and interacted with its athletes. But in performing the ad, Charles had broken American sports tradition.

"The 'I Am Not a Role Model' commercial was the most important commercial of its kind at the time, and it remains, arguably, the most important commercial," said Michael Wilbon. "And it was completely, wrongly perceived."

Charles had thought about the topic for years. Around 1989, he said he went to Nike with the idea for an ad focusing on the debate around athletes as role models. Nike thought he was nuts, he said. Also, why did Charles want to do it? He pointed to the talks he'd given at schools that were still largely segregated. At the majority-White schools, he noticed only 5 to 7 percent of the students said they wanted to play in the NBA. Instead, most of those students, he said, wanted to be doctors, lawyers, teachers, police officers, engineers, and so on. But when he'd go to majority-Black schools, nearly 100 percent of the students there said playing professional basketball was the dream. To Charles, children of color had been brainwashed to believe they could only be successful in athletics and entertainment.

In *I May Be Wrong but I Doubt It*, Charles remembered reaching out to Howard White, his friend and Nike executive, about how much this idea of athletes as role models bugged him.

No person, not even Phil Knight himself, has meant more to Charles during his time at Nike than White. A playground legend growing up in Hampton, Virginia, White, who only had *H* on his jersey at the University of Maryland, jumped to Nike in 1981 as a field representative and later became Nike's liaison for Michael Jordan, acting as an older brother figure and facilitating his relations with the company. He remains one of Jordan's closest and most trusted associates with the Jordan Brand.

In Charles, White saw one of the most caring and giving people he had ever met, someone who came off as a loose cannon in public but would visit children's hospitals on Christmas morning in private. Charles was taken by White's attention to detail and saw him as "a welcome variable" to the usually impersonal corporate world.

"Nike has given me great shoes and great money," said Charles, "but the best gift they ever gave me was the mentoring of Howard White."

Another person who was grateful for White was Jim Riswold. As creative director for Wieden+Kennedy, the Portland-based advertising agency that partnered with Nike for some of the most memorable ads in sports marketing history, Riswold was one of the best copywriters. He helped to create Charles's indelible Nike ad, at a time when the two weren't always seeing eye to eye. "I think on a few occasions [Howard] prevented Charles from strangling me, so I owe him my life," Riswold joked.

The Portland native's effect on the history of sports advertising can't be understated. He paired Jordan with Spike Lee's Mars Blackmon. We know "Bo Knows" because of Riswold. Later on, he'd help a young Tiger Woods say, "Hello, world." Riswold's brilliance was in his writing and handling of the subject matter, as well as knowing the strengths and limitations of athletes who sometimes had difficulty getting out their lines.

"Riswold took the best parts of these athletes and took them into these vehicles to sell shoes," said Joe Pytka, the director of the "Role Model" ad. "They became legends from these ads."

But Riswold disagreed with Charles's version of events. For him, the "Role Model" ad was an idea he fleshed out after reading *Outrageous!* Riswold noted Charles's repetition of the role model issue, both in his book and in interviews. "What set Charles apart is he wrote his own ads, in terms of things he said and did. Nobody gives a flying fuck what I have to say, especially 30 years later, but that was one passage in the autobiography I circled and stuck in my head," Riswold said.

At the time, Nike was planning to roll out its "Unplugged" series, a package of stripped-down ads to air around the playoffs that would be stark, gritty, and deeply personal. Charles's "Role Model" ad would be one, but he'd be joined by the likes of Jordan, Phoenix teammate Dan Majerle, and Miami's Harold Miner, nicknamed "Baby Jordan." The ad for Jordan featured the defending two-time champion musing in an empty gym, "What if my name wasn't in lights? What if my face wasn't on TV every other second?... Can you imagine it?... I can."

The series would come at a time when the company was in trouble among teen males, its most consistent demographic and easily its biggest moneymaker. Adidas had targeted inner-city teens with strong success, and Reebok unveiling a blacktop version of its popular Pump sneakers had helped cut into Nike's overwhelming dominance in the coveted demographic by nearly 20 percentage points by the start of 1993. If anyone would tip the scales of the teen male demographic more in Nike's favor, it would be the guy most likely to look and talk like them.

Phil Knight was immediately taken by the idea, as well as the plan to push Charles more to the forefront in the wake of the Olympics. Knight believed there was no danger in running the "Role Model" ad.

"It was a creative idea that had a man-bites-dog aspect to it. That was one of the first things I had heard about it, and I was in favor of it," Knight said. "The ad kept with who Charles was and what Nike's position was at the time."

At North High, Charles had epitomized the best of Nike in an hour-long shoot. Marc Perman, his longtime agent, would later say that the genius of the ad was in how Charles said the iconic lines. "If he had said it in a less evocative, more ambiguous way, people wouldn't have noticed it," Perman said. While the ad was bound to get some blowback, "Role Model" had pinched a nerve in American culture when it came to personal responsibility and celebrity worship.

"The 'I Am Not a Role Model' campaign hit like a thunderclap,"

Jemele Hill said. "Athletes just didn't say stuff like that. It was just unpopular to voice that opinion—and it showed."

Twenty-five years before Laura Ingraham of Fox News told LeBron James and Kevin Durant to not talk about politics and just "shut up and dribble," Charles was given similar instructions after the release of the Nike commercial.

"They said, 'You're going to get killed,'" he recalled in 2019. "I said, 'I can handle it, I'm a big boy.'"

No journalist took it more personally than Stan Hochman of the *Philadelphia Daily News*, a familiar dissenting voice from his time with the Sixers. Hochman's criticism of Charles would serve as a precursor for what opinionated athletes would face down the road.

"It is self-serving, stupid, almost sinister," wrote Hochman of the ad. He concluded, "If Barkley doesn't want to be a role model because he lacks the intelligence, the patience, the skills, the warmth, whatever, he doesn't have to be one. He can simply turn down the chance to shill for sneakers or deodorant or any other item. He can shut up and play hard, and the world would be a better place by far."

By the time the ad had reached millions, Charles had stirred a tremendous debate on why parents should be the ones to set the standards for their children. The ad led to a series of think pieces, columns, radio segments, and TV interviews about not just whether Charles was right regarding parents being role models but, in the public's view, if he himself should take the responsibility to be one. The *New York Times* lauded the ad as "the most subversive sneaker commercial of all time."

White acknowledged that touching the family unit was an essential part of the message, one that Charles wanted to clearly hammer home. "We thought if two parents saw that and said, 'I need to stay home and read a book with my children or check their homework,' it's meaningful," White explained. "We were trying to send people back to old family values."

ESPN's Howard Bryant recalled how much he initially disliked the ad, thinking it was an indication of an athlete shunning one of the few responsibilities asked of athletes, but his viewpoint evolved. "It's like, 'If I'm the guy who has more influence than the people who pay for your groceries, we've already lost,'" Bryant said. "We see it in our culture now, so he was so far ahead of his time." By far the most intriguing critique came from Karl Malone, his peer at power forward and Dream Team brother. In an essay in *Sports Illustrated* titled "One Role Model to Another," Malone said that while he loved and respected Charles, the Mailman noted that the decision of whether to be a role model was not Charles's to make.

"I don't think we can accept all the glory and all the money that comes with being a famous athlete and not accept the responsibility of being a role model, of knowing that kids and even some adults are watching us and looking for us to set an example," Malone wrote. "I mean, why do we get endorsements in the first place? Because there are people who follow our lead and buy a certain sneaker or cereal because we use it."

"It certainly was not a positive thing for the league," said Rod Thorn, the NBA's executive vice president. "In retrospect, if the league had control over it, the league would've never let anything like that happen."

As the avalanche of responses came in, there was a common element playing out among these discussions: Many failed to understand what Charles was saying or misinterpreted what he meant. Instead of focusing on the "I" in "I am not a role model," the real message of the ad—don't wait for a pro athlete to mentor your kid because they're famous—got lost in the debate.

"People thought he had done this to absolve himself of any responsibility so he could act however he wanted to, but to him, it was really this notion of misplaced priorities," said J.A. Adande. "There were a lot of culture wars in the '90s, and Charles turned out to be in the middle of one of them."

The way Charles was covered at the time played a role. There was a point in the early '90s when Black athletes had become more visible than ever before in mainstream culture. Black athletic excellence ranging from Barry Sanders and Jackie Joyner-Kersee to Ken Griffey Jr. signaled a new wave of representation in sports and mainstream culture at the start of the decade. Dr. Todd Boyd, the expert on race in pop culture at USC, argued that the greater exposure for Black athletes around this time triggered tension from a less diverse media skeptical of the evolution of Black people in sports across culture. From that came a passive-aggressive criticism from media members who used their respective platforms to subtly criticize Black athletes by questioning their morals and character.

Trajectories of Black athletes and the levels of their acceptance in American culture have tended to go one of two ways over the last century, Boyd explained. Sports have often provided a platform for Black athletes to take on the system—Muhammad Ali and Jack Johnson, John Carlos and Tommie Smith, Bill Russell and Kareem Abdul-Jabbar, Jim Brown, and scores of others. Speaking out about injustices also brought about attacks on their character. Ali was a self-centered war evader. Carlos and Smith were gross attention hogs. Russell was a jerk. Though thoughts and feelings would change over the decades, they were anything but embraced by a majority of the country. The reception was markedly different for icons like Jackie Robinson and Jesse Owens, who were deemed the kind of compliant and amenable Black athletes preferred by and accepted by the nation during their time. The same happened with O.J. Simpson, who Boyd noted did whatever he could not to deal with race. This was made clear in *O.J.: Made in America*, which chronicled Simpson rejecting what Black critics said was a road to equality for athletes of the time in favor of seeking White admiration and embracing ideas of White success.

So when it came to the popularity of Black athletes, specifically among young, White fans, the reaction for many parents was to judge them. The Nike ad brought those layers to the forefront. Charles wasn't afraid to turn a culture that long judged Black athletes on its head.

"All of these issues sort of informed the question of 'Are you a role model?' Another good way to phrase this is, 'Are you a good N—? Will you do as you're told? Are you going to scratch if you don't itch? Will you laugh if things aren't funny? You should be grateful for this opportunity,'" Boyd said. "Charles in that commercial says, without straight-up saying it, that this is bullshit."

In Long Island, New York, Sue Bird was twelve when she saw the ad, one she initially thought was funny because Charles was one of her role models. Then she let the vibe sink in and felt something more than laughter. "I actually remember thinking how he was like, 'This is who I am and everyone can go fuck themselves.' Even as a twelve-year-old, that's what it was to me—'This is who I am. I'm not trying to please you. I'm trying to do what I can on the basketball court and do what I can as a human,'" Bird said. "I got it loud and clear. I wasn't put off by it."

For Jay Williams, then an eleven-year-old in Plainfield, New Jersey, the ad was transformative. It enabled him to separate athlete from human. "I always used to look at some guys when I was really young like, 'I want to be like him,' or 'I want to be like this guy,' and my dad would always say, 'Well, you don't want to be that guy. You want to play like that guy.' There was a difference," Williams explained. "I think Barkley just kind of brought that to the highest degree for me to recognize that."

Since his time at Michigan, Jalen Rose has always thought of Charles as an older brother. It's why his effect on Black athletes and culture, and how it directly affected him, means so much to him thirty years later.

There were only a few exceptions of athletes speaking out in the '80s and '90s. You had Craig Hodges in Chicago and would later have Mahmoud Abdul-Rauf in Denver. The people who bucked the system were usually in college, like Jerry Tarkanian, John Thompson and the Fab Five. But then you had Charles Barkley with "I Am Not a Role Model," which stood out so much.

He became a validation for us that we could be the Fab Five and perform at an elite level at Michigan. Now, because of him, you couldn't ignore the bald heads, long shorts, black socks, and what we were doing for the culture. He'd show for guys later on, like Allen Iverson and Latrell Sprewell, that you can wear cornrows and still ball out. For Charles to do that commercial and then validate it with his performance on the floor was huge.

When you have Charles saying, "I am not a role model" and then doing what he did, professional sports were forced to embrace rap music, starting with MC Hammer and "U Can't Touch This." I remember being in gyms when you heard maybe "Whoomp! (There It Is)" or Montell Jordan's "This Is How We Do It." People were not embracing rap music. Charles helped change that culture from what he was doing in the pros.

★ ★ ★

The ad was a game changer for Nike, and helped reveal a new side of Charles, said Rob DeFlorio, then the company's global advertising director. It also opened him up to a new audience. "'Role Model,' for us, was this serious ad where Charles was going to make a statement," he said. "It wasn't a transformation, but it showed the world who he was."

Charles said the criticism he took in a moment of national fervor was all worth it if it meant starting the kind of dialogue that it did. The message did something else, too: It beat Jordan's. Though their ads came out around the same time, Jordan's spot did not hit the mark, as viewers believed the message from the best player in the world felt more like, *Just stop bugging me.* It was the rare time where Charles resonated more with people than Jordan in such an overwhelming way. Glenn Guthrie said that he, Perman, and the folks at Nike "always felt there was a market for both" Charles and Jordan, and the ad was validation of that.

Since the beginning of his rise, Jordan had been seen as the role model. As he revealed in *The Last Dance*, he never wanted to be considered one. It's a game that was too stacked against him and one he couldn't win, he said.

Jordan and Barkley understood each other. If we were lucky, they'd see each other soon.

21

The time had come to bust out a tape of General George S. Patton's Speech to the Third Army. Before Game 6 in Seattle, the Suns were up 3–2 against a SuperSonics team that had already pushed them to their limits. Charles, not one for rah-rah speeches, figured the team could channel Patton's words to inspire his teammates.

"Wade into them. Spill their blood. Shoot them in the belly. When you put your hand into a bunch of goo that a moment before was your best friend's face, you'll know what to do," actor George C. Scott said in his portrayal of the general in the 1970 film *Patton*, in an abbreviated version of the profane speech. "We're going to hold on to [the enemy] by the nose, and we're gonna kick him in the ass. We're gonna kick the hell out of him all the time, and we're gonna go through him like crap through a goose!… Thirty years from now when you're sitting around your fireside with your grandson on your knee, and he asks you, 'What did you do in the great World War II?'— you won't have to say, 'Well, I shoveled shit in Louisiana.'"

But in the battle of Game 6, the Suns lost by 16.

"It didn't do any good," guard Frank Johnson said of Charles playing the Patton pep talk.

Just one battle remained in what Kevin Johnson called the War of the Western Conference, and the Suns would have to do it without Cedric Ceballos, who reinjured his fractured left foot and was ruled out for the remainder of the playoffs. Taking a seat at the end of the Phoenix bench with four minutes to go, Charles's face lay in his left hand as he gazed up at the scoreboard. Seattle had executed its game plan to perfection: stop Charles and you stop the Suns. He had shot 4-of-14 for 13 points and 11 rebounds, and a second-quarter technical, in what resembled anything but a send-off to the Finals.

Instead, as the raucous Seattle crowd loudly indicated to the purple pests, their Sonics were far from dead. Walking off, Charles was dejected, but he still had some confidence in the tank. All he had to do was hold up his end.

"At that point," he said, "I'm just saying to myself, 'I've got to play the best game of my life and I'm going to the Finals.'"

Dan Majerle stood on top of his own bar to break the news before a packed crowd that Charles had been named MVP and a lone spotlight inside Majerle's Sports Grill pointed to a smiling Chuckster. Drinks were passed around the bar amid deafening chants of "M-V-P!"

"It was just one of those iconic nights where a kid from Traverse City, Michigan, now he's standing on his own bar announcing his teammate who is the MVP of the whole NBA," Majerle said. "It's pretty cool when you think about it."

With a sold-out America West Arena on its feet, his teammates bowing to him and a beaming Charcey pointing to the heavens from courtside, Charles, who had a cleanly shaved head for the ceremony, couldn't help but smile when commissioner David Stern read back what he had accomplished over his career—perennial all-star, MVP of the All-Star Game, Olympic gold medalist. Fresh from the headline-making Nike ad, Stern, never one to pass up a chance to rib someone publicly, praised Charles for the blueprint year he had put together, leading the team in points, rebounds, assists, and to the best record in the league. "This year, you've had a season, I guess you would say if you were looking for what an MVP season is, your season this year is a role model for an MVP season," Stern said.

For Paul Westphal, winning MVP over Michael Jordan had "legitimized his career in a way, probably more so than anything else."

"He had a year for the ages," Westphal said. "To have a front-row seat to it and have my seat belt buckled up and go for the ride along with Charles that year, it was one of the great joys of my life."

But the night turned bittersweet for Barkley, whose Suns found themselves tied in the conference finals. Coming off an exhausting seven-game series against Houston, the SuperSonics didn't put up much of a fight in a 14-point loss in Game 1. Ahead of Game 2, Charles warned that Seattle didn't "give a bleep" about any MVP award, which showed in their 103–99 comeback win in the Valley. The evening of wasted opportunities was filled with turnovers and missed free throws. Frustration bubbled over in the final eighteen seconds. Leading by one, the Suns coughed up the ball on an errant Majerle pass to Charles. The turnover left the door open for a Sam Perkins 3-pointer, which put Seattle up by 2 with 9.8 seconds to go. On the other end, Charles thought he had tied the game on a put-back bucket, but he was instead whistled for a game-clinching foul after he knocked Sonics power forward Shawn Kemp to the floor with his left elbow. The home loss was a reminder that the Sonics team wasn't going to roll over.

Sitting at his locker by balloons and bouquets of flowers, Charles couldn't focus on the MVP accolade. Instead, he outlined his disdain.

"If I'm playing checkers, and I'm losing, I'll accidentally knock the board over," he said. "There's not a worse feeling than seeing somebody else having fun at your expense."

Seattle was a mix of veterans slightly past their prime and two potential cornerstones under the age of twenty-five who management believed could change basketball forever in the city.

Perhaps no one was more hyped coming out of high school in 1988 than Shawn Kemp, a six-foot-ten star-in-the-making out of Elkhart, Indiana. A McDonald's All-American and walking highlight reel, Kemp caught the eye of Seattle president and general manager Bob Whitsitt. "I couldn't guarantee to ownership that Shawn was going to be great," said Whitsitt, "but I told them that if things came together for Shawn the way they could, he was going to have the power of Charles Barkley and the flair and dunking prowess of Dominique Wilkins."

If Kemp was misunderstood, then Gary Payton was just a hard-ass. With a father whose license plate on his 1978 Nissan Datsun 280Z simply read, "MR MEAN," Payton had gone from a brash point guard on the playgrounds of Oakland to the best player in all of college basketball. In high school, multiple police cars were sometimes needed to quell riots in between games. And everyone talked—players, coaches, fans, and the guy selling candy. When Payton arrived at Oregon State, his father recalled to *Sports Illustrated* how he gave the coaches instructions to slap his son upside the head if he got out of line. Instead, Payton would become one of the most decorated players in school history and the second pick in the 1990 Draft.

Under George Karl, the star-duo-in-training of Kemp and Payton, along with veterans like Ricky Pierce, Sam Perkins, Eddie Johnson, and Nate McMillan, turned Seattle from a .500 team a couple seasons earlier into a legitimate contender. The Payton-to-Kemp Sonic Boom alley-oop had already become a signature play for the NBA's next generation.

The Seattle Center Coliseum did not offer the warmest of welcomes to Charles, who was met with deafening boos every time he touched the ball. Early on in Game 3, as Charles headed to the bench, he felt a tap on his shoulder. When he turned around, one of the fans he had been ridiculing gave him the finger.

But the Suns mounted a dramatic offensive attack with seven players in double figures and a 104–97 win.

After an embarrassing 120–101 loss in Game 4, Charles ordered his teammates to "quit bitching" and take care of business at home. "Lots of guys talk and most of them don't know their shit from a hole in the wall," he said. "If we lose again [at home], we don't deserve to win the series."

Heading into Game 5, there was a sense in the media that Seattle had figured out Phoenix. The day before the game, Westphal, usually mild-mannered, read the splash headline on the front page of the *Arizona Republic*:

Outplayed.

Outhustled.

Outraged.

With KJ still not at 100 percent, Charles and Majerle put on a showcase. Majerle, who had been relatively quiet to that point, bombed 3 after 3 on the hapless Seattle perimeter defense. Every made 3 triggered a $50 charitable donation from Whataburger, which meant that Majerle and his eight 3-pointers, a new playoff record, was responsible for giving away hundreds of dollars to charities thanks to his hot hand.

Charles had regained his form as a methodical monster, each series feeling more rhythmic and inevitable than the last. *Dunk, jumper, free throws. Dunk, jumper, free throws. Steal, dunk. Steal, dunk.* The offensive avalanche fell on Kemp, who could do nothing to compete with Charles on the defensive end.

But the Suns found themselves trailing in the second half. An 11–0 run at the start of the quarter gave the Suns their most comfortable cushion, but Kemp erupted for 20 of his 33 points in the fourth quarter to keep them in it. He hit a turnaround jumper on Charles to pull Seattle within 1 with 34.5 seconds to go. But coming down the floor, Kevin Johnson found a wide-open Majerle for a wing 3 that seemed to hang in the air before dropping through the hoop for the playoff record and the kill shot. Dick Enberg, who was on the call for NBC, guessed that whatever they were serving at Majerle's restaurants probably came in threes. He was joined on the broadcast by Magic Johnson, who proudly said Charles was one step closer to getting the ring.

"I think sometimes we try to get other people involved instead of just getting it to me and letting *me* get everybody involved," Charles said afterward. "Well, fuck those motherfuckers. Get the ball to *me* and let *me* do it."

They'd need to do it again after a collapse in Game 6. After going for a combined 77 points two days earlier, Charles and Majerle fell flat with a combined 25 points on 8-of-25 shooting.

Kevin Johnson, a Barkley whisperer of sorts, told his friend exactly what they needed to bounce back after the Game 6 loss.

"You've never been to the Finals, right?" Johnson asked him.

After saying he hadn't, Johnson added, "You just have to play the best basketball game of your life, we'll follow."

Like it read on the Suns' shirts during pregame shootaround at the Purple Palace on June 5, 1993, one game separated them from the Finals. Billy Idol's "Rebel Yell" reverberated through an arena of over nineteen thousand screaming fans, some of whom were wearing Barkley bald caps, all of whom would remain on their feet for most of the Saturday afternoon game. At Majerle's Sports Grill, fans tried to bribe the bouncer with $100 bills for a table to watch history at the starting shooting guard's bar.

A sign inside the arena said it all: *How Bad Do You Want It?* Charles couldn't sleep the night before, his anxiousness waking him up about five times.

"The MVP is not my goal," he said. "If we don't win the world championship, I'm going to be crushed."

From the tip-off of the biggest game of his life, Charles didn't stop. Off a desperate pass from Perkins to save the ball from going out-of-bounds, Charles sprinted out of nowhere to beat Seattle forward Derrick McKey to the ball and lunged to the other end for the fast break jam.

Putbacks off offensive rebounds might as well have been set plays because Charles scored every time. He wrecked Kemp and Perkins off the ball, beating the taller men to the hoop on backdoor cuts to cash in on open slams and layups. On defense, Barkley fronted Kemp so much that the young star could never get into a rhythm, finishing with a quiet 18 points.

Coming down with a rebound meant Charles was going to swing his elbows to clear out anyone around him. Charles, in the middle of a sea of green jerseys, tumbled to the floor with the ball and dished it off late in the game before a possible turnover, bringing the sold-out crowd to its feet in appreciation. Enberg wasn't sure what he had just seen. "How does he do it?" he asked Magic over the roaring crowd.

"When Charles Barkley took over, and this is a miracle, Gary Payton stopped talking," Ceballos remembered. "And when Gary Payton stopped talking, you know Charles has done some work."

The Suns shot 64 free throws. The mark tied for the most free throws by any one team in a playoff game since the merger. (It would be matched twenty-two years later by Houston in 2015.) Their 57 made free throws in a playoff game tied the Celtics' accomplishment in a four-overtime win in 1953. Charles was a big beneficiary of the officiating, as his 19 made free throws in the second half tied the single-game playoff record. Decades later, McMillan maintained that while the Suns had an excellent team, the Sonics were screwed out of the Finals.

"We just felt that the league wanted Barkley to be in that Finals. The league didn't want us in the Finals," McMillan remembered. "I've never heard of a team shooting 64 free throws in an NBA game. The players didn't decide the game, the officials did."

Yet no one on Seattle could contain Charles Barkley. He finished with 44 points and 24 rebounds, shooting 12-of-20 from the floor and 19-of-22 from the free throw line in forty-six minutes. He joined Elgin Baylor as only the second player ever to score more than 40 points and pull down more than 20 rebounds in a Game 7. His rebounding total was 6 more than all of the Seattle starters combined, He scored 15 and pulled down half of his rebounds in the fourth quarter alone. In his embrace of Miller and Chambers walking off the court, Enberg noted the unbridled happiness of the sport's anti-hero, musing that for as angry as Charles could get at times, his smile was so electric that it could power the city.

"I tell people that 44–24 game is probably the best game I ever played in my life," Charles said.

Phoenix's 123–110 win had Jerry Colangelo in tears, his team going for its first title in the franchise's silver anniversary season. Amid the handing out of purple T-shirts, Kevin Johnson couldn't stop smiling, saying the win was "like I've dipped my hand in a honeycomb and tasted something sweet." Miller was hoarse. Chambers was rejuvenated. Ainge was beat up, but ready for the fight that awaited. Though he was already looking ahead to Chicago and all the golf he was going to play with Jordan, Charles's more pressing matter was obtaining a six-pack to drink in his Jacuzzi. After the game, he walked over to Frank Johnson.

"He said, 'Frank, I told you not to worry about it,'" the backup guard said.

The day before the game, Jordan had called him to wish him luck and urged him to take the ball to the hoop over and over again. Now he'd see him soon. But Charles got another call the night before from someone who was about to be linked to him for reasons other than basketball.

Madonna.

An avid soccer fan, chef Tony Hamati only started liking basketball because of Charles Barkley—but the free tickets to the games didn't hurt either for the star's favorite Italian restaurant manager. "When they'd score, I'd yell, *GOOOOOOOOOAAAAAAL!*" Hamati recalled. "That night, Charles came in and said, 'This is not soccer.' I told him it was the same thing."

After he cooked for King Hussein of Jordan, the royal family funded the continuation of Hamati's culinary training at the Culinary of the Sorbonne in Paris. Arriving in Phoenix in 1985, Hamati quickly became one of the premier culinary figures in the Valley. As manager at Tomaso's, the intimate Italian hotspot near Camelback Mountain, Hamati's big personality suited his high-profile patrons. Hamati took a shine to Charles from the first time Colangelo brought him into Tomaso's.

One night in late May 1993, Charles introduced Hamati to a woman the chef had never expected to meet.

"He stuck his head in and said, 'Tony, this is Madonna,'" the chef remembered. "She didn't look like Madonna, but it was actually her."

While it's unclear how Charles and Madonna connected, they had kept in touch in the weeks leading up to the playoffs. She was even spotted courtside with comedian Rosie O'Donnell and late-night host Arsenio Hall during one of the Suns' playoff games against the Lakers in early May. Hall recounted years later that it was something of an unannounced double date–type setup. "Charles Barkley was Madonna's date and I was Rosie's date," said Hall, still surprised by the arrangement.

Her public infatuation with Charles came through in an interview that year with O'Donnell, her friend and co-star in "A League of Their Own," in *Mademoiselle* magazine. The Q&A, which included the pop star asking the comedian whether getting your period or watching an episode of the daytime talk show *Sally* was more annoying, had Madonna pose another question to O'Donnell. *If you could have your choice, who would you pick to father your child: Denzel Washington, Damon Wayans, or Charles Barkley?* O'Donnell picked Wayans, saying he was the funniest and cutest to her. When she turned the question around on her friend, Madonna came to a different conclusion.

"Charles Barkley is God," Madonna said. "Denzel Washington is married, and you know what? I think Charles is probably married. See, all the good ones are taken…but that doesn't mean they can't father your children!"

After the dinner, it wouldn't take long for the media to approach Hamati, including *Inside Edition* and *Entertainment Tonight.* He claims he was offered $50,000 to spill on TV about Charles and Madonna at his restaurant. The manager had already seen a couple of the reports that framed the flirtatious couple as having played footsie, which he thought was fabricated. When speaking to Ann Gerhart in her "Tattler" column for the *Philadelphia Daily News,* Hamati denied seeing them altogether. He turned down the money offered to tell the story, even if there wasn't a lot to tell, out of what he said was loyalty to his customer and friend.

All of this was playing out right before Charles and the Suns faced off against Jordan's Bulls. A manager with The Roxy, a popular Phoenix nightclub, told the *Phoenix New Times* about how the pair danced the night away and hung out at a roped-off section. (Charles maintained that the reports were false, saying he had never shared dance moves with Madonna.) Unsubstantiated reports of Charles's limo being parked overnight outside her hotel filled newspapers.

The pop star played coy about the details of the alleged tryst, replying, "Who's Charles Barkley?" Outlets couldn't help scrutinize the potential pairing. "She's awfully short. He's awfully married. He's said he's an emotional man, can't open his eyes when he makes love. We know she's a voyeur, can't keep her eyes *closed* when she makes love," Gerhart wrote in "Tattler."

"He may retire; she'll never retire. She'll be stripping in the old-age home."

★ ★ ★

At least all the tabloid coverage gave Charles's friends great material. John Costacos, who enjoyed pranking Charles, came up with his best idea yet—and it stemmed from his girlfriend's warning: Don't get involved with Madonna unless you want to end up on the cover of a magazine. The baby daddy prank was in motion.

In 1993, nobody knew what a scanner or Photoshop was. I found photos of Madonna and found some photos of him, and scanned them side by side on a fake edition of the National Enquirer. *I had a little picture of Madonna, which said, "I'm having Charles Barkley's baby." It had a little photo of her kissing him, which I got from this artistic photo of her kissing herself in the mirror from* Life *magazine. The other headline said, "Basketball star says Madonna is his new MVP."*

My sister was going to have lunch with him at the Sheraton and I was coming in later to show it to him and get a good laugh. Charles isn't there yet, but Joann Fitzsimmons and teammate Frank Johnson, Frank's wife, and Phil Knight are all standing there with my sister. Charles was also getting his pictures taken with Phil Knight that day. I showed this thing to everyone and they started laughing. I hid behind the plants and waited.

He came back down and one of them handed [him] the National Enquirer *and he looked down at it. He just stopped and stared at it for a second and dropped an f-bomb. He looked up at everyone and put his left hand on his temple and said, "This is bad." He looked through it quickly and he stared at the cover and put his right hand on his temple and said, "Shit, this is bad." He said, "Is this a joke?" Nobody ever cracked a smile.*

I figured he had enough and I came out from behind the plants. He had a big smile on his face afterward, and he looked relieved. I think it couldn't have been more than 10 seconds, but it couldn't have been more perfect.

But the headlines and gossip columns took a toll. Speculation surrounding Charles and Madonna had become so constant that Ellen Blumhardt, his mother-in-law, had suffered a heart attack. "She has had a lot of stress from the jokes about me and Madonna [dating] and has been harassed with people calling the house. She's not doing well right now and that's a major concern," he told reporters of the heart attack, which appeared to have happened the same day as Game 7 against Seattle. "I only met [Madonna] one time when she was in Phoenix. We don't date. We don't have a relationship."

For the first time, Charles said he felt how bright and hot the limelight was for stars like Jordan and Magic Johnson. Through the Madonna coverage, Charles also got a taste of what it was like for Jordan to block out the media entirely once his gambling habits had been called into question. Charles, who admitted to being telephone pals with Madonna, would say the questions about her didn't bother him, not when he had more pressing matters at hand. Yet there was something about her celebrity he admired.

"I'm going to be on NBC at least four times, and Madonna won't be," he said ahead of the Finals. "I'll get more pub than her. Of course, she's got her movies. I've got to win a ring first, then I can make a movie. I'm on a mission."

The story of Mad-Char eventually faded, but it resurfaced less than a year later during Madonna's legendarily contentious interview with David Letterman.

The plan was for Madonna to hold Letterman's feet to the fire on some of the jokes he had made at her expense. By the time she arrived at the Ed Sullivan Theater, however, Madonna had already smoked a joint, she later admitted. Unbeknownst to the public, she was privately dating rapper Tupac Shakur, who she said had her riled up about life when she stepped on stage in a floor-length black dress and combat boots for *The Late Show with David Letterman*.

The interview featured Madonna saying "fuck" fourteen times in what became probably the most-censored late-night broadcast in television history. Madonna, who said Charles did not understand "the meaning of friendship," gave suggestive answers throughout the memorable segment.

Charles said to reporters he didn't see the Letterman interview, but was curious.

"What did she talk about?" Charles asked a radio host.

"You," the commentator replied.

Charles could only offer a one-word answer: "Good."

22

The Western Conference Champions shirt had been stuck against Charles's soaked chest for a few minutes before the question came up of whether his first appearance in the NBA Finals would mean that the world would finally love him the same way it adored Michael Jordan, the globe's greatest athlete.

"Love me?" Charles repeated. "Oh, I'm their worst nightmare: a brother who won't be quiet."

Pitting Michael against Charles in 1993 was basketball's equivalent of the Beatles against the Rolling Stones. The friendliest of pop-culture wars brought them now to the heart of the NBA championship.

"It was Michael Jordan at his best on the court and Charles Barkley at his best and entertaining everyone off the court," said J.A. Adande. "It was hard for the rest of the Finals to live up to that."

The friends had done more for each other than they cared to share. Jordan was there for Charles to tell him he needed to dress better if he was going to be taken seriously as a Black businessman in America. Charles's presence and personality was enough of a reminder for

Jordan to lighten up. "I can't express the depth of me and Michael's friendship, as far as him being my brother," Charles told ESPN in the early 2000s. "He's always been there for me—always, behind closed doors." In fact, the friendship had made headlines when it was reported the two were sighted by a local TV helicopter playing golf the day before Game 1. When the reports came back, the local outlets had mistaken Charles for NBC's Quinn Buckner. Still, some speculated that Jordan was getting close to Charles to soften him up, so that he could take another NBA title.

"That really bothered me and Michael for a long time, people saying that Michael becomes friends with guys so he can soften them up," Charles said. "I'm like, 'Dude, me and Michael never played golf.'"

Mark West felt that Charles's physicality seemed to get turned down around Jordan. "I would say, his friendship probably kept him from hitting Michael as much as he might have someone else," West said. "Because Charles would knock somebody else on their ass coming to the bucket like that. If he hit Michael, I don't think he hit him as hard as he hit somebody else... We have to live with that."

For the Bulls, winning a third consecutive title would place Jordan, Scottie Pippen, Phil Jackson, and the club in a pantheon of greatness with few peers. Jordan spoke of winning a third title as the marker for his entry into elite status with Larry Bird and Magic Johnson.

Jason Hehir, director of *The Last Dance*, described this period of the Jordan Bulls of the early '90s as "kind of Michael staggering to the finish line emotionally." Of all the opportunities to beat Chicago in the early '90s, the '93 season presented the best chance to do the unthinkable. "As far as Jordan getting beat in the Finals, that was the chance to do it," Jack McCallum said. Others around the league, such as Washington Bullets guard Rex Chapman, thought the Suns presented "a nightmare matchup" for Chicago.

Historians like Sam Smith of *The Jordan Rules* have argued that being around Jordan elevated and cultivated Charles. Yet while Jordan had an ability to sharpen his opponents, there was no question that Charles ultimately did the same in their Finals matchup. Bob Costas sought to play them up as foils before the first game.

Michael Jordan permits nothing but success. A national championship at

North Carolina. Two Olympic gold medals. Three times the NBA MVP. Twice a world champion.

Charles Barkley's road has been less satisfying. His days at Auburn brought little glory. His NBA career was largely squandered on a team that could not win. Yet this year brought a new sense of destiny. A gold medal. A new team. The MVP.

Walking out of the locker room ahead of Game 1, the team with the league's best record looked up at the inspirational quote hanging above the door. It was from Bill Russell, an eleven-time champion who offered the same pragmatic words he'd share before every contest as a coach: *The game is scheduled, we have to play it. We might as well win.*

What was a close game in the first nine minutes went the other way in methodical fashion: Pippen jumper. A B.J. Armstrong layup. Horace Grant layup. Grant turnaround jumper. Jordan jumper with 0.3 seconds left. A 10-2 run in the closing minutes of the first quarter gave Chicago a stunning 14-point lead one period into the Finals. A tentative Phoenix team blinked, and the game had already slipped from their grasp.

"I don't think we were nervous," Charles said of Game 1. "I dunno, maybe we were."

The lead got up to 20 and Jordan was feasting. A knot on the back of Jordan's wrist that had hampered his shooting in the series with the Knicks had subsided, and the star predicted that his shot would improve in Game 1. In addition to Charles winning MVP over him, a healthy Jordan found another perceived slight to inject into his veins. Ahead of the series, Jordan was reminded of how much Chicago general manager Jerry Krause loved Dan Majerle as a lockdown perimeter defender.

"Just because Krause liked him was enough for me," Jordan said years later in *The Last Dance*. "You think he's a great defensive player? Okay, fine. I'm going to show you that he's not."

But what drove the Bulls in Game 1 was their ability to press and trap a Suns team not as accustomed to varying looks on defense. When it came to guarding Charles, the Bulls had their choice of a toy box filled with all-star stoppers.

"I was covered by Horace Grant, six-foot-ten with long arms, and I'd see Scottie, six-foot-eight with long arms, coming, and I'd say, 'Oh shit,'" Charles said to *Sports Illustrated*. "And then the window was even smaller because that damn Michael was always lurking. If you didn't throw a perfect pass out of the double-team, that sumbitch would get it."

Yet the Suns didn't go away, pulling to within three points in the fourth quarter. Richard Dumas had his most dominant night of the postseason with 20 points and 12 rebounds against Pippen. Despite Johnnie Mae's best efforts coaching from the stands—"He's just gotta keep his boards, stay in the game and play some defense!" she barked at NBC's Hannah Storm—Charles and the Suns didn't have enough.

In their 100–92 loss, the Suns were overwhelmed by an all too familiar moment. Nothing prepared the Suns for playing in the Finals, Kevin Johnson said, and it cost them Game 1. "You're accustomed to 10 cameras, and now there are 200," he said. "I would advise any team that feels it can win a championship to go watch a Finals together before they get there."

Following his own poor performance, Charles refused to point fingers. It was time to eat ribs with his grandmother. It wasn't the time to panic. Not yet.

"Let's don't go crazy after one game. Let's wait until after Game 2," said Charles before heading to a quiet dinner with Johnnie Mae and some friends at Houston's. "If we lose that one, then we can go crazy."

In what had to have been a first, Johnson, not Charles, was the center of attention following the Game 1 flop. KJ was nowhere to be found at a postgame dinner with out-of-town family members. When he came out of hiding, he went outside at the crack of dawn to hear the birds chirp. He said his daily prayers before heading to the arena to watch game film before the next crucial game.

The scrutiny of the Finals was foreign to Charles, and he didn't take kindly to it. He tried to keep perspective on a Game 1 loss. "I want to win the world's championship, but I'm not like these other guys," he said. "It's not a life-or-death thing. I've got a life. Basketball is my job."

As Huey Lewis and The News finished their rendition of the national anthem, the Suns seemed calm and ready. Charles found

Storm beforehand and guaranteed a Phoenix win to the NBC reporter. The previous three teams who had lost Game 1 of the Finals at home went on to win the title—the most recent being the Bulls in 1991. Westphal stressed that they didn't need to be miracle men or play perfect. They just had to show him they weren't going to fold.

"Hey, fuck these motherfuckers," Charles barked in the huddle in the tunnel. "Let's kick their ass."

From the start of the game, a Charles jumper over Grant from the top of the key, the Suns were going to punch back. Even if he tried to downplay his disappointment, Jordan understood his friend was too prideful to have consecutive underwhelming performances—and he wasn't wrong. A barrage of jumpers and post moves gave Charles 25 points by the half, already more than he had all of Game 1, on 10-of-14 shooting. He put Grant in early foul trouble and rediscovered his smile in the process.

But Charles was doing it all himself. Amid his unsuccessful attempts at containing Jordan, Majerle's shooting had gone cold. Johnson, a goat of Game 1, was again nowhere to be found. A second-quarter flurry from Chicago had the Suns down eight at the break. With the game tied at 33, the Bulls were calculated in their half-court offense, throwing 4 or 5 passes in a run that saw them go 10-of-11 from the field in what became glorified layup and dunk drills. Grant dunk. Williams layup. Williams dunk. Jordan fast-break dunk. Another Grant dunk. Jordan driving layup.

At this point of the Chicago dynasty, the Bulls almost preferred to play on the road, winning six of their previous seven Finals games away from home.

"We had so many distractions at home," John Paxson said to *Sports Illustrated*. "Plus, Michael, as you know, loved to stick it to the visiting crowds."

After pulling to within three at the end of the third quarter, Charles was beginning to feel the effects of battling the Bulls. Following an inadvertent slap to the face from Jordan, Charles had banged his right elbow as he crashed to the floor. Icing the bruise, Charles was desperately matching Jordan play-for-play, refusing to come out.

"On the court, you never look down to see which enemies are

dead or hurt. You just continually try to run over them," said Scottie Pippen. "But I don't think anything hurt Charles."

He had 35 to Jordan's 30, but he needed help from someone, anyone. The rest of the starting lineup scored 25 for the game, or as much as Charles scored by himself in the first half. His frustration erupted late in the game when he slammed the ball on the floor, wondering what else he could possibly do on his own. He'd find support from Danny Ainge, the only member of the team with championship experience and just the fifth player in league history to play in the Finals with three different teams. His 12 points in the fourth gave him 20 off the bench for the game. But as Charles started to tire, Jordan saw an opening and went back to work—jumper, drive, drive, dunk, dunk, jumper.

Missing seven straight shots late in the fourth, the Suns were spent. But Ainge, the super sub, had one last kick. He drained a 3 over Pippen and then crossed over one of the game's best defenders for a layup to make it a one-possession contest in the final minute. Thirty seconds to go and Ainge again had the ball with a chance to tie. Pippen, who had been burned by him the previous two plays, hoped he would take the drive. But when he went up for the 3, Pippen used his long left arm to get a hand on the ball, blocking the shot and sending it the other way before getting fouled.

As the final horn sounded on a 111–108 defeat, Charles bent over and undid the strap from one of his shoes and walked off the court with his head hanging low for what he thought might be the last time that year. His dazzling performance—42 points, 13 rebounds, and 4 assists in forty-six minutes—would fall by the wayside of another Jordan masterpiece: 42 points, 12 rebounds, 9 assists, and 2 steals in forty minutes. The duel marked only the second time in NBA history that two opponents scored 40-plus in a Finals game, the first since Jerry West and John Havlicek in 1969.

Facing the press afterward, Charles acknowledged that while they weren't publicly panicking, they were in a big enough hole that they "could fit into the Grand Canyon now."

"In Game 2, I played as well as I could play," Charles remembered, "and Michael just outplayed me."

Perhaps the hardest part after Game 2 was telling Christiana the result of the game. Mornings after Phoenix wins had always been the best time for Charles, who'd phone his young daughter in Philadelphia and tell her in a gentle voice only reserved for her that Daddy and his team did a good job. Instances where he had to tell her they lost always hurt, and that was especially the case during the Finals.

He came home to find Christiana crying. Inconsolable, the four-year-old wanted to know why her daddy lost.

"She says, 'What happened?' I said, 'I don't know if I'm better than this guy,'" Charles remembered. "I had never said that before about another basketball player... I told her that night, 'I've never played against a guy I thought was better than me until tonight.'"

Before boarding the plane ride to Chicago, reality had set in for Charles: no team in the Finals had ever come back after losing the first two games at home to win the title.

The Suns were going to be a quick out if they didn't get something—anything—out of Johnson, whose poor play in the first two games made him the target of local and national scorn. Thoughtful and seeking insight, KJ turned to the printed fax messages of encouragement sent by Suns as well as two books. The first was the Bible. The other was *Tess of the d'Urbervilles*, the nineteenth-century English novel from Thomas Hardy. One of the themes in Hardy's novel was what the author called the "ache of modernism," which was described by critic Dale Kramer as "the energy of traditional ways and the strength of the forces that are destroying them." In basketball terms, the Bulls had become both the modern standard, annual and inevitable, and the Suns yearned to be the force that toppled them.

As he was trying to lose himself in *Tess*, blocking out the beating he had taken in the first two games, Johnson also needed sleep. Westphal, however, woke him up more than halfway through the flight with an idea. Removing the blanket he had placed over his head, a drowsy Johnson heard what his coach had to say. The Suns had the league's best road record and won their only regular-season meeting in Chicago, so Westphal remained optimistic. He needed to get Johnson's mind off his offensive woes to concentrate on something else. But in doing so, Johnson was getting a new defensive assignment, one that might cause him to lose some more sleep.

"Paul wakes me up and says, 'I have good news and bad news. The good news is that the series is not over. The bad news is you're going to be guarding Jordan,'" Johnson recalled. "I put the blanket on my head and on the way out of the plane, I say to Paul, 'You won't believe the nightmare I had. You told me I'd be guarding Michael.' And he says to me, 'That wasn't a dream.'"

Returning to Chicago Stadium, Jackson could smell a historic three-peat, a feat not accomplished by a team in nearly three decades. The Bulls had seemingly every tangible and intangible advantage, coming home in a series in which the Suns led for less than four of the ninety-six minutes played in the first two games. They also were facing a battered Barkley, whose right elbow was badly swollen following the second half tumble in Game 2. Charles hadn't been able to shoot in two days of practice due to a deep bruise on the bone and a swollen bursa behind the elbow. In the hours before the game, he would remain uncertain about what he'd get from a heavily wrapped elbow that had been drained and treated with anti-inflammatory shots forty minutes prior to tip-off.

"I have no idea what to expect, because right now I can't lift it above my head without tremendous pain," he said.

In the locker room leading up to the game, Storm wanted to tell Charles that she had just gotten engaged by flashing her engagement ring. "Hannah got right in front of Chuck and said, 'Look, Chuck,' and was holding out her engagement ring," remembered Ric Bucher, who was covering the series for the *San Jose Mercury News*. "Without missing a beat, Chuck says, 'Damn, Hannah, that's the biggest piece of zirconia I've ever seen!'"

The joke brought a smile to Storm's face years later. It touched her that Charles could congratulate her in his own way before the most pivotal game of the season. "He definitely felt comfortable enough to say it. He's definitely a great teaser, but in the next breath, he said, 'Congratulations, that's great!'" she said. "It was pretty funny, but also typical of him."

On the court, Phoenix's adjustments had gotten the attention of Jordan, who believed having Johnson guard him was nothing more than a gimmick from Westphal, an attempt to make the Bulls star inadvertently take away shots from his teammates by being more aggressive. Jordan said as much to the point guard before the game: *You're guarding me? I thought you wanted to win Game 3.*

Throughout the course of Game 3, Westphal barked at his team to help Johnson by double-teaming Jordan and not letting him catch the ball.

"Michael is not beating us!" a hoarse Westphal yelled in the huddle.

As Jordan was taking the game into his own hands, Charles was laboring with the bulky elbow pad, picking his spots for flashes of brilliance. Tumbling to the floor after he was fouled by Jordan on a made lefty layup, Charles was slow to get up. The Suns found themselves up by 1. Jordan was rolling with 22 points on 10-of-16 shooting, while Charles had a quieter 9-point, 6-rebound effort on just 6 shots. Even with the lead and the encouraging play from Johnson, some thought little of Phoenix's chances.

"This series is over, Bob," Bill Walton told Costas during the game. "The Bulls have been playing the clock since the first quarter of Game 1."

While the offense continued to play through Charles, everyone else picked up the slack. Dumas and West, known more for their defense, gave them something real on the offensive end for the first time. Chambers and Ainge led a bench that had otherwise been quiet. But it was Johnson who made it his game, shooting over Armstrong and beating him off the dribble for a jumper or kicking out to an open man. It was the first time Jordan had to really work on both ends.

The Suns were clinging to a 1-point lead at the start of the fourth quarter. For as frustrated as Johnson had made Jordan to that point, the fourth had belonged to Michael in the first two games. But that didn't happen at all in Game 3. In fact, Jordan and the Bulls were flat-out bad, as he went 1-for-10 in the quarter and the Suns extended the lead to 11.

Yet Phoenix's habit of fourth-quarter droughts in the Finals continued. After going scoreless for six-minute stretches in the final quarter of Games 1 and 2, the Suns were in the middle of a dry spell reaching nearly four minutes. In the process, the Bulls clawed back, highlighted by Pippen passing the ball to himself off the back of Ainge for an easy slam. A Grant dunk and free throw off a Jordan assist had capped off a 13–2 run and tied it at 103.

With two seconds separating the game clock from the shot clock, the Bulls had a chance to seal the game. The ball was in Jordan's hands for not even two seconds until Johnson miraculously batted it away from him, the kind of mistake rarely seen from His Airness. Almost immediately, he fired it down the court to an open Majerle for what looked to be a fast-break dunk with twelve seconds left in regulation. That's what would have happened if not for Johnson calling for timeout right before he found Majerle. Westphal and Johnson could only smile knowing that the right decision in the moment negated what could have been the potential game-winning play.

Westphal wanted the final moments in Charles's hands. They drew up the same play that sent San Antonio packing in the second round: give the ball to Charles and get the hell out of his way. Receiving the ball near midcourt, Charles began to penetrate. Grant forced him to his left and he gave two more dribbles and a pump-fake. His shot bounced off the back iron with one second remaining. If not for Grant failing to convert a tip-in off a perfect inbounds pass from Pippen the Suns would've lost.

At the start of the overtime period, Phoenix's offense went flat. Luckily for them, the Bulls looked spent as well. A crafty left-handed layup by Chambers with fifty-one seconds left gave Phoenix its third and fourth points of the overtime, matching Chicago's low total. A missed turnaround jumper from Jordan offered another shot to effectively end it. Putting up a short jumper, Charles missed again, but Johnson rebounded and kicked it to Ainge for an open 3-pointer at the top of the key. He missed and time expired.

Down by 4 with forty seconds left in the second overtime, the Suns looked to be cooked. One Chicago fan in particular was so confident that a sign started to hang from the balcony of the arena: *Final Sunset Wednesday Chicago Stadium*. Then, Charles banged home a short baseline jumper over Grant. Once Pippen's shot was deflected on the other end, Charles grabbed the rebound and started Phoenix's last push with ten seconds to go. Johnson found Majerle at the 3-point line. He pump-faked Armstrong, stepped in two feet and calmly knocked down the eighteen-footer to tie it with three seconds left. Charles embraced his friend, slapping him on the butt for good measure. Out of the timeout, Kevin and Frank Johnson denied Jordan the ball, which put the final shot in the hands of Pippen. The short leaner was no good, and there would be another five minutes of ball.

"You kind of wondered if this was one of those 27-inning baseball games where you're still sitting there at 3:00 in the morning, waiting for something to happen," said Bulls center Will Perdue.

In the huddle, Charles did his best to keep everyone loose heading into the third overtime. KJ hadn't sat out for a single minute. Pippen, who had played more than fifty minutes to that point, lay on the floor, holding his left leg while it cramped up. Scotty Robertson, one of the Suns' assistants, had just two tips: rebound and give up your body for the ball.

As the second-ever triple overtime game in Finals history was about to resume, Westphal was having déjà vu back to the 1976 Finals. The coach was a player for the Phoenix team that had lost to the Boston Celtics in triple overtime in Game 5 of the Finals, a 128–126 classic that long remained a what-if for Suns fans. Cedric Ceballos, injured and in street clothes, wondered the same thing from the bench: "Is this 1976 all over again?"

Down 2 after a Jordan jumper, Charles passed out of the post to find Majerle at the top of the key for his sixth 3-pointer of the game, tying a Finals record. The shot also set a new Finals record for most team 3s in a game with nine. Seconds later, Majerle stole a loose ball from Pippen's hands. He found Johnson, who found a streaking Charles rumbling toward the bucket. The big man labored but was able to glide past Jordan and beat Pippen for the slam. The dunk was by no means his hardest or most athletically impressive, but the soft two-handed flush was undoubtedly the biggest of his career.

The most important dunk would be followed by his most crucial play of the Finals. A Chambers miss resulted in a long rebound along the baseline from Stacey King, Chicago's backup center. Before he could head back down the court to play defense, Charles stayed put in the backcourt for an extra half second. Not an adept ball handler, King was trying to get rid of the ball as soon as he could. Knowing this, Charles subtly moved his shoulders to the right before making a guess: the ball was coming to Jordan underneath the Chicago basket and he was going to steal it from King. He guessed right, lunging to his left and going up for the easy deuce that put the Suns up by 5 and all but sealed the game. Even with a swollen elbow, Charles raised both arms in celebration as the sold-out crowd looked on in horror.

"I knew he was going to try and pass it to Michael," Charles said. "I just took one step the other way, and went for the steal. I was at the right place at the right time."

Three hours and twenty minutes had come and gone before the Suns could call themselves the winners of Game 3, a 129–121 marathon victory that felt like a series' worth of games rolled into one.

"It was the greatest basketball game I ever played in," Charles said.

Charles wondered how the tale of Game 3 would age over time. He thought about how he'd tell it to his daughter, exaggerating the anecdote for the ages as if he were reading out of a children's book.

"Darlin', they said my career was over. I couldn't move that night," he said to reporters the morning after the game, mimicking the storytelling voice he'd give to Christiana. "What happened was, I had my arm ripped off in a tractor-trailer accident the night before the game. I had to have major surgery. They reattached my arm just before the game. The doctor said, 'Charles, you can't go out there. You could die.'… The doctor said, 'Please, Charles, please, don't do it!' 'Doc, I'm playing. That's all there is to it.'"

Jordan was looking to spill blood in Game 4, but Charles was enjoying himself in Chicago. Taking in a game at Wrigley Field with Frank Johnson, the Suns in the stands wearing Cubs hats were more interesting than the home team and the Marlins. Jeremy Roenick had seen this side of Charles before when he had come down to the Blackhawks locker room after a game the year before to find the "bad motherfucker" who played hockey like he played basketball. Roenick didn't expect Charles to join him and his wife at a nightclub called Excalibur when he was in town, but there was Charles, rolling in at 1:00 a.m. and shooting pool with his newfound hockey brother until the place shut down. That loose approach carried over to the mandatory media sessions, where Charles was in such a good mood that he had time to share with them his ear-piercing rendition of "Oh Baby Baby I Love You" by Smokey Robinson and The Miracles.

Despite having his elbow drained for the second consecutive game, Charles was visibly at ease before Game 4, crashing NBC's on-court pregame show as he was putting up shots in the layup line. In a sit-down interview with Costas earlier in the day, he took pleasure in being described by the NBC commentator as "the villain in some melodrama," someone people can't really dislike. Toward the end of the feature, Costas posed a statement to Charles he wanted to think about.

"Charles Barkley is a great, great player," Costas started, "but Michael Jordan is in a class by himself—clearly superior to anybody else in the league."

Judging by the long, hearty chuckle from Charles, you would have thought Costas was Jerry Seinfeld. He composed himself long enough for four words: "Have another drink, Bob."

"There was nobody quite like Charles. He threw his head back and laughed at me," Costas remembered. "At that time, he could not allow himself to believe he wasn't as good as Jordan."

Knowing Jordan would be playing with a chip on his shoulder, Westphal mixed up the defensive assignment, rotating a combination of Kevin Johnson, Majerle, and Dumas to get a crack at him. Yet he'd soon learn not much could stop Jordan on June 16, 1993.

"He inflicted his will on us," Westphal said of Jordan.

In the second quarter, with the teams deadlocked, Jordan looked as if he was going to drive every time he got his hands on the ball. On one play, Jordan took Majerle off the dribble to his left, met two defenders in the lane, hung in the air, double-clutched the ball with his right hand, and scooped the ball into the hoop while drawing contact from Ainge. Another play, Jordan blew by Majerle yet again on a crossover to his left, took one dribble and skied through the air with his right finishing on a flush. Looking helpless, Ainge was again called for the foul, unsuccessful in his contact stopping Jordan from scoring 2 of his 33 first-half points.

Even with Jordan's exploits—his 14 field goals tied an NBA Finals record for most in a half—Charles's 15 points and a trio of 3s from Majerle kept it a 3-point game heading into what would be a conten-tious second half. After three and a half games and three overtimes, tensions finally started to boil over between the teams. Coming over to pull up Johnson from the floor, Charles exchanged words with Pippen and bumped his stomach into him to get the small forward away from his teammate. One fan in particular who had gotten on Charles throughout the whole game was greeted by the star yelling through his mouthpiece, "Shut the fuck up, asshole!" Later in the quarter, B.J. Armstrong, irritated by Kevin Johnson for the entirety of the series, sent the point guard flying with a shove into the cameramen sitting on the baseline. Then, after Jordan inadvertently hit Ainge in the face, the Suns reserve ripped the ball out of his hands, leading His Airness to place his right index finger squarely on the lips of his adversary. Ainge had placed his hands on Jordan at different times of the game in hope of irritating the G.O.A.T. Any civility had gone out the door. The teams had to be separated and double technical fouls were assessed, but there was also a situation in the stands that needed attention.

Colangelo, who had returned to his hometown city for the Finals, took umbrage with a Bulls fan swearing at his eighty-year-old mother. When the owner demanded the fan apologize, Colangelo said the guy refused. He remembered that for later.

"He gave me the finger after the game, and I got in a punch before security stepped in," he recalled to *Sports Illustrated* in 2013. "I had a Chicago moment."

Phoenix avoided disaster by cutting the deficit from 13 to 5 to end the third quarter. Charles was on his way to a triple-double and he made it look easy, but they needed more. With a minute left, Johnson found a streaking Charles for the open dunk to pull them within 2. After Charles baited Pippen into throwing an errant pass, the Suns had a chance. That's what they thought, at least, until Johnson bobbled an inbounds pass from Ainge, resulting in Armstrong grabbing the ball out of the air. "The ball slipped out of my hands," Johnson said. "There was no real profound reason it happened."

Sixteen seconds remained and Jordan darted past Johnson at the 3-point line and did the same with Ainge, who was the safety defender behind his teammate. The last line of defense was Charles, stepping up in the lane and raising his arms up high against his friend, hoping for the best. Flying off his left foot, Jordan flung the ball up with his right hand, as his right knee collided with Charles's chest, which sent him flying to the floor. When the ball fell through the hoop, a stone-faced Jordan raised both arms in a look of stern glee and jogged to midcourt until Armstrong caught him with a hug. Kneeling under the basket, Charles, who had been called for the foul, buried his face in his hands, knowing the game had been lost.

"Don't take it personally, Charles!" a young fan yelled from the stands.

Scoring half of his team's points, Jordan dropped 55, tied for the second-highest total ever in a Finals game, en route to a 111–105 win for the Bulls. The masterful performance yet again overshadowed Charles's dominant triple-double on the bad elbow, going for 32 points, 12 rebounds, and 10 assists in forty-six minutes. Lionel Hollins, the Phoenix assistant, summed up the game with a common sentiment from the time.

"Charles was great, but Michael was better," he said.

Long before the Bulls were on the precipice of winning a third consecutive championship, the city prepared for the violence that followed.

The celebration following the first title in 1991 against the Lakers resulted in more than one hundred arrests and the looting of dozens of stores. City officials believed the actions of its citizens to be part of a trend that had begun in Detroit during the Pistons' back-to-back championships. After the Bulls won in 1992, despite an increased police presence on the streets and the city ordering bars to shut down early and serve drinks in plastic cups, more than 1,000 people were arrested, 340 businesses were looted and 107 officers were injured. The night of June 14, 1992, was remembered as much for the arsons and the bricks and rocks that were thrown at firefighters and police as it was for Jordan outshining Clyde Drexler.

In the off-day before Game 5, the city announced it had spent $1 million on police protection and public service announcements in hope of preventing the previous year's mayhem from repeating. "Michael Jordan and Charles Barkley are fierce competitors," Chicago mayor Richard Daley said at the time. "But as they leave the court, they respect one another. That's all we're asking for."

As part of the campaign, Jordan, Paxson, and Jackson begged in the PSAs for the fans to not tear up Chicago, as clips of the previous chaos played over their pleas.

"If we make it a three-peat on the court, let's not make it a repeat on the streets," Jordan said.

In the locker room, the board had said the same three-word phrase for the time in Chicago: *Win One Game*. Ahead of Game 5, however, Westphal updated it: *SAVE THE CITY*. Though there's some dispute over who came up with the line to save Chicago—Westphal said Charles stole it from him, while the MVP maintained he thought he uttered it first. No matter who said it, the Suns followed through on their vow. They staved off Chicago, 108–98. Another 41-point gem from Jordan wasn't enough.

"Ain't gonna be no riot in this town tonight!" Charles crowed, walking off the court with 24 points, 6 rebounds, and 6 assists. In the news conference that followed, Charles made Johnson cry in laughter in replying to a question about what message he'd like to send to the people of Chicago: "Take that shit off the windows! You don't need it tonight."

He was joined by Johnson's 25-point, 8-assist bounce-back performance, and the lights-out effort from Dumas, going for 25 points on 12-of-14 shooting while being primarily guarded by Pippen. Relieved knowing he had performed his civic duty in saving Chicago, Charles threw out another D-word he thought could match the dynasty his team was contending with: *Destiny*.

"I believe it is our destiny to win the world championship," he told NBC's Rashad. "God wants us to win the world championship. I talked to him the other night."

Seemingly nothing could get Charles down on June 20, 1993, especially when he was finally able to play golf on his healed elbow for the first time. Publicly, the Suns pointed out that they had nothing to lose.

"The place is going crazy. We get Game 6 and Game 7 at home," Majerle remembered upon returning to Phoenix. "We're going to win the NBA championship."

The thousands of fans that greeted the Suns at 2:30 in the morning at Sky Harbor International Airport also believed they could do it.

If the first quarter of Game 5 was Phoenix's best of the postseason, the same could be said of the opening period of Game 6 for Chicago, which went 6-of-7 from the 3-point line to take a 9-point lead after 1. Jordan's aggressiveness to the hoop on Majerle and Johnson opened up Armstrong to bomb away. Majerle's 13 in the quarter made up for the slow start from Charles.

The chase to catch Chicago and extend the season to Game 7 started with the Bulls in control in the second quarter. A KJ drive. An Ainge 3. A Chambers jumper. A pair of free throws from Miller. Two more free throws from Chambers had tied the game.

The frustrating half continued for Charles when he picked up his third foul late in the second quarter. "Fuck, fuck, fuck!" he yelled on the block in-between free throws from Armstrong. He found the NBC camera underneath the hoop and, through his mouthpiece, barked directly into the lens, "It's bullshit!"

The Bulls blitzed the Suns to the tune of a combined 17–4 run in the final minutes of the first two quarters. Down 56–51 at the half, Phoenix knew Chicago's blistering outside shooting couldn't continue. Although Jordan had 16 and was on his way to another dominant night, the Suns were again thrilled with their defense on him, not allowing a field goal in the second period against the league's best.

The second half was a four-on-four showcase: Jordan-Pippen-Grant-Armstrong versus Charles-Johnson-Majerle-Ainge. Whatever either team could get from anyone else was extra. Chambers proved to be the fifth man in a third quarter, rebounding, shooting, and even driving past Bulls defenders in a period in which Charles remained slow to get going.

Brian McIntyre, the NBA's director of public relations, bet that the Bulls would close out and ordered NBC to start setting up their locker room for the championship celebration. Then, something happened: The Bulls stalled out. Jordan missed. Pippen missed. Cartwright had his shot blocked. A shot-clock violation on Pippen. Grant missed. In fact, they started the quarter 0-for-9 and the fatigue was more visible than ever during a dry spell of more than six minutes.

Still attracting double-teams, Charles bullied through Grant and Cartwright on his way to the hoop, tumbling to the court but popping himself back up quickly. He went to work on Williams, pump-faking and diving to the hoop for the one-handed scoop to tie the game. A Majerle 3 the next time down brought the city to its feet and gave the Suns the lead. A pair of Jordan jumpers signaled he was heating up, but it came in a quarter in which no other Bull had scored.

Up 98-94 with under a minute to go and possession of the ball, the Suns could see the light at the end of the tunnel. Charles had grabbed his 17th rebound of the game and was able to call timeout just as he was falling backward and in danger of going out-of-bounds.

Out of the timeout, Ainge curled off a screen for a long 2, and the collapsing Chicago defense forced the guard to swing the ball to Frank Johnson. He had an open seventeen-footer and a chance to seal the game, but it clanged off the rim and Jordan collected the rebound and was going the other way with forty-five seconds left. It took all of six dribbles and seven seconds for Jordan, with his tongue fully extended, to get a bucket after going untouched for ninety-four feet.

"They were so dominant in the last five minutes of games defensively, it was really hard to get a quality look on them," Ainge recalled in 2020. "Chicago was very smart defensively and they dictated who they wanted to let shoot."

The Suns up 98—96, Ainge fed the ball to Charles, desperate for a dagger. As Pippen came over to help Grant, Charles zinged it to an open Frank Johnson, who immediately swung it to Majerle, who then gave it back to Frank Johnson with the shot clock running down. After hot-potatoing it back to Majerle, the reliable shooter air-balled it into Pippen's hands as the shot clock expired. Timeout Chicago.

"We couldn't score a bucket," Hollins remembered of the Suns missing 6-of-7 shots in the final minutes. "We just couldn't do anything."

Not shooting out of the double-team in the last minute was an instant regret for Charles. He had taken the game out of his own hands.

"If we lose," he thought, "I want to lose it for us."

In the huddle, Majerle, Ainge, and West told themselves and their teammates, "No 3s, no 3s."

To this day, Jackson still doesn't know why the play he called for had the name it did: "The Blind Pig." Designed to break down a frontline's pressure defense, the set called for every player to touch the ball and spread the floor. This time, Jackson added a new wrinkle to running the triangle offense staple. Instead of taking the ball out at the usually preferred midcourt, the coach wanted his team to take it out from in front of their bench. Putting the ball in Jordan's hands that far away from the hoop would give the play the extra "thrust" needed to break down the Phoenix defense.

"The whole idea of the play was for B.J. and myself to space the floor and to get Michael in the backcourt with a running start," Paxson told *Sports Illustrated*.

Charles lightly shoved Pippen and spit some last-minute shit-talking to his fellow Dream Teamer as the crowd chanted, "Let's go Suns."

Jordan inbounded the ball to Armstrong, who passed it back to him. Guarded by Johnson, Jordan took two dribbles to his left before going behind his back, his tongue fully extended. He made one more dribble before swinging the ball across his chest. He'd find Pippen, who had flashed up from the low block to almost midcourt to receive the pass. Charles said he knew Jordan was going to get the ball back and made a split-second decision: he was going to try to jump the play to go for a steal. "I think if Scottie takes a two and makes it, it's still better than that damn Michael having it," he said.

It's a decision that would have paid off if Charles had gotten his big hands on the ball. But when he failed to make the steal, the quicker, more athletic Pippen turned to the hoop and left Charles running after him, setting off a defensive breakdown on the floor and panic in the stands over the questionable decision. Ainge rotated off his man to help defend Pippen and Charles flailed at the ball, hoping to swat it away or at least foul. Charles was again a millisecond too late. Pippen zinged the ball to his left to find Grant for what looked like an easy catch-and-shoot attempt from the baseline. Except Grant, in the middle of another woeful offensive performance, had no intentions of shooting and didn't hold on to the ball for more than tenths of a second. He knew Ainge would foul him and send him to the line. Grant wanted no part of that.

Ainge's rotation still surprised his teammates twenty years later in interviews with *Sports Illustrated*.

"The so-called smartest guy on the team, Danny, leaves his man," Johnson said.

"I don't want to rag on Danny. Instinct takes over," said Majerle.

When Paxson put up the shot, the thousands in attendance let out

Charles goes up for a dunk during a home game against the University of Georgia.
Photo Credit: R+r Sports Group/Sporting News Archive/Getty Images

Charles Barkley sits on his doorstep at Auburn University and eats a slice of pizza in a circa 1980s photo.

Photo Credit: Focus on Sport/Getty Images

Charles talks to John Glenn, a former astronaut and US senator, after a home game against Mississippi State University on March 2, 1984.

Photo Credit: George Tiedemann/*Sports Illustrated*/Getty Images

NBA commissioner David Stern, left, shakes Charles's hand after the forward was drafted fifth by the Philadelphia 76ers at the NBA Draft on June 19, 1984, in New York City.

Photo Credit: AP Images/Marty Lederhandler

Charles is upset with a call during Game 5 of the 1985 Eastern Conference Finals against the Boston Celtics at Boston Garden on May 22, 1985.

Photo Credit: Manny Millan/ *Sports Illustrated*/Getty Images

Charles poses and smiles for this photo, circa mid-1980s.

Photo Credit: Focus On Sport/ Getty Images

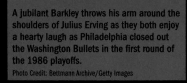

Charles just as he's about to shoot a free throw for the 76ers.

Photo Credit: Bettmann Archive/ Getty Images

Charles and his attorney Thomas Halloran, left, hold their heads down as they listen to the verdict that Charles was found not guilty on battery and disorderly conduct in his trial in Milwaukee on June 16, 1992.

Photo Credit: AP Images/Neal Lambert

Team USA's Larry Bird, left, and Charles relax on the sidelines toward the end of the July, 31, 1992, Olympic game against Brazil in Barcelona, in which Barkley scored 30 points.

Photo Credit: AP Images/Susan Ragan

John Stockton, Chris Mullin, and Charles rejoice with their gold medals after beating Croatia 117-85 in the gold medal game in men's basketball at the Summer Olympics in Barcelona on August 8, 1992.

Photo Credit: AP Images/John Gaps III

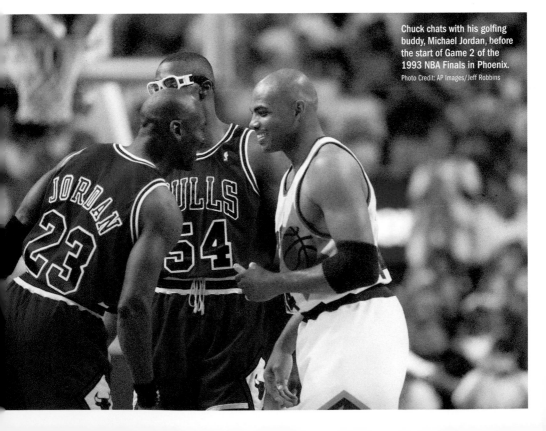

NBA commissioner David Stern presents the MVP trophy to Charles before his Phoenix Suns go up against the Seattle SuperSonics in Game 1 of the 1993 Western Conference Finals on May 24, 1993.

Photo Credit: John W. McDonough/*Sports Illustrated*/Getty Images

Chuck chats with his golfing buddy, Michael Jordan, before the start of Game 2 of the 1993 NBA Finals in Phoenix.

Photo Credit: AP Images/Jeff Robbins

Charles pulls in a rebound over Horace Grant and Scottie Pippen of the Chicago Bulls during Game 3 of the 1993 NBA Finals in Chicago.

Photo Credit: AP Images/John Swart

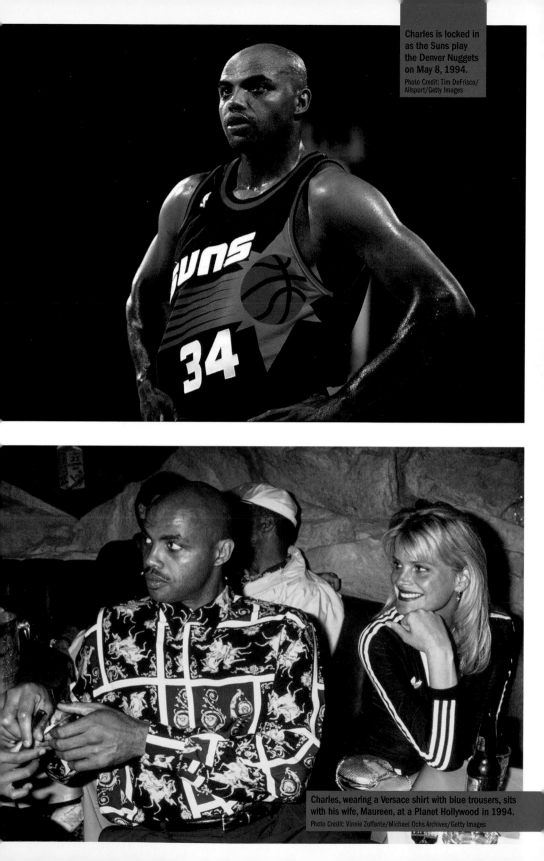

Charles laughs at a foul call with Jordan in the first half of a January 28, 1996, game at the United Center in Chicago.
Photo Credit: Brian Bahr/AFP/Getty Images

Barkley and Pippen of the Houston Rockets share a rare laugh during a game against the Sacramento Kings on February 10, 1999.
Photo Credit: The Sporting News/Getty Images

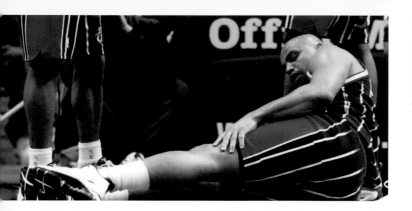

Charles holds his left leg eight minutes into his final game in Philadelphia on December 8, 1999.

Charles is joined by his daughter, Christiana, eleven, and wife Maureen as they watch his number get retired during a Philadelphia 76ers game on March 30, 2001.

Tiger Woods is interviewed by Chuck, his friend, following a news conference for the PGA Grand Slam of Golf at the Poipu Bay Golf Course on November 25, 2002, in Kauai, Hawaii.
Photo Credit: Jamie Squire/Getty Images

Charles Barkley makes his remarks at a September 2006 ceremony marking his enshrinement into the Naismith Memorial Basketball Hall of Fame in Springfield, Massachusetts. Barkley was presented for enshrinement by former Philadelphia teammate Moses Malone, left, and Jerry Colangelo, then owner of the Phoenix Suns.
Photo Credit: AP Imagesw/Stephan Savoia

Referee Dick Bavetta, right, and Chuck both take a tumble during the Bavetta/Barkley Challenge during NBA All-Star Weekend in Las Vegas on February 17, 2007.
Photo Credit: AP Images/Mark J. Terrill

Charcey Glenn dances as her son watches the 3A state championship high school basketball game in Birmingham, Alabama, on February 28, 2009.
Photo Credit: AP Images/Mark Almond/AL.com via AP

Charles tees off on the first hole during the pro-am of the Regions Charity Classic at
the Robert Trent Jones Golf Trail at Ross Bridge in Birmingham, Alabama, on May 14, 2009.

Shaquille O'Neal, Ernie Johnson, Kenny Smith, and Charles of *Inside the NBA* speak onstage at the Hammerstein Ballroom to tip-off the 2015 NBA All-Star Weekend in New York City.

Photo Credit: Stephen Lovekin/Getty Images for American Express

O'Neal, Johnson, Smith and Chuck speak at the NBA Awards on June 25, 2018, at the Barker Hangar in Santa Monica, California.

Photo Credit: Chris Pizzello/Invision/AP

Charles looks at a sculpture honoring him during its unveiling at the
Philadelphia 76ers' training facility in Camden, New Jersey, on September 13, 2019.

Photo Credit: AP Images/Matt Rourke

a collective shriek of despair. Westphal could only hold his breath knowing that his team was at the mercy of this ball.

"It seemed like it took an hour to get to the basket," the coach recounted. "And every second of the flight path, I remember thinking, 'I really hope he misses, but dang, that looks like it's going in.'"

Ainge was thinking the same. "I just went, 'Please miss! Please miss!'" he said.

The ball fell through the hoop with 3.9 seconds remaining and the Suns were down by one. The biggest shot of the season hadn't come from Jordan.

Fearing the season would end soon, "Sirius" played in a last-ditch attempt to get the crowd back in the game. On TV, Mike Fratello guessed that the Suns would look to find Charles at the top of the key. In reality, Charles said they wanted to get it to anyone who was open. When Kevin Johnson inbounded the ball to Miller from above the 3-point line, the rookie center dished it back and set a screen to force the switch on the much larger Grant. Charles looked to have a mismatch and was eyeing to post up the skinnier Pippen. But just as Johnson went up for a running fifteen-footer from about the free throw line with one second to go, Grant, who looked to have gotten beat off the dribble, came from behind, leaped and rejected the shot.

As the Chicago bench ran onto the floor, Charles began a slow walk to the locker room. The final score was 99–98, and he didn't come close to touching the ball on the final play. For the third time in four seasons, Charles would hug his tormentors from Chicago as his season came to a close. He found Pippen for a message of congratulations. He'd do the same with Jordan, who draped his arm around Charles's neck while he whispered something into his ear.

"For it to be over so quickly, that's the thing. You do something for six, seven, eight months and then it's over. In one quick jumper. Just like that," Charles said. "It's hard to take."

"By the way, how am I getting to Disney World?" he asked facetiously to the camera, days after he was asked if he could say the line—win or lose. "I ain't paying my own way."

23

The question posed to Charles on the comedy show was blunt: Are you happy?

He had millions of adoring fans, traveled all over the world, got paid an unreal amount of money to do commercials for Nike, played golf in Hawaii, and was set for life. But in his blond wig, blue sweater, and pastel yellow–collared shirt, Stuart Smalley, a caring nurturer and member of several twelve-step programs who was not a licensed therapist, followed up again if all that made him happy.

"Yeah, and the fact that I'm the best basketball player in the world," said Charles in his checkered suit and black turtleneck. "There is nobody better."

Looking down and playing with his hands, Smalley, played by *Saturday Night Live* cast member and writer Al Franken, saw an opening.

"So, I guess since, you know, you're the best basketball player in the world, then I guess you won a lot of championships then?" the self-help guru asked, eliciting oohs and aahs to go along with the laughter that filled Studio 8H in New York.

"Well," began a grinning Charles, "actually, I never won the championship."

Smalley, biting his lip and offering only a "hmm," dug into the heart of the issue that played out months before: "And Charles, how do you *feel* about not having won a championship?" He'd tell the host of "Daily Affirmation" that he was fine and not winning a title was "no big deal," but Smalley dug in.

"I guess Cleopatra isn't the only queen of De-Nial," he quipped to the faux-angry Charles.

Before the jokes on *SNL* came the affirmation from thousands of fans who appreciated Charles for almost winning a championship.

To this day, he jokingly says he doesn't know if the parade of three hundred thousand for an NBA Finals loser actually happened. That's because he didn't make it more than a block before he had to escape from the waves of people who showed up hours before and baked in the 114-degree heat just to try to get a glimpse of their almost conquering hero.

"I don't think the fans realize that we didn't win," he mused.

Riding in the back of a blue Ford Cobra convertible, Charles's car, the last one in the parade, couldn't move any further once it hit 2nd Street. The car had accidentally run over a police officer's foot, and the cop's partner pounded on the vehicle and smashed the windshield in order to stop it from moving, said George Bevans, the team's head of security. "As soon as Charles turned around the corner, they swamped him," Bevans said. "When the car stopped, that's when the people converged."

John Bloom never played football growing up, but when the time came for the team's assistant head of security to create a hole for Charles to run through to escape the crowd, he plowed through fans until they made it to the America West Arena. Once inside, Charles and the security team could laugh at almost being crushed by a sea of humanity.

"It was kind of fun, but it was kind of crazy," Charles recalled.

He joined owner Jerry Colangelo in his arena office, as the MVP sipped on a soda and overlooked a city that had rallied for a team that came up short. Following the loudest ovation of the day, Charles took the mic and explained to the understanding throngs why he had abandoned the parade only a block into his route. The loss was still raw, but it wasn't so tender that he couldn't make a promise to those who believed in him and the team.

"I want y'all to know we never expected this many people to show up today," Charles said to the roaring crowd. "We didn't come here to be runners-up. Wait till next year."

But first, he needed some rest. It was a summer of blissful inactivity for Charles, who had gone from the start of the 1991–92 season through the end of the 1993 Finals without much of a break. He wouldn't pick up a basketball for months, opting for golfing, fishing, shooting some commercials and movies, and time with Christiana. He'd also find his way back to Leeds in August 1993 for the town's "Charles Barkley Day," which had him signing autographs and refereeing a basketball game in celebration of his life-changing year.

"Can you believe it?" Charcey said of how her once undersized baby had now taken over the world.

If her son hadn't already become a towering presence in the early part of the decade, he was about to step foot into an arena where few athletes had gone before and fewer had succeeded.

Michael Jordan had stared into a mirror and tried not to laugh as he repeated the lines of daily affirmation from Smalley in front of a raucous *SNL* crowd in 1991. You know, in case Jordan had any lingering self-doubt: "Because I'm good enough, I'm smart enough, and doggonit, people like me."

Now it was Charles's turn to host the iconic show's season premiere in September 1993. Since quarterback Fran Tarkenton became the first athlete to host the show in 1977, there had been a rich history of athlete hosts, though to mixed success. For every Bob Uecker that thrived, there was a George Steinbrenner or Joe Montana that proved to be less than memorable. As the seventeenth person from the sports world to host *SNL*, Charles had a legitimate chance to be the funniest of the bunch since O.J. Simpson in 1978. He'd also be the first athlete to host since Jordan's turn in 1991, leading to yet a different kind of comparison between the Finals friends.

Although it was Charles's first time hosting, expectations were notably high considering he had been a bankable guest for the late-night shows. "You couldn't find another person like him on television. When you said his name, people smiled," said Larry King. "My God, what a thing to have." Charles could make David Letterman laugh at how he would have considered going back to school if he weren't so loaded.

For Jay Leno, it was the quickness of their exchanges. Leno valued Charles's authenticity and speed of his back-and-forths. "Charles Barkley was one of my all-time favorite guests on *The Tonight Show*," Leno said. "Charles was always prepared with great stories, and we always enjoyed having him."

Conan O'Brien lauded him for his wit, timing, and a great deadpan—as well as eyebrows that the comedian considers to be one of Charles's secret weapons: "When he trains those eyebrows on you and he gives you that very fierce look he has, it adds to the comedy of what he's saying."

Hosting *SNL*, however, would be a different animal than spending a few minutes on a late-night couch. *SNL* wanted a part of him at a time when some critics were saying the shows had fallen flat creatively. Eric Mink of the *New York Daily News*, noted that even the celebrated political sketches of the eighteenth season had been "mostly exercises in bloodless, if often hilarious, mimicry aided by makeup wizardry, rather than cutting political satire."

In his first week as a writer on *SNL*, Jay Mohr didn't bring any ideas with him into Lorne Michaels's office on September 20, 1993. For Mohr, who had come to the show after serving as host of the MTV lip-sync show *Lip Service*, this was trouble. As he wrote in his 2004 memoir *Gasping for Airtime*, Mohr was struggling to come up with anything when the likes of Franken and Adam Sandler were pitching Charles around the semicircle. Sandler, a hoops junkie, immediately gravitated to Charles. The same went for David Spade, and especially for Chris Farley, who Charles was equally fond of. Charles, for his part, captivated the cast.

"If there were ten great comedians in a room and Barkley came in the room and started telling a story, every comedian would stop talking and listen to Barkley and be happiest to hear him tell a story," Sandler recalled. "When he was sitting at the front of the table for the read-through at *SNL*, anything he said made us happy and laugh—

and how great it was when he laughed. Anytime Barkley laughed that week, we were like little kids thinking, 'Okay, I think Charles likes us.'"

A couple of the group's initial pitches fell flat, and Mohr feared that he was about to face a similar fate. He remembered one idea from writer Tom Davis in which he proposed that Charles tap-dance in an ad for Kentucky Fried Chicken. Charles brushed it off with a frosty one-word reply: *What?*

"Even if my idea—the one I had not yet conceived—sucked," Mohr wrote, "at least it wouldn't be as bad as Charles Barkley tap-dancing for chicken."

His lack of acting experience aside, the Barkley bravado was alive and well throughout rehearsals. Wally Feresten was admittedly in way over his head in his first weeks as the head cue card guy for the show. But as Charles would soon figure out, Feresten had a high threshold for stress, as well as the frequent jokes made about his hair.

"What I remember clearly from that first show is he constantly made fun of my hair. I had short spiky hair, I was twenty-eight, and it was something he locked on to," Feresten recalled. "Whenever he was standing around during rehearsal, he made fun of my hair. It got to the point that he did it so often that I would say, 'Hey, at least I have hair.' He would respond with, 'I'm bald, but if I had hair, I would not want hair like yours.' It was all good-natured, testing me to see if I could take the ribbing."

But Charles wasn't the only NBA player to grace the *SNL* stage that week. The show had brought on Muggsy Bogues, the league's five-foot-three fan favorite, to serve as both a foil and familiar face. Bogues remembered Charles being nervous in rehearsal. Bogues said Franken offered advice.

"It was all so off-the-cuff and the guy who played Stuart Smalley told him to loosen up and just be himself, 'Be Charles Barkley, the outspoken guy,'" Bogues said. "He had this look on his face and said, 'What are you trying to say, Al?'"

While Charles dominated the year in sports, there was no bigger act in the world than Nirvana. In two years, Nirvana had become a cultural phenomenon from the commercial and critical success of the band's 1991 album *Nevermind*, a rock and punk masterpiece that elevated grunge culture to new heights among young people. Through the album, considered one of the most acclaimed in the history of music, Nirvana would be the soundtrack to a generation of disaffected and cynical teens looking for someone or something to put into words what they were going through.

Some of the controversy that found the band unfolded at *SNL*. They had grown tired of people who were latching on to them due to their fame. They were even more uncomfortable when their song "Smells Like Teen Spirit" drew comparisons to Guns N' Roses, whose views on sexuality, race, and gender were at odds with their own. These concerns came to the forefront during the end credits of Nirvana's first appearance on the show in 1992. As host Rob Morrow wrapped up the show, the trio could be seen French-kissing each other in an effort to, as they later described it, "piss off the rednecks and the homophobes." The kisses caused such an uproar that *SNL* refused to air the clip in rebroadcasts of the episode. Even with all that, Nirvana would be the first band in the history of *SNL* to perform for a second time.

"We weren't trying to be subversive or punk rock," Nirvana's Kurt Cobain said of kissing his bandmates. "We were just doing something insane and stupid at the last minute."

Charles didn't know anything about Nirvana, but considered them to be nice dudes. He couldn't help but point out the unlikely pairing in his own way. Only on the *Saturday Night Live* stage could a Black basketball player who went from the projects of Alabama to being one of the most recognizable athletes in the world share the stage with the White alternative rockers from the Pacific Northwest that became the defining band of a generation.

"Knew about 'em in my neighborhood when I was growing up," he joked of Nirvana.

In recording a promo for that week's show, Charles, wearing a checkered blazer and wide smile, stood in the middle of the group as if he were their long-lost bandmate. Standing at six-foot-seven, bassist Krist Novoselic was slightly taller than Charles. The host had his hand on the right shoulder of drummer Dave Grohl, who blinked so much that he looked as if he was trying to send a distress signal into the camera. Charles playfully pointed out to his mother in the promo that her son was with her "favorite" band, and Kurt Cobain put on an awkward smile to appease Charcey, as well as all the other moms who thought they had found their inner-punk from listening once to *Nevermind*.

In another take, a grinning Grohl looked less like a hostage and more like a guy who just met his dealer at a music festival. "I'm not a role model, and these guys *really* aren't role models!" Charles pronounced, which made Cobain laugh at both the player's ridiculousness and the statement's truth.

With the *SNL* dressing rooms virtually on top of each other, Charles kept the door open to allow his friends and family to come in and out. In doing so, he started to feel for himself how the musical guests were spending their downtime three feet across the hall from him.

"Every time those guys from Nirvana opened up their door, I got like a contact high," Charles recalled. "It was like one of those big mushroom clouds came. I was scared to go to the airport... 'Do not go to the airport!'"

Whether the smoke from the ganja had anything to do with the stacks of food the production assistants brought him on set was unclear, said David Mandel, an *SNL* writer at the time. What was more obvious was that Charles was not going to step onstage in front of a live audience on an empty stomach.

"God bless him," Mandel said. "He ate a lot."

The booming baritone pipes of legendary announcer Don Pardo filled the room as Charles walked through the door, guessing that he—"one of the few non-Jewish players in the league"—wasn't the show's first choice to host.

"They did want someone from the NBA," he told the audience in his monologue, "but being Yom Kippur and all, I was the only one they could get."

In his monologue, Charles reflected on a recent game of one-on-one he had with another popular dinosaur who wanted a piece of him: Barney. In take after take, Charles pummeled Tim Gallin, the stuntman hired to wear the Barney suit. At one point, Charles elbowed Gallin so hard to the face that he knocked off Barney's head from his body. Gallin loved it.

"I was an independent contractor getting my ass kicked, but he was concerned he was going to hurt me," Gallin recounted. "He would help me up off the floor by saying, 'Hey, man, you cool?' He was very appreciative of what I was doing."

Next up was the trip to the couch. On "Daily Affirmation," "Charles B." of the "Phoenix S's," nicknames used by the sensitive shrink to protect his guest's identity, gathered that Smalley, recovering from Overeaters Anonymous, was pretty messed up. Charles was taken off guard when Bogues, referred to as "Muggsy B.," arrived to confront his friend about how his self-esteem was suffering from not living up to his own unrealistic expectations. In the sketch, Charles didn't take too kindly to seeing Bogues, whom he jokingly called "an ugly midget." Smalley and Bogues hoped to cut through Charles's brash ego and get to know his more sensitive side.

"I know how badly you wanted to beat the Bulls," Bogues said to Charles, who was about ready to crack up on national TV due to his friend's monotone delivery.

"Look at Charles. Look at him," said Smalley. "Muggsy, look at Charles. Charles, look at Muggsy."

Charles collapsed his face into his hand in an attempt to stifle laughter, almost causing Franken to also break. On-screen, Charles made his greatest professional disappointment the butt of a joke he was in on and encouraged.

The fake-crying Charles played it up as the studio audience went nuts. Franken was effusive of the pair's performance many years later, saying they played off each other so well not because of practice but due to their natural timing and recognition of the scene.

Charles introduced Nirvana's "Heart-Shaped Box" before a forty-second appearance in a "Gap Girls" sketch with Sandler, Farley, and Spade. All portraying women characters, the cast members discussed Lucy, Sandler's character, kissing a girl the night before during a game of truth or dare. Much to their surprise, the woman Lucy spoke of was at the Gap—and she was a sight to see. The towering Akeela was in a dark floral dress with long braids whose makeup hid a dark mustache. Charles's Akeela flirted a bit with Spade's Christy, comparing her to Sharon Stone, before guaranteeing to buy her a free sample down at Hickory Farms.

"He looked more beautiful than all of us," Sandler said with a laugh.

It would take seventeen years, but Charles was asked back to host *SNL* for a second time, and he crushed it again. He joked in his monologue about the lack of Black people who've hosted the show. He took mace to the eyes of Will Forte's iconic character MacGruber, who claimed he had gone through racial sensitivity training. As an overmatched contestant on a movie quote game show, he guessed that Jack Nicholson's legendary line from *A Few Good Men* was, "You can't handle *my privates!*" Teaming up with Kenan Thompson in "Scared Straight," Charles used the famous scene from the movie *Jerry Maguire* to outline how trespassing was the gateway misdemeanor that led to, well, bodily fluids in prison. "He won't say, 'Show me the money!'" Charles's character barked at cast member Bill Hader. "He'll say, 'Blow me for free!'"

"Charles just *is* funny," said Kristen Wiig, a cast member on the show between 2005 and 2012. "There's an earnestness, innocence, and true dedication to what he does on the show."

The encore in January 2010, or the two other repeat performances, wouldn't have been possible without his performance in September 1993. James Andrew Miller, the *SNL* historian and author of *Live From New York*, believed the show opened Charles to a new audience of people that couldn't care less how many rebounds he averaged. Instead, he was the guy who beat up Barney and dressed up as a Gap Girl.

"He wasn't trying to be anyone who he isn't, and didn't try to adopt a different persona," Miller said. "That genuine quality is something the *SNL* audience can appreciate."

By the end of the show, Charles, standing on stage next to Ru-Paul and with his arms around Bogues and Cobain, had conquered *SNL* and had cemented his place in '90s royalty.

"We were out of our comfort zone," Bogues recounted, "but he did it."

The episode would eventually take on a much heavier legacy. A little more than six months later, Cobain's body was discovered by an electrician who had arrived at his Seattle home to install a security system. Cobain had killed himself. He was twenty-seven years old. The *SNL* appearance with Charles was one of Nirvana's final performances on national television.

Charles's first turn hosting *SNL* was immediately deemed a success. Critics were surprised that he had "acquitted himself reasonably well" as host. The overnight Nielsen ratings saw the season premiere pull in a 9.9, good for nearly five million homes included in the survey. In Phoenix alone, more than half of the available audience tuned in to see their adopted son under the New York lights. David Casstevens wrote in the *Arizona Republic* that Charles was the perfect choice to host the show as his personality—irreverent and topical, unpredictable, and popular—represented "all the things *SNL* tries to be."

The say-whatever-is-on-his-mind star was now a legitimate crossover sensation who proved he could be great at ventures outside of basketball. There was one item he still had to achieve—and a Chicago-sized hole was about to give him his best chance to finally do it.

24

Lying stomach down after tumbling to the court twenty feet into a wind sprint, Charles no longer felt indestructible. Instead, he was scared and nervous. The thirty-year-old knew that his body was failing him.

The impromptu race on a Saturday evening at training camp in Flagstaff was against Byron Wilson, the last pick of the draft who was fighting for a spot on the team. Seeing the rookie point guard from Utah sprinting back and forth following the two-hour practice, Charles seized the chance to engage with him.

After running the length of the floor and touching the baseline underneath the basket, Charles looked uncharacteristically uncoordinated as he crashed to the hardwood. Danny Ainge joked that Charles was suffering a heart attack and needed mouth-to-mouth resuscitation. But what looked like a smile of embarrassment from afar was actually a grimace. By the time team physician Richard Emerson arrived from the Suns' hotel, Charles felt momentary numbness in the lower part of his body, and the mood in the gym turned anxious.

"I couldn't move my legs at all," he said. "It was like my legs started going into the floor. I couldn't lift my feet. This is the first time anything like this has happened to me."

It wasn't, however, the first time he had dealt with questionable health in recent weeks. Unbeknownst to many that summer, an MRI that August showed that Charles had a bulging disk that wasn't getting any better. His hamstrings, tender all throughout the Finals, made the lightest jogs and gentlest workouts deeply painful.

An injection eased his trauma so that he could get ready for the season, but by fall the pain was unbearable. The numbness was persistent and getting out of bed each morning had become a challenge.

No matter what happened during the 1993–94 season, Charles promised that he was "99.9 percent sure" it would be his last, regardless of whether he won a championship. "I know my back's not going to get better, and the more I keep playing and playing, the more it's going to hurt me down the line," he said. The prediction over a conference call with reporters was largely brushed off by the media as a joke. Teammates and coaches chalked it up to "Charles being Charles."

If the physical agony was at the front of his mind, the increased expectations following the news that rocked the sports world days earlier wasn't far behind. Michael Jordan, his brother and tormentor, had announced his retirement. Though Jordan had hinted at potentially stepping away, it was the death of his father, James Jordan Sr., who was murdered while napping in his car on July 23, 1993, that drove him to leave. Charles was there for his friend, supporting him in interviews and even filling in for him as host at his celebrity golf tournament that summer in Chicago.

From a basketball perspective, another narrative was forming: Charles was now the NBA's top dog. He was becoming Nike's, too. "The Charles Barkley Show," a running series of Nike ads, had the MVP falling from the sky to escape Dr. Joyce Brothers saying he was a role model. In another he bickers with Jordan like an old married couple of which of their shoes was superior. It was Nike's way of passing the baton to its greatest active player.

The buzz reached a new height in late 1993. You could dominate as Charles in his Sega Genesis streetball game *Barkley Shut Up and Jam!* in the morning, go see him make a cameo in *Look Who's Talking Now* in the afternoon and watch him on the Suns at night. While the video game, a foil to the popular *NBA Jam* series, was given relatively positive marks, the film bombed and was panned by critics. Gene Siskel gave zero stars to the "abysmal, embarrassing sequel," but Charles's appearance as himself, in which he goes one-on-one with toddler Julie, who carries around a Barkley buddy doll day and night, was a fun spot in an otherwise dreadful movie. "I'm always surprised by his cameo in that movie. It's such a strange thing," pondered Conan O'Brien. "I don't know how thoroughly involved Charles was, but we'd love to know why he was there and for him to break down that decision for us all."

Questionable movie decisions aside, everything was turning up Charles—and it was evident on the court. Jordan's departure signaled to many that the Suns would be the natural successors to the throne, a team that had come within two wins of a title destined to complete its mission. A second MVP was in play as well. That is, if Charles could stay healthy.

The Suns basically ran back the roster from the previous year, and the city's love for the team had only intensified. As the public wanted more of Charles, he made it a point to pull back from the social scene, if only a little. Part of that came from a home life that had become more stable after he and Maureen had reconciled. No more rumblings of dating a cheerleader or tabloids involving Madonna. It was all about Mo. He bragged about her cooking as a reason why he didn't feel the need to go out to dinner and expose himself. One day in the kitchen, she was peeling potatoes, which Charles maintained to be a real vegetable, noting that he preferred potatoes and creamed corn and that was it. Not a single green vegetable to be devoured by Charles.

Their relationship had rebounded, and the couple was in a good place. During a dinner with Nike executive Liz Dolan in Munich as part of an exhibition tournament, the couple could even laugh about the time Maureen found another woman's clothes in Charles's closet—and proceeded to throw all of the garments out the window.

"They're both telling this story, and they made it clear that things were not always easy between them, but that they loved each other," Dolan said.

It was family that made the idea of retiring after the 1993–94 season attractive to Charles. He wanted to see Christiana grow up, knowing his increased celebrity had limited his time with his only child, which he worried would hinder their relationship as she grew up. Keeping Christiana in Philadelphia so that she wouldn't have to live out of a hotel in Phoenix was the right move, but the distance had worn on him. In potentially stepping away at the age of thirty-one, he would run toward the somewhat normal life that was always far out of reach, one that involved family, sleeping in, and playing golf whenever he wanted. But it was about something else: Sir Charles was still trying to understand who Charles Wade Barkley was.

"I look forward to the time where I can spend a lot of time with her, and spend some time with myself and get to know myself better. This life is very confusing," he said. "I look forward to the day I can get some time with myself."

Life wasn't the only thing that was confusing. So was Charles's golf swing.

There are many ways to describe it. Jordan, once a regular golfing partner, diagnosed Charles as having "a sickness." *Philadelphia Magazine* declared it to be "a type of linksland Tourette's, all stopping and starting and stuttering and sputtering." Jason Sudeikis, playing golf instructor Hank Haney, one of Charles's many teachers, on *SNL*, compared it to someone who had a heart attack midswing, but who miraculously recovered. Internet posters have wisely observed that Charles looked like "a man in a closet trying to kill a snake with a broom." Swing coach Butch Harmon advised him, in jest, to take a break for two weeks before quitting the game altogether. Golfer Bryson DeChambeau agreed years later, adding that smoking cigars inside his car would be healthier for Charles than swinging the clubs.

Or, if you're looking for something more definitive, it's been called the worst golf swing on earth.

"God took this guy and gave him this incredibly embarrassing, humiliating, debilitating golf swing," said Rick Reilly, the former *Sports Illustrated* writer and longtime golf enthusiast. "There's no way a guy who is this good at everything else should suffer with this golf swing."

Years of attention amounted to what has to be the most scrutinized, clowned, and recognizable golf swing of anyone who is not a professional golfer, maybe ever. To date, YouTube videos of Charles's swing, of which there are many, have tallied over ten million views, a conservative estimate of those who've witnessed the carnage. "Damn," he once mumbled to Haney. "I'm all over the Internet." Hours of television programming have been dedicated to solving the swing. Tiger Woods spoofed the swing as part of his best-selling video game. The largest galleries at tournaments featuring Charles were there to follow someone who was regularly playing to not finish in last place. A select few in those crowds have been struck by his shots. The motion alone has become more identifiable to the non-golf fan than most of the professionals making a living on the PGA Tour.

"All men will die, all rivers will dry, and all mountains will crumble," wrote *Philadelphia Inquirer* columnist Bob Ford. "Charles Barkley's regrettable golf swing, however, will live forever."

Everyone has a golf story about Charles, like Syracuse coach Jim Boeheim, who remembers how Chuck would launch his clubs into a lake and vow never to play again if he hit a bad shot—only for him to eventually fish them out. Charles's swing amazed Dan Patrick, who didn't think his friend would keep going out, often in front of large crowds, with that hitch.

"He didn't care that you were laughing at him. He was not going to stop trying," the radio host said. "He was always like, 'I'm going to figure this out and I'm not going to stop.'"

And when Charles finally did figure out his swing many, many years later, golf got a whole hell of a lot less confusing. The same could not be said for other aspects of his life.

Charles might not have known himself as well as he would have liked at that point, but if there was one thing he did recognize, it was that his back was killing him, and soon his leg would be, too. The Suns' depth was necessary after a January 1994 game in Minneapolis. Phoenix's win came with a steep price: Charles tore his quadriceps tendon above his right knee. The preseason plan to voluntarily sit out Charles came by default, and he would miss seventeen games over the next month.

While his body and heart remained firmly on the basketball court, his mind began to wander off to the political arena. When he was to retire, he vowed to run for political office in his native Alabama, either as governor or a member of Congress. Running on a platform of better educational opportunities and an increased crackdown on crime, Charles told anyone who would listen that this was something he had thought about and was cut out for as someone who has been both poor and rich. In Birmingham, where Jordan was learning how tough it was to hit a curveball, the Double-A outfielder decorated his locker with a bumper sticker that read "Barkley for Governor."

With his political aspirations on hold for the time being, Charles finished what was, by his standards, a down year—averaging 21 points, 11 rebounds, and 5 assists in an injury-riddled season.

In the first round of the playoffs, the Suns met the Warriors in a matchup of the league's top two offensive teams. Flanked by Dream Teamer Chris Mullin and a dynamic second-year wing in Latrell Sprewell, Chris Webber was the youngest player to start in a playoff game since Magic Johnson fourteen years earlier. Charles had extra motivation in the series after a Nike ad that year featured Webber dunking on him.

"I don't think there's a person in the league who can stop a player like Charles Barkley," said Webber after his role model went for 36 points, 19 rebounds, 7 assists, and 4 steals against him in Game 1.

Fearing that his ailing back would give out on him, Charles wanted to end the series quickly so that he'd have more days off and extra time in the whirlpool.

"Charles told us, as a matter of fact, we're gonna go home, we're going to end this, sweep them, go home and rest," Oliver Miller said. "He told Paul, 'Give me the ball.'"

After he scored his team's first 12 points, Charles ran past Don Nelson and asked the opposing coach, "You gonna double me?"

"He says, 'We're not gonna double you,'" Charles recalled. "I said, 'Don, I'm gonna ask you this one more time.' He looked at me and said, 'Charles, I'm gonna tell you this one more time: we're not going to double you.'" Charles asked four times that game, and each time had the same answer: "He said, 'If you can beat us, beat us.'"

Because of that refusal, his 38 points at halftime set a new league playoff record. Keith Jennings, a reserve point guard for Golden State, realized after the first few buckets that it was going to be a bad night for his team.

"You know how in those video games like *NBA Jam*, when you can see the fire start to come up from their feet? Charles resembled that," Jennings said.

The final horn sounded, and the Suns swept the Warriors behind a career-high 56 points from Charles on 23-of-31 shooting in forty-one minutes, adding in 14 rebounds for good measure. He left to a quiet ovation from the smattering of Suns fans that made the trip to watch a supernova light up the coliseum. His 56 points were tied for the third-most scored in a playoff game in NBA history, trailing only performances from Jordan and Elgin Baylor.

"They challenged him," Ainge recalled of the series. "And the one thing I never do is challenge Charles Barkley."

Webber, who'd been named Rookie of the Year, actually thought the defensive plan against Charles had been sound. The young buck could only tip his hat to him. "It wasn't luck," Webber said. "It was incredible."

Charles was left in pain. His back had started to spasm at the half, and the soreness worsened. The win allowed some much-needed time off, but even as the second round awaited, he did take a moment, in his own way, to reflect on the level of destruction he inflicted.

"They told me I needed a cup," he quipped, "a cup to get tested [for performance-enhancing drugs]."

What started as a hug between Charles and KJ at midcourt of The Summit turned into a full-on team midcourt embrace. Joe Kleine, who had been ejected earlier in the game, even ran out of the locker room in a green T-shirt tucked into his jeans just to get in on the unlikeliest of celebrations. This is what happens in the moments after your team completes the greatest comeback in NBA playoff history against the Houston Rockets on Mother's Day of 1994.

Down by 20 with under ten minutes to play in Game 2 of the

conference semifinals, the Suns came back to win 124–117 in over-time, fueled by a 42–17 run in the fourth quarter and extra period.

The Suns were keeping true to their promise. Charles and the team vowed that, despite the inconsistent regular season, they would fin-ish the business they left unsettled the previous year.

"We're not playing to win. We're playing not to lose," he said of his team's philosophy in 1994. "We said we never want to feel like we felt last year in the Chicago game."

Going back to America West Arena, Rockets reserve guard Mario Elie heard about how Charles had predicted a possible sweep. Jim Foley, the color man for Houston's radio broadcast, called the flight to Phoenix the quietest plane ride in his decades on the job. Point guard Kenny Smith was salty because his team was now being called "Choke City." Arriving at the arena to scores of fervent Phoenix fans, Rockets center Hakeem "The Dream" Olajuwon had one message for his teammates: *It's a new day. Come ready to play.*

The Suns nearly ran the Rockets off the floor in the first quarter of Game 3, leading 29–15 against a team that missed 13 of their final 14 shots in the period. The series was seemingly over.

Then, as each quarter went on, the series flipped. "When Dream said that shit, the whole series turned around," said Earl Cureton, a reserve power forward for Houston.

The Rockets not only won Game 3 but did it by a 16-point mar-gin, thanks largely to the streaky Vernon Maxwell, who started the night 1-of-7 shooting and ended it with 34 points.

Fran Blinebury was in the locker room ahead of Game 4 when he saw Olajuwon sitting alone in a chair. Down 2–1, Olajuwon pre-dicted that all the pressure was on the Suns. "*They* must win tonight to stay alive," the center said to Blinebury. "*They* know they cannot win Game 5 in Houston."

The Rockets indeed made it two in a row in Game 4 from Ola-juwon's 28-point, 12-rebound, 8-assist masterpiece to go along with his 5 blocks. When the Suns' plane touched back down in Houston, Julie Fie, the team's longtime spokeswoman, picked up a copy of the *Houston Chronicle* to see an amendment to Blinebury's words: Phoe-nix was now Choke City West. "Julie had just gotten off the plane and showed it to Charles," Blinebury recalled. "He said, 'Well, it's hard to argue.'"

Charles was clearly injured, but refused to speak about it. He spent extra time soaking in the whirlpool to ease his back pain. Charles never asked or wanted anyone's sympathy, said Elliot Perry, a backup point guard for the Suns.

"It was just hard watching him knowing he was banged up," Perry said. "Charles didn't complain or use it as a crutch. But it's still hard for me to talk about. We still had to lean on him."

The Rockets won Game 5. Not since 1969 had there been a team that had won the first two road games of a seven-game playoff series only to lose it.

With their season on the line, Phoenix returned home and staved off elimination with a 103–89 win. Joe Proski, the Suns' trainer, was concerned about Charles's pain, but kept treating him, knowing he would regularly turn down painkillers and try to toughen it out.

"He didn't go crazy getting or wanting the injections," the trainer said. "He impressed the hell out of me. I won't say all the time, but there were some treatments he should have gotten that he didn't have, and he'd still go out there and play so well. Whatever shit he would give you was worth it." When he finally agreed to an injection for his groin from Emerson, Charles remarked to the team physician how he never had a needle that close to his stuff.

"I mean, it was *right* in there."

If they lost Game 7, it could potentially be Charles's final game. Now a shell of himself due to injury, Charles would go down shooting until there were no more bullets to be fired. Their five most reliable players—Charles, Johnson, Majerle, Ainge and A.C. Green, the free-agent signing from the Lakers—were ready for war.

From the start, Chuck was limping up and down The Summit floor, unable to mask the effect of the groin injury. Even with one of his best games of the series, his body repeatedly failed him. He couldn't run, he couldn't jump. Matt Guokas, Charles's former coach in Philadelphia, was audibly bummed out on the NBC broadcast seeing him hobbling and grimacing.

"I was just in the way," Charles said of his presence on the floor.

Meanwhile, Olajuwon was having his way with them. Fadeaway. Turnaround jumper. Dream Shake. Baseline jumper. Dunk.

"It was like we were trying to row upstream," Johnson said, "and the current just kept getting stronger."

For as well as Houston played, Phoenix was right there, down between 1 to 5 points for most of the fourth quarter. Johnson was electric again and Ainge had knocked down five 3s off the bench. But one signaled a death knell. With the shot clock down to one second, a hobbled Charles didn't make much of a defensive move on Rockets rookie Sam Cassell, who proceeded to stick the twenty-five-footer in his face.

"That long 3 with the shot clock going down is the thing that put us away," Westphal said.

Up by 7 with seconds to go, Olajuwon went for a layup. That was bullshit, Charles thought, so he did what he could to stop Olajuwon by shoving the all-world player in midair. The Dream still hit the shot, but Charles's extrahard two-handed push sent the center crashing to the parquet floor—and nearly caused an end-of-game fight with Maxwell. Charles was ejected with 7.4 seconds left, exiting through the narrow tunnel at midcourt to throngs of fans waving goodbye and cursing him out.

"This is not the way Charles is looking to end the season," observed Marv Albert.

Phoenix lost 104-94. After he shook Rockets forward Otis Thorpe's hand out of respect and urged Houston to win it all, Charles needed anti-inflammatory shots for the pain. But his ailing back, groin, and quads paled in comparison to the pain of going another year in his prime without a championship. But what would happen next was anyone's guess.

"It's simple," he started. "If the doctors can make me feel better, I'm going to play. If not, it's been a great ride."

25

Houston's Kenny Smith was soaring for a rebound that would potentially dash Phoenix's title hopes for a second straight year. But Charles wasn't about to let that happen.

Before the game, Bill Walton noted to viewers tuning in that he saw the self-doubt in Charles's eyes. His left knee was hurting. He was bruised and filled with anti-inflammatory shots. But on that night in May 1995, Charles needed the ball. Seconds later, Kevin Johnson drew contact on his way to the hoop and hit the first of 2 free throws, tying the score on his 46th point of Game 7. NBC's Greg Gumbel wondered when perfection would catch up with Johnson, who had gone 21-of-21 from the line for the game, then the most free throws made in a playoff game without a miss in league history. It turned out to be a jinx of sorts. His first miss at the stripe kept the game tied at 110 with twenty seconds to go.

Danny Ainge pounded his fists while screaming at his teammates in the huddle. Paul Westphal wanted to double-team Hakeem Olajuwon and force anyone else but him to take the shot. Out of the timeout, Ainge and Johnson double-teamed Smith before he could bring the ball past midcourt. Smith found Robert Horry, but before Charles could do anything on defense, Horry took one dribble and launched a pass into the far corner, where Mario Elie, who had gotten away from Ainge, was setting his feet.

"I hate to say it," Elliot Perry began, "but if you had to pick a guy to leave open, it would have been him."

Standing under the basket, Charles looked up as the ball, and his fate, soared through the air. He was hoping his beat-up body could leap for one more rebound.

The five-year-old daughter had to clarify something with her father: Why does everybody call you Charles Barkley?

"Well, when Daddy is playing basketball, he is Charles Barkley," the father replied.

Christiana, whose name was inspired by a Delaware shopping mall Charles passed by a few times, didn't hesitate to point out the obvious flaw in his answer. "You're my *daddy* when you're playing basketball," she said.

The only thing he loved more than being a basketball player was being a father, but excellence on the court meant time away. His mother realized early on that the sacrifice he was making echoed his own experience with Frank.

"The experience Charles had with his father I think will only make him a much better and loving father," Charcey predicted. "He would not want to do to his children what his father did to him. He's a father now, but he will be an excellent daddy when he has the real time to spend with his daughter. I know this. She loves her daddy."

The Suns of the mid '90s seemed destined for a championship. But their window was closing. Charles was inching toward retirement and winning without him felt nearly impossible. Upon the team's return to Sky Harbor International Airport after the loss in 1994, Charles was met by a chorus of five thousand begging: *Please don't go.*

The pull of the political world was real and serious. Dan Quayle was interested as early as 1994 about getting Charles in the Republican fold, when the former vice president was weighing his own run for the presidency. Charles was indeed eyeing political office using rhetoric influenced by friends like right-wing radio shock jock Rush

Limbaugh, Supreme Court justice Clarence Thomas, and Quayle, who had offered his support for Charles's "family values" message in the "Role Model" ad.

"I thought that was very poignant, and he really had an understanding of the family unit," Quayle said from his office in New York. "He had an antenna to understand that all of this, a lot of these social economic problems were really with the family."

There was also the family he had admittedly put on the back burner, and a five-year-old who didn't understand why she wasn't always seeing her father. Time with his daughter felt even more precious and urgent following the death of a four-year-old Phoenix girl named Ashley Boss, who was killed during a drive-by shooting. Boss was in her living room when she took a single bullet to the head. The tragedy shook Charles and complicated his decision even more. "If somebody ever did something like that to my daughter, I wouldn't care what happened to me…" he said, unable to finish his thought.

He agonized over the decision for a month. When he announced he would return for his eleventh season, the choice to keep playing was a heavy one. Speaking to multiple doctors, including the specialist who worked on the herniated disc of Dallas Cowboys quarterback Troy Aikman, Charles promised to dedicate himself to rigorous therapy for his back and avoid what he called the "lazy" way out in retirement.

"I never backed down from a challenge and for me to let it all end just because I didn't want to work out, I didn't think that was right," he said while choking back tears at the news conference.

A dark cloud also followed the team into the off-season. It started months earlier with one of the Suns' bench players, forward Jerrod Mustaf, being linked to an investigation for the murder of a woman who was believed to be pregnant with his child. While Mustaf was not a suspect and never charged with any crimes in the case, his cousin, Levonnie Wooten, was convicted of first-degree murder, burglary, and witness tampering for killing Althea Hayes, and sentenced to life in prison. (Strangely enough, Wooten professed his innocence in his first jailhouse interview, which was given to an unlikely pair in Charles and "Super Snake," a legendary Phoenix radio personality.) Mustaf later settled for an undisclosed amount with the woman's family in a wrongful death civil lawsuit, in which Hayes's family accused the forward of calling on his cousin to kill her.

Then, an explosive report from the alternative newspaper the *Phoenix New Times* detailed an alleged post-playoffs sex party with a few Suns at the home of Cedric Ceballos. In a widely reported allegation, a woman told Phoenix police that Oliver Miller, the second-year center, forced her to have sex during a team party shortly after the Game 7 loss to Houston. One woman's account in a police report outlined in the *New Times* accused Charles of standing at the bedroom door where Miller allegedly engaged in the unwanted sex. The players involved denied the allegations. No charges were ever filed in the case, and the claims of the woman, who stated in a police report that she declined to have a sexual assault examination, were not investigated, or substantiated by the authorities. Weeks later, Miller's wife told police that he had grabbed her around the throat during a domestic dispute. Like the sex-party allegations, no charges were filed by his wife.

Disgusted by Miller's alleged behavior and the bad publicity that came with it, Jerry Colangelo refused to match Detroit's offer sheet to the center in free agency. "When you make a mistake, you admit you made a mistake," Colangelo said. "The problem with Oliver is, he was never accountable."

The Suns were overhauled to chase Houston, which would go on to win their first championship behind the dominance of Hakeem Olajuwon. Miller and Mustaf were gone. Ceballos, another player linked to the allegations stemming from the sex party, was shipped out for a first-round pick. After trading Mark West, Phoenix made a splash in free agency by landing Danny Manning, the versatile scorer whose unquestionable talent was overshadowed only by a pair of chronically injured knees that kept him from staying on the floor. Drafting Wesley Person gave the Suns another deadeye 3-point shooter and a fellow Tiger (and the brother of college teammate Chuck) for Charles to talk to about Auburn football. The signing of Wayman Tisdale, another bucket-getter and rebounder, gave Phoenix unparalleled depth at forward.

The basketball shop quartet of Charles, Manning, Wayman Tisdale and A.C. Green was so good that the Associated Press dubbed the group "the most potent collection of forwards in NBA history."

Despite his struggles, Majerle had hit more 3-pointers over the previous two seasons than anyone else. And they still had Johnson, who was now arguably the best point guard in the game, a fearless playoff performer whose confidence was so high that he almost single-handedly dragged the Suns to the conference finals the year before. There were, however, some unresolved feelings between Charles and Johnson from the previous season that they had to play through. Donnie Nelson, who had come to Phoenix as an assistant from Golden State, only framed the unspecified strain in the ongoing, imperfect relationship as, "Kevin got his feelings hurt."

Regardless of whatever feelings the two best players had about the pecking order on the team, the Suns were undoubtedly the most talented squad in the league. But Charles knew it meant little if they couldn't finish what they started. And with that came a sense of urgency for a veteran team that knew time was running out.

"We have to win it all," Majerle proclaimed. "We're not playing to get close anymore."

Entering the $500-a-ticket, black-tie event in his name, Sir Charles donned a purple robe that required three young squires to carry its train.

This was Charles in all his glory. He was again the toast of the league, leading the Suns to a 38-10 record at the break, and would seemingly not be denied his crown this time.

"What effect did Mick Jagger have on the Rolling Stones?" asked Nelson of Charles's impact that year. "We needed a lead singer, and he was *everything*."

Royalty mattered little to Billy Crystal, who took a brief hiatus from hosting the Academy Awards for four consecutive years to rib his upcoming co-star in the 1995 romantic comedy *Forget Paris*. Behind the lectern at the Pointe Hilton, Crystal, the emcee for the occasion, gave the audience in nearby South Mountain a choice on how they wanted the Sir Charles Royal Roast to proceed: "We can have a fun entertaining evening, or we can bury this big bald spot."

Charles felt at ease at the event, and his mood had improved that season in general. The drama and off-the-court headlines that had accompanied them heading into the season quickly dissipated once the old players had been jettisoned. Winning can mask at least some of the existing problematic elements, and the Suns, not acting like they had time to kill, were victorious often in 1995. They did it despite injuries that challenged their incredible depth. Manning, the prized free agent who was the second-leading scorer behind Charles, played just forty-six games before tearing his left ACL, a result of landing on Joe Kleine's foot during practice. Johnson too was plagued with injuries. In less than two and a half seasons, the point guard had suffered a strained right ankle, lower leg contusion, strained right quadricep, strained rib cage muscle, contusion on his right knee, and come down with chicken pox.

Charles knew they needed Johnson for a shot at the playoffs, but he still teased him about his injuries relentlessly. "One day, Charles called out to Joe Proski," said columnist David Casstevens. "He said, 'Hey, Joe, give Kevin something for his yeast infection.' That was his playful dig. I winced when I heard that. I'm sure Kevin didn't appreciate it, but that was Charles's kind of humor."

All-Star Weekend in Phoenix had a little bit of everything. You could take in line dancing during a Kenny Rogers show one night and watch Bill Cosby's latest standup set the next. Even Jane Goodall, the world's foremost expert on chimpanzees, offered an invite-only lecture to owners and the players' wives. A celebrity slam-dunk contest headlined by baseball legend Cal Ripken Jr., who repeatedly struggled to dunk the ball off a high bounce, was judged by the likes of fellow Major League Baseball star David Justice, WWF champion Diesel, and Conan O'Brien, who sported rhinestone-studded high-tops with his face on one side and a bicycle horn on the other.

Perhaps the highlight of the weekend was the roast of Charles, an affair hosted by Crystal and featuring roasters from Ainge and David Robinson to Nike's Phil Knight and comedian George Wallace. (Commissioner David Stern also took a crack at his favorite problem child.) Charles had built a healthy admiration for Crystal who stuck by the Los Angeles Clippers despite decades of despair.

The two joked they would join Michael Jordan as part of an ownership group to try to buy the Clippers in hope of escaping the misery of Donald Sterling—a faux handshake agreement that even made Stern stifle laughter.

His experience on *SNL* and in commercials made him a perfect addition as himself in *Forget Paris*, where he proceeded to ream out Mickey Gordon, an NBA official played by Crystal. The comedian lauded Charles for wanting to get the argument scene right after reminding the forward that he was "playing himself, not a poet."

"That is total bullshit! You are *turrible!*" Charles barked in the movie. "You suck! You suck! *Turrible* call!"

Crystal saw a self-aware performer who knew what his audience came to see. He was, as Crystal put it, a good villain.

"The best entertainers are the ones who are most confident onstage and know who they are," Crystal said. "He always knew he wasn't Luke Skywalker. He was Darth Vader. He really played that role, but I don't think he was playing. That's just who he was."

Among the journalists surrounding Charles that week was Barry Bloom, a writer with the *San Diego Union-Tribune* who had been profiling the star for weeks. As Bloom recalled, a German reporter stuck his microphone in front of Charles to ask him about groupies, the perception that women in different cities latched on to the millionaires wherever they went. It was a topic that set off Charles and resulted in what would be the most awkward moment of the weekend. "The groupie thing is a sick subject, and you guys should get a fucking life," he replied with disdain, mumbling "motherfuckers" as he turned away.

Then, Charles looked down at Bloom, whom he liked, and said to him: "That's why I hate White people."

Knowing that his subject had been caught on a hot mic, Bloom tried to quickly clarify with Charles what he meant. "When the thing was over, I said to him, 'You don't hate White guys.' He goes, 'No, I'm just fucking with you,'" Bloom said.

But by the time the clip ran on *SportsCenter*, the comment supposedly made in jest had blown up. Charles and the Suns accused ESPN of sensationalizing the story. "It wasn't a racial slur," Charles told Jim

Gray before kissing the interviewer on the cheek. "ESPN will get over it." John Walsh, then the executive editor of the Worldwide Leader in Sports, defended the decision to run it, questioning how he could be joking when no one saw "a smile across Barkley's face."

Being called cocky and conceited was one thing, but getting labeled a racist hit differently at a time when he was considered the face of the league. For as much as he tried to escape the racist label from critics, it had resurfaced under the bright lights. The subject followed him the rest of the weekend. The Suns' secretaries were "physically drained" by the volume of calls they received about Charles. He claimed the NBA received six thousand calls in one day from people wishing that he be banned from the game. He could at least paraphrase one of the letters to Aldridge: "You fucking N——, we hate your ass."

"The thing that makes you mad is it brings out the real racists…it promotes racism to start something like that," he said. "The letters don't really bother me, [but] it upsets me a little bit, because it lets me know how many racist people are out there."

David DuPree, the *USA Today* writer who followed him in Barcelona, saw it as more fallout from his "Role Model" ad than anything else.

When Charles said, "I hate White people," he didn't mean that he hates White people. He hates the stereotypical White person and the way some Whites look at us. How some people don't want us here and openly act like they don't want us here. He hates some of the things White people have done to people of color.

Charles didn't give a shit about race. He looked into your heart and into your eyes. Sometimes, he would get frustrated when people would not know the distinction he was making.

I'll never forget him saying that trouble in America comes from two things: race and money. He would assume that people would know when he's joking and when he's serious, and would be able to judge what he meant as opposed to the actual words.

He's had to live like that, and he's never once turned away from that responsibility.

★ ★ ★

If not for the controversial comment, the rest of Charles's ninth, and most special, All-Star Weekend would have gone off without a hitch.

The fun in Phoenix was so evident that Scottie Pippen just wanted to unpack there for good. Pippen's public feud with the Bulls over his historically cheap contract had reached a boiling point with owner Jerry Reinsdorf and general manager Jerry Krause. Even though he was now the main man in Chicago following Jordan's retirement, he remained the eighty-ninth-highest-paid player in the league and the fifth-highest-paid guy on his own team. After he made his wishes clear in January 1995 that the Bulls should "trade me or trade Krause," he fueled a rumor during All-Star Weekend that he might be traded to Phoenix for Majerle, Person, and multiple draft picks. Phoenix would be "paradise" for him, even if he didn't have any "substantial evidence" to the rumor.

"Phoenix is a team that this could be their last title run," Pippen noted. "Charles isn't getting any younger."

Any rumblings would be squelched a month later. As if trying to win his first championship was hard enough, Charles, like the rest of the world, had to deal with the return of the king. Shortly after saying he would quit baseball in fear of becoming a replacement player during the major league strike, Michael Jordan announced he was a Bull again, putting the rest of the league on notice. Charles couldn't be bothered to watch his buddy's first game back on March 19, 1995, opting instead to watch college basketball and play 18 holes. He urged Jordan to come back the week before and wished him good luck, but served as the lone voice of dissent in a celebratory crowd, telling anyone around him that it would be "impossible" for Jordan to return to his previous heights.

"They've got to get to the Finals to play us again," he said. "We're going to hold up our end of the bargain. I hope he does, too."

With Pippen out of the question, the Suns turned to Richard Dumas, who had been reinstated following a drug suspension and stint in rehab. Bringing Dumas back into the fold was not an easy ask for Colangelo, who had denounced the player's substance abuse the season before. Dumas's suspension had caused the Detroit Pistons to back out of a trade that would have sent Dennis Rodman to Phoenix to pair with Charles. Colangelo recommended Dumas apologize to the city of Phoenix before he could be reinstated.

Perhaps no one was more supportive of Dumas upon his return than Charles, telling him at a team meeting, "There's nothing I won't do for you." The meeting followed an afternoon practice, sessions that featured post-workout beers—and Charles loved his beer after practice. Sure enough, Colangelo responded to Charles's words with praise and a suggestion.

"Jerry goes, 'Charles, I think that's great, and I think if you're saying you would do anything, we should take beer out of the locker room,'" Kleine recalled. "And out of this hard and long 'I'll do anything for you' talk, Charles goes, 'Well, I don't see why *that* is going to be important. If the guy is going to drink, he's going to drink.' In a manner of thirty seconds, he went from one end of the spectrum to the other."

Though Charles looked more like his dominant self, the wear and tear was getting to him, and he would miss fourteen games, including the first eleven of the season for an abdominal strain. And more time addressing his sore bones in the hot tub and with acupuncture meant Charles would inevitably need something from "Chumpy."

Jae Staats waited to hear those words: *Chumpy, come here.* Growing up in Nebraska, Staats fell hard for the Suns upon moving to Phoenix. Living close by the old coliseum, he was a regular ball boy for home games until he was promoted to bench boy, which involved folding jerseys, handing the players towels, and catering to them in the locker room. He'd read Bible verses with Johnson and take Green on an emergency trip to the dentist, before picking him up some movies at Blockbuster. When Shaquille O'Neal was in town one time, Shaq Diesel asked Staats to go get the number of a woman sitting in the stands.

Staats soon became a trusted assistant of sorts to Charles, even if Chuck refused to call the eighteen-year-old by his real name. "Maureen nudged him once and went, 'Charles, his name is Jae.' He goes, 'Well, Chumpy is better than little fucker or little shit,'" Staats said. "It was his term of endearment for me. Boy, I got used to it."

There was the time on New Year's Eve when Staats, in the middle of taping some obscure college game for the scouts, was approached by Charles for a personal ask: he needed him to shave his head. As Staats sat in front of a mirror and carefully took a razor to a head covered in shaving cream, Charles asked him about his grandparents, how he was doing in school, whether he had a girlfriend and, most importantly, if he wanted to go to his New Year's party.

After forgetting his shoes, Charles sent Chumpy to his home in Paradise Valley to retrieve them, leading Staats to see fifty pairs of Nikes stacked neatly in the corner of what he concluded was "the cleanest garage I've ever seen." But the real treat came from driving Charles's cars to get them filled up, specifically the $120,000 Mercedes-Benz convertible. Staats, who had never been in an accident, was instructed that the key and some money were in Charles's shoe before he was left with some parting words.

"He said, 'Chumpy, if you wreck it, I'll kill you,'" Staats remembered. "His tips helped me pay for my college."

The message the Suns sent to the league in their 59-win season was one of redemption. Finishing sixth in MVP voting with 23 points and 11 rebounds a game, Charles's third season with Phoenix marked the first time in franchise history that the team had at least fifty-five games in three consecutive seasons. The second-seed Suns put everyone on notice, starting with Portland. Even with Majerle's poor shooting and Johnson playing on a sore left hamstring, the Suns made easy work of the Trail Blazers, sweeping them behind a 47-point showing from Charles, who was booed every time he touched the ball in the deciding game.

Winners of eleven of their last twelve, the team was clowning on their opponents to the point that they had to open a company just to keep up with the supply and demand.

"What business are we in?" Charles asked Majerle before the start of round two.

"The butt-kicking business," he replied.

"And how's business?"

"Business is good!"

In the Houston visitors' locker room, Charles grabbed a piece of chalk and headed to the blackboard. Up 3–1, the Suns were now a game away from exorcising their red-and-yellow demons. Buttkicking Inc. was booming, but they hadn't buried the Rockets just yet. He scrawled across the board:

THEY WANT TO DIE. YOU HAVE TO KILL 'EM.

Houston's title defense that year had been inconsistent and flat. Despite a Valentine's Day trade to reunite Clyde Drexler with Phi Slama Jama frat brother Olajuwon, the Rockets were unable to rise above the sixth seed in a loaded Western Conference. Whatever momentum Houston had from a five-game upset of the Utah Jazz in the first round had evaporated against the Suns. Charles and Johnson averaged nearly 60 points in their wins. "They were so damn good," said Rockets coach Rudy Tomjanovich.

Phoenix was doing this despite Olajuwon dropping almost 30 points a game against them to that point. The Rockets cried conspiracy for the one-sided officiating and the league scheduling games on back-to-back days. Elyse Lanier, the Houston mayor's wife, called the league office to complain after Drexler was ejected during the first quarter of Game 1.

Franchise Senior and Franchise Junior, the names used by Charles for him and KJ, took advantage of defensive weak spots for a Houston lineup that stayed on the Suns' shooters and refused to double-team the big guns. The unenviable assignment of guarding Charles fell to a pair of journeymen in Chucky Brown and Pete Chilcutt. It did not go well. "I'm not ashamed to say he killed me one-on-one," Chilcutt said. "He killed a lot of guys in the league."

Fran Blinebury felt déjà vu when Olajuwon told the *Houston Chronicle* writer to pull up a chair at America West Arena so he could explain to him why it was the *Suns* that faced all the pressure. Olajuwon brushed off Green's guarantee that the Suns wouldn't lose three in a row. Drexler was fighting off a flu that had him bedridden with a 102-degree fever and hooked up to IVs all day, but his longtime friend remained confident it wasn't over. "Let's go down there and surprise 'em," Olajuwon told his teammates.

Perhaps the biggest surprise was the Suns' horrid free throw shooting. They'd gone just 20-of-34 from the stripe. Charles was the catalyst of the collapse down the stretch, missing 3 of 4 in the closing minutes of regulation, much to the pleasure of the Rockets.

"Chuck's booty hole got tight," Mario Elie observed twenty years later.

After what would have been a series-winning 3 from Person went in and out, the Rockets won in overtime to bring the series to three-two. Charles had been slowed down by a Rockets team that was now double-teaming him with Robert Horry and Brown.

While Phoenix was still in the driver's seat, the pressure tightened and their words were being used against them. Drexler could only smile knowing that Charles, who said he was taking photos with Rockets' cheerleaders after Game 4 since they wouldn't be back, would indeed have to return to The Summit.

"He said we were like Texas roaches," Tomjanovich said. "Once you step on them, you think you got them, and they keep scurrying away."

The excitement in Phoenix had turned to dread by Game 6. With a barrage of six 3s in the fourth quarter, the Rockets were the "B-film zombies who rose from the grave and terrorized a town," Casstevens said. Houston's twelve 3s had now clinched a seventh game back in the Valley. "The Suns are responsible for them being Clutch City and their mascot being named Clutch," said Bob Young of the *Arizona Republic*.

"The improbable is reality," read the front-page headline in the *Republic*.

Charles told the media that the Suns, unlike the Bulls, who had lost against Orlando that week, would win. To do so, Charles would have to do it on one good leg. He'd suffered cartilage damage in his left knee during the third quarter of Game 6, and the tendinitis caused a few bone spurs to chip off his knee cap. For as relatively healthy as he'd been all year, he was breaking down again.

Yet the Suns already had San Antonio on their minds, knowing that no team had won a Game 7 on the road since 1982. On the whiteboard before the game read their Sunday travel plans: *Practice 11:30 a.m., Bus to Airport 1:30 p.m.* After four and a half hours of treatment and an injection, Charles only started running on the knee minutes before tip-off. He told NBC that the goal for the day was to keep even with Olajuwon in the stat sheet.

Charles was in control early. Maureen anxiously crossed her fingers and Christiana cheered wildly for her daddy. He had 9 points and 15 rebounds by the half—only one board less than the entire Houston team. Still seeing double-teams, he'd throw it behind his back to a cutting Danny Schayes for an easy slam. He received a second anti-inflammatory shot and alternated between heating pads and ice packs on the knee.

With an ailing Olajuwon on the bench, Drexler and Sam Cassell helped the team claw their way back, with the Rockets shooting 24-of-33 in the second half. Frustrated over what he couldn't control in his knee, Charles tossed a full cup of water in an expletive-laden tirade in the huddle. "I don't need water," he yelled. "I need the fucking ball!"

The fourth quarter turned into a showcase between Olajuwon and KJ, who was torching Houston for a career-high 46 points and 10 assists. But when it came down to it, Elie was left open in the corner. The ball fluttered through the hoop and silenced all but a few. Charles's back was stunned at the reality he was facing. Elie turned to the Phoenix bench after his dagger 3-pointer gave the Rockets a lead with 7.1 seconds remaining.

"The first guy I looked at was Joe Kleine and blew him the kiss of death," Elie said. "He looked like he was about to cry over there."

Charles looked defeated. It's a face burned into the memory of Rudy Berumen, a season ticket holder for more than a half century. "He knew that this era was done," Berumen said. "I was devastated and thought that day would never happen."

After the teams exchanged free throws, a steal by Ainge on the inbounds pass could only get the Suns a desperation heave from three-quarters of the court. The ball bounced high off the backboard and all Charles could do was look down at the palms of his hands, wondering what more he could have done.

"What happened to Charles's party?" Olajuwon wondered aloud. "Oh well. Tell him he can come to ours."

After a remarkable stretch of 202 total wins in three regular seasons and playoffs, the Suns had unofficially joined the ranks as one of the best teams to not win a championship.

"I think we underachieved, period," Johnson said.

Though Jerry Colangelo remembered it as an outstanding period of basketball, it also felt incomplete.

"We should have won both of those years," he said decades later. "We had legitimate shots at winning the title, but we fell short."

At the center of it was Charles, who writer Frank Deford suggested would be cruelly remembered among great players as "a Nearly Man." As the Rockets went on to win back-to-back titles and become the lowest seed to ever get a ring, Charles's teams had been eliminated in the playoffs by four of the last five NBA champions. When it wasn't Jordan, it was Olajuwon—the two contemporaries taken before him from the famed 1984 Draft.

"I'll tell you the same thing I told the team after the game," Charles said to reporters. "More than likely, I have played my last game." Quietly leaving the interview room, he mumbled the obvious: "I'm fighting Father Time."

Charles would undergo surgery on his knee and rehab for his back. He would return. But others wouldn't. Ainge retired and the team traded Majerle. Westphal was replaced by a reluctant Cotton Fitzsimmons. In the season that followed, multiple players missed twenty games or more.

One of those was Johnson, who had been accused of sexually molesting a sixteen-year-old girl at his home in the summer of 1995. Johnson, who apologized to Mandi Koba but told her in a secretly recorded phone conversation that he did "not entirely agree" with her account, was not charged in the case after the Maricopa County Attorney's Office concluded the accusations did not meet a "reasonable likelihood of conviction." The allegations have lingered in recent years after Koba asserted to *Deadspin* that Johnson paid her family and their attorney more than $230,000 for her silence.

Charles was critical of the Suns' management decisions. He repeatedly told journalists how Westphal got the shaft and that he wasn't consulted on the poorly executed Majerle trade. He openly talked about the possibility of getting traded to the New York Knicks, Indiana Pacers, or Los Angeles Clippers. Thus began the open rift between Charles and Colangelo.

Finishing the year as the seven-seed at 41–41, the Suns went out with hardly a whimper against the Spurs, losing 3–1 in a season that ended again on their home floor.

"People understood that the time had come to part ways," Colangelo said.

26

Fallon Stubbs still doesn't know how her mother pulled off the perfect surprise birthday party. It had everything: a gathering at the arcade, pies from Pizza Hut, a jaunt to the local skating rink, where "Wannabe" by the Spice Girls blasted through the speakers. An eighth-grader at a magnet school in Albany, Georgia, Stubbs would become something of a gym rat at her local YMCA, where she'd befriend the people who helped Alice Hawthorne put on "the party of the year."

"It was the best party I ever had," Stubbs said in 2019. "It's still the best one and I'm thirty-seven now."

A former lieutenant in the US Army, Hawthorne was a connector in her community. She'd worked at the cable company, volunteered with the city's literacy program, and became one of the first women accepted to the local chapter of the American Legion. But Hawthorne, who had recently earned her business degree at Albany State University, was perhaps best known as the co-owner of Fallon's Hot Dog & Ice Cream Parlor, named after her daughter.

She wanted to give her daughter and shopping buddy the world. The summer of 1996 was already shaping up to be the best one yet for Stubbs. The fourteen-year-old had recently started teaching herself basketball after falling hard for the game while watching Jordan, Olajuwon, and her favorite, Charles Barkley. She hoped to make her high school team.

Stubbs watched all the Bulls games, but she was immediately drawn to Charles. He was, in her words, walking his own path. "I was one of the only people I knew who liked Charles," she said.

Knowing this, Hawthorne told her daughter in July that they were taking a road trip to Atlanta. It wasn't until her mother mentioned that they should go "check out" the Olympics that Stubbs figured out what was happening.

The best summer of the teen's life was going to be capped off with the Dream Team, the greatest gift Stubbs could have asked for in July 1996.

"It was a fucking nightmare," Charles said of his push for a second gold medal with a group of eleven future Hall of Famers.

Asked about it again years later, his opinion didn't change: "I hated it."

Charles didn't want an Olympic encore. Barcelona was the perfect team at the right moment, and everything that followed would be a letdown. Four years older and banged up in the back half of his career, he initially declined coach Lenny Wilkens's offer to join the team in late 1995. As the most mediocre and disappointing year of his tenure in Phoenix was winding down, Wilkens asked again.

"I felt he'd be great for the team," said Wilkens, who was an assistant under Chuck Daly for the '92 team. "He and I got along extremely well, and we knew we could beat everybody by about 15 or 20."

Questions surrounding the 1996 Olympics began minutes after the gold medals were placed around necks in 1992. Chris Mullin believed it would never happen again. Magic Johnson said that there might be a team as good as theirs, but everyone would be long dead and buried before that was a possibility. Jack McCallum answered his own question four years earlier.

"Will the 1996 Atlanta Games bring a Dream Team II? Or was the combination of factors that brought together twelve of the world's best players in a harmonic hoop convergence, a once-in-a-lifetime whirl?" he wrote in *Sports Illustrated*. "Bet on the latter."

The 1996 team was tasked with giving USA Basketball a much-needed facelift two years after the 1994 FIBA World Cup. Saddled with the unfortunate name of Dream Team II, the '94 squad lacked a single member of the '92 team. It was also missing widespread appeal, maturity and, most of all, respect. They were a team of all-stars and egos as talented as they were tall, but the arrogant bunch whose dignity was called into question by their opponents were dubbed an international disaster despite the easy first-place finish. Aside from Shaquille O'Neal and Reggie Miller, the 1996 team wanted nothing to do with the "Scream Team" of '94.

Wilkens quickly assembled a veteran-heavy team of players thirty or older to avoid repeating the youthful mistakes of '94. He made sure the Olympics hadn't forgotten about the original Dream Team, naming Karl Malone, Scottie Pippen, David Robinson, and John Stockton to the squad.

The prospect of having Charcey and Johnnie Mae make the two-hour drive from Leeds to Atlanta to see Charles represent the country proved too tantalizing to turn down. Yet Charles tamped down expectations.

"I don't think you can ever recapture what it was the first time," he said.

One of the first things Steve Brace learned was not to get into a verbal sparring match with the champ. The athletic trainer from Creighton University had been assigned to work with the Dream Team through the US Olympic Committee's sports medicine program, and had even moved the site of his wedding in order to work the Olympics (much to his wife's displeasure). A relative outsider, he connected with the guys in different ways—driving Anfernee Hardaway for his root canal, going to church with Robinson, talking about Islam with Olajuwon. But Charles was different.

After arriving at the team's hotel, Brace went to the luggage compartment underneath the bus to gather everyone's bags when he felt somebody push him inside. Brace didn't have a clue who pushed him until one of his students back at Creighton called him to say he was on *SportsCenter*.

"At the beginning of the show, there was a video of Charles pushing me under the bus, literally, and running off, and me popping out saying, 'What's going on?'" Brace said.

At twenty-three, Grant Hill saw playing with Charles as a chance to go back to when he was an eleven-year-old listening to Kurtis Blow list all the great players from an older generation in "Basketball." The model student athlete at Duke who took a businesslike approach as Rookie of the Year and All-Star for the Detroit Pistons, Hill's presence on the US men's team was another reminder to Charles that his best years were likely behind him. As the youngest guy on the team, Hill had seen the full breadth of Charles to that point, from punk rebel to establishment.

"He kind of became the central figure of that period," Hill said. "He was up there in age and closer to the end, but he was Charles. He was the voice."

A week into the '96 run and the team was simply trying to avoid disaster. Despite the presence of the five holdovers from '92, the '96 team couldn't avoid the similar ass kicking administered by a squad of American college all-stars. Except this time, when Dream Team III found itself down by 17 at the half in an exhibition led by All-American center Tim Duncan of Wake Forest, it was happening in front of a near-capacity crowd at the Palace at Auburn Hills instead of an empty gym in La Jolla.

"They have embarrassed the United States' Dream Team," Marv Albert declared.

The team corrected itself in the second half, ultimately winning by six. While no one seemed to panic, the '96 team had already lost some of its shine. Following the game, Wilkens stressed to the team about being conscious of who they were and what they were representing. Charles joked that they would use the wake-up call to kill Brazil because "they're not from this country."

Looking back, it's a small miracle the team got out of the exhibition run in one piece, physically and mentally.

Distractions were difficult to avoid. Bobby Cremins, the Georgia Tech coach who was an assistant under Wilkens, noticed how all the sponsors and shoe companies were pining for the players to give them exposure during what was expected to be the most-watched

Olympics in American history. O'Neal famously told reporters that all he wanted to do was have fun, drink Pepsi, and wear Reeboks. Though there was no Jordan, the assistant still likened the crowds outside the hotels to those of the Beatles.

More so than perhaps any Olympics before then, talk of the players' professional futures overshadowed what they were there to do. In the lead-up to their exhibition against China in Phoenix, several of the players—O'Neal, Miller, Gary Payton—were either up for free agency or linked to trade rumors, including Charles. A proposed three-team trade could send Chuck to Houston and bring Denver Nuggets center Dikembe Mutombo to the Suns. It was already "a done deal" in his eyes.

Fallon Stubbs' best summer ever came to an abrupt end at 1:20 in the morning on July 27. Along with forty thousand others, she and her mother were taking in the sights and sounds at Centennial Olympic Park. Soul band Jack Mack and the Heart Attack were in the middle of "I Walked Alone," and everyone was dancing.

At her mother's urging, Stubbs pulled out her Kodak point-and-shoot to take a photo.

"She was like, 'Take the picture,' and I, as a fourteen-year-old, said underneath my breath, 'I'm gonna take the damn picture!' I never ever, ever cussed at my mother," she said. "That was the last thing I ever said to the most important person in my life."

Pushing her finger down on the throwaway camera, Stubbs heard an explosion. A forty-pound crude pipe bomb hidden in a backpack had ripped through the park. Thrown to the pavement by the explosion, Stubbs rolled over to see Hawthorne in need of help. The badly wounded daughter started running to flag down medical assistance for her dying mother. Hawthorne had been hit six times by the blast, including a serious wound to her head. John Fristoe, a stagehand who had heard about the bomb threat moments before it went off, was almost paralyzed when the whiplash from the explosion collapsed a disc in his neck. He remembered seeing Hawthorne get tossed down the hill head over heels.

Team USA had just returned to the Omni Hotel after rolling China by 63 points in pool play. The explosion went off and the hotel wobbled like an earthquake, said John Stockton, who had feared for his life. "I remember looking out the window when we felt it, and seeing thousands of other people feeling it at the same time," he said.

The bombing injured 111 people and left the world in mourning.

When Stubbs awoke in her room at Georgia Baptist Hospital following surgery, her father, John Stubbs, and stepfather were crying inside her room. They broke the horrible news: Her mother had died instantly. Hawthorne was forty-four. Fallon Stubbs had few words and many tears in the days that followed. She found comfort from friends and a nurse who didn't leave the hospital during the teen's stay.

"She was visibly upset as you would expect," her stepfather said.

Another victim, a Turkish cameraman named Melih Uzunyol, also died as a result of the blast. He suffered a fatal heart attack while running to cover the explosion.

The team took a measured approach to whether they should play. Wilkens thought not playing "would be the entirely wrong response to an act of cowardice."

"We didn't mind taking the time to let these people know that they count and we were there for them," Wilkens said years later.

Charles agreed, slamming the "absurd" idea that the Olympics should be canceled following the bombing. The US Olympic Committee echoed the sentiment.

Three days after the bombing, word had gotten our that Stubbs was a big basketball fan. The Dream Team invited her to the Omni on July 30. In a wheelchair and covered in white bandages and gauze, she styled her hair in springy corkscrew curls and found the cutest outfit available. "I was fourteen and I was a lady," she remembered.

Meeting the team was surreal for Stubbs. Robinson offered her words of wisdom—"Just because you're hurt, it doesn't mean it's the end of your dream"—and O'Neal gifted her with a pair of his size-twenty-three Reeboks. Though it was a special meeting, the sadness of Stubbs' loss affected everyone, especially Anfernee Hardaway. Cremins called meeting Stubbs, presented with a signed ball from the whole team, his proudest moment of his time at the Olympics.

Decades removed from the worst day of her life, Stubbs can joke now about how part of her hoped she could be memorable enough for the younger guys on the team—Hill, Hardaway, O'Neal—to consider her a potential partner when she was older.

"Some were in their early twenties, so I thought it could eventually work out," she said through laughter. "They were tremendously sweet and accommodating, and treated me like a daughter or little sister. None of them thought I could one day be their girlfriend, so that was terrible."

Then, Charles strode into the room and Stubbs lit up. Starstruck, she could only manage three words.

You're Charles Barkley.

Stubbs's finger still doesn't bend properly and the banana-length scar on her right arm looks small compared to the one on her thigh, which is the size of "an economy-size jar of peanut butter." But her tears at the 2005 sentencing of Eric Rudolph, who faced four consecutive life terms, were not for her mother. She told Rudolph they were for *him*.

Now coaching AAU women's teams and living in Albany, Stubbs said the turning point in her life wouldn't have been possible without the kindness and love of her family and friends. And it was Charles who helped her figure out how she wanted to move on with her life and eventually find some closure.

When you go through a tragedy like that, you kind of become the tragedy itself. People always equate you with that, and you can't get out of being that person. You're always a victim—9/11, Columbine, the Olympic bombing— you can't be anything else. That's always your story that you tell.

Mind you, I hadn't played any basketball at this point, but I'm a true talker. I said, "Yo, I could beat you. I could beat you one-on-one, what's up?" I think he was shocked at first. He was like, "You could beat me?" I said, "Yeah, you might see these bandages and think I can't, but I can!" He then gave me his warmup jersey and signed it. He wrote, "You will never be able to beat me."

The jersey is up in my son's room, but the signature is gone. I have to tell people, "I promise you it's there."

I'm sure he put me in maybe the same situation he would have if it was his daughter. Meeting him altered me and what I wanted to do and who I wanted to be.

He was so sweet and nice, and he was everything I needed at that moment. He was my guy, and he didn't even know he was my guy.

In the middle of another 40-minute run-and-gun dunk fest at the Georgia Dome, more than 30,000 fans rose to their feet for the most exciting moment of the day—and it began with the unmistakable brass riff of "Y.M.C.A."

Other than Kerri Strug limping out to midcourt with the rest of her gold medal gymnastics teammates, the crowd didn't have much to get excited about in another American blowout. But Charles, who barely played following the hang with Stubbs, couldn't fight the feeling that an Olympics marred by terrorism could use a little bit of the Village People.

Clapping along to the beat during a second half timeout, and away from his teammates in the huddle, Charles went from athlete to entertainer. He threw his arms in the air to spell out *Y.M.C.A.*

"I'm ready for the 'Macarena,'" Charles said afterward. "Hopefully, they'll play it next game."

It was a light moment in a stretch of basketball remembered mostly for its redundancy. J.A. Adande observed in the *Washington Post* that the Americans were "unchallenged on the court and uncomfortable off it."

Charles didn't feel proud of the team until their 101–73 win in the semifinals against Australia, a rematch of the feisty exhibition. As Payton shit-talked Australian guard Shane Heal, who had mixed it up with Charles during an exhibition, Barkley didn't miss, going 7-for-7 in a 24-point, 11-rebound gem.

They had a date in the gold medal game against Yugoslavia, the only other unbeaten team in the field. Led by Vlade Divac, who had been recently replaced by O'Neal on the Lakers and traded to Charlotte in exchange for high schooler Kobe Bryant, the team faced a starting lineup of NBA-level talent. Yugoslavia's role as the aggressor in the Balkan conflict got them banned from the '92 Games, so making it to the gold medal game four years later was a win unto itself.

The Americans, however, were in the same no-win situation: If they won gold, it would be boring. If they lost, it would be a national disgrace. In front of more than thirty-four thousand fans, the largest crowd in Olympic basketball history, the difficult expectations were playing out in a rudderless first half that was tight despite poor showings from Divac and Sasha Danilovic, Yugoslavia's best.

Only up five at the half, the team returned to the court early to catch a glimpse of the Greatest. After returning from the 1960 Olympics in Rome, an eighteen-year-old Muhammad Ali misplaced his gold medal. Slowed by Parkinson's disease, the fifty-four-year-old forever champion strutted his way onto the court to John Williams's score from *Superman* to accept a replacement. Before the bombing, Ali was the story of the Olympics, lighting the flame during the opening ceremony and electrifying the world yet again.

Seeing Ali made the older Dream Team members feel like kids. For Charles, it was another chance to tell Ali how he was the greatest influence in his life and the most significant person who wasn't his mother or grandmother.

The meeting with Ali was a wake-up call to fight back.

Their physicality brought back the swagger missing in the first half. Charles fouled out, but the guys had him covered. Robinson, in his third Olympics, was the best player on the floor, muscling past defenders for dunk after dunk. The Admiral finished with 28 off the bench, including 10-of-14 from the line, in one of the most physically dominant performances of his Hall of Fame career. But no one could match Hardaway's raw athleticism, then considered the league's next Magic Johnson. Miller found Hardaway on an alley-oop that left his opponents breathless.

After the horn sounded on a 95–69 win, the team felt a collective sense of relief.

Charles looked down at his second gold medal with appreciation, dedicating it to Christiana. But he still knew it wasn't as sweet as the first. How could it be? It's why in speaking to the press, he suggested USA Basketball retire the Dream Team name for good.

"The Dream Team was four years ago, people seem to forget that," he said. "This time, we had a good team, a very good team, but not the Dream Team." The sentiment was echoed by Pippen years later: "I enjoyed Atlanta, I guess, but it wasn't the same. And it wasn't a Dream Team."

Part of the problem was that Charles never considered himself a legitimate leader of the team.

"Somewhere in his heart of hearts, he knows that he was not the perfect man for a leadership job, not on a team that is to be judged by history," Jack McCallum wrote in *Dream Team*.

Chuck didn't stick around for the party, leaving Atlanta that Saturday for a Sunday morning tee time in Philadelphia. He was already dreading the prospect of returning to the Valley.

"Can't go there," he joked. "Haven't you heard? Some folks in Phoenix are mad at me."

27

Right before Julie Fie was headed out of town for a much-needed vacation in June 1996, she repeated to NBC that the team's franchise player was not available for an on-camera interview.

The season had burned out in unremarkable fashion a month earlier, and Fie, the venerable spokeswoman for the Suns, hoped to squelch trade rumors surrounding Charles. If the Suns could avoid putting Charles on TV before the Olympics, they could put off the questions of the team's future for a short while longer.

So, it was a surprise to the organization on June 5, 1996, when Fie and Phoenix officials tuned into halftime of Game 1 of the NBA Finals between Chicago and Seattle to see Bob Costas interview Charles from his home in Paradise Valley.

In a black-and-white collared shirt resembling TV static, Charles, with two years remaining on his contract, relied on the same tactic he had used on Harold Katz to get out of Philadelphia. He told Costas that Colangelo made him feel "like a piece of meat." He said one of four teams would do now: Houston, New York, Chicago, or Indiana.

Management was to blame for getting rid of Barkley favorites like

Paul Westphal and Dan Majerle. Charles said Christiana was facing harassment at school. Her first-grade classmates in the Valley were asking, "How come the Suns are trying to fire your daddy?"

Fie understood that the interview marked the end.

"I begged him not to do that interview," Fie said. "I was leaving town and told NBC he wasn't going to do it. They found him anyway. It is what it is. I bet if you asked him and he thought about if he would do it again, the interview wouldn't be what he had done."

The time for acquiescing to Charles had run its course for Colangelo. The conditioning issues that plagued Charles earlier in his career reemerged as the injuries piled up, the owner said. The uncomfortable tenor of their verbal sparring signaled a sad conclusion to their partnership. Charles joked that Colangelo couldn't connect with his star at the Olympics because the owner didn't know what alias he was staying under at the Omni, which summed up where things were between the two.

"You could see the handwriting on the wall that things were going in the wrong direction," Colangelo said. "There comes a time for players when it's time to move on. It's all part of the nature of the business. And it was time for the both of us."

A little more than a week after the Olympics, Colangelo and Houston owner Leslie Alexander came to an agreement. Chucky Brown was at his home in North Carolina when he saw on his caller ID that Rockets coach Rudy Tomjanovich was calling him. "Damn" was the first word that came to Brown.

"I said, 'What's up, T?'" Brown recalled. "He said, 'Man, you know what's up.'"

On August 18, 1996, that the Suns traded Charles and a future second-round pick to the Rockets in exchange for Robert Horry, Sam Cassell, Brown, and backup big man Mark Bryant.

Charles called the shots and got his way again, saying he had to "stand up to the system" even if it meant a public relations disaster.

Charles landed in Houston that night and was whisked away by security to a limo on the tarmac.

In a sendoff note to the fans printed in the *Republic*, Charles thanked everyone from the police who protected him and the restaurant owners who fed him to Hispanic people and "the little old ladies." Yet there was a sense of sadness in leaving a place that had come to define him, knowing the void of a title and public fallout with Colangelo would follow him.

"People always remember the last thing that happened. I can't do that, because I will get depressed," he wrote. "So I choose to remember those first three years and say, 'Wow, what great years!'"

In the days following the deal, Jae Staats received a voice mail on his cell phone. The bench boy recognized the number, but paused when he realized he wasn't being summoned to pick up shoes or get his car detailed. Charles was calling to thank Jae. A quarter of a century later, Staats still has the twenty-second message saved.

This message is for Jae. Jae, this is Charles Barkley. I just called to check on you. I'm callin' all you boys, make sure y'all staying out of trouble and doing the right thing. I just called basically to say hello. I'll call you back at another time. Take care of yourself and stay out of trouble. Later.

Fresh off losing all of his basketball talent in *Space Jam* to an alien named Pound, Charles turned to God for answers on the whereabouts of his powers. Kneeling in the church, the desperate star made promises to the Big Man that ranged from unlikely to unreasonable: *No more swearing. No more technicals. No more dates with Madonna.*

Charles joked that the Michael Jordan–Bugs Bunny team-up in 1996 was "arguably the greatest sports movie ever." But Barkley's own acting in *Space Jam* was also not up to snuff for fellow thespian Shaquille O'Neal, most notably of *Kazaam* fame.

"And I thought *Kazaam* was bad. That was terrible. That was worse than *Kazaam*," O'Neal told Charles to his face. "That was awful!"

Just as Charles lost his skills in *Space Jam* so too did he now worry about meeting the same fate in Houston.

The expectations were made clear in a poster featuring their new Big Three of Charles, Hakeem Olajuwon, and Clyde Drexler standing around the two Larry O'Brien trophies from '94 and '95: Title or bust.

Yet Charles's window in Houston was limited at best. The Rockets had mortgaged their future for a chance to have three future Hall of Famers between the ages of thirty-four and thirty-five make one more run at a title, hopefully challenging Chicago's championship

3-peat. In doing so, the franchise hoped to shut up critics who had maintained the Rockets' two championships were only because of Jordan's absence over a year and a half.

The Over-the-Hill Gang brushed aside doubters as did Leslie Alexander, the owner who was quick to make the deal for Charles. Though critics argued that Alexander was in over his head.

"Les didn't know much about basketball, even if he thought he did," said Calvin Murphy, the organization's Hall of Fame point guard and longtime announcer. "He was smart enough to get people around him who knew basketball to make us a winner."

Alexander was something of a departure from Katz and Colangelo, rarely speaking to the media and only seen in public at his courtside seat with his arms folded. A star chaser, Alexander thought getting Charles was the ticket to a third title in four years.

"Charles could still do some really good things on the court, but we knew he was definitely on the downward side of his career," Tomjanovich said. "Our hope in having three superstars was Charles wouldn't need to take on the full load."

Aside from Olajuwon, Drexler, and swingman Mario Elie, much of the team had been gutted. The new squad was older, and top-heavy with big man Kevin Willis and 3-point shooter Brent Price. Charles was adjusting quickly to his new teammates, ribbing Price and forward Matt Bullard for not being the "tough White guys" that once ruled the league and asking Olajuwon to turn down the volume on one of his bright red suits.

But getting old was hell and he talked not openly about whether they could get the job done.

"We're all on the downside now," he said. "Do we have enough left? That's the question."

His first real game as a Rocket would take him back to Phoenix, fresh off a divorce that left both sides raw. But seemingly nothing would stop him from taking the court at America West. Besides, there was an invite-only party at Planet Hollywood after the game, one that included a young and impressionable Tiger Woods.

While he had long ago vowed not to play with anger, it was hard not to harbor some pent-up rage at the opening tip. The PR attacks from Suns' brass stung him and he was visibly disappointed when the fans greeted him with boos.

"They made it personal," he said.

His first game as a Rocket could have been a callback to one of his earlier Nike ads: the meek may have inherited Phoenix, but there was no way they were getting the damn ball. Each rebound, block, and putback were more emphatic than the next. By the time the game was over, he had his 20 points, but all the attention was on his career-high 33 rebounds.

"He was just so exhausted after his last rebound that game," said Houston point guard Matt Maloney. "All I could do was turn to him and say, 'This is one of the best games I've ever seen.'"

Making the trip to the unfamiliar visitors' locker room, Charles knew it was party time.

"They got what they fucking deserved!" he screamed in the hallway. He said it one more time for good measure.

When the time came for a historic first gathering of the NBA's 50 Greatest Players, Charles was nowhere to be seen. Neither was Jordan, who had made skipping All-Star Weekend media day for golf with his buddy something of a tradition well worth the five-digit fines. Despite criticism from Walt Frazier over Charles and Jordan's absence, as well the absence of many others, their peers thought the pair might have been onto something.

"I wish I was playing golf with 'em, if that's what they're doing," Boston Celtics center Bill Russell, the NBA's first standard bearer, said at the time. (Russell, who adored Charles, once joked that it was "pure instinct" for him to give Barkley the middle finger whenever he saw him.)

Yet standing on his podium in Cleveland in between contemporaries like Pippen and Karl Malone, it finally hit Charles that he had been named one of the fifty greatest to ever play the game. For all the tumult he had recently left behind in Phoenix, he wore a jacket representing Philadelphia.

But his current team gave him hope of eclipsing the others, and they were running through most of the Western Conference. An uneven mix of championship pedigree and unchallenged youthfulness, they ripped off 57 wins and the third seed in a top-heavy Western Conference. Charles's reduced role was necessary, as ankle and hip injuries forced him to miss twenty-nine games, the most of his career. He did, however, make the most of his time on the floor. His scoring dipped below 20 a game for the first time since his rookie year, but his 13.5 rebounds a night were the second highest for his career.

More importantly, the three legends were 32–8 in games they all played together. Doing so seemingly put to rest any doubts about assembling the Over-the-Hill Gang.

The first year in Houston was filled with wins, but Charles was not winning with his family. Settling into a mansion in the suburbs of Sugar Land he dubbed "the Ponderosa," Charles tried to make the most of his new setting. It wouldn't last long for Maureen, who moved with Christiana back to Phoenix because she didn't want her daughter to live in what she called a hateful area. She never specified what it was that set her off, but the years of being harassed by strangers for being in an interracial marriage had affected Maureen.

"I didn't want to raise her in Houston, in a racist environment," Maureen said in 2000. "It was terrible there."

With his family back in Arizona, Charles now had even more time for his teammates amid mutual curiosity. Charles would be dumbfounded at seeing Olajuwon, then one of three Muslims in the NBA, observe the holy month of Ramadan and kick the crap out of opponents without food or water. Before he became one of Charles's closest friends on the team, Eddie Johnson was baffled that Charles set up a surprise birthday party for him just weeks after he had signed with the team in March.

Houston Chronicle reporter Eddie Sefko likened himself to an "unofficial bodyguard" for Charles at night on road trips. Sefko found himself immersed in a nightlife scene he might otherwise not have accessed. "That's the beauty of Chuck," he said.

A lot of the time, we were in some loud, disgusting discos I didn't want to be at, but when you're with him it's fun. I can remember trying to sneak through the lobby of our hotel in San Antonio, and all I heard from across the lobby was, "Hey, get your ass over here!" You had to go and have beers with him.

In Houston, he was the kind of guy who could go out and have eight to twelve vodka-cranberry drinks, and the next night he could still kick your ass up and down the court.

When he asked me to go to Las Vegas after a game in Detroit, I said it would help him if they didn't make it a double overtime game. He said, "Trust me, it's not going to be a double overtime game." Afterward, I said, "Listen, I still have a rental car here." Well, he knew everyone in the league. He goes to a security guard at the Palace and says, "Here's this guy's keys, can you turn it in for him?" The guy said sure and Chuck gave the guy $100. We stopped and bought two cases of beer on the way to the plane. We landed in Vegas around midnight, and it was the craziest night I ever had.

It all worked out. That's just how he rolled. It just worked out.

After making short work of Kevin Garnett and Stephon Marbury's Minnesota Timberwolves in the first round, the Rockets were desperately trying to not blow a 3–1 lead against the Seattle SuperSonics. To do so, they'd have to finally get past the only team to have defeated them in the playoffs since 1993, a squad carried by a duo in Shawn Kemp and Gary Payton who were primed for a second consecutive Finals appearance.

Even in an injury-riddled transitional season, Charles felt ready.

"He was definitely a different player by then. It was scary seeing him and Olajuwon together," Kemp said. "When he got to Houston, he was a true team player."

The 96–91 win in Game 7 was validation of the trade for Charles, who finished with 20 points and 14 rebounds in forty-four minutes. Combined, Houston's Big Three of Charles, Olajuwon, and Drexler delivered big, going for 66 points, 35 rebounds, and 10 assists in Game 7. Sitting with his outstretched knees wrapped in ice packs after the game, Charles told any of his teammates who were around that they should "get another fucking job" if they were tired now.

"If we would have lost, everybody would have been on my case," he boasted, "but there's no chicken in my heart."

The Utah Jazz awaited with John Stockton and the league's MVP, Karl Malone. Five of the fifty greatest ever would share the floor in the conference finals for a likely shot at Jordan, Pippen, and the Bulls. Yet there was just one thing on his mind that afternoon: "The nightlife in Salt Lake City."

BARKLEY

★ ★ ★

The shot fell through the nylon with no time remaining, and Charles raised his arms in the air.

Eddie Johnson had already saved Houston from going down 0–3 with a 31-point performance in Game 3. Now, after hitting a game-winning 3 as time expired in Game 4, Charles caught Johnson and lifted him above his head to the chants of "EDD–IE! EDD–IE! EDD–IE!"

The Rockets had tied the series and were now two games away from the Finals.

"I'm not sure what surreal means, but I heard it on TV once and it sounded pretty damn smart. So I'd have to say surreal is the word," Barkley exclaimed.

Charles's first playoff matchup with Malone offered a different look for an individual rivalry dating back to before the first Dream Team, one filled with as much respect as animosity. In an Olympic year when Malone was set to be the breakout star, it was Charles who seized the role of American ambassador to the game. When Charles supported Magic Johnson and his HIV diagnosis, Malone threw a fuss over the prospect of competing against him. Shortly after Charles bellowed, "I am not a role model," Malone's essay in *Sports Illustrated* slammed him for not taking on the responsibilities that come with being a superstar.

Being the best 4-man was important to Malone, remembered Antoine Carr, a backup big for the Jazz.

"Once you got on the block, Karl always wanted to tell you how big he was," Carr said. "I wouldn't say he was as talented as Charles until then, but Karl turned into a beast in running the floor, and became this brute force."

Charles, for his part, took a grounded approach.

"Let's be realistic," he said. "This is our last chance, and probably Utah's. We're not young teams; we're losing something every year. We are running out of time."

Usually one to fill a whiteboard with pregame strategies, Tomjanovich kept it simple with a few words: Believe in yourselves. The problem was Utah believed in themselves more for Game 5, inching out a 96–91 victory in Salt Lake City. Malone tore up Charles in Game 5, outscoring him 29 to 10 and doubling his rebound total, 14 to 7.

The Jazz led 3–2 and were looking to close out the Rockets back in Houston.

Drexler made Game 6 his own, abusing Hornacek and Bryon Russell for 33 points. Houston was up 10 with less than three minutes left. But little by little, the Jazz clawed back.

A 3 by Russell and Greg Ostertag's surprising block on Olajuwon led to 2 free throws for Stockton on the other end. Now up 5, anxiety took hold of Rockets fans, and not even Turbo, the high-flying mascot, could settle the crowd.

Stockton had a fast-break layup to cap a 12–2 run. Suddenly, the game was tied at 98 with 1:03 to go.

On the next possession, Olajuwon, in the middle of his worst game of the series, was again blocked by Ostertag, who was enjoying his best. On the recovery, the ball would eventually find Charles, who tossed up a left-handed prayer over the seven-foot-two Ostertag with little success. But he wouldn't be denied a second time, hauling in the offensive rebound and drawing a foul before crashing to the floor in exhaustion. Houston didn't always embrace Charles, but they did in that moment, with one fan yelling out, "You the man!" right before he hit the second free throw to put them back up by 2.

The lead wouldn't last as Stockton penetrated for a hanging floater that tied it back up at 100. Drexler clanged a one-handed bank shot off the rim, and Malone called timeout with 2.8 seconds left. In the huddle, Utah coach Jerry Sloan drew up a play to set up the hot Stockton. Drexler would take on Stockton, and Charles would stay on Malone.

Walking onto the court, Charles could only smile at Carr, his friend who had entered the game for Ostertag.

As Russell was about to inbound the ball at midcourt, Malone set a devastating pick on Drexler that took him out toward the sideline. Stockton was wide open at the top of the key and Charles was now the closest man to him. In a time before switching became a popular tactic among basketball defenses, the loose switch with Charles and Drexler was late, leaving the slower forward in no-man's-land.

"Uh-oh," remarked NBC's Steve "Snapper" Jones upon seeing the breakdown in the defense.

Stockton calmly took one dribble before cocking the ball above his right shoulder for a chance at the win. Rushing in with both arms in the air, Charles turned to watch the ball.

"He knew it was going to go in," Sefko said.

An exuberant Stockton jumped up and down, showing more emotion in seconds than the thirty-five-year-old had for his entire career. His 13 points in the final three-plus minutes carried him and Malone to their first Finals appearance in a moment that would live on through replays decades later.

Depending on who you rooted for, the final play would be known as "The Shot" or "The Pick."

"I was able to get pretty good meat on him," Malone said of Drexler. "It was the best pick I set in my life."

"I was bear-hugged, not picked," Drexler said.

On the way out some fans tore up their signs reading "We Believe."

"I don't want to say we should have won," said Maloney, "but we should have won."

In the hallway underneath the arena, Charles, sweat dripping off his forehead, stood outside the door, bracing his mouth with his wrist. He'd become all too accustomed to playoff disappointment with a team he thought was good enough to win it all.

"It just happened so quickly," he said afterward.

28

At least twenty pounds overweight, a teammate asked whether Charles was in the first or second trimester of his pregnancy.

The weight concerns that followed him throughout his career had now returned along with the ridicule. The Bulls had just won their fifth title in seven years, knocking off the Jazz. Between the crushing losses and taunts Charles wondered if it was even worth it to keep playing.

Whether anyone in Houston wanted to admit it, John Stockton's shot had "changed the direction of the Rockets for Charles," said announcer Calvin Murphy. "If Stockton didn't hit that jump shot, the Rockets win that game and it's a whole different dynamic," Murphy said. "But when Stockton did, I said, 'Aww shit, here it comes.'"

But all the questions surrounding a player past his prime were put on the back burner after an early morning in Orlando—otherwise known as the time Charles threw a guy through a bar window.

"Anybody who has spent any time with me knows I meet a million people," he wrote in *I May Be Wrong but I Doubt It*, "and I've had a problem that became a serious problem with five or six crazy people."

Charles had settled into Phineas Phogg's at Church Street Station, the entertainment district in downtown Orlando, with Clyde Drexler and five or six young female friends at around 11:00 p.m. on October 25, 1997. Known for its stained-glass windows, Top 40 playlist and Nickel Beer Night, Phineas Phogg's made the area at the time a premier destination for party people of all backgrounds looking to have fun or make bad choices. In town for a preseason game against the Magic the next night, Charles and Drexler posted up at the popular bar to unwind on a Sunday night, which meant the guard kept to himself while Charles signed autographs, took photos, and bought drinks for strangers who wanted to buy him a beer. While there, the two ran into Gilbert Feliciano, a thirty-year-old Spanish reggae performer whom they had met through actor Wesley Snipes while he was filming the action thriller *Passenger 57* and asked him to join them.

Also at the bar was Jorge Lugo, who was not of legal drinking age, but had partied with six-packs all day with a group of friends following a big soccer match. A twenty-year-old construction laborer, Lugo was essentially living on the streets when he wasn't trying to make whatever money he could to send back to his family. He was also undocumented and had been arrested ten times in the city, according to the *Orlando Sentinel*, including one time in which Lugo allegedly told police that his name was "Pancho Villa."

It was about 1:45 a.m. and almost closing time. Jeffery Williams, an off-duty cop working at the bar that night, recalled that all seemed calm as people were exiting. In the middle of his police academy training, Jerry Colon had gone out to get his mind off the grueling program and happened to find himself next to Charles's table. Feliciano said the conversation that night was filled with basketball and laughter. That was about to change.

Suddenly, Feliciano noticed that when Lugo and his group looked to be exiting the bar, ice cubes were flung at their table, not hitting anyone but bothering the women standing around the NBA legends. Drexler and other witnesses said the action was unprovoked. Feliciano recalled one of the women asking Charles, "You going to let these motherfuckers throw ice at you?"

Among those in Charles's group that night was Karen Carrington, an eighteen-year-old from Deltona. Like Lugo, Carrington, as well as twenty-year-old Alexis Leiba, were underage at the bar. Carrington recalled how Charles sought to avoid a confrontation with Lugo, who she claimed was cursing at them. Charles's reasoning for avoiding conflict was that the group was clearly having fun, chanting so loudly that they were disrupting the bar, Feliciano said.

"Charles grabbed me. He said, 'Leave it alone. They're just trying to cause problems,'" Carrington said.

Then, Lugo allegedly threw a glass of ice at Charles and the women, the player told police. Multiple witnesses would say Lugo was not the one who threw the glass of ice, and Lugo later said it was one of his friends who had tossed it in Charles's direction. The glass struck Carrington in the jaw and knocked her off a chair, she told police, according to the *Orlando Sentinel*.

"She got really upset and said, 'Screw it, if you're not going to do shit, I'm going to do something,'" Feliciano said.

A ruckus broke out and two of the women stormed through the club in pursuit of Lugo and the group. After Drexler said something to Charles, Feliciano recalled, the power forward got up and blazed past onlookers to chase down Lugo, who at five-foot-two and 110 pounds was at least fourteen inches shorter. "He was running for his life," Colon said of Lugo.

Lugo, the last of his friends to exit Phineas Phogg's, was grabbed by the police officer on one side, and realized Charles had a hold of his left arm.

"Charles, I will handle this, let go," Williams said. "Charles, let me take care of this."

"I will not hurt him," Charles assured the officer. "I just want to talk to him."

By this time, a large crowd had gathered at the front of the bar to see what Charles was going to do. Feliciano had followed Drexler and the women outside. Charles looked over his shoulder as one of the women publicly challenged him in front of an increasingly rabid crowd.

"You're not gonna do shit. You're nothing but a big-ass pussy."

The taunt set him off. Williams reached for his radio to call for backup, according to the police report. As he released his grip, he felt Lugo escape. Except the twenty-year-old hadn't gotten away.

"I felt the victim being pulled from my grasp," Williams wrote in his account of the incident. "I looked up and saw [Barkley] holding the victim up in the air by his arms."

Colon heard Charles repeat a question twice to Lugo: "Do you know who the fuck I am? Do you know who the fuck I am?"

In a matter of seconds, Charles chucked Lugo through the plate glass window. Colon told reporters that Charles had approached Lugo and "flung him like he was a toy." Police later concluded that Lugo had crashed into a large mirror at the bar, which ended up smashing the plate glass window.

Amid the roaring applause from the satisfied crowd, Williams pulled Charles away from Lugo, who had slumped on the ground. A piece of glass from the broken window had struck an artery in Lugo's right arm, said Feliciano, and blood flowed from the wound like a fountain.

"You got what you deserve," Charles taunted. "You don't disrespect me. I hope you're hurt."

Williams thought he separated him from Lugo, but he was again wrong: "For all I care, you can lay there and die," Charles said.

Concerned, Feliciano took off his shirt, wrapped it around Lugo's arm and kept pressure on it until paramedics arrived.

As Lugo headed to the hospital, Charles was initially charged with resisting arrest without violence and aggravated battery, a second-degree felony with a penalty of up to fifteen years in prison. Lugo, accused of instigating the incident, was only charged with misdemeanor disorderly conduct.

Back in Houston, the city had its first significant Charles controversy, one of the biggest of them all, before he even started his second season. Jim Foley, the color man for the radio broadcast, shook his head remembering it, but didn't think much of what happened in Orlando. "I wouldn't call what Charles did 'a fight,'" Foley said.

Yet Charles wasn't disputing what he did, repeating into whatever microphone was in front of him that he was defending himself.

"Let there be no debate: If you bother me, I'm going to whip your ass," Charles said to reporters later that same day. "The guy threw ice in my face, and I slammed his ass into the window. I'm not denying that. I defended myself. He got what he deserved."

After Lugo pushed back on a paltry initial settlement offer of $5,000, the two sides brokered an out-of-court agreement that Charles acknowledged to reporters was worth $75,000, in exchange for Lugo agreeing not to prosecute. If Charles really was serious about pursuing a run for governor in Alabama, not settling would potentially dash any aspirations for office. The charges he faced, including felony aggravated battery, were later reduced to four misdemeanor counts of disorderly conduct, battery, criminal mischief, and resisting arrest without violence.

From there, Lugo's story goes dark. Feliciano heard from someone years later that Lugo was found dead near train tracks, but Feliciano was never able to confirm that.

"Whether what happened to him is urban legend or true, I really have no way of knowing," said Mark NeJame, Lugo's attorney at the time.

Charles was a senior voice in the NBA. Some rookies had started watching him when they were only seven. The time had come to grow up. Was Charles really doing this at the age of thirty-four?

As a generation led by Allen Iverson was disrupting the game and pushing boundaries in their own ways, Charles shot-putting a dude through the front window of an Orlando bar at 2:00 in the morning was not high on commissioner David Stern's wish list. Citing the harassment Christiana was getting from classmates in Phoenix over her dad's latest dustup, Charles had contemplated retirement right before the season, disappointed the league had not supported him.

The first one to reach out following what had become the most high-profile incident of his career was Jordan, who begged and pleaded with him to get a bodyguard. "He needs to keep his butt home," Jordan quipped. Stern's message was more emphatic, all but ordering Charles to find a body man if he wanted to continue going out. Barkley wondered if he had reached a point where having a fun night out with his friends was too much to ask for.

"I like going out to bars, but they said I have to walk away," said Charles, referring to the league office. "If somebody throws a drink on me, I've got to say, 'I apologize for standing in an area where you wanted to dispose of your drink.' That's how it was laid out to me."

The gun he had carried, the same firearm he never had to use, was no longer enough protection. Charles hired James Haywood, a former Houston police officer and firefighter of three decades with a black belt. Haywood became a friend, but he was also clear-eyed about his role.

"I don't think anyone would take a bullet for someone else... You'd be insane," Haywood said. "I don't think you could be paid enough to take a bullet for someone else."

Phineas Phogg's has long since shuttered, but the bar's lore took on a life of its own. Comedian Roy Wood Jr., who grew up in Birmingham and knows what Charles means to his home state, recalled drinking there. "I remember having this weird sense of accomplishment," Wood said. "Dammit, if you're drinking in the same bar where Barkley threw someone through a window, you're doing something okay."

The incident in Orlando would follow Charles for the rest of his career. A year hardly passes when it isn't brought up on TNT or in reflections on Charles's career. It wasn't until 2019 that Charles admitted on-air about how he could have handled it differently.

"I felt like, in the moment, I was mad," he said, "but now that I'm older and mature, I was wrong."

Playing with a hernia in a disappointing 41–41 season, Charles, who missed making the All-Star team for the first time in twelve years, volunteered to come off the bench behind Kevin Willis. Matt Maloney, who Charles had pushed for Houston to sign, could see his friend's cloak of invincibility dissolving.

"He was a superhero, but his injuries were tough ones to deal with," Maloney said.

But Charles was grappling with more than just injuries. The Lugo incident also raised new questions concerning Charles's drinking. Close friends and teammates offered an intervention of sorts in early 1998, when he admitted that while he wasn't an alcoholic, he did indeed have a drinking problem in terms of having too much the night before games.

"I've got to stop drinking," he said in February 1998, following a game-winning shot against Los Angeles. "If I'm going to go out and drink two beers, that's cool, but I don't think I can go out and drink six beers and six Long Island iced teas and come out and play the next morning." When asked by the *New York Times* if he knew what was in a Long Island iced tea, he replied, "I don't know. I don't make 'em. I just drank 'em."

At the same time, his political aspirations were still growing. In a *GQ* profile titled "*Governor* Barkley?," Larry Platt, one of Charles's earliest media friends in Philadelphia, detailed how his buddy's Republican makeover was layered and thoughtful—a pragmatic, moderate agenda of "pro-choice, pro–affirmative action (on a case-by-case basis), anti-tax, fervently pro-education, and tough on crime." A populist with no political experience, Charles could lambaste liberalism not doing enough for the Black community in one breath and denounce "mean-spirited" conservatives like Pat Buchanan, whom he once called a "neo-Nazi," in the next. Roger McConnell, then the chairman of the Alabama GOP, spoke of trying to convince Glenn Guthrie, Charles's most trusted adviser, to get the player to run against a seemingly vulnerable Congressional candidate in 1996 and 1998 while he was still playing.

"He was a shoo-in," McConnell said.

While his future in politics seemed bright, his on-court life was more painful. In the first round of the playoffs, Charles tore his right tricep, the result of an elbow from Antoine Carr during a second-quarter tussle against the Jazz.

"My muscles were in a little better shape than his at the time, so he took the brunt of it," Carr said. "He always claimed I messed up his golf shot, which I didn't."

Slumped in front of his locker with a swollen arm, Charles was despondent. When the Jazz finished off Houston and made it back to the Finals that year, it marked the sixth time in eight seasons that Charles's teams had been eliminated by an opponent who won the title or made it to the Finals—Michael Jordan's Bulls, Olajuwon's Rockets, and now the Stockton-and-Malone Jazz. The whole team struggled to get anything going, but Drexler's abysmal 1-for-13 shooting effort in his final game was especially demoralizing. When everyone had cleaned up and started departing the locker room in Utah,

Charles offered something of a parting shot for his Big Three mate, who announced he would retire at the end of the season to coach his alma mater, the University of Houston. The brittle relationship between Barkley and Drexler had clearly affected the team's morale.

"He goes, 'Clyde, that's the door to the real world right there,'" said the *Chronicle*'s Eddie Sefko. "I looked at Chuck and said, 'You might be careful what you say because that might be it for you, too.'"

But even with his own future in doubt, Charles gave Sefko something of a "guar-an-tee" afterward.

"Go write this," Charles said to Sefko. "Tell your readers if they want to make some money, bet on Scottie Pippen being a Rocket."

Amid the most divisive labor battle in league history, one that came as Jordan was retiring for a second time, Charles Oakley was looking for Barkley.

It started when Charles was in Atlantic City as a coach for "The Game on Showtime." A failed attempt to curb fan apathy during a battle, dubbed by Tony Kornheiser of the *Washington Post*, "between tall millionaires and short billionaires," the exhibition promoted by Patrick Ewing and agent David Falk originally wanted 90 percent of the proceeds to go to "needy" NBA players before deciding the money would go to charity. "Everything the players did from a PR standpoint was an absolute train wreck," remembered Frank Isola, the indelible beat writer for the *New York Daily News*. As part of his coaching duties, Charles felt compelled to ask Ewing if he was glad Oakley had been traded to Toronto for Marcus Camby.

"Oak was a hard worker, right?" Charles asked Ewing. "That tells you all you need to know about his game when all people can say is that he works hard."

Well, word got back to Oakley, an old sparring partner, and he was pissed. "What was this shit you were saying?" Oakley asked Barkley before a union meeting in New York in January 1999.

Then, before Charles could answer, Oakley delivered an open-handed slap that left the players stunned, said Chucky Brown, who was at the meeting. Shawn Kemp recalled the scene, and the five fingers to Barkley's face, being "pretty scary."

"It's different when it's two guys who are as soft as peanut-butter-

and-jelly or ham-and-cheese sandwiches going at it," Kemp said, "but you're talking about two Mack Trucks—and they were about to explode."

In his 2022 memoir *The Last Enforcer*, Oakley confirmed that while he did not punch Barkley, he "did, however, slap the shit out of him."

"Barkley just kept talking and I told him, next time I see him, on point, I'm coming right up to him, and I got something for him," Oakley wrote.

Barkley, understanding the mistake he'd made about fourteen months earlier in Orlando, did not strike back, allegedly telling Oakley he wasn't going to get into a brawl on the brink of the labor agreement and returned to his conversation.

Whatever it was that inspired such restraint, the 204-day lockout had ended on January 20, 1999, and a slimmed-down Charles saw the truncated fifty-game season as another real shot at a title. After ballooning to 285 in the off-season, he took the advice of Danny Manning's wife, Julie, and spent a week in December 1998 at a spiritual retreat in Calabasas, California. At the ashram that doubled as a weight-loss camp, he ate an apple for breakfast, went on a fifteen-mile hike before a lunch of salad and fruit, dedicated himself to water aerobics and weightlifting, and looked forward to daily yoga, meditation, and a bowl of soup after the spa. *Who was this guy?*

He lost seventeen pounds, strengthened his legs, and sculpted "at least one visible ab," quipped Richard Hoffer in *Sports Illustrated*. Yoga would not be a permanent activity, not after he started to have visions "of Big Macs and fries."

"I am going to have a great season," he predicted.

Charles saw the disgruntled Scottie Pippen as his ticket to a title, and the small forward had eyed Houston as his preferred landing spot the year before. For Pippen, coming to Houston was a chance to play as the well-compensated superstar that he deserved to be, and for him to prove himself outside of Jordan's shadow.

"We knew we were running out of steam, and thought he was one of the pieces that could extend this team," said Carroll Dawson, the team's general manager.

Inside the Green Room, the two-story cigar bar in Houston frequented by Charles, Pippen puffed on an El Fuente, a $65 stogie, while trashing former teammate Luc Longley—"He couldn't jump over a Sunday paper." He also talked about wanting to reestablish his dominance: winning Defensive Player of the Year, becoming MVP, and earning a championship without Jordan.

"Pippen is still Pippen, which means he must now prove that those half dozen championships were no fluke. That's what he tells himself," wrote Gene Wojciechowski in *ESPN The Magazine*. "He doesn't want to be like Mike, but you know what? Jordan would be doing the same damn thing."

The sign-and-trade completed with Chicago on January 22, 1999—Pippen and his new five-year, $67.2-million deal for Roy Rogers, a power forward who was cut and played in Italy, and a future second-round pick in Connecticut center Jake Voskuhl—was a triumph for Rockets fans and as traumatic as could be for a Bulls' base that had won six titles in eight years.

On his way to the Rockets' facility in his rented green BMW, Pippen recoiled after five men jumped out of a van near Highway 59 for the chance to shake his hand and welcome him to Houston, causing a ten-minute traffic jam.

"I thought we were getting carjacked," Pippen said.

The Big Three might have failed, but the old-guy "Superfriends" of Charles, Olajuwon, and now Pippen were seemingly destined for one last run in their twilight without a great team to stop them. As Olajuwon put it, they wanted to "make basketball fun again." Charles made it clear it was "a more cohesive group" with Pippen, and how "everybody wants it to work." Pippen was simply "just trying to fit in."

"We just hoped Scottie could keep the team at the same level as Clyde had," Eddie Johnson said. "Some of us wished Clyde wouldn't have retired, but getting Scottie was tremendous."

Questions also came up around Charles and Pippen, who were viewed more as close acquaintances than friends and who would always be connected by their mutual bond with Jordan. Aside from their many on-court battles, Pippen had accused Charles of "kissin' Michael's ass" leading up to the '93 Finals, a suggestion that left Charles bristling, according to author Roland Lazenby in *Michael Jordan: The Life*. That feeling subsided when Charles and Pippen had interest in uniting in Phoenix. The two even got Tim Grover, the famed trainer for Jordan, to move to Houston to train with them.

"Charles didn't last one week," Pippen recalled in his 2021 memoir *Unguarded*.

Charles was several days late to training camp because he was playing golf with Jordan in California, which left Pippen, in the throes of two-a-days and house-hunting, immediately disappointed. About a week into their partnership, Pippen had already started to echo Jordan's words: "I'll see where his head is, if he's willing to go for it… He's got to dedicate himself to do that."

Still, Pippen maintained that winning in Houston was "no problem." They'd find out it would take more than dedication to advance this experiment past the first round.

Antoine Carr nearly pissed himself when he heard Charles call the owner a motherfucker to his face.

After signing with Houston from Utah, Carr was walking down the hall with Charles when they saw Leslie Alexander.

"Charles goes, 'Hey, fucker, first name mother!'" Carr recalled. "I'm like, 'Whoa, did you really just say that?' And Les looked at him and just started laughing and shaking his head. I was like, 'Bro, you just called Les Alexander a motherfucker.' And all Charles could do was laugh."

His dedication to the team made such interactions acceptable. At thirty-five and fresh off arthroscopic knee surgery, Charles's off-season training with Grover and his yoga-and-apple days in California helped him bounce back quickly. He returned to his dominant form on the glass, averaging 12-plus rebounds a game.

But Pippen was another story. By March 1999, he was disgruntled by his limited role in the offense. Pippen finished with career lows in several categories, and a scoring average that dipped to 14.5 points per game.

"They wanted me to be a 3-point shooter, and watch Hakeem and Charles post up, and I was never familiar or comfortable playing that role of being a spot-up 3-point shooter," Pippen said. "That was part of one of my reasons why I didn't fit in with the Houston Rockets."

Though Pippen averaged fewer 3-point attempts per game in

Houston than he had in his previous three seasons in Chicago, he'd caught himself standing around more in Houston's post-centric offense than the constant movement of Chicago's triangle offense. Rudy Tomjanovich saw the star struggle mightily in a different system.

"We had a different way of playing and he had a continuity with the triangle," Tomjanovich said. "It was a real adjustment for him since the triangle was the only thing he knew at the time."

Pippen earned praise from younger players like Cuttino Mobley for offering mentorship, but some veterans felt that he cared more about trying to be like Mike than being a part of the team.

"He was coming in thinking, 'Hey, I'm Michael Jordan.' I mean, not really Michael Jordan, but 'I'm Scottie Pippen.' And the rest of us could feel that," said Matt Bullard, who acknowledged Pippen not being one of his favorite teammates. "When I did play with him, he wasn't trying to be a Rocket. He was just trying to be the man, and it didn't really work."

Pippen's basketball troubles spilled into his personal life when he was arrested in April on suspicion of drunk driving after his worst game as a Rocket. The misdemeanor charges were later dropped due to insufficient evidence. Charles defended him, and delightfully called Pippen "a role model." Chuck also wasn't going to let him off lightly.

"I'm going to get on the plane and take the PA and say, 'Attention, Mr. Pippen, last call for alcohol,'" Charles joked.

A 31–19 season was only good enough for the fifth seed in the Western Conference and a first-round date with the Los Angeles Lakers. Promoted as the league's next great duo, Shaquille O'Neal and Kobe Bryant had yet to unlock whatever potential they possessed. Houston saw an opening. The pressure was on.

"They're calling us the Big Three now, but if we don't stand up and perform they'll just be calling us, 'Three old people who have gone past their prime,'" Charles said.

In Game 1, Charles demolished J.R. Reid. In a Mother's Day salute, Charles yelling to The Forum crowd, "His mother can't stop me!"

His 25 points and 10 rebounds helped give the Rockets a lead late in the game. Up by two with twenty-eight seconds to go, Charles promptly fouled O'Neal off an Olajuwon miss and dared the historically bad free throw shooter to hit both to tie the game. O'Neal, with his one-handed free throw heave, clanged the first one. He'd hit the second to pull within one.

With the game clock winding down, Pippen tried to take Bryant off the dribble to his left. It was the same kind of move he had executed for years. Except this time Pippen lost the ball and it scuddled into the diving arms of Lakers guard Derek Fisher with 7.6 seconds to go. On the other end, Bryant drew a blocking foul on Rockets reserve Sam Mack that resulted in two made free throws for the twenty-year-old phenom. Out of the timeout, O'Neal rejected Mobley's last-second drive to the hoop as time expired on the unlikely Lakers' win.

Charles fired a chair against a wall on his way to the locker room. Afterward, Pippen openly questioned why Charles fouled O'Neal instead of just playing defense.

Declining to get into the back-and-forth, Charles pointed to the turnovers down the stretch, including Pippen's in the game's closing moments, as the fatal blow.

"That's not to blame anybody," he said. "We all win together and we lose together."

Not even the perfect pairing of prime Charles (30 points, 23 rebounds) and prime Pippen (37 points, 13 rebounds) in the win-or-go-home Game 3 could turn the series around. Described by NBC's Bob Costas as one of the finest playoff performances in recent years, it would only be a footnote in a largely forgettable series that ended with the Lakers winning in four games. Four years after Olajuwon swept him in the Finals, the twenty-six-year-old O'Neal rag-dolled the legend ten years his senior throughout the series. Averaging 30 points, 10 rebounds, 4 assists, and 4 blocks, O'Neal was bigger, better, faster, and stronger than Olajuwon, who was now a shell of his former self at 13 points a game. Charles and Pippen couldn't do much to offset the wide load of pain the Lakers center shoved down their throats night after night, or the emergence of Bryant.

Charles had grown accustomed to the pain of losing in the playoffs, but this one felt worse. Matt Guokas, his coach in Philadelphia who was on the call for NBC, could see Charles's anguish as he walked down the narrow tunnel for what might have been his final playoff appearance.

★ ★ ★

Carr had anticipated the early playoff loss.

I was hoping we could build a champion together, but the team ended up not having any of that.

When they added guys like Pippen and me, we were all rivals up to that point. Not just normal rivals but guys who were going hard head-to-head every year in the playoffs.

What the organization had to understand was when you take a bunch of guys from different areas who hadn't worked together, you need to give them time. Houston was not thinking about that at the time; they were in win-now mode.

No matter who you get, you can't just throw guys out on the floor and think this crew is going to be able to work together.

After going through the injury he had and to still play great, it showed he was still a beast and how much heart he had. That's the thing about Charles: he has a huge heart. But don't push him into a corner because you may go out a window.

The organization had built its future on aging stars and the gamble hadn't paid off. Pippen called the season "a big challenge" and "very disappointing for me." Due for one last payday, Charles was again leaning toward retirement after a series in which he went for 24 points and 14 rebounds a game.

If he were to return, Charles said the team was a point guard and one more wing away from being competitive at a championship level. Houston signed free agent wing Shandon Anderson away from Utah, and pulled off a coup in landing No. 2 overall pick Steve Francis, an electric point guard from Maryland who refused to play for Vancouver, in what was at the time the largest trade in NBA history.

The problem was Pippen had another idea in mind: joining the Lakers. Once Los Angeles hired Phil Jackson as coach, Pippen eyed a reunion with his old coach to run the triangle with O'Neal and Bryant. By mid-August, Pippen had requested a trade to Los Angeles just seven months after signing the biggest contract of his life with Houston, with his agent citing a plodding system that had "one of the best players in the game throwing in entry passes."

"I would be lying if I told you Scottie was not extremely frustrated playing in that system," Jimmy Sexton, Pippen's agent, said to the Associated Press. "I don't think he could make it another year like that."

Charles's scorched-earth campaign against Pippen continued throughout the off-season—despite playing together during a Nike-sponsored event in Europe. On ESPN's *Up Close*, Charles underscored how hard he'd worked to bring Pippen to Houston, and how disappointed he was in his friend. Barkley guessed Pippen wanted to go to Los Angeles because it represented the same kind of "no-lose situation" he had in Chicago. If they won, it would be due to Pippen's "leadership," he said. If they lost, Charles thought Pippen could blame Shaq and Kobe.

He called Pippen "a baby" on multiple occasions, but emphasized he wanted, and needed, that baby as his teammate.

"First, Scottie owes the Rockets' fans an apology. They've been terrific to him," Charles started. "Second, he owes the Rockets an apology. And third, he owes me an apology."

Charles concluded, "Scottie needs to stand up and be a man."

29

Scottie Pippen spoke in an even tone with a smile on his face. But his words carried venom.

I wouldn't give Charles Barkley an apology at gunpoint. He can never expect an apology from me. If anything, he owes me an apology for coming to play with his sorry, fat butt.

He's a very selfish guy. He doesn't show me the desire to want to win. That's my reason for wanting to get away from wanting to play with him anymore.

I probably should have listened to Michael a year ago when he said that Charles never will win a championship because he doesn't show any dedication.

Pippen's clapback on ESPN on September 29, 1999, had turned the league on its head, with many surprised by his audacity as well as his toxic depiction of Charles.

Among those was Michael Jordan. Within minutes of hearing Pippen's words on vacation, Jordan reached out to Charles—twice—to tell him he hadn't said anything behind his back about him or his conditioning that he hadn't said to the media or to his face.

"I don't know if Michael was madder that Scottie said all that stuff or that he dragged his name into it," Charles told Jackie MacMullan in *Sports Illustrated*. "I knew about Scottie. The whole league knew he was a guy you couldn't count on. You can fool the media and the fans, but you can't fool the players. Scottie was exposed long before this."

The destruction of the team's chemistry was all over *SportsCenter*, and there wasn't much Houston could do about it. Dawson, promoted to be the team's vice president, said he didn't have time to think about why the grouping was unsuccessful. He was focused instead on finding a trade partner days before the start of the season. Tomjanovich maintained there was no significant evidence of a rift between Charles and Pippen throughout the year but said Jackson's move to Los Angeles got Pippen mobilized.

"Scottie wanted to get back to Phil," Tomjanovich said. "We wanted him to stay, but he started to sort of leak things here and there to force the deal. And some of that was directed at Charles until we eventually did it."

Pippen's bizarre year in Houston ended three days later, not in Los Angeles but in Portland. Less than nine months after he landed in Houston, Pippen was traded to Portland on October 2, 1999, for a smattering of bench players and undeveloped prospects that yielded neither a star nor a single draft pick in return: Kelvin Cato, Walt Williams, Stacey Augmon, Brian Shaw, Carlos Rogers, and Ed Gray. Augmon and Shaw were released, and Augmon ended up re-signing with the Blazers.

Pippen claimed his sentiment against Charles wasn't personal, emphasizing in *Unguarded* that they "simply had difference approaches to the game, and there was only one way to resolve them." While the pair say they are both now cool, Barkley took some solace in witnessing Pippen's machinations. "I don't claim to be perfect. But I know I'm a good person at heart," he said at the time. "I want to win, but I want to win the right way."

The botched union with Pippen had thrown Charles into a tailspin. Before announcing that it would be his last season, Barkley was already at his wit's end. He was wounded by Pippen's insults and angry not just at Pippen but also at himself for letting his guard down and trusting someone he saw as a contemporary and a friend.

Pippen's assessment, however, wasn't shared by other teams. The Lakers, Jazz, and Sonics all expressed interest in acquiring Charles that off-season. John Stockton even called him and told him to come to Utah. "He would have made up for a lot of the mistakes elsewhere on the court," Stockton said. (Take a moment to imagine the amusing what-if of Barkley, and his hobbies of drinking and gambling, playing forty-one games a year in Salt Lake City.) It was all flattering to Barkley—and also eye-opening.

To prepare for a negotiation with Charles, Dawson rented out a room at Carmelo's, a high-end Italian restaurant in Houston, for what the Rockets executive remembered as a fourteen-course meal.

"I figured if he was eating that I'd have a better chance," Dawson said.

Though Charles had asked for $14 million, Dawson said the one-year offer at around $9 million was still too good to turn down and allowed Houston to stay under the salary cap. Charles might not get a title, but admitted he'd be a fool to turn down Houston's money.

He had also come to terms that his window for a championship, the lone accolade that people wouldn't let him forget about, had closed. Even during the early part of the season, Barkley didn't shy away from talking about what his life after basketball would look like, and the feelings that went along with it.

"I know when October and training camp and everything comes that I'm going to go through a deep depression," he said. "So I'm going to get up every morning, take my daughter to school, play golf, try to work out because I got fat potential. I've got really good fat potential. I don't want to be one of them old, fat guys."

While Barkley's rebounding was still elite, the brilliant, indefensible performances that helped cement his legacy were sporadic.

"I have to revamp my goals now," the power forward said. "The No. 1 goal is just making the playoffs."

An ugly 0-5 start to the season unsurprisingly sparked open questions about whether Barkley was ultimately to blame.

The comparisons to legends who finished their careers as sad shells of their former selves—Willie Mays at Shea Stadium, Johnny Unitas in San Diego, Muhammad Ali standing across from Larry Holmes— were too easy for local and national media.

He saw it coming. He was bracing for the inevitable. And he'd take it.

"Sooner or later, I will get blamed," Barkley said. "I understand that. I accept that. Some people have to have a scapegoat. That's part of it."

Charles's frustration reached a boiling point on November 10, 1999, against the Lakers, when Shaq fouled Charles on the low post. O'Neal, who respected Charles but had no relationship with him at that point, blocked Charles's shot and bumped his opponent's bald head. Charles swung his elbows in response, and O'Neal offered a retaliatory push. At that point, O'Neal said he recognized the old guard was testing the new guard.

"I was determined that when it came to other legends, I did not want to really be their friends," O'Neal said. "Of course, I respected Charles, but whenever I was out there playing, I was trying to rip his head off. I know he was the same way."

Then, Charles fired the ball off the head of the Lakers center, who described the motion as "one of his Charles Barkley–like stupid things."

"I was like, 'Charles, I respect you, but now I gotta knock you out,'" O'Neal recalled.

The fight was on at the Compaq Center. O'Neal landed a glancing left punch to Charles's head and Charles grabbed Shaq's right leg for a lift-and-flip move, and got in a few short punches before both hit the floor. After the pair got ejected, Charles repeated a mantra: "Can't let nobody hit me."

The tussle got the attention of two women who wanted the nonsense to stop. In the locker room, Charles and Shaq both received a three-way call. A security guard handed O'Neal the phone and did not say who it was. On the line was not just his mom, Lucille, but also Charcey. Unbeknownst to Charles and O'Neal, their mothers had become best friends—and practically sisters.

"Don't you hit my boy," Charcey told the center, according to O'Neal.

The moms never planned to call their sons and didn't take the scuffle personally, Lucille said. O'Neal's mother saw them as kids on the playground who needed to figure it out, but Charcey still demanded accountability.

"She said, 'Y'all need to stop!… We don't want y'all fighting in front of the kids,'" O'Neal recounted.

"What was that all about?" Lucille remembered asking her son. "It's a game! It's a game!"

There was also another request: Kiss and make up. Answering "yes, ma'am," O'Neal didn't dare talk back to Charcey.

"My mom called right away, and we had to meet in the tunnel and shake hands," O'Neal said, adding that they went out to dinner afterward.

The bond between their mothers created a mutual respect between them that would only strengthen over the years. But there would be no such goodwill two weeks later in Portland.

Much was made about the first meeting between Charles and Pippen since the split. At midcourt of Portland's Rose Garden, Charles and Pippen were scheduled to be the designated captains on November 26, 1999, during a pregame meeting that entailed shaking hands and agreeing to a good, clean game. When Barkley discovered Pippen was the other game captain, he declined. "I don't want to shake the blankety-blank's hand," reported Craig Sager on what Charles said. "Matt Bullard represented the team and did relay a message to Pippen from Chuck: 'If you drive the lane, you're going down.'"

There was no altercation between the two and they didn't exchange a word during Portland's 91-88 overtime win.

"I'm not disappointed we didn't talk," said Pippen. "I'm not interested in apologizing to him. As far as I'm concerned, it's over and it's behind me."

Charles would try to put it to rest in the postgame. "He said some things about me; obviously, I did not like them," he said. "But I can't sit around and whine like a little girl. It's over with."

Charles had soured on seemingly everything—his teammates, the young players of the NBA, the league's culture in general, which he felt lacked work ethic and respect.

"This game has gotten so far away from the attributes that I believe in," he said. "Guys don't want to work or learn or pay their dues anymore. All they want to do is put in the three years on their [rookie] contract and then start collecting $9 million a year. They don't want to earn it. They just want to take it."

Once brash and young, Charles sounded like a crotchety elder statesman. Given everything he'd put teammates, coaches, and executives through during the course of his career, Barkley's words were jarring.

"I'm sorry that the league has come to that," he added. "But I'll tell you, I'm glad my 16 years are up and I'm getting out. I see the stuff that goes on and they get mad when I point things out. These guys look at me and Dream as old men instead of great players they might learn something from."

After nearly two decades in the public eye, Charles was bitter. There was no stopping the unceremonious collapse of his celebrated career.

The end sounded like a sharp crack.

On a bitter cold night in 1999, Charles was introduced to the crowd in Philadelphia for the final time as a player. A full-circle moment that seemed to lack glory.

"When he came back, it was almost like a Charles we didn't recognize," said friend Mike Missanelli, the Philadelphia sports radio personality.

Eighteen games into the season, the thirty-six-year-old was firmly looking ahead to life after basketball. He was beginning to temper his expectations and channel gratitude.

"I don't think a championship would do that much for me," said a reflective Charles. "It won't make me feel like, well, now my life is complete. Trust me, my life is pretty damn complete. And I always tell people, I don't think that anybody could have had a better life than me. I really don't."

Stepping onto the floor on December 8, 1999, the Philadelphia fans who adored him then spurned him were now greeting Charles with an extended standing ovation. The harsh feelings that came with his unceremonious exit seven years earlier had subsided. The Sixers flew in Charcey and Johnnie Mae for what was to be a celebration of the franchise's finest player of recent times.

That changed seven minutes and fifty-one seconds into the first quarter.

With both teams struggling to break 20 for the quarter, Charles grabbed an offensive rebound and thought he could post up Todd MacCulloch, the Sixers' seven-foot rookie. Though he was still getting 10 rebounds a game, Charles's offense had taken a sharp turn due to his health. "I was pump-faking so much I had to go see the chiropractor like three days a week," Charles said years later about that period in his career.

As the Sixers sprinted down the floor in transition, Tyrone Hill, a journeyman power forward, drove the baseline. Never known as a shot blocker, Charles went up to redirect Hill's shot. Then, he lost his balance.

When the admittedly out-of-shape Charles landed awkwardly, he felt that something was seriously wrong. Unable to move, he immediately grabbed his left knee.

"I thought he was gonna get right back up," Hill said. "When he was down for a long period of time, I was hoping it was nothing really serious."

By the time Rockets' trainer Keith Jones came over, Charles's knee was bloody and grossly distorted. The celebratory mood inside the old Spectrum, then called the First Union Center, had turned to gloom.

"We could see that quad muscle roll up on his leg in a horrible and frightening way," said Rockets' radio announcer Jim Foley. "It was like seeing someone break a leg."

Rupturing his quadriceps tendon brought a new kind of pain—worse than any he'd experienced in the past.

"I knew it was over as soon as I saw it," Barkley said. "I saw the way the kneecap was bulging through my leg and I said, 'Well, it's been fun.'"

Barkley was grimacing, but silent. He lay immobile on the floor, talking quietly to Jones, his teammates, and coaches, with 19,109 people staring on in horror.

"You didn't hear a shriek of pain, but you saw the end of a career," recalled Phil Jasner of the *Philadelphia Daily News*. "You knew, without question, that it was over."

Barkley was helped off to the locker room, limping, with his head down and towel around his neck. He needed some time to compose himself before returning to a spot behind the Rockets' bench on crutches, wearing a knee brace. Looking down the bench, Tomjanovich held out hope that Charles hadn't played his last game, but said he was crushed knowing he likely would not call Barkley's number again.

"You're just not coming back from that," the coach said.

Charles would sign about one hundred autographs and joked with teammates and coaches, trying to lighten the mood. When the final buzzer sounded on a forgettable 83–73 win for the Sixers, Charles received another thunderous ovation as he used crutches to leave the court one final time.

On a training table, his knee was wrapped in ice when he called Maureen. Tears rolled down his cheeks as he relayed the news he was just beginning to come to terms with.

"It's over," he said to his wife.

He limped and waddled to the podium for the postgame press conference. Wearing an all-black suit, as if he were attending his own funeral, Barkley had Johnnie Mae sitting to his right. The room was packed with local and national media, many of whom had covered Barkley throughout his sixteen-year career.

In true Charles fashion he had a slight grin and a one-liner ready.

"I'm just what America needs—another unemployed Black man," he said.

He limped back to his Philadelphia hotel room after going out with his teammates to Bridget Foy's. He told Sixers star Allen Iverson, whom he had taken to task for treating the game like a birthright, that it was his league now and to cherish his time on top.

Sitting on the hotel bed, Barkley was no longer invincible. Yet fittingly, almost poetically, his career had all but ended in the city where it all began. He cried.

A red light flashed on the room phone. Barkley picked up the receiver and began to listen to the dozens of messages left for him. The first voice mail? It was Jordan.

"I'm here if you need me," his friend said.

He had scripted a much grander end. In fact, the end had begun before the season, when he had announced his sixteenth season would be his last. He had done it in grand fashion, returning to his native Alabama for a preseason game in October 1999.

That night, down a back hallway of the Birmingham-Jefferson Civic Center, Charcey had reserved a meeting hall for family and friends who made the short twenty-one-minute drive from Leeds to celebrate their hero over ribs, chicken wings, pasta salad, and cornbread. The mayors from Leeds and Birmingham stood by the entrance with the Barkley brothers and Michael Glenn, a cousin, and Charcey, eagerly awaiting the guest of honor.

"It's always special to see him play," Charcey told friends lingering by the door after the October exhibition. "Just like the first time."

Standing at half-court with his mom and grandmother, Barkley formally announced his retirement.

"It's time for me to do something else," Barkley said. "It's time for me to have some fun now. I don't think my life could get any better. But it's time to do something else."

In doing so, he also told the crowd of ten thousand that he had donated three $1 million gifts to each of his alma maters, Leeds High School and Auburn University, and to Cornerstone Schools of Alabama. In total, the donations accounted for a third of his salary that year.

Sonny Smith, his coach at Auburn, lauded his former player's "generosity and love for the area." The two had come a long way since Barkley nearly transferred out of the school.

Everyone wanted a piece of Barkley that night. He didn't have time to eat or drink. He took photos and signed balls. He never said no; it wasn't in his nature. Hugging his grandmother on the way out, he was happier than he had been in a long time.

"It's a great night for me," Barkley said to his guests. "I feel great relief and am at peace with myself."

The four months following Barkley's injury had him balancing a future in which he wanted to "learn to play the piano, finish college, and get really, really, really fat." But he was also rehabbing as much as he could to achieve one last goal on the court: to play a few minutes and leave the sport with dignity.

"My objective is to play in the last game of the year," he said. "I want to be able to walk off the court."

With his left leg still in an immobilizer, trainer Tim Grover forbade him from taking to the court until he had the cast removed. Grover, who had trained the likes of Jordan, Pippen, and Bryant, had continued working with Charles in Houston because, as he noted in his 2013 book *Relentless*, Charles was "probably the most athletically gifted individual I've ever seen." Though he trusted his trainer, Charles rejected his suggestion.

"He looked at me with that death stare and demanded a ball," Grover said. "Then he stood under the basket and dunked ten times off the healthy foot. Dunked. Ten times. One foot." He added, "The boot never touched the ground."

For the last game of the season, fans came ready with their Barkley bald caps and No. 4 jerseys for the Rockets' match-up against the Vancouver Grizzlies.

For one night, Barkley was back.

"He's done a lot for this organization and if he wants to walk off the court instead of being carried off, then I'm all for that," Tomjanovich said. "It also gives the people a chance to pay one last tribute to him."

His knee was maybe 70 percent. But nothing was going to stop him from playing in his last game on April 19, 2000.

Not everyone was going to make it easy on him. Lionel Hollins, his assistant in Phoenix who was the interim head coach for Vancouver, wanted to do whatever he could to prevent him from scoring on his team.

"I told the players, 'I don't care if it's his last moment, we're not going to let him have anything,'" Hollins recounted. "As much as I love Charles, we were not going to give him anything. He really shouldn't have been in the game."

Charles, for his part, was feeling nostalgic.

"This is a sad day for me," Barkley said. "I've been playing basketball since I was nine years old and now, I'm not going to be playing anymore. That's the only thing that makes me sad. I won't miss the limelight."

While the circumstances of his last game were not what he envisioned, Barkley was getting to enjoy himself. But first, he had to be good, at least for one more moment.

"It's important for me from a mental standpoint to get out there," he said before the game. "It's a mindset thing. It's been a grueling ordeal to get to this point. I just want to walk off under my own power." He added: "It's just something I have to do. I don't have anything else to prove."

Starting off on the bench, Charles was all smiles. His youthful vigor had returned. Almost four minutes into the second quarter, Tomjanovich got to call Charles's number for the last time. He rose from the end of the bench, snapping off his warmup pants and red shirt. At the next substitution, the crowd jumped to its feet. He was nowhere close to a hundred percent, looking nervous as he checked in. He might have been only months removed from playing, but Charles was mostly stationary and looked almost out of place on the floor.

The contest between two sub-.500 teams took a back seat to the bigger question of the night: Could Charles produce one more glimpse of greatness?

Almost immediately, the power forward tried to do just that. Off a pick and roll with Cuttino Mobley at the 3-point line, Charles rolled toward the baseline, waiting for the pass. Mobley flung the ball to an open Charles. You could hear the crowd begging Barkley to shoot. He paused for one second before launching a baseline jumper. The ball bounced off the front iron and the crowd sighed.

In the second quarter, shortly after another shot clanged off the rim, Barkley's body began to break down. A couple of possessions later, backup guard Moochie Norris got a screen from Matt Bullard at the left wing of the 3-point line. Norris slipped through two defenders and made a run at the hoop. In two dribbles, Norris got to the lane and floated a one-handed teardrop over the outstretched arm of Obinna Ekezie. Down low stood Barkley, boxing out Felipe Lopez, a guard with the same height but not nearly the same size. Charles hadn't really tested out his capacity to rebound.

Luckily, he didn't have to jump too much. The ball careened almost directly to him. With whatever spring he had left in his knees, he snared the ball from a jumping Lopez and pulled it to his hips. He wasn't going to pass it. Not now.

"Charles! Charles!" yelled Rockets' color man Calvin Murphy from the sidelines.

Barkley threw a wild pump-fake before laying it off the glass, drawing contact from Ekezie. Count the bucket. And the foul. The crowd hadn't been that loud all season.

"Charles Barkley," rumbled play-by-play man Bill Worrell, "gets a bucket in his final game!"

He was stone-faced in the seconds that followed, taking high fives from an excited Bullard and rookie Steve Francis. When he walked toward Mobley, he offered the slightest nod, before finally letting out a smile.

"About time," he told Mobley, hugging him at the free throw line. Barkley shrugged and smiled. What more could he have asked for?

Soon after he missed the free throw, Tomjanovich called Kenny Thomas's number, telling the twenty-two-year-old rookie to check in for Barkley. He had played six minutes and seven seconds, scoring 2 points and grabbing a rebound. He laughed coming off the floor to a standing ovation, with Tomjanovich wrapping his arm around his neck and Rogers giving him a bear hug.

At halftime, Dawson presented Charles with the backboard that he just grabbed his last rebound from only minutes earlier. "You really own this one," Dawson told him.

Charles then walked over to the baseline to give an interview to Sager, the TNT sideline reporter known for his warm demeanor and outlandish suits. Sager asked Charles if coming back for one night had been worth it.

"It was worth it. It was definitely worth it," he said to Sager. "I put a lot of time and effort into my rehab. Hey, my last memory was scoring a basket, not being carried off the court. That was a bonus. I really just wanted to get a rebound, and it took me a long time to get a rebound. The doctor was nervous the whole time because my knee is only about 70 percent. And that rebound came to me, so I got lucky. I couldn't have jumped to get it."

Sager reminded him that he was about to finish his career in the top-15 all-time in points and rebounds.

"Well, the big fella up there gave me some stuff that a lot of people didn't have," Charles replied. "I can't take credit for it. I want to, but I can't. God just gave me a tremendous amount of ability. I can't take credit for it though, Craig."

The Rockets lost, but no one cared. It was Barkley's night. He offered a few words to the team, saying it had a bright future with Francis and Mobley. "It's unfortunate I didn't come to Houston until I was on the downside," he told the fans. "I wish I could have played my entire career here."

His voice quavering, he gripped the microphone and pushed aside his regrets to convey his gratitude.

"Basketball doesn't owe me anything, I owe everything in my life to basketball—everything," he said. "I'm thirty-seven years old. I'm rich beyond my wildest dreams. I have great material things. I've been all over the world and it's all because of basketball."

He retreated from the standing ovation to the locker room, where his teammates were waiting for him with beer and champagne, hoots and hollers. He never won an NBA title, but this champagne was a celebration of everything Charles had accomplished.

Soaked in sweat and alcohol, Barkley talked to reporters in the locker room one last time. The regularly loud Barkley grew quieter than usual, taking on the kind of reflective, humble tone he had shown to Sager earlier in the night. All he ever wanted, he said, was to make $1 million and play in the league for ten years. His only goal was to take care of his mother and grandmother.

As cocky and insufferable as he was at times, he never expected to be talking about his own Hall of Fame career, he said. The individual numbers speak for themselves. Career averages of 22.1 points, 11.7 rebounds, and 3.9 assists in 1,073 games. He's one of the most prolific offensive rebounders in the game's history and the shortest player to ever lead the league in total rebounding. He made eleven All-Star teams and twelve All-NBA squads in sixteen seasons. Charles finished top-ten in MVP voting in nine years, including his first-place finish in 1993. As of publication, he is one of seven players in league history to record 20,000 points, 10,000 rebounds, and 4,000 assists—and by far the shortest to do so.

So, how did it happen? Even with his mistakes, and there were too many to count, his exhaustive charisma pulled him toward success and worldwide adoration.

"The difficult thing is that nothing I'll do in my life from now on will come close to what I've accomplished in basketball in the last sixteen years," he noted.

But he sure as hell had to try.

30

Charles Barkley wasn't one minute into his new career at Turner Sports before telling Peter Vecsey he was an ass who would always be ugly.

"He's been an ass a long time," he said of Vecsey seconds into TBS's opening-night broadcast on Halloween of 2000.

Ernie Johnson, the congenial host of *Inside the NBA*, paused to absorb the salvo.

Vecsey, the pithy and abrasive NBA reporter and columnist for the *New York Post*, had ripped Charles for his shortcomings on and off the court, regularly calling him, "Sir Cumference." Days before their first appearance together on TNT, Vecsey wrote in the *Post* how Charles, who had gained over seventy pounds in the months following his retirement, looked like "Richard Jewell's body double," in reference to the overweight and peculiar security guard at the '96 Olympics who was wrongly accused of planting the bomb at the Games.

Whether they knew it at the time, Charles was about to completely reshape *Inside the NBA*. Doc Rivers predicted that Charles in a studio setting "would be like Richard Pryor or Eddie Murphy doing color on basketball," and his prediction was starting to come true.

Johnson, laughing more than he ever had on air to that point, remembered the first show as strikingly different from the fine but largely milquetoast production B.C.—Before Charles. Most importantly, it was surprisingly good. Although Charles had told him in a quiet moment after that he only planned on staying at the show for "two years max," Johnson wanted to keep him there for a longer tenure.

"Everything went so well," Johnson said of the first show. "I was walking out of the studio thinking to myself, 'You know what? This is gonna be great.'"

Not everyone was in on the act. Vecsey felt on- and off-air that Turner was jumping too quickly from being a serious outlet for NBA news to one led by a former player who "talked off the top of his head without knowing shit."

Yet something else was happening: The show would now bond entertainment with the NBA, hoping to tell the story of the league better than anyone else. That couldn't be done without Charles, their new irreverent anchor.

Slamming the New York Knicks for what he perceived as unfair treatment of his friend Patrick Ewing, Charles took aim at one of his favorite targets, perhaps forgetting where he was now working.

"You guys in the media make me laugh sometimes," he started.

Johnson interrupted him to remind him of his current profession: "You're in the media now."

"Yeah," Charles retorted, "but at least I'm gonna be honest."

With that, Turner began an exciting and unpredictable new chapter in sports media.

"He became Turner Sports," said David Levy, the former president and Charles's boss. "He *is* Turner Sports."

Among the merry-go-round of hosts to lead the show was Fred Hickman, who still remembers hearing "Nature Boy" Ric Flair cutting promos one floor above in the World Championship Wrestling offices while trying to film *Inside*.

"We thought it was nuts," Hickman said, "but we made it work."

The *Inside* of today looked nothing like its earlier iterations in the late '80s and early '90s. The half-hour highlight program was traditional and scripted, with a series of hosts taking the baton. Craig Sager was there. So was Hannah Storm. Vince Cellini and Tim Brando had runs in the chair.

Around that same time, Turner hired a young broadcaster in Atlanta to do some sideline work for the NBA. Ernie Johnson Jr., who was the son of a former Major League Baseball pitcher and Atlanta Braves play-by-play man for TBS, had news anchor jobs out of college, bouncing to Macon, Georgia, and Spartanburg, South Carolina, until he landed at WSB-TV in Atlanta. After seven years delivering the news, he got a call from Turner Sports in 1989. The next year, Turner offered the thirty-two-year-old the job to be the NBA host starting in the 1990-91 season.

Cautiously confident in his own abilities, Johnson did not take for granted the opportunity, not after a childhood in which peers and adults pointed the finger at his famous father for whatever accomplishment he had achieved.

"When I took that phone call back in 1989 and said, 'Yeah, I'd love to come work with ya,' you never know how long that's going to mean," Johnson said.

The host earned high marks, but the show was invisible. The same could be said for Turner, overshadowed in the media by a blooming power in ESPN and drowned out in basketball by John Tesh's "Roundball Rock" over on NBC.

Such a facelift in sports production would start with the hiring of Mike Pearl from CBS as the network's executive producer and senior vice president. Then a ten-time Emmy winner, Pearl was already something of a TV legend by the time he landed at Turner, which came shortly after the fifty-one-year-old was the coordinating producer for the 1994 Winter Olympics in Lillehammer, one of the most-watched Games ever.

Identifying talent, and getting them to work for him, was crucial in landing Pearl. The same went for Michael Jackson, a thirty-year-old assistant to Schiller who followed him from the USOC. A former point guard for Ewing's Georgetown teams in the '80s, Jackson had become a protégé to Schiller, responsible for luring talents like John Thompson and Reggie Theus to Turner.

"The change at Turner didn't happen overnight," Pearl told the *New York Daily News* in 2003. "It took several years to give it the look and feel that it has."

Ask anyone and they'll tell you it was Tim Kiely who figured out what a studio show was supposed to feel like.

Kiely, a Pittsburgh kid whose athletic claim to fame was playing football with Dan Marino at Central Catholic High School, had produced *SportsCenter* and ESPN other programs for three years.

His ah-ha moment came in January 1993. Olympian Carl Lewis had butchered the national anthem at a Bulls–Nets game the night before, and *SportsCenter* anchor Charlie Steiner lost it.

"Dirty Harry said in one of his movies that a man's got to know his limitations," Steiner said on the show. "Carl Lewis apparently didn't see the movie."

Lewis, whose voice cracked halfway through the song and said, "Uh-oh," promised the Meadowlands crowd at Brendan Byrne Arena that he'd "make up for it now." He did not.

After the video concluded, the usually straight-faced Steiner was in hysterics, unable to compose himself to say that Lewis's version must have been written by "Francis Scott Off-Key."

Seeing this, Kiely asked for an extra fifteen seconds before the show threw to their game broadcast. His bosses proceeded to rip him a new one, he said. But Steiner's off-the-cuff commentary on Lewis was the only thing people were going to remember years later.

"That kind of got me to a point where I was like, 'Why can't we have that kind of stuff?'" he said.

Arriving at Turner gave Kiely some flexibility to do what he wanted. Johnson reminded Kiely of Craig Kilborn at ESPN—dry, quick-witted, and ridiculously funny. He admired the beautiful writing that went into his material. But Johnson, a creature of habit who Kiely said worked "like someone who thinks he might lose his job," would not give up his scripts, much to his producer's frustration. If you're throwing to highlights of a game, Kiely thought, who gives a shit if you're writing flowery prose?

Thirty seconds before they went to air one night, Kiely ordered that the prompter be turned off. Kiely only had two words of instruction to Johnson: "Just go." The announcer felt exposed on-air, even though Kiely thought he did well. An argument between the two spilled over into the men's room, where an infuriated Johnson fired his coffee mug at the wall.

"It wasn't my best night," Johnson acknowledged years later.

But Kiely got the end result he wanted: the host was on board. Now Johnson needed someone to play off in the studio. The format had been unkind to former players for decades. On NBC, considered the gold standard of basketball broadcasts for years, the rigid structure of highly scripted segments left on-air personalities from Julius Erving to Isiah Thomas sometimes difficult to watch.

"They would throw anybody on those things," said Bill Simmons, the founder and CEO of *The Ringer.* "They would put no thought into whether the person was going to be good or not, if they were comfortable, what they were going to ask them. There were just a lot of misses."

An array of talent would come in and out of the studio, but there was something about the everyman persona of Kenny Smith that struck Johnson and Kiely immediately.

The extent of the slick point guard's media training had been limited. He had received tips from his ex-wife, Dawn Reavis, who was the weekend anchor at KATV, the ABC affiliate in Little Rock, Arkansas, in the early '90s.

"She used to say, 'Critique what I'm saying when you're home watching,'" Smith said. "I would sit home and I'd be like, 'Why were your hands there? And why did you say that?' I was taping her and critiquing her, and that's how I learned about TV."

Cut by the Nets before the start of the 1997–98 season, Smith got a call from Turner. The message: *We were serious about you doing this for a living.* The thirty-two-year-old pursued the on-air gig and signed in March 1998.

"I retired prematurely, but I wanted to do television," Smith said.

"Who knows if the same opportunity would be around two or three years down the road."

Kiely helped unlock Johnson's on-air personality, then Smith became the setup man. More cameras would soon be added to capture the laid-back dynamic of Johnson and Smith's banter. Now they could talk to each other rather than at the camera. "That's what makes us feel natural," he said.

Smith also moved Kiely away from preshow production meetings for on-air talent.

"I haven't been to a production meeting in twenty years," he said in 2020. "I've only been to two ever."

Above all, Smith gave the show a respect factor.

"I can't tell you how many times his cell phone would ring after the show and it would be a current player wanting to talk to him," Kiely said. "Even if they were mad at him, they didn't stay that way for long because he had their respect."

One of them in particular thought it might be fun to join the group.

Putting Charles on TV in a full-time role seemed like a no-brainer. But initially, Barkley didn't have much interest in TV. He wanted to see his family, play golf, and kept toying with the idea of running for governor of Alabama. It was Dick Ebersol, his friend and the mastermind behind NBC Sports and their Olympics coverage, who changed his mind, he said. On NBC, Ebersol saw firsthand how Barkley affected ratings. When Adam Silver was president and COO of NBA Entertainment, he recalled Ebersol as the one pushing for the league to incorporate the perennial all-star in more TV spots.

"When Charles Barkley was still a player, I can remember that Dick was the one who said, 'Let's find ways to use him on-air,'" Silver said. "Dick Ebersol had spotted him as someone who was going to make a great broadcaster."

Turner Sports was not close to eclipsing NBC as the premier outlet for the NBA, but TNT and TBS were now airing more games than any other outlet. Though Ernie Johnson and Smith were smart and insightful, the show was still not registering with audiences. Mark

Lazarus, the president of Turner Sports, believed Charles would be a big draw, and the right fit for a cable channel rather than a network.

Lazarus made a call to Steve Mosko, a friend of Charles's from his time in Philadelphia, who connected them.

"I was all set to go to NBC," Charles said.

At a steak dinner in New York, Barkley hit it off with Lazarus and Siegel. The execs picked his brain on basketball, but Charles wanted to talk about other things. His penchant for off-topic asides would become a hallmark of his on-air personality. Lazarus got into his pitch sooner than expected—the appetizers had just arrived.

"So Mark asks, 'What do you think of our stuff?' And I say, 'You all suck. You guys don't have any fun. You're not curing cancer, you're not policemen. Have some damn fun,'" Barkley remembered.

"And Mark says, 'You think you can do that?' And I say, 'I know I can.'"

When the four-hour dinner wrapped up, Charles reeked of cigar smoke and found himself at a crossroads. NBC had been the obvious choice to that point, but Turner had changed his mind. He called his agent, Marc Perman, in the early-morning hours and told him he had a problem: Charles wanted to sign with TNT.

"He told me to sleep on it, so I slept on it," Charles recalled. "I ended up waking up at 5:00 a.m. because I couldn't sleep at all."

With the money being the same at roughly $1 million annually, Charles pondered whether NBC's relationship with the league would hinder what he could say. Whether the network would again win the broadcasting rights with the league in two years was also a question mark. Could the man with the mouth be as provocative as he wanted to be while under the league's umbrella? But Kevin Harlan initially had a different take.

"My first thought was, 'Why wouldn't you go to NBC? Why would you come to Turner?'" the play-by-play announcer said. "Not that we weren't proud of the product, but maybe he just wanted a platform that said, 'Let it rip. You can be a little off-center here, we're going to give you a wide lane and take it wherever you want to go.' I'm sure the bosses here felt it would be a perfect marriage, and that if he chose Turner, they could see everything we did kind of orbiting Charles."

That vision, and the freedom, tipped the scales in Turner's favor. Shortly after he called Perman of his decision at 6:00 a.m., Charles picked up the phone and dialed Ebersol with the news: he was headed to Turner. It was one of the toughest phone calls of his life.

In March 2000, Turner announced they had signed Charles to a two-year deal that was reported at around $2 million.

In his telling of how Turner landed Charles, he said he valued Charles's honesty and candor, and banked on viewers tuning in to see his takes.

"When I hired Charles," Lazarus said, "I told him to be himself. And I promised I'd never censor him."

That freedom to be provocative on cable was part of the reason for choosing TNT, Charles said. He wasn't sure his true voice would be heard, or given the chance to be heard, on network TV.

"Obviously," said Kiely, "when Charles came, it became nuclear."

If Charles were to break the Guinness World Record for most consecutive push-ups in a minute, he was going to do it on the floor of the TNT studio in his $1,500 custom-made suit and size-sixteen ostrich shoes.

Fifteen seconds in, he called it quits.

Smith laughed at his heavy-breathing partner on the floor, while Johnson joked that "a fifty-yard dash and a good cigar" would probably do in Charles for good. "Does anyone know CPR?" Charles asked, gasping for air on national television to the delight of the crew.

Nights like these were what made Charles and *Inside* true must-see TV in that first year—just like Ebersol had predicted. This is what the most dynamic personality to come along in sports TV since John Madden looked like—big and bold, thunderous and uproarious, unafraid and unapologetic.

That first year Charles won over the public by being his flawed self at a job he described to David Letterman as "the greatest scam going in the world." He got paid to talk shit and there was no one better.

He devised a rankings system based on the Bowl Championship

Series to help decide the presidential election between George W. Bush and Al Gore that had been deadlocked in Florida for weeks. Charles wished Bobby Knight could visit Knicks practice so he could be choked by Latrell Sprewell. At the All-Star Game in Washington, Chuck applauded Turner for not discriminating in its employment of Craig Sager, who, in his silver velvet Versace suit, looked like "a pimp doing interviews with TNT." He thought Vince Carter played like a girl and begged Steve Nash to do something about his disheveled hairdo. He was shocked to hear that journeyman forward Don MacLean was the first NBA player suspended for using steroids.

"I've seen Don MacLean naked," he remarked. "He don't use steroids!"

There was also talk of his weight in the months following his retirement. Not ashamed, Charles subjected his body to be weighed in as part of a segment called "Fat Trak." Charles, who was hoping to get back to his playing weight of 265, surprised himself, and Johnson and Smith, when he came in at 337 ½ pounds—20 more than he'd anticipated. He'd reached a point where he barely weighed less than Marv Albert and Mike Fratello combined.

His weight was regular fodder for the group: when Charles asked Johnson why a story about his weight-loss journey wasn't on the cover of *Time* magazine, the host dryly replied, "because the cover wasn't big enough." Grandmother Johnnie Mae jokingly pleaded with Johnson and Smith to stop peer-pressuring Charles to eat any of the Krispy Kreme doughnuts or drink the orange soda they'd have in the studio to taunt him.

Charles jokingly started asking Dallas Mavericks owner Mark Cuban and other guests to bring him the tiny liquor bottles from their hotel mini bars so he could cut down on his drinking. "I restrict myself to a six-pack," he claimed. But weeks later, when he took off his shirt again for an on-air weigh-in, he had reason to celebrate: he was 297 pounds.

"Charles's willingness to step on a scale on a regular basis spoke volumes about his willingness to simply be himself and to do something that would make the show better," Johnson said. He added, "That was one of the most impressive things about him early on. You could have fun with this guy who was going to be a Hall of Famer, who was one of the 50 greatest players of all time."

Charles's stardom in broadcasting was apparent to critics and fans, but Johnson and Smith were the understated supporting cast willing to run with him to wherever his words took them.

"I think the chemistry clicked a lot quicker than I thought it would," Pearl said. "A lot of that is a credit to Ernie and Kenny… There was no sulking, no crisis meetings. They recognized what he was doing for them, and they took advantage of it."

There was a part of Johnson that believed Charles would be gone once the novelty of doing the show wore off. Smith was reticent about the change. He believed that he and Johnson had started to develop a nice rhythm and wondered how adding Charles would affect their rapport.

"At first, I was a little apprehensive. But Charles came and fit in with us to create something new," Smith said. "Charles is like Mike Tyson or George Foreman, he's throwing the big punch. I'm like Sugar Ray Leonard or Roy Jones, I'm stinging with little jabs all night. And Ernie is like Angelo Dundee, he's keeping us on point."

Their chemistry came at the expense of Vecsey. Vecsey had requested to appear only on TBS and away from Charles on TNT. The ask turned out to be a huge mistake. Vecsey's contract was not renewed by Turner. He had gone after Charles, both on-air and internally, and the company made its choice known—and swiftly.

"I was gone that minute," Vecsey said. "I don't want to think about how much money I blew by asking to be moved."

The first season was lauded by critics as a master class in television, with Charles as the breakout star. In a piece titled, "His Hugeness Speaks His Mind," Richard Sandomir of the *New York Times* laid out how the man who kept the pseudonym "Homer Simpson" at hotels had given TNT's sports programming a nutty basketball version of CNN's *Crossfire*.

Inside was as much a sports show as a sketch-comedy program, said Bryan Curtis, editor-at-large and media critic at *The Ringer*. *Inside* had become a watercooler show when there were still watercoolers.

"It almost had this cult-like following, as if it were a late-night show. People talked about it in the way they would talk about the old Letterman or Conan," Curtis said. "Those who weren't huge sports fans would come up to you and say, 'Did you see what Barkley said on *Inside the NBA*?'"

The show's first Sports Emmy Award in 2001 for Outstanding Studio Show, as well as Johnson's win for Outstanding Sports Personality for a Studio Host, cemented its arrival as the preeminent show. But how long would it last?

Charles, riding the wave from *Inside the NBA*, took more chances in the early part of his TV career. On the cover of *Sports Illustrated*, he was depicted as a modern-day slave who was now unchained and free to talk about racism and all the other issues plaguing America. Around the time of the controversial yet memorable cover, he also accepted an additional role as a contributor at CNN.

When far-right conspiracy theorist Michael Savage sparred with him on immigration, the radio host questioned Charles's qualifications to debate him and bragged about being on 300 radio stations. "So you got 300 listeners," replied Charles, describing Savage as "one of them guys who is really, really smart, who's a dumbass." Savage, whose comments were echoed by Fox News host Laura Ingraham years later, said the "dumb" Barkley should focus on dribbling basketballs.

Coming to the defense of pop star Michael Jackson after he had dangled his nine-month-old baby over a hotel balcony in Berlin, Charles ripped women's rights attorney Gloria Allred for her criticism of Jackson, telling her to "go back to your office, wait on another case, and shut the hell up."

Much to his surprise, Perman told him Jackson saw his defense on TV and wanted to call and thank him. Sure enough, Charles's phone rang.

"He says, 'I just called to tell you, I heard what you said, that old, mean lady Gloria Allred was saying [bad things] about me on television. I wanted to call and say thank-you for defending me,'" Charles remembered.

Flattered by it all, Charles went from bad boy to fanboy, going on and on to the King of Pop about how much of an honor it would be to meet him in person. Except there was one problem.

"I realized that after he said what he wanted to say, he hung up," Charles said of Jackson. "And I was just rambling on about what a big fan I was."

Charles had become the biggest star in sports media in just two years. And his second career was only getting started.

31

Charles had an odd request to Tim Kiely.

"Boy, I need a fish tank," he said.

Illusionist David Blaine had fallen short in his attempt to hold his breath underwater for a record-breaking eight minutes and fifty-eight seconds. Seeing that Blaine had gone for seven minutes and eight seconds, and had to be rescued by divers, Chuck thought aloud that he could outlast a man who had spent a week submerged in a plastic sphere at Lincoln Square in New York in the lead-up to the world-record attempt.

"Get me a fish tank and a pair of goggles. I'm gonna break David Blaine's record!" he told Kiely. He added, "This crazy dude on TV is trying to hold his breath. I want to try it."

Charles had barely dunked his head into the water when Kenny Smith started cackling about him already beginning to struggle. Ernie Johnson offered whatever support he could by saying he was "almost there" at the eleven-second mark. He pulled his Milk Dud–like head out of the water after twenty-four seconds, with Johnson signaling for towels and medical attention for the physical or mental distress his colleague suffered in the fish tank.

"Kenny, you can't be making me laugh!" he yelled afterward over a graphic of Charles's head imposed on an overweight Aquaman.

This is what the biggest sports show since Howard Cosell, Frank Gifford, and Don Meredith graced the airwaves of *Monday Night Football* looked like. Charles's stunts were watched by roughly 650,000 households each week.

"Charles changed everything," said Richard Deitsch, the longtime media reporter for *Sports Illustrated* and now *The Athletic*.

Six years into the job, Charles himself was changing. The generosity he once kept secret had become more visible, like the $1 million he donated to help rebuild homes in the Lower Ninth Ward of New Orleans that were devastated by Hurricane Katrina.

In his third book, *Who's Afraid of a Large Black Man?*, Charles conducted a series of conversations with prominent figures on race. One of them was the Reverend Jesse Jackson, the civil rights movement legend who he had previously disparaged in *Sports Illustrated* for not having done enough "to make social change in the Black community" and was instead "too busy getting other women pregnant." Jackson, a former Democratic presidential candidate in 1984 and 1988, had been dismissive of Charles's political aspirations to that point, only saying, "He's a basketball player."

Their conversation, however, was eye-opening for Chuck. He saw in Jackson a tireless advocate for the Black community who, after decades, was "still delivering the message, whether or not the audience is ready to make the commitment with him."

"He had broken the stereotype of the big, dumb athlete," Jackson said in 2020. "He talks like an educated man because that's what he is."

As part of the book, he also interviewed and befriended Barack Obama, then a forty-something Illinois state senator running for the US Senate who had introduced himself to the world during his breakout keynote address at the 2004 Democratic National Convention. He was intimidated by Obama's brilliance. While campaigning in Cairo, Illinois, Obama endorsed what Charles had been saying about Black children needing role models in the classroom.

"I'm not saying this exclusively," Obama said, "but in many situations you need someone who can call you on your stuff and say exactly what Charles has been talking about, that it's not 'acting White' to read a book."

He liked Obama but believed the racial divide ran too deep for America to ever have a Black president, even if he thought a young prospect like Obama could "bring people together."

His early support of Obama coupled with his disillusionment with conservatism under President George W. Bush, a period marred by never-ending war and "a bona fide tragedy" in the widening income gap between rich and poor, caused Charles to leave the Republican Party altogether in 2006. Years later he cemented his position, telling former friend Rush Limbaugh, who claimed Charles was pandering to Obama, that he wanted to punch the hell out of him. He'd also go on to deny he was ever really a Republican.

But some things remained the same, specifically his criticism of the league. His words resonated for many. Although the segment wasn't directed at her, Sue Bird, coming off surgery and fearing that her play had plateaued in her mid-thirties, took Charles's opinion that older players coming off injury couldn't fight Father Time as inspiration. "I was like, 'No, fuck that. No way, Charles,'" she recalled during a 2020 minicamp for the US Women's National Team. "He wasn't saying it about me, but those words spoke to me and I thought, 'I'm turning my shit around.'"

One person paying attention was Kobe Bryant—and he wasn't in the mood for Charles's shit. After Bryant put up just 3 shots in the second half of a Game 7 blowout loss to Phoenix in 2006, Charles labeled the superstar's performance "very selfish," accusing him of trying to prove a point that his otherwise lifeless Lakers team couldn't do anything without him. The remarks enraged Bryant, who called Charles "stupid" for suggesting he was trying to tank the game. At around 2:00 a.m., Charles looked down at his phone inside Studio J and saw a text message. Bryant was pissed. And then another. And another. And many more.

"Kobe started texting me for the next three hours," Charles said of the twenty to twenty-five messages he received from Kobe. "We're going back and forth and he's calling me every MF, every SOB in the world, and I'm laughing as I get these. I'm like, 'Yo, man, pick up the phone and call me.' [He said], 'No, mo-fo.'"

"First of all," he texted Bryant, "I've called you the best player in the world for the last three years and you didn't exactly call and thank me. But I didn't like what you did. And I knew what you were doing."

The perception that Charles was right haunted Kobe so much that he went on *Inside* that same postseason to defend himself. The appearance of Bryant, in his light blue sweater-vest, white dress shirt, and gold tie, made Charles admit he was wrong to take his accusation to national television, a rare instance in which Chuck said he regretted publicly criticizing a player. They didn't know each other very well, but the two made the moment into an inside joke, with Charles later admitting Bryant's fiery responses were "awesome."

In some ways, showing up to *Inside* soon thereafter also helped Kobe following the sexual assault allegations in Eagle, Colorado, that had tarnished his reputation and cast a shadow on the league a couple years prior. Kobe laughed at his own image during the "Gone Fishin'" segment and promised Ernie he wasn't going to throw down with Chuck in the studio.

"I'm not gonna jump over the table and lump him upside the head or nothing like that," Bryant responded, much to the amusement of Ernie and Kenny.

It was a good thing Charles didn't get beat up on national television because he was about to be inducted into the Hall of Fame.

Six years out, Charles was starting to recognize his true legacy: every short, fat guy who plays basketball will remind fans of Charles Wade Barkley.

"That's not a bad legacy," he told friend and co-author Michael Wilbon. "There's always going to be short, fat guys."

Chuck might have been on the short list of the league's greatest players to never win a title, but he was the undisputed headlining act in a class that included Dominique Wilkins, Joe Dumars, and Geno Auriemma.

Welcoming Charles to the Hall of Fame were two of the most significant figures in his career: Moses Malone and Jerry Colangelo.

"You know, this is basically the end somewhat," Charles said at the start of his speech.

Everyone was there. John Edwards, one of his best friends from Leeds, showed up. Frank, the father he had come to accept into his life after much work, was in the building, and for many it was the first time they had seen Charles's dad in person. Charcey and Johnnie Mae joined brothers Darryl and John.

He praised all his coaches, going back to Wallace Honeycutt, his first coach in middle school who kept him busy just to keep him out of trouble. The usually even-tempered Honeycutt was overwhelmed.

"I can't believe this is happening," Honeycutt said to himself at the induction. "Is this the young kid that I used to coach?"

He thanked Sonny Smith, the man who brought him to Auburn, for making him a better man. After looking at his college transcripts, the three-year player for the Tigers joked he was a legitimate college freshman. In doing so, he noted that he didn't fulfill the promise he made to his grandmother of getting his degree.

He found Maureen in the crowd, looking stylish in a red dress, her blond curls framing her face. The only word he could think of when describing the woman he met at the TGI Friday's all those years ago was *saint*.

"If you can put up with me all these years..." Charles trailed off. "It was a lot of stuff she had to deal with when I got arrested six or seven times."

He paused before clarifying, "I was always acquitted!" The audience erupted and Maureen beamed with a toothy grin.

"You know, when I got arrested it was always in big letters," he said. "When I got acquitted, it was always in little [letters]."

Sitting beside her was Christiana, his greatest gift. At around five-foot-eleven, she'd been encouraged by her dad to play basketball. The problem? She didn't like sports. At all. With that dream dead, he could only thank his seventeen-year-old daughter in that moment for not dating. If she had, he joked, there was a good chance he'd be in jail for killing someone.

Turning to his other family, he pointed to the older brother he never had in Ernie Johnson, who announced earlier in the year that he had been diagnosed with non-Hodgkin's lymphoma since 2003.

Ernie had been shaving one day when he noticed a bump near his left ear. When he finally got it checked, he found out it was a tumor for an incurable but treatable form of cancer. The news made Johnson, a man of unshakable faith, "want to punch God right in the nose," but he vowed to put his head down, get the chemotherapy he needed and, in his words, "compete."

The news shattered Charles, who sat in silence and could only shake his head in disbelief when Ernie told him an hour before their first show since the All-Star Game. He'd call him once a week to check on him. It's why Charles was emotional in seeing Johnson, who had lost his hair from the treatment, finding the strength to make the trip to Springfield, Massachusetts, for the big night. "I told Ernie he need to be more like me and Kenny," Charles said to the crowd. "I said, 'Well, it's best you go bald because I'm not sure you want to be Black.'" He couldn't let Kenny off the hook, who was on his honeymoon: "I said, 'Kenny, it's no big deal. You're only going to get married one time.' Then I said, 'Well, this is your third marriage.' I told him to go and enjoy this one. This one might take."

Julius Erving was there, his former Philadelphia teammate and idol. Chuck remembered a nugget of wisdom from Erving: *We are caretakers of the game.* Chuck understood it now, and Dr. J applauded.

"The players viewed him by how many times he got on the court and kicked ass," Erving said. "Charles, despite being scrutinized, criticized, and judged for his failures rather than his successes, made it to the top of the heap. He became great."

Colin Cowherd could only give Charles advice he had heard so many times before: Be careful with the tables, man.

"There's a reason they build those casinos: You don't win," Cowherd told him of his well-documented trips to Las Vegas. "How about just fifteen minutes max at a table? That's enough."

"Listen, Colin, I can't die with all this money," he replied. "Can you imagine, when I'm in hell, all my family fighting over all this money? It would be a nightmare looking up."

Perhaps no athlete has ever felt more comfortable in Vegas than Charles, the life of Sin City's never-ending party. Gambling, drinking, smoking cigars, dining, women, and as much excess as you desired. Charles loved it. He was also a boxing aficionado, who rarely missed a big fight. Las Vegas had become a part of him.

"He was a player in every respect," said Norm Clarke, the long-time nightlife columnist at the *Las Vegas Review-Journal.* "Everybody wanted to be around Charles. Everybody wanted to be like Charles. He was Good-Time Charlie."

Playing blackjack with Charles was a singular experience for Mark Cuban. Long before he owned the Dallas Mavericks, Cuban was buying $10 tickets and finding his way down to floor seats, where he would yell suggestions at Charles regarding the best salad bars in the Dallas–Fort Worth Metroplex. But one summer, Charles urged Cuban to come play blackjack with a group that included Jordan, tennis great Pete Sampras, and hockey legend Mario Lemieux. But little did Cuban know that Charles was playing for $5,000 a hand. And when Cuban tried to play $100 a hand, Jordan, who playing at around $10,000 a hand, looked on in amusement: *What the fuck?*

A $1 million credit line changed that, as did Charles buying fifty bottles of tequila and handing them out like Halloween candy in what the owner remembered as "one of the best party nights ever." It didn't, however, alter Charles's fortunes at the blackjack table.

Seeing Chuck put down a $10,000 wager at blackjack and another $10,000 at craps was so anxiety-inducing for golfer Andres Gonzales that he had something of an inebriated panic attack. "It was stressing me out, man," he recalled.

Charles endeared himself to all levels of service workers in Vegas, talking to them as if they had been friends for years. Dan Le Batard once saw Charles surreptitiously slide a few hundred-dollar chips into the shirt pocket of the janitor cleaning up nearby.

Many interviewed for this book made it clear how generous of a tipper Charles is, especially compared to Jordan, who had a different attitude about money and people. Charles once recalled how Michael stopped him from giving money to a homeless man: "He smacks my hand and he says if he can say, 'Do you have any spare change?,' he can say, 'Welcome to McDonald's, how can I help you, please?'"

If casino workers got word that Chuck was in town, they'd trade their shifts so they could be on the floor at the same time. He was known for tipping hundreds, even thousands.

"He was a rock star in the casinos," Clarke said. "When Charles came in and won big, his tips were like an extra Christmas for these guys."

The three kings of Vegas—Charles, Michael, and Tiger Woods—connected in the late '90s and hit it off immediately. During his twenty-first birthday celebration, Tiger wanted to gather a group of friends for an early-morning tee time at Grayhawk Golf Club in Scottsdale. At around 7:00 a.m., he called the group and told them he couldn't make it, saying he got caught up in Vegas with Charles and Jordan.

"He ended up coming out the next day, and he looked like the mouse that the cat dragged in," a friend told *Vanity Fair* in 2010.

At the Vegas night club Light, the best-looking girls on staff were given the rest of the night off to hang out with the trio so they could keep spending money. "The girls were workin' it," said a former employee. By 2:00 a.m., Woods was sitting on top of a banquette. He wanted to be seen by not just Charles and Jordan but everyone in the young, hip crowd.

While his affinity for gambling was no secret, the depth of Charles's losses was previously unknown until 2006. As he was trying to explain what golfer John Daly was going through in his reported gambling troubles, Charles acknowledged estimated gambling losses of $10 million. That number has gone up drastically: years later, he admitted that while he had probably won $1 million ten times in Vegas, he projected that he had lost the same amount on thirty separate occasions. One night in 2006, he admitted to losing $2.5 million "in a six-hour period."

Concerns about Charles's gambling habit hit a high point in May 2008, when Wynn Las Vegas filed a lawsuit against him in district court. The casino alleged that the star had not paid back $400,000 in gambling markers given to him the year before on a Super Bowl bet. The Wynn also persuaded the Clark County District Attorney's Office to open a criminal investigation into Charles not paying off his debt.

After his attempts to reach Charles went unanswered, district attorney David Roger leaked the complaint to the *Review-Journal*. Charles paid it the next day, only to find out he owed another $40,000 for the litigation fee.

"I screwed up," he said to Ernie on *Inside*. "It was a hundred percent my fault. I'm not going to gamble anymore. Just because I can afford to lose money doesn't mean I should do it."

No one does a New Year's party quite like Charles—an annual spectacle he's hosted for years on his tab with a DJ, dancing, party favors, and ample booze.

Turner Sports president David Levy had settled into bed at his home in Westchester, New York, when he got a call from Charles in the early-morning hours of New Year's Eve 2008.

"Hey, Chuck, what's up? Happy New Year," he wished his star.

"Oh, I fucked up," Charles replied. "I'm at the police station. I was arrested."

The first thing Levy did was pull up *Deadspin* to see if the police report had been made public. Looking back at Levy from his computer screen was the mug shot of Charles—half-shaven and sweaty with a resting smile and bloodshot, watery eyes—in what the site called "easily one of the most fascinating/disturbing/mind-blowing things you'll ever read."

"Oh my God," Levy replied.

Earlier, Charles had enjoyed a feast at Mastro's City Hall of steak, lobster, mashed potatoes, and creamed corn fit for the king of sports media. The festivities of December 30, 2008, continued over at Dirty Pretty Rock Bar, where a party of four hundred people, a group that included NFL star Michael Strahan and actor Jaleel White of Steve Urkel fame, ran up a bar tab of $1,800 for about three hours.

The night, however, was far from over.

Pete Smith was on duty for the Gilbert Police Department, working with the East Valley DUI Task Force over the holiday. The job hit close to home for Smith, who had lost a squad partner in a 2006 incident involving an underage drunk driver who had run a red light and launched the officer ninety feet from his motorcycle. "You find that you're very committed when something like that happens," Smith said.

To keep him company on his December 30 birthday, Smith's fifteen-year-old daughter, Jessica, joined him on his ride-along in an unmarked patrol car around Scottsdale's Old Town, the trendy nightlife area.

At 1:26 a.m., Smith pulled over a black Infiniti QX56 for rolling through a stop sign a half block away from Dirty Pretty. Before the SUV was stopped, a woman had climbed into the passenger seat.

Smith immediately recognized the driver, as well as the strong odor of vodka coming from his breath. Charles explicitly asked if he was being pulled over because of who he was, which was not the case, Smith said.

"There were three or four cars in a line and I was the fourth car," Charles wrote in the foreword for *Dallas Morning News* columnist Tim Cowlishaw's 2013 book *Drunk on Sports*. "We all slow-rolled through a stop sign and when I did it, the flashing lights came on and the cop cars came out of the woodwork."

After the officer identified six clues of impairment, including a .149 blood-alcohol content that was nearly twice the legal limit in Arizona, Smith asked Charles where he was going. Charles, who failed the sobriety test but maintained he wasn't swerving, said he was "in a hurry to pick up the girl," and urged Smith to admit the woman with him was "hot." He wasn't going to give the cop a "bullshit answer" on how much he had to drink. Feeling a little more comfortable and congenial around the officers who were on the scene, the former player later answered why he failed to fully stop at the stop sign.

"[Barkley] asked me, 'You want the truth?' When I told him I did, he said, 'I was gonna drive around the corner and get a blow job,'" Smith wrote in the police report. "He then explained that she had given him a 'blow job' one week earlier and said it was the best one he had ever had in his life."

Once it was clear he was going to be arrested for a DUI, Charles showed concern for the female passenger, the officer recalled, and pushed for her to be released. The woman, who is not identified in the police report, was allowed to leave and walk back to the bar area, Smith said.

He was arrested on suspicion of misdemeanor DUI and impaired to the slightest degree. His car was impounded, and he was later released to a taxi.

It didn't take long for Levy to see the report on *Deadspin*, as well as *TMZ* and *The Smoking Gun*. Levy told him to come to Atlanta the next day. Charles was suspended from TNT for six weeks. After that period, Charles declined to return to the air for All-Star Weekend in Phoenix, thinking his presence would overshadow the festivities.

"I'm looking at myself thinking, 'Shit, I want him back. It's fucking big ratings,'" Levy recalled. "But I didn't because Chuck asked me not to."

Barkley would get slammed in the weeks that followed from critics wondering if the public should expect more from one of television's most handsomely paid personalities. On *Saturday Night Live*, Kenan Thompson's portrayal of Barkley had him lampooning his way-too-sweaty mug shot as looking like "Wilson floating away from Tom Hanks." But Charles and his attorneys were angered that the line about receiving oral sex was included in the police report, maintaining that it was not meant to be taken seriously.

"That was 100 percent a joke," said Charles, adding that he made the comment after he had posted bail and was waiting on a ride. "But someone decided to put it in the report and so everyone thinks I said it seriously to get out of the arrest."

Now a pastor at Redeemer Reformed Baptist Church in Phoenix, Smith maintained the night he pulled over Charles for a DUI was never personal. A member of the police force for twenty-one years, the big Suns fan was just doing his job, while trying to protect his daughter from what could have been a high-profile court date.

After the attorney turned off the tape, he asked me, "Why did you include the info about going around the corner to get a blow job?" I told him how I wanted to demonstrate Charles's level of impairment. The other half I never told him about was that my daughter was in the car. If this piece of information keeps the case out of court so my daughter isn't dragged into this situation, then so be it.

It wasn't my goal to humiliate him by including the details about the woman in the car. I can only imagine what that did to him.

I had heard it was a real low point for him. I have no idea if it modified his behavior in any way, but I hope in some way that it ended up being a positive.

Charles was fined more than $2,000, ordered to an alcohol treatment program and to install an ignition interlock device on his cars.

But it was his three-day stay in March 2009 at Maricopa County's Tent City, the infamous outdoor jail overseen by Sheriff Joe Arpaio, that raised eyebrows.

Dressing inmates in striped jumpsuits and pink underwear and having them sleep in surplus Korean War tents, Tent City was long decried by critics as cruel for keeping people in sweltering-hot conditions that could reach between 110 and 130 degrees. Arpaio's response was that if American troops in Iraq could handle such conditions, then inmates should shut up and live with it. Inmates were served green bologna and forced to listen to KJOE, the radio station that played all of the sheriff's favorite songs. Even Arpaio, a hard-liner on undocumented immigrants who was later found in a Justice Department study to have overseen the worst pattern of racial profiling in American history, once described Tent City as "a concentration camp."

At a news conference outside the jail's chain-link fence, Charles, dressed in a red-and-blue Nike tracksuit, sat beside Arpaio as he held up the book bearing his newest inmate's support and called Barkley's time at Tent City "cordial."

Though Charles's experience was hardly that of a regular inmate. As part of a work-release agreement, he would only have to be there from 8:00 a.m. to 8:00 p.m. He did not have to wear the embarrassing uniform and was not forced to eat the green bologna, and he had his own private tent. Barkley bristled at questions about why he didn't dress the part of his fellow inmates.

"If y'all really, really want to put me as low as I can go, I can do that and make you feel better," Charles said at the time. "I know when [someone is] famous, you like to see people humiliated."

The news conference in the Valley with two of the area's biggest celebrities was catnip for locals who bowed to their personalities, remembered Len Sherman, a biographer for Arpaio and Jerry Colangelo.

"It was totally a show, how could it not be?" Sherman said. "You had the most flamboyant sheriff in town and the most flamboyant sports star in a town that doesn't have a lot of either…in a flat landscape bereft of personality. It was inevitable."

Charles, who had initially endorsed Arpaio on his 1996 autobiography *America's Toughest Sheriff*, would voice his displeasure with the sheriff a year after his stint in jail. Comedian and friend George Lopez suggested on *Inside* that Charles not learn Spanish so quickly due to Arizona SB 1070, the state's immigration law allowing police to question and detain suspected undocumented immigrants. The mention of the new law, then the broadest and strictest measure against the undocumented population in the country, had Charles namechecking Arpaio in a tizzy that forced Lopez to tell him to "take it easy" before having him pivot to a Bucks-Hawks game that night.

"When I think of Charles, I like to think of him standing up against SB 1070 and the racist laws in Arizona that Joe Arpaio was promoting," said Dave Zirin of the *Nation*. "That is something worth remembering."

The incident was a learning experience for Charles, who claimed he had gotten behind the wheel "hundreds and hundreds of times" after drinking without any trouble. He stands by his belief that he wasn't drunk that night, but credits the incident for changing his outlook on a decision he had repeated for decades.

"I never thought about killing anybody," Charles said. "For me personally, I was like, 'Wow, I could actually kill somebody.'"

His broadcasting career and personal life were so unfazed that *Sports Illustrated* recognized Chuck as "The Escape Artist"—"a superhero who strolls out of the rubble of a collapsed building, calmly brushing dust off his shoulders as if nothing happened."

That power would come in his greatest period of loss.

32

They didn't have a lot to call their own in Leeds, but Daryl-Marie Barkley could count on Saturdays with her father at the Barnes & Noble in Birmingham. That was their thing: Darryl shared his love of literature with his daughter.

"I couldn't pick a book fast enough. He'd have me on his lap and always read to me," she said. "That's my favorite memory of him."

Waiting in his hospital bed to see whether he'd receive a new heart made Darryl Barkley realize how much time he had wasted on the streets. At thirty-six, Darryl's life had been riddled with health issues stemming from his previous substance abuse. The cocaine caused so much strain on his enlarged heart that he suffered two heart attacks and a stroke. His heart had been functioning at 10 percent capacity, Charles said, and had brought about complications with other organs. His ravaged body was close to falling apart.

"It had really rained on my parade," said Darryl, referring to the heart attacks and stroke. "I needed the transplant badly."

After more than a year on a waiting list, Darryl received his heart transplant in March 2003. No one was more grateful than his big brother, who was not religious but believed God played a huge role in the outcome.

"I can't describe the feeling I have that my brother gets a second chance," Charles said at the time. "I'm mostly excited for my mom and my grandma. This has really weighed on them. We almost lost him about five times."

Darryl founded HeartChange-HeartExchange Ministries to help assist transplant patients and their families at Birmingham Children's Hospital. He saw it as his second chance.

"I go around and tell kids in schools to stay positive, stay in school, and don't hang around with bad people in bad places," Darryl said to the *New York Times*. "I tell them, keep going forward and look up."

Not even the side effects from the transplant, like the migraines that sometimes forced him to stay in his bed in the dark all day, couldn't keep him away from his daughter. Though he had divorced from wife Melanie, his relationship with Daryl-Marie remained strong, the daughter said. He chaperoned all her field trips and their visits to Walmart felt epic. Daryl-Marie still thinks about the Build-A-Bear with two hearts they teamed up to create.

There wasn't much to do for spring break in Leeds, but the father and daughter planned to see a movie the Friday of that week. The ten-year-old walked a couple houses over to see her dad for what was supposed to be a fun day of buttered popcorn and fountain soda.

But when the fourth-grader got home on March 20, 2009, she found her father unconscious on the floor.

"The door was open, and I saw him lying there," Daryl-Marie remembered, "but I didn't know if he was deceased."

Almost six years to the date of the transplant that saved his life, Darryl's heart had given out. He died at the age of forty-two in the only neighborhood of the only town he'd ever known.

"He left a mark on Leeds just because everyone knew who he was," his daughter said, noting the hundreds who came to his funeral.

Darryl's death was crushing for Charles, who helped raise him as a kid and supported him through his substance abuse troubles later on. Compounding his grief, Charles had lost maternal grandfather Frank Mickens at the age of sixty-seven just months before.

Still reeling from Darryl's death, the family knew it was also about to lose its matriarch, too. Johnnie Mae, the architect behind Charles's rise to stardom, had been in failing health for some time. This reality was crushing for Shaq's mother, Lucille O'Neal, who was now like family to Charcey and Johnnie Mae.

"We looked up to Granny for everything. We looked to Granny for the way she loved on you," Lucille said. "I'd go to their church with them on Sunday morning and talk about the goodness of God, where we came from and how good life was now."

Daryl-Marie saw Johnnie Mae as doting and lenient, the kind of great-grandmother who'd still allow you to watch TV after you'd gotten in trouble at school—a far cry from the woman once unafraid to pull out a switch and discipline your backside.

Years into his run at *Inside*, Charles found ways to mention his grandmother on-air. Most of the time, he would clown on the woman he loved so much, once joking how his grandmother was so old that she had to put WD-40 on her ankles just so they could move.

"My grandmother, who's my best coach ever, she's not wrapped too tight up top," Chuck said one night on the show, much to the shock of Ernie Johnson. "My grandmother used to call me after every game and if I played bad, she'd say to me, 'Boy, you're embarrassing this damn family.' Grandma Barkley would say, 'You can't let people tell you they can stop you. You go out there and kick their butt.'"

He held on to her words forever.

Johnnie Mae England Edwards Mickens died on December 2, 2009. The former meat factory worker and proprietor of May's Beauty Shop was eighty-three. On Johnnie Mae's shared gravestone with Frank Mickens in Leeds reads an inscription from Charcey, her only daughter: *Mama I Love You—Red*.

For the second time in less than nine months, Charles lost a piece of him. First, the younger brother with the wide grin. Now, the woman who helped him find his voice.

"He looked up to her more than just about anyone and Charles was her boy," recalled Amy Shorter, his high school sweetheart.

A decade into an experiment that was only meant to last two years, *Inside the NBA* had won four consecutive Sports Emmys for its playoff coverage and Ernie the honor of Outstanding Studio Host in 2006. All the while, Charles, now a two-time Hall of Famer after being inducted as part of the '92 Dream Team, was a cultural phenomenon. He was being paid more than he ever had as a player and still working less, even with his additional role with March Madness as part of a landmark partnership with CBS.

Dan Patrick, the longtime radio and TV sportscaster, said the show has ascended into the rarified air of sports shows that have stood the test of time—institutions like *SportsCenter* of the '90s, *Pardon the Interruption*, and *College GameDay*.

"*Inside* is something we definitely hadn't seen before," Patrick said.

So, how could the best show in sports get better? Months before he was set to retire, Shaquille O'Neal had an idea: get rid of Charles or Kenny and make way for the Big Analytical.

"Matter of fact, in about three hundred days, the other guy going to be in trouble, I'm just putting it out there now," O'Neal said in early 2011, not specifying whose job he jokingly planned to take. "One of 'em gonna have to get out that seat. Big man's coming."

The big man in question was, of course, Shaq. David Levy met with him in 2011 to discuss joining the show. But questions remained. To add O'Neal, who commanded a spotlight all his own, could also disrupt an award-winning show—one that would allow its personalities to blame a zebra's escape from the circus onto the interstate as an excuse for why they were late.

The presentation Levy had in store for O'Neal was unorthodox.

"Shaq, there are companies that want you and there are companies that need you," Levy told the big fella. "We want you, but we don't *need* you."

O'Neal smiled and was intrigued. He already had a sense of how difficult it was going to be to compete with Charles. ESPN's basketball coverage had been wildly inconsistent, in large part because they didn't have the stability or verve of *Inside*. "They've always had their nose pressed up against the window of what Turner does in terms of that NBA show," said James Andrew Miller, co-author of *Those Guys Have All The Fun*. Shaq might have become ESPN's version of Charles, but being a Chuck clone was never something that appealed to him.

"Everyone who wasn't TNT was saying, 'We need another Charles, we need another Charles,'" O'Neal said. "And I'm like, 'I don't want to be another Charles.'"

Charles was immediately onboard with trying to get Shaq. Levy had this in the back of his mind as he was telling O'Neal how he already had an Emmy-winning show, almost playing hard to get.

"To put you into this mix, there's more risk on me, David Levy, and Turner than there is for you," the president said to Shaq.

The show celebrated his multiyear deal with Turner in July 2011, with an over-the-top vignette filled with cheerleaders, fireworks, pyro, and confetti as O'Neal walked onto the set. Catching a shirt shot out of a cannon, Chuck unfurled a garment that had him and the rest of the *Inside* crew dressed in togas and kneeling to The Big Aristotle, feeding him grapes, and fanning him on his throne.

But to assume his throne, O'Neal had to be heard. O'Neal had purposely mumbled throughout his career as a player, his way of shutting out the media. The problem was that had now transferred over to his career *in the media.*

"We added Shaq and it was, 'He's gonna ruin everything. He mumbles and he doesn't speak out and he's not gonna be heard,'" said executive producer Tim Kiely.

Seeing his new analyst mumble on-air, Kiely urged O'Neal to shout in order to cut through Charles. To get his point across, the producer had Ernie, Kenny, and Charles copy Shaq's mumbling delivery so that he could hear how bad it sounded. O'Neal was also not doing his homework. Smith recalled one show where O'Neal spoke about how Tyson Chandler was going to have an impact that night—not knowing that the center was injured and wasn't playing. As punishment, the trio joked how Bill Russell, then in his seventies, was going to have a great game.

The show felt off and Kiely summoned just Charles and Kenny for a rare meeting. Smith said the producer confronted them about why they were making fun of Shaq and not allowing the show to be great with him. Charles was livid but remained quiet. Smith, on the other hand, countered: When does someone come on our show and we *don't* make fun of them?

Kiely agreed: Do whatever you want to him.

"They would pull me aside and tell me, 'If you want to do what you're doing now, go to ESPN. We want you to be Shaq,'" O'Neal recalled. "I said, 'Oh, you want me to be Shaq?' Once I started loosening up, then we started cooking together."

Soon the disjointed flow of the show smoothed out and O'Neal was louder and more prepared. Kevin Harlan, TNT's play-by-play man, was most impressed at how Shaq wanted to fit in and be a role player of sorts—listening and processing before "coming at you like a locomotive." Shaq leaned more into physical comedy, tripping over himself racing Kenny to the jumbo screen.

"Charles is the catalyst for all we do. He's the big clown and I'm the second clown," O'Neal said. "I'm the comedy clown."

Once the quartet found its rhythm, it was clear that they were better with Shaq in the mix. As predicted by Levy and Lenny Daniels, the chief operating officer for Turner Sports at the time, the bombast of Charles and Shaq's repartee elevated the show.

To say it was an adjustment for CBS's Clark Kellogg to work with Charles and Kenny during the NCAA Tournament was an understatement. Kellogg leaned toward a more serious, straight-man persona. He deeply studied the schools in prep for the tournament. Charles did, well, less of that. Harlan said that Kellogg was a walking conscience compared to Charles, the walking circus. While Kellogg credited Chuck for loosening him up, he also saw what kind of person he was when his email was hacked and sent out a "I'm stuck in a foreign country, please transfer money" scam message to all of his contacts. Most people knew it was not legit, but Kellogg got a call from Charles to make sure he was okay and if he needed any money. "It floored me," Kellogg recalled. "I'm a hundred percent sure he was dead serious because he doesn't call me much."

When it came to the on-air chemistry between Charles and Shaq, the pair needed to strike a balance. Sometimes, Shaq would be the combative foil who pushed back against Charles and reminded him of his career shortcomings in every debate. Sometimes, he would play the comedic hype man. But since the beginning, their on-air arguments have followed a familiar pattern, reminiscent of an old married couple. Their verbal spats regularly generate headlines in both the blogosphere and establishment media like the *Washington Post*, the *Guardian* and *USA Today*. Charles, the man without any social media who says anyone who tweets likely lives out of their mother's basement, regularly trends on Twitter, in part because of his devolved debates with Shaq.

Charcey and Lucille O'Neal didn't need social media to hear about the shots their boys took at one another. They were usually watching, with one calling the other to talk about whatever it was they had gotten into the night before.

"We would talk to each other each day on the phone and Charcey would say, 'There they go arguing again.' I would just bust up laughing," Lucille remembered. "I started calling Shaquille and said, 'Didn't we tell y'all to play nice?'"

Howard Beck, the longtime basketball scribe now at *Sports Illustrated*, joyfully likened their banter to old men waving their fists at the clouds. They were selling the raw talk of close friends, which makes for compelling television. Their heated disagreements can take the show to a place others can't.

"I always make the distinction, and Charles will never engage in this, that the difference between him and Shaq is that Charles knows how to make fun of himself and Shaq doesn't," ESPN's Howard Bryant said. "Shaq isn't kidding when he's attacking you. They do admire each other and are friends, but you can also tell that Shaq has to win and that's not the case for Charles."

For Shaq's part, he sees it's a matter of perspective.

When it comes to certain settings, I want to know how you know something, period. If you don't know, then you shouldn't be speaking on it so adamantly.

You can give your opinion, but how do you know? I know because I've been to the Finals six times. Kenny knows because he's been there twice and won twice.

It's just like a question thing. I want to know. I'm interested when both those guys speak, but with Charles, I'm like, "How do you know?"

But here's the thing: He showed us kids how to play mean, throw elbows and play with reckless abandonment. My daddy used to tell me all the time, "You got to rebound like Barkley and get some elbows up."

So he's definitely meant a lot to me.

After a report that the Rockets and Clippers had to be separated to avoid a locker-room confrontation, Chuck and Shaq found themselves in tears and laughing uncontrollably at the thought of the two sides coming to blows.

"I played in the NBA for sixteen years and I've been on TV 18 years. It's the first time I've heard 'police presence!'" Charles said through tears, as O'Neal erupted in the background.

Charles and Shaq guessed what an emergency phone call would sound like. Ernie and Kenny were there, unable to stop the two-man bit.

"Hello, police? Chris Paul tried to beat me up!" O'Neal sputtered. "Hey, this is Blake Griffin. Chris Paul tried to get in here. Get down here and save me!"

Charles offered what he thought Griffin would sound like on a 911 call.

"I'm 6-10, 225, one of the most powerful players in the NBA," he started, "but...but Chris Paul trying to get in here and kick my ass! Get down here quick!"

On nights like this, when the duo was really letting loose and having a blast, Chuck would get text messages throughout the show.

But there was one person who wasn't going to reach out to Chuck. He hadn't done so in years.

Oprah Winfrey asked Michael Jordan, who sat next to Charles, a simple question: *Isn't it great to have someone tell you the truth?*

The friends were so close that Michael compared his arguments with him to those with his wife, Juanita. But in Charles, Jordan had a confidant who'd shared similar on-court experiences who wasn't afraid to voice his opinion.

"He's always going to tell me the truth," said Jordan, before clarifying. "His truth."

"But why do you love him?" Winfrey asked.

Not sure of what to say, Jordan paused before flashing the pitchman grin and responding with a question: "Look at him. How can you not love him?" In a sign of true friendship, His Airness then reached over and started rubbing his friend's beer belly as if he were pregnant.

"The guy was like a brother to me for, shoot, twenty-something years," Charles said in 2020.

In Jordan's second full year as majority owner of the Charlotte

Bobcats, no team in league history had looked as hopeless. En route to a 7–59 mark in a lockout-shortened 2011–12 season, the Bobcats had all but clinched the worst season for a team in the history of the NBA. No one would dare come to Charlotte in free agency, and the team had whiffed on lottery pick after lottery pick, until UConn guard Kemba Walker showed promise.

Their poor performance was historic, but the notion that it came under Jordan felt particularly jarring. Jordan wasn't supposed to be this bad at anything basketball related. Yet midway through the season, the team was last in offensive efficiency and second-to-last in defensive efficiency, which was enough for broadcaster Jeff Van Gundy to proclaim that Charlotte's coach, Paul Silas, should win Coach of the Year for miraculously winning any games, period.

One of the reasons why Charles was so adored by his media colleagues was that he was always available to talk. In March 2012, he went on *The Waddle & Silvy Show* on ESPN 1000 in Chicago to talk about all things basketball. Inevitably, Michael came up.

When asked about Michael's performance as an owner and eye for talent in 2012, Charles did not beat around the bush. Jordan's record had spoken for itself after hiring close friend and former Bulls teammate Rod Higgins as general manager. Charles mentioned one instance leading up to the 2006 Draft when Jordan, in his first year as manager of basketball operations, was leaning toward selecting Gonzaga forward Adam Morrison with the third overall pick. Charles thought there was no way that Morrison, the nice kid with the 3-point stroke, bushy hair, and wispy mustache, could play in the NBA and urged his friend to take Washington's dynamic scorer, Brandon Roy.

Charles turned out to be right in that instance: Morrison lasted only three years in the league, while Roy, who had to retire early due to a degenerative knee condition, won Rookie of the Year and was a three-time All-Star who averaged 18.8 points a game for his career. The issue for Charles wasn't about whether his friend was right or wrong, but how Jordan was getting to those conclusions.

"I think the biggest problem has been I don't know if he has hired enough people around him who he will listen to. One thing about being famous is the people around you, you pay all their bills so they very rarely disagree with you because they want you to pick up the check," Chuck said. "They want to fly around on your private jet so they never disagree with you. I don't think Michael has hired enough people around him who will disagree."

In other words, Jordan was not good at this.

At all.

"I love Michael, but he just has not done a good job," he said. "Even though he is one of my great friends, I can't get on here and tell you he's done a great job. He has not done a great job, plain and simple."

The radio show went to commercial, and Charles noticed his phone was ringing. He looked down to see who was calling him. It was Michael.

He picked up the phone and, for one of the first times in his life, he couldn't get a word in. Jordan took what he said personally.

"He is mf'ing me up and down, up and down, up and down," Chuck said. "I didn't think Michael was gonna react like that."

When he hung up the phone, Charles didn't realize it would be the last time he'd speak to a man forever connected to him, one who was akin to a brother.

The first public indication something was wrong with their friendship was when CNN's Rachel Nichols pressed him on which friends he had lost due to things he had said. Saying he'd "rather not get into that," Nichols wondered aloud if she had successfully asked Barkley a question he wouldn't answer. This was like calling Marty McFly "chicken," teasing Chuck into going a step further than he probably wanted.

"It's put a wedge between our friendship and that's been disheartening for me, too. Very disheartening," he said. "One minute we're close and now we're strained."

Knowing he had already said too much, he repeated how Jordan had too many yes-men around him and the fear among the owner's advisers to challenge him. "Might as well burn down a whole house. You started the fire now," he said to Nichols. "I've burned down the kitchen and the bedroom."

What really irked Charles was that he felt he was in the right—and Jordan's woefully mediocre run since then has only supported that.

"The thing that bothered me the most about that whole thing, I don't think I said anything that bad," he said. "The thing that really pissed me off about it later is Phil Jackson said the exact same thing."

The longer the split lasted the more people questioned whether the two would ever repair their friendship. Sam Smith, author of *The Jordan Rules*, saw the bond between Michael and Charles as overrated, a partnership blown out of proportion to make for a better story for the media. Charles was very much his own man, which didn't always vibe with what it meant to be in Jordan's bubble.

"Charles has always had a strong, independent streak about him and with Michael, if you wanted to be a part of his group, you had to subjugate yourself to Michael. I think Michael enjoyed his company, but you really didn't get the sense he was part of his group," Smith said. "As Michael's celebrity grew, these guys wanted to be around Michael's shadow and aura, and that's just not who Charles was. He didn't want to be a follower."

Kenny Smith did his part to try to squash the silence in October 2016 when Jordan, who was staying at the same hotel in New York, came down to the lobby to congratulate him on the show being inducted into the Broadcasting and Cable Hall of Fame. Kenny was standing with Charles, and it was the first time he and Michael had seen or spoken to each other since their phone call four years earlier. They all took a quick photo together. Whatever tension existed looked to be overexaggerated, Smith said, and it was all high fives.

The moment quickly went viral on Instagram with talk of appeasement, but it wasn't to be. In fact, the image reopened an unhealed wound for Charles, who told Dan Le Batard that he missed Jordan's friendship. Smith said Charles was wrong and should be the one to patch it up.

"All he has to do is make a phone call if he misses him," Kenny said. "The one thing that Charles and both Michael have is a lot of pride... [Charles] should apologize."

Four years later, with its arrival of the Michael Jordan documentary *The Last Dance*, came fresh takes on the Mike-Chuck bromance and its fallout.

On *The Waddle & Silvy Show*, the same radio program where he'd made his original comments, Charles acknowledged that the sadness over losing Jordan remained profound, but he'd come to accept it. Charles would not be the one to call Jordan, saying His Airness had his phone number and knew how to reach him.

Jordan would not apologize, and neither would he, Charles predicted. Thus, the two athletic superpowers remained in a Cold War–type standoff.

Not even Le Batard, who had once lost a Finals bet to Charles that forced him to wear a Speedo, could redirect his friend toward reconciliation.

"That's never gonna happen. You can let that go," he said to Le Batard. "That's never gonna happen. I'm too stubborn for that."

33

Three words caused the latest public uproar against Charles. Those same words also made Shaq laugh with such force that he would cry, cough, and wheeze for minutes on end.

Big. Ol'. Women.

Chuck had gone on for years about how his ass would look normal in San Antonio, which by and large, in his words, lacked skinny women. Now a spokesman for Weight Watchers, Charles joked how San Antonio would be a gold mine for the weight-loss and diet organization. To him, Victoria was a secret for the women of San Antonio, who were double-fisting churros and had to wear bloomers instead of racy lingerie.

His derogatory comments drew immediate national backlash and calls of apology from the women of San Antonio, city officials, and obesity awareness groups. Local journalists and bloggers ripped Chuck for body shaming, asking what his mother, wife, and daughter would think of what he said. Vanessa Macias, the girlfriend of Spurs legend Tim Duncan, made up tight-fitting shirts to show Chuck what he was missing.

Days later, Tim Kiely approached Charles about the public relations nightmare, O'Neal recalled. "Charles, you offended some people," said Kiely, according to Shaq. Charles tentatively agreed that he would apologize on the playoff broadcast.

What began to sound like an apology went in another direction.

"Some of you people don't like my sense of humor. Here's what I got to say: Turn off your damn television. I'm not gonna change. If you don't like me or the show, turn it off," he said. "And they want me to apologize. That's not gon' happen. That's not gon' happen." He added, "Y'all can write letters to your momma, your daddy, your uncle. I'm gonna have fun on television. You know that I'm joking around, but if y'all waiting on me to apologize, hell gonna freeze over."

Smith asked again, to remind him why his colleague needed to apologize: "For me jokin' about those big ol' women down in San Antonio."

Turner wondered how many more headlines they would grab like that if Charles made good on the suggestions he was ready to walk away. In the middle of a new diet, Chuck nearly fell asleep on a broadcast, admitting he was bored watching the games that night. He didn't even know if he would finish out his contract, which was set to expire in 2016. Turner, along with ESPN, had agreed in October 2014 to a nine-year, $24-billion extension to keep the media rights to the NBA through the 2024–25 season, an exorbitant deal that nearly tripled the previous annual average value.

The deal came with burning questions about the future of *Inside the NBA*: How do they keep the band together? And how do they both appease Charles and keep him in check?

Turner president David Levy knew they had to get creative to keep their biggest star. Starting as an advertising salesman in New York, Levy had a knack for closing deals. He came to Turner in 1986 and would be hailed within the company as the transparent communicator who let you know where you stood and how he was feeling.

Levy had solid working relationships with his on-air talent, especially Charles, whom he trusted to keep doing his job, even when players and coaches complained about him. He'd learn to do what he called "the Chuckie." If Levy didn't want Charles to bring up a specific topic on-air, he learned not to bring it up in hopes of Charles not mentioning it. If he did, there was no doubt Charles was talking about it that night.

In January 2015, Levy was joined by four of his top staffers—Lenny Daniels, Craig Barry, Tara August, and Tim Kiely—to make the trip to Charles's home in Scottsdale for the in-person pitch to stay. Levy came well equipped with a tribute video from staffers expressing their gratitude to him for making their lives better. More importantly, he carried with him $1,700 worth of wine and tequila: two magnums of 2009 Bond Estates St. Eden Napa Valley Red and two bottles of 1942 Don Julio tequila.

"We had to be dead-on that day because we had one shot as far as I was concerned," Levy recalled.

Knocking on the front door of Charles's home, a nearly nine-thousand-square-foot lot in north Scottsdale, Levy and crew were on two missions: bring back Chuck and kill all the high-end alcohol in sight.

They drank, feasted on pasta and meatballs, and smoked cigars in what Levy called "one of the greatest nights." They watched the video tribute, even if the only place in the home they could watch the DVD was on a laptop. Turner's offer included Charles essentially being part-time, so he could spend more time with his family. There was also the chance to work on media projects outside the show that focused on the Black community.

Around the time of the presentation, August, the senior vice president of talent relations, walked into the room with a giant check, the kind that would make Publishers Clearing House feel inadequate. The check was for an amount of money Charles hadn't fathomed from *Inside*.

"Chuck," said Levy, "we did some math and we believe this number, we're not one hundred percent sure, but we're pretty much sure that if you added up all the money you've made in your entire NBA career on the court, this number will be larger."

While the exact amount is unclear, a source indicated the salary was around or at $10 million a year, with one person describing the figure as "fuck-you money." When asked if that term was an appropriate description of Turner's offer, Levy replied, "I didn't say that, but yes, it was." Later on, Vince Thompson, Charles's friend from Auburn who went on to found the sports marketing agency MELT, said Charles told him his first thought when he saw the number being offered was, "That's fucking stupid." (Charles confirmed to Dan Patrick in 2022 that he makes around $20 million a year between Turner and endorsements.)

Charles looked at the check and smiled. So did Maureen. The Turner team was laughing, some nervously, not knowing what Charles would say next. He got up and shook Levy's hand.

"David," he told him, "I'm in."

And he'd be in all the way, wanting to work a full-time schedule. Chuck didn't even need his agent, Marc Perman, to hammer out any of the details. Ernie, Kenny, and Shaq were planning to come back as well, which Charles admitted put him under the gun. Leaving them now, he said, "would have been very unfair for me to do," Playing golf with Levy near his house the next morning, Charles reiterated he was all in.

"My agent never got involved. That's how much respect I have for David," Charles told *Sports Illustrated*. "At this stage of my life, I'm not concerned about money. I told my agent, 'We are not haggling or negotiating. Do the deal.'"

The ten-year deal announced in May of that year would keep the quartet intact through the length of Turner's deal with the NBA. Although Charles publicly said it wasn't about the money, the fifty-three-year-old was the wealthiest he'd ever been, making more money in one of his broadcasting contracts and arguably possessing even more fame than during his tenure in the NBA.

All the while, he didn't know how many days he had left with his mother.

For forty-five minutes, the standing-room-only audience of nearly three hundred people at the Leeds City Council meeting demanded answers. A controversial zoning ordinance that limited new home construction to a minimum of 1,500 square feet was about to be implemented, and many in attendance were concerned about what the community was becoming.

Sitting in the front row with her hand raised, a board member with the Leeds Water Works Board was loud and disruptive. She was indignant that the voices in her community were not being heard. The ordinance passed, but not without a fight. For her efforts, the manicured and well-dressed woman was thrown out after demanding transparency.

"Mayor Eric Patterson had one resident, Charcey Glenn, removed after warning her to not interrupt the council," reported the *Birmingham News* in 2010.

While her first-born was entertaining the world, Charcey had become a great and influential voice back home in Leeds. Through the Charles Barkley Foundation, Charcey and her son had contributed more than $1 million in scholarship funding to Leeds High School seniors to that point.

He talked about his grandmother's influence more, but those in Leeds saw Charcey in him. You always knew where she stood on an issue and she was going to tell you about it. Children would surround her after service at Macedonia Baptist on the street named for her oldest child, awaiting her to dole out candy from her bag before making the short walk home. If you weren't at church on Sunday, she'd ask you what it was that took precedent on the Lord's day.

In her decade working with the water board and years sitting on boards and councils around town, strangers from across the state would get wind of who her son was and asked for photos.

She never had Charles too far from her mind. Whenever he got embroiled in controversy, she'd heard from people in Leeds about how she needed to "talk to that boy and tell him to keep his mouth shut." Her response: *He ain't no damn boy, he's a grown-ass man.* If anything, she wanted to hear more of what Charles had to say—whether she agreed with him was beside the point.

"I think he should keep on talking. Seriously, he has that right, you know, and I didn't raise no fool," she said to ESPN. "You might not like what he has to say, but that's the way he was raised."

In early 2015, Martha Korman, one of Charcey's best friends, took Charcey to the hospital for pain that was initially believed to be stemming from high blood pressure. The diagnosis was grimmer than they could have anticipated: Charcey's kidneys were failing. Years of smoking had slowed the blood flow to important organs and accelerated her decline.

Back on Charles Barkley Avenue, Charcey never let on how sick she was. She didn't need to when they saw it for themselves, Lucille

O'Neal said. Decades after her grandmother bathed her and laid out her clothes as a child, the roles were reversed and it was Daryl-Marie doing the same for Charcey. Martha and Lucille were flying back and forth to Birmingham every weekend to see the woman they considered to be their sister.

The stretch was considerably hard for Charles, who was back in Leeds whenever he could get there to be with his mother. Family and friends, local and far alike, came by to give their support in the spring and summer. Charcey camped out in the living room, talking about what the future held for all of them.

"It was anticipated," Daryl-Marie said, "but her death was very hard to watch."

Charcey Mae Gaiter Glenn died of kidney failure on June 19, 2015, in the comfort of her own home.

In her obituary, the seventy-three-year-old was remembered by loved ones for her "vibrant personality and smile [that] touched many lives." Leeds had lost an icon, a Black woman who grew up in the segregated projects of the Jim Crow South and went on to become one of the most transformative and giving figures in the Alabama town's history.

It's the golden hour on an August evening and the sun is splashing the pavement on Ohio Street. Located a half mile away from the Barkley home in Russell Heights, Moton Hill Cemetery is tucked in the back of the town, with scores of plots bumping up against the greenery buffering the resting place from the traffic of Interstate 20. Don't waste your time looking for it on Google Maps. You just have to know where to go.

Toward the top of the hill headstones for grandfathers Simon Barkley and Adolphus Edwards are spread out across the field. Uncle Simon Barkley Jr., who encouraged Charles to make amends with his father, is there as well. Johnnie Mae shares a gravestone and is buried next to her husband Frank Mickens. Not far away is brother Darryl, whose grave has two hands coming together in prayer as a light shines from the heavens. Charcey's plot matches that of her late son.

The land is peaceful and quaint. The dead can rest here. Right by the flagpole in the middle of the cemetery remains an open space.

It's the prettiest spot in Leeds. The person who one day might be laid to rest there will be at home among the relatives who loved him into being.

It's through the spirit of his family that Charles was inspired to speak out on racism. He often looked back on his time in Leeds as crucial for helping him understand race in America.

In *Who's Afraid of a Large Black Man?*, he lays out how racism remains the most insidious force in our culture—a point he's repeated whenever given the chance. His goal: to have an open and thoughtful dialogue on race. He recognized no one person can end systemic racism, but he's determined to approach it head-on.

"I can't sit around and say nothing," he said. "I can, because of my position in life, try to start a more public discussion of race and how prejudice just kills us all little by little."

Charles gets emotional when he talks about Muhammad Ali. He's inspired by how Ali refused to serve in Vietnam because of the lack of respect shown for Black men expected to go kill strangers in a strange land. He's not Ali, and he's said as much, but Charles felt a similar social responsibility as a famous Black athlete. "The notion that I would say to another person I've never met before, 'I don't like that person,' that sounds insane," he said. "That sounds insane."

The advancement of Black people was on his mind as he sat across from President Barack Obama in the East Wing Library, talking about his new My Brother's Keeper initiative to shore up opportunity gaps that young men of color confront.

The Obama interview for TNT was a success for Charles, whose body of work on race and views on systemic racism have been nuanced and complex. While so much has gone into his thinking, Johnnie Mae's values continue to animate his perspective. She always encouraged Charles to judge people on their own individual merits and to find the good in people across their differences. "That's how Mama brought us up," Charcey told ESPN years before.

"All Black people ain't great. All White people ain't evil," Charles recalled Johnnie Mae saying to him.

Charles also had a deep respect for law enforcement that would also come into play.

Even when he was a player, he would read the newspaper on the plane or before practice to get caught up on current events because there was an expectation and understanding he'd be asked about it. People craved insight from athletes and they got it. And Charles was the well that never emptied.

Amid an ongoing national reckoning on race, Charles continues to share his views—some of which spark disagreement.

"He's not always trying to say the popular thing. He's gonna say what he's been saying all along… That's why a lot of people can't sit well with it," said rapper and activist Chuck D. "[The media] shouldn't ask him questions if they know the answers that are coming down. He's going to tell you the truth—his O.G. truth—and keep it moving."

He was asked by a Philadelphia radio station about Seattle Seahawks quarterback Russell Wilson, who was the subject of an article that included allegations from teammates that he wasn't "Black enough." The issue was one close to Charles's soul, and he covered much of the same ground in *Who's Afraid of a Large Black Man?* But the report frustrated Charles, who defended Wilson and claimed "there are a lot of Black people who are unintelligent, who don't have success," who are tearing down their own community if they see someone who doesn't fit their idea of what it is to be Black. Charles said he believed that Black people were singular in their thinking that "if you go to jail, it gives you street cred."

"We as Black people are never going to be successful, not because of you White people, but because of other Black people," he said.

The comments were contentious and created viral backlash. They set off a series of stories from critics questioning Barkley's reasoning. Among them was Ta-Nehisi Coates of the *Atlantic*, who months earlier had published "The Case for Reparations," the critically acclaimed essay on the historical redlining and housing discrimination and its devastating effects on the Black community. In an article titled "Charles Barkley and the Plague of 'Unintelligent' Blacks," Coates described Charles's thinking as "painful," arguing the notion that Black irresponsibility contributed to America's race problem was far from a secret, especially when it was one shared by the nation's first

Black president. The essayist chalked up Charles's words as respectability politics at its worst.

"It's worth noting that there isn't much difference between Barkley's claim that 'there are a lot of Black people who are unintelligent' and the claims of a garden-variety racist," Coates wrote.

Charles was surprised the story went national. The response reflected the mood of a country crushed by numerous fatal incidents of unarmed Black men and women killed at the hands of White police officers. The words "I can't breathe," were uttered by Eric Garner when NYPD police officer Daniel Pantaleo placed him in a prohibited choke hold in his attempt to arrest the forty-three-year-old in Staten Island on suspicion of selling single cigarettes from packs without tax stamps.

Just twenty-three days later, Michael Brown was shot and killed in the middle of a street in Ferguson, Missouri, by another White police officer, Darren Wilson, after the eighteen-year-old allegedly stole a box of Swisher Sweets.

The public anger from the cases erupted onto the streets as waves of protests unfolded across the country, with millions voicing their anger at law enforcement and a legal system that has historically discriminated against Black people. The sports world had taken notice, too, with several NBA stars wearing T-shirts during their shootarounds that read "I Can't Breathe," and five members of the St. Louis Rams taking the field for the game with their arms in the air in solidarity with "Hands Up, Don't Shoot."

That national unrest would only intensify in a nine-day period in which neither the grand jury in Ferguson nor Staten Island charged the White officers with any criminal charges in the deaths of Brown and Garner, respectively. In Ferguson, peaceful protests turned violent after the grand jury's announcement.

Seeing it play out, Charles said he again agreed with the grand jury's decision, emphasizing he was solely going off the evidence in the case. He went on the Philadelphia radio show of old friend Mike Missanelli to slam the actions of the mostly Black protesters in Ferguson and support the police working in Black neighborhoods who, according to him, were preventing those areas from going to hell.

"Them jackasses who are looting, those aren't real Black people.

Those are scumbags," Charles said. "We have to be really careful with the cops, because if it wasn't for the cops we would be living in the Wild, Wild West in our neighborhoods. We can't pick out certain incidents that don't go our way and act like the cops are all bad."

Like he did in the case of Trayvon Martin—the unarmed seventeen-year-old Black teen fatally shot by neighborhood watch volunteer George Zimmerman in Sanford, Florida—Charles doubled down on his views about Ferguson in a sit-down interview with CNN's Brooke Baldwin. He went so far as to say that Black people, as a whole, "have a lot of crooks" and that there was a reason Black people were racially profiled as much as they had been. When asked about Garner's death, he again agreed that the grand jury made the right decision and went one step further.

"I don't think that was a homicide. I think the cops were trying to arrest him and they got a little aggressive," he told CNN. "When the cops are trying to arrest you, if you fight back, things go wrong. I don't think they were trying to kill Mr. Garner. He was a big man and they tried to get him down."

If Charles's goal was to help start a dialogue, the cultural critic had succeeded—just not in the way he anticipated. His contrarian views on race and the policing of Black people were lambasted by critics who labeled his words as tone-deaf, damaging, and flat-out false.

Van Jones of CNN described Charles's comments at the time as "inflammatory" and "irresponsible." Dr. Jason Johnson, an academic and political analyst from Morgan State University, questioned Barkley's "hypocrisy about his own privilege" and demanded media outlets make Charles defend his views. CNN's Bakari Sellers was among the many who were also turned off by Charles's comments.

Despite his public breakup with the Republican party years earlier, Charles's pushback on groupthink and his takes on hot-button issues like the policing had long appealed to White conservatives. The Ferguson comments were catnip for right-wing websites that published headlines about Charles "speaking the truth about Ferguson" and lauding his shots at the media as "epic." Even Rush Limbaugh, who Charles had openly disparaged, came to his defense.

Dan Le Batard and Bomani Jones, the former duo from ESPN's *Highly Questionable*, agreed that many White people like to wave around Charles's opinions on race in a self-serving way, often putting him on a pedestal in that moment to support their own argument. Le Batard guessed these people did so not realizing "he might be dabbling in respectability politics, but ignore him when he claims, 'Yeah, that's racist.'"

But the biggest salvo came not from a media pundit but from Charles's *Inside* colleague. Kenny Smith has credited Chuck as the reason the show was able to branch out and talk about social issues. He would use that freedom to tell Charles he was penning an open letter to his broadcast brother in *USA Today* about why the Black community has so much distrust in the police and legal system. He wondered why the public gave Charles's opinions the same weight as those who've dedicated their lives to these causes. To Kenny, Charles was not qualified to hold this much authority in the debate:

What I consistently find interesting is how writers and media members view your insights in politics, and now race relations, with the same reverence as your insights in sports.

They did it in the Trayvon Martin trial and now with Mike Brown and the decision in Ferguson. It's not that you shouldn't ever have an opinion, but you are often quoted alongside the likes of Al Sharpton and even President Obama. I would hope that Sharpton or President Obama would never be referenced with you when picking the next NBA Champs!

...And you were right, Chuck, let's not discredit that there are great police officers in all neighborhoods, but let's not credit that we shouldn't have doubt.

Between Charles's pugilistic opinions and Kenny's response, Ernie Johnson promised viewers that the newest episode of *Inside* would "not be your traditional pregame show." For the next ten minutes, it was the best of what *Inside* could be, with both men making it clear it was "all right to disagree."

Charles apologized for using "scumbags"—a term he usually reserved for sportswriters he despised, like Peter Vecsey, Skip Bayless, and Phil Mushnick—but said it didn't change what happened, emphasizing that not all cops are trying to kill Black people. Kenny acknowledged Charles's point, while pushing back on how a lack of economic and educational opportunities have created distrust in police and the law in the first place. Before the end of a segment that had the two friends shake hands out of love and respect, Charles recognized the position he was in—his words used as grenades depending on whether his opinion matched up with certain politics—and wished he wasn't weaponized for one side or the other.

"You know, it's funny, I hear all these guys talking about 'my opinion.' First of all, people want to hear your opinion unless you disagree with them. That's the only thing that bothers me," Charles said. "Like if I would have came out and said—as a Black man—if I had came out and said, 'All the cops suck,' all the Black people saying, 'I love that damn Charles Barkley.' So, you're always in an awful, awkward situation."

The ten-minute segment was raw, authentic, and emotional, but also respectful, the kind of discussion between disagreeing friends that wasn't happening anywhere on television during that time. Sellers, the CNN commentator, said Charles showed he was more nuanced than people gave him credit for, adding how "people expected him to fit into a cookie-cutter image of what Black men should be and Charles doesn't do that."

A serious discussion on race and policing had become one of the basketball show's best-known moments. *USA Today* columnist Christine Brennan praised what *Inside* allowed Charles and Kenny to do as an ideal example of what open dialogue should look like. The message: Keep talking.

Chuck wasn't going to back down.

"Some people are going to agree with me," he added, "and some people are going to kiss my ass."

Charles looked like millions of others in the days after the 2016 election: shell-shocked.

Donald Trump, who ran a divisive, populist campaign filled with unhinged tweets and sound bites appealing to fear, defied expectations and conventions to become the forty-fifth president of the United States in the most stunning upset in American political history.

Two nights later, Ernie, Kenny, Shaq, and Charles struggled to process the repudiation that had just unfolded for the world to see. Kenny was disheartened at how nearly sixty-three million people voted for racism, misogyny, and narcissism. Shaq couldn't believe a guy with no political experience was about to be president. Ernie, who seemed to be on the verge of tears, was praying for America because that's what scripture told him to do. And for Charles, the guy who had played golf with the businessman at charity events in the past and once told a young boy twenty-five years earlier that he should aspire to be like Trump "because he gets all the best babes," could only hope the ugly rhetoric would be a thing of the past.

"We have to give him a chance, that's the bottom line," he said. "I respect the office of president of the United States, and we have to give him a chance. Everything he said in the past, that's water under the bridge."

That is until the river immediately flooded and swept the bridge away.

All the while, NFL quarterback Colin Kaepernick had emerged as a central figure on what had become a national conversation on athletes and free speech. Kaepernick's decision to kneel during the playing of the national anthem in protest of police brutality and racial oppression ignited a worldwide movement that had athletes of all ages, from youth leagues to the pros, taking part in the silent, peaceful protest. Trump, who never met a culture war he didn't want to stoke, called on NFL owners to fire any "son of a bitch" who kneeled and for his supporters to walk out of the games.

Years after Charles had followed the examples of Bill Russell and Kareem Abdul-Jabbar to use his platform to speak out on social issues, activism had returned to the NBA in a big way, led by superstars in LeBron James, Chris Paul, and Dwyane Wade. The WNBA had long been proactive on social issues, but their male counterparts were now catching up thanks in part to James, who was unafraid to challenge Trump on Twitter, where he called out the "bum" for his responses to the kneeling protests and the "Unite the Right" white supremacist rally in Charlottesville, Virginia, that killed one person.

This offended Fox News host Laura Ingraham, one of Trump's most dedicated defenders. After seeing a February 2018 interview featuring James and Kevin Durant in which LeBron said Trump "doesn't give a fuck" about people, Ingraham called the response "ignorant" and "barely intelligible," telling the transcendent talents to bite their tongues and obey the nation's new head man.

"Millions elected Trump to be their coach," she said on her show. "So keep the political commentary to yourself or, as someone once said, shut up and dribble."

The fallout from the phrase, which critics accused of being racially charged, cranked up the national temperature even more. Charles's response would come on a familiar stage.

His return to *Saturday Night Live* in March 2018 to host for the fourth time, the most ever for an athlete, was inflected by recent events. When Charles arrived at 30 Rock the week of the show, Bryan Tucker had an idea for a monologue to reflect the tenor of the national discussion—and remind people that the announcer had never been one to stay quiet.

Tucker, *SNL*'s co–head writer, just told Charles to start talking in the office. He wrote everything down verbatim, popping in a couple jokes, and a monologue was perfected over three days. Charles walked a little slower onstage in March 2018 than he had his previous times there. He had something to say to LeBron, someone he'd come to admire, and all the other athletes who were told to stay silent.

"I'm an athlete and athletes have been speaking out a lot this year. They've been kneeling during the anthem, refusing to go to the White House. But a lot of professional athletes are worried about [how] speaking out might hurt their career. Well, here's something that contradicts all of that: me," he said to a roaring applause. "I've been saying whatever the hell I want for 30 years, and I'm doing *great*.

"Some people don't want to hear from professional athletes, like this lady on Fox News who told LeBron James to shut up and dribble. And dribbling is like LeBron's only fourth thing he's good at—shooting, passing, and magically making his hairline come back," he observed. "Look, I got a message for people who complain about athletes: We can do a lot more than dribble."

After plugging his Chardonnay, he concluded the monologue with a message for the sport's standard-bearer.

"So LeBron, keep on dribbling and don't ever shut up," he exclaimed, "and maybe one day, you can host *SNL* for a fourth time, just like me."

The monologue hit the mark in a way other attempts hadn't. Bomani Jones said instances like this spoke to Charles's character: "We allow him to say things that are dead wrong and come back, largely because we believe in the goodness of his intentions."

34

Together, they are arguably the greatest team in the history of sports television. But individually, comedian Jeff Ross pointed out during the roast of *Inside the NBA* at All-Star Weekend 2020 what each of them are known for without each other:

Shaq is best known for missing free throws.

Ernie, in his bow tie and Jordans, is best known as the assistant coach of the quidditch team at Hogwarts, fresh off a tremendous season.

Charles is best known for missing court dates.

And Kenny is best known, well, for knowing Charles.

"Kenny Smith," Ross bellowed throughout Chicago's House of Blues. "Sounds like a name Charles Barkley gives to the cops—*'Yeah, I'm Kenny Smith.'*"

Basketball fans needed a reason to laugh over burgers and beers in February 2020. David Stern, the commissioner who helped build the NBA into a global force, died of complications from a brain hemorrhage the month before. Weeks later, Charles walked out of an early screening of *The Gentlemen* when he sensed something was wrong.

When he got home to retrieve his phone, he had more than seventy-five text messages and one hundred missed calls. Kobe Bryant was among the nine people, including daughter Gigi, who died in a helicopter crash in Calabasas, California. Dead at the age of forty-one, Bryant's passing shattered Charles, who saw him grow up before his eyes.

"It was like a death in my family," he said, noting that he couldn't stop crying the day of his passing. "He was like part of my family."

While the weekend was in memory of Bryant, the celebration of his life played out as a pandemic was taking shape. Millions descended on Chicago as the United States was unaware that the country's first coronavirus death happened just days before. Despite the World Health Organization declaring COVID-19 a global health emergency, the threat was not registering for those who packed hotels, restaurants, bars, and clubs for a glimpse of their favorite players and celebrities. This went double for the *Inside* crew, as the show was celebrating its thirtieth anniversary.

Even if there wasn't an under-the-radar public health crisis looming, the future was beginning to look unclear for TV's best quartet. David Levy, the Turner president who helped put together and maintain *Inside* while expanding NBA and MLB rights and adding NCAA Tournament rights in his thirty-three years with the company, had stepped down in the wake of the $85-billion merger between Time Warner and AT&T. (Levy would join the Brooklyn Nets as CEO, but stepped down less than two months after taking the job in what was described as a mutual parting.)

Charles didn't expect many day-to-day changes with CNN president Jeff Zucker taking over Levy's responsibilities, but Turner's biggest star acknowledged the move was "a very difficult thing," as his friend had given him complete autonomy to go wherever he needed to on-air. (Zucker resigned in February 2022 after acknowledging a romantic relationship with a fellow executive at the network.) Without Levy steering the ship, Charles was thinking aloud again about retirement—this time for good. He had originally eyed the end of the 2020 season, his twentieth with TNT, as his farewell from broadcasting, but told reporters he was looking to retire after his 60th or 61st birthday.

"I don't want to die on TV. I want to die on the golf course or somewhere fishing," he said in 2022. "I don't want to be sitting next to old fat-ass Shaq and drop dead."

Now in his late fifties, Charles could barely count on one hand the number of guys he played against who were still in the league. Warriors forward Draymond Green publicly questioned whether the "oldhead" still understood the modern-day players when he hadn't played in two decades. Charles got entangled in a feud with him.

"I said, 'Charles, you don't realize how powerful your words are,'" said Derrick Stafford, a former NBA referee and a longtime friend who said it was wrong for Barkley to advocate violence. "I bet he wanted to smack Draymond in the mouth, but he wasn't right. I said he needed to apologize because too many people are listening to him."

Yet he was as culturally relevant as he had ever been. His finances too were robust, and he was able to send all of his nieces to college. His marriage to Maureen had made it over thirty years, and his daughter, Christiana, had graduated from Villanova and Columbia's Graduate School of Journalism and followed him to Turner. A marriage of her own wasn't too far away either.

If he wanted to continue to follow the examples of Russell, Muhammad Ali, and Martin Luther King Jr., his three greatest influences not named Johnnie Mae, to shake up the world to his liking, he'd need more than his vast sea of resources.

He'd *need* time.

For as good as life had been on TNT, he publicly recognized that his run would likely soon come to an end.

"I'm not going to work fucking forever. I can promise you that," he said. "At some point, you're going to be too old to have fun and enjoy life… I don't think you can say, 'Let me just work my butt off and when I turn seventy I can enjoy life.' I don't think you got a lot of shit left after seventy."

But for now, during All-Star Weekend, the *Inside* crew was bagging on Gary Payton. Kenny pointed out that the NBA legend, nicknamed "The Glove," apparently never wore one as a father of four. Shaq later turned the tables on actors Tiffany Haddish and J.B. Smoove, who had burned them earlier in the night, in a joke so lewd it didn't make the broadcast: "JB Smoove's teeth so big, if he eat Tiffany Haddish out he gonna give her a hysterectomy." Charles bent over in laughter and Ernie's cheeks went red as he covered his face in his hands.

Smoove, however, observed that while Black might not crack, Charles was exhibit A as to how Black does indeed stretch. While he was proud of him getting the key to the city in Leeds, which the comedian said amounted to nothing but "wire cutters and a goddamn rock," Smoove gave Chuck some options for life after retirement, including banana pudding inspector and comfy chair breaker-inner.

"You got a brand-new La-Z-Boy, stiff as hell, it's all hard and stiff. He comes over there with his big fat wide ass, sits down and stands up like fifty or sixty goddamn times. Just keeps standing up like seventy times, eighty times. He's sitting down, getting up, sitting down, and getting up and work that chair until that motherfucker is comfortable as fuck," Smoove said to the joyous House of Blues crowd. "You doze off in that chair because Charles's ass has been in that chair."

Charles could only laugh and shake his head. But before he could inspect banana pudding or break in recliners, he had a lot left to give—money, support, and words, a whole lot of words.

Doug Turner didn't know how to put it to Charles: Please stop bruising my leg.

Years after politics had become the "scumbag business" that forced Charles to abandon his dreams of running for Alabama governor, he had some unfinished business back home. Running for governor was no longer a political goal that motivated him. Too many skeletons, too few zeroes in the paycheck.

Yet the thought of Roy Moore as the next senator of Alabama was too painful to envision for Charles—and that was before he was slapping the campaign manager's leg out of nerves on election night from the couch of a suite at the Sheraton Hotel in Birmingham.

"I thought he had mellowed with age, but as I'm sitting there on my iPad, he starts hitting on my leg and says, 'I'm so fucking nervous,'" Turner recalled of the man he saw kill his Pell City team decades earlier. "By the third time he did it, I was like, 'Alright, you're really hurting me.'"

Charles was rooting for Democratic candidate Doug Jones to defeat Roy Moore and take over the seat vacated by Jeff Sessions. The special election was a referendum on Alabama, a state that molded much of Charles's worldview but according to him would be dead last in every important metric "if it wasn't for Arkansas and Mississippi."

Charles knew Jones had prosecuted two members of the Ku Klux Klan responsible for the 16th Street Baptist Church Bombing in Birmingham that killed four Black girls in 1963, seven months after Charles was born. He also knew that Moore was a "white separatist" whose campaign was headed by former White House chief strategist Steve Bannon.

About a week before the contentious election, Jones got a call from a sportscaster in Birmingham with a lead: Charles wanted to help out with the campaign. If he was never going to mount a campaign of his own, then supporting Jones was the next best thing. Helping to defeat a proxy of a president he despised also played a role.

"Charles could say the things I couldn't say as a candidate. I just couldn't be that as a candidate," said Jones, describing Chuck's platform as "a wonderful bullhorn."

The night before the special congressional election came to its dramatic conclusion, Charles was back home in Alabama. He encouraged voters to get to the polls in a race that was all about turnout. "He gave people a lot of reasons to not sit at home," Jones said. "When I say he jumped in with both feet, buddy, he *jumped* in."

The early results showed Moore up by around fifty thousand votes, and Charles was nervous as hell trying to make sense of the voting projections from the *New York Times*. He remarked on the couch how he "never cared as much about anything as this." He believed the election of an alleged pedophile in Moore would hold up a narrative of Alabama and "how stupid we are." This struck Turner, who was beginning to think about Jones's concession speech all while Charles was striking him in the leg.

"He knew that it's still a part of the world so easy to look down on," Turner said. "Charles did not want his state to be embarrassed in that one shot."

Twenty minutes later, the vote shifted heavily in Jones's favor, specifically in counties that were heavily Black that had come out to overwhelmingly rebuke Moore. Jones thought it was over minutes earlier. Now he was about to become the first Democratic US Senator in the state since 1992.

Close to twenty people jammed inside a service elevator as the Associated Press was about to call the race for Jones, who now led by more than twenty thousand votes. The soon-to-be senator heard the ballroom erupt with news that his victory was near. Charles, cramped in the back of the tiny space, joined them. Before the elevator stopped, he opened up to the packed group inside the elevator about what the evening meant to him.

"Folks, let me tell you something," he said. "I've done some incredible things in my life. This is the greatest night of my life."

The night was a special one, but Jones was always vulnerable in Alabama. He'd lose to Republican Tommy Tuberville, the former Auburn football coach, in 2020. Tuberville was among the group of Republican senators who objected to Joe Biden's victory over Trump in the 2020 presidential election on January 6, 2021.

Inspired by the win in Alabama, Charles found himself in a giving mood on *Inside*, pledging $1 million to Black women in his home state to develop IT startups. But there was a catch.

"That does not mean hair salons and restaurants, Black women," he clarified, leaving a laughing O'Neal wheezing.

Kenny was not amused: "Why did you have to do an underhanded, backhanded joke?" he asked.

Charles, seeing Shaq struggling to get out words, kept it going: "We're not gonna do any more weave shops. We're going to do IT, IT—that don't mean 'it' either."

"You don't even own a computer," Kenny astutely pointed out about his friend, who needed a twelve-step program to log in to Netflix.

"I don't," Chuck confirmed, before getting serious again, "but I want to help other people be successful."

Wipe away the bluster and jokes, and Charles had been putting his money where his mouth was for years. Since his first public donation as an NBA player—$7,000 for a new basketball court in Leeds in 1990—he has given millions of dollars in scholarships, financial aid, and gifts for a wide range of causes through the Charles Barkley Foundation. Between the fiscal years of 2001 and 2019, the most recent 990 forms available, the Alabama-based nonprofit reported more than $5.93 million in contributions, gifts, and grants, averaging out to more than $312,000 annually during that period. That average more than doubled to over $630,000 annually between 2016 and 2018, according to publicly reported tax data. It's unclear whether that figure includes the additional pledges to causes he's made on-air, such as the gift to Black women in IT.

His philanthropy has focused on education and underserved communities. He has supported historically Black colleges and universities, many of which are struggling financially after years of unequal government funding.

As chair of Alabama A&M's capital campaign, John Hudson knew his alma mater needed a high-profile injection to get the word out about the school's hope in 2016 of raising almost $16 million—and he knew the right guy. Hudson had befriended Charles through Auburn tailgates and dinners. It also didn't hurt that his father was the principal of Leeds Junior High and knew Johnnie Mae.

Charles liked the idea of helping Hudson, and pledged $1 million to Alabama A&M, the largest individual gift in school history.

"I think I dropped my phone," Hudson recalled. "He did it just because he cared."

Back home in Leeds, where almost 9 percent of the population still lives below the federal government's poverty level, Charles was fighting for affordable housing. Not far from where his mother lived are dozens of dilapidated and abandoned homes overrun with weeds. Charles hoped to build ten to twenty affordable homes in their place. He would pay for it all himself, in part by auctioning off some of his basketball heirlooms: an American flag signed by the original Dream Team. The 1993 MVP trophy. His gold medal from the '96 Olympics.

Charcey and Johnnie Mae liked to display the items, but now, to Charles they were just clutter—"and I don't want that stuff crapping up my house."

He'd keep the '92 medal for Christiana, but he wanted to ship out the rest. He didn't need a trophy or gold medal to remind him of all he'd accomplished.

"It's just a long plan I've got to just keep giving back," Chuck said.

"I've been so lucky and blessed in my life, I just really want to keep doing good with all the blessings I have."

In a pandemic that has infected more than 525 million people and killed roughly 6.3 million globally as of May 2022, Charles stayed at his home in Scottsdale or his condo in Atlanta during the NBA playoffs of 2020, which took place in a strict, COVID-negative bubble.

"The one thing I've learned through this pandemic, man, we need sports," he said in conversation with Ernie on their podcast, *The Steam Room*.

"I ain't gonna lie, man. I'm sick of reality. I am so sick of just reality."

The return of sports meant Charles would be back on television. His lifestyle might have been altered, but he still came with hot takes. Though he joked about Draymond Green's "triple-single" stat line, Charles squelched their on-air beef over joint appearances on *Inside* as well as *The Arena*, where they discussed social issues on-air and had some tequila together when the cameras weren't rolling. (Green eventually signed a multiyear deal with Turner Sports that would feature the Warriors star on-air, even as an active player.) Charles pleaded with Kyrie Irving during his short-lived media boycott to "dribble a basketball [and] stop acting like you're the smartest person in the world," nearly venturing into the "shut up and dribble" territory he denounced years earlier.

He also spouted opinions that were tough to take for many, like when he didn't think the fatal shooting of Breonna Taylor at the hands of Louisville police officers deserved to be discussed alongside the deaths of Ahmaud Arbery and George Floyd. Or why the members of Congress, and not President Donald Trump, were to blame for the pro-Trump mob that stormed the US Capitol to mount an insurrection, a failed attempt to disrupt the certification of Biden as the forty-sixth president. Or how he advocated for NBA, NFL, and NHL players to receive "some preferential treatment" for the coronavirus vaccine due to how much they pay in taxes, which he ended up apologizing for later. Or how he acknowledged he was interested in joining up with LIV Golf, the Saudi Arabia-backed golf league linked to a murderous regime, and taking tens of millions of dollars if it were offered. But that was part of the package, the same way it's been in the forty-plus years since he first stepped onto the court as an Auburn freshman.

Months before the world changed, the Purple Marching Machine at Miles College gave Charles a drum-heavy pep rally fit for a dignitary. The sweltering September heat in Fairfield, Alabama, was so oppressive that you could bake a pizza on the pavement. Charles, in a blue button-down drenched in sweat from front to back, was flattered by the welcome to the HBCU, saying it reminded him of the few times he went to class.

Before he gave the school $1 million, the largest gift in its history, he was asked about what he wanted his legacy to look like. It was as quiet of a moment as he was going to get that week, with only a few people around and a couple phones pointed in his direction.

"My legacy? Like when I die, that a few people are upset, gonna be sad for a little bit. We all gonna die. Some people, we *glad* when they die, we know that," he said. "When I die, people say, 'Aww, man, that's sad,' and be sad for a little bit and keep it moving. I mean that sincerely though."

As the sweat dripped from his shiny forehead, he peppered in a joke about the fate that awaited him one day. Death will be the only thing to ever truly silence Charles Barkley. Even then, that's not a given.

"Listen, y'all know that and I'm not afraid to say it. When some people die, we be like, 'Glad that person is gone,'" he said, again making those within earshot laugh. "When I die, I hope it's like, 'Aww, man, he was a good dude,' and keep it moving. 'Cause life does not stop. It's a journey, it's not a destination.

"But that's it."

EPILOGUE

Sitting onstage in front of a crowd reflecting much of basketball's rich history, Charles is giggling like a boy as Shaq recounts how he's been mentally scarred after rubbing down the cramp on Chuck's thigh the previous night. The scene from *Inside the NBA* showed Charles bending over his chair and stretching out his thigh as Shaq came up behind him to "punch out" the cramp in an impromptu physical therapy session.

"It looked like I'm giving you a prostate check," Shaq jokes.

Charles, as he does, takes it one step further, wondering why Shaq didn't at least take him out to dinner before the suggestive pat down: "I needed a cigarette after you rubbed on me like that last night!"

A joke about Charles getting felt up by Shaq on national television was really the only way the show's formal induction into the Naismith Memorial Basketball Hall of Fame could begin. *Inside the NBA* is being presented with the Curt Gowdy Award's inaugural prize for Transformative Media in front of a crowd that includes basketball royalty such as Bill Russell, Julius Erving, Magic Johnson,

Jerry Colangelo, commissioner Adam Silver, and the family of the late Kobe Bryant.

The honor marks Chuck's third time getting inducted into the Hall. Before he joins Ernie and Shaq onstage, he borrows a napkin from fellow inductee and friend Jim Gray so he can pat the sweat off his head and gives a simple thumbs-up to another fellow inductee, Michael Wilbon, who edited his bestselling books.

But when his time comes, the sparsely filled Mohegan Sun Arena roars for *Inside*, specifically for the guy who, as Johnson puts it, "changed the landscape" in sports media.

"Yeah, Chuck!" one fan is heard yelling through their mask.

It capped off a whirlwind two-month stretch for Charles that had him returning to announcing March Madness. More importantly, he got the chance to walk Christiana down the aisle.

Ilya Hoffman had little idea what he was getting himself into when he agreed to attend a May 2016 viewing party in Manhattan for Villanova alumni to rewatch the men's basketball team's thrilling win in the national championship game the month before. Born in Moscow before immigrating to the US with his parents in the '80s, Hoffman didn't go to Villanova and wasn't sure if he'd stay at the watch party—that is, until he saw a woman who was identified as the NBA great's daughter.

"I said, Oh you mean the guy from *Space Jam*?" he recalled to the *New York Times*. "Some people might have been like, 'Oh my God, Charles Barkley.' To me it was like, 'Look at this amazing girl.'"

When he offered a few friends back to his apartment to eat six leftover slices of pizza, Christiana let Hoffman know early on that she had her father's appetite for a good time: I'm going to need two of those slices.

As Charles was preparing for a work trip in December 2019, he was surprised to see Maureen yank Hoffman into their bedroom. Hoffman needed thirty seconds to ask them for their permission to marry Christiana.

"I remember being really emotional about it," Charles recalled. "That's not something that happens all the time."

What worried Charles the most about the 120-guest wedding at a luxury resort destination in Scottsdale was not the potential spread of the coronavirus at the event. It wasn't even the father-daughter dance to Zac Brown Band's "The Man Who Loves You the Most," a song that his podcast audience helped him pick. Instead, it was the hora, the traditional Jewish celebratory dance in which Chuck would be lifted in a chair. He told Jimmy Kimmel before the wedding that he would call "all Jewish people on deck," fearing they would get hurt trying to pick him up. Thankfully, it played out without serious injury on what would be the best weekend of his life.

"He really was scared," said Christiana, "but he got in the chair, and the next thing you know he and my mom were up there. They had a blast."

There was reason for optimism in early 2021. In May, on the day before *Inside* was honored with basketball immortality, the Centers for Disease Control and Prevention announced that Americans who are fully vaccinated could go without masks or social distancing in many cases, including indoors and in large groups. The move in the spring paved the way for a full reopening of society—a hopeful moment for the nation that'd be upended months later by the delta and omicron variants.

There was so much to like in the NBA during the pandemic era—Giannis Antetokounmpo bringing Milwaukee its first title in a half century, Stephen Curry reminding everyone why he is transcendent in willing the Warriors to another ring, Nikola Jokic's groundbreaking, back-to-back MVP campaigns, nightly displays of brilliance from superstars like Joel Embiid, Luka Doncic, and Jayson Tatum. That's not even mentioning the Phoenix Suns reaching the Finals for the first time since Charles got them there twenty-eight years earlier. Charles could be comfortable knowing the Suns were no longer *turrible* but history had also repeated itself in the Valley. In an eerie callback to Charles's time in Phoenix, Chris Paul and the Suns were bounced in disappointing fashion in the second round a year after the Finals—a year they thought was theirs for the taking.

There were, however, other items people would keep turning to Charles for in the months to come, whether it was the drama surrounding Ben Simmons and James Harden, Kyrie Irving's vaccination status, the Lakers' struggles with Russell Westbrook and Anthony Davis—dubbed only as "Street Clothes"—or sounding off on Kevin Durant after a first-round sweep as a "bus rider," saying, "If you ain't driving the bus, don't walk around talkin' 'bout you a champion!" This, of course, ended with Durant feuding with Chuck, who responded by hilariously driving a bus through a security gate to conclude an episode of *Inside*. He'd also face the passing of his father, Frank, in December 2021, at the age of seventy-nine. Charles said he was "deeply sad" about the loss of his father before Christmas but was grateful he reconciled with the man he called a friend for decades.

"I just hope he rests in peace," Chuck said to Ernie.

With loss came new life. Shortly after his father's passing, Charles earned a new title: grandfather. As Christiana held baby Henry on Mother's Day, she jokingly confronted her father about how he once said "women be milking that baby thing" and argued that playing an NBA game with a sprained ankle was much more painful than childbirth. Grandpa Chuck, who smiled at the prospect of one day having a beer with Henry, blushingly walked back his comments to his daughter on national TV: "Baby, I meant them *other* women."

But the night before the Hall of Fame was set to honor its greatest class ever—headlined by Kobe Bryant, Tim Duncan, and Kevin Garnett—the crowd in Uncasville, Connecticut, only wanted to thank Charles and the *Inside* crew for making the most boring games some of the funniest nights in basketball. In return, Chuck reflects on "the greatest scam going in the world" by doing what he does often: rip on Shaq.

"You and Kobe argued all the time?" Charles said, interrupting O'Neal as he talks about the weekend's biggest honoree. "It just sounds like you [are] the common denominator, nobody likes you! You're the only thing all of us have in common."

Shaq, like a good little brother does, makes sure he gets in the final word as their segment ends: "Ernie, I love you and I appreciate you very much. And Chuck, I still hate you. Nothing has changed!"

As soon as the event ends, a crowd surrounds Charles, with each person waiting for two minutes of his time, a photo, a hug, a moment, an idea of where he's partying tonight. At Todd English's Tuscany, a refined Italian restaurant located underneath an indoor waterfall that's catty-corner from a Ben & Jerry's and a Johnny Rockets, Charles unwinds with Ernie, Tim Kiely, and some of the TNT crew. His presence is no secret to the hundreds of fans that have camped out on the opposite side of the restaurant's drawbridge just for a chance to glance at Chuck. Charles begins to sign autographs, which gives Ernie the perfect opportunity to sneak away through the throngs of people without much fanfare.

Once he's decided he's done, it's time to party. Security pushes through the crowd of masked-up fans for a seven-second jaunt to the escalators. It's a rock-star reception, as the crowd, many of whom wielding camera phones and holding out pens and memorabilia for him to sign, follows Charles, yelling every conceivable thing at him: Let me buy you a drink! Where are you gambling tonight? What about them big ol' women in San Antonio?

At the top of the escalator, a clout-chaser attempts to troll Charles by calling him "Shaq" to his face on camera. Charles has no time for the act: "Hey, all Black people don't look alike."

He's about to walk into the VIP party at Tao, the chic Asian bistro and lounge, when he stops at the front door. He's not going in without the people that helped make him.

"Where's my TNT family?" he yells out, hoping someone will respond. When Kiely needs help to get in, Charles throws his arm around his producer and brother and assures the staff that he's with him.

"This guy makes me look good on television," Charles told the bouncer of Kiely.

Knowing everyone else is inside, Chuck heads into the club for a celebration of basketball, family, and life. It might not be his party, but with the vodka flowing freely and the DJ spinning a steady diet of Beyoncé, there is little doubt he'll be the lifeblood of the gathering by the time the night turns into the morning at the casino.

He might not have been able to fly off the roof of his home as a child, but as this night and all the other nights in his life have shown us by now, there's not much else Charles Wade Barkley hasn't been able to do.

★ ★ ★ ★ ★

ACKNOWLEDGMENTS

This book would not have been possible without the contributions from hundreds of people over the course of three-plus years who helped make this dream a reality. I'd be remiss if I didn't start off by saying how working with Armen Keteyian and Jeff Benedict changed my life. I was broke and had little experience a year out of college when I cold-emailed Armen in August 2009 to introduce myself and said how I hoped to collaborate with him one day. What unfolded was a relationship with Armen and Jeff that's now spanned more than a decade, a period that's included two *New York Times* bestsellers, a Showtime documentary and too many emails and phone calls to count. They are the best and they showed me all the little things you had to do to be great—and I am forever indebted to them.

I could not have done this book without Samuel Benson, an intrepid reporter with the *Deseret News* who was invaluable to me from start to finish as my lead researcher. Sam was a Swiss Army Knife, from transcribing interviews to tracking down and obtaining police reports. He compiled notes on every significant video interview, as well as every episode of *The Steam Room* podcast through early 2021.

Sam has such a bright career ahead of him, and I'm so thankful for his work here.

Kelvin C. Bias gave such an incredible fact-checking effort here, like he did with *Tiger Woods*. Shaker Samman was as thorough and delightful as can be in fact-checking everything related to Leeds, Auburn and *Inside*. Zoe Collins Rath of the *Progress-Index* dove head-first into the 1993 Finals with a fire and energy level that I haven't seen many other young reporters have on any topic.

I'm grateful to Joe Perskie and *Real Sports with Bryant Gumbel* for providing three segments not available on streaming services. Louise S. Argianas at ESPN and ABC Sports was also immensely helpful in sending an episode of *Up Close* that's not publicly available.

My sincere appreciation goes to those in the NBA, USA Basketball and the various college athletic departments for their persistence and flexibility in coordinating in-person and phone interviews. So many other people were extremely patient with me throughout this process. There are too many to name, but I owe all of them. Special thanks to Addison Abdo, Cindi Berger, Lorrie Boula, Ginger Chan, Rishi Daulat, Howard Deneroff, Tim Donovan, Julie Fie, Heather Fluit, Todd Fritz, Mike Goings, Cindy Guagenti, Dick Guttman, Jon Jackson, Diana Koval, Eric Lindsey, Jolyn Matsumuro, Zack Miller, John Mitchell, Sandy Montag, Pete Moore, Sona Movsesian, Kathy Murphy, Patrick Rees, Raymond Ridder, Dennis Rogers, Alyssa Romano, Mike Ryan Ruiz, Heidi Schaeffer, Shakeemah Simmons-Winter, Val Small, Jon Steinberg, Derek Volner, and Ross Wooden.

Several people interviewed for this book died before it was published. To the families of Pat Dye, Larry King, Roscoe Nance, Ryan Smith, and Grant Woods: I'm so thankful to have had the chance to talk with each of them before they passed. RIP.

Though the pandemic canceled many reporting trips, I couldn't have made my multiple visits to Leeds and Auburn more fruitful if not for a group of amazing guides. Lisa Hudson was so warm and welcoming, and opened doors to crucial people in Leeds. Rayford Williams and the staff at Leeds High School understood the magnitude of the project early on, allowing me to spend hours at the school to go through old yearbooks and materials. Larry Caffee was a true mensch in showing me around the school and the old gym Charles once dominated. Margaret Little walked me through Leeds's history with immense pride and clarity. And the good folks at Rusty's Bar-B-Q allowed me to take a breath amid packed days over their pulled pork and the best banana pudding I've ever had.

At Auburn, the athletics department's communications team—namely Kirk Sampson, Cody Voga, and Shelly Poe—were incredibly accommodating and accessible. Tommy Brown, an archivist with the university, let me get lost in books on a Friday afternoon. The Leonardis, our dear family friends, and the rest of the AU Foy Hall Tailgate Team showed me what Saturdays on the Plains are all about.

Alec Harvey, the assistant director of student media at Auburn, navigated me through the *Plainsman's* extensive online library that went back decades. Bob Baker and David Hudnall were great in providing PDFs of hard-to-find articles from *The Village Voice* and *Phoenix New Times*, respectively. The same goes for the crew at Ink Global. Drew Carter of CBS 42 in Birmingham was kind enough to send video files of an Instagram Live featuring Charles from March 2020.

It's impossible to take on a book like this without thanking those who came before me in chronicling Charles's career and life. I stand on the shoulders of people who paved the way: Roy S. Johnson and Michael Wilbon. They were so kind and gracious to me during this process. Some of the best reporters out there, past and present, have done incredible work capturing the sound and color of Barkley for years. They are acknowledged here in alphabetical order, and my apologies if I've inadvertently failed to mention someone: David Aldridge, Graham Bensinger, Fran Blinebury, Christine Brennan, Mike Bruton, David Casstevens, Bob Cohn, Jeff Coplon, Jimmy Davy, Frank Deford, Richard Deitsch, Ray Didinger, David DuPree, Paul Finebaum, Roy Firestone, Bob Ford, Norm Frauenheim, Mark Heisler, Rich Hofmann, Mark Jacobson, Phil Jasner, Sally Jenkins, Curry Kirkpatrick, Jere Longman, Bill Lyon, Jackie MacMullan, Bob Mayes, Leigh Montville, Bruce Newman, Larry Platt, Rick Reilly, William Rhoden, Prentis Rogers, Richard Sandomir, Eddie Sefko, Lee Shappell, Sam Smith, Hannah Storm, Phil Taylor, Jesse Washington, Alexander Wolff, and Bob Young.

Jack McCallum took more time than I ever could have imagined giving me the lay of the land. His generosity matches his legendary status. Long before I started down this path, a quartet of biographers I admire a great deal—Peter Ames Carlin, Jonathan Eig, Dave Itzkoff, and Jeff Pearlman—provided pearls of wisdom that made me think writing a biography was doable (even if it was going to be a bit stressful).

Taking on this project wouldn't have happened without the full support of the *Washington Post*—the best place I've ever worked—and Marty Baron, Tracy Grant, Fred Barbash, and Tim Elfrink for allowing me the chance to chase Charles. *The Morning Mix* team was with me every step of the way, inspiring me to keep going through their own sheer talent, determination and a kindness you must possess to work the overnight shift: Teo Armus, Allyson Chiu, Drea Cornejo, Antonia Noori Farzan, Amber Ferguson, Meagan Flynn, Jaclyn Peiser, Andrea Salcedo, Katie Shepherd, Isaac Stanley-Becker, and Kyle Swenson. Candace Buckner, Josh Freedom du Lac, Keith McMillan, and Herman Wong provided awesome support throughout.

A group of mentors and teachers helped push me to this point, starting with my uncle, Rick Bella, a longtime reporter at the *Oregonian* who inspired and nurtured my love for journalism (and remains the best mandolinist I know). So many teachers helped push me to this point, from Cornelia Cliburn—my first journalism teacher who let me skip a pop quiz I was unprepared for to draft an article for the middle school newspaper—to professors at TCU such as the late Phil Record, Tommy Thomason, Robert Bohler, and John Tisdale. And Sandy Padwe, the legendary sports editor and my adviser at Columbia Journalism School, shaped my approach on reporting and gave me the kick in the butt I needed. He is the journalistic voice in my head, and I wouldn't have it any other way.

My agent, William Callahan at InkWell Management, took a chance on a first-time author and instilled in me the confidence to not only do this but kick ass. He's a friend who was with me from conception of the idea until now. My editor, John Glynn, was enthusiastic about the project from the jump and believed I could pull this off when a lot of other editors did not. Any writer would be lucky to have John as their editor. Eden Railsback did an amazing job keeping us organized and made sure things were run smoothly toward the end of production. Leigh Teetzel gave the book the proofread it needed in its final stages. My publisher, Hanover Square Press, was tremendous to work with, allowing me the time needed to juggle family and work. Special thanks to Walter Iooss and the National Museum of African American History and Culture for the rights to use Walter's magnificent photo of Charles from 1988 as the cover image, as well as Karen Becker and the art team for making it happen. David Potter at Harlequin offered much needed input toward the end of the process.

This book happened thanks in large part to the family and friends who supported me when this was a pipe dream. I'm thankful every day for my parents, Anne and Bill, who gave me a life I never could have imagined, one filled with unwavering love, positivity, Yankees games, lots of rigatoni, and the will to never quit on my dreams. Kevin Goll, my brother from another, and some of my closest friends in journalism—Zach Schonbrun, Ben Fearnow, Ashley Dean, Andrew Chavez, Leila Molana-Allen, Pallavi Reddy, Ashley Semler, Ryan Loughlin, Osman Noor, and Azure Gilman—encouraged me over texts, tacos and beer.

Writing can be a painfully lonely journey, but Betsy, my spouse and dancing partner in life, was the companion I needed on this path. As crazy as it was to pursue a book project while working overnight hours at a new job in the first year of our union, she urged me to go for it. She's as selfless as anyone I know, and has given my life purpose, meaning and so much joy. She's a wonderful mother to our first child, Theodore "Teddy" William Bella, who is not even a year old by the time this book came out. Teddy, may this be the start of a beautiful and extraordinary journey. We can't wait to see you author the story that is your life. We love you, son.

NOTES

When reporting what Charles said, I relied on statements he's made—in news conferences, in interviews, on television, or during other events that were recorded—and on his writings, primarily those in his three books: *Outrageous!*, *I May Be Wrong but I Doubt It*, and *Who's Afraid of a Large Black Man?* I also relied on interviews with hundreds of individuals who recounted direct conversations with him. When reporting Charles's thoughts, I relied on statements and writings in which he discussed his thinking—which there were many examples. I also conducted interviews with people with whom Chuck shared his thinking.

In instances where scenes are described, at least one person who was present or had firsthand knowledge of what happened was interviewed to help reconstruct the scene. Additionally, I pulled many quotes and dialogue from court records, police records, video footage, podcasts, and other previously published works.

Unless otherwise specified in the notes, direct quotes derive from the 374 interviews conducted by the author. Only a couple asked not to be identified. It was rare that I quoted an anonymous source, but I found their insight important to the story. I'm particularly grateful to all of those who agreed to speak to me on the record: Christian Abate, Ron Adams, J.A. Adande, John Amos, Ron Anders, Kenny Anderson, Dr. James Andrews, Darrell Armstrong, C. Jeffery Arnold, Joe Arpaio, Geno Auriemma, James Banks, Daryl-Marie Barkley, Matt Barnes, Barney Barnett, Mike Baron, Rick Barry, Howard Beck, Greg Beckwith, Scott Bedbury, Rudy Berumen, Patrick Beverley, Sue Bird, Leslie Blair, Fran Blinebury, Jim Boeheim, Muggsy Bogues, Paul and Robert Boudwin, Dr. Todd Boyd, Steve Brace, Sen. Bill Bradley, Chucky Brown,

Howard Bryant, Ric Bucher, Dan Burke, John Calipari, Victor Campbell, P.J. Carlesimo, Antoine Carr, Butch Carter, Vince Carter, David Casstevens, Darlene Cavalier, Samantha Cerio, Rex Chapman, Pete Chilcutt, Joe Ciampi, Norm Clarke, Jerry Colangelo, Connie Colla, Jerry Colon, Mike Conley Jr., Chris Connelly, Stan Cook, David Cooper, Ty Corbin, John Costacos, Bob Costas, Billy Coupland, Bobby Cremins, Billy Crystal, Mark Cuban, Billy Cunningham, Earl Cureton, Bryan Curtis, Chuck D, Johnny Dawkins, Carroll Dawson, Rob DeFlorio, Richard Deitsch, Al Del Greco, Liz Dolan, Matt Donovan, Beck Dorey-Stein, Tim Dorsey, Jack Doss, Mike Doyle, Fran Dunphy, David DuPree, Dr. Raegan Durant, Pat Dye, Pat Dye Jr., Warren Eakins, Herm Edwards, Craig Ehlo, Alex English, Julius Erving, Howard Eskin, Jeff Falletta, Gilbert Feliciano, Wally Feresten, Julie Fie, Guy Fieri, Steve Fine, Paul Finebaum, Roy Firestone, Dr. Joel Fish, Derrick Floyd, Bill Flye, Jim Foley, Bob Ford, Greg Foster, Dr. Mona Fouad, Chris Fowler, John Franke, Sen. Al Franken, Harold Franklin, World B. Free, Bill Frieder, John Gabriel, Tim Gallin, Chuck Gallina, Paul Galvan, Ted Giannoulas, Artis Gilmore, Mike Gminski, Terry Goddard, James Goldstein, Thom Gossom Jr., Russ Granik, Allen Greene, Jan Greene, David Griffin, David Grim, Tom Halloran, Tony Hamati, Kent Haney, Kevin Harlan, Tony Harris, Debbie Hartel, Hersey Hawkins, Jason Hehir, Mark Heisler, Kirk Herbstreit, Sam Heys, Fred Hickman, Brian Hill, Grant Hill, Jemele Hill, Roy Hinson, Jonathan Hock, Lionel Hollins, Wallace Honeycutt, Derrick Hord, David Housel, Phil Hubbard, John Hudson, Lisa Hudson, Andrew Hugine Jr., David Hunt, Bobby Hurley, Bobby Lee Hurt, Joe Ingles, Walter Iooss, Frank Isola, Steven Izen, the Rev. Jesse Jackson, DJ Jazzy Jeff, Keith Jennings, Chris Jent, Mayor Paul Johnson, Roy S. Johnson, Kelly Jolley, Bomani Jones, Sen. Doug Jones, Lida Jones, Popeye Jones, Van Jones, Seth Joyner, Harold Katz, Steve Kauffman, Clark Kellogg, Shawn Kemp, Bernard King, Larry King, Joe Kleine, Phil Knight, Martha Korman, Karl Krayer, Ron Kroichick, Larry Krystkowiak, Mike Krzyzewski, Jude LaCava, James Lambert, Ronie Langston, Eric Lazzari, Dan Le Batard, Norman Lear, David Levy, Nancy Lieberman, Margaret Little, Rebecca Lobo, Allen Lumpkin, Jim Lynam, Jackie MacMullan, Matt Maloney, David Mandel, Carl and Raymond Marbury, Boban Marjanovic, Beth Marshall, Donyell Marshall, Phillip Marshall, Anthony Martin, Michael Mayberry, Tharon Mayes, Jack McCallum, Mack McCarthy, Tim McCormick, Sandra McGuire, Nate McMillan, Diane McWhorter, Charlotte Meadows, Kevin Merida, Craig Miller, James Andrew Miller, Oliver Miller, Paul Millsap, Mike Missanelli, Paul Mokeski, Sidney Moncrief, Eric Montross, Leigh Montville, Warren Moon, Ricky Moore, Daryl Morey, Montal Morton, Mark Mulder, Jeff Munn, Gheorghe Muresan,

Calvin Murphy, Roscoe Nance, John Nash, Mark NeJame, Donnie Nelson, Johnny Newman, Jeff Norwood, Tommy Nunez, Conan O'Brien, Lucille and Shaquille O'Neal, Robert Parish, Paige Phillips Parnell, Dan Patrick, Bruce Pearl, Will Perdue, Elliot Perry, Josh Peter, Keith Peters, Randy Pfund, Butch Pierre, Caleb Pipes, Larry Platt, Jim Podhoretz, Scot Pollard, Terry Porter, Joe Proski, Joe Pytka, Vice President Dan Quayle, Analiese and Wayne Raath, Brent Reese, Rick Reilly, Gov. Ed Rendell, Pat Riley, Jim Riswold, Doc Rivers, Jeremy Roenick, David Roger, Jalen Rose, Nick Rousey, Jeff Ruland, Molly Rutledge, Bob Ryan, John Salley, Wimp Sanderson, Adam Sandler, Bob Sarles, Anne Schilling, Detlef Schrempf, Greg Schulte, Eddie Sefko, Bakari Sellers, Len Sherman, Amy Shorter, Rob Shuler, Jack Sikma, Dan Sims, Pete Skorich, Jan and Sonny Smith, Kim and Ryan Smith, Lydia Smith, Pete Smith, Sam Smith, Kenn Solomon, Aries Spears, Berderia Spence, Don Sperling, Jae Staats, Jerry Stackhouse, Derrick Stafford, Dawn Staley, Mark Stevenson, Shawnetta Stewart, John Stockton, Hannah Storm, Vern Strickland, Fallon Stubbs, Jon Talton, Neil Tardio, Dick Tarrant, Diana Taurasi, Parag Tembulkar, Reggie Theus, Charlene Thomas, Etan Thomas, Mark Thomashow, Vince Thompson, Rudy Tomjanovich, Jimmy Traina, Bob Trednic, Joe Trippi, Bryan Tucker, Rusty Tucker, Doug Turner, Greg Turner, Sonny Vaccaro, Macy Vandergrift, Littel Vaughn, Peter Vecsey, Dick Vitale, Steve Wallace, Donnie Walsh, Shirley Wang, Jesse Washington, Teresa Weatherspoon, Bob Weinhauer, Larry Weitzman, Rick Welts, Lang Whitaker, Bob Whitsitt, Kristen Wiig, Lenny Wilkens, Dominique Wilkins, Pat Williams, Rayford Williams, Dennis Wilson, Alexander Wolff, Roy Wood Jr., Steve Yingling, Bob Young, Trae Young, and Dave Zirin.

Prologue

Primary sources include research conducted by the author in Chicago and Northern Virginia, as well as interviews with Christian Abate, Chuck D, Dan Le Batard, Kim and Ryan Smith, Diana Taurasi, and Shirley Wang. Other sources include interviews given by Charles and his family in outlets such as *Sports Illustrated*, the *New York Times Magazine*, and NBA.com, *Outrageous!*, and a 2001 episode of *SportsCentury*.

...the seven-year-old launched himself from twenty feet off the ground...: Jeff Coplon, "Headstrong," *New York Times Magazine*, Mar. 17, 1991

"He felt like he could do just about anything...": Charles Barkley and Roy S. Johnson, *Outrageous!*, Jan. 22, 1992

"When I found out he was all right...": *Outrageous!*

"When you're a poor kid...": *Outrageous!*

...eleven-time All-Star... All-NBA selection...: Basketball Reference

"These new generations...": Interview, Jan. 14, 2021

...suggesting former Vice President Mike Pence...: Des Bieler, "Charles Barkley Says Mike Pence 'Needs to Shut the Hell Up' over NBA–China Criticism," *Washington Post*, Oct. 25, 2019

...joking about Draymond Green...: Sam Quinn, "Charles Barkley Fires Back at Draymond Green: 'He's the Worst Member of the Boy Band,'" CBS Sports, Apr. 27, 2020

...admitting that he mistook symptoms...: The Steam Room, Apr. 15, 2020

"What the fuck else...": Jack McCallum, "Behind the Interviews: Charles," JackMcCallum.net, June 18, 2012

He's hosted Saturday Night Live *the most times of any athlete...*: Dan Gartland, "Charles Barkley to Host 'SNL' for Fourth Time," *Sports Illustrated*, Feb. 20, 2018

"I'm not the one who threw somebody...": Dave McMenamin, "LeBron James Rips Charles Barkley: 'You're the NBA Bad Boy, Not Me,'" ESPN.com, Jan. 31, 2017

"I don't know why...": Instagram, BasketballNews.com, January 2021

...329 technical fouls...: Basketball Reference

"If you go looking for the next Charles Barkley...": *The Inside Story*, March 2021

"I see his picture every day...": Interview, Feb. 16, 2020

"He won the lottery...": Interview, Oct. 22, 2020

"Charles thought he was bigger than life...": *SportsCentury*, June 18, 2001

Chapter 1

Primary sources include research conducted by the author in Leeds, Alabama, as well as interviews with Leslie Blair, Lisa Hudson, Ronie Langston, Carl and Raymond Marbury, Sandra McGuire, Diane McWhorter, Amy Shorter, and Berderia Spence. Other sources include federal records publicly available on Ancestry.com that helped chart Charles's family history, records from the Alabama Department of Archives and History, *Outrageous!*, books about John Henry and Leeds, and an ESPN.com video interview with Charcey that ran around the time of her death.

The battle between John Henry and the steam hammer...: Ezra Jack Keats, *John Henry, an American Legend*, 1965

"There will never be another player like me...": *Outrageous!*

...Leeds...blossomed thanks to the discovery of...: Pat Hall and Jane Newton Henry, *Leeds (Images of America)*, Oct. 1, 2012

...Charles Bentley, a Black man, was found guilty...: Undré Phillips, "Charles Bentley, Aug. 2, 1901, Leeds," BirminghamWatch via *New York Times*, Feb. 28, 2019

Charles Barkley's family line in Leeds...: Public records from Ancestry.com

The 1870s Census is the first to include...: "African Americans and the Federal Census, 1790-1930," National Archives and Records Administration, July 2012

She worked at Lumber Jacks...: *Outrageous!*

She operated a beauty salon...: Rick Karle, "Karle's Korner: Charles Barkley's Mother: The Real MVP!," WBRC, June 23, 2015

"I was spoiled rotten...": *Outrageous!*

"My mother was a strict disciplinarian...": *SportsCentury*

The original Leeds Negro School... By the time the school opened in 1948...: Robert Russa Moton High School, National Alumni Association, *https://rrmotonhighleeds.com/welcome/history/*

"Charcey Mae was a beautiful woman...": Interview, June 26, 2019

They were a no-nonsense family...: Josh Peter, "The Barkley Doesn't Fall Far from the Tree," *USA TODAY*, Dec. 10, 2014

...her moon-shot home runs left her opponents slack-jawed...: Interview, Oct. 10, 2019

"He was just trying to get out of school...": Interview, June 26, 2019

...George Wallace approached the microphone in the portico...: "'Segregation Forever': A Fiery Pledge Forgiven, but Not Forgotten," NPR, Jan. 10, 2013

..."probably the most racist speech ever given"...: "Peggy Wallace Kennedy in Conversation with Diane McWhorter" at Politics and Prose Bookstore in Washington, DC, Jan. 7, 2020

Charles was just six pounds...: *Outrageous!*

...at Leeds's segregated hospital...: Jesse Washington, "Up from Leeds," ESPN.com, Feb. 12, 2015

...resulting in a full blood transfusion...: *Sir Charles*, NBA Entertainment, 1994

"My mom used to always joke...": *Sir Charles*

"...a slave-owner creeper...": *Lopez Tonight*, Jan. 13, 2010

"*...the most thoroughly segregated city...*": Martin Luther King Jr., "Letter from Birmingham Jail," Apr. 3, 1963

..."*one of the most vicious and tragic crimes...*": Eulogy from Sept. 22, 1963

"I know one time he hit her...": *SportsCentury*

Frank Barkley left the family..."Like me, he was young and untrained...": *Outrageous!*

Charcey then married Clee Glenn...: Public records from Ancestry.com; *Outrageous!*

"He was a father to his younger brothers...": *SportsCentury*

"Frank Barkley was one of the few mistakes...": *Outrageous!*

..."*the chairman of the board*"...: *SportsCentury*

"I'm 100 percent like her": Charles Barkley with Michael Wilbon, *I May Be Wrong but I Doubt It*, Oct. 14, 2003

"...what comes up from the gut...": *Outrageous!*

...*government bologna and cheese sandwiches one night, mayonnaise sandwiches the next...*: *Outrageous!*; Charles's Hall of Fame induction speech on Sept. 8, 2006

"... Charles'll eat every egg in the house...": *Outrageous!*

"My grandfathers were spectacular...": *I May Be Wrong but I Doubt It*

"I never had any sense...": *Sir Charles*

"He didn't ask for things...": *Outrageous!*

...*the high school cafeteria...*: WBRC

...*as a housekeeper...*: Bruce Newman, "A Double Feature All by Himself," *Sports Illustrated*, Mar. 24, 1986

"...a fantasy island in the middle of the Pacific... Scrubbing people's toilets and floors...": *Outrageous!*

...*Rennie, died during infancy...*: Obituary for Charcey Glenn in the *Birmingham News* in June 2015; obituary for Darryl Barkley in the *Birmingham News* in March 2009

"I always respected them...": *Outrageous!*

"If loving and respecting...": John Rolfe, "Charles in Charge!," *Fortune*, Feb. 1, 1991

"He just couldn't understand...": *Outrageous!*

"I would come home dead tired...": *Outrageous!*

...*Alabama implemented a statewide prohibition in 1915...*: Alabama Department of Archives and History, *https://archives.alabama.gov/govs_list/g_hender.html*

"...So, we sold alcohol...": *I May Be Wrong but I Doubt It*

"She said, 'Everybody already knows I was a bootlegger'...": "Charles Barkley Profile" (video), ESPN.com, 2015

...Leslie Blair points to the supermarket parking lot...: Interviews, Aug. 21 and 27, 2019

Charcey picked up the phone...: *Outrageous!*

Chapter 2

Primary sources include research conducted by the author in Leeds, Alabama, as well as interviews with Leslie Blair, Wallace Honeycutt, Margaret Little, Ricky Moore, Brent Reese, Amy Shorter, Lydia Smith, and Berderia Spence. Other sources include *Outrageous!*, video of Frank Barkley's appearance on ESPN's *Up Close*, and a 2016 interview Charles gave to journalist Graham Bensinger.

"We were in Mobile for a conference...": Amanda Pritchard, "Leeds Community Remembers Charcey Glenn," *St. Clair News-Aegis*, June 25, 2015

"I promised him a lot of things...": *Up Close*, 1993

"As long as I was talking to him...": *Outrageous!*

"... Charles and I both realized that it was a wasted visit...": *Outrageous!*

"I missed his companionship...": *Outrageous!*

"That was one way we had representation...": Interview, Aug. 15, 2019

In a 1971 order, Judge Sam C. Pointer...: Nikole Hannah-Jones, "The Re-segregation of Jefferson County," *New York Times Magazine*, Sept. 6, 2017

"...everyone was very leery of each other...": *Outrageous!*

...she carried a pistol in her purse...: Washington

"It wasn't easy for us...": *Outrageous!*

"It was a big sacrifice for me...": *Outrageous!*

"He was on the chubby side...": *SportsCentury*

"If something came up...": Peter

"That was my 'rep'...": *Outrageous!*

"I thought that was unbelievable...": Interview, Jan. 30, 2020

"The guy in charge of taking us to Montgomery...": Interview, Jan. 30, 2020

"The basketball coach was Black...": *Outrageous!*

"I just didn't like it…": Interview, Aug. 19, 2019

"You don't have that many kids to pull from…": Interview, Aug. 19, 2019

"…to shut his mouth…": Interview, Aug. 19, 2019

"…He kept us undefeated…": Interview, Aug. 19, 2019

"Mr. Honeycutt didn't belong to the neighborhood…": Interview, Sept. 3, 2019

"We showed them…": Interview, Aug. 19, 2019

"…he had an appetite…": Interview, Aug. 19, 2019

"…always have a plan B…": Interview, Aug. 19, 2019

Every Sunday at around ten or eleven at night…: *Outrageous!*

"Kids do stupid things…": Interview, Aug. 22, 2019

"I could hear the cops saying…": *In Depth with Graham Bensinger*, Apr. 27, 2016

"When I hit the ground…": *In Depth with Graham Bensinger*

"When classmates found out about what happened…": Interview, Aug. 22, 2019

"It was only a matter of time…": *Outrageous!*

Chapter 3

Primary sources include research conducted by the author in Leeds, Alabama, as well as interviews with Leslie Blair, Billy Coupland, Jack Doss, Jeff Falletta, Paul Finebaum, Wallace Honeycutt, Lisa Hudson, Bobby Lee Hurt, Ronie Langston, Margaret Little, Ricky Moore, Brent Reese, and Rayford Williams. Other sources include *Outrageous!*, archives of yearbooks and newspaper clippings from Leeds High School between 1977 and 1981, and a 1997 episode of *Real Sports with Bryant Gumbel.*

"…donating no less than a projected $100,000 each year…": Interview, June 18, 2019

"But make no mistake…": *Outrageous!*

"…jump that rope to death…": *Outrageous!*

"He'd jump from one side to the other…": Mike Bruton, "Barkley is driven to succeed, his way," *Philadelphia Inquirer*, Feb. 1, 1987

"…'I bet you a soda you can't'…": Interview, Aug. 19, 2019

"He dunked it without anybody knowing it…": Interview, Aug. 19, 2019

"…when I reached manhood…": *Outrageous!*

"As a student…": *Outrageous!*

…*Charles found himself the target of bullying*…: Interview, Sept. 4, 2019

…*Coupland wasn't one to cuss or fuss*…: Interview, Aug. 20, 2019

"He didn't go overboard…": *Outrageous!*

"It didn't matter if it was Charles or anyone…": Interview, Aug. 20, 2019

He went against a culture…: Interview, Jan. 30, 2020

"It was just hard for him…": *Sir Charles*

"There's really not much use…": *Outrageous!*

"I said, 'No, you can't do that…'": Interview, Aug. 19, 2019

"He wanted to be around Coach Coupland…": Interview, Jan. 30, 2020

"I realized the only way…": *SportsCentury*

"I told him he wouldn't make…": Interview, Aug. 12, 2019

"He never liked to go down there…": *Outrageous!*

"He became obsessed…": *Sir Charles*

"…'What the hell happened to you?'…": Interviews, Aug. 21 and 27, 2019

"How's that for coaching?…": Interview, Aug. 12, 2019

"I remember Charles specifically saying…": Interview, Aug. 15, 2019

"He was not like the most popular guy…": Interview, May 26, 2020

…*"some of the kids used to call him sissified"*…: *Real Sports with Bryant Gumbel*, May 1997

"They used to tell me…": Interview, July 16, 2020

…*a Hardee's roast beef sandwich and a strawberry milkshake*…: Interview, July 16, 2020

"Charles was always a hard worker…": Interview, Aug. 12, 2019

"…'Hey, come down to the gym…'": *Sir Charles*

Charles and teammates saw Austin Sanders as a legitimate…: *Outrageous!*

"Just like that, he was gone…": *Outrageous!*

"Going into my senior year…": *SportsCentury*

"I don't think any of us knew how to respond…": Interview, Aug. 20, 2019

"I guess he had that anger…": Interview, Aug. 22, 2019

…*"thousand-watt smile"*…: Mike Easterling, "All-Decade Basketball Teams: All-Time," *The Huntsville Times*, Dec. 26, 2010

"I was as tall as a tree…": Interview, Aug. 28, 2019

In a series of stories published in the Birmingham Post-Herald…: Interviews, Jan. 20 and Feb. 6, 2020; Gary Pomerantz, "Bobby Lee Hurt," *Washington Post*, July 2, 1981

Hurt has repeatedly denied all the allegations…: Interview, Aug. 28, 2019

…*if he "was ever going to have an opportunity…"*: *Outrageous!*

"I was scared, intimidated…": *Outrageous!*

Coupland…wasn't changing the game plan…: Interview, Aug. 12, 2019

"I tried to stop him…": *Outrageous!*

…*25 points…and 20 rebounds…*: Dennis Love, "Where the Sun Rose," *Arizona Republic*, May 30, 1993

"Barkley ate his lunch…": Interview, Aug. 22, 2019

…*32 points…and pulled down 16 rebounds…*: Interview, Aug. 28, 2019

"That was the time…": Interview, Sept. 3, 2019

Chapter 4

Primary sources include research conducted by the author in Leeds, Alabama, and Auburn, Alabama, as well as interviews with Stan Cook, Thom Gossom Jr., Jan Greene, Lisa Hudson, Margaret Little, Mack McCarthy, Molly Rutledge, Wimp Sanderson, Dan Sims, Jan and Sonny Smith, Macy Vandergrift, and Steve Wallace. Other sources include *Outrageous!*, public records related to the Charles Barkley Foundation, and a 1985 court ruling related to Auburn.

…*anywhere between $50,000 to $100,000 annually…*"Charcey and granny…": Interview, July 1, 2019

"If it wasn't for him…": Interview, Oct. 4, 2019

Vandergrift doubts…: Interview, Oct. 4, 2019

"He was just a total diamond…": Interview, Aug. 20, 2019

…*"flunked English in four states"…*: Ralph Wiley, "How the Tide Has Turned," *Sports Illustrated*, Feb. 2, 1987

"All my thoughts…": Interview, June 6, 2019

…*Bartow sent a letter to the NCAA…*: Danny Robbins, "Bartow Was in Fear of UCLA Booster," *Los Angeles Times*, Aug. 4, 1993

"Crap no, it wasn't civil…": Al Blanton, "A Civil Rivalry: Auburn vs. Alabama and the Battle for Hardwood Supremacy," *Saturday Down South*, 2018

…Charles said he gave a verbal commitment…: *Outrageous!*

"In my eyes…": Interview, Aug. 26, 2019

"Wimp said…": Interview, Aug. 20, 2019

"I could play against anybody, anywhere…": *Outrageous!*

"You have to find the keys…": Interview, Aug. 26, 2019

"The grandmother from the backside of the room…": Interview, Aug. 26, 2019

"I punched my assistant coach and said…": Interview, Aug. 26, 2019

…were perhaps the first unofficial basketball boosters for the school…: Interview, Dec. 3, 2019

"As we were paying our bill…": Interview, Dec. 3, 2019

…had blown the earlier opportunity to get to know Charles…: *Outrageous!*

"He camped out…": Interview, June 19, 2019

"He lived in Leeds…": Interview, June 6, 2019

The rival recruiters either got no answer…: Interviews, May 30 and June 6, 2019; *Outrageous!*

"Herb hated to lose…": Interview, June 19, 2019

"I have always had a great admiration for Herbert…": Mark Rice, "Mourners Give Coach Herbert Greene Final Applause," *Ledger-Enquirer*, July 22, 2015

"We decided what we'd do is put together…": Interview, Dec. 3, 2019

"It was a different deal back then…": Interview, Dec. 3, 2019

"Most teams use the kind of success UAB enjoyed…": *Outrageous!*

"It was truly a school of White people…": Interview, Oct. 15, 2019

In a federal ruling that decade…: US District Judge U.W. Clemon, *United States v. State of Alabama*, US District Court for the Northern District of Alabama, Dec. 7, 1985

"Charles said all he wanted…": Interview, June 6, 2019

"He hung out on the couch…": Interview, June 13, 2019

"I'd never had a recruit…": Interview, June 6, 2019

Chapter 5

Primary sources include research conducted by the author in Leeds, Alabama, and Auburn, Alabama, as well as interviews with Leslie Blair, Victor Campbell, Billy Coupland, Jeff Falletta, Ronie Langston, Amy

Shorter, Lydia Smith, Berderia Spence, Doug Turner, and Jesse Washington. Other sources include archives from Leeds High School such as old yearbooks and newspaper clippings related to the class of 1981.

"I'd be fucked…": Washington

"His grandma and I sat in the stands…": *Outrageous!*

"There was some kind of excitement…": Interview, Aug. 20, 2019

"He made a transformation…": Interview, Sept. 4, 2019

"I smoked pot like five times…": Charles Curtis, "Charles Barkley on Ezekiel Elliott: Marijuana Just Made Me Want to 'Eat Potato Chips,'" *USA TODAY*, Aug. 27, 2016

"I was so heartbroken…": Interview, July 16, 2020

"Dumb me tried to give the ball…": Interview, Aug. 12, 2019

"He scored 60 by himself…": Interview, Sept. 27, 2019

"My mother would bring the shoes to the game…": Russ Bengtson, "The Wit and Wisdom of Charles Barkley: Part II," *SLAM*, Nov. 19, 2007

…*Charles averaged 19.1 points*…: Mike Bruton, "In His Alabama Home Town, Barkley Isn't Just an NBA Star," *Philadelphia Inquirer*, Feb. 1, 1987

"I knew we had to get ahead early…": "Class 3A Wrapup," *Birmingham Post-Herald*, Feb. 27, 1981

"All of us were brokenhearted…": Interview, Aug. 20, 2019

…*the announcement from athletic director Lee Hayley*…: Leeds High School Yearbook, 1981

"Bartow was pissed…": *Outrageous!*

"Wimp tells the story…": Interview, June 6, 2019

Shortly after coming to the US from Havana in 1961…: Obituary for Raquel Caiñas Gomez, Dignity Memorial, July 2016

"She was tough…": Interview, Aug. 26, 2019

"Ms. Gomez, she was not…": Interviews, Aug. 21 and 27, 2019

A lifelong Alabamian…: Obituary for Betty Nash in the *Birmingham News* in January 2017

"She explains things…": "Betty Nash listed favorite teacher," *Leeds News*, May 28, 1981

One day, she even called him out…: Interview, Aug. 26, 2019

"I know I could speak for most people…": Interview, Jan. 30, 2020

"This was at the height of him…": Interview, Sept. 3, 2019

"I told him…": Interview, Sept. 3, 2019

"His mother and grandmother blamed him…": Interview, Aug. 15, 2019

"I was mad at Ms. Gomez…": *Phil in the Blanks*, March 2019

"I should've been a better student…": *Outrageous!*

"Our graduation song was…": Interview, Aug. 26, 2019

"Everyone was talking about the F…": Interview, Sept. 4, 2019

"Mr. Oxford turned to Charles…": Interview, Aug. 15, 2019

"She's a very fair teacher…": "Betty Nash listed favorite teacher"

…*Frank couldn't shield his anger…*: *Outrageous!*

"He ripped me…": *The Steam Room*, Jan. 7, 2022

"I just stood there for two hours straight…": *Phil in the Blanks*

He'd eventually finish summer school…: Interview, Aug. 15, 2019; *The Steam Room*, Jan. 7, 2022; *Outrageous!*

Chapter 6

Primary sources include research conducted by the author in Auburn, Alabama, as well as interviews with Samantha Cerio, Harold Franklin, Thom Gossom Jr., Jonathan Hock, David Housel, Darrell Lockhart, Phillip Marshall, Rob Shuler, Dan Sims, Sonny Smith, Vern Strickland, Vince Thompson, Steve Wallace, Dominique Wilkins, Dennis Wilson, and Alexander Wolff. Other sources include *Outrageous!*, archives from Auburn University and its student newspaper, and a 2014 episode of *SEC Storied* highlighting Barkley's time at Auburn.

…*when his friend convinced a group of Alabama guys…*: Interview, Oct. 22, 2019

"We beat them…": Interview, Oct. 22, 2019

Cerio gained national attention after…: Andrea Adelson, "The Most Important Steps: How Sam Cerio Overcame Her Horrific Gymnastic Accident," ESPN.com, July 15, 2019

"That was one of the biggest things…": Interview, Oct. 9, 2019

…*with only about 430 Black students…*: Jed Butler, "Lack of Social Life Contributes to Low Black Enrollment," *Auburn Plainsman*, Feb. 26, 1981

"One of my first reactions…": *Outrageous!*

…*Broun…had considered Black people to be better suited…*: Dwayne Cox, "Academic Purpose and Command at Auburn, 1856–1902," *Alabama Review*, January 2008

...*Draughon...didn't agree with Governor George Wallace on segregation...*: L. Anne Willis, "Desegregation at Auburn University: A Historical Look at the Uses of Media," Auburn University, Aug. 8, 2005

...*"desegregation would victimize foolish White girls..."*: Cox, *The Village on the Plain: Auburn University 1856–2006*, Apr. 8, 2016

"They didn't really want me there...": Interview, Oct. 28, 2019

...*referred to by some as the N-word walk-on*: Thom Gossom Jr., *Walk-On: My Reluctant Journey to Integration at Auburn University*, Sept. 9, 2008

"Auburn was not an inclusive environment...": Interview, Oct. 21, 2019

"Everybody got along, but you had...": Interview, June 3, 2019

"I understand that much of the way they treated me...": *Outrageous!*

Charles was weighed underwater...: Interview, Dec. 28, 2019

"His percent body fat was...": Interview, Dec. 28, 2019

"His eyes got big...": Interview, Dec. 3, 2019

"I saw him literally leap onto...": Interview, Jan. 8, 2020

"Charles intimidated Darrell so bad...": Interview, June 6, 2019

"What I learned later...": Interview, May 15, 2019

"They were so good that they impacted...": Interview, May 30, 2019

"Mr. Sims, do you remember...": Interview, Dec. 3, 2019

"He was so confident it was funny...": Rick Bragg, "AU's Barkley Talks a Good Game in Win," *Anniston Star*, Dec. 3, 1981

"He picked some winners...": Bragg

"But, conceded Smith...": Bragg

"What was happening in the SEC...": Interview, July 30, 2019

"I sat in the locker room and cried...": *Outrageous!*

...*do you work at Burger King?...*: Tom McCollister, "Freshman, Transfer Give Auburn Boost," *Atlanta Journal-Constitution*, Jan. 23, 1982

"Ahh yes, I hear everything...": *SEC Storied: Bo, Barkley, and The Big Hurt*, ESPN Films, July 24, 2014

"It doesn't bother me...": Darryal Ray, "It Isn't Over Until the Fat Boy Sings," *Alabama Journal*, Jan. 20, 1982

...*Jim Fyffe, who once remembered how Charles...*: *SportsCentury*

"I only eat twice a day...": Bob Mayes, "On and off Basketball Court, Barkley Has Devoured Auburn," *Montgomery Advertiser*, Jan. 31, 1982

The Auburn coaches weighed Barkley...: Interview, May 30, 2019

"You couldn't get it off of him…": *SportsCentury*

…*Smith and Auburn sports information director David Housel had an idea*…: Interviews, June 6, 2019, and May 5, 2020

"We were getting attention…": Interview, June 6, 2019

"Charles did not need any promotion…": Interview, May 5, 2020

"You're talking about a guy…": Interview, Aug. 5, 2019

"I try to dunk as soon as possible…": Ray

"Every time he would dunk…": *Outrageous!*

"When I first saw him play…": Interview, Mar. 6, 2020

…*averaging nearly 13 points, 10 rebounds and 2 blocks*: Basketball Reference

…*brother Darryl was struggling in school and eventually dropped out*…: Outrageous!

"Charles was never a discipline problem…": Interview, June 6, 2019

"Fuck it…": *Outrageous!*

"You've got to stay…": *Outrageous!*

"I was beginning to wonder…": *Outrageous!*

Chapter 7

Primary sources include research conducted by the author in Auburn, Alabama, as well as interviews with Jim Boeheim, Al Del Greco, Pat Dye, Paul Finebaum, Paul Galvan, Jonathan Hock, Derrick Hord, David Housel, Buck Johnson, Butch Pierre, Sonny Smith, Charlene Thomas, Vince Thompson, Greg Turner, and Dick Vitale. Other sources include *Outrageous!*, a 2014 episode of *SEC Storied* highlighting Barkley's time at Auburn, and a 1983 *Sports Illustrated* feature on the SEC.

Why don't I go over the top?…: *SEC Storied: Bo, Barkley, and The Big Hurt*

"It used to be the old joke…": Interview, Jan. 8, 2020

…*having Christmas with in-laws you can't be in the same room with*…: Interview, May 5, 2020

"In the post-integration era…": Interview, Sept. 19, 2019

"Bo was in college with me…": "Bo Jackson and Charles Barkley Speak at Barkley's Statue Unveiling," *Montgomery Advertiser*, Nov. 25, 2017

"When he came down the lane…": *SEC Storied: Bo, Barkley, and The Big Hurt*

"It was such an honor…": *SEC Storied: Bo, Barkley, and The Big Hurt*

"No matter how you look at it...": "Bo Jackson and Charles Barkley Speak at Barkley's Statue Unveiling"

"We'd get sandwiches...": *SEC Storied: Bo, Barkley, and The Big Hurt*

"Barkley got smart...": *SEC Storied: Bo, Barkley, and The Big Hurt*

...but Jackson was pushing his star player in mostly good ways...: Interview, June 6, 2019

"When you would see Bo Jackson in the stands...": Interviews, Aug. 21 and 22, 2019

"It was like the Berlin Wall coming down...": *SEC Storied: Bo, Barkley, and The Big Hurt*

...Charles, standing in front of a crowd decades younger, spits the lyrics...: Cell phone video courtesy of Dan Alexander

"With starters back including...": John McGill, "No More Fat Cats," *Louisville Courier-Journal*, Nov. 21, 1982

"Hello, I'm Charles Barkley...": *Jimmy Kimmel Live*, Feb. 15, 2018

"I like to do things to keep me excited...": Mike LoPresti, "What's the Fat Kid Doing Playing Basketball?," *GNS*, July 30, 1982

"Chuck was recruited...": *Outrageous!*

...after Barkley couldn't put up with teammate Greg Turner's snoring...: Interview, June 3, 2019

"One of the hardest-working brothers was Chuck Person...": Interview, June 3, 2019

"I was always really quiet...": *Outrageous!*

"Auburn tweaked it...": Interviews, Aug. 21 and 22, 2019

"The team with the most dunks...": *30 for 30: Phi Slama Jama*, ESPN Films, Oct. 18, 2016

"He said, 'You guys got the fat guy on the team...'": Interview, May 20, 2019

"To tell you the truth...": Darryal Ray, "Barkley Is Well Known in Houston," *Alabama Journal*, Dec. 8, 1982

"Charles lays that thing up...": Interview, May 20, 2019

"All you heard the next time was...": Interview, May 20, 2019

"We ended up losing, but...": Interview, May 20, 2019

"He put a couple of legs to me...": John Sturbin, "Coogs Topple Tigers; Look Ahead," *Fort Worth Star-Telegram*, Dec. 9, 1982

"I don't remember what the amount was...": Interview, Feb. 7, 2020

"I said, 'What do you think about Olajuwon?'…": Interview, May 1, 2020

"I thought there was no way…": Interview, July 30, 2019

"All I can remember…": Interview, May 14, 2019

"That matchup down low…": Interview, May 14, 2019

"Going against Bobby Lee fires me up…": Phillip Marshall, "Second Half Is Barkley's," *Montgomery Advertiser*, Jan. 6, 1983

Charles was tabbed as the "Wildcat Whipper"…: Curry Kirkpatrick, "They're SECond to None," *Sports Illustrated*, Feb. 21, 1983

"I remember the first time we went up against him…": Interview, Mar. 18, 2020

"It gives us confidence…": "Auburn Rocks UK 75–67," Associated Press, Jan. 17, 1983

…*"quite possibly the most amazing, dynamic and fun-to-watch collegian…"*: Kirkpatrick

Smith thought the message was clear…: Interview, June 6, 2019

…*"blasted forth like a pulling guard on an unsuspecting cornerback"*…: John McGill, "Auburn Says UK Plotted to Get Barkley Banished," *Louisville Courier-Journal*, Feb. 13, 1983

"I started feeling sorry for the kid…": Kirkpatrick

…*it was simply "my time to guard Barkley"*…: Kirkpatrick

"He had destroyed Turpin…": Interview, June 6, 2019

"Before the tip-off of the next game…": Interview, June 25, 2019

"I told him if it tastes good…": *Outrageous!*

"There was nothing left but this little pile of wrappers…": Sally Jenkins, "Barkley Puts Fierce Move on the Game," *Washington Post*, Mar. 23, 1988

"Sonny pushed Charles…": *SportsCentury*

"It was pretty well documented…": Interview, Jan. 24, 2020

"Sonny Smith came over to me and said…": Interview, Oct. 28, 2019

"It's one of the worst things when someone…": Interview, Oct. 28, 2019

…*and Barkley never got his hands on the ball*…: Charles Goldberg, "Hurt, Tide Can't Be Denied," *Anniston Star*, Mar. 7, 1983

"I said, 'Coach, I'm leaving here…'": *Outrageous!*

Chapter 8

Primary sources include research conducted by the author in Auburn, Alabama, as well as interviews with Ron Anders, Tim Dorsey, Pat Dye,

Pat Dye Jr., Bobby Lee Hurt, Phillip Marshall, Mack McCarthy, Bruce Pearl, Jan and Sonny Smith, Mark Stevenson, Vince Thompson, and Dennis Wilson. Other sources include *Outrageous!*, archives from *Sports Illustrated* and the *Montgomery Advertiser*, and the 1984 yearbook for Auburn University.

"One of the highlights for me as a coach…": Interview, Dec. 4, 2019

It was from Charles…: Interview, Dec. 4, 2019

…after he was dismissed from Tennessee for violations of…: "Bruce Pearl Told Recruits of Violation," ESPN.com, Oct. 22, 2010

Chuck Person, an associate head coach under Pearl, was arrested…: Sam Blum, "Former Auburn Assistant Chuck Person Pleads Guilty on Bribery Charges," AL.com, Mar. 19, 2019

…while his faith in God had never been stronger…: Mike Rutherford, "Why Some People Hate Bruce Pearl: A Timeline," *SB Nation*, Apr. 4, 2019

"Listen, Auburn would be idiots…": Brandon Marcello, "Charles Barkley: 'Auburn Would Be Idiots to Let Bruce Pearl Go,'" *247Sports*, Feb. 22, 2018

…a Krispy Kreme in one hand and a Bud Select in the other…: Grant Wahl, "Oh Boy," *Sports Illustrated*, Oct. 15, 2007

"I don't know anybody that's more accomplished or more grateful…": Interview, Dec. 4, 2019

…Charles pushed him out of the way and moved six hundred pounds back…: *Outrageous!*

…"when the bright lights come on, I play…": SportsCentury

…hitting him square in his chest…: SportsCentury

"Over the years, Charles had said…": Interview, June 13, 2019

He entered Sonny Smith's office and told him…: Interview, June 6, 2019

"He literally made that offer…": Interview, May 30, 2019

"He said, 'Well, tell me what you want me to do'…": *SEC Storied: Bo, Barkley, and The Big Hurt*

"We got to the point where he believed…": Interview, Apr. 10, 2020

"I was just always there for him if he needed me…": Interview, June 13, 2019

The player who had been described in newspapers as…: Bob Mayes, "AU's Barkley Expects Better Junior Season," *Montgomery Advertiser*, June 19, 1983

…but declared that he was only a teaser…: Bob Mayes, "Barkley a Key to Auburn's Fortunes," *Montgomery Advertiser*, Oct. 10, 1983

...Charles removing the famed fridge from the dorm...: Mayes

He returned to school at 14.5 percent body fat...: Interview, Dec. 28, 2019

...labeled by national media as "Fat Man"...: Jim Cour, "Fat Man Leads U.S. Win," Associated Press, July 5, 1983

..."the Eighth Wonder of the World"...: Alexander Wolff, "The Leaning Tower of Pizza," *Sports Illustrated*, Mar. 12, 1984

Missouri's Norm Stewart...still thought he was thirty pounds overweight...: Cour

"This doesn't mean I'm still not going to have fun...": Mayes

"Well, what did you do?...": Interview, May 30, 2019

...who named his dog Barkley after the junior...: *Glomerta*, Auburn University, 1984

"He became chummy to many of the guys in the fraternity...": Interview, Sept. 6, 2019

"Bo had problems hitting the backboard...": Interview, Jan. 15, 2020

...a girlfriend he lovingly called "Knucklehead"...: Wolff

"I was on the non-mandatory dean's list...": *Outrageous!*

...from switching his major from physical education to business management...: *Outrageous!*

...so he assigned assistants to accompany him to class...: Interview, June 6, 2019

...McCarthy was left befuddled when he would receive phone calls...: Interview, May 30, 2019

"I walk him to class and I kind of hang around...": Interview, May 30, 2019

...Stevenson had marveled at what Charles was able to do...: Interview, June 12, 2019

"He made it clear that he never touched the textbook...": Interview, June 12, 2019

...was telling her that he loved her in case "I don't make it home"...: Interview, Aug. 5, 2019

"He says to Cahill...": Interview, Aug. 5, 2019

It was the first time Wilbon met Charles, or even laid eyes on him...: "I Love 90s Basketball: Charles Barkley Edition," NBA on ESPN, May 30, 2020

"I just remember going there for one reason...": NBA on ESPN

...Charles pulled his back coming down for a rebound...: Ron Bliss, "Injuries Continue to Plague AU Preparation," *Montgomery Advertiser*, Nov. 20, 1983

"Some guy behind our bench…": Interview, June 6, 2019

"That kind of became a highlight photo…": Interview, Aug. 28, 2019

…*saying it reminded him of when Apollo Creed realizes*…: Interview, Jan. 8, 2020

…*often called games that unfolded involving Barkley as "a scary situation"*…: YouTube upload of a January 1984 game between Auburn and Kentucky, *https://www.youtube.com/watch?v=1Qji8vaYOXc*

"I can put my butt on Melvin's legs…": Wolff

…*Charles has a "lotta loose lip"*…: Wolff

"Isn't that how it works?…": Ron Bliss, "AU's Twin Powers Beat Twin Towers," *Montgomery Advertiser*, Jan. 14, 1984

"After that game…": Duane Rankin, "Commentary: Person Realized Barkley's Potential," *Montgomery Advertiser*, June 14, 2014

"I'm going to drive him crazy before I leave…": Phillip Marshall, "Barkley Indicates He Might Turn Pro," *Montgomery Advertiser*, Jan. 28, 1984

Chapter 9

Primary sources include research conducted by the author in Auburn, Alabama, as well as interviews with Greg Beckwith, Al Del Greco, Bill Flye, David Grim, David Housel, Phillip Marshall, Johnny Newman, Sonny Smith, Vern Strickland, Dick Tarrant, Greg Turner, and Alexander Wolff. Other sources include *Outrageous!* and YouTube videos of Auburn games during the 1983–84 season.

…*he would "lock up everybody over 12 and let kids rule the world"*…: Wolff

"He had total trust in what he said…": Interview, July 30, 2019

"P.T. Barnum didn't need anybody…": Interview, May 5, 2020

Called "Mr. Smooth" by TBS's Joe Dean…: *https://www.youtube.com/watch?v=1Qji8vaYOXc*

…*who was named the SEC Player of the Year*…: Phillip Marshall, "Tigers Open NCAA Play in Charlotte," *Montgomery Advertiser*, Mar. 15, 1984

…*Charles and Turpin shared a forceful high five*…: YouTube upload of Auburn-Kentucky game in the 1984 SEC Championship, *https://www.youtube.com/watch?v=vyrNjZjZzQA*

"He is still feeling it after all these years, too…": Larry Vaught, "Remembering the Night Kenny Walker Made Charles Barkley Cry," JustTheCats.com, June 20, 2020

"I wanted that to be my gift to Auburn…": *Outrageous!*

"One of the greatest accomplishments of my life…": *Outrageous!*

…*Charles was listed as "the most dominating player…"*: Interview, June 13, 2019

"I was expecting some big monster…": Interview, Aug. 1, 2019

"He goes, 'Coach Tarrant, I'm Charles'…": Interview, June 17, 2019

Charles even laughed the first time he saw Flye…: Interview, Aug. 1, 2019

"If you played someone with a name…": Interview, June 6, 2019

…*Tarrant delivered different messages to his team…*: Interview, June 17, 2019

"He walked over to the bench…": Interview, June 6, 2019

"He's stealing the ball, knocking guys down…": Interview, June 17, 2019

"If there were five more seconds…": Interview, June 13, 2019

"I don't know why whenever I watch the game…": Interview, May 20, 2019

Then he received a telegram from USA Basketball…: *Outrageous!*

Chapter 10

Primary sources include research conducted by the author in Northern Virginia, as well as interviews with Fran Blinebury, Jim Boeheim, Antoine Carr, Mark Heisler, Joe Kleine, Larry Krystkowiak, Mike Krzyzewski, Terry Porter, and John Stockton. Other sources include *Outrageous!*, *I May Be Wrong but I Doubt It*, *The Jordan Rules*, reporting from outlets like *Sports Illustrated* and the *Washington Post*, and parts of *The Last Dance* from 2020.

"…where the hell have you been?…": Mark Heisler, "It Was the Rage of the '84 Games," *Los Angeles Times*, May 29, 1988

"…you fat son of a bitch!…": Heisler; Sam Smith, *The Jordan Rules,* November 1991

"I heard another bang and looked over…": Interview, May 1, 2020

"Charles Barkley was a RPIA…": YouTube upload of a Bob Knight speaking engagement, *https://www.youtube.com/watch?v=ePv2YdWXjsw*

"I hate the son of a bitch…": Coplon

"When those Russians come over here…": "Morning Briefing," *Los Angeles Times*, May 14, 1984

"Barkley at 215 would be like asking Raquel Welch…": Don Pierson, "Cut from '84 Team, Barkley Rebounds," *Chicago Tribune*, June 9, 1993

"I went to the Trials intending to change everyone's mind…": *Outrageous!*

Pete Newell…had "never seen anything like these guys"…: Curry Kirkpatrick, "It Was Trial by Fire," *Sports Illustrated*, Apr. 30, 1984

Antoine Carr took time away from a $225,000 annual salary…: Interview, Apr. 16, 2020

Tisdale's terrible impression of Richard Nixon…: Kirkpatrick

…and enjoyed some time alone at The Chocolate Moose…: Jon Wertheim, "Tales of Michael Jordan and the 1984 U.S. Olympic Trials," *Sports Illustrated*, Apr. 19, 2020

"I had never seen anyone with that physique…": Interview, Mar. 19, 2020

…Charles "handles a fork as well as anybody in the world"…: Terence Moore, "Montanan Packed to Leave, Then Made the Cut," *San Francisco Examiner*, Apr. 22, 1984

"I really don't eat that much…": Michael Wilbon, "Barkley: the Great Wide Hope," *Washington Post*, Apr. 23, 1984

"…he might just cut the first exercise album…": Wilbon

…he regularly said, "I'm sorry"…: Wilbon

"Oh, no, anybody but him"…: Wilbon

Stockton…had to cool off after cocking a fist at Charles…: Interviews, Nov. 8 and 11, 2019

"He never disappointed…": Interview, May 15, 2019

"I thought he was nuts…": Interview, Nov. 4, 2019

"I had to tell him, 'Coach, there was one guy…'": *I May Be Wrong but I Doubt It*

"And he never freaking turned it off…": *The Last Dance*, ESPN/Netflix, 2020

…"the best basketball player I've ever seen play"…: *The Last Dance*

"Michael wasn't setting out to wow people…": Interview, July 8, 2019

Alford said that while Charles was good…: Steve Alford with John Garrity, *Playing for Knight: My Six Seasons with Coach Knight,* November 1989

…Charles would get him back…in Tonk…: *Outrageous!*

"I can relate very well to him…": *Outrageous!*

…USA assistant George Raveling…howled into Knight's shoulder…: Malcolm Moran, "A Powerhouse on the Court," *New York Times*, Apr. 24, 1984

"Charles was already not Bobby Knight's favorite player…": Interview, Aug. 27, 2019

…whom he called "crazy man" behind his back…: *Outrageous!*

...*"the most explosive and controversial coach..."*: *Outrageous!*

"They say if the coach screams and hollers a lot...": Phil Richards, "Applause and Affection Greet Olympic Survivors," *South Bend Tribune*, Apr. 22, 1984

"I don't know if they're going to cut him...": Interview, May 1, 2020

...*Charles took the coach's words to heart...*: Bob Knight with Bob Hammel, *Knight: My Story,* March 2002

...*he* gained *eleven back...*: *Knight: My Story*

"Everyone falls over and Knight's not laughing...": *The Jordan Rules*

...*doing a version of "the Stepin Fetchit routine"...*: *https://www.youtube.com/watch?v=ePv2YdWXjsw*

"I looked at the chart and said...": *https://www.youtube.com/watch?v=ePv2YdWXjsw*

...*"the Bobby types"...*: Kirkpatrick

...*he now appreciated and loved Knight...*: Tom Boswell, "The Playboy Interview with Charles Barkley," *Playboy*, May 1, 1993

"In a way, it was a relief...": *I May Be Wrong but I Doubt It*

...*dubbed "the bus of shame"...*: Doug Haller, "Knight, Barkley, Stockton and the Bus of Shame: Tales from the 1984 Olympic Trials," *The Athletic*, Jan. 14, 2021

"He was undaunted...": Interviews, Nov. 8 and 11, 2019

Chapter 11

Primary sources include research conducted by the author in Philadelphia and Northern Virginia, as well as interviews with Rick Barry, Billy Cunningham, Richard Deitsch, World B. Free, Russ Granik, Harold Katz, Steve Kauffman, Phillip Marshall, John Nash, Gov. Ed Rendell, and Pat Williams. Other sources include *Outrageous!*, archived reports from outlets like *Sports Illustrated*, the *Philadelphia Inquirer*, and the *Atlanta Journal-Constitution*, and video from the 1984 NBA Draft.

He began with two Denny's Grand Slam breakfasts...: Richard Deitsch, "Charles Barkley Talks Fame, Social Media at SXSW," *Sports Illustrated*, Apr. 12, 2015

...*totaling around 1,660 calories...*: Denny's Nutrition Guide, September 2021, *https://www.dennys.com/sites/default/files/2021-09/Sept_2021_Core_Nutrition_Guide.pdf*

...*"everything I could get to my face..."*: *Outrageous!*

...not marketable to mainstream America because it was too Black...: John Papanek, "There's an Ill Wind Blowing for the NBA," *Sports Illustrated*, Feb. 26, 1979

...by pointing to Marvin Gaye's rendition of "The Star-Spangled Banner"...: Pete Croatto, "The All-Star Anthem," Grantland, Feb. 16, 2013

"We were a pretty struggling organization...": Interview, July 2, 2019

"You do know if the Sixers draft you...": Deitsch

...Harold Katz...flew off the handle...: Interview, Oct. 7, 2019

Pat Williams...was rendered speechless and alarmed...: Interview, May 17, 2019

"Whatever he did before he came to Philadelphia...": Interviews, May 6 and 8, 2019

...Charles and Luchnick high-fived each other...: *Outrageous!*

...who years later would be named the SEC's Player of the Decade...: Alabama Sports Hall of Fame

"It's not like I'm going to be a brain surgeon...": *Outrageous!*

"I don't know if I'll make it in the NBA...": Phillip Marshall, "Barkley Makes It Official: He'll Enter Draft," *Montgomery Advertiser*, Apr. 29, 1984

...who had "mastered the art of 'street talk'...": *Outrageous!*

"He seemed like he could be one of the fellas...": *Outrageous!*

He'd been accused of reeling in clients through payments to coaches...: Danny Robbin and Manny Topol, "Agent Gave Money to Coaches," *Washington Post*, Apr. 3, 1988

...Luchnick improperly used their funds via a broad power-of-attorney clause...: Mike Fish and Len Pasquarelli, "Legal Disputes Plague Luchnick," *Atlanta Journal-Constitution*, Mar. 20, 1999

...Luchnick "wasn't a guy I would have hired back then"...: Interview, May 6, 2020

...Charles was snoring on the couch...: Alan Richman, "Call Him 'Round Mound' at Your Peril; Charles Barkley's Bite Is Worse Than His Woof," *People*, Apr. 27, 1987

"At 1:30 in the morning...": Richman

"The most important thing to him...": Glen Duffy, "Long Way from Home," *Philadelphia Magazine*, April 1985

...World B. Free insists Charles Barkley owes him $25...: Interview, July 24, 2020

…Cunningham…approached Pat Williams…: Interview, Oct. 8, 2019

…did not warrant more than a fifty-six-word wire story…: "76ers Trade Lloyd Free," Associated Press, Oct. 13, 1978

"The best I could get was six years down the road…": Interview, May 17, 2019

Katz acknowledged that the Sixers' pick at No. 1…: Interview, Oct. 7, 2019

…having the body of Wes Unseld and the ups of Erving…: Newman

"Harold was in awe…": Interviews, May 6 and 8, 2019

…from vacuum cleaners and brushes to TVs and lawnmowers…: Interview, Oct. 7, 2019

…had to spend $60 a week for her dieting…: Craig R. Waters, "The Fifty-Million-Dollar Diet," *Inc.*, May 1, 1982

…a personal wealth of around $100 million…: Waters

"If the word ostentatious had not existed before…": Waters

…for more than $12 million in 1981…: Thomas Rogers, "Katz Says He Paid $12 Million for 76ers," *New York Times*, July 10, 1981

"Harold was a guy who got things done…": Interview, July 19, 2019

"The one great gift Charles had…": Interview, Oct. 8, 2019

"If he ever gets down to 250…": "They've Got the Hang of It," *Sports Illustrated*, Oct. 29, 1984

"Mostly, I just stopped eating…": *Outrageous!*

"Every time I look at Charles…": Interview, July 24, 2020

"When you're poor, you get that one suit…": Scoop B Radio Overtime, April 2017, *https://www.youtube.com/watch?v=gAP2PSsTgXo*

"The Draft was the start of my amazing journey…": Scoop B Radio Overtime

…Cunningham assured Charles…: Interview, Oct. 8, 2019

…that no players of his, including Charles…: Chuck Newman, "Rockets Make Olajuwon No. 1; Sixers Take Barkley," *Philadelphia Inquirer*, June 20, 1984

"The look on my face is…": *In Depth with Graham Bensinger*

"When people go back and look at me walking…": Deitsch

"It's got to be every kid's dream…": "76ers Give Barkley Chance to Live His Dream," UPI, June 20, 1984

Lou Carnesecca…said he'd like to open a pizza concession stand…: YouTube upload of Charles Barkley being selected in the 1984 Draft, *https://www. youtube.com/watch?v=juGvOPI97yk*

"I get a lot of talk about my weight...": *https://www.youtube.com/ watch?v=juGvOPI97yk*

"I'd like to thank my mother and grandmother...": *https://www.youtube. com/watch?v=juGvOPI97yk*

...all he had to do was work hard and the money would handle itself...: George Shirk, "For Barkley, There's No Comparison," *Philadelphia Inquirer*, June 20, 1984

Chapter 12

Primary sources include research conducted by the author in Philadelphia, as well as interviews with Geno Auriemma, Billy Cunningham, Mike Doyle, Alex English, Julius Erving, Howard Eskin, Bob Ford, Phil Hubbard, Harold Katz, Jim Lynam, Jackie MacMullan, Robert Parish, Larry Platt, Bob Ryan, Pat Williams, and Alexander Wolff. Other sources include *Outrageous!*, the NBA Entertainment video of the Philadelphia 76ers' 1983 world championship season, video archives from the 1984–85 season, clips from outlets like *Sports Illustrated*, *Playboy*, and ESPN, and a 2017 interview on *The Dan Patrick Show*.

"The way I would describe Charles...": Interview, Feb. 21, 2020

...Charles said he was excited to learn from Marc Iavaroni...: *https://www.youtube.com/watch?v=juGvOPI97yk*

"When the ball bounces off the rim...": Interview, July 24, 2020

...he stayed out of Charles's way...: Julius Erving with Karl Taro Greenfeld, *Dr. J: The Autobiography*, Nov. 5, 2013

...during the Princeton Summer League...: Abbott Koloff, "Tiger in Disguise," *Daily Record*, Aug. 19, 1984

"They thought I was going to be a bust...": Newman

...traded Leo Rautins...: "76ers Sign Barkley to Multi-Year Pact," Associated Press, Sept. 26, 1984

...after a ten-hour marathon negotiation session with Katz...: Interview, Oct. 7, 2019; Phil Jasner, "Barkley Lands Whopper of a Deal," *Philadelphia Daily News*, Sept. 26, 1984

...whose goal had always been to average 10 points and 10 rebounds...: *Outrageous!*

"Charles stepped on a scale the other day...": Jasner

BARKLEY

The clause was designed to keep Charles between 255 and 265 pounds...: Jasner

"It just makes me play harder...": Ray Didinger, "Barkley Won't Let Jokes Weigh Him Down," *Philadelphia Daily News*, June 20, 1984

Irene Cara's "Flashdance... What a Feeling" blared on a loop...: *That Championship Feeling*, NBA Entertainment, 1983

"Charles viewed them both as the kind of stardom...": Interview, July 1, 2020

"What the public saw of Julius on the court...": *Outrageous!*

...Erving already had an office for his company for five years...: Interview, July 24, 2020

Working on a $10,000 monthly allowance from Luchnick...: *Outrageous!*

...but Charcey, a matriarch of the area, couldn't and wouldn't leave...: Washington

"You don't need six fancy cars...": *Outrageous!*

"Everything Larry threw up went in...": Interview, Nov. 19, 2019

"Nice going, guys...": YouTube upload of a clip from the Nov. 9, 1984, game between the 76ers and Celtics, *https://www.youtube.com/watch?v=u4oF34p3-rQ*

...the $30,500 in fines...: "Bird, Erving Fined $7,500 for Fighting," *New York Times*, Nov. 14, 1984

"I was trying to break the fight up...": *The Dan Patrick Show*, Mar. 23, 2017

"Hey, fathead...": Phil Taylor, "Moses Malone," *Sports Illustrated*, Nov. 8, 1993

"Moses was in Charles's mind...": Interviews, July 19 and 26, 2019

...the closest he came to using drugs was drinking a Coca-Cola...: "Playboy Interview: Moses Malone," *Playboy*, March 1984

He'd been homesick, and initially faced intimidation...: "Playboy Interview: Moses Malone"

...would warn him during training camp to "watch out for the freaks"...: *Outrageous!*

"I consider myself ugly...": YouTube upload of a segment from CBS Sports personality Pat O'Brien on Barkley's rookie year, *https://www.youtube.com/watch?v=FZv_aw1pxQw*

"Moses filled a gap in my life...": Taylor

"You didn't know for sure...": Interview, Jan. 9, 2020

"I pulled Moses aside and asked him...": Jackie MacMullan, "How Moses Malone Mentored a Young Charles Barkley," ESPN.com, Sept. 13, 2015

"You're fat and you're lazy...": MacMullan

"I said, 'I don't understand that'...": MacMullan

"It took me a little bit...": *Outrageous!*

"I was like, 'How you know...'": "Charles Barkley Eulogizes Moses Malone: 'He Treated Me Like a Son,'" ESPN.com, Sept. 19, 2015

"Moses was disgusted with him, really...": Interview, June 2, 2020

...*Cunningham pulled aside Charles with an incentive*...: Interview, Oct. 8, 2019

"Here's the key about Charles...": Interview, Oct. 7, 2019

"I've never been away for Christmas...": Duffy

...*he hosted Charcey, his brothers, and girlfriend Donna*...: Duffy

"I think he's still a baby...": Newman

...*he began to build a community*...: Interview, Apr. 24, 2020

Charles accepted the invite and...: Interview, Apr. 24, 2020

"We think of him completely owning...": Interviews, Aug. 26 and Sept. 3, 2019

...*it wasn't irregular for Charles to go off-script*...: Interview, May 17, 2019

"Charles didn't process getting better through repetition...": Interview, July 24, 2020

"Charles was not an easy person to coach...": Interview, Oct. 8, 2019

"It doesn't matter what you say...": Deitsch

Toney was particular about having warm milk...: *The Dan Patrick Show*

"When he got on a plane, he'd say...": Interview, July 24, 2020

...*Charles displaced the rim and backboard*...: Jere Longman, "Sixers Overpower the Warriors," *Philadelphia Inquirer*, Feb. 21, 1985

"To fix the basket...": Longman

"He says, 'I got something to say...'": *SportsCentury*

A sign inside The Spectrum during the deciding fourth game...: Alexander Wolff, "Charles in Charge," *Sports Illustrated*, May 13, 1985

...*compared his playoff run to that of Bird or Magic Johnson*...: Wolff

"I should be out there...": Wolff

As tensions mounted between MOVE...: Lindsey Norward, "The Day Philadelphia Bombed Its Own People," Vox, Aug. 15, 2019

...Sambor acknowledged he wanted to keep burning...: Lindsey Gruson, "Philadelphia Chief Says He Wanted Fire to Burn," *New York Times*, Oct. 19, 1985

"Even as a rookie...": Interview, Nov. 19, 2019

"I think everything else is just icing on the cake...": *https://www.youtube.com/watch?v=FZv_aw1pxQw*

Chapter 13

Primary sources include research conducted by the author in Philadelphia, as well as interviews with Victor Campbell, Herm Edwards, Julius Erving, Roy Firestone, Bob Ford, World B. Free, John Gabriel, Artis Gilmore, Roy Hinson, DJ Jazzy Jeff, Seth Joyner, Harold Katz, Tim McCormick, Mike Missanelli, Paul Mokeski, Sidney Moncrief, Dikembe Mutombo, Jeff Ruland, Dawn Staley, Lenny Wilkens, and Pat Williams. Other sources include *Outrageous!*, a three-part series from Ray Didinger that ran in the *Philadelphia Daily News* in 1986, stories in outlets like *Sports Illustrated*, the *Philadelphia Inquirer*, the *Washington Post*, and the *New York Times*, and YouTube uploads of playoff games from the era.

"We could really relate to him...": Interview, Apr. 30, 2020

"It didn't take long before...": Interview, June 17, 2020

...the decision had been made around Christmas...: Tom Cobourn, "Cunningham Era with 76ers Ends," *The News Journal*, May 29, 1985

...Katz wasn't sure that Matt Guokas wanted the job...: Interview, Oct. 7, 2019

"If you could not get along with Matt Guokas...": Interview, May 17, 2019

They honored him with "Charles Barkley Day"...: Ray Didinger, "Dawn of a Dream," *Philadelphia Daily News*, May 14, 1986

Johnnie Mae got a new Lincoln... Their boy bought them a satellite dish...: Didinger

...the house was about to be remodeled...: Didinger

"I'm not a bragful woman...": Didinger

"We're playing like shit...": *Outrageous!*

...Charles...held a forty-five-minute closed-door session...: Jack Cheva-

lier, "Barkley Runs Show on and off the Court," *The Morning News*, Nov. 27, 1985

…*"a star of epic proportions"*…: Newman

"He's the power forward…": Newman

…*implored Charles to read up on newspaper articles about Larry Bird*…: Ted Silary, "Briefly…," *Philadelphia Daily News*, June 28, 1985

…*took that to mean the Sixers would sign him to a lifetime contract*…: Silary

…*"a clear indication that my career…"*: Outrageous!

"He didn't wordsmith anything…": Interview, Nov. 21, 2019

"Sometimes I need the crowd to get me going…": Newman

…*Cheeks…said it was a good thing*…: Outrageous!

…*Charles would make the All-NBA 2nd Team, win the*…: Basketball Reference

"Charles is the heart of this team…": Jack McCallum, "Nothing Faint About Philly," *Sports Illustrated*, May 5, 1986

…*when he was in public with girlfriend Donna, who is White*…: Ray Didinger, "The Price of Fame," *Philadelphia Daily News*, May 15, 1986

"That stuff cuts deep…": Didinger

A good night for Charles usually meant…: Didinger

"…*five peas in a pod*…": Newman

"There was no letdown in Charles Barkley…": Interview, Aug. 1, 2019

"The Sixers were our kiss of death…": Interview, Mar. 2, 2020

Deafening chants of "Barkley sucks!" reverberated…: YouTube uploads of the 1986 playoff series between Philadelphia and Milwaukee, *https:// www.youtube.com/watch?v=-Ao9l_1yU78*, *https://www.youtube.com/ watch?v=yA0ed29gt9I*

…*describing the Bucks…as a team of role players*…: Interview, Mar. 2, 2020

…*ordered them to "kiss me where the sun don't shine"*…: Phil Jasner, "Sixers on the Ropes," *Philadelphia Daily News*, May 8, 1986

"I went up to him and said…": Interview, Nov. 12, 2019

…*Charles delivered a wild left hook to the seven-footer*…: YouTube upload of a 2019 *Inside the NBA* segment showing Charles punching Paul Mokeski, *https://www.youtube.com/watch?v=4yLEZd3v9eQ*

Don Nelson…remarked that it was the first time…: Bill Handleman, "Bucks Outslug Sixers," *Asbury Park Press*, May 8, 1986

"If you knock a guy down with one punch…": *https://www.youtube.com/watch?v=4yLEZd3v9eQ*

"If he had…": Jasner

…that didn't stop him from venturing out to a Brewers game…: Didinger

"I'm only sorry that Charles…": Didinger

…that the Bucks' forward "go bleep himself"…: McCallum

"That's not Charles Barkley…": *https://www.youtube.com/watch?v=yA0ed29gt9I*

"Lucky…": Interview, Nov. 12, 2019

…a decision would need to be "a blockbuster of a trade"…: Bill Free, "Without a Clear-Cut No.1, Sixers Play 'Let's Make a Deal,'" *Baltimore Sun*, June 15, 1986

"That put the wheels in motion…": Interview, Oct. 3, 2019

…hours after a New Orleans courtroom found John "Hot Rod" Williams…: Jere Longman, "Cavs Make Daugherty No. 1," *Philadelphia Inquirer*, June 18, 1986

…the dedicated crowd…booed lustily…: Longman

"I don't know what's going on…": Longman

"They used to call that team the Cadavers…": Interview, Nov. 27, 2019

"I'm still one of the top players…": Phil Jasner, "Moses: I'm Still the Man," *Philadelphia Daily News*, May 13, 1986

Katz didn't consult with Charles over the move…: Interview, Oct. 7, 2019

"Mentally, it screwed me up…": *Outrageous!*

…he saw the same thing play out with the "cocky" Katz…: "Malone Criticizes Katz, Vows Revenge on Court," Associated Press, June 25, 1986

"When Charles Barkley gets to be about my age…": Mike Bruton, "76ers Trade Malone and Top Pick," *Philadelphia Inquirer*, June 18, 1986

"We thought as that night ended…": Interview, May 17, 2019

"He knocks him over, dunks on Roy Hinson…": Interviews, Aug. 26 and Sept. 3, 2019

"Oh my God…": Interview, Jan. 31, 2020

"The first words out of his mouth were…": Interview, June 1, 2020

…also sold the majority of his stake in Nutrisystem…: David A. Vise, "76ers Owner to Sell Nutrisystem Stake," *Washington Post*, Feb. 6, 1986

I think I should win the MVP...: Chris Baker, "Barkley's Bark," *Los Angeles Times*, Feb. 22, 1987

...an eight-year deal worth $13 million...: Ray Frager, "Sixers Round Up a Bargain: 8 Years of Barkley for $13M," *Baltimore Sun*, Feb. 17, 1987

"It put a tremendous amount of personal pressure on Charles...": Interview, July 24, 2020

...he had not "graduated a little bit to Twinkies"...: Bruton

"One person was all about the responsibility...": Interview, June 3, 2019

"To say Charles hated his father...": Mark Heisler, "Having Fun in the Sun," *Los Angeles Times*, Apr. 28, 1993

...skipped out on the Slam Dunk Contest...: *Outrageous!*

Things soon got awkward when Campbell...: Interview, Jan. 30, 2020

"His father was ready to fight me...": Interview, Jan. 30, 2020

"We've got guys who have complained, complained...": Mike Bruton, "Barkley Takes a Shot at the Sixers' 'Complainers,'" *Philadelphia Inquirer*, Feb. 18, 1987

...this dawned on Free while he was taking a shower...: Interview, July 24, 2020

"I came in there and the next thing you know...": Interview, July 24, 2020

"He came back and put these beautiful presents...": Interview, June 30, 2020

...and was being escorted in a 1928 Packard Roadster...: "Erving Honored Again," *New York Times*, Apr. 21, 1987

...named to his first All-Star team, a repeat performance on...: Basketball Reference

"Coaches would question you about how you let Charles...": Interview, Apr. 27, 2020

...while "Going the Distance" from Rocky *played in the arena...*: YouTube upload of Game 5 of the 1987 playoff series between Philadelphia and Milwaukee, *https://www.youtube.com/watch?v=PDB1v75ukeA*

"I took the ball, and it was like...": Interview, July 24, 2020

Chapter 14

Primary sources include research conducted by the author in Philadelphia, as well as interviews with Matt Barnes, John Costacos, Billy Cunningham, Chuck D, Bob Ford, DJ Jazzy Jeff, Phil Knight, Jim Lynam, Tim McCormick, John Nash, Joe Pytka, Jim Riswold, Jalen Rose, Bob Ryan, Bakari Sellers, Dan Sims, Jerry Stackhouse, Dawn Staley, Mark Thomashow, and Sonny Vaccaro. Other sources include *Outrageous!*, a police report filed by the New Jersey State Police in August 1988, features and series that were published in outlets like *PhillySport*, *Sports Illustrated*, the *Philadelphia Daily News*, and the *Philadelphia Inquirer*, and documentaries from ESPN and *SB Nation*.

"I namechecked Charles because…": Interview, Jan. 4, 2021

He didn't want that, he thought…: *Outrageous!*

"Nike absolutely helped magnify the personality…": Interview, July 7, 2020

…the brand looked to broaden and diversify its focus…: Douglas C. McGill, "Nike Is Bounding Past Reebok," *New York Times*, July 11, 1989

The executives gathered at the McMansion in the Pacific Northwest…: *30 for 30: Sole Man*, ESPN Films, Apr. 16, 2015

…who journalist Armen Keteyian said "basically owned college basketball"…: *Sole Man*

"It was truly an honor…": "Charles Barkley: Past Meets Present in Nike Barkley Posite Max," Nike.com, Apr. 18, 2013

"There was some argument…": Interview, July 7, 2020

In "Men at Work," one of the earliest TV ads…: YouTube upload of Nike's "Men at Work" ad, *https://www.youtube.com/watch?v=IiSgsGthv0Y*

"The early version of Charles, to be blunt…": Interviews, June 3 and Oct. 3, 2019

…The meek may inherit the earth…: Nike.com

…the Air Force was the No. 1 shoe at the company ahead of Air Jordan…: Mike Bruton, "Barkley Is Driven to Succeed, His Way," *Philadelphia Inquirer*, Feb. 1, 1987

…Charles's endorsement deal was worth $500,000 a year…: Jack McCallum, "On a Mission," *Sports Illustrated*, Dec. 12, 1988

"In some ways, Charles was unlucky…": Interview, July 7, 2020

"If Jordan doesn't hit at Nike…": Interviews, June 27 and July 18, 2019

Dawn Staley had Barkleys on her feet when…: Interview, Apr. 30, 2020

Jerry Stackhouse was attracted to the style and feel…: Interview, Apr. 17, 2020

"I wore them until I had holes in them…": Interview, Oct. 18, 2019

Bakari Sellers…saw his parents save up money to buy him a pair…: Interview, Nov. 24, 2020

"I lived it by wearing Barkleys…": Interview, Sept. 11, 2020

…had developed a series of distinctive, original sports-themed posters…: Amy K. Nelson, "Poster Boys," *SB Nation*, Feb. 5, 2013

"The poster made you look cool…": Nelson

…she succeeded by asking Charles what size he wore…: Interview, Nov. 6, 2019

"I thought it captured who he was…": Interview, Nov. 6, 2019

"I told the ref his mom…": Interview, Nov. 6, 2019

This is Charles Barkley. You've reached…: Interview, Nov. 6, 2019

"The girl's mother was horrified…": Interview, Nov. 6, 2019

…known increasingly as Sir Charles…: Ira Berkow, "Sir Charles Rumbles," *New York Times*, Dec. 19, 1987

"I'm definitely as good as those guys…": YouTube upload of a 1988 segment from CBS Sports personality Pat O'Brien on Barkley's fourth season, *https://www.youtube.com/watch?v=tKU82vuR6V0*

"Shut up, you bitch… She'll get over it…": Bob Vetrone Jr., "A Career of Candor Continues," *Philadelphia Daily News*, Dec. 31, 1987

Referee Mike Mathis…ejected Charles for the third time…: Phil Jasner, "Barkley Boils over Loss to L.A., Ejection," *Philadelphia Daily News*, Dec. 30, 1987

"The team is just bad…": Jasner

"I posed the question among a group of reporters…": *Sir Charles*

…Matt Guokas…was fired right at the All-Star break…: Bob Ford, "Things Didn't Quite Work Out for Guokas and His Team," *Philadelphia Inquirer*, Feb. 9, 1988

…putting up 28.3 points per game to go along with…: Basketball Reference

…was the best player in the league not named Michael Jordan…: Interviews, May 6 and 8, 2019

Charles was dominant again…: Basketball Reference

"What the fuck do you think it is?…": Dan Steinberg, "Oprah, Popeyes and Late-Night Vacuuming: That Time Scott Brooks Lived with Charles Barkley," *Washington Post*, May 8, 2017

…to watch Oprah Winfrey…to pick up $100 worth of Popeyes…: Steinberg

"That day right there…": Steinberg

BARKLEY

Pulled over on the shoulder of the Atlantic City Expressway…: Police Report, New Jersey State Police, Aug. 17, 1988

…with reason to believe he was in possession of drugs or a weapon…: New Jersey State Police

…Simon found a loaded 9mm Heckler & Koch semiautomatic handgun…: Bruce Buschel, "It's so Hard to Be a Saint in the City," *PhillySport* (republished by *Deadspin*), January 1989

…did not have a New Jersey permit…: Buschel

…arrested on one count of possession of a controlled dangerous weapon…: New Jersey State Police

…which left the coach dumbfounded…: Interview, July 1, 2020

"I don't know why the media should make a big deal…": Phil Jasner and Gloria Campisi, "Barkley Case a Puzzle," *Philadelphia Daily News*, Aug. 19, 1988

"I would never want to kill anyone…": Buschel

…Lynam confronted him about what happened…: Interview, July 1, 2020

…the trooper's search was illegal…: Buschel

"He'll only work for the rich people… Mom, I *am* rich…": *Outrageous!*

…his agent had allegedly paid high school and college coaches…: Fish and Pasquarelli

Cliff Levingston of the Atlanta Hawks was awarded…: Fish and Pasquarelli

…using his finances as if they were "his own private pocketbook"…: Fish and Pasquarelli

…"letting an alcoholic trying to kick the habit…": Fish and Pasquarelli

…was Maurice Cheeks, who parted ways…: *Outrageous!*

"Nobody I know has gone through life…": Fish and Pasquarelli

Approximately $200,000 was invested in hotels, a car dealership…: *Outrageous!*

"I built this whole life on not being poor…": Buschel

…"that should be the extent of his involvement"…: Fish and Pasquarelli

…suspended Luchnick from representing…: "Agent Has His Certification Suspended by NBA Union," *Philadelphia Inquirer*, May 31, 1988

When Charles picked up the phone to call Glenn Guthrie…: *Outrageous!*

"Lance had Charles in big, big debt…": Interview, Dec. 3, 2019

…described as "nuclear waste" by an attorney…: Interview, Dec. 3, 2019

...he had basically nothing to show for the $1 million he had already made...: Interview, Dec. 3, 2019

...had four years' worth of back taxes and penalties...: *Outrageous!*

Luchnick was fired in March 1989...: *Outrageous!*; Mark Coomes and Pat Forde, "Gay's Records Show Many Calls to Controversial Agent," *Louisville Courier-Journal*, Dec. 15, 1995

...until Luchnick filed for bankruptcy and lost his NBA clients...: Fish and Pasquarelli

"I left my affairs totally in...": McCallum

...was born at TGI Friday's...: Ray Didinger, "Just One Big Happy Family," *Philadelphia Daily News,* June 29, 1989

...at Friday's in October 1987...: *Outrageous!*

"She grabbed my arm...": Didinger

"I didn't grab your arm...": Didinger

"You tried to stop me...": Didinger

"You're exaggerating...": Didinger

...it was a "big Black thigh"...: Dolores Tropiano, "Living as 'Mrs. Sir Charles,'" *Arizona Republic*, Feb. 19, 2000

"He chased me like a dog...": Tropiano

...growing up in Bucks County outside of Philadelphia...: *Outrageous!*

"I was the biggest tomboy...": Tropiano

Charles hands out tickets to women...: Didinger

"I thought she was stuck up...": Didinger

"Sometimes... I think she's too good...": Didinger

Maureen could keep up with Charles in a way no one had before...: Interviews, Aug. 26 and Sept. 3, 2019

...the Sixers forward had been talking about marrying Maureen...: "Barkley Is Married in Private Ceremony," Associated Press, Feb. 10, 1989

"One of the things that changed Charles was Maureen...": Interview, Oct. 8, 2019

The news delighted Charcey...: Didinger

"I said, 'You know...'": Phil Jasner, "Keeping a Secret," *Philadelphia Daily News*, Feb. 11, 1989

...Charles had actor Rob Lowe call Maureen...: W. Speers, "Sports of All Sorts," *Philadelphia Inquirer*, Jan. 7, 1989

...Why don't you stick with your own kind?...: Outrageous!

The basement of the courthouse seemed like a good place...: Associated Press

"I really think he just didn't want any publicity...": Associated Press

...at a benefit for Armenian relief in New York...: Bob Ryan, "Introducing the Barkleys," *Boston Globe*, Feb. 12, 1989

"This has nothing to do with...": Jasner

"I felt I was with a special woman...": Jasner

Chapter 15

Primary sources include research conducted by the author in Philadelphia, as well as interviews with Johnny Dawkins, Craig Ehlo, Howard Eskin, Mike Gminski, Hersey Hawkins, Jason Hehir, Harold Katz, Margaret Little, Allen Lumpkin, Jim Lynam, John Nash, Will Perdue, John Salley, Amy Shorter, and Sam Smith. Other sources include *Outrageous!*, *The Jordan Rules*, stories published in *Sports Illustrated*, the *Philadelphia Daily News*, and the *Washington Post*, the film *30 for 30: Bad Boys*, and segments from *Inside the NBA* and NBA TV.

"You were a nervous wreck... Charles was white...": Didinger

"Okay, maybe I was a *little* nervous...": Didinger

Christiana Barkley was born at eight pounds, twelve ounces...: Didinger

"I want to have a good marriage...": Didinger

A high school dropout who struggled in one year of vocational school...: Outrageous!

"Darryl had to follow a star...": Interview, Aug. 15, 2019

...the family suspected the twenty-two-year-old started using around 1988...: Outrageous!

"I had an enlarged heart since birth...": Robert Strauss, "These Athletes All Have a Gift," *New York Times*, June 21, 2004

...had been a part of the drug community "for a while"...: Strauss

...when police arrested him on a charge of selling crack...: "Barkley's Brother Arrested in Drug Sweep," Associated Press, May 10, 1989

...Leeds police brought in an undercover cop from Montgomery...: Associated Press

...Charcey, finding all the strength she had left, gave an ultimatum...: Outrageous!

The urine test showed traces of cocaine and marijuana...: Outrageous!

...a version of the same headline ran...: Associated Press

"I love my brother…": Didinger

…*suffered a stroke that left him partially paralyzed*…: Dick Weiss, "Six Shots," *Philadelphia Daily News*, Oct. 13, 1989

A blood clot on the right side of the brain…: Dick Weiss, "Barkley's Brother Stricken," *Philadelphia Daily News*, Oct. 12, 1989

"I just can't imagine being paralyzed…": Tim Potvak, "Charles Barkley Needs Those Broad Shoulders to Support Team, Family," *Orlando Sentinel*, Nov. 19, 1989

"That's what got him in trouble…": *Outrageous!*

Dear Bill…: *Outrageous!*; Interviews, Oct. 29 and Nov. 11, 2019

Michael Jordan expected them to be dicks… Scottie Pippen hated them to death…: *The Last Dance*

"Nice guys finish last…": *30 for 30: Bad Boys*, ESPN Films, Apr. 17, 2104

Mahorn thought the Pistons were joking…: *Bad Boys*

…*his client "had more tests than Ronald Reagan this year*…": "76ers Sign Mahorn," *Anniston Star*, Nov. 4, 1989

…*Mahorn threatened to play in Italy*…: "No-Show Mahorn Italy-Bound?," *Los Angeles Times*, Oct. 20, 1989

…*that Mahorn, not Charles, had the biggest butt in the league*…: Craig Neff, "Scorecard," *Sports Illustrated*, Nov. 27, 1989

"The connection he had with Rick Mahorn…": Interviews, July 19 and 26, 2019

"The team was a reflection of the city…": Interview, June 19, 2019

…*in fines totaling at least $35,000*…: David Aldridge, "Of so Many Images, Barkley's Talent Clear," *Washington Post*, May 1, 1990

…*as the $5,000 fine leveled against both Charles and*…: Sam Goldaper, "Jackson, Barkley Are Fined for Bets," *New York Times*, Jan. 12, 1990

…*were "one of the most uncomfortable things that could*…": "Charles Barkley Remembers the Late David Stern," NBA TV, Jan. 1, 2020

"When you screwed up…": NBA TV

…*Mary Walsh…called into a radio station to complain*…: "His Bark Lacked Usual Bite," *Los Angeles Times*, Feb. 19, 1989

"My wife and my momma told me…": *Los Angeles Times*

Allen Lumpkin was struck when Charles walked up to him…: Interview, July 27, 2020

"The only stipulation was…": Interview, July 27, 2020

...how Charles would "kill me if I publicized it"...: Shaun Powell, "Barkley's Always Open for a Shot," *Washington Post*, Jan. 9, 1991

...to go see Mississippi Burning, *the 1988 film...*: Interviews, Oct. 29 and Nov. 11, 2019

"We're warming up and he's like, 'Goddammit...'": Interviews, Oct. 29 and Nov. 11, 2019

...he proclaimed that no one else on the team could really fight...: *The Dan Patrick Show*, Apr. 28, 2020

"The Sixers had the real Bad Boy...": *Outrageous!*

"I don't know in my time...": NBA on ESPN

"You just tried not to get hurt...": Interview, Jan. 3, 2020

"Mahorn leans across Laimbeer and sniffs the air...": Interviews, Oct. 29 and Nov. 11, 2019

Then, Laimbeer took a swing at an interceding Charles...: YouTube upload of the April 1990 game between Philadelphia and Detroit, *https://www.youtube.com/watch?v=IE2e86u3gBQ*

"Charles is not realizing this is about to be a fight...": Interview, May 8, 2020

...but Charles declined to press charges...: Tom Moore, "Charles Barkley Pulled No Punches during Sixers' Wild 1990 Division Clincher," Tribune Media Services, May 25, 2020

"He swung at me for no reason...": *Outrageous!*

...a total of $162,500 in fines...: Jack McCallum, "Fight Night at the Palace," *Sports Illustrated*, Apr. 30, 1990

"I called David Stern and asked why he was fining me...": Interview, Oct. 7, 2019

A proud Lynam repeated some of the criticisms...: Interview, July 1, 2020

...joked that he had defended his heavyweight title...: "Charles Barkley vs. Laimbeer Fight Story—Beef History," BTM Basketball Time Machine, *https://www.youtube.com/watch?v=iltLyi7-z8o*

"Charlie was so pissed...": Interviews, Oct. 29 and Nov. 11, 2019

...when he nearly disemboweled a helpless Craig Ehlo...: Hank Hersch, "The Old Heave-Ho for Foul Play," *Sports Illustrated*, Nov. 5, 1990

"My body collided with his...": Interview, Oct. 14, 2019

"We're going to Chicago...": Interview, Jan. 3, 2020

"I can live with whatever happens...": Aldridge

...Jordan was averaging 42 points in the first two games...: Basketball Reference

"They had some good players, but...": Interview, May 26, 2020

"The first thing he does is break down...": YouTube upload of an *Inside the NBA* interview in 2001, *https://www.youtube.com/watch?v=5vuvKc5qA6s*

"Barkley's teams were still so diminished...": Interview, Dec. 11, 2019

"By the time we went to Chicago for Game 1...": *Outrageous!*

"As he turns away, he says something to Pippen...": Interview, July 1, 2020

...returned home for the funeral of his father in Arkansas...: Phil Jasner, "Barkley: Media Trying to Pull Us Apart," *Philadelphia Daily News*, May 11, 1990

"He didn't have any legs left...": Dick Weiss, "Jordan Knows Barkley's Burden," *Philadelphia Daily News*, May 14, 1990

He averaged 43 points in the five-game series...: Basketball Reference

"I never played four consecutive games...": *The Jordan Rules*

...coming in second in MVP voting despite finishing with the most first-place votes...: Basketball Reference

"I haven't let it go...": *Inside the NBA*, 2020

Chapter 16

Primary sources include research conducted by the author in Philadelphia and New Jersey, as well as interviews with Dr. James Andrews, David DuPree, Howard Eskin, Bob Ford, Tony Harris, Hersey Hawkins, Mark Heisler, Roy S. Johnson, Harold Katz, Jim Lynam, Leigh Montville, Lauren Porreca, Pat Riley, Sam Smith, Neil Tardio, and Bob Weinhauer. Other sources include *Outrageous!*, *Sir Charles*, coverage in the *Philadelphia Inquirer* and the *Philadelphia Daily News*, and video from the 1990–91 season.

Growing up in the shadows of New York City...: Interview, Oct. 1, 2019

"It was more like a playground...": Interview, Oct. 1, 2019

One of the hecklers was Craig Pistilli...: Interview, Oct. 1, 2019

A car dealer in North Jersey with a love for...: Obituary for Craig Pistilli, Settle-Wilder Funeral Home and Cremation Service, June 2018

The verbal abuse, including...racial slurs...: *Outrageous!*; Larry Platt, "Charles Barkley," *Salon*, May 30, 2000

...Pistilli ran up and down the aisle while Charles and Mahorn...: Interview, Oct. 1, 2019

Only two known camera angles exist...: "Remember When: Charles Barkley Spit on a Little Girl During an NBA Game," *NowThis* via footage from the NBA, NBC, and YouTube, *https://www.youtube.com/watch?v=Ba-ofhampSs*

...Lauren's father saw Charles start to gather his spit together...: SportsCentury

...that it wasn't his intention to spit on anyone...: *In Depth with Graham Bensinger*

The cameraman on the baseline immediately reacted...: *https://www.youtube.com/watch?v=Ba-ofhampSs*

"All of a sudden, I felt wet and gross...": Interview, Oct. 1, 2019

Her father went on the court and yelled...: Interview, Oct. 1, 2019

"As a teammate, all you could do...": Interview, Jan. 3, 2020

"The spitting incident never changed...": Interview, July 1, 2020

...Gilliam...put his arm around the girl and apologized...: Interview, Oct. 1, 2019

"It really hit me because...": Interview, Oct. 1, 2019

...who called his action "a stupid mistake"...: Phil Jasner, "Barkley: 'Stupid Mistake,'" *Philadelphia Daily News*, Mar. 28, 1991

"How do you like that...": *Outrageous!*

The mistake would cost him about $50,000...: Mike Bruton, "Barkley Suspended, Fined," *Philadelphia Inquirer*, Mar. 29, 1991

...advised the star to "cut it out"...: George Diaz, "Sir Charles Throws Another Terrific Tantrum," *Orlando Sentinel*, Jan. 22, 1993

"I didn't think I was going to make it...": *Sir Charles*

...had become a pressing concern for Neil Tardio...: Interview, Mar. 5, 2020

"He still had that round, nice, well-balanced face...": Interview, Mar. 5, 2020

...he made his pitch...over a burger at a sports bar...: Terry Lefton, "How Sir Charles Became a Winning Pitchman," *Sports Business Journal*, Feb. 21, 2011

"I knew he'd have an enduring career...": Lefton

"This is a game that, if you lose...": Phil Jasner, "Women's Groups Are Angered by Barkley's Remarks," *Philadelphia Daily News*, Nov. 26, 1990

"Naw, print it...": David Aldridge, "Barkley's Just Playing, so Why the Offense?," *Washington Post*, Apr. 6, 1995

"I'm sure the estimated...": Jasner

"This ain't no big controversy...": Bob Ford, "Sorry for Quip, Barkley Tells Women," *Philadelphia Inquirer*, Nov. 26, 1990

...Charles promised at a beef ribs restaurant in Cherry Hill, New Jersey...: Jack Chevalier, "Barkley Scores Some Points with His Radio Repartee," *The News Journal*, Oct. 31, 1990

"He was an excellent patient who...": Interview, Sept. 4, 2019

"He used to come in and get on the stationary bike...": "Jayson Williams on Playing with Charles Barkley," VladTV, *https://www.youtube.com/watch?v=_lu5QRuJ9Wc*

...Bob Weinhauer had driven to pick him up from the airport...: Interview, Oct. 30, 2019

...Bol saw a lion running across the pasture...: Leigh Montville, *Manute: The Center of Two Worlds*, Feb. 24, 1993

He watched CNN and read the New York Times *to try to learn...*: Montville

...was deeply skeptical of low-fat and 2 percent milk...: Leigh Montville, "A Tall Story," *Sports Illustrated*, Dec. 17, 1990

...Bol would often come to practice reciting taglines from...: Interview, June 11, 2019

"Charlie, let me out of the ball bag!"...: Interviews, Aug. 26 and Sept. 3, 2019

...once telling Charles that the problem with Black men in America...: Interview, July 24, 2019

..."if everyone in the world was a Manute Bol...": Montville

...lost two young children within a year...: *Outrageous!*

"Uncle Simon told me that it was time...": *Outrageous!*

"He wasn't there, we grew up poor...": *Phil in the Blanks*

"He didn't know whether the spit...": Interviews, July 19 and 26, 2019

"He was like, 'I'm sorry...'": Interview, Oct. 1, 2019

...but pushed back against the backlash, reminding people...: Bob Ford, "Barkley Regrets Spitting Incident, but...," *Philadelphia Inquirer*, Mar. 31, 1991

"He didn't give a crap about what people...": Interview, Oct. 8, 2019

...Riley...questioned in his NBC interview whether...: Interview, Jan. 12, 2021

"Emotional stability is a characteristic of a champion...": YouTube upload of a 1991 interview from *NBA on NBC*, which has since been taken down, *https://web.archive.org/web/20150509090052/https://www.youtube.com/watch?v=uFEHw4edZ98*

...and her and her family were surprise guests at the Easterseals benefit...: Stu Bykofsky, "Chuck Roast," *Philadelphia Daily News*, July 23, 1991

...of a good time was "sitting on the toilet until...": Bykofsky

...Porreca and her family heard Charles as he opened up...: Interview, Oct. 1, 2019

At some point, he realized two things...: In Depth with Graham Bensinger

"He stretched the boundaries of the things...": Interview, Jan. 27, 2020

"Lauren taught me a great deal...": *SportsCentury*

"Now that I'm a mom...": Interview, Oct. 1, 2019

...Charles had Pep Mock on the brain...: Outrageous!

"It's a little different being at war...": Phil Jasner, "War Hits Close to Home for Sixers," *Philadelphia Daily News*, Jan. 18, 1991

...donned a blue hat that read "FUCK IRAQ," which nearly caused...: Outrageous!

...with his family in the stands, including Darryl...: Outrageous!

Bill Lyon...hoped that the incident could push Charles...: Bill Lyon, "This Could Be the Incident to Turn Barkley Around," *Philadelphia Inquirer*, Mar. 29, 1991

...Phil Jackson used a quote from Thomas Jefferson to lead the scouting report...: The Jordan Rules

"What stood out about that period against Chicago...": Interview, Oct. 7, 2019

"Michael came to believe, and accept...": Interview, Dec. 11, 2019

Spending the day with Jordan and Ahmad Rashad playing craps and blackjack...: Interview, July 8, 2019

"With Jordan and Pippen...": Interview, July 1, 2020

Chapter 17

Primary sources include research conducted by the author in Philadelphia, as well as interviews with Dr. Todd Boyd, Julius Erving, Bob Ford, John Franke, Tom Halloran, Hersey Hawkins, Jemele Hill, the Rev. Jesse Jackson, Harold Katz, Larry Krystkowiak, Allen Lumpkin, Jim Lynam, Tharon Mayes, Mike Missanelli, Larry Platt, and Bob Trednic. Other sources include *Outrageous!*, Howard Stern's memoir, *Private Parts*, coverage from outlets like the *Philadelphia Daily News* and the *New York Times*, segments from *Inside the NBA*, and a 2020 episode of *The Lowe Post*.

"That's the irony of the fight he got into...": Interview, Nov. 4, 2019

...*McCarthy was a nice guy who never wanted to fight*...: Interview, Aug. 22, 2020

As Charles and Lee Anne Wooten were leaving...: Rick Gano, "Barkley Doesn't Testify," Associated Press, June 17, 1992

...*Charles said the woman he was with was Brickowski's wife*...: *The Lowe Post*, May 19, 2020

Wooten later testified in court...: Gano

"Charles... I hear you're one of the baddest dudes...": "Barkley Says He Simply Was Defending Himself," Associated Press, Dec. 24, 1991

...*he never wanted any part of Charles from the outset*...: Interview, Aug. 22, 2020

...*make them think you're crazy*...: *The Lowe Post*

He also found a triangular parking sign...: Interview, Aug. 22, 2020

"I was like, 'Is he going to start doing karate...'": Interview, Aug. 22, 2020

"He's down, and he's like...": *The Lowe Post*

He would be arrested at his hotel room...: "After Hours Fight Lands Barkley in Milwaukee Jail," Associated Press, Dec. 23, 1991

..."*police came and got the big boy last night*"...: Interviews, Aug. 26 and Sept. 3, 2019

"Can you give me a ride?...": Interviews, Aug. 26 and Sept. 3, 2019

"That guy apparently had made a comment about...": Nov. 4, 2019

...*I want to wear 32 to honor Earvin*...: Interview, July 27, 2020

"As soon as Magic announced he was HIV positive...": Interview, July 27, 2020

...*he'd whisper to Charles his appreciation*...: Anthony Cotton, "32 No Mere Number to Controversial Barkley," *Washington Post*, Nov. 17, 1991

"It's not like we're going out...": Sean Grimm, "Charles Barkley: Top 10 Moments on the Court and in the Studio," *Bleacher Report*, Aug. 16, 2010

"You really think I give a flying FUCK...": YouTube upload of Charles talking to reporters in 1991, *https://www.youtube.com/watch?v=I-T031rtyjs*

...*Charles grew tired of the city's racism*...: Keith Groller, "Racism in Philadelphia Has Barkley 'Hoppen Mad,'" *The Morning Call*, Oct. 31, 1991

"Some athletes had courage on the court...": Interview, Nov. 2, 2020

"I said, 'Dude, if I want Italian...'": *The Mike Missanelli Show*, Aug. 29, 2019

"I wanted Shaq and they gave me...": *The Mike Missanelli Show*, Jan. 22, 2013

"You liked to have your star come up...": Interview, July 24, 2020

...*become the subject of a 2:30 a.m.* SportsCenter *rumor*...: Phil Jasner, "Barkley: 'Not in the Middle of This,'" *Philadelphia Daily News*, Jan. 16, 1992

...*ended up cracking a thirty-four-year-old man in the head*...: Phil Jasner, "Double Trouble for Jayson," *Philadelphia Daily News*, Jan. 16, 1992

"I had met John Cusack...": Jasner

"I've got three more good seasons left...": *Outrageous!*

...*Charles protested that he didn't say what he had said*...: "Barkley 'Misquoted' in Own Book," Associated Press, Dec. 13, 1991

"I don't know how you can be misquoted...": Jere Longman, "Barkley Blasts His Book, Then Sticks by It," *Philadelphia Inquirer*, Dec. 13, 1991

...*this was someone who was grounded in his own Blackness*...: Interview, Jan. 27, 2020

"He understood the bar was much higher...": Interview, July 9, 2020

"Charles always had a strong conscience...": Interview, Jan. 27, 2020

...*Johnson would take the train down from New York and hit Record*...: Interview, Jan. 27, 2020

"Charles was speaking against maybe...": Interview, Jan. 27, 2020

...*as well as instruct Glenn Guthrie to see what could be done*...: Interview, Jan. 27, 2020

"How many times can you hit someone...": Alan Goldstein, "Unlike Jordan, Barkley May Be in Bind from Book," *Baltimore Sun*, Dec. 17, 1991

...*he didn't recall any book coming out on Charles*...: Interview, Oct. 7, 2019

"The public started to turn a little bit...": Interviews, Aug. 26 and Sept. 3, 2019

...*Charles's long ball had been "ill-advised"*...: Stan Hochman, "One Bad Shot after Another," *Philadelphia Daily News*, Mar. 9, 1992

"I'm a '90s...": Hochman

"Racism always exists...": Hochman

They'd slam beers together and solve the world's problems…: Interview, Apr. 24, 2020

"He was powerfully influenced by…": Interview, Apr. 24, 2020

…that killed fifty-five people…and $1 billion in property damage…: Charlie Leduff, "12 Years After the Riots, Rodney King Gets Along," *New York Times*, Sept. 19, 2004

"Charles's point was basically…": Interviews, June 27 and Sept. 23, 2019

"I think Blacks are making progress…": Chris Wilder, "Nineties N—," *The Source*, December 1992

…recently shared a hot tub with Donald Trump and some women…: Howard Stern, *Private Parts*, Oct. 7, 1993

"That's from working hard, Howard…": *Private Parts*

Naked in bed on a Friday morning, Charles passed the phone…: *Private Parts*

"Like an ant or a fly…": *Private Parts*

"They don't care…": *Private Parts*

"If I do leave him…": *Private Parts*

…with Charles taking residence at the Adam's Mark Hotel…: Stu Bykofsky, "Barkleys Split?," *Philadelphia Daily News*, Apr. 9, 1992

"It had just gotten to the point where Charles…": Interview, Jan. 3, 2020

…the Sporting News *had him on the cover with six different…*: SportsCentury

…a trip to Portland to meet with the team's general manager…: Inside the NBA, 2018

"I told them they were never gonna win…": *Inside the NBA*

…Damian Lillard presented him with a check…: Inside the NBA

…a deal seemed promising with the Lakers…: Alan Goldstein, "Barkley, Worthy Rumored Part of Blockbuster Trade," *Baltimore Sun*, Feb. 12, 1992

To celebrate, Charles started drinking around noon…: Jimmy Kimmel Live

"I'm drunk as fuck…": *The Lowe Post*

Lynam…received a letter from a fan…: Interview, July 1, 2020

"He said, 'You know, Tom…'": Interview, June 4, 2020

…the publicity and complications that came…: Interview, May 27, 2020

"Once the jury heard that…": Interview, May 27, 2020

…Trednic had told McCarthy that he would not lie on the stand…: Interview, Aug. 22, 2020

"If these dudes had beat me to a pulp…": *The Lowe Post*

…needed about ninety minutes to acquit Charles…: Rick Gano, "Jury Deliberates 1 ½ Hours, Acquits Barkley," Associated Press, June 18, 1992

"He's a good showman…": Interview, June 4, 2020

…and listed the five teams he had interest in being dealt to…: Harvey Araton, "All Is Never Quiet on Barkley Front," *New York Times*, Nov. 5, 1992

Chapter 18

Primary sources include research conducted by the author from Northern Virginia and New Jersey, as well as interviews with J.A. Adande, Kenny Anderson, P.J. Carlesimo, Vince Carter, Bob Costas, David DuPree, Russ Granik, Grant Hill, Bobby Hurley, Phil Knight, Mike Krzyzewski, Anthony Martin, Jack McCallum, Craig Miller, Bob Ryan, Detlef Schrempf, Pete Skorich, Don Sperling, John Stockton, Donnie Walsh, Lang Whitaker, and Lenny Wilkens. Other sources include the book *Dream Team*, the NBA TV documentary *The Dream Team*, coverage in outlets like *Sports Illustrated*, the *Washington Post*, and the *Philadelphia Daily News*, and an oral history of the Dream Team that appeared in *GQ* in 2012.

…a legendary combination of the Kirov Ballet…: Jackie MacMullan, Rafe Bartholomew, and Dan Klores, *Basketball: A Love Story,* September 2018

…the United States had a keen interest in funneling…: Office of the Historian, US State Department

"I don't know anything about Angola…": Tony Kornheiser, "Here, There and Everywhere," *Washington Post*, July 27, 1992

"I told old boy…": *The Dream Team*, NBA TV, 2012

…who he watched every Wednesday in Luanda…: *The Dream Team*

"Other players in Angola who play against Charles Barkley…": *The Dream Team*

Charles said he felt the Angolan hit his head…: Harvey Araton, "Barkley's Elbow Fouls a U.S. Rout," *New York Times*, July 27, 1992

David Robinson and Karl Malone… Clyde Drexler said…: *The Dream Team*

Michael Jordan would tell him that the whistling…: *The Dream Team*

…how Charles turned them into "the US bullies"…: Lang Whitaker, "The Dream Team Will Never Die: An Oral History of the Dream Team," *GQ*, June 11, 2012

"We said to Charles…": *The Dream Team*

…Barkley had become the Ugly American of the 1992 Olympics…: Martha Sherrill, "The Olympic Lip," *Washington Post*, July 29, 1992

"He was the most memorable person…": NBA on ESPN

The international basketball community had long been skeptical…: Jack McCallum, *Dream Team: How Michael, Magic, Larry, Charles, and the Greatest Team of All Time Conquered the World and Changed the Game of Basketball Forever*, 2012

A 1989 resolution from Stankovic…: Dream Team

…when two writers left Charles…off their ballot entirely…: Basketball Reference

"Don't hold 1984 against me…": *Dream Team*

…which previewed what an all-NBA Olympic starting five…: Jack McCallum, "Lords of the Rings," *Sports Illustrated*, Feb. 18, 1991

"He was so outspoken…": Interview, June 4, 2019

…and his record gave them pause…: Interview, July 2, 2019

…simply described as "a very straightforward conversation with him"…: Interview, July 2, 2019

"Right away, he said he would love to be on the team…": Interview, July 2, 2019

…he could potentially land some more endorsements…: Stan Hochman, "Barkley Tirade a Real Award Winner," *Philadelphia Daily News*, Sept. 26, 1991

"Sometimes I dream that he is me…": YouTube upload of a clip from the 1992 Olympics, *https://www.youtube.com/watch?v=NX1O2KO83Uw*

They were statesmen of basketball…: Interview, Mar. 19, 2020

"We're gonna have a little revenge in our hearts…": *The Dream Team*

…don't embarrass yourself…: Interview, May 23, 2019

"I remember Charles walking by at lunch…": Interview, May 23, 2019

Not a single point…: Interview, Mar. 19, 2020

"He was almost like *the* conscience…": Interview, July 9, 2020

…"spring break in the ghetto"…: *https://www.youtube.com/watch?v=NX1O2KO83Uw*

"My head hurt for like two days…": *The Dream Team*

…Charles was one of the first people to come see him in his room…: Interviews, Nov. 8 and 11, 2019

"He'd pick up homeless people on the street…": Interviews, Nov. 8 and 11, 2019

...Jordan and Johnson were particularly brutal toward Charles...: Interviews, July 16 and Dec. 17, 2019

"Hey, Charles who's the best two-guard...": *Dream Team*

"Can you believe that Magic Johnson has the AIDS virus?...": *I May Be Wrong but I Doubt It*

...Johnson said it was some "funny shit"...: *I May Be Wrong but I Doubt It*

..."nobody ever looks bad in a blue suit"...: Jack McCallum, "Remembering Chuck Daly," *Sports Illustrated*, May 9, 2009

"He coached the Bad Boys...": *The Dream Team*

...level of respect as if "12 Popes had come by on Easter Sunday"...: Interviews, Nov. 8 and 11, 2019

"Can I answer that?...": *The Dream Team*

...aside from the $21 beers...: *The Dream Team*

"I remember the manager saying...": Interview, July 10, 2019

"Well, I hope he stops...": Whitaker

"He goes, 'I'm retiring from basketball...'": Interview, July 15, 2019

...he didn't understand the full magnitude of what was going on...: Interview, May 16, 2019

Their battles in practice in Monte Carlo were poetry...: *Dream Team*

"I've never seen anyone...": *Basketball: A Love Story*

...It's better to be lucky than smart...: Interview, Aug. 1, 2019

He set the film of Charles...: *Sir Charles*

"Do you get the idea that, one way or another...": YouTube upload of the Dream Team's first game against Angola, *https://www.youtube.com/watch?v=E7SaPj-wJBo*

..."hasn't eaten in a couple weeks"...: Robeson

...nothing more than "a figment of the American media's imagination"...: Phil Jasner, "U.S.: Barkley's Writing a Wrong," *Philadelphia Daily News*, July 29, 1992

...thought Coimbra was "going to pull a spear on me"...: Jasner

"His answer was it would be almost disrespectful to them...": Interview, Dec. 4, 2019

...but still got a photo with him afterward...: Jasner

He'd live by the 50 percent rule...: Sherrill

"With Coimbra, that's when it was becoming evident…": Interview, Dec. 17, 2019

"I was supposed to meet him at a restaurant…": Interview, Oct. 8, 2019

…*joked that he took it upon himself to walk Las Ramblas*…: Interview, June 26, 2020

"He didn't care, man…": Interview, May 16, 2019

"They're just jealous…": Jasner

"I was mad at him…": Interview, Oct. 30, 2019

"When you hire 12 Clint Eastwoods to come in here…": David Zurawik, "Olympics' End Means the Real Contest Begins," *Baltimore Sun*, Aug. 10, 1992

"You looked at him as among the stars of the game…": Interview, July 13, 2020

Johnson called him the MVP of the team…: *The Dream Team*

…*was "the greatest compliment I ever got in my life"*…: Jack McCallum, "Ever-Glib Barkley Knows Where He Ranks in Dream Team Pecking Order," *Sports Illustrated*, July 25, 2012

…*he had "2 million reasons not to wear Reebok"*…: Donald Katz, "Triumph of the Swoosh," *Sports Illustrated*, Aug. 16, 1993

…*he didn't mind if the Nike athletes wore Reebok on the podium*…: Interview, July 7, 2020

"If I never win a championship…": *The Dream Team*

…*but Charles chose to call it a night rather than stay out*…: Interviews, Nov. 8 and 11, 2019

"It didn't look like it was getting dangerous…": Interviews, Nov. 8 and 11, 2019

…*he didn't plan on having a gold medalist over at the home*…: Interview, Feb. 25, 2020

…*Martin partnered with him on a kids' basketball hoop*…: Interview, Feb. 25, 2020

…*Charles Barkley is over at the house and we need a bunch of fried chicken*…: Interview, Feb. 25, 2020

Chapter 19

Primary sources include research conducted by the author from Northern Virginia and New Jersey, as well as interviews with David Casstevens, Jerry Colangelo, Connie Colla, David Cooper, Billy Cunningham, Matt Donovan, David Griffin, Debbie Hartel, Lionel Hollins, Mayor Paul Johnson, Jude LaCava, Oliver Miller, Joe Proski, Pat Riley, Bob Sarles, Len Sherman, and Bob Young. Other sources include coverage in outlets like *Sports Illustrated*, the *Arizona Republic*, and the Associated Press, and a YouTube series from the Phoenix Suns in 2018.

"Look, Charles, everybody…": Kent Somers, "Cotton Fitzsimmons Was Bold, Flashy—and a Winner for the Phoenix Suns," *Arizona Republic*, Oct. 14, 2018

"That was the first sign of…": Interview, July 11, 2019

"We're walking out of the arena…": Interview, June 5, 2019

…*they had what he described as a "super," or superstar in Johnson…*: Araton

"I wish we had spoken in advance…": Jerry Colangelo and Len Sherman, *How You Play the Game*, 1999

…*Colangelo went from tuxedo salesman to head of marketing…*: Rick Morrissey, "A Green Desert," *Chicago Tribune*, Aug. 9, 1999

…*he left with $200 in his pocket…*: Interview, July 17, 2019

Nick Vanos…died in a Northwest Airlines crash…: "Phoenix Suns Player Among Those Dead with PM-Plane Crash," Associated Press, Aug. 17, 1987

…*the Suns faced the single biggest drug scandal ever to hit…*: Armen Keteyian, "Dark Clouds Over Sun Country," *Sports Illustrated*, Apr. 27, 1987

…*in a case known as "Waltergate"…*: Craig Neff, "Time to Rise and Shine," *Sports Illustrated*, Nov. 23, 1987

"Out of that situation…": Interview, July 17, 2019

…*since the owner came to embody what the city hoped to be…*: Interview, July 10, 2019

"Jerry became an overarching figure…": Interview, July 10, 2019

Called "Cotton" by classmates for his wispy and fluffy hair…: Somers

"Cotton Fitzsimmons was everything to us…": Interview, Apr. 15, 2020

"I have to remind him that Superman…": Somers

Fitzsimmons's father died when he was in the fifth grade…: Dick Dozer, "Cotton's Roots," *Fastbreak* (republished by NBA.com), December 1988

"I told him I was a Bill Clinton man…": Leigh Montville, "He's Everywhere," *Sports Illustrated*, May 3, 1993

The pick was wildly unpopular…: "Phoenix Suns Since '68: Majerle Booed at Draft," Phoenix Suns, *https://www.youtube.com/watch?v=c8z3zAwTKJc*

"What don't we have? Championship flag...": *Sir Charles*

...namely that it wouldn't recognize it as a paid holiday...: "Martin Luther King Holiday in Arizona," Pima County Public Library, *https://www. library.pima.gov/content/martin-luther-king-holiday-in-arizona/*

"It had this feel as if...": Interview, June 5, 2019

...Charles ran back down and delivered a love tap...: Rick Reilly, "Hot Head," *Sports Illustrated*, Nov. 9, 1992

"That's bogus, Chuck!...": Reilly

"You didn't get touched!...": Reilly

...who saw basketball as "a chess game with soul"...: John Papanek, "A Chess Game with Soul," *Sports Illustrated*, Oct. 20, 1980

...coming off a yearlong suspension for violating the league's substance abuse policy...: Duane Rankin, "Richard Dumas Talks Drug Abuse, Playing with Charles Barkley, against Michael Jordan," *Arizona Republic*, Nov. 4, 2020

"He needs to lose weight...": Mark Heisler, "Miller Throws Weight Around," *Los Angeles Times*, Dec. 5, 1992

"I just want God to know that there's...": Interview, Dec. 23, 2019

"He pulls the ball off the glass and dribbles down the court...": *The Lowe Post*, 2018

"That right there is why we...": Jack McCallum, "The Best Finals Ever," *Sports Illustrated*, June 10, 2013

He'd read works from MLK, Plato, and Erich Fromm...: Rick Reilly, "KJ!," *Sports Illustrated*, Apr. 24, 1989

"It's like [what] Malcolm X wrote about LBJ and Goldwater...": Reilly

"Have you ever thought about wearing shoes?...": Interview, June 11, 2019

"That first year in Phoenix was about as good...": Interview, July 17, 2019

"It was like watching Babe Ruth going to play baseball...": Interview, July 1, 2019

...carved out a daily column titled, "The Barkley Beat"...: Montville

...and picked out his "Geek of the Week"...: Montville

...through the "Don't Be a Spud" public service announcement...: YouTube upload of Arizona Heart Foundation commercial, *https://www.youtube. com/watch?v=UO5L4dsBptY*

"Only one guy gets to be Elvis…": Jack McCallum, "Rising Suns," *Sports Illustrated*, Mar. 8, 1993

"He could show up at a nightclub or a restaurant…": Interview, July 23, 2019

"He brought that role of being…": *SportsCentury*

"That team was as primal of a group…": Interview, Jan. 12, 2021

…*cost him nearly $40,000…*: "Knicks hold off Phoenix," Associated Press, Jan. 19, 1993

The bad blood carried over to their return engagement…: Bob Young, "Suns Floor Knicks," *Arizona Republic*, Mar. 24, 1993

…*ripping his Armani pants…*: Interview, Jan. 12, 2021

"You can't let somebody come into your house…": Norm Frauenheim, "Johnson Makes Stand for Suns," *Arizona Republic*, Mar. 24, 1993

…*then the costliest incident in NBA history…*: Mark Heisler, "Brawl Costs Knicks, Suns $294,173.97," *Los Angeles Times*, Mar. 25, 1993

"I've gotta go home and see…": Lee Shappell, "Barkley Becomes Peacemaker as KJ, Ainge Tangle with Knicks," *Arizona Republic*, Mar. 24, 1993

"I really mean it when I say that if any one of my teams in New York…": Interview, Jan. 12, 2021

…*he'd be left with no other choice but to shoot his teammates…*: Lee Shappell, "Barkley Scores 36 against Former Team," *Arizona Republic*, Mar. 4, 1993

"When you walked into the old Spectrum…": Interview, Feb. 3, 2020

…*his former home crowd doused their departed son in chants…*: Bob Ford, "Barkley Is Given a Royal Welcome, Then Sinks Sixers," *Philadelphia Inquirer*, Mar. 29, 1993

"I haven't eaten anything today…": Timothy Dwyer, "Barkley Was Fussin' and Fumin', but There Were No Major Explosions," *Philadelphia Inquirer*, Mar. 29, 1993

"It's a madhouse…": Mark Jacobson, "The Trash-Talking, Butt-Kicking, Ball-Hogging, Love-Song Triumph of the Bad Chuck," *Esquire*, May 1, 1993

"There ain't nothing for me to fear except failing…": Jacobson

"You just never know how things…": Jacobson

She said she asked Johnson if he and his teammates could sign…: Interview, May 28, 2020

…*Hartel claimed her husband heard Charles refer to her…*: Interview, May 28, 2020

"He immediately took his beer and threw it…": Interview, May 28, 2020

She ended up quitting her job at the nursing home…: Interview, May 28, 2020

"If she'd been really upset…": "Barkley Dumps Beer on Woman," Associated Press, Apr. 22, 1993

"It did cross my mind to walk by…": Interview, May 28, 2020

…yelled at him, "Barkley, you're a fucking bum!"…: Interview, July 29, 2019

"He goes, 'I need some help…'": Interview, July 29, 2019

Charles and Maureen were separated at the time…: Frank Deford, "Barkley's Last Shot," *Vanity Fair*, February 1995

…gossip columnists reported how Connie Colla…: Ann Gerhart, "Charles' Blonde Ambitions," *Philadelphia Daily News*, June 3, 1993

…Colla maintained that was never the case…: Interview, July 9, 2020

…reported them as having an "intimate lunch"…: Interview, July 9, 2020

"Listen, Montana…": Interview, July 9, 2020

"After a while, it became obvious…": Interview, July 9, 2020

"We're gonna win the series…": "Suns Road to 1993 NBA Finals: Westy's Guarantee," NBA.com, May 4, 2020

"I've got 16,000 [career] points…": Bob Cohn, "Barkley Suns' Catalyst in Series–Tying Victory," *Arizona Republic*, May 7, 1993

After getting a stop, Charles skied for the offensive rebound…: YouTube upload of Game 5 of the 1993 series between Phoenix and Los Angeles, *https://www.youtube.com/watch?v=6CUDnK6kKVo*

…Charles, who had two anti-inflammatory injections…: Mark Armijo, "Barkley Far from Hamstrung," *Arizona Republic*, May 21, 1993

…can still hear the ringing noise in his ears…: "Phoenix Suns Since '68: Barkley Over Robinson," Phoenix Suns, *https://www.youtube.com/watch?v=9EqWW-U62Xc*

…the collective hush of the crowd was "pretty amazing"…: *https://www.youtube.com/watch?v=9EqWW-U62Xc*

"He turns around to us like…": *https://www.youtube.com/watch?v=9EqWW-U62Xc*

"Chuck wasn't afraid of the moment…": *https://www.youtube.com/watch?v=9EqWW-U62Xc*

"If you want to be successful in life…": Mark Armijo, "'Magic Needle' Helps Barkley Deliver Pain," *Arizona Republic*, May 21, 1993

Chapter 20

Primary sources include research conducted by the author from Northern Virginia and New Jersey, as well as interviews with J.A. Adande, Sue Bird, Dr. Todd Boyd, Howard Bryant, Rob DeFlorio, Jemele Hill, Phil Knight, Leigh Montville, Joe Pytka, Vice President Dan Quayle, Jim Riswold, Jalen Rose, and Mark Thomashow. Other sources include *I May Be Wrong but I Doubt It*, coverage in outlets like *Sports Illustrated* and the *New York Times*, YouTube videos of Nike commercials from the era, a 2006 episode of ESPN Classic's *The Top Five Reasons You Can't Blame…*, and a 2020 YouTube video from NBA on ESPN.

…behind North High School in Phoenix…: Montville

Stuffed chicken and tenderloin of beef were on the menu…: Montville

"They only cost $140…": Montville

"I've seen him get better at everything he's done…": Lefton

I am not a role model…: YouTube upload of Charles Barkley's "I Am Not a Role Model" commercial for Nike, *https://www.youtube.com/watch?v=NNOdFJAG3pE*

"The 'I Am Not a Role Model' commercial…": NBA on ESPN

…he went to Nike with the idea for an ad…: I May Be Wrong but I Doubt It

Nike thought he was nuts…: Phil in the Blanks

He pointed to the talks he'd given at schools…: In Depth with Graham Bensinger

…Charles remembered reaching out to Howard White…: I May Be Wrong but I Doubt It

…White, who only had H on his jersey…: "Howard White: The Man Known as 'H,'" University of Maryland Archives, Jan. 27, 2014

…and saw him as "a welcome variable" to the usually…: Sandra McKee, "Ex-Terp Carves Out Niche at Nike," *Baltimore Sun*, Nov. 26, 1998

"Nike has given me great shoes and great money…": Howard White, *Believe to Achieve*, 2003

He helped to create Charles's indelible Nike ad…: Interviews, June 3 and Oct. 3, 2019

"I think on a few occasions…": Interviews, June 3 and Oct. 3, 2019

"Riswold took the best parts of these athletes…": Interview, Aug. 8, 2019

…was an idea he fleshed out after reading Outrageous!…: Interviews, June 3 and Oct. 3, 2019

"What set Charles apart…": Interviews, June 3 and Oct. 3, 2019

"What if my name wasn't in lights?...": YouTube upload of Michael Jordan's "What If" commercial for Nike, *https://www.youtube.com/watch?v=-J48rfIEygU*

...had helped cut into Nike's overwhelming dominance...: Kim Foltz, "Reebok Fights to Be No. 1 Again," *New York Times*, Mar. 12, 1992

"It was a creative idea that had a man-bites-dog...": Interview, July 7, 2020

"If he had said it in a less evocative, more ambiguous way...": Jeff Eisenberg, "Iconic Sports Commercials: Charles Barkley's 'I Am Not a Role Model,'" *Yahoo Sports*, July 17, 2019

"...hit like a thunderclap...": Interview, July 9, 2020

"They said, 'You're going to get killed'...": *Phil in the Blanks*

"It is self-serving, stupid, almost sinister...": Stan Hochman, "Barkley Not a Role Model? Think Again," *Philadelphia Daily News*, May 9, 1993

...lauded the ad as "the most subversive sneaker commercial of all time"...: "Wreaking Havoc—and Selling Sneaks," *New York Times*, June 2, 1993

"We thought if two parents saw that and said...": "How to Achieve to Believe & Do the Impossible!," Michael Sandler's Inspire Nation, *https://www.youtube.com/watch?v=AkSM1Ep4wTA*

"It's like, 'If I'm the guy who has more influence...'": Interview, Feb. 27, 2020

"I don't think we can accept all the glory and all the money...": Karl Malone, "One Role Model to Another," *Sports Illustrated*, June 14, 1993

"It certainly was not a positive thing for the league...": "The Top 5 Reasons You Can't Blame... Charles Barkley," ESPN Classic, 2006

"People thought he had done this to absolve himself...": Interview, July 15, 2019

...the greater exposure for Black athletes around this time triggered tension...: Interviews, June 27 and Sept. 23, 2019

Trajectories of Black athletes and the levels of their acceptance...: Interviews, June 27 and Sept. 23, 2019

...which chronicled Simpson rejecting what Black critics said...: *O.J.: Made in America*, ESPN Films, June 2016

"All of these issues sort of informed the question...": Interviews, June 27 and Sept. 23, 2019

"I actually remember thinking how he was like...": Interview, Feb. 16, 2020

"I always used to look at some guys when I was really young…": NBA on ESPN

…*Jalen Rose has always thought of Charles as an older brother*…: Interview, Sept. 11, 2020

"'Role Model,' for us, was this serious ad…": Interview, May 29, 2019

…*"always felt there was a market for both" Charles and Jordan*…: ESPN Classic

…*he never wanted to be considered one*…: *The Last Dance*

Chapter 21

Primary sources include research conducted by the author from Northern Virginia and New Jersey, as well as interviews with David Casstevens, Jerry Colangelo, John Costacos, Tony Hamati, Lionel Hollins, Eddie Johnson, Shawn Kemp, Nate McMillan, Oliver Miller, Bob Whitsitt, and Bob Young. Other sources include *Sir Charles*, coverage in the *Arizona Republic*, YouTube uploads of games played in the 1993 Western Conference Finals, a special video series published by the Phoenix Suns in 2018 to commemorate the franchise's 50th anniversary, and a video of Madonna's 1994 interview with David Letterman.

Charles…figured the team could channel Patton's words…: "Frank Johnson on '93," NBA.com, June 4, 2003

"Wade into them. Spill their blood…": YouTube upload of a clip from the 1970 film *Patton*, *https://www.youtube.com/watch?v=PS5yfhPGaWE*

"It didn't do any good…": NBA.com

…*the War of the Western Conference*…: *Sir Charles*

…*Charles's face lay in his left hand as he gazed up*…: YouTube upload of Game 6 of the 1993 Western Conference Finals between Phoenix and Seattle, *https://www.youtube.com/watch?v=IX5pyoFvyO8*

"At that point…": *Sir Charles*

Dan Majerle stood on top of his own bar…: "Since '68: Sir Charles 1992–93 MVP," Phoenix Suns, *https://www.youtube.com/watch?v=0oIjAvKjOZc*

"It was just one of those iconic nights…": *https://www.youtube.com/watch?v=0oIjAvKjOZc*

…*leading the team in points, rebounds, assists, and*…: Basketball Reference

"This year, you've had a season…": YouTube upload of David Stern's presentation of the 1993 MVP Award to Charles Barkley, *https://www.youtube.com/watch?v=l596LFGOIBk*

…*had "legitimized his career in a way…"*: https://www.youtube.com/watch?v=0oIjAvKjOZc

"He had a year for the ages…": https://www.youtube.com/watch?v=0oIjAvKjOZc

…*Seattle didn't "give a bleep" about any MVP award…*: YouTube upload of Game 2 of the 1993 Western Conference Finals between Phoenix and Seattle, *https://www.youtube.com/watch?v=4ObTsi0jOb4*

"If I'm playing checkers, and I'm losing…": David Casstevens, "Sonics Show No Respect for MVP," *Arizona Republic*, May 27, 1993

"I couldn't guarantee to ownership that Shawn was going to be great…": Interview, Jan. 15, 2020

…*on his 1978 Nissan Datsun 280Z simply read, "MR MEAN"…*: Annette John-Hall, "Beavers' Payton Toning Down His Act," *Orlando Sentinel*, Jan. 9, 1990

…*were sometimes needed to quell riots in between games…*: Curry Kirkpatrick, "'Gary Talks It, Gary Walks It,'" *Sports Illustrated*, Mar. 5, 1990

…*to slap his son upside the head if he got out of line…*: Kirkpatrick

…*one of the fans he had been ridiculing gave him the finger…*: "Sonics Fan Returns Barkley's Gesture of Ill Will," Associated Press, May 29, 1993

…*Charles ordered his teammates to "quit bitching" and take care…*: Mark Armijo, "Barkley, Uh, Begs to Differ," *Arizona Republic*, May 31, 1993

"Lots of guys talk and most of them…": Armijo

…*read the splash headline on the front page of the Arizona Republic…*: Bob Young, "SuperSonics' Game 4 Rout Leaves Suns in Dark Mood," *Arizona Republic*, May 31, 1993

Every made 3 triggered a $50 charitable donation from Whataburger…: Bob Young, "Rain of 3s Sinks Sonics," *Arizona Republic*, June 2, 1993

Dick Enberg…guessed that whatever they were serving at Majerle's restaurants…: YouTube upload of Game 5 of the 1993 Western Conference Finals between Phoenix and Seattle, *https://www.youtube.com/watch?v=RxiwdejDWVU*

"I think sometimes we try to get other people involved…": Bob McManaman, "Big Boss Man: Barkley Demands (Expletive) Ball," *Arizona Republic*, June 3, 1993

"You've never been to the Finals, right?…": https://www.youtube.com/watch?v=k0IUjzyRIhQ

Billy Idol's "Rebel Yell" reverberated through an arena of over nineteen thousand screaming fans…: YouTube upload of Game 7 of the 1993 Western

Conference Finals between Phoenix and Seattle, *https://www.youtube.com/watch?v=d65qTmtWiJ4*

…fans tried to bribe the bouncer with $100 bills for a table…: Clint Williams and Susan Leonard, "Even Bribes Can't Buy Seats in Majerle's," *Arizona Republic*, June 6, 1993

"The MVP is not my goal…": *https://www.youtube.com/watch?v=d65qTmtWiJ4*

"When Charles Barkley took over…": *https://www.youtube.com/watch?v=k0IUjzyRIhQ*

The mark tied for the most free throws by any one team in a playoff game…: Basketball Reference

"We just felt that the league wanted Barkley…": Interview, June 18, 2020

"I tell people that 44–24 game…": *https://www.youtube.com/watch?v=k0IUjzyRIhQ*

…had Jerry Colangelo in tears…: Interview, July 17, 2019

…the win was "like I've dipped my hand in a honeycomb…": Bob Young, "Barkley's Best Leads the Way to West Crown," *Arizona Republic*, June 6, 1993

…was obtaining a six-pack to drink in his Jacuzzi…: Lee Shappell, "Suns Go for Gold in Silver Year," *Arizona Republic*, June 6, 1993

"He said, 'Frank, I told you…'": *Sir Charles*

…Jordan had called him to wish him luck and urged him…: *https://www.youtube.com/watch?v=d65qTmtWiJ4*

"When they'd score…": Interview, July 8, 2019

After he cooked for King Hussein of Jordan…: Jessica Dunham, "Having Cooked for Royalty, Chef Tony Hamati Knows How to Treat Scottsdale Diners," *Modern Luxury Scottsdale*, June 20, 2019

"He stuck his head in and said…": Interview, July 8, 2019

…spotted courtside with comedian Rosie O'Donnell and…: "Arsenio: I Loved My Tense Interviews with Madonna," VladTV, *https://www.youtube.com/watch?v=8529-kRZs08*

"Charles Barkley was Madonna's date…": *https://www.youtube.com/watch?v=8529-kRZs08*

If you could have your choice, who would you pick…: Steve Allen, *Vulgarians at the Gate*, 2001

"Charles Barkley is God…": Allen

…it wouldn't take long for the media to approach Hamati…: Gerhart

He claims he was offered $50,000 to spill...: Interview, July 8, 2019

...the pair danced the night away and hung out...: Robert Baird, "Sun Tracks, Program Notes," *Phoenix New Times*, June 2, 1993

Unsubstantiated reports of Charles's limo being parked overnight...: Robert Haight, "Charles in Charge," *The Sault Star*, June 20, 1993

...replying, "Who's Charles Barkley?"...: Bob McManaman, "Madonna? Met Her Once, Barkley Says," *Arizona Republic*, June 8, 1993

"She's awfully short. He's awfully married...": Gerhart

...and it stemmed from his girlfriend's warning...: Interview, Nov. 6, 2019

...Ellen Blumhardt, his mother-in-law, had suffered a heart attack...: McManaman

"She has had a lot of stress from the jokes...": Sam Smith, "Barkley: Time to Muffle Madonna Noise," *Chicago Tribune*, June 7, 1993

...who admitted to being telephone pals with Madonna...: Tom Friend, "Barkley Relishes His Prime-Time Spot," *New York Times*, June 7, 1993

"I'm going to be on NBC at least four times...": Friend

...Madonna had already smoked a joint, she later admitted...: The Late Show with David Letterman, 2009, https://www.youtube.com/watch?v=jodqIJZWFdg

...she was privately dating rapper Tupac Shakur, who she said had her riled up...: Zach Johnson, "Tupac Dumped Madonna Because She's White, His Prison Letter Reveals," E! News, July 5, 2017

The interview featured Madonna saying "fuck" fourteen times...: YouTube upload of the 1994 interview with Madonna on *The Late Show with David Letterman*, https://www.youtube.com/watch?v=PBm5kzTYfNU

...Charles did not understand "the meaning of friendship"...: https://www.youtube.com/watch?v=PBm5kzTYfNU

"What did she talk about?...": "The Barkley Beat," *Arizona Republic*, Apr. 2, 1994

Chapter 22

Primary sources include research conducted by the author from Northern Virginia and New Jersey, as well as interviews with J.A. Adande, Ric Bucher, David Casstevens, Jerry Colangelo, Bob Costas, Jason Hehir, Lionel Hollins, Jackie MacMullan, Jack McCallum, Will Perdue, Jeremy Roenick, Sam Smith, and Hannah Storm. Other sources include YouTube uploads of the 1993 NBA Finals, *The Last Dance*, coverage in

Sports Illustrated, the *Arizona Republic*, and the *Chicago Tribune*, and pod-cast interviews on *The Lowe Post*.

"Love me?...": *SportsCentury*

"It was Michael Jordan at his best...": Interview, July 15, 2019

...*he needed to dress better if he was*...: Interview, June 2, 2020

...*enough of a reminder for Jordan to lighten up*...: *Outrageous!*

"I can't express the depth of me and Michael's...": *SportsCentury*

...*playing golf the day before Game 1*...: YouTube upload of Game 1 of the 1993 NBA Finals between Phoenix and Chicago, *https://www.youtube.com/watch?v=B49tuu4o-DQ*

"That really bothered me and Michael for a long time...": "Phoenix Suns Since '68: Barkley vs MJ," Phoenix Suns, *https://www.youtube.com/watch?v=mpQec4nau0o*

"I would say, his friendship probably kept...": Sean Deveney, "Charles Barkley Wants to Clear Up Chumminess with Michael Jordan during 1993 NBA Finals," *The Sporting News*, Apr. 17, 2015

...*as "kind of Michael staggering to the finish line emotionally"*...: Interview, Jan. 13, 2020

"As far as Jordan getting beat in the Finals...": Interviews, July 16 and Dec. 17, 2019

...*Jordan elevated and cultivated Charles*...: Interview, Dec. 11, 2019

Michael Jordan permits nothing but success...: *https://www.youtube.com/watch?v=B49tuu4o-DQ*

"I don't think we were nervous...": David Casstevens, "Gore-y Describes Suns' Loss to Bulls," *Arizona Republic*, June 11, 1993

"Just because Krause liked him...": *The Last Dance*

"I was covered by Horace Grant...": McCallum

"He's just gotta keep his boards...": *https://www.youtube.com/watch?v=B49tuu4o-DQ*

"You're accustomed to 10 cameras...": McCallum

...*time to eat ribs with his grandmother*...: Michael Clancy, "Grandma, Not Madonna, Is Charles' Dinner Date," *Arizona Republic*, June 10, 1993

"Let's don't go crazy after one game...": "Jordan, Tough Defense Enough for Win in Game 1 of NBA Finals," Associated Press, June 10, 1993

...*he went outside at the crack of dawn to hear the birds chirp*...: Bob Young, "KJ on Guard," *Arizona Republic*, June 11, 1993

"I want to win the world's championship, but…": Bob Cohn, "Barkley Doesn't Like Scrutiny of Finals," *Arizona Republic*, June 11, 1993

…found Storm beforehand and guaranteed a Phoenix win…: Interview, Mar. 5, 2020

Westphal stressed that they didn't need to be miracle men…: YouTube upload of Game 2 of the 1993 NBA Finals, *https://www.youtube.com/watch?v=ntW5m8o-Cvc*

"Hey, fuck these motherfuckers…": *The Last Dance*

"We had so many distractions…": McCallum

"On the court, you never look down…": Richard Obert, "Ainge Burns Pippen Once, but All-Defense Star Turns the Tables," *Arizona Republic*, June 12, 1993

…the second time in NBA history that two opponents scored 40-plus in a Finals game…: Basketball Reference

"In Game 2, I played as well…": *The Last Dance*

"She says, 'What happened?'…": *The B.S. Report*, March 2015

…KJ turned to the printed fax messages of encouragement…: Phil Taylor, "A Happy Turn to a Horror Story," *Sports Illustrated*, June 21, 1993

…described by critic Dale Kramer as "the energy of…": Wordsworth Editions, *https://wordsworth-editions.com/blog/tess-of-the-d'urbervilles*

"Paul wakes me up and says…": McCallum

…whose right elbow was badly swollen…: David Casstevens, "Numbers Fail to Convey Heroic Tale," *Arizona Republic*, June 12, 1993

"I have no idea what to expect…": YouTube upload of Game 3 of the 1993 NBA Finals, *https://www.youtube.com/watch?v=u5e56-6Q1vg*

"Hannah got right in front of Chuck and said…": Interview, Oct. 1, 2019

"He definitely felt comfortable enough to say it…": Interview, Mar. 5, 2020

…You're guarding me?…: McCallum

"Michael is not beating us!…": *The Last Dance*

…from the balcony of the arena: Final Sunset…: *https://www.youtube.com/watch?v=u5e56-6Q1vg*

"You kind of wondered if this was one of those…": Interview, May 26, 2020

Scotty Robertson…had just two tips…: Scott Howard-Cooper, "Suns Gain Survival of Unfittest," *Los Angeles Times*, June 14, 1993

BARKLEY

Cedric Ceballos…wondered the same thing from the bench…: Bob McManaman and Pat Underwood, "Triple OTs: Suns Make History," *Arizona Republic*, June 14, 1993

"I knew he was going to try and pass it…": Bill Fay, "The Big Steal," *Tribune Wires*, June 15, 1993

"It was the greatest basketball game…": Howard-Cooper

"Darlin', they said my career…": David Casstevens, "Anecdotes to Get Better with Age," *Arizona Republic*, June 15, 1993

Taking in a game at Wrigley Field with Frank Johnson…: Paul Sullivan and Terry Armour, "Enemy? Suns Don't Feel Like One at Wrigley," *Chicago Tribune*, June 16, 1993

…to find the "bad motherfucker" who played hockey…: Interview, May 28, 2020

…his ear-piercing rendition of "Oh Baby Baby I Love You"…: Bernie Miklasz, "'Sir Charles' Is Charismatic Knight of NBA Finals," *St. Louis Post-Dispatch*, June 16, 1993

…described by the NBC commentator as "the villain in some melodrama"…: YouTube upload of Game 4 of the 1993 NBA Finals, *https://www.youtube.com/watch?v=BuxDyzSS-Rc*

"Charles Barkley is a great, great player…": *https://www.youtube.com/watch?v=OptOa8sVOM0*

"Have another drink, Bob…": *https://www.youtube.com/watch?v=OptOa8sVOM0*

"There was nobody quite like Charles…": Interview, Dec. 4, 2019

"He inflicted his will on us…": Mark Heisler, "Jordan, Doing 55, Passes Suns," *Los Angeles Times*, June 17, 1993

…his 14 field goals tied an NBA Finals record for most in a half…: Basketball Reference

"Shut the fuck up, asshole!…": *https://www.youtube.com/watch?v=BuxDyzSS-Rc*

Colangelo…took umbrage with a Bulls fan swearing…: Interview, July 17, 2019

"He gave me the finger after the game…": McCallum

"The ball slipped out of my hands…": "Jordan Provides the Offense, but Bulls' Win Characterized by Timely Defense," Associated Press, June 17, 1993

"Don't take it personally, Charles!…": *The Last Dance*

…tied for the second-highest total ever in a Finals game…: Colin Ward-Hen-

ninger, "Michael Jordan Dropped 55 Points in an NBA Finals Game 23 Years Ago," CBS Sports, June 16, 2016

"Charles was great, but...": Interview, June 5, 2019

...*more than one hundred arrests and the looting of dozens of stores*...: "Chicago Less 'Torn Up' Than in '92," *Washington Post*, June 22, 1993

...*more than 1,000 people were arrested, 340 businesses were looted*...: *Washington Post*

...*was remembered as much for the arsons and the bricks*...: "Violence, Looting as Bulls Fans Celebrate," Associated Press, June 15, 1992

"Michael Jordan and Charles Barkley are fierce competitors...": "Chicago Braces for a Violent Victory Party," Associated Press, June 18, 1993

"If we make it a three-peat on the court...": Associated Press

...*Westphal updated it:* SAVE THE CITY...: "Suns Road to 1993 NBA Finals: The Finish Line," NBA.com, June 15, 2020

...*Westphal said Charles stole it from him*...: McCallum

"Ain't gonna be no riot in this town tonight!": David Casstevens, "Suns 'Save' Chicago from Itself," *Arizona Republic*, June 19, 1993

"I believe it is our destiny to win...": *https://www.youtube.com/watch?v=BuxDyzSS-Rc*

"The place is going crazy...": "Since '68—Paxson's Shot," Phoenix Suns, *https://www.youtube.com/watch?v=IsffXQmpwDY*

The thousands of fans that greeted the Suns...: Eric Miller, Art Thomason, Kim Sue Lia Perkes, and Brent Whiting, "Thousands of Fans Jam Downtown Phoenix to Salute 'a Work of Art,'" *Arizona Republic*, June 19, 1993

"Fuck, fuck, fuck!": YouTube upload of Game 6 of the 1993 NBA Finals, *https://www.youtube.com/watch?v=kithqCmSRss*

"It's bullshit!...": *https://www.youtube.com/watch?v=kithqCmSRss*

...*and ordered NBC to start setting up their locker room*...: McCallum

"They were so dominant in the last five minutes of games...": *The Lowe Post*

"We couldn't score a bucket...": Interview, June 5, 2019

"If we lose...": *The Lowe Post*

...*the play he called for had the name it did: "The Blind Pig"*...: K.C. Johnson, "Paxson's 3-Pointer Still Unforgettable 20 Years Later," *Chicago Tribune*, June 21, 2013

"The whole idea of the play was for...": McCallum

"I think if Scottie takes a two and makes it...": McCallum

"The so-called smartest guy on the team...": McCallum

"I don't want to rag on Danny...": McCallum

"It seemed like it took an hour to get to the basket...": *https://www.youtube.com/watch?v=IsffXQmpwDY*

"I just went, 'Please miss!...'": *The Lowe Post*

...Mike Fratello guessed that the Suns would look to find Charles...: *https://www.youtube.com/watch?v=kithqCmSRss*

...Charles said they wanted to get it to anyone who was open...: YouTube upload of the news conference following Game 6 of the 1993 NBA Finals, *https://www.youtube.com/watch?v=1rcwxulhlII*

"For it to be over so quickly...": *https://www.youtube.com/watch?v=1rcwxulhlII*

"By the way, how am I getting to Disney World?...": Tom Friend, "Suns Begin Looking for the Missing Piece," *New York Times*, June 22, 1993

Chapter 23

Primary sources include research conducted by the author from Northern Virginia and New Jersey, as well as interviews with Muggsy Bogues, David Casstevens, Jerry Colangelo, Wally Feresten, Sen. Al Franken, Tim Gallin, Larry King, Jay Leno, David Mandel, James Andrew Miller, Conan O'Brien, Adam Sandler, Aries Spears, and Kristen Wiig. Other sources include YouTube uploads of *Saturday Night Live* sketches from the '90s and coverage in the *Arizona Republic*.

"Yeah, and the fact that I'm the best...": "Daily Affirmation: Charles Barkley and Muggsy Bogues," *Saturday Night Live*, *https://www.youtube.com/watch?v=VeaL_besyq8*

"So, I guess since, you know...": *https://www.youtube.com/watch?v=VeaL_besyq8*

"Well...": *https://www.youtube.com/watch?v=VeaL_besyq8*

"I guess Cleopatra...": *https://www.youtube.com/watch?v=VeaL_besyq8*

...he doesn't know if the parade of three hundred thousand for an NBA Finals loser...: "Since '68: Barkley's Parade Escape," Phoenix Suns, *https://www.youtube.com/watch?v=W33I5xoil4E*

"I don't think the fans realize...": *https://www.youtube.com/watch?v=W33I5xoil4E*

"As soon as Charles turned around the corner…": *https://www.youtube.com/watch?v=W33I5xoil4E*

…*he plowed through fans until they made…*: *https://www.youtube.com/watch?v=W33I5xoil4E*

"It was kind of fun, but…": *https://www.youtube.com/watch?v=W33I5xoil4E*

He joined owner Jerry Colangelo in his arena office…: Interview, July 17, 2019

"I want y'all to know we never expected…": "Phoenix Suns Since '68: 1993 Parade," Phoenix Suns, *https://www.youtube.com/watch?v=w4duBTJMFu0*

…*in August 1993 for the town's "Charles Barkley Day"…*: David Casstevens, "Hometown Hero: Sir Charles Basks in Heart of Little Leeds," *Arizona Republic*, Aug. 22, 1993

"Can you believe it?": Casstevens

Michael Jordan had stared into a mirror and tried not to laugh…: "Daily Affirmation: Michael Jordan," *Saturday Night Live*, *https://www.youtube.com/watch?v=xNx_gU57gQ4*

Since quarterback Fran Tarkenton became the first athlete…: Gabbi Shaw, "All 32 Athletes Who Have Hosted 'Saturday Night Live' over the Last 46 Seasons," Insider, Nov. 16, 2021

Charles could make David Letterman laugh at how…: James Herbert, "David Letterman's Top 10 Basketball Moments as Host of 'Late Show,'" CBS Sports, May 20, 2015

"Charles Barkley was one of my…": Interview, June 18, 2020

"When he trains those eyebrows on you…": Interview, Sept. 23, 2020

…*had been "mostly exercises in bloodless…"*: Eric Mink, "'SNL' Will Be Different, but at 19, Can It Be Fresh?," *New York Daily News*, Sept. 25, 1993

…*Jay Mohr didn't bring any ideas with him…*: Jay Mohr, *Gasping for Airtime: Two Years in the Trenches of Saturday Night Live*, June 9, 2004

Sandler…immediately gravitated to Charles… The same went for…: Interview, Jan. 12, 2021

"If there were 10 great comedians in a room and Barkley came in…": Interview, Jan. 12, 2021

He remembered one idea from writer Tom Davis in which…: *Gasping for Airtime*

"Even if my idea…": *Gasping for Airtime*

"What I remember clearly from that first show…": Interview, July 7, 2020

"It was all so off-the-cuff…": Interview, Nov. 7, 2019

…*"piss off the rednecks and the homophobes"*…: *Kurt Cobain: About a Son*, 2006

"We weren't trying to be subversive or punk rock…": Kevin Allman, "Nirvana's Front Man Shoots from the Hip," *The Advocate*, February 1993

"Knew about 'em in my neighborhood…": Verne Gay, "'SNL' at Age 19, a Model of Stability," *Newsday*, Sept. 22, 1993

In recording a promo for that week's show…: YouTube upload of Charles Barkley and Nirvana taping promotional ads for *Saturday Night Live* in 1993, https://www.youtube.com/watch?v=vhI-oy7-dz0

"I'm not a role model, and these guys…": *https://www.youtube.com/watch?v=vhI-oy7-dz0*

"Every time those guys from Nirvana opened up their door…": *The Dan Patrick Show*

"God bless him…": Interview, May 29, 2019

"They did want someone from the NBA…": "Charles Barkley's Monologue," *SNL* Transcripts, Oct. 8, 2018

"I was an independent contractor getting my ass kicked…": Interview, May 29, 2019

"I know how badly you wanted to beat the Bulls…": *https://www.youtube.com/watch?v=VeaL_besyq8*

Franken was effusive of the pair's performance many years later…: Interview, Aug. 19, 2020

"He looked more beautiful than all of us…": Interview, Jan. 12, 2021

…*Charles was asked back to host* SNL *for a second time…*: "Charles Barkley/ Alicia Keys," *The 'One SNL a Day' Project*, Sept. 20, 2020

"Charles just *is* funny…": Interview, Aug. 18, 2020

"He wasn't trying to be anyone who he isn't…": Interview, Nov. 24, 2020

"We were out of our comfort zone…": Interview, Nov. 7, 2019

…*he had "acquitted himself reasonably well"*…: Jim Bullard, "Barney Back on Track after a Very Busy Week," *Tampa Bay Times*, Sept. 28, 1993

…*represented "all the things* SNL *tries to be"*…: David Casstevens, "Chuck's Yucks: Barkley on 'SNL,'" *Arizona Republic*, Sept. 26, 1993

Chapter 24

Primary sources include research conducted by the author from Houston and Northern Virginia, as well as interviews with Fran Blinebury, Jim

Boeheim, Earl Cureton, Liz Dolan, Julie Fie, Keith Jennings, Chris Jent, Oliver Miller, Conan O'Brien, Dan Patrick, Elliot Perry, Joe Proski, and Rick Reilly. Other sources include coverage in the *Arizona Republic*, the *Houston Chronicle*, the *Philadelphia Inquirer*, and the Associated Press, YouTube uploads of the 1994 NBA playoffs, the 1994 book *Somebody's Gotta Be Me: The Wide, Wide World of the One and Only Charles Barkley*, and a 2005 segment from *The Oprah Winfrey Show*.

The impromptu race on a Saturday evening at training camp in Flagstaff...: Tom Friend, "The Barkley Collapse: A Scare, but No Surgery," *New York Times*, Oct. 11, 1993

Danny Ainge joked that Charles was suffering a heart attack...: Friend

"I couldn't move my legs at all...": Friend

...showed that Charles had a bulging disk...: Michael Wilbon, "Barkley: There's Nothing Funny About Playing in Pain," *Washington Post*, Oct. 17, 1993

...Charles promised that he was "99.9 percent sure" it would be his last...: Wilbon

"I know my back's not going to get better...": "A Retiring Barkley?," Associated Press, Oct. 16, 1993

Teammates and coaches chalked it up to...: Associated Press

...filling in for him as host at his celebrity golf tournament...: Julie Deardorff, "Barkley, Others Just Star-Studded Duffers," *Chicago Tribune*, Aug. 28, 1993

...to escape Dr. Joyce Brothers saying he was a role model...: YouTube upload of a Nike commercial featuring Charles Barkley and Michael Jordan, *https://www.youtube.com/watch?v=2bJ7S1KQo9E*

...zero stars to the "abysmal, embarrassing sequel"...: Gene Siskel, "'Addams Family Values' Needs the Light of Day," *Chicago Tribune*, Nov. 19. 1993

"I'm always surprised by his cameo in that movie...": Interview, Sept. 23, 2020

...which Charles maintained to be a real vegetable...: Deford

...and proceeded to throw all of the garments out the window...: Interview, June 10, 2020

"They're both telling this story...": Interview, June 10, 2020

...which he worried would hinder their relationship as she grew up...: David Casstevens, "Daughter Lights Up Barkley's Life," *Arizona Republic*, Dec. 5, 1994

"I look forward to the time...": Deford

Jordan…diagnosed Charles as having "a sickness"…: *The Oprah Winfrey Show*, October 2005

…declared it to be "a type of linksland Tourette's…": "The Continuing Adventures of Charles Barkley," *Philadelphia Magazine*, Feb. 24, 2009

Jason Sudeikis…compared it to someone who had a heart attack midswing…: "The Haney Project: Charles Barkley," *Saturday Night Live*, *https://www. youtube.com/watch?v=DdsyGXZ1e9A*

…looked like "a man in a closet trying to kill a snake with a broom"…: Philip L. Kaplan, "Sir-prise! Charles Barkley in Toledo for LPGA," *Toledo Blade*, Aug. 10, 2020

…take a break for two weeks before quitting the game altogether…: Greg Wilcox, "Chucky Gets Much-Needed Help from Tiger's Guru," *Los Angeles Daily News*, Dec. 26, 1997

…smoking cigars inside his car would be healthier for Charles…: "Quick Hitters," DraftKings, *https://twitter.com/br_betting/status/1331660831705100289*

"God took this guy and gave him this incredibly embarrassing…": Interview, June 28, 2019

"I'm all over the Internet…": Bob Ford, "Looking for another rebound," *Philadelphia Inquirer*, Mar. 8, 2009

Woods spoofed the swing as part of his…: "Tiger impersonating Charles Barkley's Golf Swing," Electronic Arts, *https://www.youtube.com/watch?v=5chdYDbYQAA*

A select few in those crowds have been struck by his shots…: YouTube upload of the 2009 Regions Charity Classic in Birmingham, Alabama, *https://www.youtube.com/watch?v=qUuhyzFSa7k*

"All men will die, all rivers will dry…": Ford

…how Chuck would launch his clubs into a lake…: Interview, May 1, 2020

"He didn't care that you were laughing at him…": Interview, May 22, 2020

…Charles tore his quadriceps tendon above his right knee…: "Torn Tendon Sidelines Barkley," Wire Reports, Jan. 10, 1994

Running on a platform of better educational opportunities and…: Larry Platt, "*Governor* Barkley?," *GQ*, May 1998

…with a bumper sticker that read "Barkley for Governor"…: "The Barkley Beat," *Arizona Republic*, Apr. 30, 1994

…Webber was the youngest player to start in a playoff game since…: YouTube upload of the 1994 first-round series between Phoenix and Golden State, *https://www.youtube.com/watch?v=wAwSpvW9994*

...after a Nike ad that year featured Webber dunking on him...: YouTube upload of a Nike commercial for Chris Webber that aired during the 1993–94 season, *https://www.youtube.com/watch?v=t9r0KVXRadc*

"I don't think there's a person in the league who can stop...": Lee Shappell, "Barkley, Suns Get Off to Good Start," *Arizona Republic*, May 1, 1994

"Charles told us, as a matter of fact...": Interview, Dec. 23, 2019

"You gonna double me?...": "Since '68: Barkley Drops 56 in Golden State," Phoenix Suns, *https://www.youtube.com/watch?v=hfEhfBhnPQQ*

"He says, 'We're not gonna double you'...": *https://www.youtube.com/watch?v=hfEhfBhnPQQ*

"You know how in those video games like...": Interview, Oct. 31, 2019

...tied for the third-most scored in a playoff game...: "56 Third Best," *Arizona Republic*, May 5, 1994

"They challenged him...": "Barkley Drops 56 Points in Great Playoff Performance," NBA.com, May 5, 2014

"It wasn't luck...": "Warriors Dare, Pay," Associated Press, May 6, 1994

His back had started to spasm at the half...: Norm Frauenheim, "Barkley Says Game Rates Only 4th Best," *Arizona Republic*, May 5, 1994

"They told me I needed a cup...": Frauenheim

...completes the greatest comeback in NBA playoff history...: "Barkley and Suns Rally over Rockets," Associated Press, May 12, 1994

"We're not playing to win...": David Casstevens, *Somebody's Gotta Be Me: The Wide, Wide World of the One and Only Charles Barkley*, October 1994

...heard about how Charles had predicted a possible sweep...: Clutch City, NBA Entertainment, 1994

...called the flight to Phoenix the quietest plane ride...: Interview, Sept. 4, 2019

...Kenny Smith was salty because his team...: Bob McManaman, "It's All Mind over Matter for Rockets," *Arizona Republic*, May 13, 1994

...It's a new day...: Interview, Oct. 27, 2019

"When Dream said that shit...": Interview, Oct. 23, 2019

"*They* must win tonight to stay alive...": Interview, Oct. 27, 2019

...picked up a copy of the Houston Chronicle *to see an amendment...*: Interview, Sept. 22, 2020

"Julie had just gotten off the plane...": Interview, Oct. 27, 2019

He spent extra time soaking in the whirlpool...: Interview, July 29, 2019

"It was just hard watching him knowing he was banged up...": Interview, Apr. 13, 2020

"He didn't go crazy getting or wanting the injections...": Interview, July 29, 2019

"I mean, it was *right* in there...": *Somebody's Gotta Be Me*

Matt Guokas...was audibly bummed out on the NBC broadcast...: YouTube upload of Game 7 of the 1994 series between Phoenix and Houston, *https://www.youtube.com/watch?v=nZsua5lDsbg*

"I was just in the way...": Chris Baker, "The Future Is Now for Barkley," *Los Angeles Times*, May 22, 1994

"It was like we were trying to row upstream...": Bob Young, "Rockets Eliminate Suns in 7," *Arizona Republic*, May 22, 1994

"That long 3 with the shot clock going down...": Young

"This is not the way Charles looking to end the season...": *https://www.youtube.com/watch?v=nZsua5lDsbg*

...Charles needed anti-inflammatory shots for the pain...: Interview, July 29, 2019

"It's simple...": "Rockets Drop Suns; Barkley May Retire," Associated Press, May 22, 1994

Chapter 25

Primary sources include research conducted by the author from Houston and Northern Virginia, as well as interviews with Dr. James Andrews, Rudy Berumen, Fran Blinebury, Chucky Brown, David Casstevens, Pete Chilcutt, Jerry Colangelo, Billy Crystal, David DuPree, Joe Kleine, Oliver Miller, Donnie Nelson, Elliot Perry, Joe Proski, Vice President Dan Quayle, Jae Staats, Rudy Tomjanovich, and Bob Young. Other sources include YouTube uploads of the 1995 NBA playoffs, a 1994 *Village Voice* article that's no longer publicly available, coverage in outlets like the *Arizona Republic*, the *Phoenix New Times*, the *Houston Chronicle*, and *Sports Illustrated*, and the 2015 NBA TV documentary *Clutch City*.

...Bill Walton noted to viewers tuning in that he saw the self-doubt...: YouTube upload of Game 7 of the 1995 series between Phoenix and Houston, *https://www.youtube.com/watch?v=7JHSqVVWP-M*

...Gumbel wondered when perfection would catch up with Johnson...: *https://www.youtube.com/watch?v=7JHSqVVWP-M*

"I hate to say it...": Interview, Apr. 13, 2020

"Well, when Daddy is playing basketball...": Casstevens

…was inspired by a Delaware shopping mall Charles passed by a few times…: *The Steam Room*, Dec. 8, 2021

"You're my *daddy* when you're playing basketball…": Casstevens

"The experience Charles had with his father…": Casstevens

…Charles was met by a chorus of five thousand…: Judi Villa and Eric Miller, "'We're Always Behind Them,'" *Arizona Republic*, May 22, 1994

…friends like right-wing radio shock jock Rush Limbaugh…: Bill Barnard, "Barkley Elects to Follow Own Path," Associated Press, Dec. 7, 1993

…Supreme Court justice Clarence Thomas…: Tom Kertes, "Charles Barkley Talks About His Republicanism," *The Village Voice*, Dec. 27, 1994

…who had offered his support for Charles's "family values" message…: Interview, Oct. 24, 2019

"I thought that was very poignant…": Interview, Oct. 24, 2019

…Ashley Boss, who was killed during a drive-by shooting…: "The Barkley Beat," Arizona Republic, May 20, 1994

"If somebody ever did something like that to my daughter…": Casstevens

"I never backed down from a challenge…": "Barkley Says He'll Be Back," Associated Press, June 29, 1994

…linked to an investigation for the murder of a woman…: "Mustaf's Cousin Reported to Be under Investigation," *Washington Post*, Aug. 15, 1993

…his cousin, Levonnie Wooten, was convicted…: "Mustaf's Cousin Gets Life," Associated Press, July 12, 1996

…an unlikely pair in Charles and "Super Snake"…: Jon Wertheim, "Jerrod Mustaf Is a Community Hero. Has Anyone Ever Googled Him?," *Sports Illustrated*, Apr. 17, 2019

…detailed an alleged post-playoffs sex party with a few Suns…: Darrin Hostetler, "After Midnight," *Phoenix New Times*, June 15, 1994

…accused Charles of standing at the bedroom door where Miller…: Hostetler

…Miller's wife told police that he had grabbed her around the throat…: "Suns' Miller Grabs by Throat in Home Quarrel, Police Report Says," *Arizona Republic*, Aug. 20, 1994

"When you make a mistake, you admit…": Bob Young, "Colangelo: Miller Supported, Wasn't 'Accountable,'" *Arizona Republic*, Sept. 23, 1994

…dubbed the group "the most potent collection of forwards in NBA history"…: "NBA Preview, 1994–95," Associated Press, Nov. 3, 1994

"Kevin got his feelings hurt…": Interview, Feb. 7, 2020

"We have to win it all…": Steve Rushin, "High and Mighty," *Sports Illustrated*, Nov. 7, 1994

Entering the $500-a-ticket, black-tie event…: Mike Wise, "Jam Session: All-Star Weekend Is Here," *New York Times*, Feb. 11, 1995

"What effect did Mick Jagger have…": Interview, Feb. 7, 2020

"We can have a fun entertaining evening, or…": Norm Frauenheim, "Crystal, Other Stars Braise Barkley," *Arizona Republic*, Feb. 10, 1995

Manning…played just forty-six games before tearing his left ACL…: Mel Reisner, "Suns' Manning Out for the Year," Associated Press, Feb. 7, 1995

In less than two and a half seasons, the point guard had suffered…: "Johnson's New Ailment: Chicken Pox," *Seattle Times*, Jan. 19, 1994

"One day, Charles called out to Joe Proski…": Interview, July 1, 2019

All-Star Weekend in Phoenix had a little bit of everything…: Leigh Montville, "February Frenzy," *Sports Illustrated*, Feb. 20, 1995

A celebrity slam-dunk contest headlined by…: Rohan Nadkarni, "Five Crazy Anecdotes from 1995 NBA All-Star Weekend," *Sports Illustrated*, Feb. 11, 2015

Perhaps the highlight of the weekend was the roast of Charles…: Frauenheim

…reminding the forward that he was "playing himself, not a poet"…: Interview, June 9, 2020

"That is total bullshit!…": YouTube upload of a clip from the 1995 film *Forget Paris*, *https://www.youtube.com/watch?v=3E4TmZG-gWI*

"The best entertainers are the ones who…": Interview, June 9, 2020

…a German reporter stuck his microphone in front of Charles…: *SportsCentury*

"The groupie thing is a sick subject…": *SportsCentury*

"That's why I hate White people…": *SportsCentury*

"When the thing was over…": *SportsCentury*

"It wasn't a racial slur…": YouTube upload of the pregame show for the 1995 NBA All-Star Game, *https://www.youtube.com/watch?v=CCY2yjihuxc*

John Walsh…defended the decision to run it…: Dave Roos, "It's Really a Gray Area," *Louisville Courier-Journal*, Feb. 15, 1995

The Suns' secretaries were "physically drained"…: David Aldridge, "Barkley's Just Playing, so Why the Offense?," *Washington Post*, Apr. 6, 1995

"You fucking…": Aldridge

"The thing that makes you mad is it…": Aldridge

David DuPree…saw it as more fallout from his…: Interview, Oct. 8, 2019

Phoenix would be "paradise" for him...: David Casstevens, "Bulls' Pippen: Phoenix Would Be 'Paradise,'" *Arizona Republic*, Feb. 11, 1995

"Phoenix is a team that this could be their last title run...": Casstevens

...opting instead to watch college basketball and play 18 holes...: Ira Winderman, "Barkley Less Than Overwhelmed," *Sun-Sentinel*, Mar. 20, 1995

"They've got to get to the Finals...": Winderman

...who had denounced the player's substance abuse...: Ian O'Connor, "Suns Down on Dumas," *New York Daily News*, Sept. 23, 1993

...to back out of a trade that would have sent Dennis Rodman to Phoenix to pair with Charles...: O'Connor

"There's nothing I won't do for you...": Interview, May 15, 2019

"Jerry goes, 'Charles...'": Interview, May 15, 2019

...Chumpy, come here...: Interview, June 18, 2019

"Maureen nudged him once and went...": Interview, June 18, 2019

...and carefully took a razor to a head covered in shaving cream...: Interview, June 18, 2019

"He said, 'Chumpy, if you wreck it...'": Interview, June 18, 2019

Finishing sixth in MVP voting...: Basketball Reference

...who was booed every time...: David Casstevens, "Barkley Loves to Be the One Others Hate," *Arizona Republic*, May 3, 1995

"What business are we in?...": Tim Crothers, "Phoenix Rising," *Sports Illustrated*, May 22, 1995

THEY WANT TO DIE...: Crothers

"They were so damn good...": Interview, Oct. 14, 2019

Elyse Lanier...called the league office to complain...: Tom Friend, "Surging Suns Have Rockets Talking About Conspiracy," *New York Times*, May 12, 1995

Franchise Senior and Franchise Junior...: Mal Florence, "If This Works, New Golf Ball Could Be Called 'Daly's Comet,'" *Los Angeles Times*, Jan. 24, 1996

It did not go well...: Interview, June 23, 2019

"I'm not ashamed to say...": Interview, Oct. 21, 2019

...to pull up a chair at America West Arena...: Interview, Aug. 27, 2019

"Let's go down there...": Interview, Aug. 27, 2019

"Chuck's booty hole got tight...": *Clutch City*, NBA TV, 2015

Drexler could only smile knowing…: Clutch City

"He said we were like Texas roaches…": Interview, Oct. 14, 2019

…were the "B-film zombies who rose from the grave…": Interview, July 1, 2019

"The Suns are responsible for them being…": Interview, July 11, 2019

"The improbable is reality…": "The Improbable Is Reality," *Arizona Republic*, May 19, 1995

…and the tendinitis caused a few bone spurs to chip off…: Bob Young, "Barkley's Knee Surgery Today," *Arizona Republic*, May 25, 1995

On the whiteboard before the game read their Sunday travel plans…: YouTube upload of Game 7 of the 1995 series between Phoenix and Houston, *https://www.youtube.com/watch?v=OmuFkFlFXgk*

…the goal for the day was to keep even with Olajuwon…: *https://www.youtube.com/watch?v=OmuFkFlFXgk*

Maureen anxiously crossed her fingers and Christiana cheered wildly for her daddy…: *https://www.youtube.com/watch?v=OmuFkFlFXgk*

"I don't need water…": *https://www.youtube.com/watch?v=OmuFkFlFXgk*

"The first guy I looked at was Joe Kleine…": Clutch City

"He knew that this era was done…": Interview, July 31, 2019

"What happened to Charles's party?…": Clutch City

"I think we underachieved…": Norm Frauenheim, "KJ Reflects Pain After Loss," *Arizona Republic*, May 21, 1995

"We should have won both of those years…": Interview, July 17, 2019

…would be cruelly remembered among great players as "a Nearly Man"…: Deford

"More than likely…": Bob Jacobsen, "Say It Ain't So, Chuck—but It Probably Is," *Arizona Republic*, May 21, 1995

…accused of sexually molesting a sixteen-year-old girl at his home…: Ryan Lillis, "Woman Speaks Publicly about Her Phoenix Molestation Allegations against Kevin Johnson," *Sacramento Bee*, Sept. 25, 2015

…who apologized to Mandi Koba but told her in a secretly recorded phone conversation…: Paul Rubin, "Phoenix Suns' Kevin Johnson Corroborates That Hug May Have Been Too Physically Intimate," *Phoenix New Times*, May 8, 1997

…did not meet a "reasonable likelihood of conviction"…: Rubin

…paid her family and their attorney more than $230,000…: Dave McKenna,

"'I'm a Grown-Up Now': The Teen Who Accused Kevin Johnson of Sexual Abuse Speaks Out," *Deadspin*, Sept. 25, 2015

He repeatedly told journalists...: John Davis, "Barkley is upset, rest sad," *Arizona Republic*, Oct. 8, 1995

He openly talked about the possibility of getting traded...: Ira Winderman, "Barkley's Trade Rumor Mill Produces Nothing of Value," *Sun-Sentinel*, Jan. 13, 1996

"People understood that the time...": Interview, July 17, 2019

Chapter 26

Primary sources include research conducted by the author from Northern Virginia and New Jersey, as well as interviews with J.A. Adande, Steve Brace, Bobby Cremins, Grant Hill, Jack McCallum, John Stockton, Fallon Stubbs, and Lenny Wilkens. Other sources include *Dream Team*, YouTube uploads of the 1996 Olympics, coverage in outlets like the *New York Times*, the *Washington Post*, and the Associated Press, and a 2011 oral history of the Olympic bombings published in *Atlanta* magazine.

"It was the best party I ever had...": Interview, June 13, 2019

A former lieutenant in the US Army...: Ronald Smothers, "Woman Who 'Lost Her Life While Celebrating the Human Spirit,'" *New York Times*, July 30, 1996

"I was one of the only people I knew who liked Charles...": Interview, June 13, 2019

"It was a fucking nightmare...": *Dream Team*

"I hated it...": *SiriusXM Bleacher Report Radio*, July 2016

...he initially declined coach Lenny Wilkens's offer to join...: Interview, Nov. 27, 2019

"I felt he'd be great for the team...": Interview, Nov. 27, 2019

Chris Mullin believed it would never happen again...: The Dream Team

Magic Johnson said that there might be a team as good as theirs...: The Dream Team

"Will the 1996 Atlanta Games bring a Dream Team II?...": Jack McCallum, "Dreamy," *Sports Illustrated*, Aug. 17, 1992

...wanted nothing to do with the "Scream Team" of '94...: Dream Team

"I don't think you can ever recapture...": "Barkley, Richmond Official Additions," Associated Press, Apr. 14, 1996

...Steve Brace learned was not to get into a verbal sparring match...: Interview, May 23, 2019

"At the beginning of the show...": Interview, May 23, 2019

"He kind of became the central figure of that period...": Interview, July 9, 2020

"They have embarrassed the United States' Dream Team...": YouTube upload of the July 1996 exhibition between the USA Men's Basketball and USA Select, *https://www.youtube.com/watch?v=8T15azF3uoM*

...to kill Brazil because "they're not from this country"...: *https://www.youtube.com/watch?v=8T15azF3uoM*

...noticed how all the sponsors and shoe companies were pining...: Interviews, May 21 and June 12, 2019

...have fun, drink Pepsi, and wear Reeboks...: Amy Shipley, "Yugos Win! (In Your Dreams)," *Miami Herald*, Aug. 4, 1996

...were either up for free agency or linked to trade rumors...: Joel Corry, "The Inside Story: How the Magic Let the Lakers Steal Shaquille O'Neal," CBS Sports, July 21, 2016

It was already "a done deal" in his eyes...: "Free-Agent Bidding Fires Up as Divac Trade Goes Through," Associated Press, July 12, 1996

"She was like, 'Take the picture'...": Interview, June 13, 2019

Hawthorne had been hit six times by the blast...: Scott Freeman, "Fallout," *Atlanta*, July 1, 2011

...was almost paralyzed when the whiplash...: Freeman

"I remember looking out the window when we felt it...": Interviews, Nov. 8 and 11, 2019

The bombing injured 111 people...: Kevin Sack, "Olympic Park Blast Kills One, Hurts 111," *New York Times*, July 28, 1996

When Stubbs awoke in her room...: Interview, June 13, 2019

"She was visibly upset...": Nick Zaccardi, "An Oral History of the Bombing That Rocked the 1996 Atlanta Games," *Sports Illustrated*, July 24, 2012

Another victim, a Turkish cameraman named Melih Uzunyol...: Freeman

...not playing "would be the entirely wrong response...": Interview, Nov. 27, 2019

"We didn't mind taking the time to let these people...": Interview, Nov. 27, 2019

...slamming the "absurd" idea that the Olympics should be canceled...: "Bomb-

ing Aftermath Unfolds in Dream Team's Backyard," Associated Press, July 28, 1996

"I was 14 and I was a lady…": Interview, June 13, 2019

Robinson offered her words of wisdom…and O'Neal gifted her…: Dean Chang and Don Gentile, "Dream Team Eases the Pain," *New York Daily News*, July 31, 1996

…affected everyone, especially Anfernee Hardaway…: Ian O'Connor, "Dreams Fade Out for Oscar," *New York Daily News*, July 31, 1996

…his proudest moment of his time at the Olympics…: Interviews, May 21 and June 12, 2019

"Some were in their early 20s, so I thought…": Interview, June 13, 2019

…the size of "an economy-size jar of peanut butter"…: Interview, June 13, 2019

She told Rudolph they were for him…: Jennifer Bayot, "A Subdued Rudolph Is Sentenced for Bombings," *New York Times*, Aug. 22, 2005

He threw his arms in the air to spell out Y.M.C.A.…: YouTube upload of a clip from the 1996 Olympics matchup between the United States and China, *https://www.youtube.com/watch?v=6iQ-sYM4CBw*

"I'm ready for the 'Macarena'…": YouTube upload of the 1996 Olympics matchup between the United States and China, *https://www.youtube.com/watch?v=9_E6PDUj1Qk*

…the Americans were "unchallenged on the court and…": J.A. Adande, "Same Old Song: U.S. Breezes," *Washington Post*, July 31, 1996

As Payton shit-talked Australian guard Shane Heal…: Russell Jackson, "The Forgotten Story of… Shane Heal v. the Dream Team," *The Guardian*, Oct. 30, 2013

Yugoslavia's role as the aggressor in the Balkan conflict got them banned…: "Yugoslavs Glad to Be in Title Game," Associated Press, Aug. 2, 1996

…strutted his way onto the court to John Williams's score from Superman…: YouTube upload of the 1996 Olympic gold-medal game between the United States and Yugoslavia, *https://www.youtube.com/watch?v=46XfV6MpPEE*

…it was another chance to tell Ali how…: *The Dan Patrick Show*, June 8, 2016

…dedicating it to Christiana…: Norm Frauenheim, "Barkley Gets Another Medal, but Still Hasn't Been Traded," *Arizona Republic*, Aug. 4, 1996

"The Dream Team was four years ago…": *Dream Team*

"I enjoyed Atlanta, I guess…": *Dream Team*

"Somewhere in his heart of hearts…": *Dream Team*

"Can't go there…": Frauenheim

Chapter 27

Primary sources include research conducted by the author from Houston and Northern Virginia, as well as interviews with Chucky Brown, Antoine Carr, Rex Chapman, Jerry Colangelo, Carroll Dawson, Julie Fie, Greg Foster, Hersey Hawkins, Eddie Johnson, Shawn Kemp, Matt Maloney, Calvin Murphy, Joe Pytka, Detlef Schrempf, Eddie Sefko, Jae Staats, John Stockton, and Rudy Tomjanovich. Other sources include coverage in outlets such as *Sports Illustrated*, the *Arizona Republic*, the *Washington Post*, and the *New York Times*, YouTube uploads of the 1997 NBA playoffs, and a recording of a voice mail left by Charles Barkley in 1996.

…she repeated to NBC that the team's franchise player was not available…: Interview, Sept. 22, 2020

…Colangelo made him feel "like a piece of meat"…: David Casstevens, "Philly II: Chuck Uses Old Speech," *Arizona Republic*, June 7, 1996

"How come the Suns are trying to fire your daddy?…": Norm Frauenheim, "Charles Clarifies NBC Interview, Well, Sort Of," *Arizona Republic*, June 8, 1996

"I begged him not to do that interview…": Interview, Sept. 22, 2020

…because the owner didn't know what alias he was staying under…: Frauenheim

"You could see the handwriting on the wall…": Interview, July 17, 2019

"I said, 'What's up, T?'…": Interview, June 23, 2020

…saying he had to "stand up to the system"…: "Barkley Traded to the Rockets," *Washington Post*, Aug. 19, 1996

…and was whisked away by security to a limo on the tarmac…: "Rockets Make Barkley Feel All Warm and Fuzzy," Associated Press, Aug. 20, 1996

In a sendoff note to the fans printed in the Republic…: "Goodbye from Charles," *Arizona Republic*, Aug. 25, 1996

"People always remember the last thing that happened…": *Arizona Republic*

…Jae Staats received a voice mail on his cell phone…: Interview, June 18, 2019

This message is for Jae…: Recording of voice mail left by Charles Barkley (courtesy of Jae Staats)

...was "arguably the greatest sports movie ever"...: The Late Show with Stephen Colbert, Mar. 11, 2020

"And I thought *Kazaam* was bad...": *Inside the NBA*, 2016

...as did Leslie Alexander, the owner who was quick to make the deal...: Michael Graczyk, "Barkley Glad to Be Wanted," Associated Press, Aug. 20, 1996

"Les didn't know much about basketball...": Interview, May 29, 2020

...getting Charles was the ticket to a third title in four years...: Graczyk

"Charles could still do some really good things on the court...": Interview, Oct. 14, 2019

...ribbing Price and forward Matt Bullard for not being the "tough White guys"...: Leigh Montville, "Listen Up!," *Sports Illustrated*, Nov. 4, 1996

"We're all on the downside now...": Montville

...an invite-only party at Planet Hollywood after the game...: John Davis, "Barkley Is Still Quick with Quip but Is Showing New Attitude," *Arizona Republic*, Nov. 2, 1996

...one that included a young and impressionable Tiger Woods...: Mario Elie (@marioelie1), Twitter, *https://twitter.com/marioelie1/status/1245531460674748418*

"They made it personal...": Norm Frauenheim, "Sir Charles rules arena," *Arizona Republic*, Nov. 3, 1996

"He was just so exhausted after his last rebound...": Interview, Oct. 22, 2019

"They got what they fucking deserved!...": Frauenheim

Despite criticism from Walt Frazier over Charles and Jordan's absence...: "Jordan, Barkley No-Shows," Associated Press, Feb. 8, 1997

"I wish I was playing golf with 'em...": Associated Press

...once joked that it was "pure instinct"...: Bill Russell (@RealBillRussell), Twitter, https://twitter.com/RealBillRussell/status/1011438471490072576

Yet standing on his podium in Cleveland in between contemporaries like...: YouTube upload of the NBA's 50 Greatest Players ceremony in February 1997, *https://www.youtube.com/watch?v=s8QG7Uppn8M*

...as ankle and hip injuries forced him to miss...: "After Loss, Rockets Reflect on Season," Associated Press, May 31, 1997

...but his 13.5 rebounds a night were the second highest for his career...: Basketball Reference

...the three legends were 32–8 in games they all played together...: Kelli Anderson, "No. 3 Houston Rockets," *Sports Illustrated*, Nov. 10, 1997

...a mansion in the suburbs of Sugar Land he dubbed "the Ponderosa"...: Davis

...she didn't want her daughter to live in what she called a hateful area...: Tropiano

"I didn't want to raise her in Houston, in a racist environment...": Tropiano

...would be dumbfounded at seeing Olajuwon...observe the holy month of Ramadan...: David Moore, "NBA's Journey of Faith and Discipline," *Dallas Morning News*, Jan. 27, 1997

...Eddie Johnson was baffled that Charles set up a surprise birthday party...: Interview, May 16, 2020

"That's the beauty of Chuck...": Interview, July 26, 2019

"He was definitely a different player by then...": Interview, Dec. 10, 2020

...going for 66 points, 35 rebounds, and 10 assists in Game 7: Basketball Reference

...they should "get another fucking job" if they were tired...: David Casstevens, "Barkley Deal Pays Off for Rockets," *Arizona Republic*, May 18, 1997

"If we would have lost, everybody would have been on my case...": Kirk Bohls, "Barkley Playing the Jazz, Not Singing the Blues," *Austin American-Statesman*, May 18, 1997

"The nightlife in Salt Lake City...": Bohls

"I'm not sure what surreal means...": Richard Hoffer, "Twilight of the Gods," *Sports Illustrated*, June 2, 1997

...Malone threw a fuss over the prospect of competing against him...: Harvey Araton, "Johnson's Return to League Isn't Welcome by Some," *New York Times*, Nov. 1, 1992

...Malone's essay in Sports Illustrated *slammed him for not...*: Malone

"Once you got on the block, Karl always wanted...": Interview, Apr. 16, 2020

"Let's be realistic...": Hoffer

...Tomjanovich kept it simple with a few words...: Interview, Oct. 14, 2019

...with one fan yelling out, "You the man!" right before...: YouTube upload of Game 6 of the 1997 playoff series between Houston and Utah, *https://www.youtube.com/watch?v=x5eDZiZoIPs*

...Charles could only smile at Carr...: *https://www.youtube.com/watch?v=x5eDZiZoIPs*

"Uh-oh…": *https://www.youtube.com/watch?v=x5eDZiZoIPs*

"He knew it was gong to go in…": Interview, July 26, 2019

…showing more emotion in seconds than the thirty-five-year-old…: Interviews, Nov. 8 and 11, 2019

"I was able to get some pretty good meat on him…": Michael Wilbon, "Malone's Pick a Winner," *Washington Post*, May 30, 1997

"I was bear-hugged, not picked…": Jody Genessy, "When John Stockton Sent the Utah Jazz to the NBA Finals," *Deseret News*, May 28, 2017

"I don't want to say we should have won…": Interview, Oct. 22, 2019

"It just happened so quickly…": Genessy

Chapter 28

Primary sources include research conducted by the author from Houston and Northern Virginia, as well as interviews with C. Jeffery Arnold, Chucky Brown, Antoine Carr, Jerry Colon, Gilbert Feliciano, Jim Foley, Bob Ford, Frank Isola, Eddie Johnson, Shawn Kemp, Matt Maloney, Calvin Murphy, Mark NeJame, Eddie Sefko, Rudy Tomjanovich, and Roy Wood Jr. Other sources include a police report filed by the Orange County Sheriff's Office in October 1997, coverage in outlets like the *Orlando Sentinel*, *Sports Illustrated*, *ESPN The Magazine*, the *Washington Post*, and the Associated Press, and YouTube uploads of the 1998 and 1999 NBA playoffs.

…whether Charles was in the first or second trimester of his pregnancy…: Gary Kingston, "Chunky Chuckster," *Vancouver Sun*, Oct. 15, 1997

"If Stockton didn't hit that jump shot…": Interview, May 29, 2020

"Anybody who has spent any time with me knows…": *I May Be Wrong but I Doubt It*

…at around 11:00 p.m. on October 25, 1997…: Police Report, Orange County Sheriff's Office, Oct. 26, 1997

Known for its stained-glass windows, Top 40 playlist and Nickel Beer Night…: Interview, May 14, 2019

…with a group of friends following a big soccer match…: Interview, Dec. 14, 2020

…Lugo was essentially living on the streets…: Interview, May 14, 2019

He was also undocumented and had been arrested ten times…: David Whitley, "Charles Barkley Fought Here and Regretted It," *Orlando Sentinel*, Oct. 28, 2017

Jeffery Williams…recalled that all seemed calm as people were exiting…: Orange County Sheriff's Office

…Jerry Colon had gone out to get his mind off the grueling program…: Interview, Dec. 14, 2020

Feliciano said the conversation that night…: Interview, Dec. 14, 2020

…ice cubes were flung at their table, not hitting anyone but…: Interview, Dec. 14, 2020

Drexler and other witnesses said the action was unprovoked…: Kenneth A. Harris and Tim Povtak, "Barkley Throws Man through Bar Window," *Orlando Sentinel*, Oct. 27, 1997

"You going to let these motherfuckers throw ice at you?…": Interview, Dec. 14, 2020

Among those in Charles's group that night was Karen Carrington…: "Chucked by Charles, He's Eyeing Lawsuit," Associated Press, Oct. 28, 1997

…as well as twenty-year-old Alexis Leiba…: Associated Press

…were underage at the bar…: Orange County Sheriff's Office

Carrington recalled how Charles sought to avoid a confrontation with Lugo…: Associated Press

Charles's reasoning for avoiding conflict was that…: Interview, Dec. 14, 2020

"Charles grabbed me…": Kenneth A. Harris and Tim Povtak, "No Apologies, Brawling, Barkley Says," *Orlando Sentinel* (republished by NeJame Law), Oct. 27, 1997

Then, Lugo allegedly threw a glass of ice at Charles and the women…: Orange County Sheriff's Office

…and Lugo later said it was one of his friends who had tossed it…: Interview, May 14, 2019

The glass struck Carrington in the jaw and knocked her off a chair…: Harris and Povtak

"She got really upset and said…": Interview, Dec. 14, 2020

…two of the women stormed through the club…: Orange County Sheriff's Office

…the power forward got up and blazed past onlookers to chase down Lugo…: Interview, Dec. 14, 2020

"He was running for his life…": Interview, Dec. 14, 2020

"Charles, I will handle this, let go…": Orange County Sheriff's Office

"I will not hurt him…": Orange County Sheriff's Office

"You're not gonna do shit…": Interview, Dec. 14, 2020

Williams reached for his radio…: Orange County Sheriff's Office

"I felt the victim being pulled from my grasp…": Orange County Sheriff's Office

"Do you know who the fuck I am?…": Interview, Dec. 14, 2020

…*Charles had approached Lugo and "flung him like he was a toy"…*: "Barkley Arrested after Altercation," Associated Press, Oct. 27, 1997

A piece of glass from the broken window had struck an artery in Lugo's right arm…: Interview, Dec. 14, 2020

"You got what you deserve…": Orange County Sheriff's Office

"For all I care…": Orange County Sheriff's Office

…*Feliciano took off his shirt, wrapped it around Lugo's arm…*: Interview, Dec. 14, 2020

…*Charles was initially charged with…*: Associated Press

"I wouldn't call what Charles did 'a fight'…": Interview, Sept. 4, 2019

"Let there be no debate…": Harris and Povtak

…*Charles acknowledged to reporters was worth $75,000…*: Henry Pierson Curtis, "Barkley to Accept Plea Deal," *Orlando Sentinel*, June 12, 1998

The charges he faced…were later reduced to…: Curtis

…*that Lugo was found dead near train tracks…*: Interview, Dec. 14, 2020

"Whether what happened to him is urban legend or true…": Interview, May 14, 2019

…*Charles had contemplated retirement right before the season…*: "Barkley Hints at Retirement," Associated Press, Oct. 30, 1997

…*who begged and pleaded with him to get a bodyguard…*: SportsCentury

"He needs to keep his butt home…": Alan Greenberg, "There Are Still Many Knocks against Barkley," *Hartford Courant*, Nov. 2, 1997

"I like going out to bars…": Bob Ford, "At Least, Barkley's Easy to Find," *Philadelphia Inquirer*, Nov. 12, 1997

"I don't think anyone would take a bullet for someone else…": Doug Lesmerises, "Total Security," *Munster Times*, Feb. 12, 1998

"I remember having this weird sense of accomplishment…": Interview, July 8, 2020

"I felt like, in the moment, I was mad…": *Inside the NBA*, 2019

"He was a superhero, but…": Interview, Oct. 22, 2019

Close friends and teammates offered an intervention of sorts...: "Barkley Says He Can't Drink, Play," Associated Press, Feb. 16, 1998

"I've got to stop drinking...": Associated Press

...if he knew what was in a Long Island iced tea...: Dave Anderson, "Has Garden Heard Last Boos for Barkley?," *New York Times*, Feb. 23, 1998

...a pragmatic, moderate agenda of...: Platt

...whom he once called a "neo-Nazi"...: Platt

"He was a shoo-in...": Platt

"My muscles were in a little better shape than his at the time...": Interview, Apr. 16, 2020

"He goes, 'Clyde, that's the door to the real world right there'...": Interview, July 26, 2019

"Go write this...": Interview, July 26, 2019

..."between tall millionaires and short billionaires"...: Tony Kornheiser, "Money Talks, Nobody's Listening," *Washington Post*, Oct. 27, 1998

...before deciding the money would go to charity...: "NBA Players' 'Gift' to Fans Comes with a Price Tag," Associated Press, Dec. 19, 1998

"Everything the players did from a PR standpoint...": Interview, Dec. 9, 2019

"Oak was a hard worker, right?...": Frank Isola, "Bark's Hot Air," *New York Daily News*, Dec. 20, 1998

"What's was this shit you were saying?...": Interview, June 23, 2020

...Oakley delivered an open-handed slap that left the players stunned...: Thomas Golianopoulos, "'An Unmitigated Disaster': An Oral History of the Lockout-Shortened 1999 NBA Season," *The Ringer*, Feb. 19, 2019

"It's different when it's two guys who are as...": Interview, Dec. 10, 2020

"Barkley just kept talking and I told him...": Charles Oakley and Frank Isola, *The Last Enforcer*, Feb. 1, 2022

...allegedly telling Oakley he wasn't going to get into a brawl...: Interview, June 23, 2020

...he took the advice of Danny Manning's wife, Julie, and spent a week...: Bob Young, "Barkley Takes Hike to Lose Weight," *Arizona Republic*, Feb. 17, 1999

...went on a fifteen-mile hike before a lunch of...: Richard Hoffer, "Ready to Roll," *Sports Illustrated*, Feb. 15, 1999

...and sculpted "at least one visible ab"...: Hoffer

"I am going to have a great season…": Jerry Bembry, "Barkley Downplays Predictions of Glory," *Baltimore Sun*, Jan. 30, 1999

"We knew we were running out of steam…": Interview, Oct. 8, 2019

Inside the Green Room…: Gene Wojciechowski, "His Turn," *ESPN The Magazine*, Feb. 12, 1999

"He couldn't jump over a Sunday paper…": Wojciechowski

"Pippen is still Pippen…": Wojciechowski

"I thought we were getting carjacked…": Wojciechowski

As Olajuwon put it, they wanted to…: YouTube upload of an interview that aired on *Inside the NBA* in 1999, https://www.youtube.com/watch?v=GuRFx4aJiMg

Charles made it clear it was "a more cohesive group"…: https://www.youtube.com/watch?v=GuRFx4aJiMg

Pippen was simply "just trying to fit in"…: https://www.youtube.com/watch?v=GuRFx4aJiMg

"We just hoped Scottie could keep the team…": Interview, May 16, 2020

…Pippen had accused Charles of "kissin' Michael's ass"…: Roland Lazenby, *Michael Jordan: The Life*, May 6, 2014

The two even got Tim Grover…: Scottie Pippen with Michael Arkush, *Unguarded*, Nov. 9, 2021

"Charles didn't last one week…": *Unguarded*

…because he was playing golf with Jordan in California…: Jeffrey Denberg, "Barkley Golfs as Rockets Practice Hard," *Atlanta Journal-Constitution*, Jan. 31, 1999

"I'll see where his head is…": Denberg

"Charles goes, 'Hey, fucker…'": Interview, Apr. 16, 2020

"They wanted me to be a 3-point shooter…": "The Rockets Wanted Me to Be a 3-Point Shooter, and That's Why I Didn't Fit," ESPN's *The Jump*, https://www.youtube.com/watch?v=XmBbmIE_Kxc

"We had a different way of playing and he had…": Interview, Oct. 14, 2019

…earned praise from younger players like Cuttino Mobley for offering mentorship…: *Milk The Clock*, Oct. 17, 2018

"He was coming in thinking…": Ben DuBose, "Matt Bullard: Scottie Pippen 'Not My Favorite Teammate' on Rockets," *USA TODAY*, May 12, 2020

"I'm going to get on the plane…": "Lane Violation: Pippen Arrested for Drunk Driving," Associated Press, Apr. 23, 1999

"They're calling us the Big Three now…": *https://www.youtube.com/watch?v=GuRFx4aJiMg*

"His mother can't stop me!…": Mark Heisler, "Barkley's Masterpiece Can't Win the Prize," *Los Angeles Times*, May 10, 1999

…*Pippen openly questioned why Charles fouled O'Neal*…: Heisler

"That's not to blame anybody…": Heisler

Described by NBC's Bob Costas as one of the finest playoff performances…: YouTube upload of Game 4 of the 1999 playoff series between Houston and Los Angeles, *https://www.youtube.com/watch?v=UgbxvmoQYGs*

Matt Guokas…could see Charles's anguish as he walked down…: *https://www.youtube.com/watch?v=UgbxvmoQYGs*

Pippen called the season "a big challenge" and "very disappointing…": Michael A. Lutz, "Adding Pippen Changes Little for Rockets," Associated Press, May 17, 1999

…*a plodding system that had "one of the best players in the game*…": "Pippen Confirms He Wants to Be a Laker," Associated Press, Aug. 13, 1999

"I would be lying if I told you…": "Pippen, Jackson to Be Reunited?," Associated Press, Aug. 13, 1999

…*Charles underscored how hard he'd worked to bring Pippen to Houston*…: "Pippen, Barkley Play the Feud," ESPN.com, Oct. 2, 1999

…*it represented the same kind of "no-lose situation*"…: "Sir Charles the Diplomat," Associated Press, Aug. 22, 1999

He called Pippen "a baby" on multiple occasions…: "Scottie Pippen's Beef with Charles Barkley Is What Happens When You Don't Listen to Michael Jordan," Secret Base, *https://www.youtube.com/watch?v=SsoddHEsU88*

"First, Scottie owes the Rockets' fans an apology…": Dale Robertson, "Rockets' Barkley to Pippen: Be a Man," *Houston Chronicle*, Aug. 20, 1999

Chapter 29

Primary sources include research conducted by the author from Houston, Philadelphia, and Northern Virginia, as well as interviews with Paul and Robert Boudwin, John Calipari, Antoine Carr, Ty Corbin, Carroll Dawson, Howard Eskin, Jim Foley, Lionel Hollins, Martha Korman, Allen Lumpkin, Jackie MacMullan, Mike Missanelli, Lucille and Shaquille O'Neal, Eddie Sefko, Sonny Smith, John Stockton, and Rudy

Tomjanovich. Other sources include YouTube uploads of the 1999–2000 NBA season, a 1999 feature by MacMullan in *Sports Illustrated*, coverage in the Associated Press, and statistics pulled from Basketball Reference.

I wouldn't give Charles Barkley an apology at gunpoint…: YouTube upload of an ESPN interview with Scottie Pippen in 1999, *https://www.youtube.com/watch?v=8-ugxfIYANA*

…Jordan reached out to Charles—twice—to tell him…: *https://www.youtube.com/watch?v=8-ugxfIYANA*

"I don't know if Michael was madder that Scottie…": Jackie MacMullan, "Michael and Me," *Sports Illustrated*, Dec. 20, 1999

Dawson…said he didn't have time to think about why…: Interview, Oct. 8, 2019

Tomjanovich maintained there was no significant evidence…: Interview, Oct. 14, 2019

"Scottie wanted to get back to Phil…": Interview, Oct. 14, 2019

Pippen claimed his sentiment against Charles wasn't personal…: *Unguarded*

"I don't claim to be perfect…": Eddie Sefko, "Barkley Blames Pippen's Insecurities for Outburst," *Houston Chronicle*, Oct. 4, 1999

The Lakers, Jazz, and Sonics all expressed interest…: "Stockton Calls Barkley to Show Jazz's Interest," Associated Press, Aug. 5, 1999

"He would have made up for a lot of the mistakes…": Interviews, Nov. 8 and 11, 2019

"I figured if he was eating that I'd have a better chance…": Interview, Oct. 8, 2019

"I know when October and training camp and everything comes…": *Inside the NBA*, 1999

"I have to revamp my goals now…": *Inside the NBA*

"Sooner or later, I will get blamed…": Landon Hall, "Pippen–Barkley Feud Not Fair so Far," Associated Press, Nov. 26, 1999

"I was determined that when it came to other legends…": Interview, Aug. 10, 2020

…who described the motion as "one of his Charles Barkley–like stupid things"…: Interview, Aug. 10, 2020

"I was like, 'Charles…'": Interview, Aug. 10, 2020

…Charles repeated a mantra: "Can't let nobody hit me…": Mark Rosner, "Lakers Outlast Rockets," *Austin American-Statesman*, Nov. 11, 1999

...their mothers had become best friends—and practically sisters...: Interview, Aug. 11, 2020

"Don't you hit my boy...": Interview, Aug. 10, 2020

The moms never planned to call their sons...: Interview, Aug. 11, 2020

"She said, 'Y'all need to stop!...'": Interview, Aug. 10, 2020

"What was that all about?...": Interview, Aug. 11, 2020

"My mom called right away, and we had to meet...": Interview, Aug. 10, 2020

When Barkley discovered Pippen was the other game captain, he declined...: YouTube upload of the 1999 NBA on TNT broadcast between Houston and Portland, *https://www.youtube.com/watch?v=1xUUYyDaO0c*

"I don't want to shake the blankety-blank's hand...": *https://www.youtube.com/watch?v=1xUUYyDaO0c*

"I'm not disappointed we didn't talk...": "Pippen-Barkley Feud Quite in Blazers' Win," Associated Press, Nov. 27, 1999

"He said some things about me...": Associated Press

"This game has gotten so far away from...": Kevin Ding, "New and Old Butting Heads," *Orange County Register*, Nov. 30, 1999

"I'm sorry that the league has come to that...": Ding

"When he came back, it was almost...": Interview, Oct. 3, 2019

"I don't think a championship would do that much for me...": YouTube upload of Charles announcing his retirement in October 1999, *https://www.youtube.com/watch?v=yU0nd9evP3w*

"I was pump-faking so much I had to...": *Inside the NBA*, 2010

"I thought he was gonna get right back up...": Celeste E. Whittaker, "Sixers Have Fond Memories of Barkley's Career," *Camden Courier-Post*, Dec. 10, 1999

"We could see that quad muscle roll up...": Interview, Sept. 4, 2019

"I knew it was over as soon as I saw it...": Doug Lesmerises, "Barkley's Painful Farewell," *Wilmington News Journal*, Dec. 9, 1999

"You didn't hear a shriek of pain, but...": *SportsCentury*

"You're just not coming back from that...": Interview, Oct. 14, 2019

"It's over...": John Smallwood, "NBA Fans Deserved Better Ending for Star," *Philadelphia Daily News*, Dec. 10, 1999

...Barkley has Johnnie Mae sitting to his right...: Smallwood

"...another unemployed Black man...": MacMullan

...after going out with his teammates to Bridget Foy's...: Interview, July 27, 2020

He told Sixers star Allen Iverson...that it was his league now...: Ken Berger, "Iverson Finds yet Another Controversy," Associated Press, Dec. 10, 1999

"I'm here if you need me...": MacMullan

...Charcey had reserved a meeting hall for family and friends who made...: Rubin E. Grant, "Family Welcome Barkley Home," *Birmingham Post-Herald*, Oct. 22, 1999

"It's time for me to do something else...": John Zenor, "Barkley Calling It Quits—Again," Associated Press, Oct. 25, 1999

...he also told the crowd of ten thousand that he had donated three $1 million gifts...: Zenor

...lauded his former player's "generosity and love for the area"...: Interview, June 6, 2019

"It's a great night for me...": Grant

...he wanted to "learn to play the piano, finish college, and...": Platt

"My objective is to play in the last game of the year...": Chris Sheridan, "Barkley to Join Turner Sports as NBA Analyst," Associated Press, Mar. 7, 2000

...Charles was "probably the most athletically gifted individual...": Tim S. Grover and Shari Lesser Wenk, *Relentless: From Good to Great to Unstoppable*, Apr. 16, 2013

"He looked at me with that death stare and demanded a ball...": *Relentless*

"He's done a lot for this organization and if he wants...": "Barkley Intends to Play Wednesday," Associated Press, Apr. 14, 2000

"I told the players, 'I don't care if it's his last moment...'": Interview, June 5, 2019

"This is a sad day for me...": "Barkley Goes Out on His Own Terms," Associated Press, Apr. 20, 2000

"It's important for me from a mental standpoint...": Michael A. Lutz, "Barkley's Farewell: Future Hall of Famers Gets to Walk Off Court," Associated Press, Apr. 20, 2000

"Charles! Charles!" yelled...: YouTube upload of clips from an April 2000 game between Houston and Vancouver, *https://www.youtube.com/watch?v=lw6dCKwKvRA*

"Charles Barkley...gets a bucket in his final game!...": *https://www.youtube.com/watch?v=lw6dCKwKvRA*

"About time," he told Mobley...: https://www.youtube.com/watch?v=lw6dCKwKvRA

"You really own this one…": "Barkley Leaves by Doing His Version of 'My Way,'" Associated Press, Apr. 20, 2000

"It was worth it…": *https://www.youtube.com/watch?v=lw6dCKwKvRA*

"Well, the big fella up there gave me some stuff…": *https://www.youtube.com/watch?v=lw6dCKwKvRA*

"It's unfortunate I didn't come to Houston until…": Associated Press

"Basketball doesn't owe me anything…": Associated Press

Career averages of 22.1 points, 11.7 rebounds, and 3.9 assists in 1,073 games…: Basketball Reference

…he is one of seven players in league history to record…: Basketball Reference

"The difficult thing is that nothing…": Associated Press

Chapter 30

Primary sources include research conducted by the author from Northern Virginia and New Jersey, as well as interviews with Chris Connelly, Mark Cuban, Bryan Curtis, Chris Fowler, Kevin Harlan, Kirk Herbstreit, Fred Hickman, Walter Iooss, David Levy, Jack McCallum, Dan Patrick, Doc Rivers, John Salley, Reggie Theus, and Peter Vecsey. Other sources include coverage in *Sports Illustrated*, the *Atlanta Journal-Constitution*, and ESPN.com, YouTube clips of *Inside the NBA*, and the 2021 docuseries *The Inside Story*.

"He's been an ass a long time…": YouTube upload of Charles Barkley's first night on *Inside the NBA* in October 2000, *https://www.youtube.com/watch?v=yyIAvpgpMV4*

…regularly calling him "Sir Cumference"…: Brian Costello, "Post Legend Vecsey Took," *New York Post*, Nov. 30, 1999

…looked like "Richard Jewell's body double"…: Peter Vecsey, "Barkley Looking Like Real Gem These Days," *New York Post*, Oct. 22, 2000

…Charles in a studio setting "would be like Richard Pryor or Eddie Murphy…": Prentis Rogers, "Rousing Last Hurrah to 'Inside the NBA' Crew," *Atlanta Journal-Constitution*, May 18, 2001

…he only planned on staying at the show for "two years max"…: *The Inside Story*

"Everything went so well…": Bill Simmons, "TNT Combo Is Pure Dynamite," ESPN.com, May 13, 2002

…a former player who "talked off the top of his head without knowing shit"…: Interview, July 14, 2020

"You guys in the media make me laugh sometimes...": *https://www.youtube.com/watch?v=yyIAvpgpMV4*

"He became Turner Sports...": Interview, June 16, 2020

...who still remembers hearing "Nature Boy" Ric Flair...: Interview, Oct. 10, 2019

"We thought it was nuts...": Interview, Oct. 10, 2019

...had news anchor jobs out of college, bouncing to...: Ernie Johnson Jr., *Unscripted*, Apr. 4, 2017

"When I took that phone call back in 1989 and said...": *The Inside Story*

...Pearl was already something of a TV legend...: Prentis Rogers, "Turner Sports Collects a Pearl," *Atlanta Journal-Constitution*, Dec. 15, 1994

...responsible for luring talents like John Thompson and Reggie Theus...: Larry Stewart, "Cheryl Miller Can't Escape from Reggies," *Los Angeles Times*, May 3, 1996

"The change at Turner didn't happen overnight...": Bob Raissman, "ABC Believes Michaels Will Be NBA 'Miracle' Worker," *New York Daily News*, Sept. 28, 2003

"Dirty Harry said in one of his movies...": YouTube upload of a *SportsCenter* segment from January 1993, *https://www.youtube.com/watch?v=3kU9XwcOIfI*

"That kind of got me to a point...": *Le Batard & Friends—STUpodity*, June 30, 2020

...who Kiely said worked "like someone who thinks he might lose his job"...: Ben Golliver, "Ernie Johnson: The Steadiest Voice in Sports," *Sports Illustrated*, Apr. 5, 2017

"It wasn't my best night...": *The Inside Story*

"They would throw anybody on those things...": *The Bill Simmons Podcast*, July 2020

"She used to say, 'Critique what I'm saying...'": *The Bill Simmons Podcast*

"I retired prematurely...": Bob Raissman, "Transition to TNT Suits Kenny Smith," *New York Daily News*, May 3, 1998

"That's what makes us feel natural... I haven't been to a production...": *The Bill Simmons Podcast*

"I can't tell you how many times his cell phone would ring...": *The Inside Story*

It was Dick Ebersol...who changed his mind...: Wesley Sinor, "Charles Barkley Tells It Like It Is," AL.com, Oct. 25, 2016

"When Charles Barkley was still a player…": John Ourand, "An Un-filtered Assessment of Today's Talent on TV," *Sports Business Journal*, May 18, 2015

Lazarus made a call to Steve Mosko…: McCallum

"I was all set to go to NBC…": Larry Stewart, "As Usual, Barkley Is Life of Party," *Los Angeles Times*, May 10, 2001

"So Mark asks, 'What do you think of our stuff?'…": McCallum

"He told me to sleep on it…": *The Inside Story*

With the money being the same at roughly $1 million annually…: "NBC's Ebersol Says Barkley to TNT Was All About the Money," *Sports Business Journal*, May 11, 2001

"My first thought was, 'Why wouldn't you go to NBC?…'": Interview, Aug. 23, 2019

…he called Perman of his decision at 6:00 a.m.…: *The Inside Story*

It was one of the toughest phone calls of his life…: McCallum

"When I hired Charles…": Jill Lieber, "Barkley Now in Starring Studio Role," *USA TODAY*, Apr. 24, 2001

"Obviously, when Charles came…": *The Inside Story*

…in his $1,500 custom-made suit and size-sixteen ostrich shoes…: Lieber

…Johnson joked that "a fifty-yard dash and a good cigar"…: Lieber

"Does anyone know CPR?…": Lieber

…he described to David Letterman as "the greatest scam going in the world"…: Ed Sherman, "They'll Let Anyone in Booth These Days," *Chicago Tribune*, Nov. 19, 2000

He devised a rankings system based on the Bowl Championship Series…: G. Allen Johnson, "Barkley Picks Bush," *San Francisco Examiner*, Nov. 13, 2000

Charles wished Bobby Knight could visit Knicks practice…: "Barkley Grows into TNT's 'Round Mound of Sound,'" Gannett News Service, Apr. 24, 2001

…looked like "a pimp doing interviews with TNT"…: YouTube upload of *Inside the NBA* at the 2001 NBA All-Star Game, *https://www.youtube. com/watch?v=wKx1A2CJsGA*

He thought Vince Carter played like a girl…: Howard Fendrich, "Barkley Provides Reasons to Chuckle," *Washington Post*, May 6, 2001

"I've seen Don MacLean naked...": Bill Fleischman, "Round Mound of Sound," *Philadelphia Daily News*, Feb. 9, 2001

...Charles subjected his body to be weighed in as part of a segment called "Fat Trak"...: Lieber

...the host dryly replied, "because the cover wasn't big enough...": YouTube upload of a 2001 segment from *Inside the NBA*, https://www.youtube.com/watch?v=-rrW_FgbBV8

Grandmother Johnnie Mae jokingly pleaded with Johnson and Smith to stop...: John McCurdy, "Funniest Moments: Charles Barkley, Eloquent Comedian," *Bleacher Report*, Feb. 8, 2009

Charles jokingly started asking Dallas Mavericks owner Mark Cuban and other guests...: Interview, July 13, 2020

"I restrict myself to a six-pack...": "Making News," *Tampa Bay Times*, Jan. 30, 2001

"Charles's willingness to step on a scale...": Golliver

"I think the chemistry clicked a lot quicker...": Ashley McGeachy, "There's No Doubt about It: Barkley Can Flat-Out Talk," *Philadelphia Inquirer*, May, 23, 2001

"At first, I was a little apprehensive...": Rogers

Vecsey had requested to appear only on TBS and away from Charles...: Interview, July 14, 2020

"I was gone that minute...": Interview, July 14, 2020

...who kept the pseudonym "Homer Simpson" at hotels had given TNT's...: Richard Sandomir, "His Hugeness Speaks His Mind," *New York Times*, May 24, 2001

"It almost had this cult-like following...": Interview, Oct. 21, 2019

...he was depicted as a modern-day slave who was now unchained...: Jack McCallum, "Citizen Barkley," *Sports Illustrated*, Mar. 11, 2002

"So you got 300 listeners...": YouTube upload of a 2003 CNN segment, https://www.youtube.com/watch?v=AAZzgTLsDYY

..."one of them guys who is really, really smart, who's a dumbass"...: https://www.youtube.com/watch?v=AAZzgTLsDYY

...telling her to "go back to your office, wait on another case, and shut the hell up"...: Brian Dakss, "Victims' Rights Lawyer: TV Fixture," CBS News, May 25, 2005

"He says, 'I just called to tell you...'": *The Steam Room*, Apr. 24, 2020

"I realized that after he said what he wanted to say...": *The Steam Room*

BARKLEY

Chapter 31

Primary sources include research conducted by the author from Northern Virginia, as well as interviews with Joe Arpaio, Geno Auriemma, Sue Bird, Norm Clarke, Jerry Colangelo, Mark Cuban, Richard Deitsch, Julius Erving, Guy Fieri, Wallace Honeycutt, David Hunt, the Rev. Jesse Jackson, Dan Le Batard, David Levy, Nancy Lieberman, Jackie MacMullan, David Roger, Len Sherman, Pete Smith, Sonny Smith, Dominique Wilkins, and Dave Zirin. Other sources include a police report filed by the Gilbert Police Department in December 2008, *Who's Afraid of a Large Black Man?*, YouTube uploads of segments from *Inside the NBA*, a YouTube upload of the 2006 Basketball Hall of Fame, coverage in outlets like *Sports Illustrated*, the *Washington Post*, and the Associated Press, and a 2020 episode of *Le Batard & Friends—STUpodity*.

"Boy, I need a fish tank...": *Le Batard & Friends—STUpodity*

Illusionist David Blaine had fallen short in his attempt...: "David Blaine's Breathtaking Stunt," CBS News, May 2, 2006

"Get me a fish tank and a pair of goggles...": *Le Batard & Friends—STUpodity*

"Kenny, you can't be making me laugh!...": *Inside the NBA* (@NBAonTNT), Twitter, *https://twitter.com/bleacherreport/status/1321596940857962496*

Charles's stunts were watched by roughly 650,000 households each week...: Steve Hummer, "Charles & Company," *Atlanta Journal-Constitution*, Jan. 22, 2006

"Charles changed everything...": Interview, Nov. 19, 2019

...like the $1 million he donated to help rebuild homes...: Larry Stewart, "Barkley Fully Supports NBA's New Dress Code," *Los Angeles Times*, Oct. 21, 2005

One of them was the Reverend Jesse Jackson...: Charles Barkley and Michael Wilbon, *Who's Afraid of a Large Black Man?*, Mar. 31, 2005

...for not having done enough "to make social change in the Black community"...: McCallum

"He's a basketball player...": Platt

...was "still delivering the message, whether or not...": *Who's Afraid of a Large Black Man?*

"He had broken the stereotype of...": Interview, Nov. 2, 2020

"I'm not saying this exclusively...": *Who's Afraid of a Large Black Man?*

...*the racial divide ran too deep for America to ever have a Black president...*: *Who's Afraid of a Large Black Man?*

...*never-ending war and "a bona fide tragedy" in the widening income gap...*: "Transcript: Charles Barkley Tells Brown 'Racism Is a Cancer,'" CNN, Oct. 27, 2008

...*caused Charles to leave the Republican Party...*: Chris Baldwin, "Charles Barkley: John Mellencamp Right, 'Conservative Means Discriminatory,'" *Travel Golf*, July 17, 2006

...*who claimed Charles was pandering to Obama...*: "Charles Barkley Supports the President," *The Rush Limbaugh Show*, Mar. 9, 2009

...*that he wanted to punch the hell out of him...*: Rick Chandler, "Charles Barkley Wants to Punch Rush Limbaugh," *Deadspin*, Mar. 12, 2009

"I was like, 'No, fuck that...'": Interview, Feb. 16, 2020

...*Charles labeled the superstar's performance "very selfish"...*: Melissa Rohlin, "Charles Barkley Says Kobe Bryant Texted Him for Three Hours after He Criticized Him On Air," *Sports Illustrated*, June 10, 2020

...*Bryant, who called Charles "stupid" for suggesting...*: Bill Plaschke, "Uncomfortable Question Returns to Haunt Kobe Bryant," *Los Angeles Times*, May 15, 2010

"Kobe started texting me for the next three hours...": "Charles Barkley Discusses Role of Sports During Social Unrest," 247Sports, *https://www.youtube.com/watch?v=q58-9cEWSR4*

"First of all...": *https://www.youtube.com/watch?v=q58-9cEWSR4*

The appearance of Bryant, in his light blue sweater-vest...: YouTube upload of a 2006 episode of *Inside the NBA*, *https://www.youtube.com/watch?v=qgjeiMBPMaE*

...*with Charles later admitting Bryant's fiery responses were "awesome"...*: *https://www.youtube.com/watch?v=q58-9cEWSR4*

"I'm not gonna jump over the table and lump him...": *https://www.youtube.com/watch?v=qgjeiMBPMaE*

"That's not a bad legacy...": Michael Wilbon, "22 Years Later, Barkley and Dumas Show They Are a Cut Above," *Washington Post*, Apr. 5, 2006

"You know, this is basically the end somewhat...": YouTube upload of Charles Barkley's Basketball Hall of Fame enshrinement speech in 2006, *https://www.youtube.com/watch?v=b2m4sXJtu3I*

"I can't believe this is happening...": Interview, Aug. 19, 2019

"If you can put up with me all these years...": *https://www.youtube.com/watch?v=b2m4sXJtu3I*

"You know, when I got arrested…": *https://www.youtube.com/watch?v=b2m4sXJtu3I*

…*who announced earlier in the year that he had been diagnosed with*…: "TNT's Ernie Johnson Reveals He Has Non-Hodgkin's Lymphoma," *Sports Business Journal*, Feb. 23, 2006

The news shattered Charles, who sat in silence and could only shake his head…: *Unscripted*

"I told Ernie he need to be…": *https://www.youtube.com/watch?v=b2m4sXJtu3I*

"The players viewed him by how many times…": Interview, July 24, 2020

"There's a reason they build those casinos…": Wil Leitner, "Charles Barkley Has Hilarious Response to Why He Loves Gambling," *The Herd with Colin Cowherd*, July 1, 2019

"Listen, Colin, I can't die with all this money…": Leitner

"He was a player in every respect…": Interview, Sept. 24, 2019

…*Cuban was buying $10 tickets and finding his way down to floor seats*…: Interview, July 13, 2020

…*in what the owner remembered as "one of the best party nights ever"*…: Interview, July 13, 2020

"It was stressing me out, man…": "Andres Gonzalez Interview: Gambling in Vegas with Charles Barkley and Why He Tweeted Tiger Woods," *GOLF's Subpar*, *https://www.youtube.com/watch?v=MM6xgKAfhqs*

…*once saw Charles surreptitiously slide a few hundred-dollar chips*…: Interview, Oct. 22, 2020

"He smacks my hand and he says…": *The Oprah Winfrey Show*

"He was a rock star in the casinos…": Interview, Sept. 24, 2019

…*saying he got caught up in Vegas with Charles and Jordan*…: Mark Seal, "The Temptation of Tiger Woods," *Vanity Fair*, Apr. 30, 2010

"He ended up coming out the next day…": Seal

"The girls were workin' it…": *Tiger*, HBO, 2021

He wanted to be seen by not just Charles and Jordan but…: *Tiger*

…*Charles acknowledged estimated gambling losses of $10 million*…: "Barkley Claims Gambling Problem Has Cost Him $10M," ESPN.com, May 3, 2006

…*he admitted to losing $2.5 million "in a six-hour period"*…: "Barkley Admits Huge Losses, Big Gains While Gambling," Associated Press, Feb. 5, 2007

The casino alleged that the star had not paid back $400,000 in gambling markers…: Jeff German, "The Wynn Sues Barkley, Claims $400,000 Gambling Debts Unpaid," *Las Vegas Sun*, May 15, 2008

…district attorney David Roger leaked the complaint to the Review-Journal…: Interview, July 2, 2019

"I screwed up…": Phil Taylor, "The Escape Artist," *Sports Illustrated*, June 2, 2008

"Hey, Chuck, what's up?…": Interview, June 16, 2020

"Oh, I fucked up…": Interview, June 16, 2020

"Oh my God…": Interview, June 16, 2020

…Charles had enjoyed a feast at Mastro's City Hall of steak, lobster…: Police Report, Gilbert Police Department, Dec. 31, 2008

…a group that included NFL star Michael Strahan and actor Jaleel White…: Dave Goldiner, "Charles Barkley Admitted He Was Looking for Sex during DUI Arrest," *New York Daily News*, Dec. 31, 2008

…ran up a bar tab of $1,800 for about three hours…: "The Cost of Partying with Urkel," *TMZ*, Dec. 31, 2008

"You find that you're very committed when something…": Interview, Mar. 9, 2020

…Smith's fifteen-year-old daughter, Jessica, joined him…: Interview, Mar. 9, 2020

At 1:26 a.m., Smith pulled over a black Infiniti QX56…: Gilbert Police Department

…a woman had climbed into the passenger seat…: Gilbert Police Department

Charles explicitly asked if he was being pulled over…: Interview, Mar. 9, 2020

"There were three or four cars in a line…": Tim Cowlishaw, *Drunk on Sports*, Mar. 17, 2013

After the officer identified six clues of impairment…: Gilbert Police Department

…said he was "in a hurry to go get that girl"…: Gilbert Police Department

"[Barkley] asked me, 'You want the truth?'…": Gilbert Police Department

…Charles showed concern for the female passenger…: Interview, Mar. 9, 2020

…was allowed to leave and walk back to the bar area…: Interview, Mar. 9, 2020

It didn't take long for Levy to see the report…: Interview, June 16, 2020

"I'm looking at myself thinking, 'Shit, I want him back…'": Interview, June 16, 2020

...as looking like "Wilson floating away from Tom Hanks"...: "Weekend Update: Charles Barkley on His DUI," *Saturday Night Live, https://www. youtube.com/watch?v=_9w0iwmvpaY*

But Charles and his attorneys were angered that the line about receiving oral sex...: Interview, Mar. 9, 2020

"That was 100 percent a joke...": "Charles Barkley: 'DUI Arrest Was Good for Me,'" *The Seth Davis Show, https://www.youtube.com/ watch?v=ICjfGf9FWjk*

Charles was fined more than $2,000...: "Charles Barkley Finishes Jail Time on DUI Charges," Associated Press, Mar. 9, 2009

...Tent City was long decried by critics as cruel...: Francisco Chairez, "The Year I Spent in Joe Arpaio's Tent Jail Was Hell. He Should Never Walk Free," *Washington Post*, Aug. 26, 2017

Arpaio's response was that if American troops in Iraq could handle...: Randy James, "Sheriff Joe Arpaio," *Time*, Oct. 13, 2009

Inmates were served green bologna and forced to listen to KJOE...: Interview, July 16, 2019

...to have overseen the worst pattern of racial profiling...: Ray Stern, "Sheriff Joe Arpaio's Office Commits Worst Racial Profiling in U.S. History, Concludes DOJ Investigation," *Phoenix New Times*, Dec. 15, 2011

...once described Tent City as "a concentration camp"...: Fernanda Santos, "Outdoor Jail, a Vestige of Joe Arpaio's Tenure, Is Closing," *New York Times*, Apr. 4, 2017

...and called Barkley's time at Tent City "cordial"...: "Charles Barkley—Tent City All-Star," *TMZ*, Mar. 7, 2009

"If y'all really, really want to put me as low...": "NBA Great Barkley Begins 3-Day Sentence in Tent City," CNN, Mar. 7, 2009

"It was totally a show, how could it not be?...": Interview, July 10, 2019

Charles, who had initially endorsed Arpaio on his 1996 autobiography...: Joe Arpaio, *America's Toughest Sheriff: How We Can Win the War Against Crime*, Mar. 1, 1996

...George Lopez suggested on Inside that Charles not learn Spanish...: Daniel Kablack, "Charles Barkley Blasts Arizona Sheriff During Halftime Utah/Denver Game," *Bleacher Report*, Apr. 29, 2010

...had Charles namechecking Arpaio in a tizzy that forced Lopez...: Kablack

"When I think of Charles...": Interview, July 15, 2019

...he had gotten behind the wheel "hundreds and hundreds of times"...: *The Seth Davis Show*

"I never thought about killing anybody...": *The Seth Davis Show*

"...a superhero who strolls out of the rubble...": Taylor

Chapter 32

Primary sources include research conducted by the author from Leeds, Alabama, and Northern Virginia, as well as interviews with Daryl-Marie Barkley, Howard Beck, Howard Bryant, Richard Deitsch, Chris Fowler, Kevin Harlan, Kirk Herbstreit, Clark Kellogg, Martha Korman, Dan Le Batard, David Levy, James Andrew Miller, Lucille and Shaquille O'Neal, Dan Patrick, Amy Shorter, and Sam Smith. Other sources include federal records publicly available on Ancestry.com, archives from *The Waddle and Silvy Show* and *The Dan Le Batard Show*, and YouTube uploads of *Inside the NBA*.

"I couldn't pick a book fast enough...": Interview, Oct. 17, 2019

...he suffered two heart attacks and a stroke...: Strauss

"It had really rained on my parade...": Strauss

...Darryl received his heart transplant in March 2003...: Lee Shappell, "Barkley's Brother Receives Donor Heart," *Arizona Republic*, Mar. 20, 2003

"I can't describe the feeling I have that my brother...": Shappell

Darryl founded HeartChange-HeartExchange Ministries to help assist...: Obituary for Darryl Barkley

"I go around and tell kids in schools...": Strauss

...like the migraines that sometimes forced him...: Interview, Oct. 17, 2019

He chaperoned all her field trips... Daryl-Marie still thinks about the...: Interview, Oct. 17, 2019

"The door was open, and I saw him lying there...": Interview, Oct. 17, 2019

"He left a mark on Leeds...": Interview, Oct. 17, 2019

...had lost maternal grandfather Frank Mickens...: Public records from Ancestry.com

"We looked up to Granny for everything...": Interview, Aug. 11, 2020

Daryl-Marie saw Johnnie Mae as doting and lenient...: Interview, Oct. 17, 2019

...his grandmother was so old that she had to put WD-40 on her ankles...: YouTube upload of a 2010 TNT broadcast, *https://www.youtube.com/watch?v=GLIg6aRPZKo*

"My grandmother, who's my best coach ever...": Peter

Johnnie Mae England Edwards Mickens died on December 2, 2009...: Obituary for Johnnie Mickens in the *Birmingham News* in December 2009

...Mama I Love You—Red...: Moton Hill Cemetery

"He looked up to her more than just about anyone...": Interview, July 16, 2020

"*Inside* is something we definitely hadn't seen before...": Interview, May 22, 2020

"Matter of fact, in about 300 days...": *Inside the NBA*, 2010

David Levy met with him in 2011 to discuss joining the show...: Interview, June 16, 2020

"Shaq, there are companies that want you...": Interview, June 16, 2020

O'Neal smiled and was intrigued...: Interview, Aug. 10, 2020

"They've always had their nose pressed up against...": Interview, Nov. 24, 2020

"Everyone who wasn't TNT was saying...": Interview, Aug. 10, 2020

Charles was immediately onboard with...: Interview, June 16, 2020

"To put you into this mix...": Interview, June 16, 2020

...an over-the-top vignetter filled with cheerleaders, fireworks...: "Shaq Joins TNT's Inside the NBA with a BIG Entrance," NBA, *https://www.youtube.com/watch?v=CCJAoezA7uM*

"We added Shaq and it was, 'He's gonna ruin...'": *The Inside Story*

...Kiely urged O'Neal to shout in order to...: Richard Deitsch, "Shaquille O'Neal Signs Multi-Year Extension to Stay with 'Inside the NBA,'" *The Athletic*, Aug. 24, 2020

...copy Shaq's mumbling delivery so that he could hear...: Le Batard & Friends—STUpodity

...where O'Neal spoke about how Tyson Chandler was going...: The Bill Simmons Podcast

...When does someone come on our show and we don't *make fun of them?...*: The Bill Simmons Podcast

"They would pull me aside and tell me...": Interview, Aug. 10, 2020

...listening and processing before "coming at you like a locomotive"...: Interview, Aug. 23, 2019

"Charles is the catalyst for all we do...": Interview, Aug. 10, 2020

…the bombast of Charles and Shaq's repartee elevated the show…: The Inside Story

…Kellogg was a walking conscience compared to Charles…: Interview, Aug. 23, 2019

"It floored me…": Interview, Nov. 19, 2019

…anyone who tweets likely lives out of their mother's basement…: Chris Barnewall, "Charles Barkley Says He Doesn't Use Social Media Because That's for 'Losers,'" CBS Sports, Feb. 15, 2018

"We would talk to each other each day…": Interview, Aug. 11, 2020

…joyfully likened their banter to old men waving their fists…: Interview, June 24, 2019

"I always make the distinction, and Charles will never…": Interview, Feb. 27, 2020

"I played in the NBA for 16 years…": "Inside the NBA: Rockets-Clippers Locker Room Drama," NBA on TNT, *https://www.youtube.com/watch?v=UzQP7u-IOxg*

"Hello, police?…": *https://www.youtube.com/watch?v=UzQP7u-IOxg*

"He's always going to tell me the truth…": The Oprah Winfrey Show

"Look at him…": The Oprah Winfrey Show

"The guy was like a brother to me…": The Waddle and Silvy Show, ESPN 1000 in Chicago, May 2020

…should win Coach of the Year for miraculously winning any games…: Kelly Dwyer, "Charles Barkley Blames Michael Jordan's Woes in Charlotte on M.J.'s Yes-Men," Yahoo Sports, Mar. 2, 2012

…Charles did not beat around the bush…: "Charles Barkley critical of Jordan," ESPN Chicago, Mar. 1, 2012

"I think the biggest problem has been…": ESPN Chicago

"I love Michael, but he just has not…": ESPN Chicago

"He is mf'ing me up and down…": "Charles Barkley on How His Role as an Analyst Affected His Relationships with NBA Legends Michael Jordan and Kobe Bryant," GOLF's Subpar, May 10, 2020

Saying he'd "rather not get into that"…: "Transcript: Unguarded with Rachel Nichols," CNN, Dec. 13, 2013

"It's put a wedge between our friendship…": CNN

"Might as well burn down a whole house…": CNN

"The thing that bothered me the most about...": *The Waddle and Silvy Show*

...*saw the bond between Michael and Charles as overrated*...: Interview, Dec. 11, 2019

"Charles has always had a strong, independent streak...": Interview, Dec. 11, 2019

Whatever tension existed looked to be overexaggerated...: "Kenny Smith: I Brought MJ and Barkley Back Together," *TMZ*, Nov. 4, 2016

...*that he missed Jordan's friendship*...: "Barkley has not mended friendship with Jordan," *The Dan Le Batard Show*, Nov. 29, 2016

"All he has to do is make a phone call...": "Kenny Smith: Barkley Should Apologize to Jordan... 'He's Wrong,'" *TMZ*, Dec. 12, 2016

...*saying His Airness had his phone number and knew*...: *The Waddle and Silvy Show*

...*who had once lost a Finals bet to Charles that forced him*...: Interview, Oct. 22, 2020

"That's never gonna happen...": "Would Charles Barkley Ever Reach Out to Michael Jordan?," *The Dan Le Batard Show*, May 11, 2020

Chapter 33

Primary sources include research conducted by the author from Leeds, Alabama, and Northern Virginia, as well as interviews with Daryl-Marie Barkley, Chuck D, Richard Deitsch, Beck Dorey-Stein, David Griffin, Jemele Hill, Lisa Hudson, Bomani Jones, Lida Jones, Van Jones, Martha Korman, Dan Le Batard, David Levy, Mike Missanelli, Daryl Morey, Lucille and Shaquille O'Neal, Larry Platt, Bakari Sellers, Vince Thompson, Bryan Tucker, and Peter Vecsey. Other sources include 990 tax forms for the Charles Barkley Foundation, coverage in outlets such as *Sports Illustrated*, the *Washington Post*, and ESPN.com, and YouTube uploads of *Inside the NBA* and *Saturday Night Live*.

...*Charles joked how San Antonio would be a gold mine*...: *Inside the NBA*, 2014

...*Victoria was a secret for the women of San Antonio*...: *Inside the NBA*

...*and calls of apology from the women of San Antonio*...: Marc Weinreich, "Charles Barkley Should Apologize for Comments, Says Obesity Awareness Group," *Sports Illustrated*, May 7, 2014

Vanessa Macias, the girlfriend of Spurs legend Tim Duncan, made up...: Cindy

Boren, "Charles Barkley Schooled by Tim Duncan's Girlfriend, Vanessa Macias," *Washington Post*, May 20, 2014

"Charles, you offended some people...": Interview, Aug. 10, 2020

"Some of you people don't like my sense of humor...": *Inside the NBA*

"For me jokin' about those big ol' women...": *Inside the NBA*

...Chuck nearly fell asleep on a broadcast, admitting he was bored...: *Inside the NBA*

...to a nine-year, $24-billion extension to keep the media rights...: "NBA Announces 9-Year TV Deal with ESPN, Turner Sports," *Sports Illustrated*, Oct. 5, 2014

...would be hailed within the company as the transparent communicator...: John Ourand, "Colleagues of David Levy Pay Tribute to Longtime Turner Executive, Culture He Created," *Sports Business Journal*, Mar. 25, 2019

He'd learn to do what he called "the Chuckie"...: Interview, June 16, 2020

...he carried with him $1,700 worth of wine and tequila...: Richard Deitsch, "Inside the Meeting That Led Charles Barkley to Re-Sign with Inside the NBA," *Sports Illustrated*, May 17, 2015

"We had to be dead-on that day...": Interview, June 16, 2020

...and smoked cigars in what Levy called "one of the greatest nights"...: Interview, June 16, 2020

"Chuck...we did some math and we believe...": Interview, June 16, 2020

"I didn't say that, but yes, it was...": Interview, June 16, 2020

...the number being offered was, "That's fucking stupid...": Interview, Jan. 8, 2020

...he makes around $20 million a year...: The Dan Patrick Show, July 25, 2022

"David... I'm in...": Interview, June 16, 2020

Chuck didn't even need his agent, Marc Perman...: Deitsch

Leaving them now, he said, "would have been very unfair...": Deitsch

"My agent never got involved...": Deitsch

"Mayor Eric Patterson had one resident, Charcey Glenn...": Anne Ruisi, "Crowd Jeers Leeds Council Vote," *Birmingham News*, Aug. 2, 2010

...had contributed more than $1 million in scholarship funding...: 990 Tax Forms for Charles Barkley Foundation, Inc., GuideStar and ProPublica's Nonprofit Explorer, *https://projects.propublica.org/nonprofits/organizations/631159820*

Children would surround her after service at Macedonia Baptist...: Washington

If you weren't at church on Sunday, she'd ask you what...: Interview, Oct. 17, 2019

...strangers from across the state would get wind of who her son was...: Interview, May 27, 2020

...about how she needed to "talk to that boy and tell him to keep his mouth shut"...: ESPN.com

"I think he should keep on talking...": ESPN.com

...Martha Korman...took Charcey to the hospital for pain...: Interview, Feb. 7, 2020

...Charcey's kidneys were failing...: Interview, Feb. 7, 2020

She didn't need to when they saw it for themselves...: Interview, Aug. 11, 2020

...and it was Daryl-Marie doing the same for Charcey...: Interview, Oct. 17, 2019

Martha and Lucille were flying back and forth to Birmingham...: Interviews, Feb. 7 and Aug. 11, 2020

...who was back in Leeds whenever he could get there...: Interview, Feb. 7, 2020

"It was anticipated...": Interview, Oct. 17, 2019

...died of kidney failure on June 19, 2015...: "Charles Barkley's Mother, Charcey Glenn, Dies in Alabama," Associated Press, June 19, 2015

...remembered by loved ones for her "vibrant personality...": Obituary for Charcey Glenn

...with scores of plots bumping up against the greenery buffering...: Moton Hill Cemetery

...he lays out how racism remains the most insidious force in our culture...: *Who's Afraid of a Large Black Man?*

"I can't sit around and say nothing...": *Who's Afraid of a Large Black Man?*

"The notion that I would say to another person...": *Who's Afraid of a Large Black Man?*

...sat across from President Barack Obama in the East Wing Library...: YouTube upload of an interview that aired on TNT during the 2014 NBA All-Star Weekend, *https://www.youtube.com/watch?v=flyFQGLn4iI*

"That's how Mama brought us up...": ESPN.com

"All Black people ain't great...": *Outrageous!*

...he would read the newspaper on the plane or before practice...: Interviews, Apr. 15 and June 16, 2020

"He's not always trying to say the popular thing…": Interview, Jan. 14, 2021

…*allegations from teammates that he wasn't "Black enough"*…: Cindy Boren, "Charles Barkley Rants about Russell Wilson Being 'Brainwashed,' Called 'Not Black Enough,'" *Washington Post*, Oct. 27, 2014

…*and claimed "there are a lot of Black people who are unintelligent…"*: Leada Gore, "'Unintelligent' Blacks 'Brainwashed' to Choose Street Cred over Success: Charles Barkley," AL.com, Oct. 25, 2014

…*"if you go to jail, it gives you street cred"*…: Breeanna Hare, "Charles Barkley: 'Brainwashed' Blacks Hold Up Success," CNN, Oct. 28, 2014

"We as Black people are never going to be successful…": Gore

…*Coates described Charles's thinking as "painful," arguing the notion*…: Ta-Nehisi Coates, "Charles Barkley and the Plague of 'Unintelligent' Blacks," *The Atlantic*, Oct. 28, 2014

"It's worth noting that there isn't much difference…": Coates

…*wearing T-shirts during their shootarounds that read "I Can't Breathe"*…: J.A. Adande, "Purpose of 'I Can't Breathe' T-Shirts," ESPN.com, Dec. 10, 2014

…*with their arms in the air in solidarity with "Hands Up, Don't Shoot"*…: "No Fines for Rams Players' Salute," ESPN.com, Dec. 1, 2014

…*Charles said he again agreed with the grand jury's decision*…: Husna Haq, "Why Charles Barkley Supports the Ferguson Grand Jury Decision," *Christian Science Monitor*, Dec. 1, 2014

…*to slam the actions of the mostly Black protesters in Ferguson*…: Interview, Oct. 3, 2019

"Them jackasses who are looting, those aren't real Black people…": Cindy Boren, "Charles Barkley Says Ferguson Rioters Are 'Scumbags,' Backs Grand Jury Decision," *Washington Post*, Dec. 2, 2014

Like he did in the case of Trayvon Martin…: Melissa Rohlin, "Charles Barkley Agrees with George Zimmerman Verdict," *Los Angeles Times*, July 19, 2013

…*Black people, as a whole, "have a lot of crooks"*…: Steve Almasy, "Charles Barkley: We Never Talk about Race until Something Bad Happens," CNN, Dec. 8, 2014

"I don't think that was a homicide…": "Transcript: @ThisHour with Berman and Michaela," CNN, Dec. 3, 2014

Van Jones…described Charles's comments at the time as "inflammatory"…: Interview, July 29, 2020

Dr. Jason Johnson…questioned Barkley's "hypocrisy about his own privilege"…:

Jason Johnson, "Charles Barkley, Wrong on Race, Ferguson and Garner," CNN, Dec. 4, 2014

...Bakari Sellers was among the many who were also turned off...: Interview, Nov. 24, 2020

...about Charles "speaking the truth about Ferguson"...: Etan Thomas, "An Open Letter to Charles Barkley," *The Nation*, Dec. 3, 2014

Even Rush Limbaugh...came to his defense...: "Charles Barkley Doubles Down," *The Rush Limbaugh Show*, Dec. 3, 2014

...many White people like to wave around Charles's opinions on race...: Interviews, May 27 and Oct. 22, 2020

Le Batard guessed these people did so not realizing...: Interview, Oct. 22, 2020

Kenny Smith has credited Chuck as the reason the show was able to branch out...: The Inside Story

To Kenny, Charles was not qualified to hold this much authority...: Kenny Smith, "Kenny Smith's Open Letter to Charles Barkley about Ferguson," *USA TODAY*, Dec. 3, 2014

...that the newest episode of Inside *would "not be your traditional pregame show"...*: YouTube upload of a 2014 broadcast of *Inside the NBA*, *https:// www.youtube.com/watch?v=RyleDw3N2u0*

...for sportswriters he despised, like Peter Vecsey, Skip Bayless, and Phil Mushnick...: The Dan Patrick Show, Feb. 19, 2015

"You know, it's funny, I hear all these guys talking about...": *https:// www.youtube.com/watch?v=RyleDw3N2u0*

...Charles showed he was more nuanced than people gave...: Interview, Nov. 24, 2020

The message: Keep talking...: Christine Brennan, "Brennan: Barkley, Smith Lead Valuable Discussion on Race," *USA TODAY*, Dec. 4, 2014

"Some people are going to agree with me...": *https://www.youtube.com/ watch?v=RyleDw3N2u0*

Kenny was disheartened at how nearly sixty-three million people...: "Our Thoughts on the Election," NBA on TNT, *https://www.youtube.com/ watch?v=7zo0Gfw9tes*

...should aspire to be like Trump "because he gets all the best babes"...: Michael Wilbon, "Not a Good Guy? Wait a Minute," *Washington Post*, Feb. 27, 1991

"We have to give him a chance...": *https://www.youtube.com/ watch?v=7zo0Gfw9tes*

...*called on NFL owners to fire any "son of a bitch" who kneeled...*: Bryan Armen Graham, "Donald Trump Blasts NFL Anthem Protesters: 'Get That Son of a Bitch off the Field,'" *The Guardian*, Sept. 23, 2017

...*where he called out the "bum" for his responses...*: Matt Bonesteel and Marissa Payne, "LeBron James Sticks Up for Stephen Curry, Calls President Trump a 'Bum,'" *Washington Post*, Sept. 23, 2017

...*LeBron said Trump "doesn't give a fuck" about people...*: Jordan Heck, "LeBron James: Donald Trump 'Doesn't Give a F— about the People,'" *The Sporting News*, Feb. 16, 2018

...*Ingraham called the response "ignorant" and "barely intelligible"...*: Emily Sullivan, "Laura Ingraham Told LeBron James to Shut Up and Dribble; He Went to the Hoop," NPR, Feb. 19, 2018

"Millions elected Trump to be their coach...": Matt Bonesteel and Des Bieler, "Fox News's Laura Ingraham to LeBron James and Kevin Durant: 'Shut Up and Dribble,'" *Washington Post*, Feb. 16, 2018

Tucker...just told Charles to start talking in the office...: Interview, Mar. 30, 2020

"I'm an athlete and athletes have been speaking out...": "Charles Barkley Athletes Monologue," *Saturday Night Live*, https://www.youtube.com/watch?v=—V6UUmWGgE

"Some people don't want to hear from professional athletes...": *https://www.youtube.com/watch?v=—V6UUmWGgE*

"So LeBron, keep on dribbling...": *https://www.youtube.com/watch?v=—V6UUmWGgE*

"We allow him to say things that are dead wrong...": Interview, May 27, 2020

Chapter 34

Primary sources include research conducted by the author from Chicago, Leeds, Alabama, and Northern Virginia, as well as interviews with Daryl-Marie Barkley, Dr. Raegan Durant, Dr. Mona Fouad, John Hudson, Andrew Hugine Jr., Sen. Doug Jones, David Levy, Jackie MacMullan, Montal Morton, Derrick Stafford, Jimmy Traina, and Doug Turner. Other sources include data from the US Census Bureau, coverage in outlets like the *Washington Post*, AL.com, and CNN, YouTube uploads of *Inside the NBA*, and episodes of *The Steam Room*.

"Kenny Smith... Sounds like a name Charles Barkley gives to the cops...": "Jeff Ross Roasts the Inside Guys," NBA on TNT, https://www.youtube.com/watch?v=RcGGFe-G3Fs

David Stern...died of complications from a brain hemorrhage...: Jordan Freiman, "David Stern, Former NBA Commissioner, Has Died at Age 77," CBS News, Jan. 2, 2020

...Charles walked out of an early screening of The Gentlemen *when he sensed...*: Jackie MacMullan, "Remembering Kobe Bryant: Relentless, Curious and Infinitely Complicated," ESPN.com, Jan. 26, 2020

Kobe Bryant was among the nine people...who died in a helicopter crash...: Greg Beacham, "Los Angeles Lakers Legend Kobe Bryant Dies at 41 in Helicopter Crash," Associated Press, Jan. 27, 2020

"It was like a death in my family...": *The Ellen DeGeneres Show*, Jan. 22, 2021

...declaring COVID-19 a global health emergency...: Merrit Kennedy, "WHO Declares Coronavirus Outbreak a Global Health Emergency," NPR, Jan. 30, 2020

David Levy...had stepped down in the wake of the...: Dade Hayes, "Turner Boss David Levy Plans Exit as Part of WarnerMedia Reorganization, Ending Tenure Marked by Sports Wins," *Deadline*, Feb. 28, 2019

...in what was described as a mutual parting...: Interview, June 16, 2020

...the move was "a very difficult thing"...: Ourand

Zucker resigned in February 2022 after acknowledging...: Brian Stelter and Oliver Darcy, "CNN President Jeff Zucker Resigns over Consensual Relationship with Key Lieutenant," CNN, Feb. 2, 2022

...he was looking to retire after his sixtieth or sixty-first birthday...: Jimmy Traina, "Charles Barkley Explains Why He Plans on Retiring in Two Years," *Sports Illustrated*, Feb. 16, 2022

"I don't want to die on TV...": Traina

Warriors forward Draymond Green publicly questioned whether...: Andrew Joseph, "Charles Barkley Apologizes for His Draymond Green Remarks: 'I Was 100 Percent Wrong,'" *USA TODAY*, May 2, 2018

"I said, 'Charles, you don't realize how powerful...'": Interview, June 23, 2020

"I'm not going to work fucking forever...": John Ourand, "Retirement for Charles Barkley?," *Sports Business Journal*, Mar. 25, 2019

...apparently never wore one as a father of four...: https://www.youtube.com/watch?v=RcGGFe-G3Fs

"JB Smoove's teeth so big, if he eat Tiffany Haddish out...": *https://www.youtube.com/watch?v=RcGGFe-G3Fs*

"You got a brand-new La-Z-Boy, stiff as hell…": *https://www.youtube.com/watch?v=RcGGFe-G3Fs*

Years after politics had become the "scumbag business"…: The Jay Leno Show, 2010, *https://www.dailymotion.com/video/xb9lbs*

"I thought he had mellowed with age, but…": Interview, Sept. 27, 2019

…*dead last in every important metric "if it wasn't for Arkansas and Mississippi"*…: "Gov. Barkley? Sir Charles Eyeing Office in Alabama," Associated Press, July 27, 2006

He also knew that Moore was a "white separatist" whose campaign…: "Charles Barkley Decries Roy Moore Links to 'White Separatist' Steve Bannon," *The Guardian*, Nov. 25, 2017

…*Jones got a call from a sportscaster in Birmingham with a lead*…: Interview, Aug. 5, 2019

"Charles could say the things I couldn't say…": Interview, Aug. 5, 2019

"He gave people a lot of reasons to not sit at home…": Interview, Aug. 5, 2019

…*make sense of the voting projections from the* New York Times…: Matthew Bloch, Nate Cohn, Josh Katz, and Jasmine Lee, "Alabama Election Results: Doug Jones Defeats Roy Moore in U.S. Senate Race," *New York Times*, Dec. 12, 2017

He remarked on the couch how he "never cared as much about anything as this"…: Interview, Sept. 27, 2019

…*Moore would hold up a narrative of Alabama and "how stupid we are"*…: Cindy Boren, "'We've Got to Stop Looking Like Idiots': Charles Barkley Tells Alabamians Not to Vote for Roy Moore," *Washington Post*, Dec. 12, 2017

"He knew that it's still a part of the world so easy to look down on…": Interview, Sept. 27, 2019

"Folks, let me tell you something…": Interview, Aug. 5, 2019

"That does not mean hair salons and restaurants, Black women…": "Chuck's Donation," NBA on TNT, *https://www.youtube.com/watch?v=2qe-RRRKUaE*

"We're not gonna do any more weave shops…": *https://www.youtube.com/watch?v=2qe-RRRKUaE*

"I don't…but I want to help…": *https://www.youtube.com/watch?v=2qe-RRRKUaE*

…*$7,000 for a new basketball court in Leeds in 1990*…: "Barkley Donates $7,000 for Court," *Montgomery Advertiser*, July 27, 1990

...and pledged $1 million to Alabama A&M...: Josh Bean, "Charles Barkley Pledges $1 million to Alabama College, but It's Not Auburn," AL.com, Nov. 29, 2016

"I think I dropped my phone...": Interview, Oct. 17, 2019

...almost 9 percent of the population still lives below the federal government's poverty level...: "Leeds City, Alabama," US Census Bureau, July 1, 2021

Charles hoped to build ten to twenty affordable homes...: Cindy Boren, "Charles Barkley Is Selling Memorabilia to Build Affordable Housing in His Alabama Hometown," *Washington Post*, Mar. 9, 2020

..."and I don't want that stuff crapping up my house"...: Boren

He'd keep the '92 medal for Christiana...: Allen Kim, "Charles Barkley Is Selling Olympic Gold Medal and MVP Award to Build Affordable Housing in Hometown," CNN, Mar. 11, 2020

"It's just a long plan I've got to just...": Giana Han, "2020 Spurs Charles Barkley to Greater Acts of Generosity," AL.com, Dec. 14, 2020

...infected more than 525 million people and killed roughly 6.3 million globally...: Chris Alcantara, Youjin Shin, Leslie Shapiro, Adam Taylor, and Armand Emamdjomeh, "Tracking Covid-19 Cases, Deaths and Vaccines Worldwide," *Washington Post*

"The one thing I've learned through this pandemic...": *The Steam Room*, July 16, 2020

Though he joked about Draymond Green's "triple-single" stat line...: Charles Curtis, "Charles Barkley Takes a Shot at Draymond Green Averaging a 'Triple Single,'" *USA TODAY*, Jan. 17, 2020

...discussed social issues on-air and had some tequila...: *The Steam Room*, Oct. 16, 2020

Green eventually signed a multiyear deal with Turner Sports...: Jannelle Moore, "Draymond Green Signs Innovative Deal to Join Barkley on TNT Postgame Show," *San Jose Mercury News*, Jan. 27, 2022

Charles pleaded with Kyrie Irving during his short-lived media boycott...: *Keyshawn, JWill & Zubin*, Dec. 17, 2020

...he didn't think the fatal shooting of Breonna Taylor...deserved to be discussed alongside...: Jason Kurtz, "Charles Barkley Is Taking Heat for His Breonna Taylor Comments," CNN, Sept. 25, 2020

Or why the members of Congress, and not President Donald Trump, were to blame...: Abby Driggers, "Here's What Charles Barkley Had to Say about Wednesday's Violent Protest," *Opelika-Auburn News*, Jan. 8, 2021

...to receive "some preferential treatment" for the coronavirus vaccine...: Chris

Bumbaca, "Charles Barkley Says Athletes 'Deserve Some Preferential Treatment' for COVID-19 Vaccination," *USA TODAY*, Jan. 15, 2021

...in joining up with LIV Golf...: Marcus Hayes, "Charles Barkley calls LIV, 9/11 outrage 'fake' at Trump tourney just minutes from Ground Zero," Philadelphia Inquirer, July 24, 2022

...he gave the school $1 million, the largest gift in its history...: Roy S. Johnson, "Charles Barkley to Donate $1 Million to Miles College," AL.com, Jan. 8, 2020

"My legacy? Like when I die...": "Charles Barkley Makes Surprise Visit to Miles College Pep Rally," Auburn Tigers on AL.com, *https://www.youtube.com/watch?v=nI4GcIsK9T4*

"Listen, y'all know that and I'm not afraid to say it...": *https://www.youtube.com/watch?v=nI4GcIsK9T4*

Epilogue

Primary sources include research conducted by the author from the 2020 Basketball Hall of Fame Enshrinement Ceremony in Uncasville, Connecticut, in May 2021. Other sources include coverage in outlets like the *New York Times* and YouTube uploads of *Inside the NBA.*

"It looked like I'm giving you a prostate check...": YouTube upload of the 2020 Hall of Fame Awards Celebration and Gala, *https://www.youtube.com/watch?v=-iJpRpW03YI*

"I needed a cigarette after you rubbed...": *https://www.youtube.com/watch?v=-iJpRpW03YI*

The honor marks Chuck's third time getting inducted...: "Charles Barkley," Basketball Hall of Fame, *https://www.hoophall.com/hall-of-famers/charles-barkley/*; "1992 United States Olympic Team," Basketball Hall of Fame, *https://www.hoophall.com/hall-of-famers/1992-united-states-olympic-team/*

Ilya Hoffman had little idea what he was getting himself into...: Tammy La Gorce, "It Was an All-Star Weekend for the Bride and Groom," *New York Times*, Mar. 19, 2021

"I said, Oh you mean...": La Gorce

...I'm going to need two of those slices...: La Gorce

"I remember being really emotional about it...": La Gorce

...the father-daughter dance to Zac Brown Band's "The Man Who Loves You Most"...: *Jimmy Kimmel Live*, Mar. 2, 2021

...he would call "all Jewish people on deck"...: *Jimmy Kimmel Live*

"He really was scared…": La Gorce

…*dubbed only as "Street Clothes"*…: YouTube upload of a 2021 episode of *Inside the NBA, https://www.youtube.com/watch?v=MQ7Q99o919g*

…*on Kevin Durant after a first-round sweep as "a bus rider"*…: "Don't Walk Around Talkin' 'Bout You A Champion!," NBA on TNT, *https://www. youtube.com/watch?v=8447VQV_JUU*

…*by hilariously driving a bus through a security gate*…: "Bus Driver Chuck Drives Inside Crew Through Security Gate," NBA on TNT, *https:// www.youtube.com/watch?v=Bs6KyuKN6BY*

…*the passing of his father, Frank, in December 2021*…: "AFGE Mourns Passing of Unionist Frank Barkley," The American Federation of Government Employees, Jan. 18, 2022

Charles said he was "deeply sad" about the loss…: The Steam Room, Jan. 7, 2022

"I just hope he rests in peace…": *The Steam Room*

…*how he once said "women be milking that baby thing"*…: "TNT Inside Crew Celebrates Mother's Day," NBA on TNT, *https://www.youtube. com/watch?v=SmQkrinhGBk*

"Baby, I mean those *other* women…": *https://www.youtube.com/ watch?v=SmQkrinhGBk*

"You and Kobe argued all the time?…": *https://www.youtube.com/watch?v=-iJpRpW03YI*

"Ernie, I love you and I appreciate you…": *https://www.youtube.com/ watch?v=-iJpRpW03YI*

…*attempts to troll Charles by calling him "Shaq" to his face*…: "Fan Spots Charles Barkley and Starts Yelling: 'Shaquille O'Neal! Yo It's Shaq!' Chuck: 'All Black People Don't Look Alike,'" Reddit (r/NBA) via Streamable, *https://streamable.com/2g4s8b*

INDEX